DIVERGENCES IN PRIVATE LAW

This book is a study of doctrinal and methodological divergence in the common law of obligations. It explores particular departures from the common law mainstream and the causes and effects of those departures. Some divergences can be justified on the basis of a need to adapt the common law of contract, torts, equity and restitution to local circumstances, or to bring them into conformity with local values. More commonly, however, doctrinal or methodological divergence simply reflects different approaches to common problems, or different views as to what justice or policy requires in particular circumstances. In some instances divergent methodologies lead to substantially the same results, while in others particular causes of action, defences, immunities or remedies recognised in one jurisdiction but not another undoubtedly produce different outcomes. Such cases raise interesting questions as to whether ultimate appellate courts should be slow to abandon principles that remain well accepted throughout the common law world, or cautious about taking a uniquely divergent path.

The chapters in this book were originally presented at the Seventh Biennial Conference on the Law of Obligations held in Hong Kong in July 2014. Another collection, entitled *The Common Law of Obligations: Divergence and Unity* (ISBN: 9781782256564), is also being published.

Divergences in Private Law

Edited by
Andrew Robertson
and
Michael Tilbury

·HART·
PUBLISHING
OXFORD AND PORTLAND, OREGON
2016

Published in the United Kingdom by Hart Publishing Ltd
16C Worcester Place, Oxford, OX1 2JW
Telephone: +44 (0)1865 517530
Fax: +44 (0)1865 510710
E-mail: mail@hartpub.co.uk
Website: http://www.hartpub.co.uk

Published in North America (US and Canada) by
Hart Publishing
c/o International Specialized Book Services
920 NE 58th Avenue, Suite 300
Portland, OR 97213-3786
USA
Tel: +1 503 287 3093 or toll-free: (1) 800 944 6190
Fax: +1 503 280 8832
E-mail: orders@isbs.com
Website: http://www.isbs.com

Hart Publishing is an imprint of Bloomsbury Publishing plc.

British Library Cataloguing in Publication Data
Data Available

Library of Congress Cataloging-in-Publication Data

Names: Conference on the Law of Obligations (7th : 2014 : Hong Kong, China) |
Robertson, Andrew, 1966– editor. | Tilbury, M. J. (Michael J.), editor.

Title: Divergences in private law / Edited by Andrew Robertson and Michael Tilbury.

Description: Hart Publishing, Oxford : 2016. | "Originally presented at the Seventh Biennial
Conference on the Law of Obligations held in Hong Kong in July 2014"—ECIP galley. | Includes
bibliographical references and index.

Identifiers: LCCN 2015038968 | ISBN 9781782256601 (hardback : alk. paper)

Subjects: LCSH: Obligations (Law)—Congresses. | Civil law—Congresses. |
Common law—Congresses.

Classification: LCC K830.A6 D58 2016 | DDC 346—dc23 LC record available
at http://lccn.loc.gov/2015038968

ISBN: 978-1-78225-660-1

Typeset by Compuscript Ltd, Shannon
Printed and bound in Great Britain by
CPI Group (UK) Ltd, Croydon CR0 4YY

PREFACE

This book had its origins in the Seventh Biennial Conference on the Law of Obligations (Obligations VII), which was co-hosted by the Faculty of Law at the University of Hong Kong and Melbourne Law School and held in Hong Kong on 15–18 July 2014. Another volume from the conference, *The Law of Obligations: Divergence and Unity*, explores a related set of issues and will be published simultaneously.

We are very grateful to the Faculty of Law at the University of Hong Kong and Melbourne Law School for supporting the conference. Particular thanks are due to Carolyn Evans and Michael Crommelin, respectively the Dean and former Dean of Melbourne Law School. The existence of the Obligations conference series owes a great deal to Michael Crommelin's warm encouragement and unstinting support from the outset in 2001. Both Michael Crommelin and Carolyn Evans have provided enthusiastic and wholehearted support for the series in general, and for this particular collaboration with the Faculty of Law at the University of Hong Kong. We are also very grateful to Michael Hor and Johannes Chan, respectively the Dean and former Dean of the Faculty of Law at the University of Hong Kong, for their generous support for the Obligations VII conference.

Our thanks also go to the staff at the Faculty of Law at the University of Hong Kong, led by the extraordinary Priscilla Wong—and including especially Daisy Lai and Tristan Wong—for the great care they took to make the conference run smoothly and efficiently and ensure that delegates were very well looked after. We also thank Eddie Leung and Alan Tsang for their efficient and attentive IT and web support.

Thanks are also due to Hart Publishing, Cambridge University Press and Kerry Holdings for their sponsorship of the conference.

Finally, we thank all who participated in the Obligations VII conference for enthusiastically embracing the conference theme and contributing to the conversation that is, in part, recorded in this book.

Andrew Robertson and Michael Tilbury
June 2015

TABLE OF CONTENTS

LIST OF CONTRIBUTORS

Louise Bélanger-Hardy is a Professor in the Faculty of Law at the University of Ottawa.

Erika Chamberlain is an Associate Professor and Associate Dean (Academic) in the Faculty of Law at the University of Western Ontario.

Paul S Davies is an Associate Professor of Law and Fellow of St Catherine's College at the University of Oxford.

Neil Foster is an Associate Professor in Law at the University of Newcastle, NSW.

Sarah Green is an Associate Professor of Law and Fellow of St Hilda's College at the University of Oxford.

Sirko Harder is a Reader in Law at the University of Sussex.

Robyn Honey is a Senior Lecturer at Murdoch University.

JW Neyers is a Professor in the Faculty of Law at the University of Western Ontario.

Robert Ribeiro is a Permanent Judge of the Hong Kong Court of Final Appeal.

Andrew Robertson is a Professor of Law at the University of Melbourne.

Alvin W-L See is an Assistant Professor in the School of Law at Singapore Management University.

Zoë Sinel is an Assistant Professor in the Faculty of Law at the University of Western Ontario.

Stephen A Smith is James McGill Professor in the Faculty of Law at McGill University.

Robert Stevens is Herbert Smith Freehills Professor of Private Law at the University of Oxford.

Michael Tilbury is a Professorial Fellow at Melbourne Law School, formerly Kerry Holdings Professor in Private Law at the University of Hong Kong.

Graham Virgo is Professor of English Private Law and Fellow of Downing College at the University of Cambridge.

Man Yip is an Assistant Professor in the School of Law at Singapore Management University.

TABLE OF CASES

All decisions of the Privy Council are cited in the Table as UK cases.

United Kingdom

Australia

Canada

Court of Justice of the European Union

European Court of Human Rights

Hong Kong

India

Malaysia

United States of America

TABLE OF LEGISLATION

Canada

France

Germany

India

Singapore

United States of America

TABLE OF INTERNATIONAL INSTRUMENTS

1

Why Diverge?

ANDREW ROBERTSON AND MICHAEL TILBURY

The common law of obligations, once a unitary body of law, is now an interrelated set of laws operating in different jurisdictions which share a great deal in the way of substantive doctrine, methodology, taxonomy, approaches, philosophies, values, principles and policies. This book studies particular divergences that have occurred within the common law of obligations. These studies offer significant insights into the nature, effects, successes and failures of the deviations in question. Our particular concern in this introductory chapter is with the forces that produce major deviations, and especially the motivations underlying decisions by ultimate appellate courts to strike out on a divergent path.

Some of the most significant causes of divergence are considered in a related volume.[1] Divergence was made possible by the abandonment of the idea of a uniform common law, the establishment of local ultimate appellate courts and the abolition of appeals to the Privy Council in several major common law jurisdictions.[2] A wide range of factors have led, and continue to lead, courts to act on that possibility, including a concern to exercise independent judgement on difficult issues and a sense of responsibility for developing and perfecting the local common law.[3] Departures are also necessitated by the need to adapt the common law to local circumstances, by the direct and indirect effects of local statutes, by constitutional structures and by distinctive local or regional human rights regimes.[4] Divergence has also been driven by different understandings of the relationship between public and private law, different understandings of the nature and function of private law,[5] and perhaps even different understandings of the foundations of the authority of the common law.[6]

At the level of particular doctrines, one cause of deviation is a concern that existing rules or principles operate unjustly or fail to achieve relevant policy goals. This is exemplified by the Canadian recognition of fiduciary duties protecting non-economic interests, which

---

[1] A Robertson and M Tilbury (eds), *The Common Law of Obligations: Divergence and Unity* (Oxford, Hart Publishing, 2015).

[2] See A Roberson and M Tilbury (eds), 'Unity, Divergence and Convergence in the Common Law of Obligations', ibid ch 1.

[3] See esp J Goudkamp and J Murphy, 'Divergent Evolution in the Law of Torts: Jurisdictional Isolation, Jurisprudential Divergence and Explanatory Theories', ibid ch 13.

[4] See Goudkamp and Murphy, ibid and Goh Y, 'A Conscious Effort to Develop a "Different" Common Law of Obligations: A Possible Endeavour?', ibid ch 4.

[5] P Cane, 'The Tort Liability of Public Authorities', ibid ch 8 and N Connolly, 'We'll Meet Again: Convergence in the Private Law Treatment of Public Bodies', ibid ch 9.

[6] D Priel, 'The Philosophies of the Common Law and their Implications: Common Law Divergences, Public Authority Liability, and the Future of a Common Law World', ibid ch 11.

is explored by Erika Chamberlain in chapter 12.[7] The expansion of the scope of fiduciary duties to encompass other interests such as bodily safety and psychological well-being facilitates the granting of remedies with respect to wrongdoing that would not otherwise be redressed, and promotes deterrence in circumstances in which it is necessary to maintain high standards of behaviour. While that divergence involves a radical departure from the traditional fiduciary paradigm, Chamberlain argues that it can be justified by reference to the values underlying fiduciary law. She also suggests that the particular willingness of the Supreme Court of Canada to develop private law in order to address social problems may be explained by the fact that the Court is routinely involved in dealing with controversial social issues under the Charter of Rights and Freedoms.[8]

Perhaps the most widely known instance of divergence between common law systems is the recovery of compensation for pure economic loss in the case of negligently constructed buildings. Sarah Green and Paul Davies regard the real cause of divergence among common law jurisdictions in this area as attributable not so much to the values underlying a particular area of law, but to the more general prioritisation of values by particular legal systems.[9] Those values may reflect formal or substantive matters. In the context of defective building cases, for example, formal matters centre on the extent to which legislation should determine the law, while substantive issues relate to whether the issue is addressed on the basis of an exclusionary rule that pure economic loss is generally irrecoverable in negligence. The response of English law, while not consistent, is to adopt a pro-defendant exclusionary approach that leaves statute law to address any unfairness caused. In contrast, most other common law systems have opted for a more flexible approach: one that is more sympathetic to plaintiffs, allowing greater room for the judicial development of the law independently of statute. Green and Davies suggest that the English isolation on this issue is attributable to the desire of the English courts to maintain 'doctrinal order' and the 'primacy of contract', while other common law jurisdictions are more concerned with the 'realties and merits' of individual cases. This accords with the thesis that a major reason why Commonwealth jurisdictions wished to see an end to the role of the Privy Council in their respective jurisdictions was because the English version of the common law that the Privy Council espoused was, in the law of obligations, one that was based on traditional doctrines that resulted in injustice in individual cases and failed to reflect appropriate standards of conduct in dealings and relationships.[10]

Deviations between the laws of common law jurisdictions may not be aimed at producing different outcomes, but may be motivated by a sense that a different mode of analysis of a particular type of legal problem is simpler, results in greater certainty, is less artificial, or more directly addresses underlying questions of justice or policy. Methodological divergence may also be motivated by a conviction that a mode of analysis followed elsewhere is flawed or inadequate. The divergence taken by Australian law in relation to duty of care analysis—which is explored in chapter 2 of this volume—arose primarily from dissatisfaction with proximity as a tool of analysis, and concern about the way in which that concept

---

[7]   E Chamberlain, 'Revisiting Canada's Approach to Fiduciary Relationships', ch 12 of this volume.

[8]   Part I of the Constitution Act 1982, being Schedule B to the Canada Act 1982 (UK), 1982, c 11.

[9]   S Green and P Davies, '"Pure Economic Loss" and Defective Buildings', ch 4 of this volume.

[10]   See P Finn, 'Unity then Divergence, The Privy Council, the Common Laws of England and the Common Laws of Canada, Australia and New Zealand' in Robertson and Tilbury, above n 1, ch 3.

had come to be understood and utilised by the Australian courts.[11] At the heart of the court's criticism of proximity is that it can be understood as a rule without content, and therefore as conferring a judicial discretion.[12] Interestingly, the abandonment of proximity and the rejection of the duty frameworks applied in other jurisdictions was not motivated by a conviction that a superior analytical device or a better method or framework had been found, but proceeded in spite of a candid acknowledgement that they had not.

Significantly less clear is the motivation for the Supreme Court of Canada's adoption of the civilian 'absence of juristic reason' approach to unjust enrichment claims, ostensibly in preference to the 'unjust factors' approach more widely followed in common law jurisdictions.[13] Like the Australian rejection of proximity, its roots seem to lie in a quest for greater guidance or constraint in judicial decision-making, or at least the appearance of greater certainty. It has been suggested that there is not much to be gained by speculating as to why, in his foundational statement of the elements of unjust enrichment, Dickson J stipulated an absence of juristic reason for the enrichment rather than the presence of a factor that made it unjust.[14] Lionel Smith has suggested that Dickson J may have been trying to bring the common law into alignment with the civil law of Quebec, but argued that it is more likely that he was seeking to alleviate concern that the application of the doctrine of unjust enrichment would involve excessive judicial discretion or appeals to individual conscience.[15] This explanation has since been endorsed by the Supreme Court,[16] though McLachlin J has noted that, in contrast with the traditional approach based on fact-specific categories, the unjust factors and absence of basis approaches both provide the flexibility needed to give effect to the equities of the particular case before the court.[17]

One of the most significant doctrinal and methodological divergences between common law jurisdictions that now presents itself is the decision of the High Court of Australia in *Andrews v Australia and New Zealand Banking Group Ltd*.[18] In that decision, which is analysed by Sirko Harder in this volume,[19] the High Court departed from what was then understood to be the law in Australia—and is still understood to be the law in other common law jurisdictions—that the penalty doctrine applies only in cases of breach of contract. Harvey McGregor has written that this is 'a straightforward, even self-evident, proposition'.[20] The High Court's disagreement with this stems from its understanding of the equitable jurisdiction in respect of penalties, which survived the judicature system, and which was not limited to breach cases, but could be engaged by, for example, the failure of a condition. The classic illustration, to which the Court appealed, was the penal bond with conditional defeasance, a popular method of contracting in early modern times. The Court's conclusion that there was nothing, in principle, to restrict the doctrine to breach cases has been

---

[11] A Robertson, 'Proximity: Divergence and Unity', ch 2 of this volume.

[12] *San Sebastian Pty Ltd v Minister* (1986) 162 CLR 340, 368 (Brennan J). See also the oft-quoted statement of Gummow J in *Hill v Van Erp* (1997) 188 CLR 159, 238 that 'used as a legal norm, [proximity] has the uncertainties and perils of a category of indeterminate reference, used with shifting meanings to mask no more than policy preferences'.

[13] See Z Sinel, 'The Methods and Madness of Unjust Enrichment', ch 10 of this volume.

[14] *Rathwell v Rathwell* [1978] 2 SCR 436.

[15] L Smith, 'The Mystery of "Juristic Reason"' (2000) 12 *Supreme Court Law Review* (2d) 211.

[16] *Garland v Consumers' Gas Co* 2004 SCC 25, [2004] 1 SCR 629, [40] (Iacobucci J for the Court).

[17] *Peel (Regional Municipality) v Canada* [1992] 3 SCR 762, 785.

[18] *Andrews v Australia and New Zealand Banking Group Ltd* [2012] HCA 30, (2012) 247 CLR 205.

[19] S Harder, 'The Scope of the Rule against Contractual Penalties: A New Divergence', ch 8 of this volume.

[20] H McGregor, *McGregor on Damages*, 19th edn (London, Sweet & Maxwell, 2014) [15-009].

the subject of intense criticism especially for its failure to provide any justification (other than an historical one) for departing from an existing understanding of the law.[21] Harder too regards the decision as flawed in its methodology, and argues that it should not be followed in other common law jurisdictions since there are other doctrines of the common law and equity, as well as legislation, that provide means for dealing with unfair contracts. Viewed from the perspective of divergence, the approach in *Andrews* can be seen as requiring an approach to common law method that reflects a particular Australian (or at least New South Wales) view of equity—one that strives to preserve equity as a distinct and living body of law within the legal system in such a way that the historical continuity of the law is maintained.[22] Whether other common law systems will place such emphasis on historical coherence is open to question.

Where the common law is codified, then the reasons for any divergences in that codification are of course a matter for the legislature rather than the courts. Whether and how the legislature has intended divergence from the common law is, however, an extremely important question in the interpretation and application of the statute. An interesting issue considered by Alvin See in chapter 11 is whether a statutory provision expressed in broad terms may be interpreted in light of, and guided by, a common law framework developed elsewhere in the common law world after the statute has come into force.[23] See suggests that it can, and explains how the modern law of unjust enrichment can provide a guiding rationale and a structure for application of section 70 of the Indian Contract Act 1872, while accommodating the dictates of the particular statutory provision.

As noted earlier, the need to adapt the common law to suit local circumstances is an important motivation for divergence. Particular local circumstances may also provide a reason to retain traditional rules in one jurisdiction while the law is modernised in others. While the presumption of advancement and the presumption of a resulting trust are considered to be in decline in English law, those presumptions have recently been reaffirmed in Singaporean law. While the presumption of advancement as between parent and child has been placed on a gender-neutral footing in Singapore, the presumption of advancement between spouses has not. These developments, as well as their motivations and implications, are explored by Man Yip in chapter 13.[24] While Mindy Chen-Wishart has argued that Confucian family values may have played a role in the Singaporean divergence in the law of undue influence, Man Yip suggests that 'Asian family values' may be a means to an end in the law of resulting trusts, and policy may be the real driver of developments. The gender-specific operation of the presumption of advancement between spouses goes hand in hand with statutory spousal maintenance obligations, which require husbands to maintain wives but not vice versa. Both may be explained on the basis of a national policy of maintaining a gendered division of labour and encouraging childbirth, although the first of these is in some tension with the national policy of promoting women's participation in the paid workforce and judicial recognition of the role of women as providers for their families.

---

[21]   See esp JW Carter, W Courtney, E Peden, A Stewart and G Tolhurst, 'Contractual Penalties: Resurrecting the Equitable Jurisdiction' (2013) 30 *Journal of Contract Law* 99.

[22]   See JD Heydon, MJ Leeming and PG Turner, *Meagher, Gummow and Lehane's Equity Doctrine and Remedies*, 5th edn (Chatswood, LexisNexis Butterworths, 2015) xxi–xxiii.

[23]   A W-L See, 'Recovery of Non-Gratuitously Conferred Benefit under Section 70 of the Indian Contract Act 1872', ch 11 of this volume.

[24]   M Yip, 'The Presumptions of Resulting Trust and Advancement under Singapore Law: Localisation, Nationalism and Beyond', ch 13 of this volume.

Just as jurisdictions may diverge, so they may converge. Louise Bélanger-Hardy provides an apt illustration in her contribution to this volume,[25] addressing what is a seemingly stark divergence between the common law jurisdictions in Canada on the one hand and the civil law of Quebec on the other. It concerns personal injury claims where the plaintiff's injury consists of mental harm standing alone, that is, where the mental harm is not ancillary to physical harm. In common law Canada, in order to succeed in such a claim in negligence or under the principle in *Wilkinson v Downton*,[26] plaintiffs must establish that their mental harm amounts to a recognisable psychiatric injury. In contrast, defendants in Quebec are liable for any 'bodily, moral or material' injury caused by their fault, and it is clear that this does not require plaintiffs to establish a recognisable psychiatric injury as an ingredient of their claim. Nevertheless, dicta in the leading common law decision of the Supreme Court of Canada, *Mustapha v Culligan of Canada Inc*,[27] have appealed to Quebec courts as setting the minimum standard for actionable mental harm in Quebec. The interpretation put on *Mustapha* by the Quebec courts has led, in turn, to suggestions that the requirement of a recognisable psychiatric injury now no longer applies in the common law in Canada. Whatever the strength of the arguments, this is indicative of the way in which the interpretation of a major case can lead away from overt divergence between laws towards their convergence.

Moves towards convergence are also apparent between common law jurisdictions, particularly in new or developing areas of law, where it is necessary for the law to adapt to novel situations. That adaptation may require the courts to mould existing principles using traditional common law methodologies. The underlying unity of the common law, both in terms of values and method, may be strong enough to ensure that convergence, or at least substantial convergence, is achieved between the laws of independent jurisdictions. This is illustrated by the application of the law of defamation in the context of Internet publication. Are Internet intermediaries (such as those who host discussion forums or blogs) to be held liable for whatever is published on them? The answer depends on identifying the publisher of the material and on whether the defence of innocent dissemination is available to the publisher so identified. As Justice Ribeiro points out in his contribution to this volume,[28] the Hong Kong and English courts have agreed that Internet intermediaries are not liable as primary publishers and so are able to avail themselves of the innocent dissemination defence before they become aware of the defamatory material. However, the English and Hong Kong courts differ in their approaches to the law after Internet intermediaries become aware of the defamatory material. The English courts have applied the 'noticeboard cases' to make intermediaries who know about and adopt the publication liable as primary publishers, while the Hong Kong courts focus on the reasonableness of the intermediaries' conduct for the purposes of applying the innocent dissemination defence. In most cases, this difference of approach will, no doubt, still lead to substantial convergence in outcome.

A similar story is evident in the law relating to non-delegable duties of care, which has assumed significance in an era of 'outsourcing', in determining whether schools or

---

[25] L Bélanger-Hardy, 'Canada's Common Law, Quebec's Civil Law and the Threshold of Actionable Mental Harm following Tortious Conduct', ch 3 of this volume.

[26] *Wilkinson v Downton* [1897] 2 QB 57.

[27] *Mustapha v Culligan of Canada Inc* 2008 SCC 27, [2008] 2 SCR 114.

[28] R Ribeiro, 'Defamation on the Internet', ch 6 of this volume.

hospitals, among others, are liable for the negligence of independent contractors to whom they have contracted out the performance of some of their functions. Formidable doctrinal issues arise in determining when a 'principal' is under a 'personal' or 'non-delegable' duty and whether the conduct in issue is within that 'personal' duty.[29] In chapter 7, Neil Foster compares the responses of the Australian and English courts to these issues.[30] His study indicates that, notwithstanding doctrinal difficulties, the overwhelming trend is towards convergence of Australian and English law, especially in the light of the decision of the UK Supreme Court in *Woodland v Essex County Council*.[31] Divergences remain, but at least two of these are justifiable or explicable. The first, namely the inapplicability in England of the law of non-delegable duties between occupiers and their visitors, is a result of statute.[32] Another is that in Australia a road authority does not owe a non-delegable duty to road users, a result that may be linked to the abolition of the so-called 'highway immunity' rule,[33] but (as Foster points out) is more convincingly explained by Australian conditions (such as the long stretches of road that need to be maintained by local councils with limited resources). A third is not easily defensible: it is the reluctance of the Australian authorities to apply the law of non-delegable duties where the conduct of the independent contractor is deliberate rather than negligent.[34] Here the hope is that, just as the UK Supreme Court referred to the Australian authorities as a basis for the development of the law in *Woodland v Essex County Council*, so the Australian courts will now refer to the English restatement in that case, as well as to other relevant Commonwealth authority, in now developing the law in Australia on a principled basis.

Robyn Honey's study of the English and Australian approaches to undue influence in chapter 14 reminds us that divergence sometimes occurs as much within a particular jurisdiction as it does between jurisdictions.[35] One can sometimes identify commonalities in strands of thinking across jurisdictions, where proponents of or adherents to a particular view of law may find more support outside their own jurisdiction than within it. Honey argues that there are three fundamental concerns underlying the law of undue influence which pull the doctrine in different directions, and which are not all adequately captured in either the Australian or English models of undue influence. That deficiency creates instability in the application of the doctrine in both jurisdictions, producing divergences within each as well as points of alignment.

The examples of divergence or convergence provided by comparative common law provide a rich database on which analysis of contemporary problems in the common law can draw. Thus, Robert Stevens' argument[36] that the decision of the High Court of Australia

---

[29] See RP Balkin and JLR Davis, *Law of Torts*, 5th edn (Chatswood, LexisNexis Butterworths, 2013) [26.24]–[26.36].

[30] N Foster, 'Convergence and Divergence: the Law of Non-delegable Duties in Australia and the United Kingdom', ch 7 of this volume.

[31] *Woodland v Essex County Council* [2013] UKSC 66, [2014] AC 537.

[32] Occupiers Liability Act 1957 (UK) s 2(4)(b). For the position in Australia, see Balkin and Davis, above n 29, [26.34].

[33] *Brodie v Singleton Shire Council* [2001] HCA 29, (2001) 206 CLR 512.

[34] Esp *New South Wales v Lepore* (2003) 212 CLR 511, which is probably not the last word on this issue, nor on vicarious liability in these situations (where the topic has also been considered by the final courts of appeal in Canada, England and New Zealand: see Balkin and Davis, above n 29, [26.54]–[26.55]).

[35] R Honey, 'Divergence in the Australian and English Law of Undue Influence: Vacillation or Variance?', ch 14 of this volume.

[36] R Stevens, 'Rights Restricting Remedies', ch 9 of this volume.

in *Andrews*, which has been mentioned above,[37] should not be followed in other common law jurisdictions is grounded in the premise that the scope of the penalty doctrine can only be delimited by identifying its rationale. In his view, that rationale requires a recognition that the obligation to pay damages is a 'monetised form of the primary obligation of performance' that cannot be inconsistent with the primary obligation.[38] A clause imposing liability on breach of contract for an amount that is excessive in comparison to the value of the primary obligation at least runs the risk of being inconsistent in this sense. In contrast, a sum of money payable on the occurrence of a condition is not capable of being inconsistent in this way: the situation simply cannot be analysed in terms of primary and secondary obligations.

A similar approach is evident in Jason Neyers' study of the nature of the tort of public nuisance in Canadian and English law.[39] Conceptualising the tort as limited to the enforcement of private rights (akin to easements or profits) associated with passage on the highway and with fishing, Neyers confronts two of the difficult issues that have plagued the development of the tort: the meaning of the requirement of 'special damage' and the question of the availability in the tort of personal injury damages. Analysing the sometimes divergent approaches of the courts in England and Canada, Neyers argues that the rights-based analysis of public nuisance that he offers gives coherence to the tort by requiring that the special damage requirement is best understood as 'actual damage', which sometimes encompasses the recovery of personal injury damages.

Divergent uses of the concept of unconscionability,[40] both within and between particular jurisdictions, are analysed by Graham Virgo in his contribution to this volume. Unconscionability is used to justify equitable intervention in a variety of different contexts and in relation to a variety of different kinds of behaviour. Virgo proposes a taxonomy of unconscionability which distinguishes between its different meanings, and explains why each is used when it is, in order to promote more precise, consistent and comprehensible usage. Virgo proposes a threefold classification, which distinguishes between references to the defendant's state of mind, the defendant's behaviour (assessed in light of his or her awareness of relevant circumstances) and the conscience of the court, which involves the exercise of discretion in accordance with established principles. Of particular interest in the present context is the High Court of Australia's embrace of unconscionability as the foundation, and basis for determination, of restitutionary claims such as the action to recover money paid under a mistake of fact. Like the Australian divergence in the law of penalties, this deviation from the common law mainstream is grounded in history. Like the Canadian divergence in the law of unjust enrichment, it also seems to be grounded in a fear of an excessive flexibility or discretion in unjust enrichment analysis. As Virgo indicates, however, it is difficult to see an unelaborated standard of unconscionability as the path to greater certainty and consistency in the determination of restitutionary claims.

One of the best-known divergences between the United States and Commonwealth jurisdictions in the field of private law is in the extent to which the common law and equity are

---

[37] Above n 18.

[38] Stevens, above n 36, also analyses *Transfield Shipping Inc v Mercator Shipping Inc (The Achilleas)* [2008] UKHL 48, [2009] 1 AC 61 in terms of a wider theory that primary obligations determine the form of the (secondary) duty of next-best compliance.

[39] J Neyers, 'Divergence and Convergence in the Tort of Public Nuisance', ch 5 of this volume.

[40] G Virgo, 'Whose Conscience? Unconscionability in the Common Law of Obligations', ch 15 of this volume.

understood to have been merged to form a single body of law. Whether the two bodies of law remain separate, and ought to remain separate, remain contentious questions in Commonwealth jurisdictions. Differing views about the distinctiveness of equity provide fertile ground for particular doctrinal divergences between common law jurisdictions. In the final chapter of this volume, Stephen Smith asks whether is there is anything distinctively equitable about awards of specific relief, other than their origins in the Court of Chancery.[41] We are accustomed to describing these remedies as 'equitable', and to assuming that because they are discretionary and subject to special bars and defences they can only properly be understood by reference to their origin. In fact, Smith argues, what is distinctive about awards of specific relief is neither their origin nor their special equitable nature, but that they concern matters that are within the more or less exclusive control of the defendant. They must therefore be enforced by way of an incentive, namely the threat of punishment, rather than execution by court officials. The crucial distinction is therefore between executable and non-executable rulings, which does not require any reference to the distinction between the common law and equity. Executable rulings can be carried out by court officials without the participation of the defendant, whereas non-executable rulings concern matters that are within the more or less exclusive control of the defendant and must therefore be enforced by the threat of punishment. The distinction arose in a dual system, in part because of it, but reflects a natural distinction between impersonal directives to do things that can be done without the defendant's participation and personal directives to do things that cannot.

---

[41] S Smith, 'Form and Substance in Equitable Remedies', ch 16 of this volume.

2

Proximity: Divergence and Unity

ANDREW ROBERTSON

In 1986 a joint judgment of four justices of the High Court of Australia maintained that '[t]he relationship of proximity is an integral constituent of the duty of care concept'.[1] From its place as an 'integral constituent' of duty, proximity is considered to have fallen so far in Australian law that six justices of the High Court have declared that 'the demise of proximity as a useful informing principle' in the determination of duty of care questions 'is now complete'.[2] The expression, we are told, 'has been discarded from the Australian judicial lexicon' because it is not a useful tool of analysis and does no more than to point to the need for something more than foreseeability of damage to establish a duty of care.[3] As we will see, however, the concept of proximity, as conventionally understood, has in fact been utilised as a tool of analysis in the High Court of Australia throughout the period of its supposed demise and up to the present day.[4] While the High Court has properly rejected the idea of proximity as a comprehensive determinant of the duty question, that rejection has cleared the way for a return to the narrower and more focused concept articulated by Lord Atkin in *Donoghue v Stevenson*[5] and applied elsewhere in the common law world. The extensive continued use of the substance of the proximity concept in the High Court of Australia makes it very unclear what, exactly, has been rejected. On one view, which is well supported by reasoning in the High Court of Australia, what has replaced the requirement of proximity is the 'sufficiently close relationship test'.[6]

The Australian experience with proximity provides an interesting study in methodological divergence. That the much-maligned concept of proximity has continued to be used in spite of its ostensible rejection tells us something about its utility as a tool of analysis. It also points to a fundamental unity in this area of the common law of obligations and reminds us of the importance of shared concepts. This first part of this chapter will analyse the nature of proximity as conventionally understood, and its place in duty

---

[1] *San Sebastian Pty Ltd v Minister* (1986) 162 CLR 340, 355 (Gibbs CJ, Mason, Wilson and Dawson JJ).
[2] *Miller v Miller* [2011] HCA 9, (2011) 242 CLR 446, [59] (French CJ, Gummow, Hayne, Crennan, Kiefel and Bell JJ) [60].
[3] ibid.
[4] This is fully explained in section III below, but has also been discussed by others, notably P Vines, 'The Needle in the Haystack: Principle in the Duty of Care in the Law of Negligence' (2000) 23 *University of New South Wales Law Review* 35; N Katter, '"Who Then in Law Is My Neighbour?" Reverting to First Principles in the High Court of Australia' (2004) 12 *Torts Law Review* 85; D Tan, 'The Salient Features of Proximity: Examining the *Spandeck* Formulation for Establishing a Duty of Care' [2010] *Singapore Journal of Legal Studies* 459.
[5] *Donoghue v Stevenson* [1932] AC 562, 580–82.
[6] *Moorabool Shire Council v Taitapanui* [2006] VSCA 30, (2006) 14 VR 55, [21] (Maxwell P).

of care analysis. The second part will examine the particular role of proximity in each of the other major, non-US common law countries, namely England, Canada, Singapore and New Zealand. The third part of the chapter will consider the purported rejection of proximity in Australia, the enduring role of the concept in decisions of the High Court of Australia and the alternative modes of analysis that have been proposed.

I. Understanding Proximity

The Nature of the Inquiry

According to the classical definition, a relationship of proximity sufficient to establish a duty of care exists where one person is so closely and directly affected by another's act or omission that the second person ought to have the first in contemplation, with the 'ought' question to be judged by reference to whether neglect of the plaintiff's interest by the defendant would be regarded by 'general public sentiment' as 'moral wrongdoing for which the offender must pay'.[7] The proximity question thus has three elements: the *closeness and directness* of the effect of the defendant's conduct on the plaintiff; the question whether the defendant *ought* to have had the plaintiff in contemplation; and the idea that the 'ought' question is to be judged by reference to perceived *community standards*. Of course the word 'proximity' does not accurately or comprehensively describe the underlying idea, but in this respect proximity is in the good company of other well-established labels for doctrinal concepts such as 'consideration', 'estoppel' and 'remoteness'.

The application of the principle of proximity does not simply involve an abstract question of closeness and directness, or speculation as to how particular conduct would be judged by general public sentiment. Those questions can only be answered on the basis of an intensive analysis of the distinctive factual features of the case being decided and comparison with the features of comparable cases.[8] Lord Pearce famously said in *Hedley Byrne & Co v Heller & Partners Ltd* that the width of the law of negligence 'depends ultimately on the courts' assessment of the demands of society for protection from the carelessness of others'.[9] But as Lord Diplock said in *Home Office v Dorset Yacht Co Ltd*, Lord Pearce's reference to the 'courts' in the plural is significant: the law of negligence develops through a comparison of the characteristics that are common to the type of conduct and relationship before the court and the types of conduct and relationships which have previously been accepted as giving rise to a duty of care.[10] The identification of those factual characteristics or 'salient features' that denote sufficient proximity is therefore fundamentally important to the development and application of the concept of proximity.[11] The 'area of demarcation

---

[7] ibid 580 (Lord Atkin).
[8] See, eg, *Marc Rich & Co AG v Bishop Rock Marine Co Ltd (the 'Nicholas H')* [1996] 1 AC 211, 236 (Lord Steyn).
[9] *Hedley Byrne & Co v Heller & Partners Ltd* [1964] AC 465, 536.
[10] *Home Office v Dorset Yacht Co Ltd* [1970] AC 1004, 1058.
[11] *Caltex Oil Australia Pty Ltd v The Dredge 'Willemstad'* (1976) 136 CLR 529, 575–76 (Stephen J).

between what is and is not a sufficient degree of proximity' is marked out by 'the piecemeal conclusions arrived at in precedent cases'.[12]

The Factors to be Considered

The proximity inquiry involves a consideration of the directness of the different mechanisms by which the kind of conduct engaged in by the defendant might harm the plaintiff or someone similarly situated.[13] That depends in particular on a consideration of two related issues. First, it depends on the defendant's control of the risk of harm, including in particular the extent of the defendant's role in creating the risk or source of harm. The conduct of a person who creates a source of danger has a closer and more direct effect on others than one who merely controls a danger that arose otherwise, and of course the greater the degree of control one has, the more closely and directly one's conduct affects others.[14] Secondly, it is necessary to consider the nature of any antecedent relationship between the parties, whether the defendant assumed responsibility for a particular task affecting the plaintiff, and whether the defendant knew or ought to have known that the plaintiff would rely on anything said or done by the defendant.[15]

The 'Ought' Question

In more routine situations of course the case law provides significant guidance as to when sufficient proximity does and does not exist.[16] Through the elucidation and application of the above-mentioned factors, the case law also identifies and provides guidance on the factual characteristics to be taken into account in cases that lie beyond the established categories.[17] There is, however, no avoiding the fact that in some cases the courts must make a judgement as to whether in particular circumstances one person ought to take account of the interests of another.[18] Whether a person in the defendant's position 'ought' to have been mindful of the interests of a person in the plaintiff's position is a question of interpersonal responsibility, or what one person can reasonably expect of another. The court is ultimately required to make an assessment as to whether neglect of the relevant interest in the given

---

[12] ibid 576. Stephen J was referring to the emergence of proximity in particular classes of case involving economic loss, but his comments are of general applicability.

[13] See C Witting, 'The Three Stage Test Abandoned in Australia—Or Not? (2002) 118 *LQR* 214, 218–19.

[14] See, eg, *Sutradhar v Natural Environmental Research Council* [2006] UKHL 33, [2006] 4 All ER 490, discussed in section II below.

[15] As to why the assumption of responsibility issue must be framed in this way, rather than as a question whether the defendant assumed a responsibility to take care to avoid or prevent injury (as suggested by Deane J in *Sutherland Shire Council v Heyman* (1985) 157 CLR 424, 497–98), see A Robertson and J Wang, 'The Assumption of Responsibility' in K Barker, R Grantham and W Swain (eds), *The Law of Misstatements: 50 Years on from Hedley Byrne v Heller* (Oxford, Hart Publishing, 2015) 49–83.

[16] As McLachlin CJ said in *Childs v Desormeaux* 2006 SCC 18, [2006] 1 SCR 643, [15], this 'simply captures the basic notion of precedent'.

[17] *Caltex Oil Australia Pty Ltd v The Dredge 'Willemstad'* (1976) 136 CLR 529, 575 (Stephen J).

[18] As WK Fullagar, 'Liability for Representations at Common Law' (1951) 25 *Australian Law Journal* 278, 278 said, proximity was not 'intended to make, and it does not make, everything nice and easy. It must call, in some cases, for a very nice appreciation, and weighing against one another, of the factors of a situation.'

circumstances would generally be understood in the community as moral wrongdoing for which the defendant must pay. The court's perception of current community standards is thus at the heart of the proximity inquiry.[19] The idea behind this appears to be that the law of negligence is directed towards the community welfare purpose of maintaining civil peace through the provision of civil recourse for particular interpersonal wrongs.[20] The pursuit of that purpose depends on giving effect to what are thought to be commonly accepted ideas about how people ought to be behave in relation to one another, and when a person ought to be made to answer for the consequences of his or her wrongdoing.[21]

The concept of proximity clearly does not provide a precise criterion or rigid formula that can be applied mechanically to a given fact situation. As Deane J has observed, this consideration did not escape Lord Atkin or other proponents of proximity, but the utility of common law concepts is not determined by their capacity to provide a 'formularized criterion of liability'.[22] Deane J accepted that the nature of the considerations to be taken into account in determining whether there is sufficient proximity will vary across different classes of case, as will their relative weight, and novel cases raise difficult questions that 'may involve value judgments on matters of policy and degree'.[23] Concern about cases being determined by 'individual predilections ungoverned by authority'[24] may be allayed by the idea that the proximity requirement controls the *categories* of case in which duties are recognised and operates as 'a question of law to be resolved by the process of legal reasoning by induction and deduction'.[25] The development of the law by reference to categories does not obviate the need to make difficult decisions on questions of interpersonal responsibility, but simply allows those decisions to be made across categories of fact situations rather than on the facts of each individual case.[26]

A significant problem with Lord Atkin's definition of proximity is that it is framed as though the closeness and directness of the effect of one person's conduct on another is sufficient, on its own, to determine whether the first person ought to have the second in contemplation. It assumes, in other words, that proximity exhausts the interpersonal responsibility question. There are, however, a number of situations in which one person's conduct may have a close and direct effect on another, but a duty cannot be justified as a matter of interpersonal responsibility, and so one cannot say that the defendant 'ought' to have had the plaintiff in contemplation. The 'ought' question therefore depends on the consideration of a number of factors in addition to closeness and directness. Because duty of care questions arise in relation to a wide range of different kinds of harm, different kinds of risk-creating conduct and different kinds of relationships, the factors to be taken into

---

[19]   See, eg, *Tame v New South Wales; Annetts v Australian Stations Pty Ltd* [2002] HCA 35, (2002) 211 CLR 317, [14] (Gleeson CJ) and *King v Philcox* [2015] HCA 19, (2015) 89 ALJR 582, [89] and [92] (Nettle J).

[20]   A Robertson, 'On the Function of the Law of Negligence' (2013) 33 *OJLS* 31; See *Toh Siew Kee v Ho Ah Lam Ferrocement (Pte) Ltd* [2013] 3 SLR 284, [87] (VK Rajah JA).

[21]   See Robertson, above n 20, 47–48

[22]   *Sutherland Shire Council v Heyman* (1985) 157 CLR 424, 497.

[23]   *Jaensch v Coffee* (1984) 155 CLR 549, 585.

[24]   ibid, quoting *HC Sleigh Ltd v South Australia* (1977) 136 CLR 475, 514 (Jacobs J).

[25]   ibid 585. See also *Hedley Byrne & Co Ltd v Heller & Partners Ltd* [1964] AC 465 (HL), 524 (Lord Devlin); *Hargrave v Goldman* (1963) 110 CLR 40, 65 (Windeyer J); *Burnie Port Authority v General Jones Pty Ltd* (1994) 179 CLR 520, 543 (Mason CJ, Deane, Dawson, Toohey and Gaudron JJ).

[26]   See Vines, above n 4, 46.

account in determining whether a person in the defendant's position ought to be mindful of the interests of someone on the plaintiff's position necessarily vary from case to case.

Whether a person in the defendant's position ought to be mindful of a particular interest of a person in the plaintiff's position depends on the following factors in addition to the closeness and directness of the effect of the first person's conduct on the second. First, it depends on the reasonable foreseeability of the kind of harm in question. Where a person in the defendant's position could not reasonably foresee the risk of harm to the plaintiff it cannot be said that he or she 'ought' to have the plaintiff in contemplation.[27] The foreseeability requirement is therefore an essential element of the 'ought' question. Secondly, the 'ought' question depends on the nature of the protected interest in question (ie freedom from bodily harm, property damage, psychiatric injury or pure economic loss). It may be said that greater attention must be paid to the avoidance of bodily or psychiatric injury than property damage, and that greater attention must be paid to avoiding property damage than pure economic loss, and this may be justified on the basis of perceptions of public sentiment as to the relative importance of the interests in question.[28] Thirdly, it depends on the court's assessment of the proper scope and limits of the defendant's autonomy, and the extent to which a person in the plaintiff's position can reasonably be expected to protect himself or herself from the harm in question. This is of course closely tied up with proximity: the less direct the effect of the defendant's conduct on the plaintiff, the more likely the defendant's freedom of action will be protected. It also depends, however, on whether the defendant may be said to be acting in pursuit of his or her own legitimate interests, even where his or her conduct has quite a direct effect on the plaintiff.[29] Fourthly, it is necessary to consider whether the posited duty would be inconsistent with the contractual matrix in which the parties interacted.[30] Fifthly, it depends on whether imposing a duty would be unreasonably burdensome for a person in the defendant's position, in a way that cannot be taken into account through the standard of care (ie whether it would be unreasonably burdensome to impose any duty at all).[31] Sixthly, it depends on whether the posited duty would conflict with a duty owed by the defendant to another party.[32]

It is therefore clear that whether a person 'ought' as a matter of interpersonal responsibility to be mindful of the interests of another does not depend always or entirely on how closely and directly his or her conduct affects another or others. This necessarily affects the place of proximity within the broader duty inquiry. The proximity inquiry could be reformulated in this light so that A is considered to be in a relationship of sufficient proximity with B if a person in B's position is so closely and directly affected by the actions of a person in A's position that, taking all other relevant factors into account, A ought to have the relevant interest of B in contemplation. But this is somewhat unwieldy and artificial given that closeness and directness may not be the decisive factor. It would therefore be better to

---

[27] See D Owen, 'Figuring Foreseeability' (2009) 44 *Wake Forest Law Review* 1277.

[28] See, eg, *Brookfield Multiplex Ltd v Owners—Strata Plan No 61288* [2014] HCA 36, (2014) 88 AJLR 911, [121]–[123] (Crennan, Bell and Keane JJ) for discussion of 'the crucial distinction between physical injury and economic loss' which means that the common law protects the former even in circumstances where it does not protect the latter.

[29] See A Robertson, 'Policy-based Reasoning in Duty of Care Cases' (2013) 33 *Legal Studies* 119, 127.

[30] See A Robertson, 'Justice, Community Welfare and the Duty of Care' (2011) 127 LQR 370.

[31] ibid 383–84.

[32] ibid 380–83; Robertson, above n 29, 127–28.

understand proximity not as a separate element in itself, but rather as one of several factors to be taken into account in determining whether a person in the defendant's position ought, as a matter of interpersonal responsibility, to have had a person in the plaintiff's position in contemplation. It may be the most important of those factors, but can neither incorporate the other factors nor obviate the need to consider them.

Proximity and Community Welfare

The concept of proximity must also be understood within the broader context of the duty of care inquiry as a whole.[33] Whether a duty of care should be recognised in a given situation depends on three questions: first, whether it would be just as between those who would owe the duty and those to whom it would be owed to recognise the duty (the interpersonal responsibility or justice question); secondly, whether it would be workable to recognise a duty of care in the circumstances in question;[34] and, thirdly, whether the interests of the broader community require that the duty not be recognised (the community welfare question). Proximity forms the core of the interpersonal responsibility or justice question. Whether it is just that one person should be expected to be mindful of another person's interests when engaging in particular activity depends primarily, but not exclusively, on how closely and directly the activity affects that other person. As we will see, the proximity inquiry cannot involve any consideration of the community welfare question, which must be considered at a separate stage of the duty inquiry. A framework for assessing duty can either establish a structured relationship between interpersonal justice and community welfare, as the two-stage framework applied in Canada, Singapore and New Zealand clearly does,[35] or can leave the mediation between considerations of justice and community welfare to be determined by the judge in each case.[36]

II. Proximity in the Common Law Mainstream

England

Although it has been criticised in English cases,[37] the concept of proximity remains an integral component of the standard framework for assessing duty of care questions in cases

---

[33] See Robertson, above n 30; A Phang, CL Saw and G Chang, 'Of Precedent, Theory and Practice—The Case for a Return to Anns' [2006] *Singapore Journal of Legal Studies* 1.

[34] Some fundamentally important considerations, such as whether the claim is justiciable and whether recognition of a duty would create inconsistency, incoherence or incongruity in the law, are concerned with workability rather than interpersonal justice or community welfare.

[35] See *Cooper v Hobart* 2001 SCC 79, [2001] 3 SCR 537; *Fullowka v Pinkerton's of Canada Ltd* 2010 SCC 5, [2010] 1 SCR 132, [18]; *Spandeck Engineering (S) Pte Ltd v Defence Science and Technology Agency* [2007] SGCA 37, [2007] 4 SLR(R) 100; *See Toh Siew Kee v Ho Ah Lam Ferrocement (Pte) Ltd* [2013] SGCA 29, [2013] SGCA 29; *Anwar Patrick Adrian v Ng Chong & Hue LLC* [2014] SGCA 34, [2014] 3 SLR 761; *North Shore City Council v Attorney-General* [2012] NZSC 49, [2012] 3 NZLR 341, and section II below.

[36] See Robertson, above n 20, 35–37 and Robertson, above n 30.

[37] See, eg, *Stovin v Wise* [1996] 923, 932 (Lord Nicholls of Birkenhead); *Alcock v Chief Constable of South Yorkshire Police* [1992] 1 AC 310, 411 (Lord Oliver of Aylmerton).

not involving assumptions of responsibility. As observed most recently by Lord Toulson JSC in *Michael v Chief Constable of South Wales Police*,[38] the framework articulated by Lord Bridge in *Caparo Industries plc v Dickman* has come to be regarded as a blueprint for deciding cases in English law, even though Lord Bridge took pains to show that he did not intend it as such. The *Caparo* framework requires, as necessary ingredients of a duty of care, foreseeability of damage, a relationship of proximity and a situation in which it is fair, just and reasonable for the law to impose a duty.[39] The House of Lords and Supreme Court have tended not to apply the *Caparo* framework, but instead have focused on the particular issues presented by individual cases. After being somewhat neglected in the House of Lords in the 1990s and early 2000s, the concept of proximity has become much more prominent in the last ten years.[40] Proximity featured prominently in the reasoning in *D v East Berkshire Community Health NHS Trust*[41] and *Mitchell v Glasgow City Council*.[42] The crux of the majority decision in *Michael v Chief Constable of South Wales Police* that police do not owe duties of care to potential victims of crime was the statement of Toulson JSC that

> the duty of the police for the preservation of the peace is owed to members of the public at large, and does not involve the kind of close or special relationship ('proximity' or 'neighbourhood') necessary for the imposition of a private law duty of care.[43]

The application of the proximity principle through the factors discussed in the previous section of this chapter is nicely illustrated by the decision of the House of Lords in *Sutradhar v Natural Environmental Research Council*, which was based squarely on insufficient proximity.[44] The issue in that case was whether the British Geological Survey (BGS), in preparing and issuing a report on the hydrochemistry of newly created irrigation wells in Bangladesh, owed a duty either not to cause or to prevent physical injury to people who consumed water from similar wells constructed by international organisations at around the same time to provide drinking water in that country. The report was funded by the British Overseas Development Agency and was undertaken as part of a broader project designed to increase food production in Bangladesh. The BGS did not test for or report on the presence of arsenic. It was alleged that this gave local health authorities the impression that water from irrigation wells, and the similar drinking-water wells, was safe, and inhibited local health authorities from testing the water and preventing the mass poisoning that occurred. The House of Lords upheld a decision granting summary judgment to the defendant.[45] Lord Hoffmann held that '[t]here must be proximity in the sense of a measure of control over and responsibility for the potentially dangerous situation'.[46] The source of danger here was the supply of drinking water in Bangladesh and the BGS had no control

---

[38] *Michael v Chief Constable of South Wales Police* [2015] UKSC 2, [2015] 2 WLR 343, [106].

[39] *Caparo Industries plc v Dickman* [1990] 2 AC 605.

[40] J Hartshorne 'Confusion, Contradiction and Chaos within the House of Lords post Caparo v Dickman' (2008) 16 *Tort Law Review* 8, 12–13.

[41] *D v East Berkshire Community Health NHS Trust* [2005] UKHL 23, [2005] 2 AC 373.

[42] *Mitchell v Glasgow City Council* [2009] UKHL 11, [2009] 1 AC 874.

[43] *Michael v Chief Constable of South Wales Police* [2015] UKSC 2, [2015] 2 WLR 343, [120] (Lord Toulson JSC, with whom Lord Neuberger of Abbotsberry PSC, Lord Mance, Lord Reed and Lord Hodge JJSC agreed).

[44] *Sutradhar v Natural Environmental Research Council* [2006] UKHL 33, [2006] 4 All ER 490.

[45] ibid. Lord Walker of Gestingthorpe agreed with Lord Hoffmann, while Lord Nicholls of Birkenhead and Lord Mance agreed with both Lord Hoffmann and Lord Brown.

[46] ibid [38].

over or responsibility for that supply.[47] Lord Brown held that 'the essential touchstones of proximity are missing'.[48] Lord Brown compared the facts of the present case with those of the authorities relied upon and found that here 'there is nothing like the *directness and immediacy between the defendant's role in events and the claimant's injuries* which characterise each of those cases'.[49] The claimants were not so closely and directly affected by the defendant's actions that the defendant ought to have had them in contemplation because the defendant did not create the immediate source of danger and exercised no real control over it. The mechanism by which the defendant's conduct was said to affect the claimants was indirect, and depended on decisions and actions taken by other institutions.

Canada

The Canadian courts at all levels almost invariably determine duty of care questions by reference to a two-stage test developed from *Anns v Merton London Borough Council*.[50] At the first stage, a prima facie duty of care is established if the requirements of reasonable foreseeability and proximity are satisfied. At the second stage, the court considers whether policy considerations going beyond the relationship between the parties negate the prima facie duty of care.[51] Proximity here is given its classical meaning: it is necessary that the plaintiff is so closely and directly affected by the plaintiff's actions that the defendant ought to have the plaintiff in contemplation in conducting his or her affairs.[52] Insufficient proximity has provided the basis for the denial of duties of care in recent decisions of the Supreme Court of Canada,[53] and the proximity requirement has been closely scrutinised in cases in which duties have been upheld.[54] Proximity is understood in Canadian law not only as the core element of the duty inquiry, but also as the foundation of the law of negligence, as the court made clear in *Childs v Desormeaux*:

> Legal neighbourhood is 'restricted' to 'persons who are so closely and directly affected by my act that I ought reasonably to have them in contemplation as being so affected when I am directing my mind to the acts or omissions which are called in question.' This concept, sometimes referred to as proximity, remains the foundation of the modern law of negligence.[55]

Singapore

In *Spandeck Engineering (S) Pte Ltd v Defence Science & Technology Agency* the Singapore Court of Appeal undertook a major review of the method by which duty of care questions

---

[47] ibid.

[48] ibid [48].

[49] ibid [47] (emphasis added).

[50] *Anns v Merton London Borough Council* [1978] AC 728.

[51] *Cooper v Hobart* 2001 SCC 79, [2001] 3 SCR 537.

[52] ibid [32]–[36] (McLachlin CJ and Major J), quoting *Donoghue v Stevenson* [1932] AC 562, 580–81 and *Hercules Managements Ltd v Ernst & Young* [1997] 2 SCR 165, [24] (La Forest J).

[53] *Childs v Desormeaux* 2006 SCC 18, [2006] 1 SCR 643, [47] (McLachlin CJ for the court); *Alberta v Elder Advocates of Alberta Society* 2011 SCC 24, [2011] 2 SCR 261, [73] (McLachlin CJ for the court).

[54] *Fullowka v Pinkerton's of Canada Ltd* 2010 SCC 5, [2010] 1 SCR 132, [25]–[55] (Cromwell J for the court).

[55] *Childs v Desormeaux* 2006 SCC 18, [2006] 1 SCR 643, [10] (McLachlin CJ for the court), citing *Donoghue v Stevenson* [1932] AC 562, 580 (Lord Atkin).

were to be answered in Singaporean law.[56] The outcome of that review was that a two-stage approach very similar to that followed in Canada is to be applied to determine duty of care questions in negligence cases of all kinds in Singapore. On the Singaporean approach, reasonable foreseeability is treated as a preliminary threshold requirement. If that preliminary requirement is satisfied, the court at the first stage considers whether there is relationship of proximity, which establishes a prima facie duty. At the second stage the court considers whether that prima facie duty should be negated on the basis of policy considerations. Proximity therefore constitutes the heart of the Singaporean approach to duty. In the *Spandeck* case the court justified the retention of the proximity requirement, notwithstanding well-known criticisms of the concept,[57] on the following basis:

> If indeed the 'proximity' concept is merely a label or an artificial exercise in judicial creativity, then one must ask why the concept is still resorted to or utilised in the various tests. Its very presence suggests that it has some substantive content that is capable of being expressed in terms of legal principles. Rather than denouncing it as a mere 'label', the courts should strive to infuse some meaning into it, if only so that lawyers who advise litigants and even law teachers can make some sense of the judicial formulations.[58]

The court in *Spandeck* emphasised the importance of differentiating policy considerations from the first-stage requirement of proximity, although it did not make entirely clear the basis on which that distinction was to be drawn. The court said that 'value judgments which reflect differential weighing and balancing of competing moral claims and broad social welfare goals', if pertinent and relevant, were better addressed as policy considerations rather than subsumed within proximity so that the reasons could be openly expressed.[59] The court did note, however, that proximity imports 'the whole concept of the necessary relationship between the claimant and the defendant described by Lord Atkin in *Donoghue v Stevenson*'.[60] More recently, VK Rajah JA has confirmed that the proximity stage of the analysis is concerned with questions of interpersonal justice,[61] and this is reflected in the Court of Appeal's extensive analysis of proximity in *Anwar v Ng Chong & Hue LLC*.[62]

New Zealand

The New Zealand courts, like those in Canada and Singapore, follow a refined version of the *Anns* approach to determining novel duty of care questions. In *North Shore City Council v Attorney-General* Blanchard, McGrath and William Young JJ (with the concurrence of Tipping J) reviewed that approach in light of criticisms of it in the High Court of Australia

---

[56] *Spandeck Engineering (S) Pte Ltd v Defence Science and Technology Agency* [2007] SGCA 37, [2007] 4 SLR(R) 100.

[57] Such as that of Lord Oliver of Aylmerton in *Alcock v Chief Constable of South Yorkshire Police* [1992] 1 AC 310, 411: '[I]n the end, it has to be accepted that the concept of "proximity" is an artificial one which depends more upon the court's perception of what is the reasonable area for the imposition of liability than upon any logical process of analogical deduction.'

[58] *Spandeck Engineering (S) Pte Ltd v Defence Science and Technology Agency* [2007] SGCA 37, [2007] 4 SLR(R) 100, [80] (Chan Sek Keong CJ for the court).

[59] ibid [85].

[60] ibid [79].

[61] See *Toh Siew Kee v Ho Ah Lam Ferrocement (Pte) Ltd* [2013] SGCA 29, [2013] 3 SLR 284, [87]–[90].

[62] *Anwar v Ng Chong & Hue LLC* [2014] SGCA 34, [2014] 3 SLR 761.

and elsewhere.[63] Their Honours accepted that there was some force in the criticisms (eg of the extent to which proximity provides practical guidance), but reaffirmed the two-stage approach as providing the most helpful mechanism for analysis.[64] At the first stage, foreseeability provides 'at best' a mechanism for screening out claims that must obviously fail.[65] Attention then turns to proximity, which is 'usually the hardest part of the inquiry' and 'enables the balancing of the moral claims of the parties: the plaintiff's claim for compensation for avoidable harm and the defendant's claim to be protected from an undue burden of legal responsibility'.[66] At the final stage of the inquiry the court considers whether, notwithstanding foreseeability and proximity, it should find that no duty of care exists because of factors external to the relationship between the parties. This is clearly a limited exclusionary rule, as it is in Canada and Singapore:

> At this last stage of the inquiry the court looks beyond the parties and assesses any wider effects of its decision on society and on the law generally. Issues such as the capacity of each party to insure against the liability, the likely behaviour of other potential defendants in reaction to the decision, and the consistency of imposition of liability with the legal system more generally may arise.[67]

Thus in New Zealand, as in Singapore and Canada, the concept of proximity has recently been reaffirmed as an integral element of the duty of care inquiry and undoubtedly constitutes the substantive core of duty analysis. In English law proximity is an integral element of the most commonly followed approach to the determination of duty of care questions, and is decisive in some cases at the highest level.

III. Proximity in Australian Law

Criticism and Abandonment

The distrust of the concept of proximity that led to its banishment from the Australian judicial lexicon is at least partly attributable the development and application of an expanded notion of proximity which operated as a general determinant of the duty of care question. The idea that proximity provides an all-encompassing basis for determining whether a duty of care is owed perhaps reached its high point in *Gala v Preston*.[68] In that case Mason CJ, Deane, Gaudron and McHugh JJ concluded that the driver of a vehicle was not in the relationship of proximity with a passenger with whom he was engaged in a dangerous joint illegal enterprise, and held that the requirement of proximity encompasses 'policy considerations' and other factors such as 'the appropriateness and feasibility of seeking to define the concept of a relevant duty of care'.[69] There is, however, considerable force in the criticism of Brennan J that the proximity requirement as conventionally understood was clearly

---

[63] *North Shore City Council v Attorney-General* [2012] NZSC 49, [2012] 3 NZLR 341, [147]–[161].
[64] ibid [147]–[155].
[65] ibid [157].
[66] ibid [158]–[159].
[67] ibid [160].
[68] *Gala v Preston* (1991) 172 CLR 243.
[69] ibid 253. See also ibid 260 (Brennan J).

satisfied on those facts,[70] that the reasons for denying the duty lay elsewhere, and that no purpose was served by seeking to shoehorn those reasons into the concept of proximity.[71] If the proximity inquiry is made to accommodate broader considerations of policy, then it simply becomes a question whether, all things considered, a duty should be recognised.[72] The concept of proximity is then, as Brennan J said, 'surplus to the reasoning'.[73]

Brennan J's powerful criticism in *Gala v Preston* of the expanded notion of proximity was followed by a strong critique of the narrower, more orthodox version of the concept in *San Sebastian Pty Ltd v Minister*.[74] Brennan J said in *San Sebastian* that whether a duty of care exists in a particular case must be determined by 'legal rules', and a legal rule is 'a rule that prescribes an issue of fact on which a legal consequence depends'.[75] Because of its variable content, the notion of proximity cannot be treated as a particular proposition of law that can be applied in the resolution of a particular case.[76] While some legal rules import community standards such as reasonableness, they nevertheless require the determination of issues of fact.[77]

> But proximity is not a community standard by reference to which issues of fact can be determined, nor is it a particular proposition of law excluding a right to relief otherwise open on the facts of a case. If proximity were misunderstood as being a particular proposition of law expressing a touchstone for resolving a particular case, the judge would be required to define its legal content according to some notion of whether it was appropriate to impose a duty of care in that case. A rule without specific content confers a discretion. The discretion might be described as a judicial discretion and the discretion might be reviewed on appeal but such a rule nonetheless confers a discretion. Damages in tort are not granted or refused in the exercise of a judicial discretion.[78]

Brennan J developed this line of criticism further in *Bryan v Maloney*, where he expressed concern that if proximity is treated as a criterion of legal liability without an a priori definition of its elements, then duty questions arising in cases out of the mainstream can only be determined by courts.[79] Brennan J found it unacceptable that proximity might involve 'value judgments on matters of policy and degree' because 'the law of negligence should be capable of application in solicitors' offices'.[80] A notion of proximity which involved no more than the evaluation of the circumstances favouring or not favouring recovery 'would be a juristic black hole into which particular criteria and rules would collapse and from which no illumination of principle would emerge'.[81]

The move away from proximity gathered pace in *Hill v Van Erp*.[82] In that case Dawson J abandoned the idea to which he had subscribed in *Burnie Port Authority v General*

---

[70] ibid 261 (Brennan J): 'Here the parties are driver and passenger in a car. There are few more familiar examples of a proximate relationship.'

[71] ibid 259–61.

[72] Robertson, above n 30, 377–79.

[73] *Gala v Preston* (1991) 172 CLR 243, 261 (Brennan J).

[74] *San Sebastian Pty Ltd v Minister* (1986) 162 CLR 340, 367–69.

[75] ibid 367–68.

[76] ibid 368.

[77] ibid. Brennan J also accepted the relevance of 'contemporary community standards' in the determination of duty of care questions in *Hawkins v Clayton* (1988) 164 CLR 539, 556.

[78] ibid.

[79] *Bryan v Maloney* (1995) 182 CLR 609, 653.

[80] ibid.

[81] ibid 655.

[82] *Hill v Van Erp* (1997) 188 CLR 159.

Jones that proximity was the '"general conceptual determinant and the unifying theme" of the categories of case in which a duty of care arises'.[83] Dawson J accepted that proximity remains useful as a reminder that something more than foreseeability may be required, but rejected the idea that it describes the process of reasoning that is required or identifies an element that is common to all categories of case in which duties are recognised.[84] Toohey J adhered to the idea that proximity is useful as a general conception in opening up new categories, but noted that it does not identify a common underlying element with any precision.[85] Like Dawson J, Toohey J maintained that proximity analysis involved the drawing of analogies and the examination of policy considerations in order to determine whether new categories should be recognised or existing categories expanded.[86] McHugh J had joined the plurality judgment in *Gala v Preston* in spite of having written a paper before his appointment to the High Court in which he rejected proximity as a criterion for determining whether a duty is owed.[87] The problem presented in *Hill v Van Erp* 'reinforced' his 'scepticism as to whether the concept of proximity gives any real guidance in determining the existence of a duty of care in difficult and novel cases'.[88] Gummow JJ preferred to explain his reasoning on the duty question without reference to the concept of proximity which, he said, may provide a conceptual umbrella or unifying theme, but 'used as a legal norm, has the uncertainties and perils of a category of indeterminate reference, used with shifting meanings to mask no more than policy preferences'.[89]

In *Sullivan v Moody* a unanimous High Court held that to ask whether there was a relationship of proximity between the parties in that case provides no assistance in answering the question whether a duty of care is owed.[90] 'That is so whether it is expressed as the ultimate test of a duty of care, or as one of a number of stages in an approach towards a conclusion on that issue.' Their Honours accepted that the concept expresses the nature of what is at issue and gives focus to the inquiry, but does little to explain the reasoning process.[91] In *Imbree v McNeilly* Gummow, Hayne and Kiefel JJ noted that the High Court had 'rejected proximity as a satisfactory tool for determining whether a defendant owed a duty of care' and had denied 'the utility of that concept as a determinant of duty'.[92]

The place of proximity in Australian law in light of these judgments and others along similar lines arose for consideration in *Caltex Refineries Pty Ltd v Stavar*.[93] One of the issues for the New South Wales Court of Appeal in that case was whether the President of the Dust and Diseases Tribunal had erred in using proximity to assess whether the defendant owed

---

[83] ibid 177, quoting a statement by Deane J in *Stevens v Brodribb Sawmilling Co Pty Ltd* (1986) 60 CLR 16, 53, which had been adopted in *Burnie Port Authority v General Jones Pty Ltd* (1994) 179 CLR 520, 543 (Mason CJ, Deane, Dawson Toohey and Gaudron JJ).

[84] *Hill v Van Erp* (1997) 188 CLR 159 177–78.

[85] ibid 189–90.

[86] ibid.

[87] MH McHugh, 'Neighbourhood, Proximity and Reliance' in PD Finn (ed), *Essays on Torts* (1989) 5–42.

[88] *Hill v Van Erp* (1997) 188 CLR 159, 210.

[89] ibid 238, citing McHugh, above n 87.

[90] *Sullivan v Moody* (2001) 207 CLR 562, [48] (Gleeson CJ, Gaudron, McHugh, Hayne and Callinan JJ).

[91] ibid. More recently, in *King v Philcox* [2015] HCA 19, (2015) 89 ALJR 582, [80] Nettle J quite properly treated the fact that it 'gives focus to the inquiry' as a significant virtue of proximity and a reason to utilise it.

[92] *Imbree v McNeilly* (2008) 236 CLR 510, [41], [46].

[93] *Caltex Refineries Pty Ltd v Stavar* [2009] NSWCA 258, (2009) 75 NSWLR 649.

a duty of care to the plaintiff, who had contracted malignant mesothelioma by inhaling asbestos dust and fibres carried home from the defendant's oil refinery on her husband's clothing. In an extempore judgment the President had made reference to the concept of proximity discussed in the plurality judgment in *Gala v Preston*. The Court of Appeal found that this did not constitute an error. Allsop P noted that the High Court has rejected proximity as a general determinant, but held that proximity still falls within the factual analysis the court was required to undertake 'as part of the evaluative judgment of the appropriateness of legal imputation of responsibility'.[94] The President had followed that approach so there was no error in his reasoning. Similarly, Basten J held that the Australian courts have departed from the language of proximity not because the concept is erroneous, but because it is unhelpful.[95] There was no error in making reference to proximity, although there might have been an error if the President had treated proximity as a general determinant of the duty of care.[96] The subsequent judgment in *Miller v Miller* of French CJ, Gummow, Hayne, Crennan, Kiefel and Bell JJ exhibited a greater hostility to proximity than was recognised in *Caltex Refineries Pty Ltd v Stavar*. As noted above, their Honours declared that 'the demise of proximity as a useful informing principle in this area is now complete'. Proximity 'has been discarded from the Australian judicial lexicon' because 'it has been found not to be useful'.[97] Their Honours said:

> It is not useful because it neither states, nor points to, any relevant principle that assists in the resolution of disputed questions about the existence of a duty of care, beyond indicating that something more than foreseeability of damage is necessary.[98]

The Endurance of Proximity

While proximity is said to have become 'a metaphor under threat'[99] from the mid-1990s onwards, and to have been 'already dispatched' by 1999,[100] the concept has continued to play a role from the mid-1990s up to the present day in deciding duty of care issues concerned with pure economic loss, indirectly inflicted physical injury and psychiatric injury. These cases show that proximity as traditionally understood can, in at least some fact situations, be applied to determine the interpersonal responsibility element of the duty of care inquiry in Australian law. Proximity provided a useful tool of analysis in all of these cases because they were all cases in which basic questions of interpersonal responsibility were in issue. In each case it was necessary to determine whether it was fair to expect a person in the position of the defendant to be mindful of a particular interest of a person in the position of the plaintiff.

---

[94] ibid [106].
[95] ibid [190].
[96] ibid [191].
[97] *Miller v Miller* [2011] HCA 9, (2011) 242 CLR 446, [60].
[98] ibid.
[99] *Brookfield Multiplex Ltd v Owners—Strata Plan No 61288* [2014] HCA 36, (2014) 88 AJLR 911, [21] (French CJ).
[100] ibid, citing *Perre v Apand Pty Ltd* [1999] HCA 36, (1999) 198 CLR 180, [74] (McHugh J).

Pure Economic Loss

Hill v Van Erp

The fact that four justices of the High Court in *Hill v Van Erp* adopted the view that proximity has limited utility has been seen as a decisive step in the demise of proximity, 'at least as a universal identifier of the existence of a duty of care'.[101] The strongest criticism, and that which has since been most quoted, was that of Gummow J, who said that he eschewed use of the term proximity in explaining the path of his reasoning.[102] The issue was whether a solicitor retained to prepare a will owed a duty, in the course of its preparation and execution, to take reasonable care not to cause economic loss to an intended beneficiary. The solicitor asked the husband of the intended beneficiary to attest the execution of the will, causing the intended dispositions to fail. Although Gummow J preferred to explain his reasons without reference to proximity, those reasons read like orthodox proximity analysis. The 'complex of factors' in addition to foreseeability of harm that combined to justify a duty of care included the fact that the solicitor was retained for the purpose of enhancing the economic position of the beneficiary, the solicitor's control over the realisation of the testamentary intentions of the testatrix, 'and the closeness of the connection' between the solicitor's actions and the direct legal effect of those actions on the plaintiff through failure of the gifts.[103] The only departure from orthodox proximity reasoning was Gummow J's addition of community welfare reasons for recognising a duty:

> There is also the public interest in the promotion of professional competence and the avoidance of disappointment of the wishes and expectations of testators and beneficiaries by negligent actions of solicitors.[104]

Gummow J's addition of a consideration of public interest weighing in favour of duty may be seen by some as desirable. One of the criticisms of proximity is that it operates as a mask for policy considerations and that it is better for those policy considerations that are taken into account to be articulated openly rather than hidden in amorphous legal concepts such as proximity.[105] On the other hand the structured, sequential approaches to analysing the duty question followed elsewhere in the common law world accord a particular place in the inquiry to considerations of public interest. A structured approach does not allow considerations of public interest to be added as makeweight considerations in favour of recognising a duty of care. Under the frameworks adopted in England, Canada, New Zealand and Singapore, considerations of public interest weighing in favour of duty are taken into account at a stage of the inquiry that is separate from the proximity analysis. They become relevant only if there are considerations of public interest weighing against the recognition of duty which necessitate a balancing process.[106] If considerations of justice require the

---

[101] *Pyrenees Shire Council v Day* [1998] HCA 3, (1998) 192 CLR 330, 414 (Kirby J).

[102] *Hill v Van Erp* (1997) 188 CLR 159, 238.

[103] ibid 234.

[104] ibid, citing *Gartside v Sheffield, Young & Ellis* [1983] NZLR 37, 51.

[105] J Fleming, *Law of Torts*, 7th edn (Sydney, Law Book Company, 1987), approved by McHugh, above n 87, 13, and Gummow J in *Hill v Van Erp* (1997) 188 CLR 159, 238.

[106] See Robertson, above n 30, 394.

recognition of a duty of care, and there are no community welfare reasons to deny a duty, then community welfare reasons in favour of recognising a duty are simply irrelevant.

Perre v Apand Pty Ltd

Perre v Apand Pty Ltd[107] was another pure economic loss case in which the concept of proximity was held to be indeterminate, devoid of content and unhelpful.[108] The issue in that case was whether a potato crisp manufacturer supplying experimental potato seeds to growers in South Australia owed a duty not to cause economic loss to nearby growers and associated entities through the supply of diseased seed which disqualified nearby growers from selling their crops in the lucrative Western Australian market. The supplier knew that Western Australia was a lucrative market for South Australian growers and that regulations prohibited the importation of potatoes grown within 20 km of a known outbreak of the disease within the last five years. The court found that the duty was owed, and the notion of proximity provides a good explanation as to why that was so. On one hand, the interest in question was economic and the effect of the defendant's conduct on the plaintiffs was indirect, taking effect through regulations in another state which affected the capacity of the plaintiffs to sell their products in that state. On the other hand, the defendant created the source of harm in pursuit of its own profit, knowing that it might affect the plaintiffs in the way that it did. The defendant had a very significant measure of control over the risk, while the plaintiffs had no means of knowing that the risk existed and no means of protecting themselves against it. Although the case is sometimes regarded as a step in the demise of proximity, the notion of proximity was recognised in different ways in different judgments as framing the central issue.

McHugh J devoted a section of his judgment to '[t]he demise of proximity as a unifying theme', and concluded that the reason 'proximity can not be the touchstone of a duty of care is that it "is a category of indeterminate reference par excellence"'.[109] McHugh J noted that since 'the fall of proximity' no authoritative statement has been made as to the correct approach to the determination of duty of care questions and '[p]erhaps none is possible'.[110] After concluding that the incremental approach was the most satisfactory, McHugh J went on to consider the reasons for imposing or denying a duty of care:

> In determining whether the defendant owed a duty of care to the plaintiff, the ultimate issue is always whether the defendant in pursuing a course of conduct that caused injury to the plaintiff, or failing to pursue a course of conduct which would have prevented injury to the plaintiff, *should have had* the interest or interests of the plaintiff in contemplation before he or she pursued or failed to pursue that course of conduct.[111]

Earlier in his judgment McHugh J had recognised that 'in some cases judges cannot escape applying notions of "current ideas of justice or morality" in determining the duty question' but said they 'should be invoked only as criteria of last resort when more concrete reasons, rules or principles fail to provide a persuasive answer to the problem'.[112]

---

[107] *Perre v Apand Pty Ltd* [1999] HCA 36, (1999) 198 CLR 180.
[108] ibid [9] (Gleeson CJ), [27] (Gaudron J), [70]–[78] (McHugh J) and [330] (Hayne J).
[109] ibid [70]–[78].
[110] ibid [76].
[111] ibid [100], citing *Donoghue v Stevenson* [1932] AC 562, 580 (Lord Atkin).
[112] ibid [82].

McHugh J thus embraced all but the 'closeness' aspect of Lord Atkin's proximity inquiry. The closeness aspect was, however, emphasised by Gummow J in his judgment in *Perre v Apand*. Gummow J adopted the approach articulated and followed by Stephen J in *Caltex Oil Australia Pty Ltd v The Dredge 'Willemstad'*.[113] Stephen J had 'isolated a number of "salient features" which combined to constitute *a sufficiently close relationship* to give rise to a duty of care owed to Caltex for breach of which it might recover its purely economic loss'.[114] In fact for Stephen J the factors demonstrated 'a close degree of proximity' between the defendant's conduct and the economic loss suffered, which Stephen J regarded as necessary 'to entitle the plaintiff to recover its foreseeable economic loss'.[115] Gummow J noted that a similar approach justified the recognition of a duty of care in *Hill v Van Erp* and the denial of a duty of care in *Esanda Finance Corporation Ltd v Peat Marwick Hungerfords*,[116] where:

> The pleading was bad because it did not allege facts adequate to carry the auditors into a sufficiently close relationship with the creditors or financiers of the company so as to found the element necessary to constitute a duty of care to the appellant.[117]

The unnamed 'element' referred to by Gummow J is clearly proximity. Gummow J also approved the statement by Stephen J in *Caltex v Willemstad* that guidance in determining the requisite degree of proximity can be derived from the broad principle that underlies the law of negligence. The guiding principle is that identified by Lord Atkin, namely that liability for negligence is 'no doubt based on a general public sentiment of moral wrongdoing for which the offender must pay'.[118] Stephen J said:

> Such a sentiment will only be present when there exists a degree of proximity between the tortious act and the injury such that the community will recognize the tortfeasor as being in justice obliged to make good his moral wrongdoing by compensating the victims of his negligence.[119]

Lord Atkin's notion of 'general public sentiment' was also recognised by Kirby J in *Perre v Apand*. Kirby J said that the boundary of liability for negligence is set by the question whether the alleged tortfeasor ought to be under an obligation to take care to protect the plaintiff against the risk that ensured. 'Inescapably, the answer to that question will reflect "a general public sentiment of moral wrongdoing for which the offender must pay".'[120]

Physical Injury

It is said that a person who is close enough to do physical damage to the person or property of another is close enough to be held liable for the consequences.[121] The existence of a duty

---

[113] *Caltex Oil Australia Pty Ltd v The Dredge 'Willemstad'* (1976) 136 CLR 529, 576–77.

[114] *Perre v Apand Pty Ltd* [1999] HCA 36, (1999) 198 CLR 180, [201]. An identical form of words appeared in *Woolcock Street Investments Pty Ltd v CDG Pty Ltd* [2004] HCA 16; (2004) 216 CLR 515, [22] (Gleeson CJ, Gummow, Hayne and Heydon JJ).

[115] *Caltex Oil Australia Pty Ltd v The Dredge 'Willemstad'* (1976) 136 CLR 529, 576–77.

[116] *Esanda Finance Corporation Ltd v Peat Marwick Hungerfords* (1997) 188 CLR 241.

[117] *Perre v Apand Pty Ltd* [1999] HCA 36, (1999) 198 CLR 180, [202].

[118] *Donoghue v Stevenson* [1932] AC 562, 580, quoted in *Caltex Oil (Australia) Pty Ltd v The Dredge 'Willemstad'* (1976) 136 CLR 529, 575 (Stephen J).

[119] *Caltex Oil*, ibid 575.

[120] *Perre v Apand Pty Ltd* [1999] HCA 36, (1999) 198 CLR 180, [232] citing *Jaensch v Coffey* (1984) 155 CLR 549, 607 (Deane J), in turn citing *Donoghue v Stevenson* [1932] AC 562, 580 (Lord Atkin).

[121] *Canadian National Railway Co v Norsk Pacific Steamship Co* [1992] 1 SCR 1021, 1153 (McLachlin J); *Tame v New South Wales; Annetts v Australian Stations Pty Ltd* [2002] HCA 35, (2002) 211 CLR 317, [46] (Gaudron J).

of care is generally only a live issue where the injury is inflicted by an indirect mechanism, whether or not the defendant's involvement can properly be characterised as a mere omission. In such cases the closeness and directness of the effect of the defendant's conduct on the plaintiff will be a telling criterion, as *Sutradhar v Natural Environmental Research Council*[122] and the following cases show.[123]

Agar v Hyde

The issue in *Agar v Hyde*[124] was whether a member of the International Rugby Football Board (IRFB) owed a duty to rugby players to take reasonable care to monitor and alter the laws of the game to prevent injury to those players. While playing rugby the plaintiffs suffered spinal injuries which they claimed were attributable to deficiencies in the laws relating to scrum formation. The laws were later changed to prevent injuries of the kind the plaintiffs suffered. The High Court held that it was not arguable that an individual board member owed a duty of care to every person who played rugby under the laws made by the IRFB. Changes to the laws could not be proposed by individual members, but only by a Member Union or Committee of the Board, and required a 75 per cent majority of votes at a board meeting. Whether the laws promulgated by the IRFB were followed in a particular match was a decision for the association organising it, and depended on decisions made at 'club, regional, state and national level'.[125] The application of the laws in a particular match turned, in significant respects, on the officials controlling the match.[126] The IRFB did not therefore have any legal or practical control over the way the game was played. 'There were too many intervening levels of decision-making between the promulgation by the IRFB of laws of the game and the conduct of the individual matches in which the respondents were injured.'[127] Gaudron, McHugh, Gummow and Hayne JJ held that, when a board member attended a meeting,

> the law of negligence did not require him to conclude that thousands, perhaps hundreds of thousands, of rugby players were so closely and directly affected by his presence as a board member that he ought to consider whether he should propose an amendment to the laws of the game to protect each player from injury. Unless it did, no duty of care to the respondents could arise.[128]

Although that is a slightly circuitous way of putting it, it is clear from this statement that, unless the plaintiff is so closely and directly affected by the defendant's conduct that the defendant ought to consider the risk of injury to the plaintiff, then no duty can arise. Gaudron, McHugh, Gummow and Hayne JJ were therefore saying that without proximity in its traditional formulation there can be no duty of care in Australian law. Gleeson CJ, in a

---

[122] Discussed above, text accompanying nn 44–49.

[123] It is also worth noting that in *Jones v Bartlett* [2000] HCA 56, (2000) 205 CLR 166, Gummow and Hayne JJ returned to Lord Atkin's speech in *Donoghue v Stevenson* in order to justify and delineate a landlord's duty of care to a tenant with respect to the safety of the demised premises. Their honours observed that the basis of a landlord's duty in a residential tenancy is that: 'The relationship between landlord and tenant is so close and direct that the landlord is obliged to take reasonable care that the tenant not suffer injury.'

[124] *Agar v Hyde* [2000] HCA 41, (2000) 201 CLR 552.

[125] ibid [79].

[126] ibid [80].

[127] ibid [81].

[128] ibid [70], citing *Donoghue v Stevenson* [1932] AC 562, 580 (Lord Atkin).

separate judgment, held that it was undeniable that rugby players are 'so closely and directly affected by what the IRFB does that members of the Board ought to have them in contemplation, but neighbourhood in that sense is not the issue in this case'.[129] That seemed to be contradicted by the statement made by Gleeson CJ in the following paragraph that the control exerted by individual board members (who had no power to amend the rules) was remote from the players, extending at most to participation in laying down the conditions of a sporting contest in which people might chose to participate. Gleeson CJ also found that the duty was uncertain in content, would create liability that was 'practically indeterminate' and would create a legal responsibility that would not be in conformity with 'the circumstances of life in this community'.[130] In those circumstances, it is difficult to see how players could be said to be so closely and directly affected by the actions of board members that the board members ought to have the players' physical safety in contemplation, such that a failure to do so would be regarded in the community as wrongdoing for which board members must pay. The conclusion reached by Gleeson CJ seemed to be precisely the opposite of that.

Graham Barclay Oysters Pty Ltd v Ryan

In *Graham Barclay Oysters Pty Ltd v Ryan* the relevant issue was whether the State of New South Wales and the Great Lakes Council owed a duty to take reasonable care to prevent people from contracting illness through the consumption of contaminated oysters produced by farms operating within the State and the Great Lakes Shire.[131] The plaintiffs contracted hepatitis A from eating contaminated oysters grown at Wallis Lake, which was within the Great Lakes Shire. The outbreak occurred after lakes had become contaminated with faecal waste. That waste had come primarily from inadequately treated human effluent entering the lake from land-based sources following a period of heavy rain, but discharge from boats may also have contributed. The High Court held that neither the State nor the Council owed a duty of care to oyster consumers. It is instructive to focus on the reasons that led Gummow and Hayne JJ to find that the Council did not owe such a duty. The crucial factor for Gummow and Hayne JJ was the Council's lack of control over the relevant risk of harm. The element of control is of fundamental importance in determining whether a public authority owes a duty of care because 'a form of control over the relevant risk of harm, which … is remote in a legal and practical sense does not suffice to found a duty of care'.[132]

The Council had wide-ranging powers with respect to the regulation of sewerage systems, which it could exercise for the promotion of public health and environmental protection. It also had wide-ranging powers to conduct testing to identify sources of pollution and to prevent and remove pollution. Gummow and Hayne JJ held that the fact that the Council had power to monitor pollution levels and to intervene to protect the environment was an insufficient foundation for a duty of care to oyster consumers.[133] The Council lacked the requisite degree of control over the risk of harm that eventuated. It had no control over the immediate source of harm, which was the oysters themselves. Its relationship with

[129] ibid [20].
[130] ibid [23].
[131] *Graham Barclay Oysters Pty Ltd v Ryan* [2002] HCA 54, (2002) 211 CLR 540.
[132] ibid [150].
[133] ibid [154]

oyster consumers was indirect, and was mediated by the intervening conduct of the commercial enterprises involved in the oyster-growing industry.[134]

> The conduct of the Council did not 'so closely and directly [affect]' oyster consumers so as to warrant the imposition of a duty of care owed by the former to the latter. There were 'too many intervening levels of decision-making' between the conduct of the Council and the harm suffered by the consumers.[135]

As in *Agar v Hyde*, the reasoning of Gummow and Hayne JJ in *Graham Barclay Oysters v Ryan* with respect to the Council was thus classically proximity-based. The Council's lack of control over the risk of harm meant that its conduct had an insufficiently direct effect on oyster consumers to establish a duty. McHugh J expressed his reasons in the same way. McHugh J held that the Council owed no duty of care to consumers because

> [t]here was simply no relationship between the Council and oyster consumers sufficient to create a duty of care. ... There was no close and direct relationship between oyster consumers and the Council such that it had a duty to take care for the safety of each and every one of them.[136]

McHugh J was, however, reluctant to use the term proximity for the criterion he deployed. He said:

> This Court no longer sees proximity as the criterion of a duty of care. But no duty of care can arise unless the relationship between the parties is one of neighbourhood in Lord Atkin's sense as stated in *Donoghue v Stevenson*. To create a duty, the relationship between the public authority and persons affected by the conduct of the authority must be "so closely and directly affected by [its] act [or omission] that [it] ought reasonably to have them in contemplation as being so affected" when it directs its mind to the relevant conduct in question.[137]

McHugh J's first sentence sits uncomfortably with the remainder of the paragraph. If no duty can arise unless the relationship between the parties is one of neighbourhood in Lord Atkin's sense, and if, in order to create a duty, the persons to whom the duty is said to be owed must be so closely and directly affected by the act or omission of public authority that it ought reasonably to have them in contemplation, then proximity is an essential criterion of a duty of care. The only way to make sense of the passage is to emphasise McHugh J's use of the definite article in the first sentence, and read it as referring to the discredited and rejected idea of proximity as the universal determinant of duty which incorporates all relevant considerations including policy. While proximity is *a* criterion of duty, may be considered an essential criterion and is often the determinative criterion, as it was in this case, it is clearly not the only criterion.

Also pertinent is that McHugh J set out in his judgment a framework for determining whether a public authority owes an affirmative duty of care in a situation not previously recognised as giving rise to a duty.[138] The essence of that framework is that where the elements of foreseeability, control, vulnerability and knowledge of a risk of harm to the plaintiff are present, a duty of care will usually be recognised unless the duty would impose

---

[134]   ibid [153].
[135]   ibid [154], citing *Agar v Hyde* [2002] HCA 54, (2000) 201 CLR 552, [70] and [81]; [2000] HCA 41.
[136]   ibid [99].
[137]   ibid, citing *Donoghue v Stevenson* [1932] AC 562, 580 (Lord Atkin). The alterations to Lord Atkin's text are McHugh J's.
[138]   ibid [84]–[85].

liability with respect to core policy-making or quasi-legislative functions or a supervening policy reason requires the denial of duty. If any of the elements of foreseeability, control, vulnerability or knowledge is absent, or if the duty would impose liability with respect to core policy-making or quasi-legislative functions or a supervening policy reason requires the denial of duty, then there will usually be no duty. This framework is in substance identical to the two-stage framework currently applied in Canada, Singapore and New Zealand based on *Anns v Merton London Borough Council*,[139] under which considerations of justice or interpersonal responsibility set up a prima facie duty of care which may be denied on justiciability or policy grounds.[140] The only difference is that the requirement of proximity is replaced in McHugh J's version of the *Anns* framework by the elements of control, vulnerability and knowledge (actual or imputed) of a risk of a harm to a specific class of persons that included the plaintiff.

Sydney Water Corporation v Turano

Another physical injury case in which proximity played a significant role was *Sydney Water Corporation v Turano*.[141] The question in that case was whether a water authority laying a water main beside a public road owed a duty in carrying out its works to take reasonable care not to cause injury to future road users by undermining the stability of nearby trees.[142] The water main was laid in such a way that it diverted drainage from a nearby culvert, causing water logging of the surrounding soil, which facilitated the development of a pathogen, which entered the root system of a tree, which fell on the plaintiff and her family as they were driving along the road approximately 20 years later. The High Court held, in a single judgment, that Sydney Water's challenge to the duty of care was to 'the reasonableness of the conclusion that Sydney Water should have had in its contemplation, as persons closely and directly affected by its conduct in laying the water main, persons on or near Edmondson Avenue in 2001'.[143] That challenge was successful. French CJ, Gummow, Hayne, Crennan and Bell JJ held that no duty of care was owed, either because injury to the class of persons in question was not reasonably foreseeable or 'because there was not a sufficiently close and direct connection between [the defendant and the plaintiff] for her to be a "neighbour" within Lord Atkin's statement of the principle'.[144]

Psychiatric Injury

Proximity has also operated as the decisive interpersonal question justice in determining whether one person owes another a duty not to cause reasonably foreseeable psychiatric injury.

---

[139] *Anns v Merton London Borough Council* [1978] AC 728.
[140] See the cases cited above n 35, and the discussion in section II of this chapter.
[141] *Sydney Water Corporation v Turano* [2009] HCA 42, (2009) 239 CLR 51.
[142] The level of abstraction at which the duty question should be framed in this case and the scope of the alleged duty were contentious questions but were not clearly resolved: see ibid [44]–[53].
[143] ibid [44].
[144] ibid [53].

Tame v New South Wales

In *Tame v New South Wales; Annetts v Australian Stations Pty Ltd*[145] the High Court was concerned with two cases involving psychiatric injury. In the first a police officer incorrectly recorded that the plaintiff had been found to have a high blood alcohol reading following an accident. The false entry was communicated to the plaintiff's insurer, but the error was promptly corrected and a formal apology issued. In the second case the plaintiffs alleged that they had allowed their 16-year-old son to be employed by the defendant as a jackaroo on the faith of assurances given by the defendant that their son would be closely supervised and well cared for. The plaintiffs claimed to have suffered psychiatric injury when they learned of his disappearance and, months later, of his death in disturbing circumstances as a result of being exposed to danger in the course of his employment.

Before dealing with the two cases Gleeson CJ quoted Lord Atkin's foundational statement on proximity, and reflected that the existence of a duty of care is determined by 'the reasonableness of a requirement that a defendant should have certain persons, and certain interests, in contemplation'.[146] This, he went on to explain, was to be 'judged in the light of current community standards' since 'conceptions of legal responsibility adapt to social conditions and standards'.[147] In the *Tame* case Gleeson CJ found that it was not reasonable to require the police officer to have the plaintiff's mental health in contemplation because he could not reasonably be expected to foresee the risk of harm.[148] In the *Annetts* case the Chief Justice found that there was a relationship between the parties 'of such a nature that it was reasonable to require the respondent to have in contemplation the kind of injury to the applicants that they suffered'.[149] Like Gleeson CJ, Gummow and Kirby JJ did not refer to the closeness and directness of the effect of the defendant's actions on the plaintiff as an aspect of the duty inquiry, but their Honours did accept that the court was concerned with the general public sentiment of wrongdoing for which the defendant must, in justice, pay.[150]

Gaudron J rejected the notion that a duty not to cause psychiatric injury was owed only to those who directly perceive a distressing phenomenon on the basis that such a limit would not be in conformity with the principle that 'a duty of care is owed to those who should be in the contemplation of the person whose acts or omissions are in question as persons closely and directly affected by his or her acts'.[151] Instead, a duty not to cause psychiatric injury will be owed wherever there is some special feature of the relationship between the parties 'such that it can be said that the latter should have the former in contemplation as a person closely and directly affected by his or her acts'.[152] On the facts of *Annetts*, Gaudron J expressly found this requirement to be satisfied.[153] In the middle of this discussion Gaudron J observed that the notion of proximity 'has not served as a unifying doctrine' that allows us to identify precisely the relationships in which one person should

---

[145] *Tame v New South Wales; Annetts v Australian Stations Pty Ltd* [2002] HCA 35, (2002) 211 CLR 317.
[146] ibid [9].
[147] ibid 14, in the second instance quoting *Donoghue v Stevenson* [1932] AC 562, 619 (Lord Macmillan).
[148] ibid [29].
[149] ibid [37].
[150] ibid [185]. Both McHugh J (ibid 107) and Hayne J (ibid [250], [257] and [268]) expressly rejected the notion that proximity constituted an independent element of the duty of care inquiry.
[151] ibid [51], citing *Donoghue v Stevenson* [1932] AC 562.
[152] ibid [52].
[153] ibid [54].

have another in contemplation as closely and directly affected by his or her actions.[154] But whatever Gaudron J found wanting in the notion of proximity, in her judgment it provided the basis for determining the scope of the duty not to cause psychiatric injury, and the basis for identifying a duty of care on the facts before the court in *Annetts*. While Callinan J did not analyse the nature of proximity, the reason he found a duty to be owed in the second case was 'by reason of the relationship of proximity' identified in the pleadings.[155]

Gifford v Strang Patrick Stevedoring Pty Ltd

The concept of proximity was at its most prominent in *Gifford v Strang Patrick Stevedoring Pty Ltd*.[156] Although the word 'proximity' was not used by any of the judges,[157] the concept of proximity in its full traditional sense was treated by McHugh, Gummow, Kirby and Callinan JJ as the core determinant of the existence of a duty not to cause psychiatric injury. The issue in *Gifford v Strang* was whether an employer owed a duty not to cause psychiatric injury to teenaged children of an employee fatally injured at work, where the children did not directly perceive the accident or its aftermath, but suffered psychiatric injury when told of it afterwards. Gleeson CJ reiterated the view he expressed in *Tame* that the central issue was whether it was reasonable to require the defendant to have the plaintiffs in contemplation, bearing in mind the nature of the plaintiff's interest and the burden such a duty would place on the defendant.[158] Given the close relationship that children generally have with their parents, it is not unreasonable to require an employer who places an employee at physical risk to have the psychiatric interests of the employee's children in contemplation.[159]

In *Tame*, McHugh J concluded from an analysis of the foundational cases that 'neighbour = person closely and directly affected = proximity', but held that it was wrong to treat proximity as a substantive and independent requirement.[160] Remarkably, given this and his previous criticisms and rejections of the concept, McHugh J held in *Gifford v Strang* that whether the respondent owed a duty to prevent psychiatric injury to the plaintiffs in the present case

> depends on whether the children were 'neighbours' in Lord Atkin's sense of that term. Were they so closely and directly affected by Strang's relationship with their father that Strang ought reasonably to have had them in contemplation when it directed its mind to the risk of injury to which it was exposing their father?[161]

McHugh J held that nervous shock is such a widely known phenomenon that a wrongdoer exposing a person to the risk of fatal harm ought reasonably to have all those in a close and loving relationship with that person in contemplation.[162] Each of them is 'the neighbour of

---

[154] ibid [53].

[155] ibid [357].

[156] *Gifford v Strang Patrick Stevedoring Pty Ltd* [2003] HCA 33, (2003) 214 CLR 269.

[157] The word appeared only once, when Gleeson CJ (ibid [11]) quoted a passage from *Jaensch v Coffey* (1984) 155 CLR 549, 555 (Gibbs CJ).

[158] *Gifford v Strang Patrick Stevedoring Pty Ltd* [2003] HCA 33, (2003) 214 CLR 269, [8]–[9].

[159] ibid [12].

[160] *Tame v New South Wales; Annetts v Australian Stations Pty Ltd* [2002] HCA 35, (2002) 211 CLR 317, [107], after considering statements in *Donoghue v Stevenson* [1932] AC 562; *Heaven v Pender* (1883) 11 QBD 503 and *Le Lievre v Gould* [1893] 1 QB 491.

[161] *Gifford v Strang Patrick Stevedoring Pty Ltd* [2003] HCA 33, (2003) 214 CLR 269, [46], citing *Donoghue v Stevenson* [1932] AC 562, 580.

[162] ibid [47].

the wrongdoer in Lord Atkin's sense'.[163] Similarly, Gummow and Kirby JJ held that the relationship between the employer and the employee's children attracted the neighbourhood principle identified by Lord Atkin. The children were so closely and directly affected by the employer's conduct that the employer ought to have had them in contemplation, and neglect of their interests would be regarded by general public sentiment as wrongdoing for which the offender must pay.[164] That conclusion was justified by the facts that the employee was exposed to the risk of death in the pursuit of the employer's commercial interests, that psychiatric injury to the employee's children was a consequence of the employee's death which the employer ought to have foreseen, and that the employer exercised a significant degree of control over the risk of harm to the employee and the consequent risk of harm to the children, who had no way of protecting themselves against the risk.[165] Callinan J adhered to the approach he followed in *Tame*, which was based on identifying a relationship of proximity 'within the classic formulation of Lord Atkin in *Donoghue v Stevenson*'.[166]

King v Philcox

In *King v Philcox* the plaintiff witnessed the aftermath of an accident in which his brother was fatally injured, but only subsequently learned that his brother was trapped and dying in the car he had seen.[167] The incident caused him to develop a depressive illness. The Full Court of the Supreme Court of South Australia held the driver who was responsible for the accident liable to pay damages for negligence to the plaintiff. There were two grounds of appeal to the High Court: first, that no duty of care was owed and, secondly, that an award of damages was barred by the Civil Liability Act 1936 (SA), section 53. The High Court unanimously held that section 53 prevented damages being awarded since, relevantly, the plaintiff was not 'present at the scene of the accident when the accident occurred'. The Court unanimously held by way of obiter dicta that the first ground of appeal had not been made out and the court below had not erred in finding that a duty of care had been owed.[168]

Of relevance to the present discussion is the central role of proximity in the reasoning of Nettle J on the duty of care issue. Nettle J explained that while proximity is no longer considered determinative of the duty of care issue, it usefully directs attention to the relationship between the parties, the relevant factual circumstances, and the factors pointing for and against the conclusion that it is reasonable for a duty to arise.[169] Nettle J carefully compared the causal and temporal proximity between the accident and the mental harm on the present facts with those in *Jaensch v Coffey* and the psychiatric injury cases discussed above. His Honour held that:

> In terms of contemporary standards of liability and responsibility, it is not unreasonable that a driver should have in contemplation not only an accident victim who suffers physical injury caused by the driver's negligence but also a close relative of the victim, such as a sibling, who might suffer

---

[163] ibid.

[164] ibid.

[165] ibid [87]–[90].

[166] ibid [118].

[167] *King v Philcox* [2015] HCA 19, (2015) 89 ALJR 582.

[168] ibid [28]–[31] (French CJ, Kiefel and Gageler JJ), [32] (Keane J), [75]–[103] (Nettle J).

[169] ibid [80], citing *Sullivan v Moody* [2001] HCA 59, (2001) 207 CLR 562, [48] (Gleeson CJ, Gaudron, McHugh, Hayne and Callinan JJ) and *Tame v New South Wales; Annetts v Australian Stations Pty Ltd* [2002] HCA 35, (2002) 211 CLR 317, [14] (Gleeson CJ).

mental harm the result of what he or she sees and learns of the victim's physical injuries in the aftermath of the accident. As has been recognised or assumed by courts in the United Kingdom, Canada and the United States and in some States in Australia, *such a relative is a person who is so closely and directly affected by the driver's negligence that the driver should have them in contemplation as potentially so affected.*[170]

An Enduring and Unifying Concept

The series of decisions discussed above can be understood to have rehabilitated the concept of proximity in Australian law, returning it to its classical formulation and restoring it to its proper place at the centre of any duty of care inquiry. These cases show that proximity is a unifying concept, operating as the core determinant of the duty question in cases involving both public and private actors, a wide range of protected interests (namely the interests in freedom from bodily, psychiatric and economic harm), and a wide range of relationships. In light of these cases, it is surely incorrect to say either that proximity has been discarded by the High Court or that it has been found not to be a useful principle.

Alternatives to Proximity

If proximity no longer operates as the core question in duty of care analysis in Australian law, then what has replaced it? One possibility favoured by some commentators would be to abandon altogether the idea of a general approach to duty,[171] on the basis that Lord Atkin was wrong to suggest that there must be a 'general conception of relations giving rise to a duty of care'.[172] Although justices of the High Court of Australia have at times been sceptical of the idea of a general conception, and the Court is said to have rejected the use of 'any particular formula or methodology or test' to determine whether a duty of care exists in particular circumstances,[173] this has not yet resulted in the fragmentation of the duty inquiry in Australian law.[174]

One influential interpretation of the recent case law is the statement of Allsop P in *Caltex v Stavar* that, as a control on reasonable foreseeability of harm (which alone is insufficient to establish a duty of care),[175]

> the proper approach is to undertake a close analysis of the facts bearing on the relationship between the plaintiff and the putative tortfeasor by references to the 'salient features' or factors affecting the appropriateness of imputing a legal duty to take reasonable care to avoid harm or injury.[176]

Allsop P provided a non-exhaustive list of 17 considerations of the kind that are relevant to the task of identifying the existence, scope and content of a duty. The listed factors included

---

[170] ibid [89] (emphasis added, citations omitted).
[171] See, eg, B Hepple, 'Negligence: The Search for Coherence' (1997) 50 *Current Legal Problems* 69.
[172] *Dongohue v Stevenson* [1932] AC 562, 580.
[173] *Caltex Refineries (Qld) Pty Ltd v Stavar* [2009] NSWCA 258, (2009) 75 NSWLR 649, [102] (Allsop P).
[174] Though see, eg, *Hill v Van Erp* (1997) 188 CLR 159 177 (Dawson J).
[175] *Caltex v Stavar* [2009] NSWCA 258, (2009) 75 NSWLR 649, [106].
[176] ibid [102]. See also *Apache Energy Ltd v Alcoa of Australia Ltd (No 2)* [2013] WASCA 213, (2013) 45 WAR 379, [134] (Buss JA).

all of those that would be involved in proximity analysis, but also included proximity itself: one of the listed factors was 'the proximity or nearness in a physical, temporal or relational sense of the plaintiff to the defendant'.[177] Allsop P noted that formulae such as 'proximity' and 'fairness' 'do not encapsulate the task' but 'fall within it as part of the evaluative judgment of the appropriateness of legal imputation of responsibility'.[178] In addition to the factors involved in proximity analysis discussed earlier in this chapter, the considerations identified by Allsop P include any indeterminacy of liability, the effect of recognising a duty on 'the autonomy or freedom of individuals', the existence of conflicting duties and the desirability or need for 'coherence in the structure and fabric of the common law'.[179]

A second interpretation sees the most authoritative exposition of the current Australian approach as that developed in a series of sole and joint judgments by Gummow J, based on the judgment of Stephen J in *Caltex v Willemstad*.[180] As noted above, that approach is to consider whether it is possible to isolate a number of salient features which combine to constitute a sufficiently close relationship to create a duty of care. That method was articulated by Gummow J in *Perre v Apand*,[181] with the concurrence of Gleeson CJ, and was subsequently adopted (though not applied) in the plurality judgment in *Woolcock Street Investments Pty Ltd v CDG Pty Ltd*.[182] That approach has been called the '"sufficiently close relationship" test', and it has been said that a determination that there is a sufficiently close relationship justifies a conclusion that the case exemplifies 'a particular manifestation of the notion of a relationship of proximity'.[183] Thus, although the plurality in *Woolcock* insisted that proximity is 'no longer seen as the "conceptual determinant" in this area',[184] and despite the fact that McHugh J in the same case described proximity as a 'discarded doctrine' which was 'rejected in *Sullivan*',[185] the conventional notion of proximity lies, on one view, at the heart of the new approach developed in that case.

The two principal difficulties with the multifactorial approach are that it lacks structure and, in the first of the above two formulations, that it lacks focus.[186] An intensive examination of the facts bearing on the relationship between the parties must be directed towards a particular question. As Kirby J has pointed out: 'Somehow in the end accumulated facts must be turned into an "ought".'[187] It is not enough to ask whether a duty should

---

[177] *Caltex v Stavar* [2009] NSWCA 258, (2009) 75 NSWLR 649, [103].

[178] ibid [106].

[179] ibid [103].

[180] This approach was developed in *Hill v Van Erp* (1997) 188 CLR 159, 233–34 (Gummow J), *Pyrenees Shire Council v Day* [1998] HCA 3, (1998) 192 CLR 330, 389 (Gummow J); *Perre v Apand Pty Ltd* [1999] HCA 36, (1999) 198 CLR 180, [198], [201] (Gummow J); *Agar v Hyde* [2000] HCA 41, (2000) 201 CLR 522, [70] (Gaudron, McHugh, Gummow and Hayne JJ); *Graham Barclay Oysters Pty Ltd v Ryan* [2002] HCA 54, (2002) 211 CLR 540, [154] (Gummow and Hayne JJ); *Woolcock Street Investments Pty Ltd v CDG Pty Ltd* [2004] HCA 16, (2004) 216 CLR 515, [22] (Gleeson CJ, Gummow, Hayne and Heydon JJ).

[181] *Perre v Apand* [1999] HCA 36, (1999) 198 CLR 180, [198], [201].

[182] *Woolcock Street Investments Pty Ltd v CDG Pty Ltd* [2004] HCA 16, (2004) 216 CLR 515, [22] (Gleeson CJ, Gummow, Hayne and Heydon JJ).

[183] *Moorabool Shire Council v Taitapanui* [2006] VSCA 30, (2006) 14 VR 55, [21] (Maxwell P), quoting *Hill v Van Erp* (1997) 188 CLR 159, 238 (Gummow J).

[184] *Woolcock Street Investments Pty Ltd v CDG Pty Ltd* [2004] HCA 16, (2004) 216 CLR 515, [18] (Gleeson CJ, Gummow, Hayne and Heydon JJ).

[185] ibid [37], [73].

[186] It is significant that in *King v Philcox* [2015] HCA 19, (2015) 89 ALJR 582, [80] Nettle J prefaced his proximity-based analysis of the duty of care question by quoting the acknowledgement in *Sullivan v Moody* [2001] HCA 59, (2001) 207 CLR 562, [48] that proximity 'gives focus to the inquiry'.

[187] *Graham Barclay Oysters Pty Ltd v Ryan* [2002] HCA 54, (2002) 211 CLR 540, [242].

be recognised, because that 'should' question can be considered by reference to an unworkably wide range of different considerations of interpersonal justice and community welfare. This is related to the structure problem, which is that the multifactorial approach does not provide a method by which the different considerations can be evaluated and weighed against one another.[188] It has been said of the Canadian approach to duty that 'the underlying question is whether a duty of care should be imposed, taking into account all relevant factors disclosed by the circumstances' and it may not matter at what stage in the analysis a particular factor is considered.[189] The unstructured version of the multifactorial approach puts this to the test by combining all potentially relevant considerations into a single list of factors, which are to be assessed together to determine whether a duty should be imposed.

IV. Conclusions

The proximity principle may be considered something of an embarrassment for the common law of obligations. It is remarkable that parties' rights and obligations in relation to interactions involving fundamental personal and economic interests should be determined by reference to a question as abstract as how closely and directly one person's conduct affects another in a given situation, and by direct consideration of the question whether in particular circumstances one person ought to have the interests of another in contemplation. A legal principle that requires judges to determine how the community would view particular conduct depends on the existence of a relevant community standard and on the capacity of judges to identify it. We might console ourselves that duty questions are reasonably well settled for most areas of human interaction, that a substantial body of case law provides a level of certainty at least as to the factual features to be focused upon in novel cases, and that the courts generally resolve duty questions at the level of broad categories. But the courts seem to be faced with an endless series of factual variations at and beyond the edges of recognised duty and non-duty situations. The Australian courts have routinely considered duty questions entirely on the basis of the particular facts before them, without considering whether the law recognises a notional duty operating across a particular category or type of relationship,[190] although there has been a recent indication that this may be changing.[191]

There can be no doubt that the High Court of Australia was right to reject the notion of proximity as a criterion that is capable of providing a complete answer to the duty of care question. What is interesting about the Australian experience, however, is that the development and subsequent abandonment of that universal criterion left a void, which in many instances has been filled by proximity in its traditional formulation. This has occurred

---

[188]   On the importance of this, see Robertson, above n 30.

[189]   *Cooper v Hobart* [2001] SCC 79, [2001] 3 SCR 537, [27] (McLachlin CJ for the court).

[190]   See, eg, *Cole v South Tweed Heads Rugby League Club* [2004] HCA 29, (2004) 217 CLR 469, [9] (Gleeson CJ): it is unnecessary to formulate 'some general proposition', '[t]he question is whether there was such a duty in the circumstances of this case'.

[191]   *Brookfield Multiplex Ltd v Owners—Strata Plan No 61288* [2014] HCA 36, (2014) 88 AJLR 911, [172]–[174], where Gageler J insisted on applying principles capable of general application in order to determine the existence and scope of a duty of care in the category of case in question.

despite trenchant criticism of that orthodox notion of proximity and a professed rejection of the concept. As remarkable as the endurance of proximity is McHugh J's revival of the two-stage duty framework. Having, in *Perre v Apand*, 'rejected arbitrary exclusions, proximity, impairment of precise legal rights and *Anns* and *Caparo* as suitable determinants of duty',[192] McHugh J only a few years later set out a framework for determining whether a public authority owes an affirmative duty of care which in substance replicates the modified versions of the *Anns* framework now applied in Canada, Singapore and New Zealand.

The endurance of proximity in Australian law in spite of its well-known shortcomings as a legal principle, in spite of attempts to abandon it, and in spite of the energy devoted to finding an alternative, evidences the utility of the concept as a determinant of duty. The problem that needed to be addressed in Australian law did not lie with the concept of proximity as traditionally understood, but with the fact that the word had come to be used in an expanded sense to refer to an all-encompassing basis for determining whether a duty of care is owed. The closeness and directness of the defendant's conduct on the plaintiff is a decisive consideration in some cases. Proximity in its traditional formulation provides a helpful focus for the question of interpersonal responsibility that lies at the heart of the duty determination. As Christian Witting has observed, an ultimate question is needed in duty analysis to give the various factors and features their salience and to provide a basis on which they can be weighed against one another.[193] If proximity serves a useful purpose such as this, but cannot provide a comprehensive answer to the duty question, then this suggests that greater attention needs to be paid in Australian law to identifying and explaining the broader framework of the duty inquiry and the place of proximity within it.

The Australian experience teaches the obvious lesson that well-established common law concepts cannot easily be abandoned. The divergence considered in this chapter is not a substantive deviation. It does not involve the recognition of rights and obligations not recognised in other common law jurisdictions or the denial of rights and obligations that are recognised elsewhere.[194] Rather, it is a methodological divergence. Methodological divergences are desirable from the point of view of the development of the common law as a whole because they represent doctrinal experiments that may be followed elsewhere if they prove to offer more workable, meaningful, substantive analysis than those they replace.[195] Criticism and rejection of established concepts and frameworks is a necessary part of doctrinal development, but must go hand in hand with the identification of new and better concepts and frameworks. Where no better concept or analytical framework is available, it is surely preferable to seek to understand, develop and refine shared concepts and analytical methods than to abandon them.

---

[192] *Perre v Apand Pty Ltd* [1999] HCA 36, (1999) 198 CLR 180, [93] (McHugh J).

[193] Witting, above n 13, 218.

[194] The rejection of proximity is not in itself likely to lead to different outcomes because, as was noted in *North Shore City Council v Attorney-General* [2012] NZSC 49, [2012] 3 NZLR 341, [155] (Blanchard, McGrath and William Young JJ), the features or factors focused upon by the Australian courts are not substantially different from those taken into account in analysis which is more explicitly focused on proximity.

[195] On the idea of doctrinal divergence as experimentation, cf A Beever, 'How to Have a Common Private Law: The Presuppositions of Legal Conversation' in A Robertson and M Tilbury (eds), *The Common Law of Obligations: Divergence and Unity* (Oxford, Hart Publishing, 2015).

3

Canada's Common Law, Quebec's Civil Law and the Threshold of Actionable Mental Harm Following Tortious Conduct

LOUISE BÉLANGER-HARDY[*]

I. Introduction

In common law systems, compensation for mental harm[1] following tortious conduct poses a number of challenges. In common law Canada, given that the law is still evolving and thus susceptible to change and reorientation, it seems logical and even desirable to turn to the Province of Quebec and its civil law system to seek another viewpoint. Indeed, some of the scholars who favour more flexibility in mental harm compensation rules have remarked on the civil law's more open approach vis-à-vis claims based on mental harm and on the fact that this openness does not necessarily lead to excessive litigation.[2]

This being said, it must be recognised that not all civil law jurisdictions adopt the same approach. Quebec's civil law is a mixed legal system and although some of its roots lie in the French legal system, which is known for its victim-oriented legal culture,[3] the influence of the common law is very present.[4] This makes Quebec's perspective particularly

---

[*] The author wishes to acknowledge the assistance of Isabelle Brideau JD, LLL and Jamil-Daniel Beauchamp-Dupont, JD, LLL.

[1] Given the nature of the present inquiry, the expression 'mental harm' has been retained because it is wide enough to include emotional, psychological or psychiatric damage. A similar definition was adopted by the Scottish Law Commission, *Damages for Psychiatric Injury* (Scot Law Com No 196, 2004) recommendation 3(a): 'any harm to a person's mental state, mental function or mental well-being, whether or not the harm amounted to a medically recognised medical disorder'.

[2] On civil law systems, see P Handford, *Mullany & Handford's Tort Liability for Psychiatric Damage*, 2nd edn (Sydney, Law Book Co, 2006) 99–101. On the floodgates issue, see JS Borghetti, 'The Culture of Tort Law in France' (2012) 3 *Journal of European Tort Law* 158–59.

[3] Borghetti, above n 2, 158.

[4] For an overview of the links between the French and the Quebec systems, see JEC Brierley and RA MacDonald, *Quebec Civil Law—An Introduction to Quebec Private Law* (Toronto, Edmond Montgomery, 1993) 6–14; S Normand, 'An Introduction to Quebec Civil Law' in L Bélanger-Hardy and A Grenon (eds), *Elements of Quebec Civil Law: A Comparison with the Common Law of Canada* (Toronto, Thomson Carswell, 2008). For an overview of the influence of the common law on Quebec's extracontractual liability rules, see M Tancelin, *Des obligations en droit mixte du Québec*, 7th edn (Montreal, Wilson & Lafleur, 2009) 440ff.

interesting in a debate on convergence and divergence of the law[5]—at least within the Canadian context.

The focus of this chapter is on the threshold of actionable mental harm. Currently, for certain torts such as negligence or intentional infliction of mental harm, most Canadian common law courts insist on physical symptoms or a recognisable psychiatric illness (RPI) when mental harm is not ancillary to physical injury. However, the Civil Code of Quebec (CCQ) does not impose such limits on actionable mental harm.[6] In other words, there appears to be a fairly clear divergence in applicable legal principles between Canada's two legal traditions.

Given this context, it is perhaps surprising that some Quebec courts have relied on common law decisions when adjudicating claims for compensation for stand-alone mental harm. In particular, these courts have cited *Mustapha v Culligan of Canada Ltd*,[7] the Supreme Court of Canada's only 'modern' common law judgment on mental harm in the negligence context. At first glance, this situation is puzzling as *Mustapha* is a typical common law decision which emphasises the need for restraint in compensation (especially via the concept of foreseeability). While Quebec law defines actionable mental harm broadly and does not insist on proof of an RPI, the analysis of civil law cases reveals that nevertheless there are built-in limits to compensation. Therefore, at times, setting the threshold of actionable mental harm is necessary, especially when claims are based on harm that seems insignificant. This is when civilian courts have turned to *Mustapha* for guidance.

Of particular interest in this process is the difference in the interpretation the courts have given to the *Mustapha* decision. Indeed, Canadian common law courts have interpreted the Supreme Court's words on actionable harm as confirming the orthodox position that an RPI is required, while Quebec courts have relied on the decision for the proposition that mental harm must amount to more than mere upsets or annoyances of daily living to be indemnified.

Although this points to a clear divergence in approaches, the position taken in this paper is that, in fact, this is not the case. Correctly interpreted, *Mustapha* does not endorse the RPI limit. Rather, the decision emphasises that, to be actionable, mental harm must cross the 'more than mere upset' lower threshold. In other words, the proposition is that, following *Mustapha*, there is a possible 'convergence' between the civil and common law systems. More accurately perhaps, at a minimum, there is a commonality of preoccupations within the two systems as they both attempt to delineate what constitutes actionable mental harm.

Comparing legal systems and approaches is always challenging. The structure and organisation of legal principles and rules are not symmetric. This must be taken into

---

[5] This chapter does not pretend to be a formal exercise in comparative law. The terms convergence and divergence are given a general meaning, ie where convergence means 'leaning in a common direction' and divergence has the opposite meaning; see L LeBel and PL Le Saunier, 'L'interaction du droit civil et de la common law à la Cour suprême du Canada' (2006) 47 *Cahiers de droit* 179, 228. On the challenges of comparing the common law and the civil law, see P Legrand, 'European Legal Systems Are not Converging' (1996) 45 *ICLQ* 52, 64–74.

[6] Civil Code of Québec (CCQ), Art 1457: 'Every person has a duty to abide by the rules of conduct incumbent on him, according to the circumstances, usage or law, so as not to cause injury to another. Where he is endowed with reason and fails in this duty, *he is liable for any injury he causes to another by such fault and is bound to make reparation for the injury, whether it be bodily, moral or material in nature.* He is also bound, in certain cases, to make reparation for injury caused to another by the act or fault of another person or by the act of things in his custody' (emphasis added).

[7] *Mustapha v Culligan of Canada Ltd* 2008 SCC 27, [2008] 2 SCR 114.

consideration. For instance, Quebec civil law does not differentiate between intentional and non-intentional wrongs.[8] Rather, a general principle imposes liability for damage caused by fault.[9] Some of the civil law cases discussed below deal with negligence while others do not; common lawyers will recognise actions similar to nuisance and malicious prosecution. The asymmetry between tort law and extracontractual liability makes comparison somewhat awkward but not impossible as the present inquiry focuses on a notion common to both systems: the concept of damage.

The analysis is divided in Parts II and III of this chapter. Part II discusses the common law's traditional approach to the threshold of actionable mental harm issue, the *Mustapha* decision and the subsequent responses from common law and civil law courts. Part III explores two related topics. Section III.A considers the extent to which Quebec's civil law limits actionable mental harm, thereby pointing to elements of convergence with the common law, while section III.B proposes an interpretation of the *Mustapha* decision which rejects the orthodox view that actionable mental harm must amount to an RPI and favours a more flexible approach based on the mere upset threshold. The argument is that such an interpretation is another element of convergence between the two legal systems.

II. The Threshold of Actionable Mental Harm: Post-*Mustapha* Interpretations by Common Law and Civil Law Courts

In Canadian tort law the issue of actionable mental harm is particularly important in relation to the torts of negligence and of intentional infliction of mental suffering.[10] In both cases the traditional principle can be set out quite simply. In cases where there is independent or stand-alone mental harm, not ancillary to physical injury, compensation will be awarded only if the mental harm manifests as physical symptoms (a heart attack, a miscarriage) or as an RPI. Canadian courts generally accept that a mental injury amounts to an RPI when a psychiatrist finds that the plaintiff's injury is a diagnosable mental disorder,[11] usually by reference to diagnostic criteria found in texts such as the American Psychiatric Association's DSM-V[12] or the World Health Organization's ICD-10.[13] However, in *Mustapha*, a negligence case, the Supreme Court appeared to move away from this traditional approach.

---

[8] Quebec's law of obligations encompasses contractual and extracontractual liability. The latter is the equivalent of tort law. The first civil code, adopted in 1866, included a distinction between intentional (delict) and non-intentional wrongs (quasi-delict) but was eliminated when the CCQ was adopted in 1991.

[9] CCQ, Art 1457, above n 6.

[10] Regarding the tort of intentional infliction of mental harm, one needs to establish the existence of 'visible and provable illness': see *Wilkinson v Downton* [1897] 2 QB 57. It is important to note that mental harm which occurs in the context of other torts such as assault or the new Ontario tort of 'intrusion upon seclusion' is not subject to restrictions as to the type of actionable harm: see *Jones v Tsige* 2012 ONCA 32, 118 OR (3d) 241.

[11] See, eg, *Devji v District of Burnaby* 1999 BCCA 599, 180 DLR (4th) 20 [83] where the Court wrote: 'The medical distinction between psychiatric injury and ordinary grief or distress turns on diagnosis of a psychiatric illness'; *Healey v Lakeridge Health Corporation* 2010 ONSC 725 [120]–[138], [166]–[170], [2010] OJ No 417 (QL).

[12] American Psychiatric Association, *Diagnostic and Statistical Manual of Mental Disorders: DSM-V*, 5th edn, text revision (Washington, American Psychiatric Association, 2013).

[13] *The ICD-10 Classification of Mental and Behavioural Disorders, 2010*, online: World Health Organization, www.who.int/classifications/icd/en/bluebook.pdf.

The facts of the case are well known. The plaintiff suffered a severe mental illness after seeing a dead fly and the remnants of a second one in the sealed water bottle delivered to his home by the defendant, Culligan of Canada Ltd. The action succeeded at trial but was rejected both by the Ontario Court of Appeal and eventually by the Supreme Court as the plaintiff's mental harm was seen as too remote.[14]

The extent of Mr Mustapha's mental injuries was not at issue before the Supreme Court as there was clear evidence of a debilitating psychiatric injury. Nonetheless, the Supreme Court commented, obiter, on the threshold of actionable mental harm. After stating that 'the distinction between physical and mental injury is elusive and arguably artificial in the context of tort',[15] the Court noted the need to distinguish between a 'psychological disturbance that rises to the level of personal injury' and 'psychological upset'.[16] The Court then wrote:

> Personal injury at law connotes serious trauma or illness .... The law does not recognize upset, disgust, anxiety, agitation or other mental states that fall short of injury. I would not purport to define compensable injury exhaustively, except to say that it must be serious and prolonged and rise above the ordinary annoyances, anxieties and fears that people living in society routinely, if sometimes reluctantly, accept. … Quite simply, minor and transient upsets do not constitute personal *injury*, and hence do not amount to damage.[17]

For the purpose of the discussion herein, it is significant to note that the Court did not directly mention or discuss the phrase 'recognisable psychiatric illness'. This has led some plaintiffs to argue that *Mustapha* had moved the threshold from an RPI to something less, for instance, a 'serious and prolonged' injury.[18]

Common law lower courts have not been receptive to this argument. Two key decisions will be discussed here to illustrate the courts' approach. In *Kotai v Queen of the North (Ship)*,[19] passengers started a class action for negligence after the ferry on which they were travelling sank off the British Columbia coast one night. Many of them suffered solely from stand-alone mental harm which did not reach the threshold of psychiatric injury. The plaintiffs submitted they were entitled to compensation as long as their mental harm was 'serious and prolonged'. In their view, the Supreme Court in *Mustapha* 'put forward a different and less stringent test as to the kind or degree of damages that will be compensable at law provided the other elements [of the tort of negligence] are satisfied'.[20] The Court disagreed and held that *Mustapha* did not change the law on the threshold of mental harm.[21] Indeed, the need to prove an RPI 'introduced a degree of objectivity and certainty to the law through the mechanism of expert medical evidence'.[22]

The Ontario Court of Appeal came to a similar interpretation of *Mustapha* in *Healey v Lakeridge Health Corp*,[23] a class action negligence case by patients who received notices

---

[14] *Mustapha v Culligan of Canada Ltd* 2008 SCC 27, [2008] 2 SCR 114, [14]: the psychiatric injury was not foreseeable by a 'person of ordinary fortitude'.
[15] ibid [8].
[16] ibid [9].
[17] ibid (emphasis added by the court; legal citations omitted).
[18] ibid.
[19] *Kotai v Queen of the North (Ship)* 2009 BCSC 1405, [2009] BCJ No 2022 (QL).
[20] ibid [59].
[21] ibid [65].
[22] ibid [68].
[23] *Healey v Lakeridge Health Corp* 2011 ONCA 55, 103 OR (3d) 401.

of potential exposure to tuberculosis. The appeal dealt with the claims of the 'Uninfected Persons' class and the derivative claims of family members. The plaintiffs argued that *Mustapha* had significantly lowered the threshold for compensation and that their injury only had to meet the 'serious and prolonged' threshold. The Court doubted that *Mustapha* intended to introduce a fundamental change to a 'well-established, though at times contested, rule'[24] and held that an objective threshold was required. Accordingly, there were 'strong policy reasons for imposing some sort of threshold … [g]iven the frequency with which everyday experiences cause transient distress, the multi-factorial causes of psychological upset, and the highly subjective nature of an individual's reaction to such stresses and strains'.[25] The interpretation of *Mustapha* described in *Kotai* and *Healey* has generally been followed by lower Canadian common law courts since 2008.[26]

Before turning to a more thorough analysis of the threshold issue, Quebec decisions citing *Mustapha* will be considered. Seven cases have been identified. While two of them will be discarded as they respectively deal with contract law[27] and the definition of foreseeability,[28] the other five are relevant and will be examined more thoroughly.

The first case, *Cyr v Ste-Adèle (City of)*,[29] involved a motion to certify a class action against the defendant town for failing to take precautionary measures to prevent contamination of the drinking water supplied to the neighbourhood in which the plaintiff lived. The plaintiff allegedly suffered mental harm upon learning that a bird and two raccoons had been found dead in the reservoir close to her home. The Court was mostly concerned with causation between the omission to maintain the reservoir and the mental harm, especially given that the plaintiff's evidence did not establish actual contamination of the water supply. Commenting on the nature of the mental harm apparently suffered, the Court, noting the 'highly subjective' nature of the injury,[30] quoted from *Mustapha* and the Supreme Court's passage on psychological harm reproduced above.[31] The Court concluded that even if the plaintiff's mental injury could be proven, the motion to certify the class action had to be dismissed as there was no evidence that other members of the class were similarly affected.

---

[24] ibid [61].

[25] ibid [65].

[26] There are exceptions where a more flexible threshold has been retained. See, eg, *Lodge v Fitzgibbon* 2011 NBQB 226, 378 NBR (2d) 202 [99]. For an analysis of the post-*Mustapha* common law decisions, see L Bélanger-Hardy, 'Reconsidering the "Recognizable Psychiatric Illness" Requirement in Canadian Negligence Law' (2013) 28 *Queen's Law Journal* 583.

[27] *Hébert v Placements et assurances Renauld Gagner inc* 2008 QCCQ 5370 where a woman sought damages when the defendant failed to change the beneficiary on a life insurance policy. The Court rejected the defendant's argument that *Mustapha* (still before the Court of Appeal for Ontario at the time) applied to a civil law case.

[28] *Commission de la santé et de la sécurité du travail v Deshaies & Raymond inc* 2013 QCCS 1062 [19]. In that case, the Commission alleged that the defendant contractor failed to comply with regulatory requirements about worker training before undertaking work where the danger of asbestos dust was possible. The Superior Court of Quebec relied on *Mustapha* for an explanation of the expression 'susceptibles d'émettre' (which it equated with reasonable foreseeability).

[29] *Cyr v Ste-Adèle (City of)* 2009 QCCS 2827.

[30] ibid [56]. Interestingly, the Court pointed out, at [57], that '[m]ême si certains éléments de la responsabilité civile en Ontario peuvent différer de ceux au Québec, l'obligation d'établir un lien direct entre la faute et le préjudice de même que son caractère prévisible est la même' (even if some elements of civil liability in Ontario differ from those in Quebec, the obligation to establish a direct link between fault and harm, as well as the foreseeable nature of the harm, is the same). As an aside, the comment on foreseeability is curious as foreseeability is an element of *contractual* liability only: see JL Baudouin, P Deslauriers and B Moore, *La responsabilité civile*, 8th edn (Cowansville, Yvon Blais, 2014) 374.

[31] *Mustapha v Culligan of Canada Ltd* 2008 SCC 27, [2008] 2 SCR 114, [9].

In *Chartrand v Ferme DSR Dussault inc*[32] the plaintiff started an action for compensation for mental harm and anxiety allegedly suffered as a result of a demand letter sent to her by the defendants' lawyer. There was a long-standing conflict between the parties about land usage and compliance with environmental regulations. The demand letter requested that the plaintiff inform environmental authorities that facts previously received about a spill allegedly caused by the defendants were incorrect. In considering the plaintiff's claim for *abus de procédure*,[33] the Court discussed the thin-skull rule since there was evidence the plaintiff had suffered from anxiety and other health issues for a number of years prior to the events leading to the action. After noting that a predisposition to illness could not be used to reject the claim and that any aggravation caused by the tortious conduct could be indemnified, the Court quoted from *Mustapha* and the paragraph reproduced above and concluded the plaintiff's claim had to be dismissed: there was no causal link between the demand letters and the harm suffered. The Court attributed the plaintiff's stress to her own legal action against the defendants.

In *Regroupement des citoyens contre la pollution v Alex Couture inc*[34] the defendant corporation moved to quash a class action by a group of citizens complaining of nuisance linked to strong smells emanating from the defendant's rendering plant. The plaintiffs argued the nuisance caused injury to their health, physical integrity, well-being and quality of life. The court rejected the defendant's argument whereby expert opinion was essential to assess the nature of the harm. In the Court's opinion, the evaluation of the harm would properly occur at the trial on the merits. The trial court would assess if the injury was recognised by the law and compensable, or whether it amounted to 'other mental states that fall short of injury', referring to *Mustapha*.[35]

In *Mazzonna v DaimlerChrysler Financial Services Canada Inc/Services financiers DaimlerChrysler inc Mazzonna*[36] the petitioner sought certification of a class action against the defendant DaimlerChrysler Financial Services for negligence in the handling and subsequent loss of personal information located on a data tape lost during shipping. The petitioner described her damage as anxiety, inconvenience and fear due to loss of personal information which made her a potential target for fraud and theft. The Court agreed that prima facie there was negligence. However, in its opinion there was no compensable injury and certification was denied. The Court noted that no identity theft had occurred and that the only steps taken by the plaintiff to relieve her anxiety were to keep a minimal balance in her account and check it from time to time to make sure there was nothing amiss. The Court quoted *Mustapha*[37] as the source of 'guidance on the distinction between minor and transient upsets on the one hand and compensable injury on the other'. The Court noted:

> While the appeal in *Mustapha* was from a judgment of the Ontario Court of Appeal and while there may be differences in the contractual and delictual (tort) rules of both jurisdictions, the Court

---

[32]   *Chartrand v Ferme DSR Dussault inc* 2013 QCCQ 3935.

[33]   A cause of action similar to abuse of process at common law.

[34]   *Regroupement des citoyens contre la pollution v Alex Couture inc* 2011 QCCS 4262.

[35]   ibid [68]. The full phrase quoted by the Court (drawn from *Mustapha v Culligan of Canada Ltd* 2008 SCC 27, [2008] 2 SCR 114, [9]) reads as follows: 'The law does not recognise upset, disgust, anxiety, agitation or other mental states that fall short of injury.'

[36]   *Mazzonna v DaimlerChrysler Financial Services Canada Inc/Services financiers DaimlerChrysler inc* 2012 QCCS 958.

[37]   *Mustapha v Culligan of Canada Ltd* 2008 SCC 27, [2008] 2 SCR 114, [9].

finds no reason to conclude that the distinction between a compensable damage as opposed to an ordinary 'annoyance' of life should not apply in Quebec Law.[38]

The same approach was followed in the last case under study, *Fortin v Mazda Canada Inc*,[39] a class action to recover various forms of damages linked to a design defect in the locking system of various Mazda vehicles. One of the claims had to do with the inconvenience and trouble the car owners had to go through in order to get the locking system repaired. The Court rejected this claim and quoted from *Mazzonna* (and the reference therein to *Mustapha*) with approval to conclude that inconveniences and worries of ordinary life were not usually considered as 'compensable damages'.[40]

Although in the five cases discussed above, the line of reasoning—from the civil law to the common law—is not always clearly defined, the decisions lead to a number of observations not only about the way both legal traditions perceive mental harm as an injury but also about the type of threshold the law should retain when it comes to mental harm indemnification. Indeed, the analysis will reveal that there may be more convergence of the law between the two legal systems than one would believe at first glance.[41]

III. Of Thresholds, Convergence and Damage

Limiting Actionable Mental Harm within Quebec Civil Law: One (Small) Step towards Convergence with the Common Law?

According to Article 1457 CCQ, liability depends on proof of fault, causation and injury. Of course, a court can rely on any of these elements to reject a claim for compensation. For instance, in *Cyr*[42] the Court's analysis focused on causation.[43] However, it is the notion of injury that is most relevant to a discussion about the threshold of actionable mental harm.

---

[38] *Mazzonna v DaimlerChrysler Financial Services Canada Inc/Services financiers DaimlerChrysler inc* 2012 QCCS 958, [61]–[62].

[39] *Fortin v Mazda Canada Inc* 2014 QCCS 2617.

[40] ibid [150] ('les désagréments et les angoisses ordinaires de la vie ne sont généralement pas des "dommages indemnisables"').

[41] One must recognise that drawing convincing conclusions from only five cases may be a bit difficult especially given that the analysis is not very detailed, except perhaps in *Mazzonna* and *Fortin*. It must also be noted that four of the decisions were rendered in the context of class actions or motions for certification. With these limitations in mind, this paper nevertheless attempts to draw certain parallels in the challenges facing both common law and civil law systems when it comes to mental harm claims in tort.

[42] *Cyr v Ste-Adèle (City of)* 2009 QCCS 2827.

[43] A thorough study of causation as a limiting tool in mental harm cases in a civil law setting is beyond the scope of this paper. For an example of the use of causation in stand-alone mental harm cases, see *Syndicat des cols bleus regroupés de Montréal, (SCFP, section locale 301) v Coll* 2009 QCCA 708. The case involved a class action by persons who suffered inconvenience due to an illegal walkout by blue-collar employees in Montreal. A demonstration in the centre of the city caused traffic jams and the claimants were subjected to long delays. The Court of Appeal, overturning the Superior Court's decision to partially allow the action, noted that there was no evidence of any injury on the record and the only complaint was of delay. The Court found it 'difficult to see how only the inconveniences caused by being stuck in a traffic jam could constitute an injury directly attributable to the illegal strike. ... The inconveniences suffered by the motorists ... were not the logical, direct, and immediate consequence of this alleged fault': ibid [78]–[80].

The Code does not provide a definition of what constitutes an injury under Article 1457. This is not particularly surprising given that, in theory, all types of losses or damages can be compensated. There are no substantial indicators of what injury consists of, only qualifiers.[44] Doctrinal works and judicial pronouncements reveal that an injury must be direct,[45] certain[46] and legitimate[47] for compensation to occur.[48] The Code does, however, propose categories of actionable injury: bodily, moral and material.[49] Under the old version of the Code, injury was either material or moral, categories loosely corresponding to pecuniary and non-pecuniary losses. According to one author, under the new classification, the focus has moved from the consequences of the wrongful act to the source of the claim.[50]

The transition to the tripartite division of injury has been a difficult process and there is sometimes confusion about the exact meaning of 'bodily injury' and about the classification of mental harm within the new scheme. Significantly, it appears that mental harm falls either under the 'bodily injury' category (if the mental harm flows from a physical injury) or under the 'moral injury' category (if there is stand-alone mental harm).[51] In this sense, an injury to the dignity of the person is a 'moral injury' as is an injury to the extrapatrimonial interests of a corporate body.[52] What a general review of recent cases reveals is that when the mental harm flows from a physical injury, courts conclude quickly that there is 'bodily injury' and focus on the calculation of damages.[53] Cases of stand-alone mental harm have been more challenging.

In a 1996 decision the Supreme Court of Canada gave a definition of 'moral injury' as including 'loss of enjoyment of life, esthetic prejudice, physical and psychological pain and suffering, inconvenience, loss of amenities, and sexual prejudice'.[54] As can be seen, the definition is very wide and includes psychological pain, suffering and inconveniences. The Code does not define moral injury and there is little guidance from doctrinal studies.[55]

---

[44] Tancelin, above n 4, 540 § 748.

[45] Baudouin, Deslauriers and Moore, above n 30, 374: 'Tous les dommages directs, indépendamment de leur caractère de prévisibilité, devraient être accordés' (All direct injuries, independently of their foreseeability, should be compensated).

[46] ibid 397: the injury, present or future, must have already occurred or will probably occur.

[47] ibid 404: this refers to the notion that the victim's injury must not be illegal or illicit.

[48] Tancelin, above n 4, at 545–48.

[49] See the second sentence in CCQ Art 1457, above n 6: 'He is liable for any injury he causes to another by such fault and is bound to make reparation for the injury, whether it be bodily, moral or material in nature.'

[50] D Gardner, *Le préjudice corporel*, 3rd edn (Cowansville, Yvon Blais, 2009) 29.

[51] See, in the doctrine, Tancelin, above n 4, 556 § 773, and in the case law, *Schreiber v Canada (Attorney General)* 2002 SCC 62 [63]–[64]; *Andrusiak v Montréal (City of)* [2004] RJQ 2655, 2004 CanLII 32989 (CA) [17]–[18] (Baudouin J). There are consequences to the characterisation. For example, the limitation periods for claims arising from 'bodily injury' are not necessarily the same as those arising from 'moral' or 'material' injury. See Gardner, above n 50, at 33ff for a thorough discussion of these consequences.

[52] Tancelin, above n 4, 548–49. Mental harm suffered following defamation or harassment are forms of moral injury, see Gardner, above n 50, 30–31.

[53] See, eg, *Loiselle v Bernard* 2008 QCCS 1616.

[54] The key issue was not the threshold of harm but rather whether the functional approach applied to the evaluation of moral injury; see *Quebec (Public Curator) v Syndicat national des employés de l'hôpital St-Ferdinand* [1996] 3 SCR 211, [63]. This was a class action by mentally disabled patients who suffered harm, including mental harm, when the unionised employees of a hospital in which they were living participated in illegal strikes and failed to provide appropriate care.

[55] A notable exception is JF Lehoux, 'Pour une approche plus méthodique des dommages psychologiques non pécuniaires' in Service de la formation continue du Barreau du Québec 2006, *Le préjudice corporel* vol 252 (Cowansville, Yvon Blais, 2006) 53. See also S Morin, *Le dommage moral et le préjudice extrapatrimonial* (Cowansville, Yvon Blais, 2011) 224–35.

In this context, the key question for a court is to determine what type of mental harm amounts to bodily or moral injury.

Two comments must be made here. First, the civil law of Quebec does not insist that mental harm amount to an RPI. Plaintiffs may be encouraged to rely on mental health experts to substantiate their claim,[56] and many in fact do so,[57] but there is no requirement that the mental harm be an RPI or even be 'severe and prolonged', to borrow the Supreme Court of Canada's words in *Mustapha*.[58]

Second, there is a requirement in civil law that the injury reach a minimal threshold. The maxim *de minimis non curat lex* applies in Quebec just as it does in the common law provinces.[59] The challenge is that since moral injury is given a wide definition which includes inconveniences, it is difficult at times to determine when inconveniences amount to a compensable head of damages and when they do not. Although the matter has not been fully researched for this chapter, it appears that there are few cases where the maxim has been relied on to reject claims based on mental harm.[60] In fact, it has been argued that Quebec courts should rely on the maxim more often especially in cases where claimants in class actions seek compensation for mere inconveniences.[61] Interestingly, none of the five civil law cases discussed above relied on the de minimis maxim, preferring instead to quote from *Mustapha* to reinforce the notion that not all mental harm is actionable.

The civil law cases discussed above have a common thread: the plaintiff's mental harm is more akin to a form of inconvenience than a serious injury. For example, in *Cyr* the court is clearly concerned with the 'peculiarity' of the harm,[62] while in *Mazzonna* the judge qualifies the damage as 'negligible' inconveniences[63] which were 'not enough to meet the threshold, however prima facie, of the existence of "compensable damages"'.[64] Noting that four out of five decisions were not favourable to the plaintiffs, it seems correct to point out that *Mustapha* was relied on to justify limiting the claims. The courts apparently sought judicial reinforcement of the notion that compensable mental harm must amount to more than mere upsets and general annoyances of daily living. Otherwise, why would these courts refer to the Supreme Court's statement on the threshold of actionable mental harm? The reliance on the Supreme Court decision could point to the paucity of civil law precedents enunciating explicitly a threshold of harm, a situation that is perhaps unsurprising in a system relying on a general extracontractual liability clause—Article 1457 CCQ—as a basis for the obligation to indemnify for harm.

---

[56]   See Lehoux, above n 55, 72.

[57]   See, eg, *Loiselle v Bernard* 2008 QCCS 1616.

[58]   Lehoux, above n 55, 67, states that under Quebec law it is not possible to define psychological harm by simply referring to the DSM-V.

[59]   J Hétu, 'De minimis non curat praetor: une maxime qui a toute son importance!' (1990) 50 *Canadian Bar Review* 1065. The rule has been discussed in the context of an interesting article on class actions based on inconveniences, annoyances and frustrations in Quebec: CA Carron and AC Garin, 'A Trifle Inconvenient, Class Actions for Inconvenience and Stress under Quebec Civil and Canadian Common Law: A Comparative Study' in TL Archibald and RS Echlin (eds), *Annual Review of Civil Litigation 2011* (Toronto, Carswell, 2011) 415.

[60]   Carron and Garin, above n 59, 420 fn 22, who refer to only one recent case (2004). The others date back to the 1960s and 1970s. However, see *Thibault v Gestion immobilière Lafrance et Mathieu inc* 2011 QCCQ 4506 (CanLII) [17] relying on the de minimis rule to reject a claim for compensation for inconveniences.

[61]   Carron and Garin, above n 59, 420–21.

[62]   *Cyr v Ste-Adèle (City of)* 2009 QCCS 2827 [56]: 'la singularité du préjudice subi'.

[63]   *Mazzonna v DaimlerChrysler Financial Services Canada Inc/Services financiers DaimlerChrysler inc* 2012 QCCS 958, [57].

[64]   ibid [58].

Interestingly, from a common law perspective, none of the civil law decisions examined herein has associated *Mustapha* with the need to prove an RPI. This is to be contrasted with the post-*Mustapha* common law cases where the contrary view has been adopted. On this point, there is, at first glance, clear divergence between the two legal systems as to where the line should be drawn in terms of actionable mental harm flowing from tortious acts. What this chapter will now argue is that the civil law courts' view of *Mustapha* is also the way the common law courts should properly interpret the Supreme Court's decision.

A Different Interpretation of *Mustapha*: A Step towards Convergence?

This author has argued in detail elsewhere[65] that in light of the judicial treatment of the nature of actionable mental harm in Canadian common law since the early twentieth century, *Mustapha* could and should be interpreted in a flexible way, in the sense that the preferred threshold should not require the identification of an RPI. A short summary of the argument is presented here in order to explore the possible convergence of Canadian common and civil law on the threshold issue.

In order to understand what is proposed, it is essential to emphasise that when common law courts or doctrinal works mention the obligation to prove an RPI they almost always do so in conjunction with the rule whereby there can be no compensation for mere upsets or distresses of life. A plaintiff must establish that the harm goes beyond the emotions that are part and parcel of human life, such as distress, grief, anxiety, and is, in fact, an RPI.[66] This orthodox view treats mental harm as an either/or proposition.

However, a tortious act can cause a wide spectrum of mental reactions, some of which rise above mere upset but fall short of an RPI. In that sense, there is an upper threshold (the RPI) and a lower threshold (the need that harm be more than 'mere upset'). Some Canadian courts have recognised the middle ground between both thresholds[67] and the argument is that the Supreme Court in *Mustapha* has endorsed this position or, at least, has raised doubts about the continued primacy of the orthodox view.

In *Mustapha* the Court did not endorse the RPI threshold as it is presently understood in Canadian law but chose instead to emphasise the notion that compensable harm must amount to more than mere upsets of life. According to this interpretation, it is argued that the use of the phrase 'serious and prolonged' simply provided another way of defining the lower threshold rather than articulating a new upper limit or 'merely stat[ing] the [RPI] test in different words'.[68]

The suggestion that *Mustapha* be understood as enunciating a 'lower threshold' of actionable mental harm is consistent with how the law has historically developed in Canada at

---

[65] The study was done through two companion articles. For the first, see Bélanger-Hardy, 'Reconsidering', above n 26, and for the second, see 'The Recognizable Psychiatric Injury Threshold in Canadian Negligence Law: A Policy-Based Appraisal' (2013) 36 *Dalhousie Law Journal* 103.

[66] R Mulheron, 'Rewriting the Requirement for a "Recognized Psychiatric Injury" in Negligence Claims' (2012) 32 *OJLS* 77, 78 (describing this threshold as the 'Traditional Rule').

[67] See, eg, Southin JA's decision in *Rhodes v Canadian National Railway* (1990) 50 BCLR (2d) 273 (CA) and in *McDermott v Ramadanovic Estate* (1988) 27 BCLR (2d) 45 (SC).

[68] Mentioned by the Court in *Kotai v Queen of the North (Ship)* 2009 BCSC 1405, [2009] BCJ No 2022 (QL) [60], while referring to defendant's counsel's argument that *Mustapha* 'merely state[d] the test in different words' and used the expression 'serious trauma and illness' to refer to an RPI.

least until 1970, and is supported by the fact that the Supreme Court has never explicitly endorsed the RPI requirement in decisions prior to *Mustapha*.[69]

In previous work,[70] after a discussion of the policy considerations underlying the setting of a limit along the spectrum of possible mental reactions to a tortious act, a model based on a 'no compensation for mere upsets' threshold was proposed as it appears most apt to strike the correct balance between deterring legal actions based on 'mere upsets' of life and recognising the legitimacy of 'mid-spectrum' mental harm. The idea of revisiting the threshold and lowering the upper limit of actionable harm has been suggested at times in legal precedents[71] and doctrinal works.[72] Moreover, there are strong public policy reasons militating in favour of such an approach.[73]

Given this suggestion to rely only on a 'lower threshold' to limit the scope of actionable stand-alone mental harm, the Quebec cases discussed above provide a useful example of how the criterion could work in practice. The courts were able to successfully weed out claimants whose alleged mental distress did not appear to amount to injury at law, and supported their decision to do so by referring to the 'lower threshold' described in *Mustapha*.

Coming back to the notion of convergence, the juxtaposition of the proposed interpretation of *Mustapha* with the interpretation civil law courts have given of the decision points to a possible rapprochement regarding the threshold issue. In both legal systems, stand-alone mental harm would not be compensated unless it reached a minimal threshold: the injury would have to 'rise above the ordinary annoyances, anxieties and fears that people living in society routinely, if sometimes reluctantly, accept'.[74] Beyond this, injury crossing the threshold could be compensated. In essence, the suggestion is that the common law should converge, in the sense of leaning in a common direction,[75] towards the civil law's interpretation of *Mustapha*.

From the civil law perspective, it is important to recognise that only a small number of cases have relied on the obiter dicta in *Mustapha*. Questions arise as to the possible integration of the decision in a civil law system. How does a threshold of actionable harm, albeit a low threshold, fit within the *civiliste* culture which favours compensation of injury? The rare reliance on the de minimis maxim[76] in civil liability cases could indicate a certain reluctance to limit the scope of actionable harm although it must be recalled that even civil

---

[69] This idea is developed fully in Bélanger-Hardy, 'Reconsidering', above n 26, 598–610. Briefly, the RPI formula is associated with the British case *Hinz v Berry* [1970] 2 QB 40 (CA). The article argues that Canadian courts were historically content to rely on the 'no compensation for mere upsets' rule or to link mental harm to a physical injury, no matter how slight, and which they occasionally found even in instances of stand-alone mental injury cases. Following *Hinz*, some Canadian courts started to insist on an RPI. Although there is no doubt that this case was the catalyst for introducing the phrase 'recognisable psychiatric illness' in Canadian tort vocabulary, a detailed examination of the concurring judgments in the decision raises serious doubts as to the Court's intent to affect a dramatic change in the law.

[70] Bélanger-Hardy, 'Policy', above n 65, 130–33.

[71] For pre-*Mustapha* decisions, see n 67. For post-*Mustapha* cases see Bélanger-Hardy, 'Reconsidering', above n 26.

[72] See especially D Butler, *Damages for Psychiatric Injury* (Annandale, Federation Press, 2004); Mullany and Handford, above n 2; H Teff, *Causing Psychiatric and Emotional Harm: Reshaping the Boundaries of Liability* (Oxford, Hart Publishing, 2009); Mulheron, above n 66.

[73] These are reviewed in detail in Bélanger-Hardy, 'Policy', above n 65. The article concludes that some of the perceived advantages of the RPI rule, in particular predictability, are debatable and that insistence on the traditional formula raises issues of access and fairness.

[74] *Mustapha v Culligan of Canada Inc* 2008 SCC 27, [2008] 2 SCR 114, [9].

[75] See comment n 5.

[76] See Carron and Garin's analysis, above n 59, and comments in n 60.

law systems have some built-in limits to liability. What seems fairly obvious is the apparent need for clearer principles to assist courts in identifying actionable moral injury at least when 'inconveniences' are involved.[77] The need for more guidance is highlighted by the fact that, in these instances, some civil law courts have resorted to *Mustapha*, a common law decision.

All of this shows the importance of recognising that the issue of a threshold of actionable mental harm is part of a wider inquiry into the concept of damage, on the one hand, and the scope of civil liability for tortious acts, on the other. Both topics raise crucial questions for both common law and civil law systems.

IV. The Wider Debate on Damage: Convergence of Preoccupations and Concerns

At the outset, it must be said that, from the perspective of the common law, in-depth studies of the concept of damage are few, but this may be slowly changing as evidenced by a recent article on the topic.[78] In Quebec, although doctrinal works usually dedicate an important part of discussions on liability to the notion of injury (*préjudice*), they tend to focus heavily on issues linked to damages[79] and less so on the theoretical analysis of the concept of injury.[80] There is even less on moral injury although a recent study has addressed the issue.[81] Recent works have highlighted a number of issues about terminology and the need for further definition and clarification of key concepts.[82]

Beyond definitional concerns, however, more research is required on what constitutes damage (and injury), and by extension moral harm. Speaking of damage in general, Nolan suggests that it is 'impossible to define damage for the purposes of a negligence action without falling into circularity' and that the 'extension of damage beyond physical harm to encompass harms such as psychiatric injury ... makes the task of definition harder still'.[83] In his opinion part of the solution lies in the rights-based analysis of tort law. This would be an interesting avenue to explore further from a mental harm perspective. In his discussion Nolan describes personal injury as a 'form of damage' that includes physical and psychological injury, both of which are underpinned by the notion of impairment.[84] Suggestions

---

[77]   Carron and Garin, above note 59, 55–56 and *Fortin v Mazda Canada Inc* 2014 QCCS 2617, [150].

[78]   See D Nolan, 'Damage in the English Law of Negligence' (2013) 4 *Journal of Tort Law* 259.

[79]   See, eg, Baudouin, above n 30, where approximately 80% of the pages dedicated to the analysis of injury (préjudice) deal with damages.

[80]   Tancelin, above n 4, 546, who speaks of the insufficiency of theoretical analysis; Morin, above n 55, 21.

[81]   See Morin, above n 55. The seminal work on mental harm in tort in the common law world is that of Mullany and Handford, above n 2.

[82]   At common law, discussing the notion of damage in general, Nolan, above n 78, 265–67 notes concerns about equating damage and loss. At civil law Morin, above n 55, 9 explains that in practice, Quebec courts interchange terms such as damage, injury, loss and even damages. Indeed, according to this author, there appears to be an astounding variety of terms and expressions employed in Quebec to describe mental harm (more than 20 different expressions are used): ibid 225 fn 481.

[83]   Nolan, above n 78, 265.

[84]   ibid 270. He discusses briefly (at 273–76) the RPI threshold in the context of English law, expressing the view it should not be abandoned and recognising that French law is much more open as it pertains to claims based on emotional harm.

of this type are a good start and point to the need for an in-depth exploration of the notion of damage in terms of its emotional, psychological and psychiatric components.

In Quebec, as explained above, 'moral injury' has had to be redefined within a tripartite classification based on a distinction between bodily, moral and material injury. Morin argues that the confusion which sometimes arises in the case law about moral injury could be resolved by a better understanding of the distinction between damage (*dommage*) and injury (*préjudice*).[85] The suggestion will need to be examined more closely as currently the two terms are almost always employed as synonyms both by Quebec courts and in doctrinal works.[86]

Beyond issues related to the concept of damage itself, from a comparative perspective it is interesting to consider the debate currently taking place in France in the context of the Europeanisation of civil liability laws.[87] Of interest is the fact that some of the reform projects would bring France's civil liability rules closer to a model based on a differentiated protection of interests similar to the Germanic model.[88] The topic is complex and cannot be fully discussed here except to say that the adoption of a model based on the protection of interests is seen as an 'instrument on which a hierarchy of damages could be based'.[89] Whether a hierarchy would lead to a more restricted view of mental harm is hard to tell, as it appears the intention generally is to protect physical and mental integrity.[90]

Although these discussions are taking place in Europe, the concerns are not foreign to Canada. One Quebec author has recently spoken of 'forces of contraction' within conceptualistic civil law systems such as those in Quebec and France, and 'forces of expansion' in casuistic systems such as the common law[91] brought about by the pressure to constantly redefine what constitutes actionable harm in modern societies. The same author has assessed the extent to which a relative conception of extracontractual liability[92] should be imported in Quebec to restrict the scope of liability. Although she concludes that the general liability principle (and conceptualist technique) should not be dramatically changed in that province, she recognises that the tools provided by the Code may not be as efficient at weeding out unmeritorious claims as those of other systems.[93]

This in an interesting perspective from which to consider the civil law cases described above and the guidance the courts sought from *Mustapha*. In this context, it appears that

---

[85] Morin, above n 55, 232.

[86] See Baudouin, above n 30, 363.

[87] For a good summary of the situation, see P Brun and C Quézel-Ambrunaz, 'French Tort Law Facing Reform' (2013) 2 *Journal of European Tort Law* 78; Borghetti, above n 2, 176–79 who explains that there are two competing doctrinal projects to reform civil liability law in France: the Catala project and the Terré project. See P Catala (ed), *Avant-projet de réforme du droit des obligations et de la prescription* (Paris, La documentation française, 2005) and F Terré (ed), *Pour une réforme du droit de la responsabilité civile* (Paris, Dalloz, 2011).

[88] See especially Terré, above n 87, 75ff.

[89] Our translation of 'offrir un instrument pouvant justifier une hiérarchie entre les différents dommages' in C Grare-Didier, 'Du Dommage' in Terré, above n 87, 133.

[90] eg, Brun and Quézel-Ambrunaz, above n 87, 83, write: 'There is certainly a general movement in Europe that could rapidly lead to a consensus on the pre-eminence properly to be accorded to the compensation of bodily damage.'

[91] M Lacroix, 'La relativité aquilienne en droit de la responsabilité civile—Analyse comparée des systèmes germanique, canadien et québécois' (2013) 59 *McGill Law Journal* 425, 450.

[92] Which, based on the theory of Aquilian relativity, tends to circumscribe the scope of civil liability: ibid 431–36.

[93] In her view the solution lies in the development of a stronger link between wrongfulness (illicéité) and the standard of conduct, as well as in a better understanding of the notions of causation and injury.

further inquiries into the threshold of actionable mental harm issue—at least under the theme of convergence of legal systems—should perhaps take into account the climate in which the traditionally victim-oriented civil law systems are currently discussing the scope of extracontractual liability. The hope is that the 'openness' towards victims will not totally disappear as such a quality is particularly important in the context of compensation for mental harm where claimants are sometimes viewed with suspicion.

V. Conclusion

The objective of this chapter was to consider possible points of intersection between the Canadian common law and Quebec's civil law regarding thresholds of actionable mental harm in the tort/extracontractual liability context. The starting point was the Supreme Court of Canada's decision in *Mustapha*. While common law courts have viewed the Court's comments as affirming the need for plaintiffs to prove an RPI, some civil law courts have quoted from the decision to confirm the principle according to which there can be no compensation for the mere upsets and annoyances of daily life.

This apparent divergence in interpretation was questioned in light of a more flexible interpretation of the Supreme Court's pronouncements on the threshold issue which, if adopted by Canadian courts, would create a rapprochement between Canada's two legal traditions regarding the manner in which mental harm is apprehended. More specifically, the hope is that the common law will move away from the RPI requirement towards a new threshold of harm based on a 'no compensation for mere upsets' formula. Meanwhile, Quebec courts seem to be searching for guidance on how to differentiate between mere inconveniences and actionable harm. Relying on the 'more than mere upsets' threshold could be helpful in this regard. Whether this heralds a degree of convergence towards the common law remains to be seen.

Ultimately, even if one was to reject the notion of convergence within Canadian law as too tenuous, it is clear that there is a convergence in preoccupations and concerns not only about mental harm but, more generally, about the concept of damage, its definition and its scope. In this context, encouraging a more meaningful dialogue between Canada's two legal traditions could be beneficial to mental harm claimants in both systems when they seek to assert their right to fair compensation.

4

'Pure Economic Loss' and Defective Buildings

SARAH GREEN AND PAUL S DAVIES

Recovery for pure economic loss in negligence has for some time been a thorny issue across the common law world. On one view of the case law, it would seem that jurisdictions differ as to whether this type of loss is one with which negligence should be concerned. Yet every jurisdiction recognises that pure economic loss should, in certain circumstances, be recoverable in negligence. Those circumstances exhibit more similarities than they do differences. The real cause of divergence, it seems, lies in the values prioritised by different judicial systems. The most significant divergence within the common law world lies not in the protection of a limited right not to suffer pure economic loss as the result of another's negligence, but in the manner in which contentious issues such as this are addressed. More specifically, the disagreement centres on two points; one formal and one substantive. The formal issue is the extent to which recovery should be determined by legislation, as opposed to a common law at liberty to set its own parameters. The substantive, and somewhat inter-related, issue is whether the question is one of duty or of damage and, if the latter, when such damage is deemed to occur. For example, does the inquiry proceed from an a priori doctrinal assumption that anything classed as 'pure economic loss' is not recoverable, thereby requiring claimants to establish that their situation is exceptional, or does the court treat such cases as standard negligence inquiries, meaning that if a claimant can establish that the defendant owed her a duty of care, breached it and caused her loss of a reasonably foreseeable type, she can recover? As might be predicted, those jurisdictions that favour the latter approach are also those that tend to look less to the legislature to define their boundaries. At the risk oversimplifying the legal landscape, it would seem that England is leading the charge for the exclusionary-rule-statutory-exception route, whilst almost every other system[1] has plumped for common law flexibility.[2]

This leads inevitably to a question of why jurisdictions diverge in this way. The familiar conservatism of English law may be explained partly by deference to its own tradition and endowment, but also by the need (perceived or actual) to safeguard the hallowed certainties of its commercial rules—not an export to be undervalued. It might also be the case that

---

[1] With the exception of Malaysia: see *Government of Malaysia v Cheah Foong Chiew* [1993] 2 Malayan Law Journal 439.

[2] Although see recently *Brookfield Multiplex Ltd v Owners Corporation Strata Plan 61288* [2014] HCA 36, (2014) 313 ALR 408 [134] (Crennan, Bell and Keane JJ), discussed below, text to nn 46 and 61.

the overcrowded island over which its revered but infamously scarce court resources must preside leads to a default tendency to limit, rather than to expand, litigation opportunities. What is clear is that, viewed through the lens of pure economic loss debates, English courts diverge from their common law counterparts in ways which transcend the specific issues of the instant question.

What is 'Pure Economic Loss'?

This is the pivotal question, and one which suggests that substantive disagreements about whether to allow recovery for a certain type of loss in negligence do not go to the heart of the issue. This is because there is no consensus, not only between jurisdictions but also within them, as to what counts as 'pure economic loss' and what does not: a particular form of damage, classed by one court as 'purely economic' might be classified by another (in another place, or in another era within the same jurisdiction)[3] as 'property damage' or 'consequential economic loss'. Divergent results across national boundaries suggest heterogeneous values; divergent definitional criteria suggest heterogeneous methods.

> Exemplary and nominal damages aside, a plaintiff awarded monetary redress for damage to his property is essentially being compensated for economic loss. It is in his pocket, not in his person, that he has suffered. The distinction between 'pure' economic loss and economic loss flowing from deprivation of the use of property is especially thin. ... Perhaps even more metaphysical is the debate about the complex structure concept—whether a house is one whole item of property or an assembly of integrated parts. That anything should turn on this, that it should be a subject of grave discussion in the highest court of a land, gives it curiosity value and the charm going with fine points of law. As a touchstone for answering practical questions it may not turn out to be reliable. A result suggested, though possibly not actually decided, by opinions in *Murphy* is that if a contractor supplies only part of a house, such as the electrical system or boilers or steel framing, he owes a duty of reasonable care to successive owners to safeguard them from economic loss caused by damage to other parts of the building; yet not if he supplies the whole house. The smaller the role, the greater the responsibility. It must be respectfully questioned whether such a distinction can survive.[4]

In England, in the 1970s, for instance, it seemed crystal clear to Lords Wilberforce, Salmon, Diplock, Simon and Russell that latent defects in a building amount to physical property damage.[5] Less than two decades later, Lords Mackay, Keith, Bridge, Oliver and Jauncey were equally convinced that it could be nothing of the sort, and could only be classed as 'pure economic loss'.[6] In the High Court of Australia, only five years subsequently, however, Brennan J declared that 'it is artificial to classify defects in a building as pure economic loss. Defects in a building are physical defects and the cost of their rectification is consequential on their existence.'[7] In *Invercargill City Council v Hamlin*[8] Lord Lloyd made explicit reference to the divergent interpretations of 'pure economic loss' within common

---

[3] Compare *Anns v Merton Borough Council* [1978] AC 728 (HL) and *Murphy v Brentwood DC* [1991] AC 398 (HL).

[4] R Cooke, 'An Impossible Distinction' (1991) 107 *LQR* 46, 50.

[5] *Anns v Merton Borough Council* [1978] AC 728 (HL).

[6] *Murphy v Brentwood DC* [1991] AC 398 (HL).

[7] *Bryan v Maloney* (1995) 182 CLR 609 (HCA) 643. This is particularly notable since the judgment of Brennan J in *Council of the Shire of Sutherland v Heyman* (1985) 157 CLR 424 (HCA) was influential in the House of Lords' about turn in *Murphy v Brentwood DC* [1991] AC 398.

[8] *Invercargill City Council v Hamlin* [1996] AC 624 (PC).

law systems, when he said, after referring to a series of New Zealand cases in which recovery had been granted for reduction in value alone:

> These cases ... are important because they extended the principle[9] to cases where there was no physical damage as such, nor any certainty that there would be. It was enough that the value of the premises had been reduced. Whether it is right to describe such cases as 'pure' economic loss may not matter very much. They do not depend on pure economic loss in the sense of *White v Jones* [1995] 2 AC 207 or *Henderson v Merrett Syndicates Ltd* [1995] 2 AC 145. For in the building cases the economic loss is suffered by reason of a defect on a physical object.[10]

With respect to Lord Lloyd, whether it is right to describe such cases as 'pure' economic loss matters very much indeed. There are certain situations, most notably those arising in situations akin to the famous English case of *Hedley Byrne v Heller*,[11] in which the loss concerned is, and can only be, described as purely economic, since the facts involve nothing to which a physical injury of any kind can be caused. Where there exists, however, a tangible thing that is physically different in the real world from how it would have been in the counterfactual world in which the defendant had not been negligent (situations which we shall refer to as 'physical defect' cases), the issue has proven to be more difficult. Consequently, the malleability of the concept of pure economic loss, as it is currently understood, is ripe for judicial tailoring to purpose. There are three reasons for recommending a less protean definition, by demarcating clearly between cases of genuine pure economic loss and those concerning intrinsic physical defects:

— the common law does not benefit from the mercurial nature of the current concept of 'pure economic loss';
— the two types of loss currently classified as being 'purely economic' do not exhibit sufficient similarities to justify the use of such an umbrella term; and
— an alternative means of classification is both available and easily applicable.

One of the arguments of this paper, therefore, is that the common law should recognise a dichotomy between (i) genuine pure economic loss cases, such as those in the *Hedley Byrne* line, in which no physical thing has been affected, and (ii) physical defect cases, which are concerned with tangible things, the value of which has been reduced by a defendant's negligence. Such recognition would both provide a more intuitive means of dealing with physical defect cases, and distinguish substantive points of divergence within the common law from mere differences of interpretation. In order to illustrate this, we will consider two of the areas most affected by the current definitional elision:[12] defective property and accrual

---

[9] The principle of recovery for pure economic loss, derived from *Bowen v Paramount Builders (Hamilton) Ltd* [1975] 2 NZLR 546 (HC).

[10] *Invercargill City Council v Hamlin* [1996] AC 624, 636 (PC).

[11] *Hedley Byrne v Heller* [1964] AC 465 (HL): a case which involved negligent investment advice, and in which no tangible asset of the claimant's was involved.

[12] Another obvious point of divergence, although not one dealt with here, lies in the differing interpretations of relational economic loss, such as those discussed in *Leigh and Sillavan Ltd v Aliakmon Shipping Co Ltd* [1986] 1 AC 785 (HL), *Caltex Oil (Australia) Pty Ltd v The Dredge 'Willemstad'* (1976) 136 CLR 529 (HCA) and *Shell UK Ltd v Total UK Ltd* [2010] EWCA Civ 180, [2011] QB 86. As these involve physical changes to tangible things, they too could be classified under the dichotomy outlined herein as physical defect cases, as opposed to genuine pure economic loss cases, but raise further, difficult issues. See generally K Barker, 'Relational Economic Loss: The Search for Rational Limits' in S Degeling, J Edelman and J Goudkamp (eds), *Torts in Commercial Law* (Sydney, Thomson Reuters Australia, 2011).

of actions. It is in these two types of cases that we can see most clearly how jurisdictional identities and instincts influence means far more than they do ends.

Defective Property

The defective property issue is probably the most well known of the situations about which common law systems appear to disagree.[13] Where a defendant's negligence has caused a building to be defective, but that defect has not (yet) damaged anything external to its own fabric, the position of English courts, as a result of *Murphy v Brentwood District Council*,[14] is that a claimant cannot make good this loss through the tort of negligence. In overturning the earlier House of Lords decision in *Anns v Merton London Borough Council*,[15] English law thereby embarked upon a path that turned out to be too narrow for most of its common law counterparts to follow.[16] In *Invercargill CC v Hamlin*,[17] for example, the Court of Appeal of New Zealand found the local council liable for its inspector's negligent approval of defective foundations, and declined to follow the House of Lords' approach in *Murphy*. Significantly, this decision was later endorsed by the Privy Council on the basis that the defective property situation was one 'especially unsuited for the imposition of a single monolithic solution'.[18] On the specific question of the duty of care, Lord Lloyd said:

> In a succession of cases in New Zealand over the last 20 years it has been decided that community standards and expectations demand the imposition of a duty of care on local authorities and builders alike to ensure compliance with local byelaws. …Whether circumstances are in fact so very different in England and New Zealand may not matter greatly. What matters is the perception.[19]

Canada, Australia and Singapore have all taken some sort of pro-liability approach to the matter of defendants whose negligence has caused a claimant to find herself in possession of a building worth less in market terms than she had expected it to be.

---

[13] *Brookfield Multiplex Ltd v Owners Corporation Strata Plan 61288* [2014] HCA 36, (2014) 313 ALR 408 [176] (Gageler J): 'Markedly divergent approaches to whether a builder should be recognised to have such a duty of care to a subsequent owner have now prevailed for more than two decades in other common law jurisdictions. In the United Kingdom, a duty of care has been rejected. In Canada, a duty of care has been recognised, limited to the cost of remedying dangerous defects in the building. In New Zealand, a duty of care has been recognised, extending to the cost of remedying all latent defects. There is no reason to consider any one of those approaches to result in a greater net cost to society than any other. Provided the principle of tortious liability is known, builders can be expected to accommodate it in the contractual terms on which they are prepared to build and subsequent owners can be expected to accommodate it in the contractual terms on which they are prepared to purchase.'

[14] *Murphy v Brentwood DC* [1991] AC 398 (HL).

[15] *Anns v Merton London Borough Council* [1978] AC 728 (HL).

[16] 'Their Lordships' view in that regard seems to us … to have rested upon a narrower view of the scope of the modern law of negligence and a more rigid compartmentalisation of contract and tort than is acceptable under the law of this country': *Bryan v Maloney* (1995) 182 CLR 609 (HCA) 629 (Mason CJ). Although the High Court of Australia in *Brookfield Multiplex Ltd v Owners Corporation Strata Plan 61288* [2014] HCA 36, (2014) 313 ALR 408 found that there was no duty of care on the facts of the case before it, it made no move to overrule *Bryan* and in fact expressly preserved its authority. For more on this, see below, text to nn 32 and 61.

[17] *Invercargill CC v Hamlin* [1994] 3 NZLR 513 (CA).

[18] *Invercargill City Council v Hamlin* [1996] AC 624 (PC) 640 (Lord Lloyd).

[19] ibid 642. Although see Lord Keith in *Murphy v Brentwood DC* [1991] AC 398 (HL) 432.

In *Winnipeg Condominium Corporation No 36 v Bird Construction Co Ltd*[20] the Supreme Court of Canada held a builder[21] liable to a remote purchaser[22] for the costs of repairing intrinsic and dangerous defects caused by negligent construction, and in *Spandeck Engineering v Defence Science & Technology Agency*[23] the Singapore Court of Appeal imposed liability on developers for the same type of loss. In *Bryan v Maloney*[24] the Australian High Court went a step further in imposing liability for the cost of remedying non-dangerous defects.[25] The reasons given for preferring this approach to that of the House of Lords in *Murphy* can be summarised as follows (in no particular order):

—   There is no principled distinction to be made between requiring a defendant to pay for physical damage which has resulted from her negligence, and requiring that defendant to pay for remedial work necessary to prevent such damage occurring.[26]
—   It is bizarre for the law to create a disincentive to repair dangerous defects.[27]
—   Refusing to impose liability on the basis of an analogy with defective chattels is unconvincing, given that defective chattels can be discarded in a way that defective buildings generally cannot.[28]
—   It is reasonably foreseeable that a negligently designed or constructed building will cause personal injury or property damage, leading to a conclusion that there is sufficient proximity between the claimant and defendant on these facts.[29]
—   There has been an assumption of responsibility by the defendant, and reliance on the same by the claimant.[30]
—   There is no issue of indeterminacy in these cases, given the limited class of claimants, the limited cost of remedial work required and the finite useful lives of such buildings.[31]

These arguments are all characterised by judicial pragmatism and a clear view of the practical implications of imposing liability.

---

[20] *Winnipeg Condominium Corporation No 36 v Bird Construction Co Ltd* [1995] 1 SCR 85. This approach had already been adopted by the court in the earlier decision of *City of Kamloops v Nielsen* [1984] 2 SCR 2, which pre-dated *Murphy v Brentwood DC* [1991] AC 398 (HL).

[21] New Zealand has adopted the same approach for builders as well as local authorities: see *Rolls Royce New Zealand Ltd Carver Holt Harvey Ltd* [2005] 1 NZLR 324 (CA).

[22] ie one not in contractual privity with the defendant.

[23] *Spandeck Engineering v Defence Science & Technology Agency* [2007] SGCA 37. See also *RSP Architects Planners & Engineers v Ocean Front Pte Ltd* [1996] 1 SLR 113.

[24] *Bryan v Maloney* (1995) 182 CLR 609 (HCA).

[25] Also allowed to some extent by *Invercargill City Council v Hamlin* [1996] AC 624 (PC), and not ruled out by the reasoning of LaForest J in *Winnipeg Condominium Corporation No 36 v Bird Construction Co Ltd* [1995] 1 SCR 85.

[26] *Winnipeg Condominium Corporation No 36 v Bird Construction Co Ltd* [1995] 1 SCR 85; *Bryan v Maloney* (1995) 182 CLR 609 (HCA) 628.

[27] *Winnipeg Condominium Corporation No 36 v Bird Construction Co Ltd* [1995] 1 SCR 85, 116; *Bryan v Maloney* (1995) 182 CLR 609 (HCA) 649.

[28] *Winnipeg Condominium Corporation No 36 v Bird Construction Co Ltd* [1995] 1 SCR 85, 119; *Bryan v Maloney* (1995) 182 CLR 609 (HCA) 625.

[29] *Winnipeg Condominium Corporation No 36 v Bird Construction Co Ltd* [1995] 1 SCR 85, 115; *Bryan v Maloney* (1995) 182 CLR 609 (HCA) 623, 624, 627.

[30] *Invercargill City Council v Hamlin* [1996] AC 624 (PC) 638–41; *Bryan v Maloney* (1995) 182 CLR 609 (HCA) 624, 627. See also *Byron Avenue* [2010] NZCA 65 [59]

[31] *Winnipeg Condominium Corporation No 36 v Bird Construction Co Ltd* [1995] 1 SCR 85 125–26; *Bryan v Maloney* (1995) 182 CLR 609 (HCA) 623.

Were the reasons given for reaching the opposite result in *Murphy* to be summarised in a similar way, they would look like this:

—   The tort of negligence does not permit recovery for pure economic loss outside of the parameters of *Hedley Byrne*, and these facts do not fit that model because the twin requirements of assumption of responsibility and reliance have not been met.[32]
—   Holding defendants liable on these facts would be tantamount to providing an indefinitely transmissible warranty of quality for buildings, which might then also be adopted for chattels.[33]
—   This particular type of loss is purely economic and, as such, is a matter for contract and not tort.[34]
—   The need for common law liability in such situations has been superseded by the passing of the Defective Premises Act 1972.[35]

This latter reason was probably the most significant reason for the House of Lords' change of direction from *Anns* to *Murphy*:

> By section 1 of the Defective Premises Act 1972 Parliament has in fact imposed on builders and others undertaking work in the provision of dwellings the obligations of a transmissible warranty of the quality of their work and of the fitness for habitation of the completed dwelling. But besides being limited to dwellings, liability under the Act is subject to a limitation period of six years from the completion of the work and to the exclusion provided for by section 2. It would be remarkable to find that similar obligations in the nature of a transmissible warranty of quality, applicable to buildings of every kind and subject to no such limitations or exclusions as are imposed by the Act of 1972, could be derived from the builder's common law duty of care or from the duty imposed by building byelaws or regulations.[36]

This statute is also the reason often used to justify the divergence in common law approaches to the defective property issue.[37] The Defective Premises Act 1972, however, tells us two important things. First, its very existence is evidence of a perceived need to protect remote purchasers of residential houses from the type of loss currently described as 'purely economic' without resort to contract or first party insurance. Second, in section 6(2), the statute itself tells us that: 'Any duty imposed by or enforceable by virtue of any provision of this Act is in addition to any duty a person may owe apart from that provision.'

Despite Lord Bridge's views to the contrary, therefore, the existence of similar duties at common law would not be so very remarkable. This is particularly so given that the Defective Premises Act, whilst significant in its recognition of a right protected in so responsive a

---

[32]   *Murphy v Brentwood DC* [1991] AC 398 (HL) 479, 480, 483, 486. The existence of these dual factors was however, one of the ways in which the High Court of Australia distinguished the facts of *Brookfield Multiplex Ltd v Owners Corporation Strata Plan 61288* [2014] HCA 36, (2014) 313 ALR 408 from *Bryan v Maloney* (1995) 182 CLR 609 (HCA).

[33]   *Murphy v Brentwood DC* [1991] AC 398 (HL) 430, 469.

[34]   ibid 475, 479.

[35]   ibid 419, 433, 441, 451 and 457, and the approved building scheme guarantees, such as the National House-Building Council scheme, which offer some form of protection for purchasers. The NHBC, however, has now stopped submitting schemes for approval: E Peel and J Goudkamp, *Winfield and Jolowicz on Tort*, 19th edn (London, Sweet & Maxwell, 2014) [10-058].

[36]   *Murphy v Brentwood DC* [1991] AC 398 (HL) 480–81 (Lord Bridge).

[37]   eg *Invercargill City Council v Hamlin* [1996] AC 624 (PC) 642; Cooke, above n 4, 69–70.

way in other common law systems, has been subjected to trenchant criticism because of the very limited protection it offers.[38] Spencer has described it as

> a measure which adopts excessively cumbrous means to achieve relatively modest ends; which is drafted in terms which are long-winded, ugly and obscure; and which ultimately changes little—a poor show in view of the complications it creates in the process.[39]

The primary problem with the Act is that it limits liability to defects arising within six years of the completion of the work. Whilst this prevents claims from realising negligence's fear of indeterminacy, it also blunts the statute's teeth. And for no good reason. Given that the average UK house price is now £280,000,[40] it is reasonable for purchasers to expect a longer useful life than half a dozen years. What is more, there was no need to put an arbitrary time limit on such claims in order to prevent liability of an indeterminate amount for an indeterminate time to an indeterminate class[41] because there is no danger of a floodgates problem arising where loss is related (howsoever it is classified) to physical property. As has been recognised elsewhere in the common law world,[42] liability will naturally be limited to the cost of remedying the defects, during the useful life of the building, and in relation to those with sufficient title to that property when the defects 'occur'.[43] These intrinsic limits to such a claim exist because the loss is not really purely economic, but is instead parasitic upon the state of the subject matter of property rights. Since the natural limits of the property nexus apply, the indeterminacy question should never have arisen in the first place.

Consequently, judicial deference to the Defective Premises Act seems neither necessary nor constructive in this context. Not only is it clear that this statute does too little for those at whom it is aimed, but it explicitly restricts itself to 'dwellings', leaving those who acquire defective buildings intended for any other purpose with no protection outside of the law of contract. That the House of Lords felt this to be appropriate says much about its priorities. By contrast, *Bryan*, *Winnipeg*, *Invercargill* and *Byron Avenue* are all decisions which look a lot like practical justice: the courts in those cases recognised the realities of the factual situations before them, and allowed these, rather than legal formalities, to guide their decisions. As Laura Hoyano has observed:

> The Canadian Supreme Court has emphasised that incrementalism preserves the flexibility which is the particular strength of the common law, even though 'absolute logical formulations' of legal principle may be unattainable as a consequence. In their view, any resulting uncertainty in a particular area of negligence will be short-lived as the jurisprudence develops, and is the price which should be willingly paid in preference to the insistence on 'doctrinal tidiness' of exhaustive and definitive rules which the Supreme Court found to be the motivating spirit in *Murphy*.[44]

---

[38]   JR Spencer, 'The Defective Premises Act 1972—Defective Law and Defective Law Reform' (1974) 33 *CLJ* 307; I Duncan Wallace, 'Negligence and Buildings: Confusion Confounded' (1989) 105 *LQR* 46.

[39]   Spencer, above n 38, 307.

[40]   http://www.ons.gov.uk/ons/rel/hpi/house-price-index/february-2015/stb-february-2015.html#tab-Average-house-prices-in-countries-and-regions.

[41]   Cardozo J's famous articulation in *Ultramares Corp v Touche* 174 NE 441 (NY 1932) of the prospect against which the tort of negligence is always vigilant.

[42]   eg, La Forest J in *Winnipeg Condominium Corporation No 36 v Bird Construction Co Ltd* [1995] 1 SCR 85, 124-26 [48]–[50].

[43]   For more on this point, see below 'Accrual of Action'.

[44]   L Hoyano, 'Dangerous Defects Revisited by Bold Spirits' (1995) 58 *MLR* 887, 893.

There is clearly a difficult relationship between the common law of tort and statute in this area.[45] This again reared its head in *Brookfield Multiplex Ltd v Owners Corporation Strata Plan 61288*,[46] in which the High Court of Australia expressed the view that the courts should be slow to extend any protection to be found in statutory schemes.[47] This approach might appeal to those who consider that 'consumer protection' should be best left to the legislature, rather than judges. But it allows interested groups to influence the legislative process, perhaps leading to weaker legislation which fails adequately to protect consumers' rights in particular.[48] It may be that common law solutions should be preferred since they can be more flexible; for example, by recognising that consumers have a right protected by tort law that builders do not negligently cause dangerous defects in property.[49]

In any event, the reluctance to allow recovery for defective buildings under the general law of tort is not obviously warranted. First, it is hard to see why *Hedley Byrne* principles do not apply on the facts of a typical case, since private individuals buying homes have very little choice, or at least any sense that they might want to exercise a choice, but to rely on local authorities to ensure that building regulations are observed. Such reliance has, elsewhere in the English common law of negligence, been deemed to be sufficient grounds for a claim where a claimant has been 'arbitrarily denied a benefit which was routinely provided to others',[50] a description fitting the facts of *Murphy*. The answer might lie in the fact that the power of the local authority to act, or even its public duty to act, does not necessarily create a private right upon which the claimant can rely.[51] But such an explanation does not assist defendant builders and, moreover, if *Hedley Byrne* reasoning can justify the result in *Smith v Eric Bush* on the basis of reliance,[52] it is not at all clear why the same should not have happened in *Murphy*. In *Smith* liability was imposed on a valuer for pure economic loss caused to the purchaser of a house by its negligent valuation. This was done despite the fact that the valuation, complete with disclaimers of which the purchaser was aware, was prepared not for the purchaser, but for the mortgagee of the property concerned. These facts are arguably a step *further* removed from the *Hedley Byrne* model, as it was then understood, than those in *Murphy*, and yet were deemed by the House of Lords to fall within its remit. It seems odd that a negligent builder cannot be liable for economic loss in tort, yet surveyors and architects who negligently give bad advice to a purchaser about the property can be so liable. The apparent applicability of *Hedley Byrne* principles to *Murphy* is also evidenced by the fact that John Spencer, writing in 1974, thought it obvious that, even had the House of Lords deemed the loss in *Anns* to have been purely economic, as opposed to property

---

[45] See too *Kamloops v Nielsen* [1984] 2 SCR 2, 35 (Wilson J); *Sutherland Shire Council v Heyman* (1985) 157 CLR 424 (HCA) 481 (Brennan J).

[46] *Brookfield Multiplex Ltd v Owners Corporation Strata Plan 61288* [2014] HCA 36, (2014) 313 ALR 408.

[47] ibid [134] (Crennan, Bell and Keane JJ), [186] (Gageler J).

[48] cf S Deakin, A Johnston, B Markesinis, *Markesinis and Deakin's Tort Law* (Oxford, Oxford University Press, 2012) 292.

[49] eg, *Winnipeg Condominium Corporation No 36 v Bird Construction Co Ltd* [1995] 1 SCR 85.

[50] See Lord Hoffmann in *Stovin v Wise* [1996] AC 923 (HL) 953, and the use made of this in the claimant's favour in the New Zealand Court of Appeal's decision on facts similar to *Murphy* in *Byron Avenue* [2010] NZCA 65 [59]. For critical discussion of a notion of 'general reliance', see D Nolan, 'The Liability of Public Authorities for Failing to Confer Benefits' (2011) 124 *LQR* 260, 275.

[51] See, eg, R Stevens, 'Salvaging the Law of Torts' in PS Davies and J Pila (eds), *The Jurisprudence of Lord Hoffmann* (Oxford, Hart Publishing, 2015).

[52] *Smith v Eric Bush* [1990] 1 AC 831 (HL) esp 871–72 (Lord Jauncey).

damage, the claimant could nonetheless have been successful on the basis of *Hedley Byrne*.[53] The House of Lords' classification of the claimant's loss in *Murphy* as purely economic, and its consequent denial of recovery, is therefore doubly capricious; even were such loss to be regarded as being purely economic, recovery should nevertheless have been granted through an application of *Hedley Byrne*.

Second, the objection to the creation of an effective transmissible warranty, a concern correlative to the Court's desire to keep contract and tort as parallel entities, is based on concerns that are both exaggerated and misled. Whilst warranties now look at home in the law of contract, they are by no means thoroughbred, and in fact grew up alongside the tort of deceit.[54] In any event, there is nothing intrinsically contractual about the concept of a warranty and, subject to the constant spectre of indeterminacy, to which we shall return below, a transmissible warranty of quality is only a bad thing if viewed from the point of view of negligent producers and service providers. A tort of negligence formed with only the interests of defendants in mind would be a very simple construct indeed. What is more, the fear that such a warranty, even if it were to apply to buildings, would somehow be automatically transmuted into a rudiment of personal property law, is inexplicable. If the veil between the worlds of personal and real property were so thin, then arguably the whole property damage versus pure economic loss debate could quickly be resolved by reference to section 1(c) of the Torts (Interference with Goods) Act 1977, which defines as one instance of wrongful interference with goods 'negligence so far as it results in damage to goods *or to an interest in* goods'. The italicised words might preclude the need for semantic hand-wringing over how to classify latent defects in property since, physically manifest or not,[55] defects in property affect one's interest in it. On the other hand, it might be argued that the property itself is simply not worth as much as the claimant envisaged, and that no interest in the goods has been damaged: the damage was inherent in the goods purchased.[56] In any event, however, decisions across the common law world demonstrate that the distinct characteristics of real property and its acquisition, significance and logistics mean that legal rules formed in relation to it have no natural applicability to personal property.[57]

Third, the strict separation of contract and tort does a greater service for textbook writers than it does for the common law. Whilst it is clear that double recovery should be avoided, the argument against a claimant having a choice of avenue for that recovery is not nearly so strong. The House of Lords itself, perhaps against its natural instincts, accepted as much when it decided *Henderson v Merrett Syndicates*,[58] in which Lord Goff said:

> [I]n the instant case, liability can, and in my opinion should, be founded squarely on the principle established in *Hedley Byrne* itself, from which it follows that an assumption of responsibility coupled with the concomitant reliance may give rise to a tortious duty of care irrespective of whether there is a contractual relationship between the parties, and in consequence, unless the contract precludes him from doing so, the plaintiff, who has available to him concurrent remedies in contract and tort, may choose that remedy which appears to him to be the most advantageous.[59]

[53] Spencer, above n 38, 311 fn 17.
[54] Cooke, above n 4, 59 and W Holdsworth, *History of English Law*, vol VIII (London, Methuen, 1937) 68.
[55] For more on this, see below 'Accrual of Action'.
[56] cf *Sutherland Shire Council v Heyman* (1985) 157 CLR 424 (HCA) 504–05 (Deane J).
[57] See, eg, *Winnipeg Condominium Corporation No 36 v Bird Construction Co Ltd* [1995] 1 SCR 85, 119; *Bryan v Maloney* (1995) 182 CLR 609 (HCA) 625.
[58] *Henderson v Merrett Syndicates* [1995] 2 AC 145 (HL).
[59] ibid 194.

LeDain J, speaking for a unanimous Supreme Court of Canada, put the argument in remarkably similar terms:

> A concurrent or alternative liability in tort will not be admitted if its effect would be to permit the plaintiff to circumvent or escape a contractual exclusion or limitation of liability for the act or omission that would constitute the tort. Subject to this qualification, where concurrent liability in tort and contract exists the plaintiff has the right to assert the cause of action that appears to be most advantageous to him in respect of any particular legal consequence.[60]

If the existence of a contract between claimant and defendant, which offers a remedy for the problem in hand, does not negate the presence of a duty of care in negligence, it is not at all clear why the *absence* of such contractual protection should do so. Whilst it is true that tort should not undermine a contractual agreement with which its operation would conflict, it seems odd to equate the fact that a claimant secured no contractual protection against a particular loss with a contractual position which militates against the imposition of a tortious liability. Other common law jurisdictions have interpreted the claimant's failure to secure his or her own contractual protection as being evidence of the claimant's relative vulnerability.[61] English courts, on the other hand, have regarded such a failure as a reason not to offer any alternative protection.[62] This shows a divergence in approach: the English judicial priority seems to be keeping doctrinal order and the primacy of contract,[63] whereas the priority elsewhere in the common law world seems to be evaluating the realities and merits of particular cases.

Accrual of Action

There is also marked divergence within the common law on the question of *when* a negligence claim relating to defective property accrues. The leading English decision remains that of the House of Lords in *Pirelli General Cable Works Ltd v Oscar Faber & Partners*.[64] The claimants hired the defendants, a firm of consulting engineers, to advise on and design an addition to their factory premises, which included a chimney. The chimney was built in 1969, but the material used was unsuitable and cracks developed at the top of the chimney by April 1970. These were discovered by the claimants in 1977. In 1978 the claimants issued proceedings against the defendants for their negligent design of the chimney. Even though it was found that the claimants could not with reasonable diligence have discovered the cracks before 1972, it was held that the claim was barred as it was not brought within six years of the accrual of the cause of action.[65] Lord Fraser thought he was bound by an earlier

---

[60] *Central Trust Co v Rafuse* [1986] 2 SCR 147.
[61] See *Williams v Mount Eden Borough Council* [1986] 1 NZBLC 102 [551] (Casey J). See also L Hoyano, above n 44, 892, text to fn 33, and *Brookfield Multiplex* [2014] HCA 36, (2014) 313 ALR 408 [30], [58] and [185]. The judgments in the latter case provide an excellent example of the way in which Australian courts deal with the question as one of duty, (which is determinable by the facts of a particular case), as opposed to damage (which is determined absolutely and in an a priori sense as irrecoverable): see in particular [58], [60], [69] and [185].
[62] *Murphy v Brentwood DC* [1991] AC 398 (HL) 475.
[63] See too, eg, *Brookfield Multiplex Ltd v Owners Corporation Strata Plan 61288* [2014] HCA 36, (2014) 313 ALR 408 [132] (Crennan, Bell and Keane JJ)
[64] *Pirelli General Cable Works Ltd v Oscar Faber & Partners* [1983] 2 AC 1.
[65] Limitation Act 1939 (UK) s 2(1).

decision of the House of Lords in *Cartledge v E Jopling & Sons Ltd*,[66] a case concerning personal injuries, which held that 'time begins to run whether or not damage could be discovered'.[67] Lord Fraser considered that the same principle applied in the context of property damage. His Lordship insisted that the defect itself was insufficient for the cause of action to arise, since that may never lead to any damage to the building; rather, the cause of action accrued when the damage occurred, which happened with the cracks coming into existence, even though the cracks were undiscovered and undiscoverable.[68] However, Lord Fraser further commented that he agreed with Lord Reid in *Cartledge* 'that such a result appears to be unreasonable and contrary to principle, but I think the law is now so firmly established that only Parliament can alter it'.[69]

Pirelli is a difficult decision. It placed the onus squarely on Parliament to alleviate the harsh regime that applied such that a cause of action could arise and be lost before it was discoverable by a claimant. Thankfully, legislation was soon passed.[70] But courts in other jurisdictions were less willing to allow the common law to deprive claimants of a remedy. For example, in *Kamloops v Nielsen*[71] the Supreme Court of Canada had to decide a similar issue at the same time as *Pirelli*; in fact, *Pirelli* was handed down after oral argument in *Kamloops* had been heard. Wilson J said:

> There are obvious problems in applying *Pirelli*. To what extent does physical damage have to have manifested itself? Is a hairline crack enough or does there have to be a more substantial manifestation? And what of an owner who discovers that his building is constructed of materials which will cause it to collapse in five years' time? According to *Pirelli* he has no cause of action until it starts to crumble. But perhaps the most serious concern is the injustice of a law which statute-bars a claim before the plaintiff is even aware of its existence. Lord Fraser and Lord Scarman were clearly concerned over this but considered themselves bound by *Cartledge*. The only solution in their eyes was the intervention of the legislature.[72]

By contrast, the Canadian court did not wish to impose upon the legislature in the same manner, and instead found that time only began to run from the point at which the damage was reasonably discoverable.[73] A similar approach has been adopted elsewhere in the Commonwealth.[74]

One aspect of the decision in *Pirelli* that might underlie a strict approach to the time of accrual is that the claim was framed in tort in order to circumvent the fact that the claim for breach of contract was time-barred.[75] As outlined above,[76] there is a divergence of views about how contract and tort should relate to one another in the context of concurrent

---

[66] *Cartledge v E Jopling & Sons Ltd* [1963] AC 758 (HL).
[67] ibid 772 (Lord Reid). Compare *Sparham-Souter v Town and Country Developments (Essex) Ltd* [1976] QB 858 (CA).
[68] *Pirelli General Cable Works Ltd v Oscar Faber & Partners* [1983] 2 AC 1 (HL) 16.
[69] ibid 19.
[70] Latent Damage Act 1986 (UK).
[71] *Kamloops v Nielsen* [1984] 2 SCR 2.
[72] ibid 40 (delivering the judgment of herself and Ritchie and Dickson JJ).
[73] See too *Central Trust Co v Rafuse* [1986] 2 SCR 147, 224 (Le Dain J): 'There is no principled reason, in my opinion, for distinguishing in this regard between an action for injury to property and an action for the recovery of purely financial loss caused by professional negligence, as was suggested in *Forster v Outred*, at pp 765–66.'
[74] eg *Sutherland Shire Council v Heyman* (1985) 157 CLR 424 (HCA) (Australia); *Invercargill City Council v Hamlin* [1996] AC 624 (PC) (New Zealand).
[75] *Pirelli General Cable Works Ltd v Oscar Faber & Partners* [1983] 2 AC 1, 12.
[76] See text to n 58.

claims. It may be that such claims—which might be called 'contorts'[77]—deserve their own distinct rules.[78] Or that the stricter contract rules of remoteness and limitation should also govern the tort claim.[79] But this is another area of the law where it is not clear why English courts treat tort law as if it were subservient to contract. If the rules in remoteness or limitation are more generous in tort than contract, this could be for good reason. As Lord Walker said in a speech given in Queensland, 'the tendency towards the assimilation of concurrent remedies in contract and tort may be in danger of going too far'.[80] Whilst it might be that the tendency in England to give priority to contract over tort results from a desire to maintain the integrity of the former owing to its international significance, this is not a reason to which any explicit concession is made in this context. It can, therefore, only function as a speculative explanation.

Perhaps the most difficult aspect of *Pirelli* is that it treats the relevant claim as one for property damage. This was consistent with the decision of the House of Lords in *Anns v Merton*, but not with the subsequent decision in *Murphy*. If, as *Murphy* currently dictates, the claim should be understood as one for pure economic loss, it is not clear that time should begin to run from the same date, namely when the cracks came into existence. In *Murphy* Lord Keith explained *Pirelli* as based upon the defendant's assumption of responsibility in a similar manner to *Hedley Byrne v Heller*, but did not say whether or not the decision remains good law as regards the accrual of a cause of action in tort. *Pirelli* is still applied in England such that time does not begin to run from the defect itself, but from when the damage comes into existence.[81] Nevertheless, in *Abbott v Will Gannon and Smith Ltd* Tuckey LJ asked:

> So what is the present state of the law of England? With three House of Lords' cases[82] to guide us it ought to be possible to give a clear answer to this question, but I regret that I feel unable to do so with any confidence.[83]

This is lamentable, particularly given judges' concern to promote clarity and certainty. Ultimately, the facts of *Abbott* were essentially indistinguishable from *Pirelli*, so the Court of Appeal considered itself bound by precedent to follow the decision of the House of Lords.

However, in *Abbott* Tuckey LJ expressed the view that if the Court of Appeal was not bound by *Pirelli*, he would have held that 'pure economic loss' did not occur when the physical damage appeared, but only when the defect 'manifested itself in some way which would affect the value of the building, measured either by the cost of repairs or depreciation in market value'.[84] This approach is consistent with the view that, until the defendant

---

[77] S Hedley, 'Negligence—Pure Economic Loss—Goodbye Privity, Hello Contorts' (1995) 54 *CLJ* 27.

[78] J O'Sullivan, 'The Meaning of "Damage" in Pure Financial Loss Cases: Contract and Tort Collide' [2012] *Professional Negligence* 248.

[79] A Burrows, *Remedies for Torts and Breach of Contract*, 3rd edn (Oxford, OUP, 2004) ch 6: cf *Yapp v Foreign and Commonwealth Office* [2014] EWCA Civ 1512 [119] (Underhill LJ).

[80] R Walker, 'Pure Economic Loss: The Problem of Timing' (2012) 20 *Torts Law Journal* 77, 82 (citing *Wardley Australia Ltd v Western Australia* (1992) 175 CLR 514 (HCA) 531).

[81] eg *Abbott v Will Gannon and Smith Ltd* [2005] EWCA Civ 198, [2005] BLR 195; *Robinson v PE Jones (Contractors) Ltd* [2011] EWCA Civ 9, [2012] QB 44.

[82] *Pirelli General Cable Works Ltd v Oscar Faber & Partners* [1983] 2 AC 1 (HL); *Murphy v Brentwood DC* [1991] AC 398 (HL); *Ketteman v Hansel Properties* [1987] AC 189 (HL).

[83] *Abbott v Will Gannon and Smith Ltd* [2005] EWCA Civ 198, [2005] BLR 195 [17].

[84] ibid [20].

is 'hit in his pocket', there is no damage capable of forming the gist of a negligence claim. Yet it may be questioned whether this is consistent with the House of Lords' decision in *Murphy*; if 'pure economic loss' arises because the property is defective, the cause of action would arguably accrue upon completion of the work, meaning that the claimant could sue the defendant as soon as the work was finished. This might seem logical when analysing the cause of action itself, but it would have harsh results in the context of limitation: time would begin to run from a point even earlier than in *Pirelli*, and claims could continue to arise and disappear before claimants could reasonably discover their existence.[85] Given that, post-*Murphy*, such claims are likely to fail, the danger of limitation issues affecting the substantive law is much reduced, but the situation remains a vivid illustration of the difficulties caused by too promiscuous a use of the 'pure economic loss' label.

In most other jurisdictions not constrained by House of Lords authority *Pirelli* would be decided differently, and with a greater regard for the merits of individual cases.[86] In *Invercargill City Council v Hamlin* the Privy Council had to decide an appeal from New Zealand on an accrual of action question based upon similar facts to *Pirelli*. The Privy Council discussed developments elsewhere in the common law world, and ultimately found that the date of physical damage was not the point at which the cause of action accrued in New Zealand; rather, time began to run from the date of discoverability of the defect, as this was the moment when the claimant suffered a loss. Lord Lloyd said:

> It is regrettable that there should be any divergence between English and New Zealand law on a point of fundamental principle. Whether the *Pirelli* case [1983] 2 A.C. 1 should still be regarded as good law in England is not for their Lordships to say. What is clear is that it is not good law in New Zealand.[87]

The point at which a cause of action arises does seem to be an issue of fundamental principle on which divergence across the common law world is surprising. Surely one would expect a claim in tort to accrue at the same point irrespective of the jurisdiction. So why is there divergence? English law's traditionally restrictive approach to claims of this nature may set it at odds with other jurisdictions reluctant to follow the 'tortuous path'[88] along which English law has developed. It may be that English law differs from its common law brethren simply because the decision of the House of Lords in *Pirelli*, which continues to bind English courts but not others, treated as property damage that which was later shoehorned into the category of 'pure economic loss'. Yet that seems too simplistic, and indeed *Pirelli* has been endorsed in Hong Kong in *The Bank of East Asia Ltd v Tsien Wui Marble Factory Ltd*.[89] This decision, by a bare majority of the Hong Kong Court of Final Appeal, seems to highlight the importance of a particular jurisdiction's limitation regime to deciding when a cause of action accrues. However, the date at which

---

[85] *The Bank of East Asia Ltd v Tsien Wui Marble Factory Ltd* [1999] HKCFA 6, (1999) HKCFAR 349 [244] (Bokhary PJ).

[86] eg *Kamloops v Nielsen* [1984] 2 SCR 2 (Canada); *Sutherland Shire Council v Heyman* (1985) 157 CLR 424 (HCA) (Australia); *Invercargill City Council v Hamlin* [1996] AC 624 (PC) (New Zealand).

[87] *Invercargill City Council v Hamlin* [1996] AC 624 (PC) 649 (it is notable that Lord Keith was also on the Board).

[88] *The Bank of East Asia Ltd v Tsien Wui Marble Factory Ltd* [1999] HKCFA 6, (1999) HKCFAR 349 [164] (Ching PJ).

[89] ibid.

the cause of action accrues is important to every limitation regime, and is not defined by statute. It is defined by the common law, and relevant beyond the confines of limitation.[90] The Privy Council in *Invercargill* was surely right to observe that divergence in this area is 'regrettable'.

In *Tsien Wui Marble Factory* the Bank of East Asia sued its nominated subcontractor and its architect for defective cladding works that were done in 1983 on the bank's headquarters building—a tower block 23 storeys high standing on a podium of 5 storeys. The defective cladding was potentially dangerous; the building was on a busy street, so slabs of granite cladding detaching from the upper floors could obviously have serious effects. Claims were brought in tort against the subcontractors in 1994 and the architects in 1996. The issue for the courts was whether the six-year limitation period for tort claims had expired. This required the court to determine when the bank first sustained loss or damage consequent upon the negligent conduct of the defendants. Findlay J at first instance had found that the bank had suffered 'pure economic loss', but that this only arose when the defect became first known or manifest in 1993, so the claims were not time-barred. This was overturned by the Court of Appeal, which held that economic loss was sustained as soon as the building was completed. A bare majority of the Court of Final Appeal dismissed the appeal, insisting that the bank's claim arose when the physical damage occurred.

Litton PJ noted the 'divergence' in the common law world,[91] but held that Hong Kong should follow *Pirelli*. He considered the Hong Kong laws on limitation to have followed a very similar path to their English counterparts, such that English cases should be followed in order to avoid wreaking 'violence'[92] on the statutory regime.[93] Ching PJ emphasised that discoverability does not cause damage, which must have been inflicted before the date of discoverability,[94] and that the bank had not discharged the burden of establishing that 'pure economic loss' first occurred within the limitation period. Nazareth PJ agreed, despite recognising 'an immediate, if superficial attraction of a moral nature' towards a rule that economic loss only arose when the defect was discoverable.[95]

Bokhary PJ and Lord Nicholls NPJ dissented. Both were persuaded by the approach adopted in *Invercargill*. Bokhary PJ thought that *Pirelli* should be confined to instances of physical damage,[96] and for 'pure economic loss' to have a sensible meaning it could only arise where the claimant could have been aware of the defect. He said:

> I do not think that there can be any doubt that any layman would condemn as an absurdity, injustice and mockery the notion of someone having something which lawyers call a 'cause of action' but which secretly comes about and just as secretly goes away before the victim of a legal wrong can go to a court for a remedy.[97]

---

[90] *Nykredit Mortgage Bank PLC v Edward Erdman Group Ltd* [1997] 1 WLR 1627.

[91] *The Bank of East Asia Ltd v Tsien Wui Marble Factory Ltd* [1999] HKCFA 6, (1999) HKCFAR 349 [59].

[92] ibid [118].

[93] Although the Defective Premises Act 1972 (UK) has no counterpart in Hong Kong.

[94] *The Bank of East Asia Ltd v Tsien Wui Marble Factory Ltd* [1999] HKCFA 6, (1999) HKCFAR 349 [154]: 'it is clear that the discovery or discoverability of damage cannot in itself amount to damage'. See too *Pirelli General Cable Works Ltd v Oscar Faber & Partners* [1983] 2 AC 1 (HL) 16 (Lord Fraser).

[95] *The Bank of East Asia Ltd v Tsien Wui Marble Factory Ltd* [1999] HKCFA 6, (1999) HKCFAR 349 [268].

[96] ibid [245].

[97] ibid [244].

Lord Nicholls NPJ similarly insisted that 'physical damage to the building and financial loss to the owner are not necessarily linked'[98] and robustly held that the statutory regime did not affect the fundamental issue for the common law about when a cause of action accrued:

> [T]his legislation cannot be regarded as having frozen the common law as thus enunciated, and *Pirelli* has already been overtaken. *Pirelli* treated the onset of physical damage to the building as the relevant damage in cases of claims for negligence in the design or construction of buildings. As already noted, that analysis of the relevant damage is no longer regarded as satisfactory. To treat *Pirelli* as still the guiding principle in this field would be to take a retrograde step for which I can see no justification.[99]

The judges in the Hong Kong Court of Final Appeal showed divergence and convergence both amongst themselves and with the common law. This highlights the difficulties associated with identifying the damage and hence accrual of a cause of action as 'pure economic loss' in negligence. The law in Hong Kong is now aligned with that in England and Wales, but differs from the general approach in the common law world. This may be because the statutory regime regarding limitation in Hong Kong closely mirrors its English counterpart, such that a similar date of accrual is sensible. But this treats the date on which the cause of action accrues as relevant only to limitation, which it is not.[100] This is another illustration of the different approaches of different judges in different jurisdictions to the relationship between judge-made law and statute. For example, England has endeavoured to adopt a restrictive approach to the common law in the hope and expectation that statute will ensure appropriate protection for those who deserve it. Judges elsewhere have taken it upon themselves to provide redress through the common law, regardless of statute. Given the pressures on parliamentary time, and the fact that legislation does not always follow where judges deem it necessary, it may be fortunate that English law has reached the equilibrium it has. Every jurisdiction has its own particular challenges, and in *Invercargill* the Privy Council recognised that '[t]he ability of the common law to adapt itself to the differing circumstances of the countries in which it has taken root, is not a weakness, but one of its great strengths'.[101] But although this might influence questions of policy in the context of situations where a claim ought to be recognised, it is less convincing to suggest that this can explain divergence on important points of principle, such as when a cause of action accrues. Moreover, the desire of the Hong Kong Court of Final Appeal to seek convergence with English law may lead to only transient unity; if the English courts drift away from *Pirelli*, that would leave the law of Hong Kong somewhat isolated in the common law world.

Lord Walker has suggested that the root cause of divergence in this area is that 'other Commonwealth countries were more robust in developing a judge-made rule as to discoverability'[102] and refused to 'accept the injustice' inherent in *Cartledge v Jopling & Sons Ltd* and *Pirelli*.[103] Indeed, even approaches to the question of when a cause of action

---

[98] ibid [269].
[99] ibid [276].
[100] eg, *Nykredit Mortgage Bank Plc v Edward Erdman Group Ltd* [1997] 1 WLR 1627 (HL).
[101] *Invercargill City Council v Hamlin* [1996] AC 624 (PC) 640.
[102] Walker, above n 80, 89.
[103] ibid 88.

for genuine pure economic loss accrues differ generally across the common law. This is unfortunate.[104] In *Wardley Australia Ltd v State of Western Australia*,[105] for instance, the plurality in the High Court of Australia said:

> If, contrary to the view which we have just expressed, the English decisions[106] properly understood support the proposition that where, as a result of the defendant's negligent misrepresentation, the plaintiff enters into a contract which exposes him or her to a contingent loss or liability, the plaintiff first suffers loss or damage on entry into the contract, we do not agree with them. In our opinion, in such a case, the plaintiff sustains no actual damage until the contingency is fulfilled and the loss becomes actual; until that happens the loss is prospective and may never be incurred. A deferred liability may stand in a different position but there is no occasion here to discuss that matter.[107]

Wardley indicates a general tendency of Australian courts to find that time should begin to run at a later rather than earlier date. By contrast, English judges have expressed the view that time should begin to run earlier rather than later.[108] But it is unclear why the common law should diverge on this point. It is suggested that allowing claims to be brought within a given period which begins to run from the date at which the economic loss was discoverable or ascertainable[109] does not represent a significant injustice.[110] Indeed, this is the position taken by the English Law Commission.[111] But it is not obvious that the limitation tail should be able to wag the substantive dog.[112] It may be better if English law were to maintain consistency on the accrual point, but the legislative regime on limitation of actions nevertheless requires reform.[113] In other jurisdictions, judges have taken greater initiative in finding that causes of action arise at a later date in order to arrive at a satisfactory law on limitation.

Concluding Remarks

These points of divergence within the common law highlight the inevitable difficulties caused by judicial vacillation between the values of certainty and flexibility. A common law with either one of these as its master is bound at least to be coherent and defensible, but one with divided loyalties is apt only to confuse and mislead. For the most part, the issue of recovery in physical defect cases in negligence seems like an effective barometer, not so

---

[104] eg *The Bank of East Asia Ltd v Tsien Wui Marble Factory Ltd* [1999] HKCFA 6, (1999) HKCFAR 349 268, [230] (Bokhary PJ): 'As to when the cause of action accrues, uniformity of approach across the board as far as possible is certainly desirable. Nevertheless each class of case must be analysed with care in order to ensure that it is approached in a way that matches the true nature of the cause of action involved.'

[105] *Wardley Australia Ltd v State of Western Australia* (1992) 175 CLR 514 (HCA).

[106] *Forster v Outred & Co* [1982] 1 WLR 86 (CA); *DW Moore and Co v Ferrier* (1988) 1 WLR 267 (CA); *Islander Trucking Ltd v Hogg Robinson Ltd* [1990] 1 All ER 826 (QB); *Bell v Peter Browne and Co* [1990] 2 QB 495 (CA).

[107] *Wardley v Western Australia* (1992) 175 CLR 514 (HCA) [26] (Mason CJ, Dawson, Gaudron and McHugh JJ).

[108] *Nykredit Mortgage Bank PLC v Edward Erdman Group Ltd* [1997] 1 WLR 1627 (HL) 1623 (Lord Nicholls). See too *Law Society v Sephton & Co* [2006] UKHL 22, [2006] 2 AC 543 [28].

[109] Meaning a loss of a chance which was quantifiable and more than speculative: *Forster v Outred & Co* [1982] 1 WLR 86 (CA), *Wardley v Western Australia* (1992) 175 CLR 514 (HCA); Burrows, above n 79, 53–62.

[110] cf *Abdulla v Birmingham City Council* [2012] UKSC 47, [2012] ICR 1419 (Lord Sumption).

[111] Law Commission, *Limitation of Actions* (Law Com No 151, 1998).

[112] O'Sullivan, above n 78, 263.

[113] This would have the merits of being a consistent and transparent means of dealing with the issue.

much for the divergence of values across common law systems, but for the divergence of methods. It may be that in this area English courts pay greater heed to tradition, history and doctrine than they do to the inherent malleability of concepts such as duty of care and damage in negligence,[114] and that the reverse is true in much of the rest of the common law world. Were this awareness to have a reliable predictive function, it would give rise to the question of why divergence within the common law matters. The model founders, however, because English courts have not used the tools of negligence in any uniform way, leading to a divergence within their own methods. This paper has examined one of the most obvious examples of this: the House of Lords' reclassification of physical defect cases as instances of 'pure economic loss', compounded by both its subsequent denial of recovery notwithstanding the principle it had formulated earlier in *Hedley Byrne v Heller*, and the problems posed by that reclassification for the rules it had already established regarding accrual of actions. Whilst, over time, judicial approaches even within a system are bound to shift direction to some degree, it is perhaps the default rigidity of English law which makes such arbitrary variations more obvious. The greater flexibility which characterises most other common law systems is at least a point of internal convergence, which gains in consistency what it lacks in certainty.

At present, the 'pure economic loss' label is used somewhat disingenuously by English courts, as an apparent means of guarding against the imposition of liability without having finely to delimit the boundaries of the duty of care. The existence of the Defective Premises Act 1972 and the Latent Damage Act 1986, for example, as well as recent judicial dicta,[115] indicate that there are more shared values than the rationes decidendi of common law judgments, looked at in isolation, would suggest. Were 'pure economic loss' as a moniker to be formally limited to cases not involving physical defects, the approaches of different common law jurisdictions could at best be made easier to reconcile and, at worst, present more transparent reasons for their differences. The making of such a distinction would also help in rationalising the accrual of action cases, and the issue of when a claim arises could be tackled head-on, without the need for obfuscatory sleights of hand in classifying actions as a means of pre-determining their outcome.

---

[114] For the extent of this, see D Nolan, 'Deconstructing the Duty of Care' (2013) 129 *LQR* 559 and D Nolan, 'Damage in the English Law of Negligence' (2013) 4 *Journal of European Tort Law* 259.

[115] See, eg, above n 46.

5

Divergence and Convergence in the Tort of Public Nuisance

JW NEYERS*

I. Introduction

Writing in 1941, William Prosser stated that 'there is perhaps no more impenetrable jungle in the entire law than that which surrounds the word "nuisance"'.[1] While much work has been recently done by Donal Nolan[2] and Allan Beever[3] to elucidate how the tort of private nuisance can been seen to be a be 'a thoroughly coherent cause of action' centred on protecting rights in land,[4] little work has been done on rationalising that part of the tort jungle known as public nuisance. This deficiency is undoubtedly based on the fact that most people would regard such a project as a fool's errand that is 'nigh-on impossible'.[5] As Denning LJ said in *Morton v Wheeler*: 'As all lawyers know, the tort of public nuisance is a curious mixture. It covers a multitude of sins.'[6] While there is superficially much truth to Lord Justice Denning's comments, I wish to suggest that with a little effort the tort of public nuisance, like its private nuisance sibling, can be seen to be a thoroughly coherent cause of action. In order to do so, and in keeping with the theme of divergence and convergence, this chapter will proceed as follows. First, it will examine areas of the law where English and Canadian courts have come to divergent results in relation to controversial issues in the tort of public nuisance. Second, for each it will suggest a point of convergence—namely what answers the courts should supply from this point forward if they are to recognise more explicitly the coherent core at the heart of the tort of public nuisance. The topic areas to be

* This research was funded in part by a grant from the Foundation for Legal Research. I would like to thank Allan Beever, Andrew Botterell, Ben McFarlane, John Murphy, Donal Nolan and Stephen Pitel for their comments on drafts of this chapter, and Aaron Farough and Alison Dover for their research assistance. The usual disclaimer applies.
[1] WL Prosser, *Handbook of the Law of Torts* (St Paul, West Publishing Co, 1941) 549. See also, FH Newark, 'The Boundaries of Nuisance' (1949) 65 *LQR* 480, 480: 'Twelve years of lecturing on the Law of Tort have led to the conclusion that the tort of nuisance is the least satisfactory department of that subject.'

[2] D Nolan, '"A Tort against Land": Private Nuisance as a Property Tort' in D Nolan and A Robertson (eds), *Rights and Private Law* (Oxford, Hart Publishing, 2011) 457.

[3] A Beever, *The Law of Private Nuisance* (Oxford, Hart Publishing, 2013).

[4] Nolan, above n 2, 457.

[5] J Murphy, *The Law of Nuisance* (Oxford, Oxford University Press, 2010) 20.

[6] *Morton v Wheeler* (CA, No 33 of 1956, 31 January 1956 unreported) 2.

covered are the divergence between the two jurisdictions in regard to the conceptualisation of the tort, the issue of whether special damage requires a difference in kind from the damage suffered by the general public or whether a difference in degree will suffice, and the recoverability of damages for personal injury. The methodology employed will be conceptual and interpretative rather than historical.[7]

II. Divergence and Convergence in Conceptualisation

According to the orthodox English understanding, the tort of public nuisance and the crime of the same name are indistinguishable (save for the fact that the tort requires proof of special damage in order to be actionable). Thus, most English textbooks start their discussion of public nuisance with assertions that what distinguishes this tort from private nuisance is that it is also a crime.[8] While this might at first blush appear to be a rather unimportant point of emphasis, given that many well-established torts have both a criminal and tortious nature,[9] the significance of the link is this: the commission of the crime is seen as 'both a necessary and a sufficient condition for civil liability for public nuisance', whereas for all other torts 'the commission of a crime is neither a necessary nor a sufficient condition for tort liability'.[10] Thus, as John Murphy states in his treatise on nuisance: 'In order for there to be an actionable *tort* of public nuisance ... two things must be shown: first, that a public nuisance simpliciter has been committed; and secondly, that the claimant has suffered particular damage in consequence.'[11] In *R v Rimmington*, Lord Bingham explained this interrelationship as follows:

> Unusually, perhaps, conduct which could found a criminal prosecution for causing a common nuisance could also found a civil action in tort. Since, in the ordinary way, no individual member of the public had any better ground for action than any other member of the public, the Attorney General assumed the role of plaintiff, acting on the relation of the community which had suffered. This was attractive, since he could seek an injunction and the abatement of the nuisance was usually the object most desired ... . It was, however, held by Fitzherbert J, as early as 1536 ... that a member of the public could sue for a common or public nuisance if he could show that he had suffered particular damage over and above the ordinary damage suffered by the public at large. To the present day, causing a public nuisance has been treated as both a crime and a tort, *the ingredients of each being the same.*[12]

---

[7] On the appropriateness and requirements of interpretative theory, see SA Smith, *Contract Theory* (Oxford, Oxford University Press, 2004) 36; A Beever and C Rickett, 'Interpretive Legal Theory and the Academic Lawyer' (2005) 68 *MLR* 320.

[8] See, eg, RA Buckley, *The Law of Nuisance* (London, Butterworths, 1996) 67 ('A public nuisance is a criminal offence at common law. ... A private nuisance on the other hand is merely a tort'); P Giliker and S Beckwith, *Tort*, 4th edn (London, Sweet & Maxwell, 2011) [10-002] ('Whilst private nuisance seeks to protect private rights, public nuisance is primarily a crime'); D Nolan, 'Nuisance' in K Oliphant (ed), *The Law of Tort*, 2nd edn (London, Butterworths LexisNexis, 2006) 1169 ('Public nuisance is a crime that may also give rise to tort liability'); S Deakin, A Johnston and B Markesinis, *Markesinis and Deakin's Tort Law*, 6th edn (Oxford, Clarendon Press, 2007) 551 ('Public nuisance is first and foremost a crime').

[9] See NJ McBride and R Bagshaw, *Tort Law*, 4th edn (Harlow, Pearson Education, 2012) 639.

[10] TW Merrill, 'Is Public Nuisance a Tort?' (2011) 4(2) *Journal of Tort Law*, art 4, 11.

[11] Murphy, above n 5, 154 (emphasis in original). See also, Beever, above n 3, 103.

[12] *R v Rimmington* [2005] UKHL 63, [2006] 1 AC 468 [7].

The definition employed by the courts[13] for both the tort and crime has been taken from *Archbold: Criminal Pleading, Evidence and Practice* and is as follows:

> A person is guilty of a public nuisance (also known as common nuisance), who (a) does an act not warranted by law, or (b) omits to discharge a legal duty, if the effect of the act or omission is to endanger the life, health, property or comfort of the public, or to obstruct the public in the exercise or enjoyment of rights common to all Her Majesty's subjects.[14]

Although Canadian courts and commentators have paid lip-service to the orthodox English conception,[15] they have rarely taken it seriously. Thus when deciding public nuisance cases, Canadian courts have merely asked whether an activity unreasonably interferes: (i) with 'the rights of the public generally to live their lives unaffected by inconvenience, discomfort or other forms of interference',[16] or (ii) with 'the public's interest in questions of health, safety, morality, comfort or convenience'.[17] However, if the English conception were correct, the Canadian courts should have also been asking further questions since the codified Canadian criminal offence of common nuisance has since 1892 been more onerous than its English equivalent (ie it has required proof of additional elements by the Crown to secure a conviction).[18] The modern wording of the section on common nuisance is now as follows (though earlier versions were not significantly different in their essence):

> 180. (1) Every one who commits a common nuisance and thereby
>
> (a)   endangers the lives, safety or health of the public, or
> (b)   causes physical injury to any person,
>
> is guilty of an indictable offence and liable to imprisonment for a term not exceeding two years.
>
> (2) For the purposes of this section, every one commits a common nuisance who does an unlawful act or fails to discharge a legal duty and thereby
>
> (a)   endangers the lives, safety, health, property or comfort of the public; or
> (b)   obstructs the public in the exercise or enjoyment of any right that is common to all the subjects of Her Majesty in Canada.[19]

Thus, in general terms, in order to secure a conviction a Canadian prosecutor has always had the additional burden of proving two things that an English one would not. First, the prosecutor must prove that the act which constitutes the nuisance was independently 'unlawful' (as opposed to merely being 'not warranted by law').[20] Second, the prosecutor must prove that this illegal interference (such as with a public right) endangered the 'lives,

---

[13] See ibid [45].

[14] J Richardson, *Archbold: Criminal Pleading, Evidence and Practice* (London, Sweet & Maxwell, 2010) 2864.

[15] See, eg, *Stein v Gonzales* (1984) 14 DLR (4th) 263 (BCSC) [3]; *Hickey v Electric Reduction Co of Canada* (1970) 21 DLR (3d) 368 (Nfld SC) [6]–[9] (applying English criminal law); PH Osborne, *The Law of Torts*, 3rd edn (Toronto, Irwin Law, 2007) 379 (claiming that the Canadian criminal code definition 'captures the common law meaning of public nuisance').

[16] *Ryan v Victoria (City)* [1999] 1 SCR 201 [52] citing GHL Fridman, *The Law of Torts in Canada*, vol I (Agincourt, Carswell, 1989) 168.

[17] *Ryan v Victoria (City)* [1999] 1 SCR 201 [52], citing L Klar, *Tort Law*, 2nd edn (Scarborough, Carswell, 1996) 525.

[18] See Criminal Code of Canada 1892, c 29, s 191.

[19] Criminal Code, RSC 1985, c C-46.

[20] *British Columbia (AG) v Victoria (City)* (1920) 52 DLR 325 (BCCA); *R v Gilbertson and Fuller* (1930) 53 CCC 286 (Sask CA); *R v Thornton* [1993] 2 SCR 445.

safety or health of the public' or caused 'physical injury to any person'.[21] Accordingly, if the English conception were truly followed in Canada a tort plaintiff would have to prove double illegality, namely that the defendant committed (i) the crime of common nuisance by committing (ii) another independently unlawful act.[22] As Canadian commentators have pointed out, however, no 'action for public nuisance has ever failed because the defendant's conduct has not been proven criminal'.[23]

In fact, in the rare case where questions of lack of independent illegality have been averted to, the courts have not allowed this to defeat the plaintiff's action. Two examples will suffice.[24] The first is *Manitoba (Attorney General) v Campbell*.[25] In that case, the Attorney General sought an interim injunction ordering the defendant to dismantle a large steel tower on his land on the basis that it was a public nuisance that interfered with the landing of planes at night. Although the tower's existence caused the federal transport authority to withdraw permission for night flights, it did not breach any municipal, provincial or federal enactment or regulation.[26] Despite this, the presiding judge ordered the tower's removal as the court found that the defendant was merely 'indulging in a frustrated tantrum' to try to force the airport authority to purchase his land.[27]

The second example is *British Columbia (Attorney General) v Couillard*.[28] In that case, the Attorney General sought an interim injunction to restrain the activities of prostitutes in the West End of Vancouver as a public nuisance. The defendant prostitutes resisted the injunction partly on the basis that their activities were not unlawful under the relevant Criminal Code provisions existing at the time. The presiding judge granted the injunction and had this to say about the prostitutes' argument:

> For reasons which are not material to this application, it is apparent that a small group of prostitutes have assumed, quite incorrectly, that causing public inconvenience for the purpose of prostitution is lawful subject only to prosecution under the Criminal Code. Authorities ... suggest that there may be some practical problems in the prosecution of soliciting under the Criminal Code at the present time, but that does not mean that public misconduct is lawful. It is not, and if it amounts to a public nuisance anywhere in the province, it may be enjoined upon a proper application being made by the Attorney General.

> Those who would defile our city must understand that in addition to the criminal law, the citizens of this country are protected by the common law which is a statement of the accumulated wisdom of history. But it is a dynamic force which is always ready to respond to the reasonable requirements of civilisation.[29]

---

[21] See *R v Reynolds* (1906) 11 CCC 312 (NSSC) (an indictment which merely alleges an obstruction of a public highway is insufficient to charge the criminal offence unless it also alleges physical injury or threat of physical injury). See also *R v Schula* (1956) 115 CCC 382 (Alta CA); *R v Thornton* [1993] 2 SCR 445.

[22] For a rare case where this could easily be done, see *Little v Smith* (1914) 20 DLR 399 (Ont CA) where the defendant left a hole in the ice unattended in contravention of the criminal code and the plaintiff's horse fell in while using the frozen bay as a highway.

[23] J Cassels, 'Prostitution and Public Nuisance: Desperate Measures and the Limits of Civil Adjudication' (1985) 63 *Canadian Bar Review* 764, 782. For a similar view, see L Klar *Tort Law*, 5th edn (Toronto, Carswell, 2012) 751.

[24] Klar, above n 23, 751 also points to *Chessie v JD Irving Ltd* (1982) 42 NBR (2d) 192 (CA), stating that 'the decision was made without any regard to the criminality requirement' and *Ryan v Victoria (City)* [1999] 1 SCR 201 stating that there 'was no suggestion ... that the tracks were illegal or the defendant's acts were in any other way criminal'. The facts of *Ryan v Victoria* are discussed below, text to n 182.

[25] *Manitoba (Attorney General) v Campbell* (1983) 24 Man R (2d) 70 (QB).

[26] ibid [6].

[27] ibid [10].

[28] *British Columbia (Attorney General) v Couillard* (1984) 11 DLR (4th) 567 (BCSC).

[29] ibid [26]–[27].

Thus, if only by happenstance, Canadian courts have come to the conclusion that 'while public nuisance may also be a crime' it is now also an independent tort action with its own set of doctrinal requirements.[30]

With the difference between the two systems identified, we can now examine whose conceptualisation of public nuisance—the English or Canadian—should be adopted by the courts going forward. It is submitted that the English conceptualisation of the matter is deeply problematic and should be rejected for at least three reasons. First, allowing recovery violates the general English law principle, authoritatively affirmed in cases such as *Lonrho Ltd v Shell Petroleum Co Ltd (No 2)*[31] and *OBG Ltd v Allan*,[32] that there is no liability for merely causing loss through the commission of a criminal offence or other unlawful action.[33] As JR Spencer notes:

> The courts may be wrong in refusing to accept the idea that damages should be generally recoverable for losses caused by breaches of the criminal law, but as long as they do so, giving the plaintiff damages for any type of loss merely because the defendant has caused it by committing the crime of public nuisance is anomalous.[34]

Second, allowing recovery for private individuals also violates the private law rule that an injury to another's rights, even if it causes loss to you, does not give you a cause of action.[35] Since the gravamen of the crime is conceived to be interference with public rights, only the holder of that right, ie the public, represented by the Attorney General, should be able to sue. As Nicholas McBride and Roderick Bagshaw note: 'In a classic example of the dangers of reaching the right conclusion but for the wrong reasons, the judges did *not* say', but of course should have said, 'that public nuisances were not civilly actionable because committing a public nuisance involved a wrong to the public, and not any particular claimant.'[36]

---

[30] See *British Columbia v Canadian Forest Products* 2004 SCC 38, [2004] 2 SCR 74 [67]–[68]; *Ryan v Victoria (City)* [1999] 1 SCR 201 [52]. See also *Susan Heyes Inc (cob Hazel & Co) v Vancouver (City)* 2011 BCCA 77, [37]: 'Public nuisance is the unreasonable interference with the use and enjoyment of a public right.'

[31] *Lonrho Ltd v Shell Petroleum Co Ltd (No 2)* [1982] AC 173 (HL). For a Canadian analogue, see *Canada v Saskatchewan Wheat Pool* [1983] 1 SCR 205.

[32] *OBG Ltd v Allan* [2007] UKHL 21, [2008] 1 AC 1. For a Canadian analogue, see *AI Enterprises Ltd v Bram Enterprises Ltd* 2014 SCC 12, [2014] 1 SCR 177.

[33] See *Halsbury's Laws of England*, 5th edn (2010) vol 97, para 493. There is, of course, the tort of unlawful means conspiracy that allows for the recovery of losses caused via the commission of crimes, but even in that tort it is not the criminality alone which allows relief. Instead it is the combination of criminality and conspiracy which is the gravamen of liability. Of course, this makes little sense but it is what the House of Lords decided in *Revenue and Customs Commissioners v Total Network SL* [2008] UKHL 19, [2008] 1 AC 1174 [221] ('it appears that the law of tort takes a particularly censorious view where conspiracy is involved'). The position is the same in Canada: see *Canada Cement LaFarge Ltd v British Columbia Lightweight Aggregate Ltd* [1983] 1 SCR 452. For a better understanding of the unlawful means conspiracy tort as a manifestation of the rules of joint tortfeasance, see R Stevens, *Torts and Rights* (Oxford, Oxford University Press, 2007) 248–51; JW Neyers, 'The Economic Torts as Corrective Justice' (2009) 17 *Torts Law Journal* 162, 199–200.

[34] JR Spencer, 'Public Nuisance: A Critical Examination' (1989) 48 *CLJ* 55, 83.

[35] See Stevens, above n 33, 173: 'The only person who can enforce a right is the right-holder, and persons who suffer loss because of the infringement of someone else's right do not have standing to sue. Privity is a principle most commonly considered within the law of contract, but it is applicable to all rights.' See also BC Zipursky, 'Rights, Wrongs, and Recourse in the Law of Torts' (1998) 51 *Vanderbilt Law Review* 1, 3: 'For all torts, courts reject a plaintiff's claim when the defendant's conduct, even if a wrong to a third party, was not a wrong to the plaintiff herself. For example, an injured plaintiff can win in fraud only if she was defrauded, in defamation only if she was defamed, in trespass only if her land rights were violated, and so on. Courts reach these results even where the defendant acted tortiously, the plaintiff suffered a real injury, and the plaintiff's injury was reasonably foreseeable.'

[36] McBride and Bagshaw, above n 9, 640 (emphasis in original). See also the discussion of Newark, above n 1, 483.

Third, there is the practical problem that under this view of public nuisance, if the crime were abolished or replaced, the tort would go with it. As Murphy notes:

> Perhaps ironically, one of the strongest arguments that can be made in favour of retaining the common law crime of public nuisance is the fact that, without it, there would be no prospect of an individual obtaining a civil law remedy in respect of such interferences.[37]

And the prospect of losing the common law crime is a possibility, at least, if the recommendations of the Law Commission were to be adopted by the British government.[38]

Having rejected the English conception, it is submitted that the Canadian view of public nuisance as a tort that exists independently of the crime is the better view. While the Canadian courts have the form of liability correct (ie liability arises from the violation of a private right), much complaint can be made about the vague and imprecise content that is ascribed to this independent tort. As mentioned above, the Canadian courts see public nuisance as a tort which interferes with 'the rights of the public generally to live their lives unaffected by inconvenience, discomfort or other forms of interference'.[39] As others have noted, a tort of this nature is extraordinarily wide, protecting a right not to have one's life unreasonably interfered with.[40] If taken seriously it would have the potential to swallow much of the law of torts and undercut the well-defined causes of action that currently protect our rights to bodily integrity, property and reputation.[41] As Spencer rhetorically asked: 'With such a broad concept in existence, backed with such broad remedies, what need have we of any other … torts … ?'[42] In some ways these growing pains are to be expected, since as the Supreme Court of Canada noted in *Ryan v Victoria (City)*, public nuisance is 'a poorly understood area of the law'.[43] With that said, is there a way forward that avoids these problems of over-breadth and vagueness?

In a 1985 article in the *Canadian Bar Review*, Jamie Cassels asserted that since criminality could not serve as the lynchpin of the tort of public nuisance, it was crucial for courts and lawyers to delineate the right or rights that could undergird the tort rather than merely to provide some vague 'catalogue of social interests such as health, safety, comfort and morality which may qualify for protection'.[44] In other words, public nuisance was 'a remedy in search of a right'.[45]

What right or rights might be at the heart of the tort of public nuisance? As is the case with any interpretive exercise, the most natural place to begin is with the leading Anglo-Canadian cases and the articles and textbooks explaining those cases. Among these sources, there is general agreement that obstruction of highways (ie dedicated roads or navigable waterways)[46]

---

[37] Murphy, above n 5, 154.

[38] Law Commission, *Simplification of Criminal Law: Public Nuisance and Outraging Public Decency* (Law Com CP 193, 2010) 73.

[39] *Ryan v Victoria (City)* [1999] 1 SCR 201 [52].

[40] OM Reynolds, 'Public Nuisance: A Crime in Tort Law' (1978) *Oklahoma Law Review* 318, 339.

[41] See Murphy, above n 5, 25–26. For a similar view, see Beever, above n 3, 103.

[42] Spencer, above n 34, 55.

[43] *Ryan v Victoria (City)* [1999] 1 SCR 201 [52].

[44] Cassels, above n 23, 783.

[45] ibid 783. See also Murphy, above n 5, 25: 'What seems to be missing is a more fundamental notion of what it is that public nuisance protects.'

[46] From this point forward, I will use the term 'highway' to refer to both roads and navigable waterways since the law in relation to them is 'essentially the same': see RFV Heuston and RA Buckley (eds), *Salmond and Heuston on the Law of Torts*, 21st edn (London, Sweet & Maxwell, 1996) 82. See also *Drake v Sault Ste Marie Pulp Co* (1898)

is the core case of public nuisance.[47] Moreover, upon examining the cases of high authority in both England and Canada discussing obstruction, it becomes clear which rights the courts are protecting, namely the public's right to pass and repass (or to navigate) on the highway.[48] Interestingly, the courts often described this right as one in the nature of, or akin to, an easement.[49] It is said 'to be akin' since unlike an easement proper, this easement does not require a dominant tenement but rather is enjoyed by all subjects.[50] As Lord Hope noted in *DPP v Jones*: 'A public right of way is similar to … an easement of way', and is 'exercisable by anyone whether he owns land or not'.[51] Thus the leading cases see the core case of public nuisance as protecting rights akin to easements that people have over public, as opposed to private, property.

Are there any other 'cognate' rights which the Anglo-Canadian common law recognises?[52] While there appear to be no other rights in the nature of easements, there is one in the nature of a profits à prendre[53] that is clearly established by the highest authority in both

---

25 OAR 251 (CA) 258 (Moss JA): 'The river is a highway and as regards obstructions there appears to be no distinction between it and a highway on land'; *Ireson v Holt Timber Co* (1913) 18 DLR 604 (Ont CA) 612: 'It is admitted … that the river is a navigable river; it is consequently in the same position as a common or public highway.'

[47] See, eg, *R v Rimmington* [2006] 1 AC 468 (HL) [6] (Lord Bingham): 'Interference with the use of a public highway or a public navigable river provides the best and most typical example [of a public nuisance].' See also, McBride and Bagshaw, above n 9, 642 ('The rights which are most often relied on in public nuisance cases are the right to free passage along public highways and the right to free navigation along a public river'); Klar, above n 23, 748 (public nuisance was 'originally designed to deal with obstructions of public rights of way'); Spencer, above n 34, 81 ('Claims for damages based on public nuisance … are almost always highway cases'); Nolan, *The Law of Tort*, above n 8, 1171 (the most 'important … category of public nuisances concern obstruction of the highway'); Giliker, above n 8, [10-045] (the tort of public nuisance's 'most common use, however, is in relation to claims for unreasonable interference with the claimant's use of the highway').

[48] See, eg, *Vancouver (City) v Burchill* [1932] SCR 620, 6 (Rinfret J): 'It is idle to say that the municipality has no … rights upon its streets. It holds them as trustee for the public. The streets remain subject to the right of the public to "pass and repass"; and that character, of course, is of the very essence of a street.' See also *Tate & Lyle Food & Distribution Ltd v GLC* [1983] 2 AC 509 (HL) 537; *Jacobs v London City Council* [1950] AC 361 (HL) 375; *DPP v Jones* [1999] 2 AC 240 (HL) 253–55; *Steamship Eurana v Burrard Inlet Tunnel and Bridge Co* [1931] 1 AC 300 (PC) 305; *Hickman v Maisey* [1900] 1 QB 752 (CA).

[49] Beyond *DPP v Jones* [1999] 2 AC 240 (HL), see *Harrison v Duke of Rutland* [1893] 1 QB 142 (CA) 154 (Lopes LJ) ('The easement acquired by the public is a right to pass and repass at their pleasure for the purpose of legitimate travel'); *Wood v Esson* (1884) 9 SCR 239, 252 (Henry J) (the plaintiff 'had, without doubt, the right of easement over the navigable waters'); *Ward v Grenville (Township)* (1902) 32 SCR 510, 528 (Davies J) (the right of navigation is 'in the nature of a public easement'); *Tanguay v Canadian Electric Light Co* (1908) 40 SCR 1, 20 (Girouard J) ('These rivers are called public rivers, because at common law they are subject to a servitude or easement in favour of the public to navigate or float over the same'); *Quyon Milling Co v EB Eddy Co* [1926] SCR 194, 196 (Rinfret J) (the right of navigation 'is not a paramount right but an easement'); *Saumur v Quebec (City)* [1953] 2 SCR 229, 325 (Kerwin J) ('The right of the public in a highway is an easement of passage only—a right of passing and repassing'); *Upper Ottawa Improvement Co v Ontario (Hydro-Electric Power Commission)* [1961] SCR 486, 501 (Locke J) (there is nothing inconsistent between riparian rights and 'the exercise by the appellant of the easement or right of passage for its timber').

[50] *DPP v Jones* [1999] 2 AC 240 (HL) 268–69.

[51] ibid 268–69.

[52] *Attorney General for British Columbia v Attorney General for Canada* [1914] AC 153 (PC) 172. See also *Anderson v Alnwick DC* [1993] 1 WLR 1156 (Div Ct) 1166: 'The right to fish is closely linked with the public's right to navigate on the seas.'

[53] As is said in R Megarry and W Wade, *The Law of Real Property*, 8th edn (London, Sweet & Maxwell, 2012) [27–069] the 'public right which most closely resembles a profit is the right of the public to fish in the sea and all tidal waters'. See also: *Reference re British Columbia Fisheries (British Columbia)* (1913) 47 SCR 493, 513 (Anglin J) ('waters in fact navigable though non-tidal should be deemed navigable in law, and publici juris in the same sense as tidal waters, there would … exist in them the same public right of piscary which exists in tidal waters'); *Attorney*

jurisdictions.[54] As such, it is usually included in any list of core public rights.[55] This right is the right enjoyed by all subjects to fish in public waters. As was stated in *Neill v Duke of Devonshire*:

> But though the King is owner of this great waste, and as a consequence of his propriety hath the primary right of fishing in the sea … yet the common people of England have regularly the liberty of fishing in the sea … as a common of piscary, and may not without injury to their right be restrained of it.[56]

Similarly in *Attorney General for British Columbia v Attorney General for Canada*, Viscount Haldane held that:

> [T]he subjects of the Crown are entitled as of right not only to navigate but to fish in the high seas and tidal waters alike … . The right into which this practice has crystallised resembles in some respects the right to navigate the sea or the right to use a navigable river as a highway.[57]

Moreover, this right to fish in public waters has been protected by the tort of public nuisance (much like the right to pass and repass).[58] Thus, it appears that the conceptual core of the tort of public nuisance is the protection of rights, akin to easements and profits, that subjects enjoy over public property (ie property currently or once vested in the Crown[59] or dedicated to the public) that arise merely by being resident in the jurisdiction.[60] This too was the conclusion of Cassels who noted 'that at the core of public nuisance lies a concern to protect the use and enjoyment of public resources and facilities'.[61]

Three things follow from this realisation. The first is that academics and courts[62] have been wrong to claim that private nuisance and public nuisance 'have almost nothing in

---

General for British Columbia v Attorney General for Canada [1914] AC 153 (PC) 168 ('a common of piscary'); *Johnston v O'Neill* [1911] AC 552 (HL) 605 ('a public common of piscary'); *Loose v Lynn Shellfish Ltd & Ors* [2014] EWCA Civ 846 [5] ('The general public enjoys a right to fish in tidal waters … as a public common of piscary').

[54] See, eg, *Malcolmson v O'Dea* (1863) 10 HLC 593; *Attorney General for British Columbia v Attorney General for Canada* [1914] AC 153 (PC); *R v Gladstone* [1996] 2 SCR 723; *Isle of Anglesey County Council v Welsh Ministers* [2010] QB 163 (CA). For a historical discussion, see R Barnes, 'Revisiting the Public Right to Fish in British Waters' (2011) 26 *International Journal of Marine & Coastal Law* 433.

[55] See *Halsbury's Laws of Canada—Torts* (2012 Reissue) §59: 'the term "public rights" … [includes] the right to fish in public waters, the right to navigate public waters free from obstruction and the right to travel a highway unimpeded'. See also the similar list given in W Estey, 'Public Nuisance and Standing to Sue' (1972) 10 *Osgoode Hall Law Journal* 563, 564.

[56] *Neill v Duke of Devonshire* (1882) 8 App Cas 135, 177 quoting from Lord Hale, *De Jure Maris, Pars Prima*, c 4.

[57] *Attorney General for British Columbia v Attorney General for Canada* [1914] AC 153 (PC) 169.

[58] See, eg, *Leconfield v Lonsdale* (1870) LR 5 CP 657; *Whelan v Hewson* (1871) 6 IR 283 (Ex Ct); *Jan de Nul (UK) Ltd v NV Royale Belge* [2000] 2 Lloyd's Rep 700 (QB) aff'd on other grounds, [2002] 1 Lloyd's Rep 583 (CA); *McRae v British Norwegian Whaling Ltd* [1927–31] Nfld LR 274 (SC); *Fillion v New Brunswick International Paper Co* [1934] 3 DLR 22 (NBCA); *Hickey v Electric Reduction Co of Canada* (1970) 21 DLR (3d) 368 (Nfld SC). But not in Australia: see *Ball v Consolidated Rutile Ltd* [1991] Qd R 524.

[59] As was stated in *Gann v Free Fisheries of Whitstable* (1864–65) 11 HL Cas 192, 208: 'If the Crown therefore grants part of the bed or soil of an estuary or navigable river, the grantee takes subject to the public right.' See also *Wood v Esson* (1884) 9 SCR 239; *Cunard v Canada* (1910) 43 SCR 88; *Friends of the Oldman River Society v Canada (Minister of Transport)* [1992] 1 SCR 3 [69]–[71].

[60] It appears that even Newark might have agreed with this analysis. As he stated: cases in 'which plaintiffs who have been particularly incommoded in the use of the highway … have recovered damages in an action on the case for nuisance' are ones of which 'we have no complaint and nothing more to say': Newark, above n 1, 484.

[61] Cassels, above n 23, 784.

[62] See *In Re Corby Group Litigation* [2009] QB 335 (CA) [27]. This aspect of the decision is discussed below: see text to n 163.

common, except that each causes inconvenience to someone'[63] or that the 'relation between the two torts exists at the level of nomenclature rather than at the level of juridical essentials'.[64] In fact, on the conceptualisation presented here the two torts are analogues of each other. Private nuisance protects rights that people have both over their own land and the privately held land of others (such as easements and profits); public nuisance protects rights that people have (in the nature of easements and profits) over public land (as defined above). On this view, the tort of public nuisance is 'public' both in this aforementioned sense and in the sense that every member of the public enjoys these rights simply because they are subjects of the Crown. Second, even if the crime of public (or common) nuisance were abolished tomorrow in either jurisdiction, this would not abolish the tort of public nuisance, just as the abolition of any other crime (such as theft, assault or defamatory libel) would not abolish its corresponding tort. And third, since easements and profits are the only non-possessory, non-security common law property rights that one can hold in the land of another,[65] and since the cases have definitively determined that navigation and fishing are the only public rights in existence,[66] public nuisance claims are limited to substantial interferences with (i) passing and repassing on the highways or (ii) fishing in public waters (unless, of course, the courts were to recognise new varieties of easements or profits that arise merely by being a subject of the Crown).

Now might be the appropriate place to deal with some criticisms of the proposed view of the tort of public nuisance just presented. The first criticism that might be raised is that there has been no discussion of the role of the Attorney General in enforcing these public rights.[67] However, and to be clear, nothing that has been said about the scope of the tort of public nuisance is meant to apply to, or in any way limit, the powers of the Attorney General, as the representative of the public, to protect public resources through injunctions or tort law actions[68] or to enjoin criminal behaviour that threatens the private rights of the public.[69] Those cases raise very different issues and one of the failings of the literature and jurisprudence to date has been a reluctance to separate those issues (relating to the powers of the Attorney General to protect the patrimony of the public) from a determination of the content and scope of the rights (of passage and fishing) protected by the tort of public nuisance.

The next criticism that might be made is that the theory presented above cannot be correct because cases of high authority have stated that the public rights of navigation and

---

[63] Prosser, above n 1, 552. See also JPS McLaren, 'Nuisance Law in Canada' in AM Linden (ed), *Studies in Canadian Tort Law* (Toronto, Butterworths, 1968) 325: public nuisance 'has no obvious connection with interference with interests in land'; B Bilson *The Canadian Law of Nuisance* (Toronto, Butterworths, 1991) viii ('these torts have little in common').

[64] Murphy, above n 5, 155. See also, *Salmond and Heuston*, above n 46, 54: 'Public and private nuisance are not in reality two species of the same genus at all.'

[65] See Megarry and Wade, above n 53, [27-001]. For a discussion of the closed list or *numerus clausus* principle, see B McFarlane, *The Structure of Property Law* (Oxford, Hart Publishing, 2008) 137–38, 342–43; B McFarlane, '*Keppell v Bailey* (1834); *Hill v Tupper* (1863): The *Numerus Clausus* and the Common Law' in N Gravells (ed), *Landmark Cases in Land Law* (Oxford, Hart Publishing, 2013) 1.

[66] See *Blundell v Catterall* (1821) 5 B & Ald 268; *Lord Fitzhardinge v Purcell* [1908] 2 Ch 139; *Denaby and Cadeby Main Collieries Ltd v Anson* [1911] 1 KB 171 (CA).

[67] For discussion of these issues, see Estey, above n 55, 563; Law Reform Commission of British Columbia, *Civil Litigation in the Public Interest* (LRC 46, 1980).

[68] See *British Columbia v Canadian Forest Products* 2004 SCC 38, [2004] 2 SCR 74.

[69] As to these powers, see *Gouriet v Union of Post Office Workers* [1978] AC 435 (HL); *Grant v St Lawrence Seaway Authority* [1968] OR 298 (CA); *Civil Litigation in the Public Interest*, above n 67.

fishing are not proprietary (and therefore cannot be akin to easements or profits). For example, in *Attorney General for Canada v Attorney General for Quebec* Viscount Haldane declared that 'the right of fishing' in public waters is 'a public and not a proprietary right'.[70] While this might at first appear to be a major obstacle, it is clear that what was meant by the judges was that these public rights were not to be interpreted as giving a form of full ownership over the property impressed with the easement or profit.[71] Thus, the public right to fish did not give the public the right to use 'kiddles, weirs, or other engines fixed to the soil' since the solum was vested in the Crown.[72] Similarly, in relation to the right of navigation the Supreme Court of Canada has held that a person exercising that right cannot complain that the natural velocity of a river's current has been lessened by the actions of a riparian owner since only other riparian owners have a right to a particular flow of the river.[73] As was explained by Lord Gordon in *Orr Ewing v Colquhoun*:

> The rights of the public are of a limited nature. They possess no right of property in the water itself. They have a right to the use of it only for the purpose of navigation. They have no rights as regards the flow of the water or the withdrawing of water, if the right of navigation is not affected.[74]

Thus, there is nothing illogical in stating that the public rights of passage and fishing are akin to easements and profits (and are proprietary in that sense) but are not proprietary in the sense that their existence connotes an interest equivalent to full ownership of the affected public land.

III. Divergence and Convergence in Special Damage: Particularity

Having discussed the differences between England and Canada in relation to the conceptualisation of public nuisance, I now propose to examine two differences in relation to the concept of special damage. In this section I will explore the issue of particularity; in the next section I will turn to a discussion of the matter of whether damages for personal injuries are recoverable.

As Gilbert Kodilinye reminds us, 'It is an established principle that an individual who is adversely affected by a public nuisance may not sue in tort unless he can show that he has suffered [special damage] over and above that suffered by the general public.'[75] Although 'the requirement of proof of [special] damage is so entrenched that it is unlikely to be uprooted except by legislative intervention',[76] what constitutes special damage for this purpose has

---

[70]   *Attorney General for Canada v Attorney General for Quebec* [1920] 1 AC 413 (PC) 421.

[71]   See *Friends of the Oldman River Society v Canada (Minister of Transport)* [1992] 1 SCR 3 [69] (La Forest J) ('the right of navigation is not a property right, but simply a public right of way').

[72]   *Attorney General for British Columbia v Attorney General for Canada* [1914] AC 153 (PC) 171; *Attorney General for Canada v Attorney General for Quebec* [1920] 1 AC 413 (PC) 422.

[73]   *Upper Ottawa Improvement Co v Ontario (Hydro-Electric Power Commission)* [1961] SCR 486.

[74]   *Orr Ewing v Colquhoun* (1877) 2 App Cas 839 (HL) 871.

[75]   G Kodilinye, 'Public Nuisance and Particular Damage in the Modern Law' (1986) 6 *Legal Studies* 182, 182.

[76]   ibid 182.

been clouded with uncertainty 'for more than four centuries'[77] and is 'far from a clear-cut concept'.[78] Similarly, as Spencer notes: 'Few points in civil law are more obscure than the meaning of "special damage"'.[79] According to the most traditional formulation of the test, the damage will qualify as special if it is substantial, direct and particular.[80] One of the main debates in relation to the concept of special damage between England and Canada is what 'particularity' requires: does it mean that the plaintiff must prove that his or her injury is different in kind from that suffered by the rest of the public or does it merely require the plaintiff to prove that the damage is greater in extent or degree?

In the Canadian context, 'the proposition that the plaintiff must show a different kind of damage from that suffered by the public has been frequently applied … to deny standing to sue'.[81] For example in *Hickey v Electric Reduction Co of Canada*[82] the defendant was alleged to have destroyed a commercially viable fishing ground in Placentia Bay through the discharge of poisonous material from its phosphorous plant. The defendant was sued in public nuisance by local fishermen for interfering with their right to fish. The plaintiffs' case was dismissed on a preliminary motion as disclosing no cause of action. The reasoning of the court, which relied on the similar cases of *McRae v British Norwegian Whaling Ltd*[83] and *Fillion v New Brunswick International Paper Co*,[84] was that the plaintiffs' claim was destined to fail because they could not show that they suffered damage that was different in kind than that suffered by the rest of the public. As the court held:

> The plaintiffs' right, as one of the public, to fish may be affected to a greater extent than that of others, but they have no ground of complaint different from anyone else who fishes or intends to fish in these waters.[85]

Thus, the court found that the plaintiffs had suffered 'differently from the rest of the public only in degree' and that the case was therefore not maintainable.[86]

A similar result was reached in *Stein v Gonzales*.[87] In that case, the plaintiffs were proprietors of businesses located in the Granville Street area of downtown Vancouver and sought an order enjoining local prostitutes from working in the nearby streets and alleys. The plaintiffs claimed that these activities were causing them particular damage in the form of loss of custom since the deteriorating neighbourhood made 'their premises less desirable

---

[77] *Walsh v Ervin* [1952] VLR 361 (SC) 367.

[78] Murphy, above n 5, 140.

[79] Spencer, above n 34, 74.

[80] *Benjamin v Storr* (1874) LR 9 CP 400, 406, which ironically 'could have been regarded as one of private nuisance', see Buckley, above n 8, 74. See also *Overseas Tankship UK Ltd v Miller Steamship Co Pty 'The Wagon Mound No 2'* [1967] 1 AC 617 (PC) 635–36; *Ireson v Holt Timber Co* (1913) 18 DLR 604 (Ont CA), 608–09; *BC Express Co v Grand Trunk Pacific Ry Co* (1916) 27 DLR 497 (BCCA).

[81] Kodilinye, above n 75, 189.

[82] *Hickey v Electric Reduction Co of Canada* (1970) 21 DLR (3d) 368 (Nfld SC).

[83] *McRae v British Norwegian Whaling Ltd* [1927–31] Nfld LR 274 (SC).

[84] *Fillion v New Brunswick International Paper Co* [1934] 3 DLR 22 (NBCA).

[85] *Hickey v Electric Reduction Co of Canada* (1970) 21 DLR (3d) 368 (Nfld SC) [10] quoting from *McRae v British Norwegian Whaling Ltd* [1927–31] Nfld LR 274 (SC) 283–84.

[86] *Hickey v Electric Reduction Co of Canada* (1970) 21 DLR (3d) 368 (Nfld SC) [11] quoting from *Fillion v New Brunswick International Paper Co* [1934] 3 DLR 22 (NBCA) 26.

[87] *Stein v Gonzales* (1984) 14 DLR (4th) 263 (BCSC).

to guests and prospective tenants'.[88] Relying on *Hickey*, McLachlin J[89] denied the plaintiffs' application. Her reasoning was as follows:

> The right to carry on business in Vancouver is a public right, just as the right to fish in Placentia Bay was a public right. Any member of the public may pursue this right … . The rights which the plaintiffs claim have been infringed are rights which they possess as members of the public, and they have suffered the same damage which any other citizen who exercised those rights would suffer. The finances of many businesses in the area may be adversely affected by the defendants' activities. … But the injuries suffered, insofar as they are of the same type as those suffered by other members of the public exercising their public rights, remain public injuries in the eyes of the law.[90]

Thus, as noted at the outset, modern Canadian courts have generally held that plaintiffs must prove that the damage they suffered was different in kind from that suffered by the rest of the public in order successfully to sue in public nuisance (though as might be expected one can find authority going the other way).[91]

Unlike their Canadian brethren, however, English 'courts seem to have been much less concerned with the distinction between kind and degree of harm'.[92] As pointed out by Denise Antolini,[93] in the anonymous case of 1535 establishing the special damage exception for private actions, Fitzherbert J emphasised degree rather than kind of harm:

> I agree well that each nuisance done in the King's highway is punishable in the Leet and not by an action, unless it be where one man has suffered *greater hurt or inconvenience* than the generality have; but he who has suffered such *greater displeasure or hurt* can have an action to recover the damage which he has by reason of his special hurt.[94]

Similarly, in *Metropolitan Board of Works v McCarthy*[95] Lord Penzance noted that the language of the older cases, such as *Iverson v Moore*[96] and *Ashby v White*,[97] emphasised extent over type. As his Lordship stated: 'The Judges do not say a damage of a *different kind or description* from that suffered by other subjects, but "more than" or beyond

---

[88]   ibid [10].

[89]   Currently Chief Justice of the Supreme Court of Canada.

[90]   *Stein v Gonzales* (1984) 14 DLR (4th) 263 (BCSC) [13]. Of course, McLachlin J was wrong (at [13]) to claim that the 'right to carry on business in Vancouver is a public right'. There can be no public right to trade in a capitalist economy since there is no concomitant duty on anyone to respect that right. People have a liberty to trade, not a right: see *Allen v Flood* [1898] AC 1 (HL); Murphy, above n 5, 27, 142–43; JW Neyers, 'Rights-Based Justifications for the Tort of Unlawful Interference with Economic Relations' (2008) 28 *Legal Studies* 215, 220–22.

[91]   See, eg, *Gagnier v Canadian Forest Products Ltd* (1990) 51 BCLR (2d) 218 (SC) where Low J refused to dismiss a case summarily on the basis of *Hickey* or *Stein* since there were three older decisions of Ontario appellate courts going the other way in relation to the right of navigation, namely *Crandell v Mooney* (1878) 23 UCCP 212 (CA), *Rainy River Navigation Co v Ontario and Minnesota Power Co* (1914) 17 DLR 850 (Ont CA) and *Rainy River Navigation Co v Watrous Island Boom Co* (1914) 26 OWR 456 (CA). As McLaren notes, 'these decisions make it clear that financial loss incurred by commercial concerns engaged in shipping enterprises on navigable waterways by obstructions to navigation, amounts to "special damage". There is no difference in principle between financial loss flowing from interference with the commercial uses of the right to navigate and the right to fish in public waters': JPS McLaren, 'The Common Law Nuisance Actions and the Environmental Battle—Well-Tempered Swords or Broken Reeds?' (1972) 10 *Osgoode Hall Law Journal* 505, 514.

[92]   Kodilinye, above n 75, 189 and the discussion at 190.

[93]   DE Antolini, 'Modernizing Public Nuisance: Solving the Paradox of the Special Injury Rule' (2001) 28 *Ecology Law Quarterly* 755, 792.

[94]   *Anon* YB Mich 27 Hen 8, Mich, f 26, pl 10 (1535) (emphasis added).

[95]   *Metropolitan Board of Works v McCarthy* (1874) LR 7 HL 243, 263.

[96]   *Iverson v Moore* (1699) 1 Ld Raym 486 (KB).

[97]   *Ashby v White* (1704) 1 Bro Parl Cas 61.

their fellow-citizens.'[98] Lord Denning took a similar view in *Southport Corporation v Esso Petroleum Co Ltd*, holding that 'if any person should suffer greater damage or inconvenience from the oil than the generality of the public, he can have an action to recover damages on that account'.[99] Finally in the more recent case of *Jan de Nul (UK) Ltd v NV Royale Belge* Moore-Bick J held that: '[A]ny significant interference with an individual's commercial operations ... resulting from the obstruction to navigation would in my judgment represent damage over and above that suffered by the public at large and would be sufficient to support an action.'[100] Thus, on the evidence it appears that England is a difference in degree, rather than a difference in kind, jurisdiction.[101]

With this difference outlined, which position should Anglo-Canadian courts adopt on a going-forward basis: kind, degree or some other test? When I was a young law student, an erudite professor once told me that the answer to any long-standing legal problem was most likely hidden in a *Harvard*, *Yale* or *Columbia Law Review* article published prior to 1930 and that all one had to do to enlighten oneself was to find it.[102] And so it is with this problem. In a largely forgotten two-part article, published in 1915, Jeremiah Smith (who was one of 'the leading torts theorists of the late nineteenth century')[103] argued that Anglo-American courts had misinterpreted the then-existing case law and been led astray by sterile and misleading appeals to concepts such as 'kind' or 'degree' of damage.[104] As he stated:

> But all these expressions ... are objectionable, as giving some color to the erroneous idea that the damage must be exclusive, ie that the plaintiff must be the only one to suffer damage of that description from the same cause.[105]

Instead of appeals to kinds and degrees, Smith argued that the better understanding of the special damage rule was that a plaintiff could bring an action in public nuisance 'consequent upon his exercise of a public right being interfered with, and distinct from the [mere] fact that it is interfered with' provided that the plaintiff could prove that he or she suffered actual pecuniary loss.[106] Thus, public nuisance was similar to private nuisance or negligence in that it was not a tort actionable per se; 'actual loss, proved as a matter of fact, is the gist of the private action'.[107] If the courts needed to hear this truth explained in terms of 'kind' it could be done as follows:

> Taking the expression 'the general public' in its broadest signification, it seems to us that the alleged rule might be understood to mean only that the plaintiff must prove actual damage to himself, as distinguished from the theoretical damage which, in contemplation of law, is supposed to be

[98] *Metropolitan Board of Works v McCarthy* (1874) LR 7 HL 243, 263 (emphasis in original).

[99] *Southport Corporation v Esso Petroleum Co Ltd* [1954] 2 QB 182, 197.

[100] *Jan de Nul (UK) Ltd v NV Royale Belge* [2000] 2 Lloyd's Rep 700 (QB) [44]. This point was not challenged on appeal: [2002] 1 Lloyd's Rep 583 (CA).

[101] See Antolini, above n 93, 859; Kodilinye, above n 75, 193; *Markesinis & Deakin's Tort Law*, above n 8, 553, but see Murphy, above n 5, 146 (arguing that the authorities are mixed but 'that a significant difference in degree *should* suffice').

[102] That professor was David Stevens who was at that time at McGill University and is now a partner at a leading Toronto firm.

[103] See GE White, 'The Integrity of Holmes' Jurisprudence' (1982) 10 *Hofstra Law Review* 633, 643, cited in Antolini, above n 93, 807.

[104] J Smith, 'Private Action for Obstruction to Public Right of Passage' (1915) 15 *Columbia Law Review* 1, (1915) 15 *Columbia Law Review* 142.

[105] ibid 11.

[106] ibid 11, quoting F Pollock, *The Law of Torts*, 6th edn (London, Stevens and Sons Ltd, 1901) 612.

[107] ibid 13, citing *Piscataqua Navigation Co v New York*, NH & HRR 89 F 362 (D Mass, 1898) (Brown J).

sustained by the entire community. Actual damage certainly differs in kind from mere theoretical damage. The statement, thus interpreted, would amount to this,—A defendant cannot escape liability for causing actual damage to an individual, on the ground that he has also, by the same obstruction, caused theoretical damage to all citizens of the State. This, instead of stating an additional requirement, would be merely a clumsy and roundabout way of repeating (re-stating) the actual damage test.[108]

This test of actual damage was adopted by Prosser[109] (who then retreated from it as American cases hardened around the difference in kind limitation espoused in *Hickey* and *Stein*)[110] and through Prosser found its way into the Fleming treatise.[111] The position was also supported by Kodilinye in his oft-cited article on the subject. As he stated: '[A]n alternative course to applying one or other of the above tests would be to abandon altogether the distinction between "kind" and "degree" of damage and to allow recovery to any person who suffers actual damage.'[112]

While Smith's view has much to recommend it, it needs supplementation in order to provide a full understanding of the concept of special damage. As mentioned above, the traditional view requires the damage to be direct and substantial, as well as particular.[113] In relation to directness, Smith thought that this requirement was unjust:

> To require that the damage, though actual, must not be consequential is to allow a defendant to escape because the damage, though distinctly traceable to the defendant's tort, did not follow immediately upon the commission of the tort. This ground is untenable.[114]

In relation to substantiality, Smith argued:

> It is virtually asserted that the law should require something more ... than actual damage of the smallest amount. But how much more? Here is the difficulty. There is no satisfactory way of fixing the quantum. The proposed rule is unworkable.[115]

Although Smith thought both of those limitations to be without merit, they are actually implicit in his test since they concern, not matters of fact relating to loss, but rather the question of whether the rights protected by the tort have been infringed. One needs to have *injuria* before we can get to questions of *damnum*, as Smith's test makes clear.

On this rights-based view of public nuisance, directness is merely a concern for the basic private law principle that only the holder of right may sue for its violation.[116]

---

[108] ibid 18.

[109] Prosser, above n 1, 572.

[110] See WL Prosser, 'Private Action for Public Nuisance' (1966) 52 *Virginia Law Review* 997, 1008–13. For a history of Prosser's change of attitude, see Antolini, above n 93, 813–49.

[111] C Sappideen and P Vines (eds), *Fleming's The Law of Torts*, 10th edn (Pyrmont, NSW, Lawbook Co, 2011) 491: 'There is a clear modern tendency to reject the elusive distinction between difference in kind and in degree, and to allow recovery if the obstruction causes more than mere infringement of a theoretical right which the plaintiff shares with everyone else.' For a similar view, ie that actual loss is the key to understanding this area, see GHL Fridman, 'The Definition of Particular Damage in Nuisance' (1953) 2 *University of Western Australia Law Review* 490, 503.

[112] Kodilinye, above n 75, 190. See also PH Osborne, *The Law of Torts*, 4th edn (Toronto, Irwin Law, 2011) 400: 'the time may be ripe to dispense with terminology of kind and degree completely and allow a claim for damages for actual ... economic loss'; AM Linden and B Feldthusen, *Canadian Tort Law*, 9th edn (Toronto, LexisNexis Canada, 2011) 575; Stevens, above n 33, 32.

[113] See authority cited above n 80.

[114] Smith, above n 104, 13–14.

[115] ibid 14.

[116] See discussion above n 35.

The enforcement of this principle is thus a requirement of doing justice between the parties rather than its antithesis.[117] Thus, in these circumstances directness means that the plaintiff cannot sue if someone else's right to navigate or fish was infringed[118]—a classic example being a road obstruction that causes business losses in the form of lost custom. This loss would be consequential on a violation of the *customers'* rights to pass and repass and would therefore not be direct. Although it has been customary in recent times[119] to criticise the Exchequer Chamber and House of Lords decisions in *Ricket v Directors of the Metropolitan Railway Company*,[120] they impeccably lay out this fundamental and principled distinction.[121] As Murphy argues: 'quite why' modern courts think that a plaintiff 'should be able to hitch his claim to the infringement of others' rights is unclear; although if he had been prevented from plying his trade because he himself had been obstructed … the objection to his action succeeding' of course disappears.[122] Thus, if the concept is correctly understood, there is nothing 'obscure' and 'shrouded in mystery',[123] or 'specious' and 'peculiarly Canadian'[124] about what is meant by directness in public nuisance—it is merely a question of privity.[125]

Similarly, concerns of substantiality go not to quantum, as Smith seemed to think, but to whether the interference that the plaintiff actually encountered violated his or her rights (since a public nuisance requires substantial interference as a condition of actionability). This makes sense for two reasons. First, it is consistent with the law relating to private

---

[117] As Peter Benson notes: 'Each part of private law has—and must have—its own suitably specified idea of privity': see P Benson, 'Should *White v Jones* Represent Canadian Law: A Return to First Principles' in JW Neyers, E Chamberlain and SGA Pitel (eds), *Emerging Issues in Tort Law* (Oxford, Hart Publishing, 2007) 141, 184.

[118] For a forceful application of the privity principle, see *Denaby and Cadeby Main Collieries Ltd v Anson* [1911] 1 KB 171 (CA), where the English Court of Appeal refused to enjoin a harbour master from removing the plaintiff's permanently moored ship. The plaintiff had claimed that it had a right to remain since its coal-supply ship was necessary for others to enjoy their rights of navigation (coal being a necessity for the operation of steamships). The court refused the injunction since the plaintiff had to base its claim to stay in the harbour on its own right of navigation (which it could not do since it was permanently moored rather than passing and repassing) rather than on the rights of navigation of others.

[119] See, eg, *Colour Quest Ltd v Total Downstream UK Plc* [2009] EWHC 540, [439]–[458] for an outline of the cases that might be said to be inconsistent with *Ricket*. As a result of these, Steel J comments at [458]: '[T]he decision in *Ricket* is now in a state of some disrepair.' See also *Wildtree Hotel v Harrow LBC* [2001] 2 AC 1 (HL) 9 where Lord Hoffmann states that *Ricket* 'was explained and distinguished in later cases in your Lordships' House until it became very difficult to say for what proposition, if any, it remained authority'.

[120] *Ricket v Directors of the Metropolitan Railway Company* (1865) 5 B & S 156 (Ex Ch), (1868) LR 2 HL 175.

[121] See Stevens, above n 33, 186–87 for a similar view. Smith (above n 104, 163 n 124) was critical of *Ricket* since he thought that 'the storekeeper had a right, *as against third parties*, that the third persons should not, by tortious interference, influence the choice to be made by the customers' (emphasis in original). The right protected in Anglo-Canadian law is not so wide but rather requires the third person to interfere intentionally with the customer–storekeeper relationship by use of unlawful means so as to cause the storekeeper loss: see *OBG Ltd v Allan* [2007] UKHL 21, [2008] 1 AC 1; *AI Enterprises Ltd v Bram Enterprises Ltd* 2014 SCC 12, [2014] 1 SCR 177. Moreover, even if a right as wide as that posited by Smith existed, why would that properly ground a claim in public nuisance as opposed to whatever tort was said to protect that right?

[122] Murphy, above n 5, 27. For examples of cases where the business losses were direct, and therefore rightly recoverable, see *Rose v Miles* (1815) 4 M & S 101, 105 ER 773; *Tate & Lyle Food & Distribution Ltd v GLC* [1983] 2 AC 509 (HL) 537; *Blundy Clarke v North Eastern Railway* [1931] 2 KB 334 (CA); *Drake v Sault Ste Marie Pulp and Paper Co* (1898) 25 OAR 251 (CA); *Crandell v Mooney* (1878) 23 UCCP 212 (CA); *Rainy River Navigation Co v Ontario and Minnesota Power Co* (1914) 17 DLR 850 (Ont CA); *Rainy River Navigation Co v Watrous Island Boom Co* (1914) 26 OWR 456 (CA).

[123] As Kodilinye claims, see above n 75, 193–94.

[124] Estey, above n 55, 572, 569.

[125] For more detailed discussion, see JW Neyers and J Diacur, 'What (Is) a Nuisance?' (2011) 90 *Canadian Bar Review* 215.

easements and profits which also require substantial interference to be actionable.[126] Second, it recognises that the rights to navigate and to fish are shared amongst all of the public and therefore the legal system's rule must accommodate the shared use of all its subjects. As was held by the court in *Crandell v Mooney*:

> Every person has an undoubted right to use a public highway, whether upon the land or water, for all legitimate purposes of travel and transportation; and if, in so doing … he necessarily and una-voidably impedes or obstructs another temporarily, he does not thereby become a wrongdoer, his acts are not illegal, and he creates no nuisance for which an action can be maintained.[127]

Thus, when Smith's understanding of particularity is combined with a rights-based under-standing of directness and substantiality, we have a coherent regime of legal liability that protects a subject's undoubted rights to navigate and fish in public spaces.

While a rule centred on protecting the rights of navigation and fishing from actual dam-age is coherent, one might object that adopting this view would eviscerate the rationales or policies behind the special damage rule. What are these rationales? In a very helpful survey, Antolini outlines the three well-accepted rationales, which she describes as sover-eignty, triviality and multiplicity.[128] The rationale of sovereignty represents the view that since the rights involved are public, it is primarily the duty of the public's representative to enforce these rights and to control the ensuing litigation so that it is, all things considered, conducted in the public interest.[129] As Prosser noted: 'The plaintiff did not and could not represent the King and vindication of royal rights was properly left to his duly constituted officers.'[130] Shades of this type of reasoning can be found in the position taken by Baldwin CJ in the 1535 case[131] and in *Stein v Gonzales*, where McLachlin J held that the policy behind the rule is 'that the public and criminal jurisdiction of the court is not to be usurped in a civil proceeding'.[132] On the view of public nuisance presented above, however, the concept of sovereignty does not apply. The rights involved are private rights in the nature of ease-ments and profits, so the Crown has no say in how they should be enforced or whether that enforcement would be in the public interest, just as the Crown would have no say in how private easements or profits were enforced (beyond, of course, the generalised rules of civil procedure applying to all actions). Moreover, if it were true that individuals enforcing these rights would jeopardise an overwhelming public interest (such as the construction of an important highway or bridge), that public interest might be protected by deeming the

---

[126] See *Colls v Home and Colonial Stores Ltd* [1904] AC 179 (HL); *Nicholls v Ely Beet Sugar Factory Ltd (No 2)* [1936] Ch 343 (CA); *Fallowfield v Bourgault* (2003) 68 OR (3d) 417 (CA); Nolan, 'A Tort against Land', above n 2, 464.

[127] *Crandell v Mooney* [1873] UCCP 212, 221 citing *Davis v Window*, 51 Maine 297 (1863, SJC). See also *Harper v GN Haden & Sons* [1933] Ch 298 (CA) 320: 'The law relating to the user of highways is in truth the law of give and take. Those who use them must in doing so have reasonable regard to the convenience and comfort of others, and must not themselves expect a degree of convenience and comfort only obtainable by disregarding that of other people. They must expect to be obstructed occasionally. It is the price they pay for the privilege of obstructing others.'

[128] Antolini, above n 93, 886. See also *Civil Litigation in the Public Interest*, above n 67, 31–36; McLaren, above n 91, 515.

[129] Antolini, above n 93, 887.

[130] Prosser, above n 110, 1007.

[131] *Anon* YB Mich 27 Hen 8, Mich, f 26, pl 10 (1535) (emphasis added): 'It seems to me that this action does not lie to the plaintiff for the stopping of the highway; for the King has the punishment of that.'

[132] *Stein v Gonzales* (1984) 14 DLR (4th) 263 (BCSC) 265.

interference to be lawful via statute—the defence of statutory authority being as much a defence to a public nuisance as it is to a private one.[133]

The rationale of triviality is that without a rigorous special injury rule, courts would be inundated with 'busybodies' who would clog the court system with unmeritorious or frivolous claims.[134] Under the theory proposed, there are both conceptual and pragmatic answers to this concern. On the conceptual side, and as noted above, the rights protected by the tort of public nuisance are not protected from all interferences, but being claims in nuisance are only protected from substantial interference. Thus, to win a case there must be a modicum of seriousness to the claim that would not be necessary, for example, in torts actionable per se.[135] On the pragmatic side, Antolini notes that trivial claims are unlikely to be brought since plaintiffs 'have little incentive to sue ... given the real and intangible costs of litigation'.[136] As Smith, who 'had over twenty years of experience as a judge and practitioner' before becoming an academic,[137] adds:

> The law as to costs ... furnishes a very strong reason why such suits will not be frequent. The costs recoverable generally fall far short of making the plaintiff whole. They do not begin to equal the fees which he has to pay his counsel. If he does not recover a substantial sum by way of damages, he is sure to be out of pocket by the litigation, although he has been the prevailing party.[138]

Moreover, even if obdurate plaintiffs bring hopeless or vexatious claims, modern civil procedure allows judges and defendants to deal with these actions prior to a full trial using motions to strike and summary judgment applications in appropriate circumstances and to penalise vexatious plaintiffs through enhanced cost awards.[139] As McLaren remarks: '[I]f there are trivial claims, it is surely not beyond the capacity of the courts to expose and discourage them.'[140] However, as the Law Reform Commission of British Columbia noted, it should always be remembered that rules denying the ability to have one's day in court cannot be too rigidly enforced since 'one man's busybody may be another's saviour'.[141]

Having examined sovereignty and triviality we now arrive at the rationale of multiplicity. This concern was famously expressed by Baldwin CJ in the anonymous case of 1535:

> It seems to me that this action does not lie to the plaintiff for the stopping of the highway; for the King has the punishment of that ... and so there is no reason for a particular person to have an *accion sur son cas*; for if one person shall have an action by this, by the same reason every person shall have an action, and so he will be punished a hundred times on the same case.[142]

---

[133] See *Ryan v Victoria (City)* [1999] 1 SCR 201; *Steamship Eurana v Burrard Inlet Tunnel and Bridge Co* [1931] 1 AC 300 (PC); *R v Pease* (1832) 4 B & Ad 30, 110 ER 366.

[134] *Civil Litigation in the Public Interest*, above n 67, 31.

[135] See, eg, *Whaley v Kelsey* [1928] 2 DLR 268 (Ont CA) (stairs and verandah built so as to encroach on the sidewalk was not a public nuisance in light of municipality's offer to widen the footpath). See also *R v Betts* (1850) 16 QB 1022.

[136] Antolini, above n 93, 890.

[137] Ibid 809.

[138] Smith, above n 104, 6.

[139] See *Civil Litigation in the Public Interest*, above n 67, 60.

[140] McLaren, above n 91, 515.

[141] *Civil Litigation in the Public Interest*, above n 67, 61.

[142] *Anon* YB Mich 27 Hen 8, Mich, f 26, pl 10 (1535) (emphasis added). See also *Paine v Partrich* (1691) Carth 191, 90 ER 715, 717 (Gregory J); *Winterbottom v Lord Derby* (1867) LR 2 Exch 316, 321 (Kelly CB) ('If we were to hold that everybody ... who chooses to incur some expense in removing it, might bring his action on the case for being obstructed, there would really be no limit to the number of actions that might be brought'); *Fillion v*

At first blush the concern seems misguided since, in modern law, a tort proceeding is not seen primarily as a vehicle for punishment but rather as one that undoes violations of plaintiffs' rights through the award of appropriate (usually compensatory) damages.[143] Putting that aside, and assuming that the last line read 'and so defendants will be liable in damages to multiple parties for the same wrong', why is this problematic? As *Fleming's The Law of Torts* argues:

> The mere fact that a great number of people have cause of complaint is not otherwise recognised as a disqualification from bringing suit; indeed if the [plaintiffs] could establish their standing to sue for private nuisance, it would not matter how many there were who shared the same plight.[144]

Similarly, Smith asks, 'what special claim have the defendants to pity'?[145] These defendants have violated the rights of subjects to navigate or fish in a substantial way and caused these plaintiffs to suffer actual pecuniary loss, so 'their acts were tortious'.[146] He continued, citing *Davis v County Commissioners*:[147]

> If a rule of public policy denying remedy, 'shall become necessary, it certainly should be applied only when found necessary for the protection of the public and of the courts, and should not be given to a wrongdoer to defend himself from the natural consequences of his wrong'.[148]

Although in times past courts might have been overwhelmed by large cases involving multiple plaintiffs and therefore needed protection, it must be remembered that the modern law in both jurisdictions has a multitude of procedural mechanisms for dealing with such claims. These include the ability to have representative or mass proceedings, to order joinder/consolidation of actions and to certify class actions in appropriate circumstances.[149] Thus, the protection of the courts is ensured without resort to a more limited kind or degree restraint to special damages. Moreover, Smith thought that for pragmatic reasons

> the danger of a multiplicity of suits is very much overestimated. ... Where the damages recoverable are likely to be small, a prudent lawyer will generally refuse to sue in behalf of an impecunious client; and, if the applicant for his services is solvent, an honest lawyer will inform the applicant that he will lose money by suing, even though he should prevail. Under these circumstances, comparatively few suits are likely to be brought.[150]

A similar view was expressed by the Law Reform Commission of British Columbia which stated: 'In our opinion the fear of multiple litigation is exaggerated. ... Public apathy, and the expense and inconvenience of litigation are inhibiting factors.'[151] Thus, given the limited

---

New Brunswick International Paper Co [1934] 3 DLR 22 (NBCA) 26 (Baxter J) ('it is inexpedient that there should be multiplicity of actions and ... where a nuisance or injury is common to the whole public the remedy is by indictment but ... no private right of action exists unless there is a special or particular injury to the plaintiff').

[143] See A Ripstein, 'As if it had Never Happened' (2007) 48 *William and Mary Law Review* 1957.

[144] *Fleming's The Law of Torts*, above n 111, 490. For a similar view: see Kodilinye, above n 75, 182; Newark, above n 1, 483: 'But this is no reason at all. If a hundred private wrongs have been done a hundred private actions may well be brought.'

[145] Smith, above n 104, 5.

[146] ibid 5.

[147] *Davis v County Commissioners* (1891) 153 Mass 218, 225 (Allen J).

[148] Smith, above n 104, 5.

[149] See Antolini, above n 93, 889.

[150] Smith, above n 104, 6.

[151] *Civil Litigation in the Public Interest*, above n 67, 59.

nature of recovery suggested above (that is available only in cases where there is a direct and substantial interference with rights that leads to a particular and actual loss), the rationales usually given for limiting special damages to those that are different in kind or degree should not preclude Anglo-Canadian courts from adopting a more coherent formulation of the special damage rule. In other words, as McLaren argued, 'one wonders whether this "floodgates" type of thinking has any more validity here than in other areas of tort law in which it has been utilised to prevent or delay progressive development'.[152]

IV. Divergence and Convergence in Special Damage: Personal Injury

Having examined the concept of special damage in general terms, I now turn to the question of whether damages for personal injury are recoverable using the tort of public nuisance. As with the other two areas examined in this chapter, there is a divergence of opinion between English and Canadian courts.

Although personal injuries are generally seen as representing the clearest example of special damage,[153] for several generations commentators on English law have been suggesting that damages for personal injuries should not be recoverable using the tort of public nuisance.[154] Several reasons have been offered for this conclusion. The first reason given is that the awarding of damages for personal injury in public nuisance is ahistorical since prior to about 1840 such actions were conceived as actions in negligence.[155] Second, it has been pointed out that, in practice, liability for personal injuries for a public nuisance almost invariably involves an examination of whether the defendant was negligent.[156] Even in situations where liability appears to be strict, such as in *Wringe v Cohen*, the facts surrounding the case—visible disrepair for three years[157]—suggest that the result would not have been any different if it had been decided on negligence principles.[158] A third reason for denying recovery for personal injuries is that this would bring public nuisance in line

---

[152] McLaren, above n 91, 515.

[153] As Gregory Hall and Margaret Pun argue, 'the point [that personal injury equals special damage] is effectively trite': GS Pun and MI Hall, *The Law of Nuisance in Canada* (Markham, Ont, LexisNexis Canada, 2010) 50.

[154] See, eg, Newark, above n 1; *Salmond and Heuston*, above n 46, at 89 ('In theory the proper remedies for personal injuries caused by … a public nuisance should be the actions of trespass and negligence'); GHL Fridman, *Torts* (London, Waterlow Publishers, 1990) 219 ('It would appear that this variety of nuisance [ie personal injury via obstruction] is firmly involved with proof of negligence and may indeed be nothing more than another form of negligence liability').

[155] *In Re Corby Group Litigation* [2009] QB 335 (CA) [14]; Newark, above n 1, 485–86.

[156] For example, if a plaintiff sues because he or she was injured as a result of a falling tree (or other natural object), it must be proven that the defendant had knowledge or means of knowledge of the danger and failed to take reasonable precautions to avert that danger: see *Caminer v Northern & London Investment Trust* [1951] AC 88 (HL).

[157] *Wringe v Cohen* [1940] 1 KB 229 (CA) 229.

[158] See Buckley, above n 8, 82–83. As others have pointed out, the fact that a defendant is not liable for damage resulting from 'the act of a trespasser, or by a secret and unobservable operation of nature, such as a subsidence under or near the foundations of the premises' (see *Wringe v Cohen* [1940] 1 KB 229 (CA) 233) means that 'that the rule in *Wringe v Cohen* has been substantially assimilated to ordinary fault liability': see *Markesinis and Deakin's Tort Law*, above n 8, 556.

with more recent developments in relation to private nuisance[159] and the rule in *Rylands v Fletcher*,[160] where the House of Lords have denied the ability of plaintiffs to recover damages for personal injury.[161] Thus, as FH Newark pointed out, the continued allowance of damages for personal injury in public nuisance 'is equally offensive to the legal historian and the jurisprudent'.[162]

Despite these entreaties, the English courts have been reluctant to follow this path (largely as we will see on the basis of the orthodox 'crime-in-tort' conceptualisation of public nuisance). The leading case is *In Re Corby Group Litigation*.[163] In that case, the Court of Appeal was asked to strike out the public nuisance claims of 18 litigants. These plaintiffs alleged that remedial work undertaken by Corby Borough Council on polluted lands that it had acquired for reclamation and redevelopment had caused them to suffer personal injury in the nature of limb deformities. The mechanics of these injuries were that their mothers, who lived close to the redevelopment site, had been exposed to toxic materials that the council had allowed to escape from the work site, thereby harming the plaintiffs while they were in utero. The case of the defendant was that the public nuisance claim should be struck out since personal injuries were not a recoverable head of damage for that tort. While conceding that 'it has long been accepted' that such damages were recoverable,[164] the defendant argued that the issue had never been the 'subject of a reasoned decision' and that such recovery was inconsistent with the recent developments in relation to private nuisance and the rule in *Rylands v Fletcher* mentioned above.[165] The court ultimately came to the conclusion that, given the long line of English Court of Appeal authority supporting such recovery, this was not the proper case to strike out the claim and change the law. As Dyson LJ noted: 'I readily accept that the House of Lords may decide to take that course. But it is not open to this court to do so.'[166]

More interestingly, however, the Court indicated that it would not have been inclined to change the law had it been competent to do so.[167] Its analysis was as follows. Damages for personal injuries were not recoverable in private nuisance because private nuisance is a tort that protects one's use and enjoyment of land.[168] The right protected by public nuisance, however, was very different. As Dyson LJ argued:

> It seems to me that it is at least arguable that Professor Newark was wrong to describe a public nuisance as a 'tort to the enjoyment of rights in land'. The definition of the crime of public nuisance

---

[159] See *Hunter v Canary Wharf Ltd* [1997] AC 655 (HL) 707–08 (Lord Hoffmann): 'So far as the claim is for personal injury, it seems to me that the only appropriate cause of action is negligence. It would be anomalous if the rules for recovery of damages under this head were different according as to whether, for example, the plaintiff was at home or at work.'

[160] *Rylands v Fletcher* (1868) LR 3 HL 330. In *Transco plc v Stockport Metropolitan Borough Council* [2004] 2 AC 1 (HL) [35] Lord Hoffmann said: 'In some cases in the first half of the 20th century plaintiffs recovered damages under the rule for personal injury. ... But I think that the point is now settled by two recent decisions of the House of Lords: *Cambridge Water Co v Eastern Counties Leather plc* [1994] AC 264, which decided that *Rylands v Fletcher* is a special form of nuisance and *Hunter v Canary Wharf Ltd* ... which decided that nuisance is a tort against land. It must, I think, follow that damages for personal injuries are not recoverable under the rule.'

[161] See the arguments of the defendants in *In Re Corby Group Litigation* [2009] QB 335 (CA) [10]–[12].

[162] Newark, above n 1, 488.

[163] *In Re Corby Group Litigation* [2009] QB 335 (CA).

[164] ibid [10].

[165] See text surrounding n 160.

[166] *In Re Corby Group Litigation* [2009] QB 335 (CA) [23].

[167] ibid [24].

[168] ibid [13].

says nothing about enjoyment of land and some public nuisances undoubtedly have nothing to do with the interference with enjoyment of land.[169]

His Lordship then continued:

> The essence of the right that is protected by the crime and tort of public nuisance is the right not to be adversely affected by an unlawful act or omission whose effect is to endanger the life, safety, health etc of the public. ... In these circumstances, it is difficult to see why a person whose life, safety or health has been endangered and adversely affected by an unlawful act or omission and who suffers personal injuries as a result should not be able to recover damages. The purpose of the law which makes it a crime and a tort to do an unlawful act which endangers the life, safety or health of the public is surely to protect the public against the consequences of acts or omissions which do endanger their lives, safety or health. One obvious consequence of such an act or omission is personal injury.[170]

Thus, in England damages for personal injuries are recoverable, not only for accidents on the highway, where recovery was 'more or less traditional',[171] but also in any case of public nuisance.

In Canada the exact position of the courts is more difficult to pin down. While at one time the courts followed the traditional English position that accidents on or near the public highways could alternatively be pleaded in either negligence or public nuisance,[172] after 1960 claims in public nuisance for personal injuries caused on the highway became less frequent as negligence came to be the dominant cause of action.[173] In Alberta this trend was accelerated by the decision of the Alberta Court of Appeal in *Abbott v Kasza*.[174] In that case, the plaintiff sued the defendant for property damage (caused to his tractor-trailer) suffered in consequence of an obstruction in the highway (created by the defendant's tractor-trailer). In relation to the plaintiff's claim in public nuisance, Clement JA held as follows:

> The claim against the [defendants] was laid in the alternative in nuisance. I am of the opinion that in respect of vehicles using a highway there is now left no distinction between a cause of action alleging obstruction of the highway and one framed in negligence, and that our jurisprudence is not enriched by seeking to maintain any distinction between them in today's society.[175]

After *Kasza* Alberta courts consistently decided these issues using negligence principles.[176] As the court said in *Tibbits v Molloy*, no matter how the issue is pleaded, 'the measure of responsibility for nuisance is that of negligence'.[177] In the rest of Canada, however, plaintiffs

---

[169] ibid [27].

[170] ibid [29]–[30].

[171] BL Laskin, 'Tort—Nuisance or Negligence—Collision on Highway with Standing Truck' (1944) 22 *Canadian Bar Review* 468, 469. Bora Laskin went on to become Chief Justice of the Supreme Court of Canada.

[172] See, eg, *Gloster v Toronto Electric Light Co* [1906] 38 SCR 27; *Prentice v Sault Ste Marie (City)* [1928] SCR 309; *Jones v Shafer Estate* [1948] SCR 166 (citing *Maitland v Raisbeck* [1944] 1 KB 689 (CA)).

[173] See, eg, *Northland Greyhound Lines Inc v Bryce* [1956] SCR 408 decided a mere eight years after *Jones v Shafer* in which public nuisance was not even mentioned despite the fact pattern (ie a fatal collision with a parked vehicle on the highway) being essentially the same.

[174] *Abbott v Kasza* (1976) 71 DLR (3d) 581 (Alta CA).

[175] ibid [29].

[176] See, eg, *Kuipers v Gordon Riley Transport 1967 Ltd* (1976) 1 CCLT 233 (Alta SC-TD); *Marchuk v Scott* (1978) 8 Alta LR (2d) 237 (Dist Ct); *Tiessan v Scott*, [1979] AJ No 439 (CA); *Kleysen Transport v Northern Ind Carriers Ltd* (1981) 32 AR 541 (QB); *Simpson v Bender* (1995) 34 Alta LR (3d) 370 (QB); *Wickberg v Patterson* (1997) 145 DLR (4th) 263 (Alta CA); *Bannerman v Freeborn* 2004 ABQB 857.

[177] *Tibbits v Molloy* (1989) 94 AR 176 (QB) [9].

still occasionally made,[178] and succeeded with,[179] public nuisance claims for personal injuries even though some judges did so 'with some reluctance'[180] or attempted to incorporate negligence-like principles into the analysis.[181]

Thus when leave was given by the Supreme Court in *Ryan v Victoria* there was hope that the Court might address this divergence of approach.[182] The facts of the case were as follows. The plaintiff was injured while attempting to cross railway tracks which ran across the centre of a street in downtown Victoria. The mechanics of the injury were that the front tyre of the plaintiff's motorcycle became stuck in a 'flangeway gap'[183] that ran alongside the inner edge of the rails and which was one-quarter of an inch wider than the plaintiff's front tyre. This caused the plaintiff to be thrown from the vehicle and seriously injured. In consequence, he sued the railway company in both negligence and public nuisance. At the time, railway operators were protected by a special common law rule that said that they could not be found liable in negligence if they discharged their statutory obligations and complied with the orders of the relevant regulator.[184] It therefore seems likely that the public nuisance claim was added as one way for the plaintiff to escape the consequences of that rule. Rather than follow the lead given in *Kasza* (and banish public nuisance from these types of cases), the Supreme Court abrogated the special railway rule and found the defendant liable in *both* negligence and public nuisance. Interestingly, the public nuisance discussion is short—running to only five paragraphs[185]—and mentions nothing about the debates over the proper interrelationship between nuisance and negligence or whether personal injuries are recoverable under the tort of public nuisance. Canadian law is therefore left in a slightly ambiguous position: is public nuisance a useful standalone tool for recovering personal injuries or, given the fact that the defendant in *Ryan v Victoria* was also found negligent, are the two actions virtually indistinguishable in requiring a plaintiff to point to negligent conduct (no matter what cause of action is actually pleaded)?[186]

---

[178] See, eg, *Chessie v JD Irving Ltd* (1982) 42 NBR (2d) 192 (CA) (citing *Ware v Garston Haulage Ltd* [1944] KB 30 (CA)) in which the court held that a plaintiff injured after colliding into a wharf while snowmobiling on a frozen river had suffered special damage and therefore was entitled to sue in public nuisance. The plaintiff's claim failed on the basis that the obstruction was not unreasonable (since wharves are necessary for navigation and that particular wharf was not unusually dangerous).

[179] See, eg, *Alexander v Harrison* (1967) 2 OR 318 (CA); *Black v James D McRae & Son* (1969) 1 OR 213 (CA); *Goodwin v Pine Point Park* (1974) 7 OR (2d) 134 (CA).

[180] *Albion v Cochrane* (1969) 2 OR 184 (Co Ct) [7].

[181] See, eg, *Ross v Wall* (1980) 23 BCLR 294 (CA) [5]–[6] stating that liability for the collapse of an awning into the highway required 'the test of knowledge or means of knowledge accepted in the speeches of the House of Lords' in *Sedleigh-Denfield v O'Callaghan* [1940] AC 880 (HL), thereby rejecting the strict liability position espoused in *Wringe v Cohen* [1940] 1 KB 229 (CA).

[182] *Ryan v Victoria (City)* [1999] 1 SCR 201.

[183] As Major J explained (at [7]): 'When railway tracks run across a street or highway at grade, the rails are normally embedded in the pavement so as not to impede traffic. A groove called a "flangeway" is installed alongside the tracks in order to prevent derailments while permitting the running rails to remain flush with the road surface.'

[184] See *Grand Trunk Railway Co v McKay* (1903) 34 SCR 81; *Paskivski v Canadian Pacific Ltd* [1976] 1 SCR 687.

[185] Of the five paragraphs, three are devoted to explaining the proper understanding of the defence of statutory authority in Canadian law, which was unclear at the time as a result of the court being divided in *Tock v St John's Metropolitan Area Board* [1989] 2 SCR 1181. For a discussion, see N Rafferty, 'Tortious Liability of Railways: Defences of Statutory Compliance and Statutory Authority' (1999) 44 *Canadian Cases on the Law of Torts* (2d) 55; J Levitt, 'Statutory Authority Defence to Nuisance Actions: Alive but not Well' (1999) 5 *Digest of Municipal & Planning Law* 81.

[186] WE McNally, B Cotton and P Fischer, 'Is the Tort of Public Nuisance Still a Useful Tool for the Plaintiffs' Personal Injury Bar?', Bottom Line Research and Communications, www.bottomlineresearch.ca.

In light of the current state of the English and Canadian law, future Anglo-Canadian courts are left with essentially three choices in dealing with the recovery of personal injuries in public nuisance. The first is to follow the position set out in *Corby*, namely that personal injuries are always recoverable (provided the other elements of the traditional expansive definition of the action are met). The second is to follow the position set out in *Kasza*, and adopted by the High Court of Australia,[187] that personal injuries are never recoverable in public nuisance.[188] This, of course, would not mean that the plaintiff would have to suffer them without remedy. Instead, a plaintiff whose complaint was that his or her right to personal integrity was unintentionally violated would be required to sue in ordinary negligence and prove all the requisite elements. The third choice would be to adopt some hybrid or intermediate rule that says that *sometimes* personal injuries are recoverable and that *sometimes* they are not (with the 'sometimes' part of the formula to be given some specified content).

If the view of public nuisance presented above is correct (ie that the tort only protects rights in the nature of easements and profits that subjects enjoy over public land), then it is clear that the first option is a non-starter. If a fact pattern such as that in *Corby* were to be decided by a court not bound by its own precedents, the result should be that the plaintiffs lose on their public nuisance claim. The plaintiffs' rights to navigate on the public highway were not substantially interfered with, nor were their rights to fish in public waters. On the facts of *Corby*, therefore, it was recovery in negligence or nothing since the only right that was possibly violated was the right to personal integrity.[189] Allowing recovery in public nuisance would be both unnecessary and unhelpful as the common law already has well-defined causes of action which protect this right in a way, it would be hoped, that accommodates the just positions of both plaintiffs and defendants. In other words, we do not need two torts with the same fault/conduct element protecting the same right in potentially different ways—that is not a recipe for legal certainty or for treating like cases alike.[190] The fact that this was not seen by the Court of Appeal in *Corby* is, of course, largely attributable to the court's reliance on the overly wide 'crime-in-tort' conceptualisation of public nuisance criticised earlier in this chapter.

Does that mean that choice two—namely holding that personal injuries are an unrecoverable head of damage—is the winner? The answer is no, since choice two focuses on a type of loss rather than on the way in which that loss was brought about. On account of this failure, choice two is too wide and too indiscriminate in its application. Just as the tort of negligence does not have a problem with awarding economic losses that are consequential on the violation of our rights to personal integrity or property (yet finds that the award of

---

[187] At least in regard to highway defects: see *Brodie v Singleton Shire Council* (2001) 206 CLR 512, (HCA) [55]: '[I]t is the law of negligence which supplies the criterion of liability in such cases.' For a discussion of the nuances of Australian law, see K Barker et al, *The Law of Torts in Australia*, 5th edn (South Melbourne, Victoria, Oxford University Press, 2012) 225.

[188] This is also the position taken by the House of Lords in relation to private nuisance: see discussion above at text surrounding n 159. For criticism of this position, see Nolan, above n 8, 1198 and Beever, above n 3, 154.

[189] The litigation in *Corby* was ultimately settled, as McBride and Bagshaw, above n 9, 653 explain: '[A]t a subsequent trial, the claimants demonstrated that the defendant was responsible for a public nuisance, and that the toxic materials … had the ability to cause the type of limb defects … complained of. In April 2010, the defendant dropped plans to appeal, and reached a settlement with the claimants.'

[190] See Beever, above n 3, 103, and the discussion above at text surrounding n 40.

non-consequential or 'pure' economic losses requires special justification),[191] the tort of public nuisance should not have a problem with awarding damages for personal injuries provided that the personal injuries were consequential on the violation of the rights protected by the tort.[192] Thus, if personal injuries are caused by an obstruction to the public highway, recovery should be allowed. The classic example of this is a plaintiff who suffers personal injuries as a result of crashing into a vehicle which has been parked or left on the highway. The test for recovery on this set of facts will often appear (to the uninitiated) to be a form of negligence in disguise, since questions of reasonableness are at issue, but this is not the case. As Locke J stated in *Jones v Shafer Estate*:

> In determining whether there was here an actionable nuisance, it is necessary to determine whether the use to which the highway was put by the defendant was reasonable under the circumstances, and this question is to be distinguished from the question as to whether the defendant took reasonable care which must be determined on the count for negligence.[193]

Why did the Supreme Court of Canada think it necessary to determine if the use was reasonable? Because if the use was reasonable, then the defendant could merely be said to be exercising his or her right to pass and repass on the highway. As was discussed above, the cases hold that the exercise of this right could not be a wrong to the plaintiff (at least from the perspective of the tort of public nuisance)[194] since everyone's right to use the highway is subject to everyone else's right to do the same.[195] If, however, the vehicle was left for too long, then its presence ceased to be an exercise of the defendant's right of use—it instead became an obstruction and a public nuisance. Therefore, if the plaintiff suffered personal injuries crashing into a vehicle that was reasonably on the highway, there should be no recovery for personal injuries in public nuisance (since the right to pass and repass was not violated). However, if the plaintiff crashed into a vehicle that was an obstruction, then there should be recovery for personal injuries since these would be consequential on a violation of the right to pass and repass. Put differently, for the third option the concept of rights-infringement gives 'sometimes' its definitive content. On this view of the law, findings of liability for personal injury in the tort of public nuisance:

1. would be justified in cases such as *Ware v Garston Haulage Ltd*,[196] *Marsden Kooler Transport Ltd v Pollock Estate*,[197] *Ryan v Victoria, Dymond v Pearce*[198] and *Chessie v JD Irving Ltd*[199] since the highway was obstructed;

---

[191] As to the justification for this difference between consequential and pure economic loss, see: P Benson, 'The Basis for Excluding Liability for Economic Loss in Tort Law' in D Owen (ed), *Philosophical Foundations of Tort Law* (Oxford, Oxford University Press, 1995) 427; A Beever, *Rediscovering the Law of Negligence* (Oxford, Hart Publishing, 2007) chs 7–8; Stevens, above n 33, ch 3.

[192] For a similar view in relation to private nuisance, see Nolan, above n 8, 1198 and Beever, above n 3, 154.

[193] *Jones v Shafer Estate* [1948] SCR 166,178.

[194] It could be negligent vis-à-vis the plaintiff's right to personal integrity but that is a different matter.

[195] See *Crandell v Mooney* (1878) 23 UCCP 212; *Harper v GN Haden & Sons* [1933] Ch 298 (CA).

[196] *Ware v Garston Haulage Ltd* [1944] KB 30 (CA).

[197] *Marsden Kooler Transport Ltd v Pollock Estate* [1953] 1 SCR 66.

[198] *Dymond v Pearce* [1972] 1 QB 496 (CA).

[199] *Chessie v JD Irving Ltd* (1982) 42 NBR (2d) 192 (CA).

2. would not be justified in cases such as *Corby*, *Mint v Good*[200] and *Morton v Wheeler*[201] since the personal injuries were not consequential on any obstruction whatsoever, or in cases such as *Maitland v Raisbeck*[202] and *Jones v Shafer* since the vehicles, although on the highway, had not yet become obstructions.

V. Conclusion

Writing in 1989, Spencer concluded his critical examination of the tort of public nuisance by stating that 'if we abolished civil liability for damages for public nuisance the law of tort would be no less fair, and clearer and simpler as a result'.[203] In essence, this statement was prompted by Spencer's concern that an overly broad definition of the tort (which was wholly parasitic on the English crime) made for a regime of liability that was impossible to rationalise with the general structure and principles of Anglo-Canadian tort law. The purpose of this chapter has been to suggest that if one looks past certain surface features and commitments there is a more limited but coherent core to the tort of public nuisance— that the tort exists to protect private rights akin to easements and profits that every subject enjoys over public property. Moreover, it has sought to show: (i) that a regime of liability based around this core is consistent with tort law's principles, and (ii) that this regime of liability is implicit in English and Canadian cases of the highest authority. In other words, through an examination of the divergence of English and Canadian views (in relation to the conceptualisation of the tort, the issue of particularity in regard to special damage, and the availability of damages for personal injuries) the way has been paved for these courts to converge around a shared and coherent understanding of the tort of public nuisance. Thus, in contradistinction to Spencer's claim, abolishing the tort of public nuisance would indeed make the law appreciably less just and fair even if it did make it marginally clearer and simpler.

---

[200] *Mint v Good* [1951] 1 KB 517 (CA).
[201] *Morton v Wheeler* (CA, No 33 of 1956, 31 January 1956 unreported).
[202] *Maitland v Raisbeck* [1944] 1 KB 689 (CA).
[203] Spencer, above n 34, 83.

6

Defamation on the Internet

ROBERT RIBEIRO*

I. Introduction

The law of defamation seeks to protect individuals against unwarranted harm to their reputation. The Internet has created new ways of damaging reputations. The law must therefore seek appropriate responses. In doing so, it must avoid damaging free expression on the Internet.

The Act of Publication

A person's reputation consists of what others think of her or him. That reputation is harmed when someone publishes a statement to others which, as Lord Atkin famously put it, tends to lower the individual concerned 'in the estimation of right-thinking members of society generally'.[1] The act of publication is what does the damage. It is that act which is at the heart of the law of defamation.

Common law principles have largely been developed in relation to publications in the print medium. With the advent of mass circulation newspapers in the nineteenth century, much greater injury could be caused by a defamatory statement. This was accentuated in the twentieth century by the development of radio and television.

Those traditional forms of mass media take what has been called a 'one-to-many' form of communication. Information originating from a single source is published to many recipients. The originating entity has editorial control over content and the power and opportunity to decide whether the item should be published.

The Internet, however, has provided new ways to communicate and—inevitably—new ways of publishing defamatory matter. I shall touch on two aspects that have raised novel and difficult legal issues. First, I will deal with the liability of Internet intermediaries who provide platforms for exchanges among their users. Secondly, I shall consider the liability of those who provide Internet search engines.

* I would like to thank Mr Frank Choi Fai-ki, a Judicial Assistant at the Court of Final Appeal, for his valuable assistance in preparing this paper. I would also like to thank Mr Andrew McLeod, Stipendiary Lecturer in law at Lady Margaret Hall, Oxford, for his insights into the Australian position.

[1] *Sim v Stretch* (1936) 52 TLR 669 (HL) 671.

II. Liability of Internet Intermediaries

Internet intermediaries play a role that is essential to the functioning of the Internet as we know it. To quote Professor Jack Balkin, they are entities which

> do not necessarily broadcast but facilitate the speech of others, and instead of being a one-to-many, they are many-to-many forms of communication. They include not only broadband companies, but also a whole range of online service providers, like YouTube, Blogger, and their parent company Google; social networking sites like MySpace and Facebook; Flickr, a photo-sharing service owned by Yahoo; and virtual worlds like Second Life. These online service providers offer platforms through which people can find content, create new content, transform existing content and broadcast the content to others … a key element of their business models is providing widespread, democratized, access to media and encouraging participation. That is because their business models depend on user-generated content.[2]

Such interactivity is now ubiquitous. There are discussion forums and blogs expressing and inviting views on every conceivable subject. Online editions of newspapers encourage readers to comment on articles. Television presenters ask viewers to 'tweet' their reactions. Customers are invited to review books, products, restaurants, hotels and so forth. But what happens if the reviews or comments contain statements defamatory of some person? Often the authors may be unknown or not worth suing. Should the person who provided the platform hosting their comments be held liable as publisher of the defamatory statements? How is the balance to be struck between free expression and protection of reputation in such cases?

As it happens, the issue of intermediary liability reached the Hong Kong Court of Final Appeal a year ago in a case called *Oriental Press Group v Fevaworks*.[3] It is interesting to compare its approach with that adopted by the English Court of Appeal in *Tamiz v Google Inc*,[4] which had been decided some five months earlier.

The *Oriental Press Group* Case

The defendants in the *Oriental Press Group* case maintained a website which hosted one of the most popular discussion forums in Hong Kong, known as the 'Golden Forum'. This forum often had some 30,000 users online, with over 5,000 messages being posted each hour. Anyone could browse the site but only registered members could post items on the forum. There were rules, including a prohibition of defamatory posts, but no attempt was made to edit or filter posts before they appeared on the forum. Two administrators were employed to remove objectionable content. Violation of the rules could result in suspension or termination of membership.

The *Oriental Press Group* case arose out of three discussion threads posted in 2007, 2008 and 2009, respectively. They contained highly defamatory statements accusing the plaintiffs

---

[2] J Balkin, paper prepared for the Global Constitutionalism Seminar, Yale Law School, 2010, adapted from Jack M Balkin, 'Media Access: A Question of Design' (2008) 76 *George Washington Law Review* 933.

[3] *Oriental Press Group Ltd v Fevaworks Solutions Ltd* [2013] HKCFA 47, (2013) 16 HKCFAR 366.

[4] *Tamiz v Google Inc* [2013] EWCA Civ 68, [2013] 1 WLR 2151.

of involvement in drug trafficking and money laundering and even complicity in murder. The defendants were unaware of those posts until the plaintiffs threatened proceedings concerning the 2007 and 2008 statements. The defendants removed the 2008 posts from the website about 3½ hours after receiving the complaint. But the 2007 posts were not taken down until some eight months later. The defendants themselves subsequently discovered the 2009 statements and immediately took them down, about 12 hours after they had been posted.

The plaintiffs were awarded $100,000 damages for the 2007 statements—an award that the defendants did not appeal. However, the plaintiffs' claims regarding the 2008 and 2009 posts were dismissed at trial and their appeal to the Court of Appeal failed. The issue of whether such an intermediary should be held liable for the defamatory posts of its forum users therefore came before the Court of Final Appeal.

The Court approached the case by asking whether the forum hosts qualified as publishers of the libel and, if so, whether they could rely on the common law defence of innocent dissemination. This is a defence established at the turn of the twentieth century to mitigate the harshness of the strict, pre-existing rules on publication. A defendant had previously been held liable as a publisher if by an act of any description he could be said to have intentionally assisted in conveying the defamatory statements to a third party. It did not matter that he did not know that the article contained the offensive words and it was irrelevant that he had acted with reasonable care.[5] All who participated in the process of distribution were jointly and severally liable for the entire damage suffered by the plaintiff, regardless of the degree of responsibility each had for the publication.[6]

The innocent dissemination defence was formulated in the judgment of Romer LJ in a case called *Vizetelly v Mudie's Library*,[7] reported in 1900. His Lordship held that a person who was not the printer[8] or the first or main publisher of a libellous work, but who had taken a subordinate part in its dissemination, had a defence if he could show that he did not know that the work disseminated contained the libel and that his lack of knowledge was not due to any negligence on his part.

This defence has been adopted in jurisdictions including Australia, New Zealand, Canada and Hong Kong. It has two central features. First, it is only available to secondary publishers; those considered 'first or main publishers' cannot rely on it. Secondly, in relation to secondary publishers, it replaces strict liability with liability only where they knew or ought reasonably to have known that the article contained the defamatory matter.

The Court held in the *Oriental Press Group* case[9] that knowledge and control provide the criteria for differentiating between the two classes of publishers. A primary publisher is someone who knows or can easily acquire knowledge of the content of the article being published (although he may not know that it is defamatory as a matter of law). He also has

---

[5] *Vizetelly v Mudie's Select Library* [1900] 2 QB 170, 179; *Godfrey v Demon Internet Ltd* [2001] QB 201, 207 per Morland J; *Dow Jones & Co Inc v Gutnick* (2002) 210 CLR 575 [25].

[6] A Mullin, R Parkes and G Busuttil, *Gatley on Libel and Slander*, 12th edn (London, Sweet & Maxwell, 2013) [6.11].

[7] *Vizetelly v Mudie's Select Library* [1900] 2 QB 170, 180. It drew on the earlier decision of Lord Esher MR in *Emmens v Pottle* (1886) 16 QBD 354 (CA).

[8] As to printers, see *Oriental Press Group Ltd v Fevaworks Solutions Ltd* [2013] HKCFA 47, (2013) 16 HKCFAR 366 [79] and [80].

[9] ibid [76].

editorial control plus the ability and opportunity to prevent publication. On that basis, the Court concluded that the forum providers were not first or main publishers but were subordinate publishers eligible to rely on the defence.

On the facts, the Court decided that *before* they were notified of the plaintiffs' complaint, the defendants were protected. Since there was no realistic means of vetting for libel the 5,000 messages posted every hour, the Court was satisfied that they did not know and, without negligence on their part, did not have any reason to suppose that the libels had been posted.

But what about their position *after* they received complaints about the defamatory posts? In an Internet case such as *Oriental Press Group* the discussion thread is likely to receive 'hits' and so to be published afresh to persons accessing that content after the complaint has been received but before the libellous material is removed. Is the innocent dissemination defence available to the intermediary in such circumstances?

The Court of Final Appeal decided that this defence is available, provided that the intermediary proves that upon learning of the defamatory posts, he took all reasonable steps to take them down as soon as reasonably practicable. The standard of reasonableness was therefore applicable both before and after becoming aware of the offending posts. The Court concluded that the 2008 and 2009 statements were taken down sufficiently promptly to retain the protection of the innocent dissemination defence and dismissed the plaintiffs' appeal.

Tamiz v Google Inc

The English Court of Appeal adopted a somewhat different approach in *Tamiz v Google Inc*.[10] Google Inc ('Google'), a Delaware corporation with its main place of business in California, was the intermediary sued. On a website it owned, known as Blogger.com, Google provided a platform for users to create blogs expressing their own views and inviting the comments of others. Google did not exercise any prior control over what appeared on Blogger.com, but it had rules about permitted content and was able to remove or block access to offending material to which its attention was drawn.

In April 2011 Mr Tamiz complained that a blogger had defamed him on Blogger.com. Google forwarded his complaints to the blogger who voluntarily removed the offending comments some 3½ months after the complaint was made. Mr Tamiz sued Google for libel in respect of the period before removal and sought permission to serve the claim out of the jurisdiction. The issue was whether there was an arguable claim against Google to justify granting such permission.

Richards LJ, writing for the Court of Appeal, held that Google was not a primary publisher since it did not create or have any prior knowledge of, or effective control over, the content of the blog.[11] He doubted whether Google could be regarded as a subordinate publisher but nevertheless held that *before* receiving Mr Tamiz's complaint, Google had a defence at common law because it did not know and would not, by exercising reasonable care, have known that the publication was defamatory. It seems to me that that defence is

---

[10] *Tamiz v Google Inc* [2013] EWCA Civ 68, [2013] 1 WLR 2151 (Lord Dyson MR, Richards and Sullivan LJJ).
[11] ibid [25].

in substance the innocent dissemination defence although it was not described as such. His Lordship also held that Google had an unassailable defence under section 1 of the UK's Defamation Act 1996 which gives statutory form to the common law defence.[12]

Similar statutory provisions exist in each of the Australian States and Territories.[13] New Zealand has the equivalent in section 21 of its Defamation Act 1992. But Hong Kong has not enacted such a provision. However, those provisions do not alter the common law defence and do not affect the present discussion.

Although the courts in *Tamiz* and *Oriental Press Group* converged in substance on *pre*-notification liability, they diverged on the question of *post*-notification liability. As we have seen, in Hong Kong, the Court of Final Appeal extended the innocent dissemination defence to afford a reasonable time for taking down the offending words, but Richards LJ turned to quite a different principle. He drew on a line of cases involving notice boards and graffiti.

Three well-known cases illustrate that principle. The first is the 1937 decision of the English Court of Appeal in *Byrne v Deane*.[14] A member of a golf club who objected to fruit machines on the premises had them taken away by the police on the ground that they were unlawful gambling machines. Someone then pinned a sheet on the club's notice board attacking (in verse) the member who had reported the fruit machines. There was a rule that no notice should be posted without the club secretary's consent. The plaintiff claimed that he was defamed by the notice and sued the proprietors of the club, one of whom was the club secretary. No one had sought her consent to put up the notice, but she had allowed it to remain on the notice board since she could see no harm in it. The English Court of Appeal noted that posting the notice without consent was an act of trespass, but concluded that after its discovery, the secretary had adopted it and made herself responsible for its publication.[15]

Next, there is the 1952 decision of the California District Court of Appeal in *Isabelle Hellar v Joe Bianco*.[16] Someone had scrawled a defamatory message on the wall of the men's lavatory in a bar. The judge described it as 'libellous matter indicating that the appellant was an unchaste woman who indulged in illicit amatory ventures'. The message included the appellant's telephone number. After someone called Ms Hellar at that number, her husband telephoned the bartender giving him 30 minutes to remove the offending words. The bartender said he was too busy and would get round to removing it in due course. Applying *Byrne v Deane*, the Court held that 'by knowingly permitting such matter to remain after reasonable opportunity to remove the same, the owner of the wall or his lessee [was] guilty of republication of the libel'.

The third example is the 1991 case of *Urbanchich v Drummoyne Municipal Council*,[17] in the Supreme Court of New South Wales. The plaintiff was the leader of an extreme

---

[12] Defamation Act 1996 (UK) s 1(1): 'In defamation proceedings a person has a defence if he shows that (a) he was not the author, editor or publisher of the statement complained of, (b) he took reasonable care in relation to its publication, and (c) he did not know, and had no reason to believe, that what he did caused or contributed to the publication of a defamatory statement.'

[13] ACT: Civil Law (Wrongs) Act 2002, s 139C; NSW: Defamation Act 2005, s 32; NT: Defamation Act 2006, s 29; Qld: Defamation Act 2005, s 32; SA: Defamation Act 2005, s 30; Tas: Defamation Act 2005, s 32; Vic: Defamation Act 2005, s 32; WA: Defamation Act 2005, s 32.

[14] *Byrne v Deane* [1937] 1 KB 818 (CA).

[15] The defendants, however, escaped liability because the words did not bear a defamatory meaning.

[16] *Isabelle Hellar v Joe Bianco* 244 P 2d 757 (Cal App, 1952).

[17] *Urbanchich v Drummoyne Municipal Council* (1991) Aust Torts Reports §81-127 (NSWSC).

right-wing group who sued the Urban Transit Authority for libel on the basis that posters purporting to depict him in the company of Adolf Hitler and others in Nazi uniforms had been glued onto bus shelters controlled by the Authority. Although asked to remove them, the posters were allowed to remain in place for at least a month. Hunt J held that there was a sufficient case to go to the jury since the plaintiff might be able to establish liability by showing that the defendant had consented to or ratified the continued presence of the defamatory statement on its property enabling others to read it.[18]

In *Tamiz* Richards LJ thought that provision of a platform for bloggers was equivalent to the provision of a notice board.[19] He held that if Google allowed defamatory matter to remain on a Blogger.com blog after being informed of its presence, it might be found to have made itself a publisher of the material.[20]

Divergence and Convergence in the Views of the Two Courts

In the *Oriental Press Group* case the Hong Kong Court of Final Appeal considered the *Byrne v Deane* approach unsuitable for dealing with Internet intermediaries. It took the view that such intermediaries *do* participate in a real sense in the dissemination of items posted on the platforms provided. They register users as members, lay down rules for participation and encourage visitors to browse the site. They often rely on advertising income and aim to maximise traffic on their sites. It is legitimate to make the availability of the innocent dissemination defence conditional on them proving that they did not know and did not have reasonable grounds to be aware of the defamatory matter posted by their users.

However, proprietors of premises such as the golf club, the bar and the bus shelters are in quite a different position. People who deface their walls with graffiti or pasted posters, or who pin scurrilous items onto their notice boards contrary to club rules, are trespassers. Such occupiers are not treated as publishers of the defamatory messages unless the plaintiff proves that they adopted or ratified the defamatory statements. The *Byrne v Deane* line of authority is not concerned with innocent dissemination. It is concerned with persons who are not participants in the dissemination of statements by others but who, by their ratifying conduct, convert themselves into publishers of the defamatory graffiti or notices. If they know about and adopt the publication of the libellous content, they become primary publishers, leaving no room for the defence of innocent dissemination.

In *Tamiz* the Court of Appeal appears to have considered it possible effectively to adopt *both* the innocent dissemination defence (applying it to the period before Google became aware of the posts) and the *Byrne v Deane* approach (applying it after notice was received). But it seems to me that those two principles cannot comfortably be combined. They address different issues, apply different standards in judging the defendant's conduct, and impose different burdens of proof.

---

[18]   ibid 193.

[19]   *Tamiz v Google Inc* [2013] EWCA Civ 68, [2013] 1 WLR 2151 [33].

[20]   ibid [34]. Some support for the *Tamiz* approach can be found in two earlier first instance interlocutory decisions: *Sadiq v Baycorp (NZ) Ltd* [2008] NZHC 403 [48] (after citing *Byrne v Deane*, Doogue AJ said that he could see 'no reason why a parallel process of reasoning should not be applied to the presence on websites of defamatory material'); *Davison v Habeeb* [2011] EWHC 3031 [38] (after considering *Byrne v Deane*, Judge Parkes QC likened the website Blogger.com to 'a gigantic notice board').

Notwithstanding such divergence, however, a large measure of convergence can be seen in the outcome of the *Tamiz* and *Oriental Press Group* decisions. Both courts rejected the suggestion that the Internet intermediaries were primary publishers subject to strict liability. They both held that the enormous volume of traffic on their discussion platforms meant that the intermediaries were not negligent in failing to detect and remove the defamatory material before they were made aware of the libellous matter since they could not reasonably have been expected to filter or edit the posts beforehand. Both courts then went in search of an appropriate principle for dealing with the intermediaries' position *after* they became aware of the objectionable material. It was only at that point that their approaches diverged. But there was nonetheless convergence as to the practical outcome. Both courts held that liability was avoided if the intermediary promptly took down the offending posts after becoming aware of the offensive matter.

Looking to the future, the question of what constitutes reasonable conduct is likely to be a frequent issue. It will often be reasonable to adopt a notice and take-down policy. But sometimes it may not be good enough just to sit back and wait for complaints. If, for instance, the intermediary knows that someone has been repeatedly targeted for defamatory attacks on its platform, the standard of reasonableness may require a more proactive stance.

Some platforms may be inherently likely to attract defamatory statements. For example, in *Kaplan v Go Daddy Group*,[21] a decision of the New South Wales Supreme Court, a customer dissatisfied with his car dealer started a blog provocatively called 'www. hunterholdensucks.com' and encouraged others to share their views. Unsurprisingly, some extremely negative comments were elicited, defamatory of the dealer. Similarly, in *Wishart v Murray*,[22] a decision of the New Zealand High Court, the defendants set up a Facebook page campaigning for a new book to be boycotted, making seriously defamatory allegations against one of the authors. The creators of such sites might reasonably be required to exercise particular care given the obvious risk of attracting defamatory comments.

Reasonableness may also depend on the quality of the information provided by the complainant. A vague complaint which does not enable the intermediary readily to identify the offending posts or to understand why they are said to be objectionable may well sustain the intermediary's defence. At the same time, the intermediary might reasonably be expected to provide an accessible procedure for reporting abuse.

Even after receiving a complaint, an Internet intermediary may be unable to tell whether a post is defamatory or, if defamatory, whether it is lawful. How could they, for example, know whether the statement is true or is a matter of honest comment? An intermediary may therefore be inclined to play it safe and so automatically take down all posts which are made the subject of complaint. But it is an important social value that certain kinds of wrongdoing should be publicly exposed. Freedom of expression embraces the making of defamatory statements if they are true or represent honest comment on matters of public interest. A simple notice and take-down rule is therefore less than ideal.

In some jurisdictions the vulnerable intermediary is given statutory protection. In the United States section 230 of the Communications Decency Act 1996[23] confers a general

---

[21] *Kaplan v Go Daddy Group* [2005] NSWSC 636.
[22] *Wishart v Murray* [2013] NZHC 540.
[23] 47 US Code § 230(1), 1996: 'No provider or user of an interactive computer service shall be treated as the publisher or speaker of any information provided by another information content provider.'

immunity on Internet intermediaries against being treated as publishers of content created by someone else. However, such a blanket immunity may be thought to go too far, giving insufficient weight to the protection of one's reputation. A more nuanced approach can be found in sections 5 and 10 of the United Kingdom's Defamation Act 2013, which came into operation on 1 January 2015. Those sections, together with regulations made under the Act, require plaintiffs to pursue the originator of an offending post and restrict actions against Internet intermediaries to cases where the plaintiff cannot identify the originator. Those provisions do not do make the common law principles irrelevant since website operators who are unable to identify the originators cannot avail themselves of the new statutory defences. It remains to be seen how those provisions operate.

III. Liability of Providers of Internet Search Engines

I turn next to deal with my second topic which concerns liability for defamatory content generated by the use of Internet search engines. I have so far been discussing the difference between primary and secondary publishers. A third category involves entities sometimes referred to as 'mere conduits' or 'passive facilitators'. These include entities such as the Post Office and operators of telephone networks. Although their services may be used to publish libels, they are not themselves regarded as publishers at common law and often have statutory immunity. They provide the means for one person to communicate with another but play no active role regarding the content of those exchanges.

Internet service providers (ISPs) have been held to fall within this third category. In *Bunt v Tilley*,[24] a decision of the English High Court which has been widely accepted,[25] Eady J struck out an action brought by a plaintiff against three ISPs whose only role was to afford the persons posting the defamatory matter a connection to the Internet. Issues have arisen as to whether the provider of an Internet search engine such as Google or Yahoo should also be classed as a mere conduit or whether it should instead be deemed a publisher at common law potentially liable for defamation.

The Internet is of course a global network of computers comprising tens of billions of web pages, and search engines are an essential means for locating content on the World Wide Web. In *Metropolitan International Schools v Designtechnica*[26] Eady J explained how a search engine operates in the following terms:

> What happens is that Google compiles an index of pages from the web and it is this index which is examined during the search process. … [The] index is compiled and updated purely automatically (ie with no human input). The process is generally referred to as 'crawling' or the 'web crawl'.

> When a search is carried out, it will yield a list of pages which are determined (automatically) as being relevant to the query. The technology ranks the pages in order of 'perceived' relevance—again without human intervention.

---

[24] *Bunt v Tilley* [2007] 1 WLR 1243 (QB).

[25] eg in *Crookes v Newton* 2011 SCC 47, [2011] 3 SCR 269; *Davison v Habeeb* [2011] EWHC 3031 (QB); *Tamiz v Google Inc* [2013] EWCA Civ 68, [2013] 1 WLR 2151 [33]; *Wishart v Murray* [2013] NZHC 540, [2013] 3 NZLR 246; and *Oriental Press Group Ltd v Fevaworks Solutions Ltd* [2013] HKCFA 47, (2013) 16 HKCFAR 366.

[26] *Metropolitan International Schools Ltd v Designtechnica Corpn* [2009] EWHC 1765, [2011] 1 WLR 1743 (QB) [11]–[12].

Search results take the form of hyperlinks to web pages. To make the search process more user-friendly, there is usually displayed alongside some indication of the contents of the linked website. This might be a text excerpt, an image or a snapshot of the site. These previews are often called 'snippets'. The initial series of cases brought against search engine providers have concerned 'snippets' said to be defamatory.

O'Kroley v Fastcase Inc[27] in the US District Court in Tennessee provides a good illustration. Mr Colin O'Kroley decided to do what is sometimes called a 'vanity search' on Google. In other words, he performed a search for his own name and, to his horror, the snippet that the search produced showed 'his name in a sentence fragment separated by an ellipsis from another sentence fragment including the words "indecency with a child"'. He sued Google on the ground that the snippet wrongfully suggested that he had been accused or convicted of that crime.

The snippet was probably defamatory, but the linked web page was not. If one clicked on the hyperlink, one would have seen from the web page that Mr O'Kroley's name appeared at the start of an innocuous entry in a digest of legal cases, but the Google excerpt had also captured the words at the tail end of the preceding entry which referred to a child indecency case. The Court dismissed Mr O'Kroley's action on the basis of Google's immunity under section 230 of the Communications Decency Act 1996.

Where no such immunity exists, is the search engine provider liable for publishing the defamatory snippet? Is the position different after it receives a complaint and becomes aware of the offending search result?

The case law (outside the United States) is at present far from definitive. However, some divergence has emerged between Eady J's decision in 2011 in the *Metropolitan International Schools* case and the decision of Beach J in 2012 in the Supreme Court of Victoria in *Trkulja v Google (No 5)*.[28]

The *Metropolitan* case was one in which the plaintiff sued Google, alleging that both the snippet and the linked website were defamatory, in suggesting that it was involved in a 'scam'. Eady J was not sympathetic. His Lordship noted that Google does not choose the search terms which the user inputs and stressed the absence of human intervention in producing the search result. He decided that Google was not a publisher at common law because, in his view, it had not authorised or caused the snippet to appear on the user's screen in any meaningful sense. He held in effect that by providing the search engine, Google had acted as a mere conduit or facilitator akin to an ISP.[29] That remained the case, in his Lordship's view, even after receiving complaints about defamatory snippets and content.

Eady J emphasised the technical difficulties involved since, unlike a website host, a search engine provider cannot simply press a button to ensure that the offending words will never reappear in a search snippet. Whatever the search engine provider might do, the offending website would remain in existence. And if the author of the defamation should post the same matter on other websites, the search engine might well find them and create similar snippets. Against that background, Eady J held that it would be unrealistic to

---

[27] *O'Kroley v Fastcase Inc* 2014 WL 2197029 (M D Tenn).
[28] *Trkulja v Google Inc LLC (No 5)* [2012] VSC 533.
[29] *Metropolitan International Schools Ltd v Designtechnica Corpn* [2009] EWHC 1765, [2011] 1 WLR 1743 (QB) [50]–[51].

attribute responsibility for publication to Google, whether on the basis of authorship or acquiescence.[30]

In *Trkulja v Google (No 5)* Beach J declined to follow *Metropolitan. Trkulja* also involved snippets (this time in the form of photo images) and linked web page content both said to be defamatory. His Honour took the view that while Internet search engines operate in an automated fashion, they 'operate precisely as intended by those who own them and who provide their services'.[31] He added:

> To say as a general principle that if an entity's role is a passive one then it cannot be a publisher, would cut across principles which have formed the basis for liability in the newsagent/library type cases and also in those cases where someone with power to remove a defamatory publication chooses not to do so in circumstances where an inference of consent can be drawn.

Beach J's view is, however, not the last word on the topic in Australia. In the Federal Court, in *Rana v Google Australia*,[32] a case decided in 2013, Mansfield J reviewed the authorities, including Beach J's judgment, and held that whether or not a search engine can be considered a publisher of defamatory material 'is not settled in Australia'.

Which is the preferable approach? The approach of Eady J or of Beach J? In my view, there is merit in both positions, but I think it important to distinguish between liability for a defamatory snippet on the one hand and liability for providing a link to a third party's defamatory website on the other.

To take snippets first, Eady J likened a search engine provider to a passive facilitator of a communications network. But the analogy is not very convincing since, unlike mere conduits or passive facilitators, a search engine provider *does* deal with content, crawling and indexing websites, and generating snippets which point the way to websites of interest by reference to their content. Indeed, in a case such as *O'Krole* the underlying web pages are inoffensive and it is only because of the way the search snippet is displayed that the plaintiff's reputation is injured. The publisher of such injurious content can only be the search engine provider.

At the same time, with respect, I think that Beach J overstates the case by suggesting that the search engine provider's intentional use of pre-programmed algorithms should be equated with an intention to publish the defamatory content in a snippet. If that approach were taken, the provider would be deemed a primary publisher and attract strict liability, which would plainly be unwarranted.

Beach J in fact appears to suggest that search engine providers should be treated as secondary rather than primary publishers. I would tentatively be inclined to agree with that classification in relation to snippets. Secondary publishers do not actually know and do not intend to publish the defamatory matter. They avoid liability if, relying on the innocent dissemination defence, they can show that, without negligence on their part, they did not know of the defamatory matter disseminated and, on becoming aware of it, took steps to excise the defamatory result as soon as reasonably practicable.

Eady J's approach is more apposite for dealing with cases where the snippet itself is not defamatory but where the search provides a hyperlink to a website which *is* defamatory of the plaintiff. In such cases, the search engine does not create any autonomous offensive

---

[30] ibid [64].
[31] *Trkulja v Google Inc LLC (No 5)* [2012] VSC 533 [27].
[32] *Rana v Google Australia Pty Ltd* [2013] FCA 60 [58].

content but functions merely as a location tool. It indicates where already existing content, made available by third parties on the Internet, can be found. In that situation, the analogy with a mere conduit or passive facilitator is far more compelling. Until recently, I think one would confidently have rejected any suggestion that the search engine provider is liable in that situation. Authority in support could be found in the decision of the Canadian Supreme Court in *Crookes v Newton*,[33] where Abella J held that a defendant who embedded a hyperlink in his article, linking it to another article containing defamatory matter, did not thereby publish the defamation contained in the second article.

I said 'until recently' because the debate could be opened up by the recent decision of the Grand Chamber of the European Court of Justice (ECJ) involving Google, Spain.[34] It is a decision which has stirred up much controversy by asserting that 'a right to be forgotten' exists by virtue of a European data protection law. It is not a libel case but plainly has implications that may be relevant.

The problem started once again with a 'vanity search'. In November 2009, Mr Mario Costeja González made a Google search for his own name and this produced links to the electronic version of a newspaper, displaying two pages which had originally been published more than ten years earlier. Those pages advertised an auction of property owned by Mr González which had been attached as part of proceedings against him for recovery of social security debts. He was agitated by the search results because those proceedings had long been resolved and he regarded the information about them as entirely irrelevant (and no doubt embarrassing). It was not a case of libel since there was nothing false or inaccurate about the fact that his property had been attached and advertised. In fact, the advertisements had been placed by the lawful order of the Ministry of Labour and Social Affairs. That was why his claim against the newspaper to take down those web pages failed.

However, with the support of the Spanish Data Protection Agency, Mr González persuaded the ECJ (acting contrary to the opinion of its Advocate General)[35] to make the search engine provider liable. The ECJ declared that a user such as Mr González had the right to demand that Google should remove from search results relating to his name links to a third party's web pages containing information regarding him which is 'inadequate, irrelevant or excessive in relation to the purposes of the [data] processing [concerned]'.[36] The Court did, however, acknowledge that this 'right to be forgotten' could be overridden in cases where 'the preponderant interest of the general public' supported retention of the relevant information in the search results.[37]

Mr González was not complaining about Google publishing a defamatory snippet or other defamatory content about him. The search engine was, in this case, merely functioning as a location tool. The information objected to was in the website located. Nevertheless, the ECJ upheld Mr González's right to be forgotten against Google (subject to a public interest exception) even though the publication was perfectly accurate and lawful. Given

---

[33] *Crookes v Newton* 2011 SCC 47, [2011] 3 SCR 269.
[34] Case C-131/12 *Google Spain SL, Google Inc v Agencia Española de Protección de Datos (AEPD)* and *Mario Costeja González* (13 May 2014).
[35] Case C-131/12 *Google Spain SL, Google Inc v Agencia Española de Protección de Datos (AEPD)* and *Mario Costeja González (rep)* Opinion of AG Jääskinen (25 June 2013).
[36] Case C-131/12 *Google Spain SL, Google Inc v Agencia Española de Protección de Datos (AEPD)* and *Mario Costeja González* (13 May 2014), [92].
[37] ibid [81], [97] and [99].

such a result, it would not be surprising to hear it argued that the courts should be all the more willing to adopt the same approach where the located website contains defamatory matter. We shall have to wait and see whether such claims materialise.

The *Google, Spain* case may have other implications arising out of Google's reaction to the judgment rather than the judgment itself. I have touched on the difficulties faced by an intermediary trying to decide whether a take-down request alleging defamation is justified. Such difficulties are at least as great in relation to the right to be forgotten. How is the search engine provider to know whether the search result is inadequate, irrelevant or excessive? How does it judge whether it is in the public interest that the information should remain available? Additionally, search engine providers face technical difficulties in trying to devise an effective means of blocking objectionable search results. But given Google's reaction, the courts might be less deterred by such practical problems from imposing liability.

Google has indicated that it is exploring ways of complying with the ECJ judgment and that it intends 'to assess each individual request and balance the rights of the individual to control his or her personal data with public's right to know and distribute information'.[38] This is so even though the *Financial Times* reported on 3 June 2014 that in the first four days Google received more than 41,000 removal requests.[39] By 4 July it was reported that more than 70,000 removal requests involving over 250,000 links had been received, with requests continuing to be made at the rate of around 1,000 per day.[40] Google's willingness to undertake such a demanding task may encourage some courts to discount the technical and practical problems and be more prepared to impose liability.

I hasten to add that I am not by any means encouraging actions against search engine providers when they are acting merely as location tools. I mention *Google, Spain* only because search engine liability has already engendered divergent views and the ECJ decision may well contribute to the evolving picture.

IV. Concluding Remarks

At the beginning of this chapter I spoke of defamation law seeking a balance between the right to reputation and the right to free expression. In Internet cases, that balance must accommodate a far more complex constellation of rights, freedoms and policies. The courts are not simply concerned with the originator's defamation and the victim's injured reputation. They must assess the liability of all kinds of Internet intermediaries who are in some way involved in the publication of defamatory statements by third persons. The courts must be careful not to cause collateral damage to the general right to free expression and information. They must not impose liabilities which threaten the viability of entities which provide facilities essential for using the Internet. Defamation decisions by the courts may have implications not only for free expression and rights to reputation, but also for

---

[38] www.google.fr/policies/faq/.

[39] Of these reportedly, 31% concerned frauds or scams; 20% concerned arrests or convictions for violent or serious crimes; and 12% concerned arrests for child pornography.

[40] Rhiannon Williams, 'Google Asked to Remove over 250,000 Links', www.telegraph.co.uk/technology/google/10945451.

privacy and data protection rights, as well as rights to protection of electronic commerce, in countries where such protection exists.

The Internet has other dimensions raising legal problems which I have not had time to explore. These include problems arising out of its global and borderless reach and the enduring nature of matter circulating in cyberspace. For example, conflicting rules exist in different jurisdictions as to whether repeated publications of the same defamatory statement each constitute a fresh cause of action, or whether the single publication rule should apply. The choice of rule has implications for limitation periods and possibly on the multiplicity of actions. Remedies and enforcement may obviously pose problems where relevant parties are abroad, especially if they are in jurisdictions offering statutory immunity.

In an ideal world, one might hope to see a series of carefully calibrated statutes sensitively addressing each of those complex concerns and providing a coordinated and balanced policy. But of course life is seldom ideal and one cannot necessarily count on the legislature. In the absence of applicable statutes, the courts have had to fall back on the common law. It may seem odd that they have had recourse to centuries-old cases and have considered the possible value as precedents, of such matters as graffiti on lavatory walls and versified notices pinned onto golf club notice boards. But it is a hallmark of the common law that the courts seek to adapt established principles to solve novel problems. The cause of action asserted by the plaintiff is itself a creature of the common law and invites a common law response.

Convergence or divergence in the courts' decisions in this area has depended on which principles were selected, on whether the principles were extended and on how they were actually applied. By and large, there has been convergence in adopting the standard of reasonableness and in accepting notice and take-down policies by intermediaries as prima facie reasonable. But, as I have stated, that is not an ideal solution and limited statutory immunities such as those conferred by the UK's Defamation Act 2013, restricting actions against intermediaries to cases where the originator of the libel cannot be identified, are attractive. Such a scheme can obviously only be introduced by legislation. The common law has shown itself resourceful, but the limits of judicial intervention and the need for supportive legislation in this area must be recognised.

7

Convergence and Divergence: The Law of Non-Delegable Duties in Australia and the United Kingdom

NEIL FOSTER[*]

I. Introduction

In general, as is well known, while an employer can be held vicariously liable for wrongs committed by an employee in the course of their employment, a 'principal' is not vicariously liable for the actions of an independent contractor.[1] The High Court of Australia noted in *Hollis v Vabu*: 'It has long been accepted, as a general rule, that an employer is vicariously liable for the tortious acts of an employee but that a principal is not liable for the tortious acts of an independent contractor.'[2]

There was an attempt by McHugh J in the High Court in the early part of the twenty-first century to reformulate the rules relating to liability for the actions of non-employees, where his Honour argued that the actions of 'representative agents' ought to create vicarious liability.[3] But the majority of the High Court firmly rejected this view, and an attempt by Kirby J to revive this theory in *Sweeney v Boylan Nominees Pty Ltd* also failed.[4]

However, despite the general rule precluding vicarious liability for independent contractors, it has long been accepted that there are some specific situations where the courts have recognised what is called a 'non-delegable duty of care' ('NDD'). In these situations liability may be imposed on a principal for the wrongful actions of a contractor.

While the outcome of a finding of non-delegable duty is similar to vicarious liability (in that one party is being held strictly liable for harm committed by another with whom

---

[*] I would like to thank colleagues who commented on this chapter at the Obligations VII conference for sharpening my thinking on some areas, especially Andrew Burrows, Nick McBride and John Murphy (although none of them should be held responsible for any remaining errors).

[1] See *Salsbury v Woodland* [1970] 1 QB 324, 336G (where Widgery LJ describes the proposition as 'trite law').

[2] *Hollis v Vabu* [2001] HCA 44, (2001) 207 CLR 21 [32] (footnotes omitted).

[3] ibid, and *Scott v Davis* [2000] HCA 52, (2000) 204 CLR 333.

[4] *Sweeney v Boylan Nominees Pty Ltd* [2006] HCA 19, (2006) 226 CLR 161. For comment on this case, see N Foster, 'Vicarious Liability for Independent Contractors Revisited: *Sweeney v Boylan Nominees Pty Ltd*' (2006) 14 *Torts Law Journal* 219; J Burnett, 'Avoiding Difficult Questions: Vicarious Liability and Independent Contractors in *Sweeney v Boylan Nominees*' (2007) 29 *Sydney Law Review* 163; D Rolph, 'A Carton of Milk, A Bump to the Head and One Legal Headache: Vicarious Liability in the High Court of Australia' (2006) 19 *Australian Journal of Labour Law* 294.

they have a contract), there is a clear conceptual difference between the two doctrines.[5] The difference may best be described as follows.

Assume a wrongdoer W, a victim V, and an allegedly liable 'superior' party S, who has some supervisory power over W, and for whom W was acting. V wants to recover monetary compensation from S for the harm caused by W, often because W will not have adequate resources to meet a claim in full.

In cases of *vicarious liability*, the main question is whether there is a relationship between S and W, of a sort that will make S legally responsible for W's actions (eg is W an employee of S?).[6]

However, in cases of *NDD*, the action is conducted on the assumption that W is (usually) an independent contractor acting under directions from S (not an employee), and the main question is as to the relationship between S and V (not S and W). Is there a relationship of some sort between S and V that imposes a 'non-delegable duty' on S to see that reasonable care is taken for the safety of a person in V's situation?

Hence there is a clear difference in focus in the relevant issues in the two types of claims, which hinges on the question as to which is the relevant legal relationship to impose liability on S.

Recently in the UK Supreme Court decision in *Woodland* Lord Sumption noted that in a case involving a hospital Lord Denning had adopted this sort of approach:

> Denning LJ considered that the critical factor was not the hospital's relationship with the doctor or surgeon, but its relationship with the patient, arising from its acceptance of the patient for treatment.[7]

With that overall background in place, we turn briefly in section II to justify these propositions from the authorities. Differences that have emerged between the common law of England and Australia are then examined. After reviewing areas of divergence and convergence between the two jurisdictions in sections III–V, the chapter then identifies in section VI some 'misreadings' of the principle that have created confusion in recent years. It then explores in more detail in section VII one of the main areas for operation of the principle, the NDD owed by an employer to employees. Section VIII considers the important question of how the principle may apply to 'intentional torts', and section IX notes some outstanding problems in determining the reach of the principle through the concept of 'collateral negligence'.[8]

---

[5] See, eg, *Woodland v Essex County Council* [2013] UKSC 66, [2014] 1 AC 537 [33]: 'They are conceptually quite different' (Lady Hale).

[6] There are of course some other relationships that will give rise to vicarious liability. One is a commercial partnership arrangement: see, eg, *National Commercial Banking Corporation of Australia Ltd v Batty* (1986) 160 CLR 251 (HCA); *Dubai Aluminium Co Ltd v Salaam* [2002] UKHL 48, [2003] 1 All ER 97. Other possibilities are not explored in detail here.

[7] *Woodland v Essex County Council* [2013] UKSC 66, [2014] 1 AC 537 [15], citing *Cassidy v Ministry of Health* [1951] 2 KB 343 (CA).

[8] There are some interesting specific issues raised about NDD under Australian tort reform legislation, especially relating to the Civil Liability Act 2002 (NSW), s 5Q which this chapter will not be able to deal with. See *Galea v Bagtrans Pty Ltd* [2010] NSWCA 350, [2011] *Australian Torts Reports* ¶ 82–078, esp [65]–[71]; *Withyman bht Withyman v NSW and Blackburn* [2013] NSWCA 10 [132], and *Echin v Southern Tablelands Gliding Club* [2013] NSWSC 516 [104]. See also D Villa, *Annotated Civil Liability Act 2002 (NSW)*, 2nd edn (Sydney, Lawbook Co, 2013) [1A.5Q.080].

II. General Principles of Non-Delegable Duty

Gleeson CJ in *NSW v Lepore*[9] gave a general overview of the area as follows:

> Lord Blackburn referred to the inability of a person subject to a certain kind of responsibility to 'escape from the responsibility attaching on him of seeing that duty performed by delegating it to a contractor'. His Lordship's reference to a responsibility of 'seeing' a duty performed has echoes in later judicial statements. The concept was taken up in relation to the duty of an employer to take reasonable care for the safety of a workman. … Lord Wright described the duty as 'personal', and said that it required the provision of competent staff, adequate material, and a proper system of effective supervision. … [To] describe a duty of care as 'personal' or 'non-delegable' [means] that the person subject to the duty has a responsibility either to perform the duty, or to see it performed, and cannot discharge that responsibility by entrusting its performance to another.[10]

The terminology of 'non-delegable duty', then, comes from idea that there are certain duties owed to others, the performance of which cannot lawfully be passed on to someone else (in the sense that even if in fact there is an attempt to delegate the obligation to someone else, a court will still hold the original duty-holder liable.)

It is important, however, to remember that the *content* of the duty will still need to be examined. In most cases (usually negligence claims) it will be a duty of 'reasonable care', not one of 'strict liability' from the point of view of the immediate wrongdoer, W.[11]

Thus the content of the duty ('reasonable care', if it is a negligence claim) can be distinguished from the question of who has been delegated to perform the duty. True, the doctrine of NDD may appear from the point of view of the duty-holder (the principal) to be strict liability (because no amount of personal care on the part of the duty-holder will avoid liability if the delegate is careless), but in truth for a breach of duty in negligence to be established there must still be a failure of due care by somebody (for whose actions the principal will be held responsible).

Is this so, however? Some have suggested that the use of the word 'personal' to describe a duty of care in this area implies that whenever there has been a failure to provide, say, a safe system of work, then S, the principal, can be held liable, even if W, the engaged contractor, was not at fault.

It seems that some confusion arises in this area flowing from the way the courts have used this word, sometimes with almost completely opposite meanings. 'Personal' can mean 'something that the employer was obliged themselves to actually do and failed to do'—so it is clear that an employer is obliged themselves to directly set up a safe system of work. Or 'personal' can be used to mean 'something that an employer is bound to see is done by somebody, no matter who actually carries out the job', in which case in the NDD area it refers to the obligation to 'ensure that reasonable care is taken' (by someone). In the second sense a breach of the employer's 'personal' duty happens when a contractor fails to take

---

[9] *NSW v Lepore* [2003] HCA 4, (2003) 212 CLR 511.

[10] ibid [20], citing *Dalton v Angus* (1881) 6 App Cas 740, 829 (Lord Blackburn), and *Wilsons and Clyde Coal Co v English* [1938] AC 57 (HL) 84 (Lord Wright) (adopting (at 73) the statement in *Bain v Fife Coal Co* 1935 SC 681, 693 (Lord Thankerton)).

[11] See *NSW v Lepore* [2003] HCA 4, (2003) 212 CLR 511 [290]–[291] (Kirby J, citing A Barak, 'Mixed and Vicarious Liability—A Suggested Distinction' (1966) 29 *MLR* 160, 160–61, and J Fleming, *The Law of Torts*, 9th edn (Sydney, LBC Information Services, 1998) 434).

reasonable care; and in that case it is strict liability as far as the employer is concerned. But in this second case there will still be no liability unless the contractor has themselves been careless.

It would be preferable, given the contrasting meanings of the word 'personal', for some clearer terminology to be adopted. One might speak of the duty of an employer to themselves carry out a responsibility as 'direct', with the duty to see that *someone* carries out a responsibility (even if they do not it themselves) as their 'indirect' duty. However, it is important to realise that the courts in the NDD context have regularly used the word 'personal' to describe this second, 'indirect', duty, and not to read into the word the meaning it may have in other contexts.[12]

The comments of Mason J in *Kondis v State Transport Authority*[13] support the view that NDD imposes liability for a failure of due care by someone else, not simply for failure to produce a particular 'state of affairs'. His Honour refers to the principle in these terms: '[T]he respondent's duty to provide a safe system of work was non-delegable and the respondent was liable for *any negligence on the part of its independent contractor* in failing to adopt a safe system of work.'[14]

These remarks are consistent with the comments of the members of the House of Lords in *Wilsons & Clyde Coal Co Ltd v English*,[15] which is usually regarded as establishing the action for workplace negligence based on NDD. Lord Thankerton commented:

> The duty may not be absolute, and may be only a duty to exercise due care, but, if, in fact, the master entrusts the duty to some one else instead of performing it himself, he is liable for injury caused through *the want of care of that some one else*, as being, in the eye of the law, his own negligence.[16]

A similar point was made by Lord Wright, although he referred to the duty of an employer to provide a safe system of work, etc, as 'absolute'. However, he qualified his remarks as follows:

> When I use the word absolutely, I do not mean that the employers warrant the adequacy of the plant, or the competence of fellow-employees, or the propriety of the system of work. The obligation is *fulfilled by the exercise of due care and skill*. But it is not fulfilled by entrusting its fulfillment to employees, even though selected with due care and skill.[17]

Given these clear statements about the need for carelessness by the contractor, and the fact that no decision in this area has succeeded in the absence of such carelessness, this requirement seems well established, and the second sense of the word 'personal' referred to above (in the sense of an 'indirect' duty which is breached by the carelessness of someone else) is seen to be the orthodox meaning.[18]

---

[12] This matter will be taken up further in section VI below.

[13] *Kondis v State Transport Authority* (1984) 154 CLR 672 (HCA).

[14] ibid 688 (emphasis added), 694 (Deane J agreeing with the judgment of Mason J, and citing *Voli v Inglewood Shire Council* (1963) 110 CLR 74 (HCA) 95 (Windeyer J)).

[15] *Wilsons & Clyde Coal Co Ltd v English* [1938] AC 57 (HL).

[16] ibid 73, citing with approval the remarks in *Bain v Fife Coal Co* 1935 SC 681, 693 (emphasis added).

[17] *Wilsons & Clyde Coal Co Ltd v English* [1938] AC 57 (HL) 78 (emphasis added). See also ibid 88 (Lord Maugham).

[18] See also *Galea v Bagtrans Pty Ltd* [2010] NSWCA 350, [2011] Aust Torts Reports 82-078 [5]: '[T]he employer is liable for any breach of the duty whoever was retained by Adecco to perform it' (Allsop P). Also more recently, Meagher JA in *AF Concrete Pumping Pty Ltd v Ryan* [2014] NSWCA 346 [29]: 'If … an employee as part of the duties of his employment assists an independent contractor of the employer to undertake a particular task, and does so under its supervision and control, the employer's non-delegable duty to provide a safe system of work

What if the NDD relates to a tort other than negligence? There are not many examples of this, but it seems fairly clear that in this case whatever standard of behaviour is appropriate to that other tort will be engaged as the standard required of the wrongdoer W—though the duty-holder's (S's) responsibility will still be strict.[19]

An example may be taken from the operation of the tort of breach of statutory duty.[20] If a statutory duty to ensure safety is cast upon the occupier of premises, and if an employee is injured due to a breach of that duty, the occupier cannot avoid liability by noting that the breach was due to the actions of a contractor.[21] If the duty is a strict duty, not requiring demonstration of fault, then there will be liability for the actions of the contractor, even if the contractor is not at fault.[22]

One thing is clear: the doctrine of NDD is a principle of attribution of liability, not a separate tort action. Christian Witting's argument to the contrary[23] was rejected by Kirby J in *Leichhardt Municipal Council v Montgomery*.[24] NDD is not a free-standing tort, but a part of the liability rules that attach to torts, to determine who will be held responsible for wrongdoing.

In Australia one of the leading cases, already noted, is *Kondis v State Transit Authority*,[25] where a principal was held to owe an NDD to his employee, and hence was held strictly liable for harm to the employee caused by a careless crane operator who was a contractor. Kirby J set out the main circumstances in which an NDD had been previously held to be owed in Australia as follows: 'employer/employee; hospital/patient; school authority/pupil; and occupier/contractual entrant in circumstances involving extra-hazardous activities'.[26]

There may be other situations which are possibly recognised under the law of Australia as giving rise to an NDD, as discussed below. *Leichhardt Muncipal Council v Montgomery* makes it clear, however, that there is in Australia no NDD owed by a local 'roads authority' to members of the public who may be harmed by the actions of contractors engaged to work on the roads.[27] This is contrary to the position in England, where such a duty is well

---

extends to the performance of that task. If the *contractor fails* to adopt a safe system of work, the employer is liable for *that failure*' (emphasis added).

[19] J Murphy, 'The Liability Bases of Common Law Non-Delegable Duties—A Reply to Christian Witting' (2007) 30 *University of New South Wales Law Journal* 86, 99; see also generally J Murphy, 'Juridical Foundations of Common Law Non-Delegable Duties' in J Neyers, E Chamberlain and S Pitel (eds), *Emerging Issues in Tort Law* (Oxford, Hart Publishing, 2007) ch 14.

[20] For general background to the tort, see N Foster, 'The Merits of the Civil Action for Breach of Statutory Duty' (2011) 33 *Sydney Law Review* 67.

[21] See *Braham v J Lyons & Co Ltd* [1962] 3 All ER 281 (CA) 283E–F (Lord Denning MR).

[22] See K Stanton, P Skidmore, M Harris and J Wright, *Statutory Torts* (London, Sweet & Maxwell, 2003) [8.027], and *Hosking v De Havilland Aircraft Co Ltd* [1949] 1 All ER 540. See also M Jones (gen ed), *Clerk & Lindsell on Torts*, 20th edn (London, Sweet & Maxwell, 2010) [6-58].

[23] C Witting, 'Breach of the Non-Delegable Duty: Defending Limited Strict Liability in Tort' (2006) 29(3) *University of New South Wales Law Journal* 33.

[24] *Leichhardt Municipal Council v Montgomery* [2007] HCA 6, (2007) 230 CLR 22 [72]–[73], citing Murphy, 'Liability Bases', above n 19.

[25] *Kondis v State Transport Authority* (1984) 154 CLR 672 (HCA).

[26] *Leichhardt Municipal Council v Montgomery* [2007] HCA 6, (2007) 230 CLR 22 [110], citing *Stevens v Brodribb Sawmilling Co Pty Ltd* (1986) 160 CLR 16 (HCA) 44; *Gold v Essex County Council* [1942] 2 KB 293 CA) 304; *Cassidy v Ministry of Health* [1951] 2 KB 343 (CA) 363; *Albrighton v Royal Prince Alfred Hospital* [1980] 2 NSWLR 542 (CA); *Ellis v Wallsend District Hospital* (1989) 17 NSWLR 553 (CA); *Commonwealth v Introvigne* (1982) 150 CLR 258 (HCA) 269–73, 274–75; and *Burnie Port Authority v General Jones Pty Ltd* (1994) 179 CLR 520 (HCA) 550–54, 556–57; cf *Stevens v Brodribb Sawmilling Co Pty Ltd* (1986) 160 CLR 16, 29–30.

[27] *Leichhardt Municipal Council v Montgomery* [2007] HCA 6, (2007) 230 CLR 22 [123].

established.[28] For the purposes of comparing the development of the law in the two juris-dictions, it is worth pondering why there has been a divergence on this point. There are one or two other areas where the law on this topic continues to be different. In addition, it seems fairly clear that up until the recent decision in *Woodland*[29] the law of Australia clearly rec-ognised some categories of relationships as generating an NDD, which were not recognised in the UK. Some suggestions are briefly made below as to why this was the case, although in light of recent developments we now see an arguably welcome greater convergence between the two jurisdictions.

III. Divergence: Road Authorities

The liability of road authorities for carelessness committed by their contractors goes back many years in the UK. The liability was usually closely connected with the law of public nuisance. If that law recognised a right of members of the public to free access along pub-lic roads, and a local body or other authority interrupted that access by carrying out road works, then the courts took the view that the privilege to do road works would be accom-panied by a duty to see that it was done without carelessness, even if the work was done by a contractor.

Indeed, one view of the case that has been described as the earliest reported example of NDD,[30] *Pickard v Smith*,[31] may have been drawn from this area of public nuisance. Smith operated the refreshment rooms at a railway station, and contractors engaged in delivering coal for him left a hole open into which Pickard fell. In finding that Smith should be held liable for the carelessness of his contractors, Williams J drew the analogy with a public road and the railway station where passengers would be expected to walk:

> No sound distinction in this respect can be drawn between the case of a public highway and a road which may be and to the knowledge of the wrongdoer probably will in fact be used by persons law-fully entitled so to do.[32]

In *Salsbury v Woodland*[33] this principle was accepted, but on the facts was held not to be applicable where the work being done was on a property adjacent to the highway, and a tree that had been carelessly cut down fell onto the highway.

---

[28] See P Handford, 'Non-Delegable Duties: Making Straight the Highway' (2007) 15 *Tort Law Review* 71; C Witting '*Leichhardt Municipal Council v Montgomery*: Non-Delegable Duties and Roads Authorities' (2008) 32 *Melbourne University Law Review* 332.

[29] *Woodland v Essex CC* [2013] UKSC 66, [2014] 1 AC 537.

[30] ibid [6] (Lord Sumption); and see also Murphy, 'Juridical Foundations', above n 19, 381. In *Kondis v State Transport Authority* (1984) 154 CLR 672, 684 Mason J also identifies *Pickard* as one of the earliest sources of the doctrine, while adding that 'the concept seems to have been derived from earlier cases dealing with duties imposed by statutes: eg, *Hole v Sittingbourne and Sheerness Railway Co* (1861) 6 H & N 488 [158 ER 201]'.

[31] *Pickard v Smith* (1861) 10 CB (NS) 470.

[32] ibid 479. Other English cases holding road authorities liable for the actions of contractors included *Penny v Wimbledon Urban District Council* [1898] 2 QB 212 (CA), *Holliday v National Telephone Company* [1899] 2 QB 392 (CA), and others up to and including *Rowe v Herman* [1997] 1 WLR 1390 (CA).

[33] *Salsbury v Woodland* [1970] 1 QB 324 (CA).

A major divergence from this view in the law of Australia, then, was seen in the unanimous decision of the High Court in *Leichhardt Muncipal Council v Montgomery*[34] holding that there was no NDD in these circumstances. The reasons offered by members of the Court for differing from the previous English authorities varied. For some the turning point was to be found in the previous decision in *Brodie v Singleton Shire Council*.[35] In that case the High Court had abolished the 'highway immunity rule' holding roads authorities not liable for 'non-feasance'; however, the Court also declared that the law of public nuisance as it applied to highway accidents had been 'subsumed' in the general law of negligence.

The abolition of the highway immunity had no direct impact on the rule concerning an NDD owed by highway authorities; one was a defence, the other was an extension of liability.[36] But it seems that the decision to remove the law of public nuisance from the area could be seen as removing the 'personal duty' owed by authorities under that area of tort law, and hence (while not compelling the conclusion) supporting the decision that no longer would the law of Australia allow for such a principle.

Kirby J was the only member of the Court who attempted to find a more general set of principles integrating the various decisions on NDD, and having done so concluded that the case of highway authorities did not fit these general principles. Relying fairly heavily on John Murphy's 2007 paper,[37] his Honour suggested that an NDD (at least where not previously supported by clear authority) should only be found in cases where the following factors were present:

(1)   The creation of a substantial risk due to the 'enterprise' carried out by the defendant; coupled with
(2)   An assumption of responsibility toward the claimant;
(3)   (these factors usually only being found where the plaintiff is particularly 'vulnerable'); and
(4)   Usually there will be a clear reason for imposition of a *positive* duty to take care for the safety of the claimant.[38]

Here road works were said not to be especially risky, and members of the road-using public were not particularly vulnerable or especially dependent, in contrast to the established categories for NDD, patients/employees/pupils (and possibly prisoners).[39] Another factor was the fact that the main previous authorities on the topic at the High Court level, *Kondis*[40] and *Burnie Port Authority v General Jones Pty Ltd*,[41] had not explicitly authorised this category of NDD.

It is also possible that geographical and social factors prevailing in Australia may have influenced the decision. As opposed to England, Australia is a very large place with long

---

[34]   *Leichhardt Municipal Council v Montgomery* [2007] HCA 6, (2007) 230 CLR 22
[35]   *Brodie v Singleton Shire Council* [2001] HCA 29, (2001) 206 CLR 512.
[36]   A distinction, it has to be said, elided somewhat confusingly by Hayne J in *Montgomery*, who refers to 'that complex of rules, described as "the highway rule"': ibid [148] and [158]. Whatever the High Court was doing in *Brodie*, it had nothing to do with the rules about non-delegable duty: ibid [69] (Kirby J).
[37]   Murphy, 'Juridical Foundations', above n 19.
[38]   *Leichhardt Municipal Council v Montgomery* [2007] HCA 6, (2007) 230 CLR 22 [117]–[120].
[39]   ibid [123].
[40]   *Kondis v State Transport Authority* (1984) 154 CLR 672 (HCA).
[41]   *Burnie Port Authority v General Jones Pty Ltd* (1994) 179 CLR 520.

stretches of road which often need to be maintained by local councils with sometimes very limited resources.

> The typical village and county responsibilities for road works in England, reflected in the late nineteenth century cases cited by the respondent, produced a legal environment that was quite different from that which generally obtained in Australia in relation to the repair and maintenance of roads.[42]

To add to the liability of councils, responsibility for the carelessness of contractors, as well as for that of their own employees, may have been thought to impose too great an economic burden. Kirby J also commented:

> The use of non-employee contractors has greatly expanded in Australia in recent times, due to the privatisation of many activities formerly performed by governments and their agencies, and the resulting 'out-sourcing' of functions to independent contractors that operate for their own profit.[43]

It is interesting that, here, 'outsourcing' is used as a reason for not imposing an extended liability on councils. But in the reasoning of Lord Sumption in *Woodland*[44] the growth of this phenomemon plays a different role. His Lordship commented (having concluded already that schools ought now to have an NDD to see that reasonable care is taken for their pupils):

> It is important to bear in mind that until relatively recently, most of the functions now routinely delegated by schools to independent contractors would have been performed by staff for whom the authority would have been vicariously liable. The recognition of limited non-delegable duties has become more significant as a result of the growing scale on which the educational and supervisory functions of schools are outsourced, but in a longer historical perspective, it does not significantly increase the potential liability of education authorities.[45]

'Outsourcing' here is seen as a reason for concluding that the imposition of an NDD will not be too onerous, as until recently many of the activities in which schools will now be held liable for the carelessness of contractors would in any event have been provided by employed staff, for whom the schools would have been vicariously liable.

For Kirby J, then, an increase in outsourcing will mean an increased financial burden for councils if they are held to have an NDD; whereas for Lord Sumption an increase in outsourcing will simply shift liability which already exists from one area to another, and not result in a significant overall burden. Determining which of these two respected judicial officers is correct is not easy; it may depend on whether outsourcing results in an actual increase in work being done, or simply shifts works around within the overall workforce. The fact that this question does not have an obvious answer might be thought by some to support the view that this (as opposed to a more traditional legal question) is not really a relevant issue for judges to be deciding. And it must be said that neither Kirby J nor Lord Sumption make this issue a central plank of their respective arguments.

Following *Leichhardt*, in *Rail Corporation of NSW v Fluor Australia Pty Ltd*[46] McDougall J held that a railway infrastructure authority (responsible for maintaining railway lines) did

---

[42] *Leichhardt Municipal Council v Montgomery* [2007] HCA 6, (2007) 230 CLR 22 [101] (Kirby J).

[43] ibid [98].

[44] *Woodland v Essex County Council* [2013] UKSC 66, [2014] 1 AC 537. The details of this decision are discussed in section IV below.

[45] ibid [25].

[46] *Rail Corporation of New South Wales v Fluor Australia Pty Ltd* [2008] NSWSC 1348.

not owe an NDD to train operators who used the lines. The operator of the trains, the SRA, was not relevantly 'vulnerable', in that it could have negotiated appropriate contractual promises about maintenance of the lines. Nor was the repair of railway lines, or the operation of the lines, inherently 'hazardous'. The similarity of the case with a claimed NDD owed by highway authorities meant that an extended NDD in this case was not appropriate given the decision in *Montgomery*—his Honour noted that 'in essence, a railway track is no more than a highway on which trains, rather than motor vehicles, travel'.[47]

IV. Other Differences Between English and Australian NDD Law

There are some other differences between the law of England and the law of Australia in this area.

Occupiers

At one stage it seems to have been thought that there was a general NDD applying to an occupier of land who allowed others to enter that land. It seems clear, at least, that such a rule applied to 'contractual entrants' to land, who paid for the privilege of access, although it may have extended to others. In *Woodward v Hastings Corporation*[48] a school was held to be liable for careless sweeping of an icy step carried out by a contracted cleaner. The injured pupil was treated as an 'invitee' but not said to be there under a contract. The decision of the House of Lords in *Thomson v Cremin*[49] seems to lay down a broad non-delegable liability owed by occupiers to invitees. Viscount Simon LC commented:

> The shipowner's responsibility for the safety of the structure is not indeed absolute, but, on the principle of *Indermaur* v. *Dames,* he owes to the invitee a duty of adequate care. If adequate care was not exercised in fitting and securing the shore, it would be no answer (as the appellant's counsel candidly admitted) to say that the shipowner employed an independent contractor at Fremantle to do the work.[50]

The worker who had been injured here was not viewed as a 'contractual entrant'.

However, the situation in England has now been changed by the enactment of the Occupiers Liability Act 1957 (UK), which explicitly states that there is no liability for the carelessness of contractors.[51]

---

[47] ibid [110]–[113]. See also, for another decision following *Montgomery* in a roads context, *Browning v Bitupave Limited* [2008] NSWSC 19.

[48] *Woodward v Hastings Corporation* [1945] KB 174 (CA).

[49] *Thomson v Cremin* [1956] 1 WLR 103n, [1953] 2 All ER 1185 (HL).

[50] ibid 106. The decision is characterised in *Clerk & Lindsell*, above n 22, [12-56] fn 243 as 'rather Delphic' but seems clear enough. See also the judgment of Lord Wright at 110, which clearly refers to previous decisions such as *Pickard v Smith* (1861) 10 CB (NS) 470, 142 ER 535 in holding that the duty to an 'invitee' is non-delegable. One unusual feature of the decision, however, is that it was delivered in 1941 but does not seem to have been reported until the 1950s.

[51] See R Stevens, *Torts and Rights* (Oxford, Oxford University Press, 2007) 119–20.

The law of Australia on the topic seems to be that contractual entrants at least are still owed an NDD. While the old common law rules establishing differential standards for different classes of entrants were abolished in *Australian Safeway Stores Pty Ltd v Zaluzna*,[52] the rule imposing an NDD in the special case of contractual entrants seems to have survived, as is apparent from *Calin v Greater Union Organisation Pty Ltd*[53] and *Hoyts Pty Ltd v Burns.*[54]

The difference between the jurisdictions at this point, then, stems from a specific legislative reform on the one hand, and a refinement of the common law on the other which has left in place what might be called a remnant of the former rules.

Prisoners and Others in Detention?

It has been said that the law of Australia recognises an NDD owed by prison authorities to those held in custody. *Howard v Jarvis*[55] was cited as authority for this proposition by Finn J in *S v Secretary, Department of Immigration & Multicultural & Indigenous Affairs*,[56] where it was held that the Commonwealth government owed an NDD to persons detained as illegal immigrants.

However, in *Leichhardt Municipal Council v Montgomery*[57] Kirby J, in reviewing the existing categories of NDDs, mentioned this category, but with somewhat less confidence than other categories.[58] His Honour's doubts on the topic are reinforced when it is noticed that *Howard v Jarvis*[59] does refer to a duty on the part of a gaoler to take reasonable care, but does not seem explicitly to go further and speak of ensuring that 'reasonable care be taken'.[60]

This question, then, may need to be revisited, especially since the *Montgomery* decision illustrates the reluctance of the High Court to expand the category of relationships where an NDD exists, even where other lower courts have said so, if the High Court itself has not previously authorised it. On the other hand, it is submitted that the matters mentioned by Finn J, and the general criteria being adopted for the question in *Montgomery* and *Woodland*,[61] would support an NDD owed by a government authority to those in detention, especially in circumstances where it is becoming increasingly common to 'outsource' such responsibilities.[62] There seem to be no English decisions directly on point at the moment.

---

[52] *Australian Safeway Stores Pty Ltd v Zaluzna* (1987) 162 CLR 479 (HCA).
[53] *Calin v Greater Union Organisation Pty Ltd* (1991) 173 CLR 33 (HCA).
[54] *Hoyts Pty Ltd v Burns* [2003] HCA 61, (2003) 201 ALR 470 [32] (Kirby J).
[55] *Howard v Jarvis* (1958) 98 CLR 177 (HCA).
[56] *S v Secretary, Department of Immigration & Multicultural & Indigenous Affairs* [2005] FCA 549 esp [209].
[57] *Leichhardt Municipal Council v Montgomery* [2007] HCA 6, (2007) 230 CLR 22.
[58] See ibid [111] n 162, and [124]: 'possibly prisoners in relation to prison authorities'.
[59] *Howard v Jarvis* (1958) 98 CLR 177 (HCA).
[60] In *New South Wales v Bujdoso* [2005] HCA 76, 80 ALJR 236 [44] the High Court commented that 'a prison authority, as with any other authority, is under no greater duty than to take reasonable care'. But since that case hinged on the question of the exercise of due care 'directly' by state authorities, the remark does not seem to be determinative on the NDD issue.
[61] *Woodland v Essex County Council* [2013] UKSC 66, [2014] 1 AC 537.
[62] Although it will be, as noted above, a matter for debate as to whether this factor counts in favour of, or against, such a duty.

Former Divergences: Hospitals and Schools

The law of Australia has recognised an NDD owed by schools to their pupils, and hospitals to their patients, for some time. In *Commonwealth of Australia v Introvigne*[63] the Commonwealth government had contracted with the State of New South Wales to provide teachers for a school in the ACT.[64] When a student was injured due to lack of appropriate supervision in the playground, the High Court held that the Commonwealth was in breach of an NDD.

In *Fitzgerald v Hill*[65] the decision in *Introvigne* was extended slightly to cover the situation of a child injured in a recreational activity, while under the supervision of a business owner. In a 'martial arts' class, the instructor was supervising some boys on a run along a road and failed to take sufficient care to prevent a passing car from running into the plaintiff, then eight years old. The court held that the owner and operator of the business, a Mr Ivanov, had an NDD which was breached by the instructor (who was not an employee).[66] Until the recent *Woodland* decision,[67] however, the liability of schools for harm to pupils in England was not accepted as being non-delegable.[68]

The liability of hospitals is another area which has been accepted generally as being non-delegable in Australia, while there has previously been reluctance to move in that direction in many English decisions. In *Ellis v Wallsend District Hospital*[69] it was held that a hospital owes an NDD to its patients in relation to the healthcare it undertakes to provide, so that if a surgeon is negligent, then the hospital will be liable irrespective of whether the surgeon is an employee or an independent contractor. In *Ellis*, however, the hospital was found not to be liable because the patient had selected the particular surgeon, who had only used the premises of the hospital as the venue for the operation. The negligence of the surgeon was outside the specific 'undertaking' of the hospital.[70]

In England, however, while comments supporting such a duty were made in *Gold v Essex County Council*[71] by Lord Greene MR, and in *Cassidy v Ministry of Health*[72] by Denning LJ, those remarks were often regarded as obiter and were not generally followed.

With the changes made by *Woodland*, though, the law of Australia and England now seems very similar. It is time, then, to turn to that decision.

---

[63] *Commonwealth of Australia v Introvigne* (1982) 150 CLR 258 (HCA).

[64] In the more usual case, of course, the teachers would have been Commonwealth employees for whose carelessness the Commonwealth would have clearly been vicariously liable. But at the time the ACT, a smallish Territory, relied heavily for some of its infrastructure on support from the surrounding state of NSW.

[65] *Fitzgerald v Hill* [2008] QCA 283.

[66] See also *Harris v Trustees of the Roman Catholic Church for the Archdiocese of Sydney* [2011] NSWDC 172, with very similar facts to the *Woodland* case to be discussed below. The plaintiff was a student at a Roman Catholic school, who had gone on a school skiing excursion. The ski instructor had been careless, leading to the plaintiff's injury, and the school was found liable due to its NDD, for the carelessness of the ski instructor.

[67] *Woodland v Essex County Council* [2013] UKSC 66, [2014] 1 AC 537.

[68] See the review of previous authority in the Court of Appeal's decision in *Woodland v Essex County Council* [2012] EWCA Civ 239, [2013] 3 WLR 853 (over-ruled in *Woodland v Essex CC* [2013] UKSC 66, [2014] AC 537).

[69] *Ellis v Wallsend District Hospital* (1989) 17 NSWLR 553 (CA).

[70] For other examples of the application of a NDD in relation to a hospital, see *Sherry v Australasian Conference Association (trading as Sydney Adventist Hospital)* [2006] NSWSC 75 esp [550]–[552]; *Australian Capital Territory v Crowley* [2012] ACTCA 52, [378] (though in the circumstances, as the plaintiff there had not been admitted to care, such a duty was not owed).

[71] *Gold v Essex County Council* [1942] 2 KB 293 (CA).

[72] *Cassidy v Ministry of Health* [1951] 2 KB 343 (CA).

V. Convergence

The Decision in *Woodland*

The facts of the case were summed up well in the Court of Appeal judgment in *Woodland v Essex County Council*[73] by Kitchin LJ:

> The appellant suffered her terrible injuries in the course of a swimming lesson which she attended together with other members of her class at the Gloucester Park swimming pool in Basildon. The swimming pool was run by the Basildon Council, and the arrangements under which the children had their swimming lessons were organised by Ms Beryl Stotford trading as Direct Swimming Services. The life guard and the swimming teacher supervising the lesson in which the plaintiff suffered her injuries were employees of Ms Stotford, not the authority.

The appellant sued a number of parties, but the issue at stake in the case was this: could Essex County Council, the school authority, be held responsible under the doctrine of NDD for the carelessness of the life-guard and the swimming teacher? (There was also a claim based on the direct failure of the Council to select a competent swimming teaching contractor, but that issue had not been tried when these proceedings took place.)

At first instance Langstaff J held that a school which sends a pupil off to swimming lessons does not owe an NDD to the pupil in those circumstances, and hence cannot be held directly liable for carelessness of the swimming instructor (not employed by the school).[74]

On appeal to the English Court of Appeal,[75] the majority, Tomlinson and Kitchin LJJ, over a strong dissent from Laws LJ, agreed with the trial judge that in the circumstances the school did not owe an NDD to a pupil who was injured due to carelessness of those conducting a swimming lesson off-site.

On final appeal in *Woodland v Essex County Council*,[76] however, the Supreme Court as a whole held that schools do indeed owe an NDD to pupils, and hence that the matter needed to be sent back for trial, on the basis that the local authority running the school might be held liable for negligence by the contracted swimming instructors whose carelessness may have given rise to Miss Woodland's injuries.

Lord Sumption set out five criteria to be applied to determine if an NDD is owed:

(1) The claimant is a patient or a child, or for some other reason is especially vulnerable or dependent on the protection of the defendant against the risk of injury. Other examples are likely to be prisoners and residents in care homes.

(2) There is an antecedent relationship between the claimant and the defendant, independent of the negligent act or omission itself, (i) which places the claimant in the actual custody, charge or care of the defendant, and (ii) from which it is possible to impute to the defendant the assumption of a positive duty to protect the claimant from harm, and not just a duty to refrain from conduct which will foreseeably damage the claimant. It is characteristic of such relationships that they involve an element of control over the claimant, which varies in intensity from one situation to another, but is clearly very substantial in the case of schoolchildren.

---

[73] *Woodland v Essex County Council* [2012] EWCA Civ 239, [2013] 3 WLR 853 [78].
[74] *Woodland v The Swimming Teachers' Association* [2011] EWHC 2631.
[75] *Woodland v Essex County Council* [2012] EWCA Civ 239, [2013] 3 WLR 853.
[76] *Woodland v Essex County Council* [2013] UKSC 66, [2014] AC 537.

(3)   The claimant has no control over how the defendant chooses to perform those obligations, i.e. whether personally or through employees or through third parties.

(4)   The defendant has delegated to a third party some function which is an integral part of the positive duty which he has assumed towards the claimant; and the third party is exercising, for the purpose of the function thus delegated to him, the defendant's custody or care of the claimant and the element of control that goes with it.

(5)   The third party has been negligent not in some collateral respect but in the performance of the very function assumed by the defendant and delegated by the defendant to him.[77]

Lady Hale agreed in an essentially concurring judgment, citing in support an article by Beuermann.[78] It might be noted that there is some similarity between Lord Sumption's criteria and those suggested by John Murphy in 2007,[79] and then taken up by Kirby J in *Montgomery*.[80]

Lord Sumption referred in detail to High Court of Australia decisions on the point and agreed that the approach taken in *Introvigne*[81] and *Kondis*[82] was generally correct.

While the decision directly reframed the English law of NDD in relation to schools, in doing so Lord Sumption for the majority said very clearly that an NDD should also arise in hospital cases: '[T]he time has come to recognise that Lord Greene in *Gold* and Denning LJ in *Cassidy* were correct in identifying the underlying principle.'[83]

Dangerous Activities?

An area of NDD not previously mentioned is the situation of 'dangerous activities'. In this area, while it is not perfectly clear, there may now also be convergence between the law of England and the law of Australia.

In England it is well accepted that one situation where an NDD will arise is where, to quote Lord Sumption, 'the defendant employs an independent contractor to perform some function which is either inherently hazardous or liable to become so in the course of his work'.[84]

The most commonly cited 'modern' example of this principle is *Honeywill and Stein Ltd v Larkin Brothers (London's Commercial Photographers) Ltd*.[85] As others have noted, the decision came at a time when it was thought that 'extra-hazardous' activities might generally lead to strict liability in tort, a view that has now been rejected in both England and Australia.[86]

---

[77]   ibid [23].

[78]   ibid [33], citing C Beuermann, 'Vicarious Liability and Conferred Authority Strict Liability' (2013) 20 *Torts Law Journal* 265.

[79]   See Murphy, 'Juridical Basis', above n 19.

[80]   *Leichhardt Municipal Council v Montgomery* [2007] HCA 6, (2007) 230 CLR 22.

[81]   *Commonwealth of Australia v Introvigne* (1982) 150 CLR 258 (HCA).

[82]   *Kondis v State Transport Authority* (1984) 154 CLR 672 (HCA).

[83]   *Woodland v Essex CC* [2013] UKSC 66, [2014] AC 537 [23]. See more recently *Nyang v G4S Care & Justice Services Ltd* [2013] EWHC 3946 (QB), where the judge ruled that this was indeed the effect of the decision, holding that someone who had undertaken to provide medical care was liable for the carelessness of a doctor whom they had engaged.

[84]   *Woodland v Essex CC* [2013] UKSC 66, [2014] AC 537 [6].

[85]   *Honeywill and Stein Ltd v Larkin Brothers (London's Commercial Photographers) Ltd* [1934] 1 KB 191 (CA).

[86]   *Read v Lyons* [1947] AC 156 (HL); *Stevens v Brodribb Sawmilling Co Pty Ltd* (1986) 160 CLR 16 (HCA). See comment in Stevens, above n 51, 343–44; *Clerk & Lindsell*, above n 22, [6-67].

However, this category of NDD seems to be one that in theory is still accepted. In *Biffa Waste Services Ltd v Maschinenfabrik Ernst Hese GmbH*,[87] where the Court accepted that the trial judge was correct to have considered the application of *Honeywill*, it referred to the case as 'a much-criticised decision which however is binding on this court as it was on him'.[88] In the circumstances of that case, involving welding near inflammable material, the Court of Appeal ruled that the activity was not 'extra-hazardous' and commented that the principle 'should be applied only to activities that are exceptionally dangerous whatever precautions are taken'.[89]

In Australia, as noted above, the principle of strict liability for 'extra-hazardous' operations generally was rejected in *Stevens v Brodribb*.[90] However, in its later decision in *Burnie Port Authority v General Jones Pty Ltd*[91] the High Court enunciated a principle of NDD that applied in similar circumstances. The Port Authority had employed a contractor to carry out welding work near some particularly inflammable material, which caught alight and burned down a warehouse. The Court held that in the circumstances the Authority was liable for the action of the contractor. In doing so it overruled the old and well-established action based on the case of *Rylands v Fletcher*[92] (which held a landowner strictly liable for the escape of 'dangerous' matter from his land to another's). (*Rylands*, in fact, is also an example of the application of the NDD principle, the work there having been done by contractors.)

The High Court, having abolished *Rylands*, formulated a principle of NDD in this area as follows:

> [A] person who takes advantage of his or her control of premises to introduce a dangerous substance, to carry on a dangerous activity, or to allow another to do one of those things, owes a duty of reasonable care to avoid a reasonably foreseeable risk of injury or damage to the person or property of another. In a case where the person or property of the other person is lawfully in a place outside the premises that duty of care both varies in degree according to the magnitude of the risk involved and *extends to ensuring that such care is taken*.[93]

As an aside, it may be that the series of cases which holds that where operations on the defendant's land cause structural damage to the plaintiff's land (such as undermining support for land), then the defendant will be liable for the carelessness of contractors, should now be characterised as an example of this sort of 'dangerous activity'.[94]

As with *Honeywill* in England, it cannot be said that the principle in *Burnie Port Authority* has been extensively used since it was first formulated. One example of the use of the principle is *A D & S M McLean Pty Ltd v Meech*.[95] There the Victorian Court of Appeal extended the principle of 'dangerous activities' to hold that an owner of land who allows the agistment of animals on the land (in that case horses) owes an NDD to road-users

---

[87] *Biffa Waste Services Ltd v Maschinenfabrik Ernst Hese GmbH* [2008] EWCA Civ 1257.

[88] ibid [63].

[89] ibid [78].

[90] *Stevens v Brodribb Sawmilling Co Pty Ltd* (1986) 160 CLR 16 (HCA).

[91] *Burnie Port Authority v General Jones Pty Ltd* (1994) 179 CLR 520.

[92] *Rylands v Fletcher* (1868) LR 3 HL 330.

[93] *Burnie Port Authority v General Jones Pty Ltd* (1994) 179 CLR 520, 556–57 (emphasis added).

[94] See *Dalton v Angus & Co* (1881) 6 App Cas 740; more recently *Pantalone v Alaouie* (1989) 18 NSWLR 119 (SC).

[95] *A D & S M McLean Pty Ltd v Meech* [2005] VSCA 305.

who may be injured by the escape of the animals. Hence, the court ruled, the owner will be liable even if the cause of the escape was carelessness by someone other than themselves or an employee. In its decision the Victorian court followed the earlier decision of the NSW Court of Appeal in *Simpson v Blanch*.[96] With respect to both courts, it may be doubted that agistment of horses would normally be described as 'dangerous activity'. The authority of these cases may need to be tested, it seems, in light of the later High Court decision in *Montgomery*.[97]

Corkhill gives a detailed analysis of what amounts to a 'dangerous' activity for the purposes of the rule in *Burnie*.[98] He notes *Meech* but also points to two other decisions of State courts finding insufficient danger in 'crowd surfing at a concert'[99] and in 'erecting scaffolding',[100] and concludes that it is difficult to predict what will be regarded as sufficiently dangerous to create an NDD.

He concludes by suggesting the following guidelines (incorporating material from US decisions), namely that consideration should be given to:

— The magnitude of the foreseeable risk of some harm from the nature of the activity itself;
— The gravity of the possible harm if the risk eventuates;
— Whether or not the substance is 'commonly used' or the activity is ordinarily engaged in;
— The 'inappropriateness' of the substance or activity to the place where used or carried on;
— The value to the community of the substance or activity weighed up against its danger.[101]

These seem to be sensible matters which a court might take into account.

A claim that an NDD arose based on 'dangerousness' initially succeeded in *Hall v Adventure Training Systems Pty Ltd*.[102] The plaintiff was a naval reservist who while using a 'high ropes course' designed for physical training, fell due to a faulty rope and was injured. Transfield had a contract to maintain the course and inspect it; it had arranged for a contractor, ATS, to undertake this work on its behalf. The question that arose was whether, where the rope failed due to the careless inspection by a contractor, Transfield was liable—ie, did it owe a 'non-delegable duty' to users of the rope course?

After considering *Leichhardt* and *Burnie*, Harrison AJ held that Transfield did owe an NDD to users of the course, based on the *Burnie* criteria of the dangerous nature of the activities and the vulnerability of the users.[103]

However, on appeal in *Transfield Services (Australia) v Hall; Hall v QBE Insurance (Australia)*[104] the decision that an NDD was owed was overturned. The majority judgment was given by Campbell JA, with whom Beazley JA and McClellan CJ at CL agreed on this point.[105]

---

[96] *Simpson v Blanch* (1998) Aust Torts Rep ¶ 81-458.
[97] *Leichhardt Municipal Council v Montgomery* [2007] HCA 6, (2007) 230 CLR 22.
[98] See A Corkhill, '"Dangerous" Substances and Activities in the Context of a Non-delegable Duty of Care' (2007) 15 *Torts Law Journal* 233.
[99] *Newcastle Entertainment Security Pty Ltd v Simpson* (1999) Aust Torts Rep ¶ 81-528.
[100] *Complete Scaffold Services Pty Ltd v Adelaide Brighton Cement Ltd* [2001] SASC 199.
[101] Corkhill, above n 98, 261.
[102] *Hall v Adventure Training Systems Pty Ltd* [2007] NSWSC 817.
[103] ibid [89].
[104] *Transfield Services (Australia) v Hall; Hall v QBE Insurance (Australia)* [2008] NSWCA 294, [2008] *Aust Torts Reports* ¶ 81-979.
[105] Although their Honours disagreed with Campbell JA on another point, the interpretation of an indemnity clause, which meant that in the end Mr Hall received compensation for his injury from the contracted company, ATS.

His Honour explored the background of the concept of 'extra-hazardous activities' and noted the rejection of this notion as a general determinant of a duty of care in the decision of the High Court in *Stevens v Brodribb Sawmilling Co Pty Ltd.*[106] However, he then re-examined the majority decision in *Burnie Port Authority* which, as noted above, seems to provide a clear indication of a possible NDD in such cases, and ended up confining the decision very closely to 'cases like *Rylands v Fletcher*'.[107]

With respect, this approach seems to unduly 'read down' the words of the High Court in *Burnie*, which state the principle in much broader terms. It seems arguable that *Burnie* does indeed support the existence of an NDD in cases of a 'dangerous' substance or activity, not artificially limited to cases that would formerly have been decided under *Rylands v Fletcher*.[108] Their Honours did not explicitly limit the principle to situations where there was an 'escape' of something from one property to another.

Campbell JA also noted that, even if there were a duty in relation to hazardous acitivities, 'inspecting ropes' was not such an activity.[109]

However, the liability in *Burnie* arises where a person 'takes advantage of his or her control of premises to introduce a dangerous substance [or] to carry on a dangerous activity'.[110] It is submitted that it is the 'activity' in general which leads to the duty, rather than a minute dissection of the individual aspects of the activity. If the activity of 'operating a high ropes course' can be regarded as dangerous, then the duty will arise. It is not to the point that some of the specific actions that may take place under the broad heading of the 'activity' may in other contexts not be regarded as themselves dangerous.

To illustrate the point, take the facts of *Burnie*. Liability in that case was imposed because of the introduction of highly inflammable material into an area, and the later authorisation of welding activities in that area. The combination of these two elements made the activity of welding dangerous. The fact that on some other worksites the mere operation of a welding device might not be regarded as 'extra-hazardous' was not to the point.[111]

Similarly, it could be argued that the overall activity of operating a 'high ropes course' involves such a high degree of foreseeably grave danger to those using the course (which will include those whose job it is to check the course from time to time) that it is reasonable to impose a non-delegable or personal duty on the company concerned to ensure that reasonable care is taken in maintenance, whether the task is undertaken by employees or contractors. Nevertheless, just as the English courts have recently given a very limited operation to the *Honeywill* principle, it seems that Australian courts are reading the *Burnie* principle very narrowly.[112]

---

[106] *Stevens v Brodribb Sawmilling Co Pty Ltd* (1986) 160 CLR 16 (HCA).

[107] *Transfield Services (Australia) v Hall; Hall v QBE Insurance (Australia)* [2008] NSWCA 294, [2008] *Aust Torts Reports* ¶ 81-979. [90].

[108] *Rylands v Fletcher* (1868) LR 3 HL 330.

[109] *Transfield Services (Australia) v Hall; Hall v QBE Insurance (Australia)* [2008] NSWCA 294, [2008] *Aust Torts Reports* ¶ 81-979 [107].

[110] See the passage from *Burnie Port Authority v General Jones Pty Ltd* (1994) 179 CLR 520, 556–57, text to n 93 above.

[111] The decision of the English Court of Appeal in *Biffa Waste Services Ltd v Maschinenfabrik Ernst Hese GBMH* [2008] EWCA 1257 may be described as such a case—'welding as such is not ultra-hazardous': ibid [81].

[112] For other recent decisions where NDD claims in novel circumstances have failed in recent years, see *Aircraft Technicians of Australia Pty Ltd v St Clair* [2011] QCA 188; *N M Rural Enterprises Pty Ltd v Rimanui Farms Ltd* [2013] NSWSC 309; *The Owners—Strata Plan No 51077 v Meriton Apartments Pty Ltd* [2014] NSWSC 129.

VI. Misreadings of the NDD

As noted above, NDD is a form of strict liability that operates when S, the 'principal', is *not* at personal fault. That is why it developed. It is therefore a fundamental category mistake to discuss NDD through the lens of what the principal should have done 'directly'. That is not how the doctrine operates. Yet in a number of recent decisions it seems that the courts have been misled by the designation of the principle as a 'personal duty', to discuss the behaviour of the duty-holder.

This seems (with respect) to have happened in the decision of Court of Appeal in Western Australia in *Placer (Granny Smith) Pty Ltd v Specialised Reline Services Pty Ltd*.[113] The decision may serve as one example of some common misreadings of the NDD doctrine.

The injured employee here was a Mr Murphy, employed by SRS; he was injured when a crane being operated by a Mr Leach (employed by another company, Drake) dropped a heavy load on him. Placer were the general occupiers of the site (a gold mine). Placer and Drake accepted liability (Leach's action of moving the load over some unprotected workers was clearly careless, and Placer conceded it ought to have coordinated activities more carefully).

The issue was, however, whether SRS, the employer, could be held liable (for the purposes of being required to make a contribution to the damages being paid by the other companies). At first glance the situation is so like *Kondis*[114] that it is hard to believe that they could be distinguished; in fairly similar circumstances in that previous decision the High Court had found SRA, the employer of the worker Mr Kondis, liable under the NDD principle for the carelessness of a crane operator who dropped part of a load onto Mr Kondis.

But unfortunately both the trial judge and the Western Australia Court of Appeal seem to have been confused about different aspects of NDD, and in the end the Court held that the employer SRS was *not* liable. The decision is hard to explain.

It should not be to the point, of course (as reference to *Kondis* would show) that the employer had *itself* behaved without fault; the issue is whether the employer can be held liable under the law of NDD for carelessness by one of the *other* participants.

There was one relevant distinction from *Kondis*, which was that SRS had not directly 'engaged' either Placer or Drake to do work for it; but the fact is that SRS placed Murphy in a situation where his safety depended on decisions made by both other companies, and in general the effect of the NDD doctrine seems designed to be to impose liability in those circumstances.

In particular, it seems that the Court went wrong when Pullin JA said: 'It [NDD] remains a duty to exercise reasonable care.'[115] This is true if it is referring to the nature of the obligation. But it is fundamentally misleading if it is intended to characterise the NDD as a duty of 'direct' action by the employer. As noted above, the duty is best described as a duty 'to see that reasonable care is taken' by whomever *else* has been entrusted with the supervision of the employee. NDD does not only impose a duty to directly *take* reasonable care onto the duty-holder.

---

[113] *Placer (Granny Smith) Pty Ltd v Specialised Reline Services Pty Ltd* [2010] WASCA 148.
[114] *Kondis v State Transport Authority* (1984) 154 CLR 672 (HCA).
[115] *Placer (Granny Smith) Pty Ltd v Specialised Reline Services Pty Ltd* [2010] WASCA 148 [19].

This then led to much (arguably irrelevant) focus on what SRS had done to ensure its workers were safe. All that was irrelevant because SRS, under the NDD principle, should be held responsible for what Drake or Placer had done, not for its own lack of care.

There was a question raised in the case about whether there was liability for a 'casual act of negligence'—but (as discussed below) the only way to make sense of this exception is to regard it as applying to carelessness which is *unrelated* to the task that was entrusted to the other party; and here driving a crane carefully was clearly part of that task.

With the greatest of respect, Pullin JA wrongly attempts to distinguish *Kondis* by saying that liability was found there because of the 'employer's breach of its personal duty of care to provide a safe system of work'.[116] Again, this is true, but seems to be misinterpreted—the High Court clearly meant (as illustrated by previous quotations from the case, noted above) that the 'personal' duty was breached *through* the carelessness of the contractor.[117] It may be that the habit of using the word 'personal' is one of the problems here, as noted above. When it is used in the NDD context, it is usually used to distinguish 'vicarious' liability, which is a clear example of 'transferred' liability. But to say that NDD is 'personal' means simply that the duty is to 'see that reasonable care is taken', and it is a duty that results from the relationship between the principal S and the victim V, rather than from the relationship of S and the wrongdoer W. It is not intended to depart from the fundamental principle that NDD is strict liability from the principal's perspective.

In brief, then, *Placer* is a very unsatisfactory decision and may need to be corrected in the future; but there was no appeal to the High Court.

Another case involving a similar misreading of the strict liability nature of the NDD principle is *Cassley v GMP Securities Europe LLP*.[118] Mr Cassley died in a light airplane crash. His dependants were suing his employer GMP, who had sent him on a survey flight for the purposes of a mining project in Africa; the light plane on which he was flying had been chartered by the firm Sundance Resources Ltd. While Coulson J accepted that GMP owed an NDD to its employee,[119] when analysing the question of 'breach' his Lordship focused on what GMP had done 'directly'[120] rather than asking whether Cassley was placed under the authority of another company, and hence whether GMP was then strictly liable for the carelessness of that *other* company.[121]

---

[116] ibid [65]–[67].

[117] It is true that in *Kondis* members of the court also found on the facts of that case that the employer had been 'directly' careless in some respects. But they carefully distinguished this 'direct' carelessness as an alternative finding, not the same thing as the strict liability for the actions of a contractor imposed under the NDD doctrine. See Mason J in *Kondis v State Transport Authority* (1984) 154 CLR 672 (HCA) 678: 'Leaving to one side for the moment the possibility of the respondent being negligent independently of the negligence of Clissold [the contractor], the question then becomes whether, in such circumstances, the respondent is liable to the appellant for an admitted act of negligence on the part of an employee of an independent contractor.' Later, after discussing the NDD doctrine, his Honour turned (at 688) to the question of a 'direct' breach of duty by the employer and found that also established. But the clear ratio of the decision is that there was liability for the contractor's breach under NDD.

[118] *Cassley v GMP Securities Europe LLP* [2015] EWHC 722 (QB).

[119] ibid [216].

[120] ibid [217]ff.

[121] As it turned out, since the other company, Sundance, had also been found not to have behaved negligently (see ibid [309]ff), the ultimate outcome of the case would not have been different. But it is submitted that the wrong route was taken to that outcome, for reasons outlined in the text.

VII. Recent Developments of NDD in Workplace Contexts

The employer's duty in the law of negligence to see that reasonable care is taken to provide a safe working environment for his or her employees, then, cannot be satisfied by delegation to a contractor. This is another area where the law of England and that of Australia are in agreement. To quote Mason J in *Kondis v State Transport Authority*: '[T]he respondent's duty to provide a safe system of work was non-delegable and the respondent was liable for any negligence on the part of its independent contractor in failing to adopt a safe system of work.'[122]

In England this principle was applied in *McDermid v Nash Dredging and Reclamation Co Ltd*.[123] In this area the laws of England and Australia seem identical.

The courts have long held that this obligation applies even if a worker is 'loaned out' to another or placed by a 'labour hire firm'. In *White v Malco Engineering Pty Ltd*[124] White was employed by Skilled Engineering, and made available as a forklift driver to Malco. Skilled Engineering was held to still owe a duty to White as his employer.

In *Thomas v Sydney Training & Employment Ltd*[125] the training organisation which employed Thomas (who had been placed under the supervision of another company) was held to be Thomas's employer and to have an NDD.[126]

It should be noted that, while an employer may be found to be liable in NDD on the basis of a breach of duty by someone supervising its employee, it may be appropriate in a particular action for 'contribution' among tortfeasors to apportion all the damages to the immediate supervisor.[127] Hence in many cases the NDD will in practice only need to be relied on where the supervisor is unavailable to be sued.

A slightly unusual (but clearly correct) case involving the NDD owed to employees was *Sneddon v Speaker of the Legislative Assembly*,[128] which involved a claim made by a former staff member of a State MP, Milton Orkopolous. The staff member alleged she had been bullied as a result of complaints made about the member's behaviour (which proved to be true, leading to his conviction of a number of offences). The Speaker of the Legislative Assembly was the 'employer' of staff members allocated to MPs. On this question, the court ruled that the Speaker, as the employer, was liable for the actions of the Member which led to the employee's psychological harm.[129]

The relationship of employer to employee, then, will create the 'non-delegable duty'. One further complication, however, arises when consideration is given to the relationship between a labour hire worker placed by his or her employer to work with a host, and the host itself. Is duty of a 'host' to a labour hire worker 'non-delegable'?

---

[122] *Kondis v State Transport Authority* (1984) 154 CLR 672, 688.

[123] *McDermid v Nash Dredging and Reclamation Co Ltd* [1987] AC 906.

[124] *White v Malco Engineering Pty Ltd* [1999] NSWSC 1055 [467].

[125] *Thomas v Sydney Training & Employment Ltd* [2002] NSWSC 970.

[126] ibid [142] (Cooper AJ). See also *TNT Australia Pty Ltd v Christie* [2003] NSWCA 47 [67]–[68]; *Pieter Hoekstra v Residual Assco Industries Pty Ltd* [2004] NSWSC 564 [37]–[46]; *Shields v Gurcinoski t/as Perfect Air Refrigeration Air Conditioning & Heating* [2006] ACTSC 109 [33]–[35].

[127] *Hodge v CSR Limited* [2010] NSWSC 27; *Barns v Parlin Pty Ltd* [2010] WADC 92.

[128] *Sneddon v Speaker of the Legislative Assembly* [2011] NSWSC 508. The subsequent appeal in *Sneddon v NSW* [2012] NSWCA 351 did not disturb this finding of an NDD owed by the Speaker—see paras [139], [141] noting the finding.

[129] ibid [224]–[226].

Yes, at least in some cases, according to *TNT Australia Pty Ltd v Christie*.[130] In this case Mr Christie was a 'long-term' worker who had been working on the premises of TNT along-side its employees, and had been effectively 'integrated' into TNT's workforce. TNT was held liable for injuries suffered by Mr Christie because *another* contractor it had engaged to maintain machinery had done so carelessly. Mason P commented:

> Judge Delaney was correct to have concluded that TNT was in a position analogous to that of an employer as regards [its] (non-delegable) duty of care to the plaintiff. TNT exercised day-to-day control over the plaintiff's work activities, treating him to all intents the same as its employees as regards work on the factory floor. ... TNT's relationship was more than that of an occupier of the factory. In all respects relevant to the imposition of a duty of care the plaintiff was in an identical position to that of the four TNT employees with whom he worked.[131]

A possible complication which has emerged in recent years, however, is the question whether the NDD of an employer applies when the employee is sent to work on different premises, which are completely under the control of someone else. In *DIB Group Pty Ltd t/ as Hill & Co v Cole*,[132] Mr Cole was a truck-driver delivering fuel to premises occupied by DIB; he was injured when he stepped on a loose pit lid and fell into a pit. The trial judge found that DIB as occupiers of the premises ought to have fixed the loose lid, and this was not challenged on appeal. But what was in issue was whether Cole's employer, Lewingtons, was *also* liable for the injury. This came down to the issue whether the employer could be said to be in breach of an NDD.

Basten JA, in a very careful judgment, made a number of suggestive points. He said that the term 'non-delegable' is not a very good one, as it is unclear what is meant by 'delegation'.[133] His Honour preferred, he said, the term used in *Wilsons and Clyde Coal Co v English*:[134] the question is, what is the 'personal' duty of the employer? (The use of the term 'personal duty' was also endorsed more recently by Lord Sumption in *Woodland*,[135] although as already noted, can itself lead to some confusion.)

Basten JA noted that a number of problems arise when this personal duty is applied to circumstances outside the immediate control of the employer. For example, in *Davie v New Merton Board Mills Ltd*[136] it was held that an employer is not 'personally' liable for a defect in equipment that has been supplied by an outside manufacturer.[137] Accepting that there is liability for carelessness of a contractor on the employer's premises, as in *Kondis*, this still leaves a number of difficult questions where an employee is injured elsewhere. Basten JA commented: 'The application of these principles has given rise to differing views in cases where the employer is not in control of the premises or place on which or at which the worker is injured.'[138]

---

[130] *TNT Australia Pty Ltd v Christie* [2003] NSWCA 47.
[131] ibid [41]. See also [178] (Foster AJA agreeing).
[132] *DIB Group Pty Ltd t/as Hill & Co v Cole* [2009] NSWCA 210.
[133] ibid [27].
[134] *Wilsons and Clyde Coal Co* [1938] AC 57 (HL).
[135] *Woodland v Essex CC* [2013] UKSC 66, [2014] AC 537 [4].
[136] *Davie v New Merton Board Mills Ltd* [1959] AC 604 (HL).
[137] *DIB Group Pty Ltd t/as Hill & Co v Cole* [2009] NSWCA 210 [32].
[138] ibid [39].

Some cases where liability of an employer was found for an incident occurring on other premises involved the employer having actual knowledge of conditions on the premises.[139] Arguably, however, that was not a true application of 'non-delegable duty' but a culpable direct failure of the employer to take due precautions against a known hazard.

In the end in *DIB* his Honour came to the following conclusion:

> The employer's duty, however effected, to adopt safe systems of work and to provide proper plant and equipment, will operate differently on its own premises and in circumstances over which it has full control, as compared with premises under the control of others and circumstances over which it does not have control.[140]

His Honour suggested that, just as in *Davie* the employer was not liable for the carelessness of a manufacturer, an employer who sent his or her employee off to other premises might not be liable for harm caused by some defective condition of those premises of which the employer was not aware.

In this particular case, even if it had been reasonable to expect the trucking company to conduct a 'risk assessment' inspection of the premises where the truck was to unload, the trial judge had found that the loose pit lid would not have been noticed.[141] Hence in this situation there was no liability on the employer.

It has to be said that if this view were adopted it would amount to a fairly fundamental restatement of the law of NDD owed by employers, and would seem not to sit very happily with some of the cases noted previously. The decision may represent a trend toward the crafting of a limitation of the NDD to situations where the employer would (apart from the engagement of some third party) have 'control' over the circumstances of work. But it leaves a high degree of uncertainty. It may be that, if the more nuanced theory of Beuermann noted below were adopted, NDD applies where the employee has been 'placed under the authority' of a contractor; this would explain why no NDD was found in *DIB*. In sending an employee to a number of locations to make deliveries, there is no intention that he or she be placed under the supervisory authority of the occupiers of those locations.

However, in many cases where a worker is sent somewhere else to work the employer will still, of course, have a personal (direct) obligation to provide proper safety systems and equipment. In *Pacific Steel Constructions Pty Limited v Barahona; Jigsaw Property Group Pty Limited v Barahona*[142] the company Pacific Steel, employer of Mr Barahona, was found to be in breach of its duty of care by sending a worker to another site without providing him with proper safety equipment.

A clear difference between the approach in the *DIB* case and that in *Barahona* is that in *DIB* the issue was really one of the 'condition of the premises' (an unobservable hole in the ground), whereas in *Barahona* the issues related to a system of work that should have been known to the employer.[143] This is not, then, despite the phrase being used at one point, an example of the principle of 'non-delegable duty'. It is an example of a culpable direct failure on behalf of the employer.

---

[139] *Bourke v Hassett* [1998] VSCSA 24.
[140] *DIB Group Pty Ltd t/as Hill & Co v Cole* [2009] NSWCA 210 [54].
[141] ibid [61].
[142] *Pacific Steel Constructions Pty Limited v Barahona; Jigsaw Property Group Pty Limited v Barahona* [2009] NSWCA 406.
[143] ibid [128].

The contrast between these two approaches can be seen in two other decisions. The first is one which clearly recognises the orthodox difference between a directly culpable failure and liability imposed under NDD. The second seems again to confuse the two different bases for liability.

In *Glynn v Challenge Recruitment Australia Pty Ltd*[144] the plaintiff was employed by a 'labour supply' service, CRA. He was sent to work for the host company Concrete Demolition Contractors Pty Ltd ('CDC'). He was injured when he fell off a ladder that had not been properly secured by the CDC foreman, Mr Madden. The court held that CRA was liable on two independent grounds: (i) through culpable direct breach of its duty of care because it had not provided proper training in working at heights; but also (ii) because it was liable for the negligence of the CDC supervisor in sending the plaintiff up an unsecured ladder, due the non-delegable nature of the duty. Giles JA commented:

> Mr Madden [the CDC foreman] failed to ensure that 'either he or some other worker was available to stabilise the ladder'. … The failure was in the system of work, which did not properly attend to securing the ladder, and it was a *breach of the defendant's non-delegable duty* of care; the injury was in law caused by the negligence. There was *also a direct breach* by the defendant in its failure to instruct the plaintiff as to the use of ladders, negligence which may also in law have caused the injury in that, properly instructed, it may be that the plaintiff would not have assumed that Mr Madden was holding the ladder and would have gone up the ladder only when it was secured; but it is not necessary to rest the defendant's liability on that breach.[145]

In *Pollard v Baulderstone Hornibrook Engineering Pty Ltd*[146] a driver who was employed by a 'labour hire firm', Dependable, was allocated to work for Pioneer. He was injured when cleaning his truck at a Pioneer depot. Pioneer conceded liability. McColl JA (for the Court of Appeal) held that Dependable was also liable, as it had not discharged its NDD, because it had effectively not considered at all what system of work Pioneer had adopted for the drivers: 'Dependable *must have known* that Pioneer's system of work exposed the appellant to different site conditions throughout the day.'[147]

It will be noted that, while a 'non-delegable duty' is referred to, the focus on what the employer should have known and done means that the orthodox doctrine is not being applied. It would be less confusing if, when 'direct' liability is being considered, the language of 'non-delegable duty' were not used.

A recent important article by Beuermann[148] suggests that the doctrine of NDD in the workplace has been developed to deal with the risk of abuse of authority. She prefers the term 'conferred authority strict liability', as she argues that the doctrine only applies where an employer (S) has conferred authority on an independent contractor (W) to control the activities of an employee (V). This description does indeed seem to fit most of the employment cases where an NDD has been found to exist.

---

[144] *Glynn v Challenge Recruitment Australia Pty Ltd* [2006] NSWCA 203.

[145] ibid [48] (emphasis added). The comments of Giles JA here, it may be noted, support this chapter's suggested use of the word 'direct' when referring to liability for something that the employer themselves should have done. For another recent case where the NDD principles were correctly applied, see *Galea v Bagtrans Pty Ltd* [2010] NSWCA 350, [2011] *Australian Torts Reports* ¶ 82-078.

[146] *Pollard v Baulderstone Hornibrook Engineering Pty Ltd* [2008] NSWCA 99.

[147] ibid [58] (emphasis added).

[148] C Beuermann, 'Tort Law in the Employment Relationship: A Response to the Potential Abuse of an Employer's Authority' (2014) 21 *Torts Law Journal* 169.

It also explains the fact that in *Davie v New Merton Board Mills Ltd*,[149] where a worker was injured by a negligently manufactured tool, the employer was not held liable under the NDD principle for the carelessness of the manufacturer (as there was no sense in which the worker had been placed 'under the authority' of the manufacturer).[150]

As will be discussed below, this theory may also provide some guidance in determining whether the contractor was acting outside the 'scope' of the relevant relationship—the issue of so-called 'collateral' negligence.

VIII. NDD and Intentional Torts

A question that, it is submitted, has been answered in an unsatisfactory way in Australia so far is whether there can be liability under the NDD principle for commission of an intentional tort.

The issue came up in *NSW v Lepore*,[151] where the intentional wrongful act was the alleged sexual assault of a student by a teacher. Kirby J declined to rule on this issue as the teacher was an employee;[152] with respect this seems correct, but the rest of Court went on to decide the point. The decision of the majority was effectively that there can be no breach of an NDD by an intentional wrongful act.[153]

With respect to Lord Sumption, his Lordship's comments on this aspect of *Lepore* in *Woodland*[154] are liable to be misread. His Lordship in discussing *Lepore* said:

> Several of [the High Court's] members thought that vicarious liability was a simpler route to liability than a non-delegable duty of care. Nonetheless, by a majority of 4–3 (Gaudron, McHugh, Gummow and Hayne JJ) the Court held that the schools owed a non-delegable duty.[155]

While Gaudron and McHugh JJ did support the operation of NDD in the circumstances of the case (involving the intentional tort of battery), Gummow and Hayne JJ did not, refusing to extend the principle to an intentional act of sexual assault. Their Honours did not, however, express any doubt about the principle in *Introvigne* generally applying to carelessness; and so Lord Sumption is correct that on the question of an NDD applying between schools and pupils in relation to carelessness, *Lepore* supports that principle. But there was a 4–3 majority in the decision holding that NDD could not be applied to a case of intentional wrongdoing.[156]

This will lead to different outcomes in case of a workplace assault depending on the employment status of the worker committing the assault. It is an odd and unjust outcome.

---

[149] *Davie v New Merton Board Mills Ltd* [1959] AC 604 (HL).
[150] Beuermann, above n 148, 179.
[151] *NSW v Lepore* (2003) 212 CLR 511.
[152] ibid [295].
[153] ibid [38] (Gleeson CJ); [265] (Gummow and Hayne JJ); [339] (Callinan J, agreeing with Gleeson CJ).
[154] *Woodland v Essex CC* [2013] UKSC 66, [2014] AC 537.
[155] ibid [21].
[156] For the dissents see [136] (McHugh J), [293], [309]–[314] (Kirby J), and [127] (Gaudron J).

This aspect of *Lepore* has been cogently criticised as 'indefensible' by Stevens.[157] It is illogical to extend NDD to negligent acts and deny its application to intentional torts.[158]

Hence we are left in Australia with the unsatisfactory situation that an intentional tort cannot be brought home to a principal through the NDD principle, although negligence can. If the recent UK decision in *Woodland*[159] were accepted in Australia, however, that may change the situation.

Lord Sumption summarises the main principles of NDD in his judgment:

> Both principle and authority suggest that the relevant factors are the vulnerability of the claimant, the existence of a relationship between the claimant and the defendant by virtue of which the latter has a degree of protective custody over him, and the delegation of that custody to another person.[160]

None of these matters depend on the harm committed to the child who is owed such a duty being committed by carelessness as opposed to an intentional act of assault. Similarly, none of the five factors noted above in *Woodland*[161] explicitly addresses the type of intention behind the wrong. A child being cared for in a school, for example, is 'vulnerable' to intentional sexual assault; the school has assumed a duty to 'protect the claimant from harm' of all sorts; the child has no control over how that duty is realised; the school will commonly have delegated to the wrongdoer the care of the child. Even the fifth and final point, which refers to the wrongdoer being '*negligent* not in some collateral respect but in performance of the very function assumed by the defendant and delegated by the defendant to him' (emphasis added), while it uses the word 'negligent', is really aimed at the question of whether the wrongdoer was behaving wrongfully in a core or a 'collateral' area.

Indeed, it may be that this type of flexibility in understanding the wording used is what Lady Hale is referring to in her concurring judgment, where she notes that her agreement is 'subject of course to the usual provisos that such judicial statements are not to be treated as if they were statutes and can never be set in stone'.[162]

In her reference to Beuermann's article,[163] her Ladyship specifically picks up the point that it would have been possible in previous cases dealing with sexual assault of children to have adopted the logic of 'non-delegable duty' (what Beuermann refers to as 'conferred authority strict liability') rather than the principle of vicarious liability.[164]

It is submitted that this would be a sensible development of the law, and it is one that ought to be considered by the High Court of Australia. There is no opportunity here to develop the point in any detail, but it is arguable that the development of the law in the area of vicarious liability for child sexual abuse by clergy, in the recent decision of the UK Supreme Court in *Various Claimants v The Catholic Child Welfare Society* ('*CCWS*'),[165] has taken the law in unhelpful directions. The criterion for vicarious liability accepted in that

---

[157] Stevens, above n 51, 122–23.

[158] Some of the problems created by the view that NDD cannot apply to an intentional tort can be seen in the decision in *Nationwide News Pty Ltd v Naidu; ISS Security Pty Ltd v Naidu* [2007] NSWCA 377.

[159] *Woodland v Essex CC* [2013] UKSC 66, [2014] AC 537.

[160] ibid [12].

[161] ibid [23], text to n 77 above.

[162] *Woodland v Essex CC* [2013] UKSC 66, [2014] AC 537 [38]. See also her Ladyship's similar remarks at [28].

[163] ibid [33], citing Beuermann, above n 78.

[164] Referring to 'previous cases concerning harm suffered by school pupils', the 'child sexual assault cases' discussed by Beuermann: ibid 273.

[165] *The Catholic Child Welfare Society v Various Claimants* [2012] UKSC 56, [2013] 2 AC 1.

decision, of a relationship 'akin to employment',[166] is so vague and potentially broad that it risks allowing a wide and uncontrolled expansion of strict liability for the wrongs of third parties.[167] However, most if not all child sexual assault cases involving churches and schools would clearly fall within the criteria accepted now in *Woodland*[168]—and accepted in Australia since *Introvigne*[169]—for the existence of an NDD. That principle would provide a clear and appropriately limited avenue for recovery of compensation for the harms inflicted by persons in trusted positions of authority, without unduly stretching the boundaries of vicarious liability in yet another uncontrolled expansion.

Tan offers a similar comment in his case note on *CCWS*, suggesting that NDD would provide a better basis for action in child abuse cases:

> Perhaps the doctrine of non-delegable duty can better give effect to the policy reasons for finding liability through the imposition of a *direct* and *primary* duty on the enterprise to protect highly vulnerable parties from harm regardless of the status of the person undertaking work on its behalf.[170]

IX. Collateral Negligence?

Finally, more work needs to be done on the question of defining the type of 'collateral' negligence or wrongdoing that will mean that the principal is not liable for harm committed by the contractor, despite other elements of the NDD principle being satisfied.

An employer is only vicariously liable for wrongs committed by an employee 'in the course of employment', and the rules as to this issue are fairly well developed. There must clearly be a similar limitation on the liability of a principal for a tort committed by a contractor, where the principal has an NDD. The precise scope of the limitation, however, is unclear.

The limitation is sometimes stated to be that the principal will not be liable for the 'collateral negligence' of a contractor. The sense seems to be that there is some negligence of a contractor that would be outside the scope of the obligation undertaken by the principal to the person who was harmed. But defining this limit seems difficult, and some of the older cases offered to illustrate it seem no longer to be valid. Balkin and Davis, for example, offer the example of *Padbury v Holliday & Greenwood Ltd*,[171] where a principal was held not responsible for harm caused by a hammer falling from a window ledge onto a pedestrian, the carelessness of the contractor in leaving the hammer being said to be 'collateral' to the task of installing a window.[172]

---

[166] ibid [47], citing the decision of the Court of Appeal in *E v English Province of Our Lady of Charity* [2013] QB 722.

[167] See, eg, the decision in *Cox v Ministry of Justice* [2014] EWCA Civ 132 [43] where prison authorities were held vicariously liable for the carelessness of a prisoner, on the basis that while assisting in unloading a truck his relationship with the authorities was 'akin to employment'.

[168] *Woodland v Essex CC* [2013] UKSC 66, [2014] AC 537 [23].

[169] *Commonwealth of Australia v Introvigne* (1982) 150 CLR 258 (HCA).

[170] D Tan, 'For Judges Rush in Where Angels Fear to Tread …' (2013) 21 *Torts Law Journal* 43, 57. As noted previously, it would be better to use the word 'direct' to refer to actual negligence or wrongdoing, rather than to the sort of strict liability imposed by the NDD principle. But apart from this matter of terminology, I would endorse Tan's comments.

[171] *Padbury v Holliday & Greenwood Ltd* (1912) 28 TLR 494 (CA).

[172] RP Balkin and JLR Davis, *Law of Torts*, 5th edn (Australia, LexisNexis Butterworths, 2013) [26.35].

But why is that so? If the person harmed was someone to whom the employer owed an NDD (perhaps under the English 'highway' rules) it is hard to see why the carelessness is 'outside the scope' of the contractual undertaking. Surely carelessness in handling tools is the sort of thing that is entirely foreseeable.

Sachs LJ made a similar point in *Salsbury v Woodland*,[173] referring to the contrasting results in *Padbury* (no liability where a tool dropped) and another decision, *Walsh v Holst & Co Ltd*,[174] where liability was established: 'How, in *Walsh* … could one distinguish between a falling half-brick and a falling cold chisel?'[175] The whole concept of 'collateral negligence' is criticised for its lack of clarity by Callinan J in his judgment in *Montgomery*.[176]

Perhaps the best that can be said is that the limits of the notion are unexplored, and would benefit from further work. One promising line of inquiry, however, is suggested by Beuermann.[177] She argues that, if her theory that NDD is based on 'conferred authority' is correct, then the scope of liability should be limited to circumstances where the (ostensible) authority conferred by the employer or other party is being exercised. This seems to be a good test which would give the right result, so long as the notion of 'ostensible authority' is not read too narrowly—for example, in a case of intentional child abuse, if intentional torts could be sued for in NDD, then child abuse by a teacher would be covered so long as it occurred within the overall 'authority' relationship established.

X. Conclusion

This chapter has outlined a number of issues of convergence and divergence in Australia and England in the area of attributed liability for the actions of non-employees under the principle known as 'non-delegable duty'. It has noted that, while the principle enjoys a long pedigree, it is being misunderstood in some court decisions. Nevertheless, when the elements and limits of the principle are noted from the major common law decisions that developed it, the doctrine is an important part of the tort liability system.

Recent clarification of the area in the UK in the *Woodland*[178] decision seems to go a long way to set it again on a principled basis, and suggests that if the High Court of Australia is prepared to revisit the question of its application to intentional torts, a revitalised NDD analysis may be a preferable way of dealing with the difficult tort issues presented by institutional sexual abuse of children. Finally, more work needs to be done on defining with increased clarity the boundary line beyond which wrongdoing by a contractor will be outside the scope of the contractual engagement entered into by the principal and be viewed as merely 'collateral' rather than central to the contractual purpose.

---

[173] *Salsbury v Woodland* [1970] 1 QB 324 (CA).
[174] *Walsh v Holst & Co Ltd* [1958] 1 WLR 800 (CA).
[175] *Salsbury v Woodland* [1970] 1 QB 324 (CA) 348H.
[176] *Leichhardt Municipal Council v Montgomery* [2007] HCA 6, (2007) 230 CLR 22 [179].
[177] Beuermann, above n 148, 182.
[178] *Woodland v Essex CC* [2013] UKSC 66, [2014] AC 537.

8

The Scope of the Rule Against Contractual Penalties: A New Divergence

SIRKO HARDER

I. Introduction

All major common law countries have a judge-made rule according to which a contractual stipulation of a penalty is unenforceable or void. During the twentieth century it became widely accepted that this rule applies only where the impugned obligation is triggered by a breach of contract or by an event that cannot occur without breach. In *Andrews v Australia and New Zealand Banking Group Ltd*[1] the High Court of Australia departed from the common understanding by holding that the penalty doctrine may apply where the event triggering the impugned obligation is not a breach of contract and may occur without breach. This has created a divergence in the common law world. This chapter will discuss the decision and its possible impact in other common law countries.

II. The Breach Requirement Outside Australia

In England and Wales it is well established that the penalty doctrine applies only where the impugned obligation is triggered by a breach of contract or by an event that cannot occur without breach.[2] This breach requirement was the premise of the decision by the House of

---

[1] *Andrews v Australia and New Zealand Banking Group Ltd* [2012] HCA 30, (2012) 247 CLR 205.

[2] *Bridge v Campbell Discount Co Ltd* [1962] AC 600 (HL) 613–14 (Viscount Simonds), 614–15 (Lord Morton); *United Dominions Trust (Commercial) Ltd v Ennis* [1968] 1 QB 54 (CA) 67, 69; *Export Credits Guarantee Department v Universal Oil Products Co* [1983] 1 WLR 399 (HL) 402–03; *Euro London Appointments Ltd v Claessens International Ltd* [2006] EWCA Civ 385, [2006] 2 Lloyd's Rep 437 [16]–[17], [23]–[24]; *M & J Polymers Ltd v Imerys Minerals Ltd* [2008] EWHC 344 (Comm), [2008] 1 Lloyd's Rep 541 [41]; *Office of Fair Trading v Abbey National plc* [2008] EWHC 2325 (Comm), [2009] 1 All ER (Comm) 717 [20]; *Lehman Brothers Special Financing Inc v Carlton Communications Ltd* [2011] EWHC 718 (Ch) [45]. It has been suggested that the breach requirement came about by accident: JD Heydon, MJ Leeming and PG Turner, *Meagher, Gummow and Lehane's Equity: Doctrines and Remedies*, 5th edn (Chatswood, LexisNexis, 2015) [18-040]–[18-045].

Lords in *Dunlop Pneumatic Tyre Co Ltd v New Garage and Motor Co Ltd*,[3] where the focus was on the difference between a contractual penalty and liquidated damages.[4]

One of the first English cases in which the breach requirement was crucial is *Associated Distributors Ltd v Hall*,[5] which involved a minimum payment clause in a hire-purchase contract. Such a clause requires the hirer-purchaser to pay a minimum percentage (50 per cent in *Hall*) of the total rent payable under the contract if the contract comes to an end (through breach by the hirer-purchaser or otherwise) before the instalments of rent paid have reached the minimum percentage. The hirer-purchaser in *Hall* exercised his contractual right to terminate the contract after paying only one instalment of rent. The English Court of Appeal held that the rule against penalties did not apply to the hirer-purchaser's obligation to make the minimum payment in that case because that obligation had been triggered by an event other than a breach of contract.[6]

A recent illustration of the breach requirement in English law is *Berg v Blackburn Rovers Football Club & Athletic plc*,[7] where the impugned clause gave the defendant a right to terminate prematurely the fixed-term employment of the plaintiff and obliged the defendant in that event to pay to the plaintiff a sum equal to the plaintiff's salary for the unexpired balance of the fixed period. The argument that this obligation constituted a contractual penalty was rejected on the ground that the event triggering the obligation was not a breach of contract but the exercise of the contractual right to terminate the contract.[8]

The breach requirement has also been endorsed by courts in Canada,[9] Hong Kong,[10] Ireland,[11] New Zealand,[12] Northern Ireland[13] and Scotland.[14] There are differences between the jurisdictions of the United States, but both the Uniform Commercial Code and the Restatement (Second) on Contracts include the breach requirement.[15] Australian courts

---

[3] *Dunlop Pneumatic Tyre Co Ltd v New Garage and Motor Co Ltd* [1915] AC 79 (HL).

[4] A Gray, 'Contractual Penalties in Australian Law after *Andrews*: An Opportunity Missed' (2013) 18 *Deakin Law Review* 1, 4–6; G Baker and M Sheldon, 'A Timely Look at the Law of Penalties' (2012) 23 *Journal of Banking and Finance Law and Practice* 141, 146.

[5] *Associated Distributors Ltd v Hall* [1938] 2 KB 83 (CA).

[6] ibid 87–88.

[7] *Berg v Blackburn Rovers Football Club & Athletic plc* [2013] EWHC 1070 (Ch), [2013] IRLR 537.

[8] ibid [33]–[34].

[9] *Boisonault v Block Bros Realty Ltd* (1987) 47 Man R (2d) 148 (QB); *Doman Forest Products Ltd v GMAC Commercial Credit Corp—Canada* 2007 BCCA 88, (2007) 65 BCLR (4th) 1 [121]–[125]; *Homburg LP Management Inc v Lappin* 2009 NSSC 346, (2009) 182 ACWS (3d) 750 [12]–[15]. The breach requirement was also the premise of the decision in *Elsley v JG Collins Insurance Agencies Ltd* [1978] 2 SCR 916.

[10] *Philips Hong Kong Ltd v Attorney General of Hong Kong* [1993] 1 HKLR 269 (PC) 277–78; *Re Mandarin Container* [2004] 3 HKLRD 554 (CFI) 557–58.

[11] *O'Donnell and Co Ltd v Truck and Machinery Sales Ltd* [1998] 4 IR 191 (SC).

[12] *Camatos Holdings Ltd v Neil Civil Engineering (1992) Ltd* [1998] 3 NZLR 596 (HC) 606. The question of whether the penalty doctrine is confined to cases of breach was expressly left open in *Isac New Zealand Ltd v Managh* [2013] NZHC 3242 [117].

[13] *Lombank Ltd v Kennedy* [1961] NI 192 (CA) 211–13, 217–18.

[14] *Bell Brothers (HP) Ltd v Aitken* 1939 SC 577 (IH) 588, 589, 591; *Granor Finance Ltd v Liquidator of Eastore Ltd* 1974 SLT 296 (CSOH) 298; *EFT Commercial Ltd v Security Change Ltd* 1992 SC 414 (IH) 428, 431, 432–34. A legislative relaxation of the restriction has been recommended by the Scottish Law Commission, *Penalty Clauses* (Scot Law Com No 171, 1999) pt 4.

[15] Uniform Commercial Code (US) § 2-718; *Restatement (2d) of Contracts* § 356.

too endorsed the breach requirement[16] before the High Court of Australia disapproved it in *Andrews v Australia and New Zealand Banking Group Ltd* ('*Andrews*').[17]

III. The Litigation in *Andrews* and *Paciocco*

The class action in *Andrews* concerned various fees ('exception fees') that banks charged their customers. For example, honour fees (or overdrawn fees) were charged when a cheque, direct debit or withdrawal of money overdrew the customer's account, and dishonour fees were charged when the customer attempted to overdraw the account but the bank declined the payment.

At the time of writing, four decisions had been made in the litigation: the first decision by the trial judge (Gordon J in the Federal Court of Australia),[18] the decision by the High Court of Australia on appeal against the trial judge's first decision,[19] the second decision by the trial judge,[20] and the decision by the Full Court of the Federal Court of Australia on appeal against the trial judge's second decision.[21] After the High Court's decision, the name of the case changed to *Paciocco v Australia and New Zealand Banking Group Ltd* ('*Paciocco*').

Gordon J's first decision was a ruling on the preliminary question of whether each of 17 types of exception fees was capable of being characterised as a penalty. After a detailed examination of the history of the rule against penalties, including the recent English and Australian cases, Gordon J concluded that the rule was confined to obligations triggered by a breach of contract.[22] She went on to examine which fees were payable on breach of contract and found this to be the case only for four types of fees, all of which were late-payment fees charged when a credit card holder failed to make the minimum repayment by the due date.[23] She regarded the other 13 types of fees as not being capable of being characterised as a penalty, on the ground that the events rendering those fees payable involved no breaches of contract but the exercise of an option by the customer.[24]

The plaintiffs appealed Gordon J's decision in respect of those 13 types of fees, and the appeal was removed to the High Court of Australia.[25] The High Court held that the rule

---

[16] *Interstar Wholesale Finance Pty Ltd v Integral Home Loans Pty Ltd* [2008] NSWCA 310, (2008) 257 ALR 292 [106]; *Kowalczuk v Accom Finance Pty Ltd* [2008] NSWCA 343, (2008) 77 NSWLR 205 [162]; *Ange v First East Auction Holdings Pty Ltd* [2011] VSCA 335, (2011) 284 ALR 638 [85]. An exception was *AMEV-UDC Finance Ltd v Austin* (1986) 162 CLR 170, 197–98 (Deane J).

[17] *Andrews v Australia and New Zealand Banking Group Ltd* [2012] HCA 30, (2012) 247 CLR 205.

[18] *Andrews v Australia and New Zealand Banking Group Ltd* [2011] FCA 1376, (2011) 211 FCR 53.

[19] *Andrews v Australia and New Zealand Banking Group Ltd* [2012] HCA 30, (2012) 247 CLR 205

[20] *Paciocco v Australia and New Zealand Banking Group Ltd* [2014] FCA 35, (2014) 309 ALR 249.

[21] *Paciocco v Australia and New Zealand Banking Group Ltd* [2015] FCAFC 50, (2015) 321 ALR 584.

[22] *Andrews v Australia and New Zealand Banking Group Ltd* [2011] FCA 1376, (2011) 211 FCR 53 [7]–[80].

[23] ibid [5], [243], [259], [268], [312].

[24] ibid [5].

[25] Transcript of Proceedings, [2012] HCATrans 104 (11 May 2012). The appeal would normally have been heard by the Full Court of the Federal Court of Australia. Pursuant to the *Judiciary Act 1903* (Cth) s 40(2), (4), a cause pending in the Federal Court may be removed to the High Court if this is in the interest of the parties and the public. This extraordinary step was taken in *Andrews* because the Full Federal Court would have been bound by *Interstar Wholesale Finance Pty Ltd v Integral Home Loans Pty Ltd* [2008] NSWCA 310, (2008) 257 ALR 292 as authority for the breach requirement.

against penalties is not confined to cases of breach of contract, and that the 13 types of exception fees in question were not incapable of characterisation as penalties only because they were not charged upon breach of contract by the customer.[26] This decision will be scrutinised later in this chapter.

The case went back to Gordon J, although with a different person as the representative of the class and with 72 types of exception fees.[27] With regard to each type of fees, Gordon J needed to decide whether the obligation to pay the fees was unenforceable by virtue of the penalty doctrine as formulated by the High Court.[28] Gordon J held that the late-payment fees were so unenforceable, but not any other type of fees. Her second decision thus produced the same outcome as her first.

Both parties appealed Gordon J's second decision. The Full Court of the Federal Court of Australia held that none of the fees were unenforceable by virtue of the penalty doctrine; the late-payment fees were not extravagant or unconscionable by reference to the greatest loss that could conceivably have followed from a breach by the customer, and the other fees constituted a payment in exchange for an additional right of the customer.[29] At the time of writing, the plaintiffs were seeking special leave from the High Court of Australia to appeal the Full Court's decision.

IV. The Decision by the High Court of Australia in *Andrews*

In *Andrews* the High Court of Australia held that a contractual obligation may constitute a penalty even if the event triggering the obligation is not a breach of contract and may occur without breach. The decision was made in a joint judgment by all five judges in the Court.

The Court started by examining the equitable jurisdiction to relieve against penalties in English law before the nineteenth century. It made the following observations.[30] A common instrument at that time was the penal bond with conditional defeasance.[31] It contained an obligation to pay a certain sum of money, accompanied by a condition in the nature of a defeasance, the performance or occurrence of which discharged the obligation. The purpose of the bond was to secure performance of the condition, but instead of a promise to perform the condition, there was a promise to pay a certain sum of money if the condition was not performed. While the obligation to pay contained in the bond was enforceable at law, equity limited recovery to the loss suffered by the obligee as a result of the non-performance of the condition, but only where such loss could be properly compensated in money. Over time, the equitable jurisdiction to relieve against penalties extended to provisions in simple

---

[26] *Andrews v Australia and New Zealand Banking Group Ltd* [2012] HCA 30, (2012) 247 CLR 205.

[27] *Paciocco v Australia and New Zealand Banking Group Ltd* [2014] FCA 35, (2014) 309 ALR 249.

[28] The plaintiffs also relied on certain statutes. None of the fees was held to be unenforceable by virtue of any of those statutes.

[29] *Paciocco v Australia and New Zealand Banking Group Ltd* [2015] FCAFC 50, (2015) 321 ALR 584. The Full Court upheld Gordon J's decision that none of the fees were unenforceable by virtue of any statute.

[30] *Andrews v Australia and New Zealand Banking Group Ltd* [2012] HCA 30, (2012) 247 CLR 205 [33]–[44].

[31] The development of the penal bond in medieval and early modern times is traced by Joseph Biancalana, 'The Development of the Penal Bond with Conditional Defeasance' (2005) 26 *Journal of Legal History* 103. A historical account going back to Roman times is provided by WH Loyd, 'Penalties and Forfeitures' (1915) 29 *Harvard Law Review* 117. See also the articles cited by Gray, above n 4, 2 n 5.

contracts, without changing the nature of the jurisdiction. In simple contracts, therefore, the scope of the penalty doctrine is not limited to stipulations that are contractual promises broken by the promisor.[32]

The Court went on to reject the proposition, made in previous Australian cases,[33] that the penalty doctrine has disappeared from equity by becoming a rule of the common law. The Court made the following observations.[34] In early modern times, the common law courts in England developed assumpsit as an action to enforce agreements not under seal (simple contracts). By the seventeenth century, those courts had developed rules mirroring the equitable rules on penalties. Statutes of 1696 and 1705 reinforced that approach.[35] However, the developments in the practice of the common law courts did not supplant the equitable jurisdiction. There is 'no reason in principle why the scope of the equitable doctrine should be restricted to those cases today where, hypothetically, an assumpsit action would have lain at common law in the nineteenth century'.[36] To the extent that the common law courts had developed rules mirroring the equitable rules on penalties, there was no conflict or variance between the common law and equity for the purpose of the Judicature legislation. In any event, under the Judicature legislation, it is equity, not the law, that is to prevail.

The Court thus took the view that an equitable jurisdiction to relieve against contractual penalties still exists today.[37] The details of the penalty doctrine as set out by the Court will be discussed later in this chapter.

V. Methodological Flaws in the High Court's Reasoning

Irrespective of the substantive merits or demerits of extending the scope of the penalty doctrine beyond cases of breach, the reasoning of the High Court of Australia in *Andrews* involved several methodological flaws.

First, the Court was adamant that the Judicature legislation did not lead to a demise of the equitable jurisdiction to strike down as penalty a contractual obligation not triggered by breach. But the Court cited no Australian or English case in which such an obligation was in fact struck down as a penalty under the Judicature system. Indeed, no such case seems to exist.[38] There were a few judicial statements supporting the jurisdiction under the

---

[32] *Andrews v Australia and New Zealand Banking Group Ltd* [2012] HCA 30, (2012) 247 CLR 205 [45]. In this chapter, the 'promisor' is the party subject to the alleged penalty, and the 'promisee' is the party benefiting from the alleged penalty.

[33] *Citicorp Australia Ltd v Hendry* (1985) 4 NSWLR 1, 23, 39; *AMEV-UDC Finance Ltd v Austin* (1986) 162 CLR 170, 191 (Mason and Wilson JJ); *Harris v Digital Pulse Pty Ltd* [2003] NSWCA 10, (2003) 197 ALR 626 [59] (Spigelman CJ); *Ringrow Pty Ltd v BP Australia Pty Ltd* [2003] FCA 1297, (2003) 203 ALR 281 [97]; *Interstar Wholesale Finance Pty Ltd v Integral Home Loans Pty Ltd* [2008] NSWCA 310, (2008) 257 ALR 292 [99].

[34] *Andrews v Australia and New Zealand Banking Group Ltd* [2012] HCA 30, (2012) 247 CLR 205 [53]–[63].

[35] Administration of Justice Act 1696 (8 & 9 Will 3, c 11); Administration of Justice Act 1705 (4 & 5 Anne, c 16).

[36] *Andrews v Australia and New Zealand Banking Group Ltd* [2012] HCA 30, (2012) 247 CLR 205 [62] (French CJ, Gummow, Crennan, Kiefel and Bell JJ).

[37] The same view had been taken by W Newland, 'Equitable Relief against Penalties' (2011) 85 *Australian Law Journal* 434, 439–44.

[38] JW Carter, W Courtney, E Peden, A Stewart and GJ Tolhurst, 'Contractual Penalties: Resurrecting the Equitable Jurisdiction' (2013) 30 *Journal of Contract Law* 99, 132.

Judicature system, but they were all made in minority judgments[39] or judgments reversed on appeal.[40]

Moreover, dicta rejecting the jurisdiction were made by three of the five judges in the High Court's 1986 decision in *AMEV-UDC Finance Ltd v Austin*.[41] Dawson J observed that an obligation not triggered by breach cannot be a penalty,[42] and Mason and Wilson JJ said that the equitable rule against penalties had 'withered on the vine' in the absence of English (and, by implication, Australian) cases in which the equitable rule against penalties had been invoked under the Judicature system.[43]

In *Andrews* the High Court simply said that Mason and Wilson JJ had overlooked that the only relevant effect of the Judicature system was upon the court system, not substantive doctrine.[44] But Mason and Wilson JJ did not suggest that the equitable rule against penalties had been abolished by the Judicature legislation. What they suggested, in effect, is that the rule had become defunct through disuse.[45] In *Andrews* the High Court ought to have explained why it thought that this was not the case.

Secondly, the High Court in *Andrews* said that there is no reason in principle why the equitable rule against penalties should be confined to cases of breach when it was not so confined 200 years ago. That argument completely ignores that the past 200 years have seen a huge transformation in society and economy and indeed contract law. The Court was not prepared to consider even the possibility that those changes have impacted upon the equitable rule against penalties.

Thirdly, and related to the last point, the High Court in *Andrews* purported simply to maintain the scope of the equitable rule against penalties, in defence against supposed attempts to limit it. In fact, the Court dramatically increased the scope of the rule. Simply maintaining its scope would mean applying the rule to those types of agreement in relation to which it was developed. But the Court extended the rule to the myriads of new types of agreement that have emerged over the past 200 years. It is one thing to say that the equitable rule against penalties, as developed in early modern times, applies to penal bonds where they are still used today. It is a totally different thing to say that the equitable rule against penalties, as developed in early modern times, somehow applies to bank fees, franchise agreements, hire-purchase contracts, 'take or pay clauses' and all other modern forms of agreement. The High Court did not simply preserve an existing doctrine; it created a new doctrine.

Crucially, the High Court in *Andrews* gave the impression that the New South Wales Court of Appeal in *Interstar Wholesale Finance Pty Ltd v Integral Home Loans Pty Ltd*[46] had changed the then existing law by restricting the scope of the rule against penalties to cases of

---

[39] *Bridge v Campbell Discount Co Ltd* [1962] AC 600 (HL) 629–31 (Lord Denning); *AMEV-UDC Finance Ltd v Austin* (1986) 162 CLR 170, 197–200 (Deane J).

[40] *Integral Home Loans Pty Ltd v Interstar Wholesale Finance Pty Ltd* [2007] NSWSC 406, (2007) Aust Contract R 90-261 [74]; rev'd *Interstar Wholesale Finance Pty Ltd v Integral Home Loans Pty Ltd* [2008] NSWCA 310, (2008) 257 ALR 292.

[41] *AMEV-UDC Finance Ltd v Austin* (1986) 162 CLR 170.

[42] ibid 214.

[43] ibid 191.

[44] *Andrews v Australia and New Zealand Banking Group Ltd* [2012] HCA 30, (2012) 247 CLR 205 [68].

[45] A principle may become inoperative by being ignored for a long time: JW Salmond, 'The Theory of Judicial Precedents' (1900) 16 LQR 376, 383; quoted in *PGA v The Queen* [2012] HCA 21, (2012) 245 CLR 355 [24].

[46] *Interstar Wholesale Finance Pty Ltd v Integral Home Loans Pty Ltd* [2008] NSWCA 310, (2008) 257 ALR 292.

breach. In fact, that decision merely pronounced how Australian law had been understood to be for several decades. It is the High Court's decision in *Andrews* that effectively changed the law.[47] While the High Court is free to change any judge-made rule, such a dramatic change as that made by the Court in *Andrews* requires a justification of the change on policy grounds, engaging with the current conditions in Australia, and should not simply be based on the English law of the eighteenth century.[48] In that respect, the High Court's decision in *Andrews* stands in stark contrast to other recent decisions by the Court on important rules of private law, in which the Court extensively discussed policy considerations, engaged with scholarly work, and reviewed the state of the law in a number of other (civil law and common law) countries.[49] The Court did none of these in *Andrews*.[50]

Methodology matters. A decision needs a proper methodological basis in order to be persuasive and to be applied correctly and consistently. A flawed methodology may obscure the 'message' sent by a decision. The sole reliance on history and the absence of any policy discussion in the High Court's decision in *Andrews* may impact upon the effect of that decision. For example, the flawed methodology employed by the High Court permitted Australian courts to maintain the classification as an option of a clause in a loan contract that provides for what is in substance the penalty rate of interest to be the normal rate and further provides for a reduction of the interest rate if the principal and the reduced rate are paid on time. It was said as early as 1801:

> It is a well-known rule in equity, that if a mortgage covenant be to pay 5l. per cent. and if the interest be paid on certain days then to be reduced to 4l. per cent. the Court of Chancery will not relieve if the early day be suffered to pass without payment; but if the covenant be to pay 4l. per cent. and if the party do not pay at a certain time it shall be raised to 5l. there the Court of Chancery will relieve.[51]

In 1919 Isaacs J in the High Court of Australia described this rule as anomalous but felt obliged to apply it because it had been 'firmly established' in equity.[52] The rule was subsequently endorsed in many Australian cases,[53] albeit begrudgingly at times.[54] In short, while Australian courts disapproved of the rule as a matter of policy, they felt obliged to apply it as a matter of history. Shortly after the High Court rendered its decision in *Andrews*,

---

[47] Gray, above n 4, 17.

[48] ibid; Carter et al, above n 38, 111, 128, 132. The High Court's methodology is defended by PS Davies and PG Turner, 'Relief against Penalties without a Breach of Contract' (2013) 72 *CLJ* 20, 23–24.

[49] In particular *Cattanach v Melchior* [2003] HCA 38, (2003) 215 CLR 1 (concerning 'wrongful birth' claims); *Harriton v Stephens* [2006] HCA 15, (2006) 226 CLR 52 (concerning 'wrongful life' claims); *Tabet v Gett* [2010] HCA 12, (2010) 240 CLR 537 (concerning liability for the lost chance of a better medical outcome).

[50] Its decision in *Andrews* reflects a recent trend in the High Court of being preoccupied with doctrine and neglecting policy considerations: Carter et al, above n 38, 128–30; P Finn, 'Internationalization or Isolation: The Australian *Cul de Sac*? The Case of Contract Law' in E Bant and M Harding (eds), *Exploring Private Law* (Cambridge, Cambridge University Press, 2010) 47.

[51] *Astley v Weldon* (1801) 2 Bos & Pul 346, 353; 126 ER 1318, 1322–23 (Heath J). Lord Hatherley gave the same example in *Wallingford v Mutual Society* (1880) 5 App Cas 685 (HL) 702.

[52] *Brett v Barr Smith* (1919) 26 CLR 87, 94.

[53] See, eg, *O'Dea v Allstates Leasing System (WA) Pty Ltd* (1983) 152 CLR 359, 366–67 (Gibbs CJ), 386 (Brennan J); *Acron Pacific Ltd v Offshore Oil NL* (1985) 157 CLR 514, 518, 520; *Kowalczuk v Accom Finance Pty Ltd* [2008] NSWCA 343, (2008) 77 NSWLR 205 [162]; *Summer Hill Business Estate Pty Ltd v Equititrust Ltd* [2011] NSWCA 149 [46]–[47] (Young JA).

[54] *David Securities Pty Ltd v Commonwealth Bank of Australia* (1990) 23 FCR 1, 29; *Kellas-Sharpe v PSAL Ltd* [2012] QCA 371, [2013] 2 Qd R 233 [2]–[3]; [41]–[49]; [57]–[59].

some commentators took the view that the rule under discussion might not survive that decision.[55] In fact, Australian courts have continued to apply the rule.[56] The High Court's decision in *Andrews* has proved to be no obstacle, since that decision was solely concerned with history, not policy. The Court effectively said that, in relation to the penalty doctrine, the current law of Australia is the same as the English law of 200 years ago. As the quotation above demonstrates, the rule that the penalty doctrine does not apply where a higher interest rate is specified as the normal rate and punctual payment will lower the rate was firmly entrenched in English law 200 years ago. The survival of the rule is in line with the High Court's 'resurrection' of the old penalty law.

VI. The Penalty Doctrine in Australia after *Andrews*

It will now be investigated what the current Australian law on contractual penalties is. The first question to consider is whether there are now two rules against penalties, one at common law and one in equity, or whether there is a single 'amalgamated' rule. In its description of the current law the High Court in *Andrews* set out only one test for determining whether a contractual stipulation is a penalty.[57] This might suggest a single rule. However, the key point that the Court was at pains to make was the survival of the equitable rule against penalties *in addition to* the common law rule against penalties, the survival of which went without saying. There can be no doubt that the Court envisaged the coexistence of two rules.[58]

However, it seems to be equally clear that the Court regarded the common law rule as insignificant since it does not apply to any clause to which the equitable rule would not apply, whereas the equitable rule applies to clauses to which the common law rule does not apply, namely obligations not triggered by breach.[59] It is not entirely clear whether the Court took the view that the two rules have the same consequence, but if not, the equitable rule would prevail under the Judicature system.[60] This must include the omnipresent equitable discretion not to grant relief,[61] and established equitable defences such as

---

[55] K Dharmananda and L Firios, 'Penalties Arising without Breach: The Australian Apogee of Orthodoxy' [2013] *Lloyd's Maritime and Commercial Law Quarterly* 145, 149; P Easton, 'Penalties Percolating through the Construction Industry: Andrews v Australia and New Zealand Banking Group Ltd' (2013) 29 *Building and Construction Law Journal* 233, 245; B Taylor, 'The High Court's Expansion of the Doctrine of Penalties in Andrews v ANZ Banking Group' (2013) 28 *Australian Banking and Finance Law Bulletin* 106, 109.

[56] *Lachlan v HP Mercantile Pty Ltd* [2015] NSWCA 130 [41] (without reference to *Andrews*); *Abraham v Abraham* [2015] NSWSC 785 [39]–[40]. The need for a separate decision by the High Court to abolish the rule is seen by Heydon, Leeming and Turner, above n 2, [18-075].

[57] *Andrews v Australia and New Zealand Banking Group Ltd* [2012] HCA 30, (2012) 247 CLR 205 [10].

[58] *Paciocco v Australia and New Zealand Banking Group Ltd* [2015] FCAFC 50, (2015) 321 ALR 584 [19], [25]; *PT Thiess Contractors Indonesia v PT Arutmin Indonesia* [2015] QSC 123 [150]; E Ovey, 'Bank Charges Litigation: The View from Two Hemispheres' (2014) 29 *Butterworths Journal of International Banking and Financial Law* 435, 437. The co-existence of two rules was also assumed in *IPN Medical Centres Pty Ltd v Van Houten* [2015] QSC 204 [196].

[59] The High Court did not restrict the equitable rule to cases other than breach: *Paciocco v Australia and New Zealand Banking Group Ltd* [2014] FCA 35, (2014) 309 ALR 249 [15]; Carter et al, above n 38, 108, 114.

[60] This is implicit in *Paciocco v Australia and New Zealand Banking Group Ltd* [2015] FCAFC 50, (2015) 321 ALR 584 [27].

[61] Easton, above n 55, at 241.

acquiescence, delay and laches.[62] Thus, the common law rule adds nothing to the equitable rule, which explains why the Court set out only the equitable rule in its description of the current law.

The Court stated the penalty doctrine in the following way:

> In general terms, a stipulation prima facie imposes a penalty on a party (the first party) if, as a matter of substance, it is collateral (or accessory) to a primary stipulation in favour of a second party and this collateral stipulation, upon the failure of the primary stipulation, imposes upon the first party an additional detriment, the penalty, to the benefit of the second party. In that sense, the collateral or accessory stipulation is described as being in the nature of a security for and in terrorem of the satisfaction of the primary stipulation. If compensation can be made to the second party for the prejudice suffered by failure of the primary stipulation, the collateral stipulation and the penalty are enforced only to the extent of that compensation. The first party is relieved to that degree from liability to satisfy the collateral stipulation.[63]

Since the High Court was rejecting the breach requirement, the primary stipulation may be the occurrence or non-occurrence of a stipulated event where the promisor made no promise as to the occurrence or non-occurrence of the event.[64] Later in its judgment the Court contrasted a collateral stipulation with an alternative stipulation,[65] which contains an additional obligation as price for some service or privilege.[66] Thus, the first step in applying the new penalty doctrine in Australia is to determine whether, as a matter of substance, the impugned stipulation is an alternative stipulation or whether it is collateral (or accessory) to a primary stipulation and imposes an additional detriment upon the failure of the primary stipulation.[67] The distinction between an alternative and a collateral stipulation will be explored later in this chapter.

If the impugned stipulation is collateral and not alternative, it will be necessary to consider what the High Court observed in the passage quoted. It has been said that this passage contains a description rather than a definition and should not be used as though it was a formula to be rigidly applied.[68] That may be true. But until the High Court considers the penalty doctrine again, Australian courts are required to apply the Court's decision in *Andrews* and must carefully consider what was said in that decision.

In the passage quoted the High Court observed that a collateral stipulation is 'prima facie' a penalty.[69] The phrase 'prima facie' indicates that a collateral stipulation is not always a penalty. Therefore, once the impugned stipulation has been identified as being collateral, it is necessary to look at the factors that nonetheless prevent the stipulation from being a

---

[62] A Ottaway, 'Relief Against Penalties: The Restoration of Equity's Jurisdiction' (2013) 51(2) *Law Society Journal* 55, 58.

[63] *Andrews v Australia and New Zealand Banking Group Ltd* [2012] HCA 30, (2012) 247 CLR 205 [10] (French CJ, Gummow, Crennan, Kiefel and Bell JJ) (footnotes omitted).

[64] ibid [12], [42], [65]–[67].

[65] The Court did not actually use the phrase 'alternative stipulation', but it cited the section 'Stipulations not Penalties—Alternative Stipulations' by John Norton Pomeroy, *A Treatise on Equity Jurisprudence*, 5th edn, vol 2 (San Francisco, Bancroft-Whitney, 1941) § 437.

[66] *Andrews v Australia and New Zealand Banking Group Ltd* [2012] HCA 30, (2012) 247 CLR 205 [79]–[80].

[67] ibid [10]; *Paciocco v Australia and New Zealand Banking Group Ltd* [2015] FCAFC 50, (2015) 321 ALR 584 [199]. It has been suggested, though, that the question of whether the impugned stipulation is alternative can only be decided in the course of deciding whether it is instead a penalty or liquidated sum: Heydon, Leeming and Turner, above n 2, [18-105].

[68] *GWC Property Group Pty Ltd v Higginson* [2014] QSC 264 [37].

[69] *Andrews v Australia and New Zealand Banking Group Ltd* [2012] HCA 30, (2012) 247 CLR 205 [10].

penalty. Unfortunately, the High Court failed to set out those factors in a clear and comprehensive manner.

The Court did say that 'the penalty doctrine is not engaged if the prejudice or damage to the interests of the second party by the failure of the primary stipulation is insusceptible of evaluation and assessment in money terms'.[70] Thus, one factor preventing a collateral stipulation from being a penalty is the impossibility of compensating the promisee for the prejudice suffered as a result of the failure of the primary stipulation. It has been critically suggested that the High Court allowed difficulties in assessing loss to prevent a collateral stipulation from being a penalty.[71] However, it seems that the Court demanded more than mere difficulties of assessment.[72] The promisee's prejudice must be 'insusceptible' of evaluation in money terms. It is the nature of the prejudice that matters. An example may be the prejudice suffered by the state as a result of the delayed completion of a public infrastructure project.[73]

Some commentators take the view that the fact that the promisee's prejudice is insusceptible of evaluation in money terms is the only factor that can prevent a collateral stipulation from being a penalty.[74] If this was correct, a collateral stipulation could never be enforced beyond the promisee's actual loss where that loss can be assessed in money terms, even if the stipulation constitutes a genuine pre-estimate of the promisee's loss in the event that the primary stipulation fails.

However, the High Court in *Andrews* also made the following observation:

> The formulation of that distinction between a penalty and a pre-estimate of liquidated damages which was made by Lord Dunedin in *Dunlop* has been described as a product of centuries of equity jurisprudence. It was recently applied by this court in *Ringrow Pty Ltd v BP Australia Pty Ltd*. But the present dispute requires attention at an anterior stage of analysis, namely identification of those criteria by which the penalty doctrine is engaged.[75]

This passage indicates a second factor preventing a collateral stipulation from being a penalty.[76] The High Court was saying that its decision in *Andrews* was concerned only with

---

[70]   ibid [11] (French CJ, Gummow, Crennan, Kiefel and Bell JJ), citing as example *Waterside Workers' Federation of Australia v Stewart* (1919) 27 CLR 119. This statement has been described as 'critical to the tempering of the [penalty] doctrine's future development': Easton, above n 55, 238–39.

[71]   Carter et al, above n 38, 122.

[72]   See *Paciocco v Australia and New Zealand Banking Group Ltd* [2014] FCA 35, (2014) 309 ALR 249 [46]–[47].

[73]   Philip Davenport and Helen Durham, *Construction Claims*, 3rd edn (Annandale, Federation Press, 2013) 132–33; Heydon, Leeming and Turner, above n 2, [18-160]. Thus, the enforceability of a clause obliging a contractor in a public infrastructure project to pay a certain amount per day of delay follows simply from the impossibility of calculating loss of public utility, and need not be based on a characterisation of the clause as a genuine pre-estimate of loss, although the latter approach was taken in *Philips Hong Kong Ltd v The Attorney-General of Hong Kong* (1993) 61 BLR 41 (PC) 60; *State of Tasmania v Leighton Contractors Pty Ltd* [2005] TASSC 133, (2005) 15 Tas R 243 (FC) [38].

[74]   Philip Davenport, 'Andrews v ANZ and Penalty Clauses' (2012) Issue 147 *Australian Construction Law Newsletter* 32, 34; Philip Davenport, 'A Possible End to Time-Bar Clauses: The Penalty Doctrine and Construction Contracts' (2013) 51(2) *Law Society Journal* 58; Davenport and Durham, *Construction Claims*, above n 73, 314–25; Ludmilla K Robinson, 'Fees? Not So Simple: *Andrews and Ors v Australia New Zealand Banking Group Ltd* [2012] HCA 30 (6 September 2012)' (2012) 16 *University of Western Sydney Law Review* 161, 165–66, 172–73.

[75]   *Andrews v Australia and New Zealand Banking Group Ltd* [2012] HCA 30, (2012) 247 CLR 205 [15] (French CJ, Gummow, Crennan, Kiefel and Bell JJ) (footnotes omitted).

[76]   *Zomojo Pty Ltd v Hurd (No 2)* [2012] FCA 1458, (2012) 299 ALR 621 [459]; *Paciocco v Australia and New Zealand Banking Group Ltd* [2015] FCAFC 50, (2015) 321 ALR 584 [22], [25]; *PT Thiess Contractors Indonesia v PT Arutmin Indonesia* [2015] QSC 123 [181]; R Manly, 'Breach No Longer Necessary: The High

the type of clause which falls within the scope of the rule against penalties, and that its decision was not to affect the rules laid down in *Dunlop Pneumatic Tyre Co Ltd v New Garage and Motor Co Ltd* ('*Dunlop*')[77] and *Ringrow Pty Ltd v BP Australia Pty Ltd* ('*Ringrow*')[78] in relation to the circumstances in which a clause that falls within the scope of the rule against penalties is in fact a penalty. Those two cases concerned the way in which the penalty doctrine is to be applied in cases of breach.

In *Dunlop* Lord Dunedin laid down the following rules.[79] A sum of money to be paid by a contract-breaker in the event of breach is a penalty unless it constitutes a genuine pre-estimate (as at the time of the making of the contract) of the loss likely to be suffered by the other party as a result of the breach. A genuine pre-estimation is presumed to be absent where the sum is extravagant and unconscionable in amount compared to the greatest loss that could conceivably follow from the breach. The fact that a precise pre-estimation of the loss was almost impossible at the time of the making of the contract does not prevent the stipulated sum from being a genuine pre-estimate but makes it in fact probable[80] that the sum is a genuine pre-estimate.

In *Ringrow* the High Court of Australia proceeded on the basis, not challenged by either party, that the *Dunlop* test continued to apply in Australia,[81] but the Court added that an agreed sum is not a penalty unless it is 'extravagant and unconscionable in amount'[82] and 'out of all proportion to damage likely to be suffered as a result of breach'.[83] The Court also confirmed that an obligation other than one to pay money (eg an obligation to transfer property) may constitute a penalty.[84]

The High Court's observation in *Andrews* that all those rules continue to apply means at least that they continue to apply in the circumstances for which they were pronounced in *Dunlop* and *Ringrow*, namely where the event triggering the impugned obligation is a breach of contract.[85] What is not entirely clear is whether the Court was prescribing an application of the rules (necessarily in a modified form) also in cases in which the event triggering the impugned obligation is not a breach of contract. The Court's reference to 'liquidated damages' in the last passage quoted may suggest that it was not, for the term

---

Court's Reconsideration of the Penalty Doctrine' (2013) 41 *Australian Business Law Review* 314, 322; B Mason, 'Revitalising a Withered Vine: Equity's Penalty Doctrine' [2013] *Lloyd's Maritime and Commercial Law* Quarterly 233, 246. See also J Bond, 'Contrary to What You Might Have Heard, a Properly Drafted Contractual Time Bar Will Not Attract the Penalty Doctrine' [2013] *The Arbitrator and Mediator* 69, 71; Andrew Chew, David Starkoff and Mark Sheldon, 'The Effect of Andrews v ANZ: Going beyond Bank Fees—It's about Performance Too!' [2013] *International Construction Law Review* 187, 197; Davies and Turner, above n 48, 23; Easton, above n 55, 246; Jeffrey Goldberger, 'Australian Contract Law: A Case Law Update' (2012–13) 26 *Commercial Law Quarterly* 8, 28; Steven Klimt and Narelle Smythe, 'When Is a Penalty Clause Not a Penalty Clause' (2012) 146 *Australian Construction Law Newsletter* 51; Alex Ottaway, 'Relief Against Penalties: The Restoration of Equity's Jurisdiction' (2013) 51(2) *Law Society Journal* 55, 58; Ovey, above n 58, 437; Taylor, above n 55, 109.

[77] *Dunlop Pneumatic Tyre Co Ltd v New Garage and Motor Co Ltd* [1915] AC 79 (HL).
[78] *Ringrow Pty Ltd v BP Australia Pty Ltd* [2005] HCA 71, (2005) 224 CLR 656.
[79] *Dunlop Pneumatic Tyre Co Ltd v New Garage and Motor Co Ltd* [1915] AC 79 (HL) 86–88.
[80] But not inevitable: *Zomojo Pty Ltd v Hurd (No 2)* [2012] FCA 1458, (2012) 299 ALR 621 [461].
[81] *Ringrow Pty Ltd v BP Australia Pty Ltd* [2005] HCA 71, (2005) 224 CLR 656 [12].
[82] ibid [32] (Gleeson CJ, Gummow, Kirby, Hayne, Callinan and Heydon JJ).
[83] ibid [27] (Gleeson CJ, Gummow, Kirby, Hayne, Callinan and Heydon JJ), quoting *AMEV-UDC Finance Ltd v Austin* (1986) 162 CLR 170, 190 (Mason and Wilson JJ).
[84] *Ringrow Pty Ltd v BP Australia Pty Ltd* [2005] HCA 71, (2005) 224 CLR 656 [21].
[85] *Director of Consumer Affairs v Tassoni* [2014] VSC 21 [15], [25]; *GWC Property Group Pty Ltd v Higginson* [2014] QSC 264 [39]; *Grocon Constructors (Qld) Pty Ltd v Juniper Developer No 2 Pty Ltd* [2015] QSC 102 [54]–[63]; *IPN Medical Centres Pty Ltd v Van Houten* [2015] QSC 204 [197].

'damages' denotes a response to a breach of contract (or other civil wrong).[86] However, in the same passage, the Court described the rules as 'a product of centuries of equity jurisprudence', and the Court did not regard the equitable rule against penalties as being confined to cases of breach.

It is more likely that the High Court in *Andrews* was prescribing an application of the *Dunlop* and *Ringrow* rules whenever equity's penalty doctrine is engaged.[87] But those rules must then be modified in cases in which the event triggering the impugned obligation is not a breach of contract. Since there may be no breach in those cases, the amount that serves as reference point in deciding the question of proportionality cannot be the loss likely to result from breach, but must be the loss likely to result from the failure of the primary stipulation.[88]

It is further necessary to look at the dates as at which the elements discussed are to be determined. As already mentioned, *Dunlop* laid down that the question of whether the impugned stipulation is a genuine pre-estimate of the promisee's loss is to be determined as at the date of the contract. This rule continues to apply in Australia after *Andrews*.[89] The question of whether the impugned stipulation is alternative or collateral must also be determined as at the date of the contract.[90]

It has been suggested that the question of whether the prejudice suffered by the promisee as a result of the failure of the primary stipulation is susceptible of assessment in money terms must also be determined as at the date of the contract.[91] However, the High Court in *Andrews* said that '[i]t is the availability of compensation which generates the "equity" upon which the court intervenes; without it, the parties are left to their legal rights and obligations'.[92] This should mean that if, at the time of the trial, the promisee's prejudice is insusceptible of assessment in money terms, the equity upon which the court relieves against penalties is not generated. Thus, a clause cannot be classified as a penalty where an assessment of the promisee's prejudice in money terms was possible at the time of the contract but has become impossible by the time of the trial. In those circumstances, it is not feasible to apply the consequence of the penalty doctrine (identical at common law and in equity), which is the unenforceability of the impugned stipulation beyond the amount

---

[86] *F & K Jabbour v Custodian of Israeli Absentee Property* [1954] 1 WLR 139, 143–44; *Cassell & Co Ltd v Broome* [1972] AC 1027 (HL) 1070 (Lord Hailsham LC); Harvey McGregor, *McGregor on Damages*, 19th edn (London, Sweet & Maxwell, 2014) [1-001], [1-004].

[87] *Cedar Meats (Aust) Pty Ltd v Five Star Lamb* [2014] VSCA 32 [52]; *Paciocco v Australia and New Zealand Banking Group Ltd* [2015] FCAFC 50, (2015) 321 ALR 584 [22], [25]; Mason, above n 76, 246.

[88] *Paciocco v Australia and New Zealand Banking Group Ltd* [2015] FCAFC 50, (2015) 321 ALR 584 [25], [95]; Ottaway, above n 76, 57.

[89] *Paciocco v Australia and New Zealand Banking Group Ltd* [2015] FCAFC 50, (2015) 321 ALR 584 [95], [147]; *Director of Consumer Affairs v Tassoni* [2014] VSC 21 [25]; *GWC Property Group Pty Ltd v Higginson* [2014] QSC 264 [39].

[90] See *Paciocco v Australia and New Zealand Banking Group Ltd* [2015] FCAFC 50, (2015) 321 ALR 584 [23]–[24], [199]; Heydon, Leeming and Turner, above n 2, [18-105].

[91] Bond, above n 76, 71, 74; Andrew P Downie, 'Time Bars after Andrews v ANZ' (2014) 30 *Building and Construction Law Journal* 7, 17; D Dragovic, M Cole and C Woo, 'Are Time Bars Unenforceable as Penalties—The Importance of Looking at the Contract as a Whole' (2014) Issue 154 *Australian Construction Law Newsletter* 18, 20; RJ Manly, 'Substance over Form: Australia's Highest Court Reconsiders the Penalty Doctrine' (2013) 7 *Construction Law International* 19, 24. Perhaps also *Paciocco v Australia and New Zealand Banking Group Ltd* [2014] FCA 35, (2014) 309 ALR 249 [46].

[92] *Andrews v Australia and New Zealand Banking Group Ltd* [2012] HCA 30, (2012) 247 CLR 205 [11] (French CJ, Gummow, Crennan, Kiefel and Bell JJ).

of the promisee's actual loss. Conversely, where an assessment of the promisee's prejudice in money terms was impossible at the time of the contract but has become possible by the time of the trial, the clause is capable of being classified as a penalty. However, in those circumstances, it will be difficult to show that the impugned clause does not constitute a genuine pre-estimate of the promisee's loss.

The High Court's outline of the equitable penalty doctrine may thus be distilled into the following algorithm.[93] It must first be asked whether the impugned stipulation is alternative or collateral. If it is alternative, it cannot be a penalty. If it is collateral, it must be asked whether the prejudice suffered by the promisee as a result of the failure of the primary stipulation is susceptible of evaluation in money terms at the time of trial. If it is not, the impugned stipulation cannot be a penalty. If it is, it must be asked whether the impugned obligation is extravagant and unconscionable and out of all proportion to a genuine pre-estimate of the loss likely to be suffered by the promisee as a result of the failure of the primary stipulation. This is judged as at the time of the contract.

Prior to *Andrews*, the High Court of Australia had said that a penalty clause is wholly unenforceable or void.[94] That approach leaves the promisee with an entitlement to damages assessed under common law principles.[95] In *Andrews* the Court said that a collateral stipulation that constitutes a penalty is to be enforced (only) to the extent of the loss suffered by the promisee as a result of the failure of the primary stipulation.[96] But the Court also approved a statement, made in an earlier case,[97] that equity would not award to the promisee an amount greater than that awarded as common law damages.[98] Nevertheless, where the failure of the primary stipulation does not involve a breach of contract by the promisor, the penalty clause provides the promisee with an entitlement to compensation that might not exist in the absence of the clause.[99] Since equitable relief is always at the discretion of the courts, the High Court's pronouncement as to the consequence of classifying a clause as a penalty can only be a general rule. A court must be able to tailor relief against a penalty clause to the circumstances of the individual case.[100]

Furthermore, the rule that a penalty clause be partially enforced works only for obligations to pay money. The High Court in *Andrews* emphasised that a detriment other than an obligation to pay money may constitute a penalty,[101] but said nothing on the consequences of classifying such a detriment as a penalty. It is therefore unclear whether the promisor

---

[93]   See *Zomojo Pty Ltd v Hurd (No 2)* [2012] FCA 1458, (2012) 299 ALR 621 [459].

[94]   *IAC (Leasing) Ltd v Humphrey* (1972) 126 CLR 131, 142 (Walsh J); *Pigram v Attorney-General (NSW)* (1975) 132 CLR 216, 221, 230; *O'Dea v Allstates Leasing System (WA) Pty Ltd* (1983) 152 CLR 359, 372 (Gibbs CJ); *AMEV-UDC Finance Ltd v Austin* (1986) 162 CLR 170, 192; *Ringrow Pty Ltd v BP Australia Pty Ltd* [2005] HCA 71, (2005) 224 CLR 656 [14].

[95]   *Scandinavian Trading Tanker Co AB v Flota Petrolera Ecuatoriana* [1983] 2 AC 694 (HL) 702; *GWC Property Group Pty Ltd v Higginson* [2014] QSC 264 [42].

[96]   *Andrews v Australia and New Zealand Banking Group Ltd* [2012] HCA 30, (2012) 247 CLR 205 [10]. The loss may include the costs of demanding payment, including the costs of the proceedings: *Paciocco v Australia and New Zealand Banking Group Ltd* [2014] FCA 35, (2014) 309 ALR 249 [48], citing *Johnes v Johnes* (1814) 3 Dow 1, 20; 3 ER 969, 975 (HL).

[97]   *AMEV-UDC Finance Ltd v Austin* (1986) 162 CLR 170, 190 (Mason and Wilson JJ).

[98]   *Andrews v Australia and New Zealand Banking Group Ltd* [2012] HCA 30, (2012) 247 CLR 205 [65]. See *GWC Property Group Pty Ltd v Higginson* [2014] QSC 264 [46]–[48].

[99]   Carter et al, above n 38, 115–16.

[100]   Davies and Turner, above n 48, 23. The court may combine relief against a penalty with an order of specific relief against the promisor: Heydon, Leeming and Turner, above n 2, [18-200].

[101]   *Andrews v Australia and New Zealand Banking Group Ltd* [2012] HCA 30, (2012) 247 CLR 205 [12].

can free herself from the impugned obligation by offering compensation in money to the promisee, or whether the promisee can enforce the impugned obligation if she offers to pay the amount by which the value of the promisor's performance exceeds the promisee's loss. This is a matter of the court using its discretion to tailor equitable relief to the circumstances of the individual case.

Prior to *Andrews*, Australian courts had said that the promisor bears the onus of proving that the impugned clause is a penalty.[102] The High Court in *Andrews* said nothing expressly on that matter. There can be no doubt that the promisor must prove that the impugned stipulation is collateral and not alternative, and that it is extravagant and unconscionable and out of all proportion to a genuine pre-estimate of the loss likely to be suffered by the promisee as a result of the failure of the primary stipulation.[103] It seems that the promisor must also prove that the prejudice suffered by the promisee as a result of the failure of the primary stipulation is susceptible of evaluation and assessment in money terms. As mentioned before, the High Court in *Andrews* declared that: 'It is the availability of compensation which generates the "equity" upon which the court intervenes; without it, the parties are left to their legal rights and obligations.'[104]

Less clear is the onus of proof in relation to the amount of loss actually suffered by the promisee as a result of the failure of the primary stipulation. Since the High Court's decision in *Andrews*, two trial judges have expressed different views on this issue. Gordon J in *Paciocco* placed the onus upon the promisee,[105] but the opposite view was taken in another case.[106] Since the promisee is usually in a much better position than the promisor to provide evidence on the promisee's circumstances, the promisee ought to bear at least some evidentiary obligations.[107]

VII. The Distinction Between Alternative and Collateral Stipulations

As mentioned earlier, a key question under the penalty doctrine as enunciated by the High Court of Australia in *Andrews* is whether the impugned obligation is alternative or collateral. This issue will now be explored.

All that the High Court said in that respect is that a collateral stipulation imposes an additional detriment upon the failure of the primary stipulation,[108] whereas an alternative

---

[102] *Multiplex Constructions Pty Ltd v Abgarus Pty Ltd* (1992) 33 NSWLR 504 (SC) 527.

[103] *Active Tree Services Pty Ltd v Electrical Resource Providers Pty Ltd* [2014] WASCA 6 [19]–[20]; *Paciocco v Australia and New Zealand Banking Group Ltd* [2015] FCAFC 50, (2015) 321 ALR 584 [148], [230]. The parol evidence rule does not apply in this context: *Paciocco v Australia and New Zealand Banking Group Ltd* [2015] FCAFC 50, (2015) 321 ALR 584 [209], [212], [225]; *Grocon Constructors (Qld) Pty Ltd v Juniper Developer No 2 Pty Ltd* [2015] QSC 102 [116].

[104] *Andrews v Australia and New Zealand Banking Group Ltd* [2012] HCA 30, (2012) 247 CLR 205 [11] (French CJ, Gummow, Crennan, Kiefel and Bell JJ).

[105] *Paciocco v Australia and New Zealand Banking Group Ltd* [2014] FCA 35, (2014) 309 ALR 249 [48]. The Full Court of the Federal Court of Australia did not address the issue.

[106] *Love v Brien* [2012] WASC 457 [68].

[107] Mason, above n 76, 233, 252.

[108] *Andrews v Australia and New Zealand Banking Group Ltd* [2012] HCA 30, (2012) 247 CLR 205 [10]. An example is the retrospective increase in rent on the termination of a lease by the landlord for breach by the tenant: *GWC Property Group Pty Ltd v Higginson* [2014] QSC 264 [37].

stipulation contains an additional obligation as the price for some service or privilege.[109] The court said[110] that the distinction is illustrated by the decision of the majority in the New South Wales Court of Appeal in *Metro-Goldwyn-Mayer Pty Ltd v Greenham* ('*Greenham*').[111] That case, which had never been judicially cited prior to *Andrews*, will now be scrutinised.

A distributor of films and the owner of a cinema (the 'exhibitor') entered into two contracts for the hire of certain films for certain periods. Both contracts contained the same standard terms, which provided as follows. The exhibitor 'shall' exhibit the films in his cinema at the times specified in the relevant contract, and 'shall not' exhibit a film at any other place or time without the distributor's written consent. If the exhibitor without such consent exhibits a film at a place or time not authorised by the relevant contract, the exhibitor shall pay as hire for each such exhibition four times the amount of the normal hire. The distributor may terminate the contract if the exhibitor commits any breach of the contract in relation to (among others) the time or place at which a film may or may not be used.

On 12 occasions, without the distributor's written consent, the exhibitor exhibited films at times not authorised by the contract. The distributor claimed an amount of four times the normal hire for each of those screenings. The exhibitor argued that the obligation to pay four times the normal hire was an unenforceable penalty.

The trial judge agreed with that argument. So did Wallace P in the New South Wales Court of Appeal, who reasoned as follows.[112] The standard terms obliged the exhibitor not to exhibit films at a place or time not authorised by the contract. That obligation could be enforced through an injunction. The exhibitor did not have an option to exhibit films at other places or times. Such an option was inconsistent with the distributor's right to terminate the agreement in the case of unauthorised screenings. Since the obligation to pay four times the normal hire was not a genuine pre-estimate of the distributor's loss, it was a penalty.

The other two appellate judges held that the penalty doctrine was not engaged. Jacobs JA opined that the exhibitor had an option to show the film at additional times for an additional hiring fee, even though it may have been intended that additional showings were 'strongly discouraged'.[113] He pointed out that the day and place of exhibition goes to the whole root of a contract for the exhibition of films.[114] Holmes JA opined that additional showings were 'covered by the agreement' and not a breach of it,[115] although they could have been prevented through an injunction.[116] The distributor had the choice between preventing additional showings through an injunction and claiming the increased hire.[117]

Thus, of the four judges involved at the two instances in *Greenham*, only two opined that the impugned clause was not a penalty, and those two judges gave different reasons. Yet, it is

---

[109] *Andrews v Australia and New Zealand Banking Group Ltd* [2012] HCA 30, (2012) 247 CLR 205 [79]–[80]. In *Paciocco v Australia and New Zealand Banking Group Ltd* [2015] FCAFC 50, (2015) 321 ALR 584 [401], Middleton J seems to have additionally required for a stipulation to be alternative that it is not out of all proportion to the attainment of the benefit or right for the promisor. This cannot be right as it requires courts to assess the adequacy of consideration.

[110] *Andrews v Australia and New Zealand Banking Group Ltd* [2012] HCA 30, (2012) 247 CLR 205 [80], [82].

[111] *Metro-Goldwyn-Mayer Pty Ltd v Greenham* [1966] 2 NSWR 717 (CA).

[112] ibid 719–21.

[113] ibid 723.

[114] ibid.

[115] ibid 726.

[116] ibid 727.

[117] ibid.

the reasons of those two judgments that the High Court in *Andrews* referred to as the source of guidance in distinguishing between alternative and collateral stipulations. Unfortunately, the reasons of both judgments are problematic.

Jacobs JA in *Greenham* opined that the exhibitor had enjoyed the option of conducting additional showings for an increased hire. In the terminology used by the High Court in *Andrews* Jacobs JA classified the payment of an increased hire as an alternative to the prohibition of additional showings. The problem is that he also observed that the purpose of the significant increase in hire may have been to 'strongly discourage' additional showings. This comes close to saying that the increased hire was a security for, and in terrorem of, the adherence to the number of showings set out in the contract. But this is exactly how the High Court in *Andrews* described a collateral stipulation.

Even more problematic are the reasons given by Holmes JA in *Greenham*, who opined that additional showings were not a breach of contract even though they could have been prevented through an injunction. This makes no sense. Additional showings could not have been prevented through an injunction unless the exhibitor was obliged not to run additional showings. But if such an obligation existed, additional showings constituted a breach of contract.

It is not necessary here to form a conclusive view on whether the obligation to pay four times the normal hire in *Greenham* should or should not have been classified as a penalty under the law as it was then understood to be. Suffice to say that the reasons given by the majority in the New South Wales Court of Appeal cannot be described as manifestly more persuasive than those given by Wallace P. It is ironic that the High Court in *Andrews*, in a decision intended to widen the scope of the penalty doctrine, said that guidance as to the scope ought to be taken from two previous judgments that were arguably wrong in not applying the penalty doctrine even in the narrow scope that the doctrine was thought to have at the time of those judgments.[118]

One consequence of restricting the penalty doctrine to cases of breach is the possibility of circumventing the doctrine by using the form of an option to achieve the same purpose as a penalty clause.[119] It might be thought that the High Court's rejection of the breach requirement removed that possibility of circumvention. But this is put in doubt[120] by the fact that the High Court expressly endorsed the judgments of Jacobs JA and Holmes JA in *Greenham* and quoted[121] Jacobs JA's reference to an option.[122] It has been suggested that 'contract drafters, in seeking to evade the application of the new penalties doctrine, will simply exchange one set of drafting techniques for another',[123] and that 'the overall effect of the High Court's decision entrenches, rather than removes, the importance of form'.[124]

---

[118] Carter et al, above n 38, 127.

[119] See S Harder, 'The Relevance of Breach to the Applicability of the Rule against Penalties' (2013) 30 *Journal of Contract Law* 52, 56–58.

[120] Easton, above n 55, 240.

[121] *Andrews v Australia and New Zealand Banking Group Ltd* [2012] HCA 30, (2012) 247 CLR 205 [82].

[122] *Metro-Goldwyn-Mayer Pty Ltd v Greenham* [1966] 2 NSWR 717, 723.

[123] Carter et al, above n 38, 125. See also E Peel, 'The Rule against Penalties' (2013) 129 *LQR* 152, 155; P Saprai, 'The Penalties Rule and the Promise Theory of Contract' (2013) 26 *Canadian Journal of Law and Jurisprudence* 443, 464 n 60.

[124] Chew, Starkoff and Sheldon, above n 76, at 200.

On the other hand, the High Court in *Andrews* described the first step in the penalty enquiry as the question of whether, 'as a matter of substance',[125] the impugned stipulation is collateral to a primary stipulation. The phrase 'as a matter of substance' indicates that substance must prevail over form.[126] The problem is that the courts have always said that substance prevails over form in distinguishing an indulgence or option from a penalty,[127] yet form has often prevailed. It is therefore difficult to determine whether the High Court's decision will change the classification of any type of clause that had previously been classified as providing an option. A negative answer is suggested by the fact that the Full Court of the Federal Court of Australia has since classified as alternative stipulations exactly those types of bank fees that Gordon J in her first decision in the *Andrews/ Paciocco* litigation had classified as providing an option. It remains to be seen how the High Court itself will classify the fees if and when the matter comes before it.

The problem may be illustrated by looking at the facts of *Ange v First East Auction Holdings Pty Ltd* ('*Ange*'),[128] decided prior to *Andrews*. The defendant agreed to consign certain paintings to the plaintiff, an auctioneer of fine art, for sale by auction. The contract required the defendant to pay a 'withdrawal fee' if she withdrew the paintings from sale, the amount of the fee rising with the passing of time between the making of the contract and the withdrawal. The defendant withdrew the paintings from sale, and the plaintiff demanded payment of the withdrawal fee. Regarding the penalty doctrine as being confined to cases of breach (as it was then understood to be),[129] the trial judge held the penalty doctrine inapplicable on the ground that the withdrawal of the paintings from auction had not constituted a breach by the defendant since the contract had not prohibited the defendant from withdrawing the paintings.[130] The plaintiff's appeal was dismissed.[131]

It might be thought that, on the same facts, the penalty doctrine would be engaged today since the trial judge placed emphasis on the absence of breach and since the penalty doctrine is no longer confined to cases of breach. However, the structure of the contract in *Ange* is similar to that of the contract in *Greenham*. Following the majority's approach in the latter case, it may well be argued today that a withdrawal fee such as that present in *Ange* is not a collateral stipulation but is an alternative stipulation that contains an additional obligation for a service or accommodation, namely the right to withdraw.[132] If the High Court's endorsement of the majority's approach in *Greenham* is taken seriously, a withdrawal fee such as that present in *Ange* will still be outside the scope of the penalty doctrine.[133]

---

[125] *Andrews v Australia and New Zealand Banking Group Ltd* [2012] HCA 30, (2012) 247 CLR 205 [10] (French CJ, Gummow, Crennan, Kiefel and Bell JJ).

[126] Equity examines the parties' real intentions: Heydon, Leeming and Turner, above n 2, [18-105].

[127] See, eg, *O'Dea v Allstates Leasing System (WA) Pty Ltd* (1983) 152 CLR 359, 368 (Gibbs CJ), 400 (Deane J); *Acron Pacific Ltd v Offshore Oil NL* (1985) 157 CLR 514, 520 (Deane J); *David Securities Pty Ltd v Commonwealth Bank of Australia* (1990) 23 FCR 1, 28–29.

[128] *Ange v First East Auction Holdings Pty Ltd* [2011] VSCA 335, (2011) 284 ALR 638.

[129] *First East Auction Holdings Pty Ltd v Ange* [2010] VSC 72 [157]–[158].

[130] ibid [152]–[153].

[131] *Ange v First East Auction Holdings Pty Ltd* [2011] VSCA 335, (2011) 284 ALR 638 [85]–[95]. The trial judge and the Victorian Court of Appeal did take different views on whether the amount of the withdrawal fee was out of all proportion to a genuine pre-estimate of the plaintiff's loss.

[132] The opposite view is taken by Manly, above n 76.

[133] See also K Barnett, 'Bank Fees May Be Illegal Penalties' (2012) 37 *Alternative Law Journal* 283: 'Although the judgment appears to be an expansion of the previous law, it may be that its effect is less radical than it first appears, because of the exception carved out for "alternative stipulations".'

By contrast, a different outcome may today be reached on facts such as those present in *Acron Pacific Ltd v Offshore Oil NL*.[134] A group of companies owed money to a group of creditors. In order to settle a dispute about the terms of the debts, the creditors and the debtors entered into a deed (the moratorium deed) in which the debtors acknowledged that the debts were owing and unconditionally repayable on demand, and agreed to pay interest at a certain commercial rate. The creditors promised not to enforce the debts during the moratorium, which was one year unless terminated earlier. The moratorium was to terminate on the happening of any of certain events, one of which was the giving of notice of termination by a creditor in the event of breach by a debtor. Breaches occurred, and the creditors gave notice of termination three months after the date of the deed. The debtors argued that the clause that permitted a creditor to terminate the moratorium in the event of breach by a debtor was an unenforceable penalty clause since it provided for the same consequence regardless of the gravity of the breach.

The High Court of Australia regarded the penalty doctrine as inapplicable on the ground that the creditors had given a 'qualified indulgence', an indulgence qualified by the right to terminate for breach.[135] The Court was saying, in other words, that the penalty doctrine did not apply because the creditors, instead of providing a qualified indulgence, had been free not to provide any indulgence at all. This argument is problematic since it could be applied to any clause that is alleged to constitute a penalty. It could always be said that the promisee, instead of entering into the contract with the impugned clause, was free not to enter into the contract at all. Today, in the wake of the High Court's decision in *Andrews*, a clause such as that present in *Acron Pacific Ltd v Offshore Oil NL* may engage the penalty doctrine. It is arguable that the clause permitting termination of the moratorium is a collateral stipulation, the primary stipulation being the debtors' obligations under the moratorium deed. The clause on its own cannot be an alternative stipulation since there is no additional service or accommodation. The only way of avoiding an application of the penalty doctrine today is to attach the label 'alternative stipulation' to the whole 'package' consisting of the indulgence and its qualification. This is what the High Court in *Acron Pacific* effectively did. But it is unclear whether this approach is still permitted after *Andrews*.

An important effect of the High Court's decision in *Andrews* is that the impugned clause can no longer be classified as involving an option or indulgence on the mere ground that there is no obligation, and thus no breach, on the part of the promisor. *Andrews* requires an examination of the commercial context of the impugned clause. This may have an impact, for example, on the classification of 'take or pay' clauses, which involve the following circumstances. The promisee promises to supply periodically to the promisor certain goods in an amount requested by the promisor for the relevant period, and the promisor promises to pay a certain price per item on each delivery. It is envisaged that the promisor will order a certain minimum quantity in each period, and a clause in the contract provides that the promisor must pay the price for the minimum quantity even in a period in which the promisor ordered no goods or less than the minimum quantity.

In England and Wales, where the penalty doctrine is still confined to cases of breach, the applicability of the doctrine to a 'take or pay' clause depends solely upon whether the promisor is obliged to order at least the minimum amount in each period, in which case

---

[134]   *Acron Pacific Ltd v Offshore Oil NL* (1985) 157 CLR 514.
[135]   ibid 519 (Mason ACJ, Wilson, Brennan and Dawson JJ).

the doctrine is engaged,[136] or whether the promisor is obliged to pay at least the price of the minimum quantity without being obliged to order the minimum quantity, in which case the penalty doctrine is not engaged.[137]

In the wake of *Andrews* an Australian court today cannot deny the applicability of the penalty doctrine to a 'take or pay' clause on the mere ground that the promisor was not contractually obliged to order a minimum quantity.[138] This is demonstrated by the post-*Andrews* case *Cedar Meats Pty Ltd v Five Star Lamb Pty Ltd*.[139] The plaintiff, which operated an abattoir, agreed to provide the defendant, a producer of lamb, with manufacturing, processing and packaging services for lamb products. The contract set out daily volumes of lamb to be provided by the defendant and the price per head to be paid by the defendant. A clause in the contract (the 'minimum payment clause') provided that if daily volume fell more than 25 per cent below the agreed daily volume, the defendant would pay a minimum of 75 per cent of the agreed daily volume and price for those days. When the defendant delivered less than 75 per cent of the agreed daily volume, the plaintiff sought to enforce the minimum payment clause. The defendant argued, inter alia, that this clause was a penalty.

Under English law, the applicability of the penalty doctrine in those circumstances would depend solely upon whether the defendant was obliged to deliver at least 75 per cent of the agreed daily volume or whether the defendant was obliged to pay for 75 per cent of the agreed daily volume without being obliged to deliver it. Sifris J in the Supreme Court of Victoria did not take that approach but asked, following *Andrews*, whether the minimum payment clause was collateral to secure performance of a primary obligation or whether it was a payment in return for the provision of further services or accommodation.[140] In that context, he examined the commercial context of the minimum payment clause.[141]

Sifris J observed that the cost of new equipment which the plaintiff had acquired to fulfil the contract with the defendant had been low and had already been reflected in the price per head to be paid by the defendant. The upfront costs were low while the operational costs were high. He contrasted this with a gas supply contract where the upfront costs (of laying the pipeline) are very high and the operational costs are very low. He classified the minimum payment clause in the instant case as a collateral stipulation and eventually as a penalty, having found that the payment to be made by the defendant under the clause greatly exceeded the loss suffered by the plaintiff as a result of the shortfall in delivery, since the clause took no account of the significant cost savings flowing from the shortfall.[142]

---

[136] *M & J Polymers Ltd v Imerys Minerals Ltd* [2008] EWHC 344 (Comm), [2008] 1 Lloyd's Rep 541 [41], [44]; *E-Nik Ltd v Department for Communities and Local Government* [2012] EWHC 3027 (Comm), [2013] 2 All ER (Comm) 868 [25]. These decisions are criticised by B Holland and PS Ashley, 'Enforceability of Take-or-Pay Provisions in English Law Contracts—Revisited' (2013) 31 *Journal of Energy and Natural Resources Law* 205, 211–17.

[137] *Associated British Ports v Ferryways NV* [2008] EWHC 1265 (Comm), [2008] 2 Lloyd's Rep 353 [17], [50]; affirmed, without discussion of the issue, in [2009] EWCA Civ 189, [2009] 1 Lloyd's Rep 595.

[138] Dharmananda and Firios, above n 55, 148.

[139] *Cedar Meats Pty Ltd v Five Star Lamb Pty Ltd* [2013] VSC 164; rev'd on other grounds [2014] VSCA 32.

[140] *Cedar Meats Pty Ltd v Five Star Lamb Pty Ltd* [2013] VSC 164 [103]–[104].

[141] ibid [108].

[142] ibid [107]. The Victorian Court of Appeal left the issue of excessiveness open, but also took the view that the minimum payment clause was a collateral stipulation, and the penalty doctrine thus engaged, whether or not there was an actual obligation to deliver 75% of the agreed daily volume: [2014] VSCA 32 [51].

VIII. The Possible Impact of *Andrews* on Certain Common Clauses

In *Andrews* the High Court of Australia said that every 'collateral' stipulation is prima facie a penalty. Some commentators fear that certain clauses which are common in practice and, prior to *Andrews*, had been thought to be outside the scope of the penalty doctrine may now have to pass the 'genuine pre-estimate of loss' test to be enforceable. This fear is unwarranted insofar as it overlooks that factors other than being a genuine pre-estimate of loss may prevent a collateral stipulation from being a penalty, in particular the insusceptibility of assessing in money terms the prejudice suffered by the promisee as a result of the failure of the primary stipulation.[143]

One clause under discussion is a clause that entitles the promisee in a certain event (in particular breach of contract by the promisor) to withhold a performance which would otherwise be due. Some commentators have suggested that such a clause may constitute a collateral stipulation and thus prima facie a penalty.[144] It is necessary to distinguish three types of clause. The first type provides that in the event of termination of the contract the promisor loses rights not yet accrued at the time of termination. Such a clause is incapable of being a penalty because it merely restates the effect of termination under the general law.[145]

The second type of clause purports to deprive the promisor of a right already accrued. Prior to *Andrews*, it had been established that such a clause is capable of being a penalty.[146] Many of the cases in which this rule was laid down involved clauses in contracts for construction work which purported to deprive the (sub)contractor of part of the accrued fee in the event of delay or breach in general.[147] Some cases involved other types of contract.[148] A clause that purports to deprive the promisor of a right already accrued remains capable of being a penalty in Australia after *Andrews*.

The third type of clause provides that a certain right of the promisor does not accrue until the occurrence of a certain event, for example the completion of work by the promisor. In other words, the clause makes the relevant event a condition precedent of the promisor's right. In English cases[149] and pre-*Andrews* Australian cases[150] such a clause has been

---

[143] See Heydon, Leeming and Turner, above n 2, [18-055].

[144] Davenport and Durham, *Construction Claims*, above n 73, 320–22; Easton, above n 55, 244.

[145] *Interstar Wholesale Finance Pty Ltd v Integral Home Loans Pty Ltd* [2008] NSWCA 310, (2008) 257 ALR 292 [79]–[84]. See also *SCI (Sales Curve Interactive) Ltd v Titus Sarl* [2001] EWCA Civ 591, [2001] 2 All ER (Comm) 416 [47]–[56].

[146] *Integral Home Loans Pty Ltd v Interstar Wholesale Finance Pty Ltd* [2007] NSWSC 406, (2007) Aust Contract R ¶ 90-261 [14] (Brereton J): '[T]he deprivation of rights that have already accrued under the contract may be penal in operation.'

[147] *Commissioner of Public Works v Hills* [1906] AC 368 (PC) 375–76; *Bysouth v Shire of Blackburn and Mitcham (No 2)* [1928] VLR 562 (FC) 573–74, 585; *Gilbert-Ash (Northern) Ltd v Modern Engineering (Bristol) Ltd* [1974] AC 689 (HL) 698, 711, 723.

[148] *The 'Fanti' and the 'Padre Island'* [1989] 1 Lloyd's Rep 239 (CA) 262, 265; *General Trading Co (Holdings) Ltd v Richmond Corp Ltd* [2008] EWHC 1479 (Comm) [113].

[149] *Eshelby v Federated European Bank Ltd* [1932] 1 KB 423 (CA) 429–30, 431–32; *Euro London Appointments Ltd v Claessens International Ltd* [2006] EWCA Civ 385, [2006] 2 Lloyd's Rep 436 [18]–[21]; *El Makdessi v Cavendish Square Holdings BV* [2013] EWCA Civ 1539, [2013] 2 CLC 968 [123]. See also *Nutting v Baldwin* [1995] 1 WLR 201 (Ch) 208.

[150] *Bysouth v Shire of Blackburn and Mitcham (No 2)* [1928] VLR 562 (FC) 574; *Helicopters Pty Ltd v Bankstown Airport Ltd* [2010] NSWCA 178, (2010) 15 BPR 28,593 [39]–[44]. See also *Agricultural and Rural Finance Pty Ltd v Gardiner* [2008] HCA 57, (2008) 238 CLR 570 [37].

considered incapable of being a penalty. On principle, a clause making a certain event a condition precedent of a right of the promisor ought to be capable of being a penalty where the event would not be a condition precedent of the promisor's right under the general law. This characterisation may be achieved in post-*Andrews* Australian law.[151] The stipulation of the event may be regarded as the primary stipulation, and the stipulation that makes the accrual of the promisor's right dependent upon the event may be regarded as a collateral stipulation.

Another clause under discussion is a time-bar clause in construction contracts. Such a clause absolves the principal from liability for claims made by the contractor after a certain deadline. In its widest form, a time-bar clause may stipulate that the principal will not be liable for any claim by the contractor unless the contractor lodges the claim with the principal a certain number of days after the date the contractor became aware of the event on which the claim is based.[152] Some commentators have argued that such a time-bar clause contains two stipulations: the right to make a claim prior to the deadline (the primary stipulation), and the barring of any claim not notified within time (the collateral stipulation).[153] If the prejudice suffered by the principal as a result of the contractor's delay in bringing a claim is susceptible of evaluation in money terms,[154] the time-bar clause will be a penalty unless it constitutes a genuine pre-estimate of that loss.

Other commentators have argued that a time-bar clause cannot be a penalty if it provides that the promisor's claim does not accrue unless the promisor lodges the claim before the deadline.[155] Those commentators rely on the cases mentioned before, according to which the penalty doctrine does not apply to clauses that make a certain event a condition precedent of a certain right. However, as also said before, the High Court's decision in *Andrews* could be used to bring such a clause within the scope of the penalty doctrine where the event would not be a condition precedent of the right under the general law.[156] The deadlines stipulated in time-bar clauses would not apply under the general law.

Nevertheless, the penalty doctrine may not apply to time-bar clauses for a different reason. Instead of splitting a time-bar clause into two stipulations, it may be possible to identify just one stipulation, namely the barring of any claim not notified within time. *Because of* that stipulation, the contractor is forced to lodge a claim prior to the deadline. Thus, the requirement of lodging a claim prior to the deadline is the consequence, rather than the prerequisite, of the stipulation that the claim is barred.[157] Since that stipulation is the only stipulation, it cannot be collateral to another stipulation and thus cannot even prima facie be a penalty. This is not to say that a time-bar clause may not be unfair on the

---

[151] See Peel, above n 123, 368–69.

[152] See, eg, *John Goss Projects Pty Ltd v Leighton Contractors* [2006] NSWSC 798 [66].

[153] Davenport, 'Andrews v ANZ', above n 74, 34, 36–37; Davenport, 'A Possible End to Time-Bar Clauses', above n 74, 58–59; Davenport and Durham, *Construction Claims*, above n 73, 315–16; Easton, above n 55, 243–44.

[154] The view that it normally is so susceptible is taken by Davenport, 'Andrews v ANZ', above n 74, 35. The opposite view is taken by Downie, above n 91, 19; Dragovic, Cole and Woo, above n 91, 20.

[155] Bond, above n 76, 73–74; Downie, above n 91, 16; Dragovic, Cole and Woo, above n 91, 20; S Steele and M Brookes, 'The Impact of Andrews v ANZ on Time Bar Clauses in Construction Contracts' (2014) 26 *Australian Construction Law Bulletin* 10, 10–11.

[156] Downie, above n 91, 17 argues that the High Court in *Andrews* did not intend its decision to have that effect.

[157] See, in a different context, *Re New South Wales Bar Association* [2014] NSWSC 1695, (2014) 315 ALR 146 [71] (Brereton J): '[T]he consequence of failure to comply with the deadline was no more than the ordinary consequences of missing a deadline, namely the loss of the opportunity that was available until the deadline. No penalty is incurred; the opportunity to which the deadline applied simply ceases to be available.'

contractor and should never be subject to control by the law. However, that control ought to occur through an unfair-terms regime[158] rather than the crude penalty doctrine.

IX. Lessons for Other Common Law Countries

Should courts in other common law countries adopt the penalty concept laid down by the High Court of Australia in *Andrews*? This depends upon the impact of the concept in practice, which has yet to be worked out. There are three possibilities.

First, the impact of the concept could be far less than initially anticipated. In particular, as demonstrated earlier, the notion of an alternative stipulation may turn out to be the Achilles heel of the High Court's penalty concept. In many circumstances, the practice of disguising a penalty as an option might be able to continue in the form of disguising a collateral stipulation as an alternative stipulation. If that were in fact to happen, an adoption of the High Court's penalty concept in other common law countries would be possible but also largely pointless.

At the other extreme, in applying the High Court's penalty concept, Australian courts might keep the notion of an alternative stipulation in narrow confines and classify as penalty many clauses hitherto enforceable. Such an approach would no doubt cause disquiet among contracting parties and should not be followed in other countries. After all, 'the courts of equity never undertook to serve as a general adjuster of men's bargains'.[159]

Finally, the effect of the High Court's decision in *Andrews* may turn out to be somewhere in the middle between the two extremes, leading to a change that is noticeable but not dramatic. In that case, the desirability of courts in other common law countries following the High Court's decision in *Andrews* would depend upon the details of its effects.

Irrespective of all of this, however, it must be doubted that the blunt penalty doctrine is the right instrument to deal with unfair contract terms in the twenty-first century. Other instruments are more flexible and more suited to fulfil that task. First, some doctrines of the common law and equity are superior to the penalty doctrine in that respect. As the New South Wales Court of Appeal said in *Interstar Wholesale Finance Pty Ltd v Integral Home Loans Pty Ltd*:

> The role or place of equity and relieving parties from injustice or unconscionable bargains or from unfair forfeitures is most effectively brought about by judging the operation of the clause or provision in the light of principles of relief against forfeiture, unconscionable bargains, any found obligation of good faith or such other consideration.[160]

---

[158] Or perhaps the doctrine of relief against forfeiture: Easton, above n 55, 243.

[159] *Bridge v Campbell Discount Co Ltd* [1962] AC 600 (HL) 626 (Lord Radcliffe). It would be even more dramatic if the penalty doctrine applied to the exercise of regulatory or statutory powers. However, an application of the penalty doctrine outside contract law has been rejected: *Re New South Wales Bar Association* [2014] NSWSC 1695, (2014) 315 ALR 146 [71]. See also *Re 4 Yearly Review of Modern Awards* [2015] FWCFB 1549 [25]–[26].

[160] *Interstar Wholesale Finance Pty Ltd v Integral Home Loans Pty Ltd* [2008] NSWCA 310, (2008) 257 ALR 292 [159] (Allsop P speaking for the court). A penalty doctrine solely based on unconscionable conduct is advocated by William Day, 'Penalty Clauses Revisited' [2014] *Journal of Business Law* 512, 516–17.

Secondly, many common law countries have legislation empowering the courts to strike down unfair contract terms at least in business-to-consumer contracts. Finally, particularly offending clauses could be addressed by specific legislation. For example, there could be specific legislation regulating bank fees.[161] All these instruments are superior to the penalty doctrine. Indeed, a comprehensive use of all other instruments may render the penalty doctrine redundant.[162]

X. Conclusion

In *Andrews v Australia and New Zealand Banking Group Ltd* the High Court of Australia held that the penalty doctrine may apply where the event triggering the impugned obligation is not a breach of contract and may occur without breach. This is a divergence from the position in other common law countries. The High Court based its decision solely on a brief excursus into legal history and eschewed any engagement with policy considerations. This methodological flaw undermines the persuasiveness of the decision and may hamper its interpretation. The decision fuels doubts as to the propriety of using the blunt penalty doctrine to combat unfair terms in the twenty-first century. Ironically, therefore, a decision that intended to make the penalty doctrine more relevant may eventually lead to its demise.

---

[161] See Baker and Sheldon, above n 4, 148.
[162] Peel, above n 123, 156.

9

Rights Restricting Remedies

ROBERT STEVENS

I. Introduction

This paper concerns the way in which the present places limits upon the future.

Twenty-five years ago I arrived at the University of Oxford as an undergraduate. Since that time I have changed. My hair is now more grey than sandy blond. Exams have been studied for and taken. I am paunchier than I was, but can probably run further. A beard has sprouted. Career successes and failures. Marriage and divorce. Deaths. Children born and growing. I am not the same.

Despite the changes that have occurred I am still, recognisably, Robert Stevens. Even if we do not believe that the future is pre-ordained, we can recognise that the person I was placed limits upon who I now am or could have been. Sadly I was never, it is now clear, going to play centre-forward for England. I could not have acquired either the looks or abilities of a movie star. However much I practised, I was never going to be a great dancer. An optimistic five foot eight inches is all I am ever going to be.

In the law our failure to fulfil our obligations changes them, but they remain in an important sense the same. What our obligations are places limits upon what they can be if unperformed.

Our Law in Common

Comparing systems with different legal traditions is an exciting but dangerous business. Superficially different rules concerning, say, privity of contract may give rise to few differences in result because of other compensating differences in other areas of the law.[1] Conversely, procedural differences may in practice give rise to fundamentally different results hidden behind rules that appear on their face to be in substance the same. The linguistic barriers to understanding are often not the hardest to overcome.

Comparing the reasoning and results from decisions in different common law systems is less exciting and dangerous, but usually of more direct practical utility. Today we are entering a Golden Age, with the law of other jurisdictions instantly available to us. If we

---

[1] See, eg, the German law of privity of contract, discussed in B Markesinis, H Unberath and A Johnston, *The German Law of Contract: A Comparative Treatise*, 2nd edn (Oxford, Hart Publishing, 2006) ch 4.

ever lived in an era of chauvinism, we do not do so now, with no jurisdiction either having, or being thought by anyone to have, a monopoly on wisdom. Nationalism in law is at best embarrassing.

It is true that in some times and places courts go through happy periods of productivity, with their pronouncements subsequently coming to be recognised as particularly authoritative. The New York Court of Appeals dominated by Cardozo CJ went through such an era in the 1920s, any Australian court with Dixon CJ as a member of it could not have failed to have done so, and the last years of the judicial House of Lords containing the complementary talents of Lords Hoffmann and Bingham also falls into this elite club.

The downside of our not possessing any single authoritative body whose judgments are binding on the rest is that common law systems are subject to the tiresome centripetal forces that argue that the peculiar circumstances of one system (typically weather, history, geographical size or population density) mean that it can ignore the others.[2] The upside is that we are free to treat the decisions from other jurisdictions as persuasive; they only have such force as their merits deserve.

In this chapter I wish to examine two decisions, one each from the ultimate appellate courts of England and Australia, and to argue that there are good reasons, uncanvassed before those courts, why other jurisdictions should not follow their lead. These decisions are that of the House of Lords in *The Achilleas*[3] concerning remoteness of damage for breach of contract, and that of the High Court of Australia in *Andrews v Australia and New Zealand Banking Group*[4] in relation to the rule against penalties. In both cases I shall argue that there are related reasons for thinking that the underlying rationales for the rules in play may justify different results. In both, the question was the extent to which our primary rights constrain the content of any secondary obligations.

The Next Best Thing

If I promise to give a lecture starting at 4.30 pm, but am running late, what should I do once that time has been and gone? Does my obligation disappear once it cannot be fulfilled? Outside the law, the answer is clear. Whatever reason entailed that I was obligated in the first place (here whatever reason meant that I am obliged to keep my promise) continues to have force after the obligation has been breached. I must now do the next best thing to perfect compliance that is possible. I must try to deliver the lecture as close to 4.30 as is possible (4.31, 4.32. 4.33, etc). I must apologise for my failure to conform with the terms of my original obligation, and the further away I am from perfect compliance the worse my wrongdoing. It would be to compound my initial wrong if, at 4.31, I were to give up and go and read a book instead.

Is this the same obligation throughout? (Or, synonymously, has the right of the promisee remained unchanged?) Clearly what I am obliged to do has changed its form over time. An obligation to lecture at 4.30 is not formally the same as an obligation to lecture

---

[2] eg, the Australian rejection of any special rule for the spread of a fire as based upon the different conditions in modern-day Australia compared to medieval England: see *Burnie Port Authority v General Jones Pty Ltd* (1994) 179 CLR 520, 534.

[3] *Transfield Shipping Inc v Mercator Shipping Inc (The Achilleas)* [2008] UKHL 48, [2009] 1 AC 61.

[4] *Andrews v Australia and New Zealand Banking Group* [2012] HCA 30, (2012) 247 CLR 205.

at 4.35, coupled with an apology for the late start. However, the underlying reason for the promisor's obligation at these different moments in time is still the same throughout. That is whatever reason or reasons originally meant I was obliged to keep my promise. From that perspective it is the form not the substance that has changed.

The reason that underlies the primary obligation places limits upon the form any obligation of next best compliance can take. This is just as true of obligations not to punch someone on the nose as it is of promissory obligations to be at a particular place at a particular time. A caterpillar may be transformed into a butterfly, which appears to be a startlingly different thing, but it cannot be transformed into a water buffalo. Being late for a lecture may entail particular care is taken that it goes well when delivered, but it does not require the lecturer to sell his worldly goods and give the proceeds away as penance.

This concept of next best compliance seems to underlie the quantification of damages for wrongdoing in all of private law. The locus classicus for the quantification of damages in the law of torts is Lord Blackburn's formulation from *Livingstone v Rawyard's Coal*:

> [W]here any injury is to be compensated by damages, in settling the sum of money to be given for reparation of damages you should as nearly as possible get at that sum of money which will put the party who has been injured, or who has suffered, in the same position as he would have been in if he had not sustained the wrong for which he is now getting his compensation or reparation.[5]

Identical is the equivalent formulation for the quantification of damages in the law of contract in *Robinson v Harman* by Parke B:

> The rule of common law is that where a party sustains a loss by reason of a breach of contract he is, so far as money can do it, to be placed in the same situation, with respect to damages, as if the contract had been performed.[6]

Notice that neither formulation necessarily confines damages to a claim for *consequential loss*. Although the duty of next best compliance often, indeed usually, will entail that the wrongdoer makes good any consequential loss the victim has suffered, the justification for damages is not necessarily dependent upon such loss being suffered. The reason for the duty of next best compliance is because the duty of best compliance can no longer be fulfilled, not because any consequential loss has necessarily been suffered. We should not therefore be surprised that the law frequently awards damages because a wrong has been suffered, regardless of proof of any consequential loss.[7]

The idea of next best compliance, or the continuity of the reason underlying the primary duty with the secondary duty of repair, has found favour with a number of theorists who do not in other ways have much in common.[8] On this view, there should be, and is,

---

[5] *Livingstone v Rawyards Coal* (1879–80) LR 5 App Cas 25 (HL) 39.

[6] *Robinson v Harman* (1848) 1 Exch 850, 855.

[7] See further R Stevens, *Torts and Rights* (Oxford, Oxford University Press, 2007) ch 3; R Stevens, 'Damages and the Right to Performance: A *Golden Victory*?' in J Neyers, R Bronaugh and S Pitel (eds), *Exploring Contract Law* (Oxford, Hart Publishing, 2009) ch 7.

[8] N MacCormick, *Legal Right and Social Democracy* (Oxford, Clarendon Press, 1982) 212; E Weinrib, *The Idea of Private Law* (Oxford, Oxford University Press, 1995) 135; J Raz, 'Personal Practical Conflicts' in P Baumann and M Betzler (eds) *Practical Conflicts: New Philosophical Essays* (Cambridge, Cambridge University Press, 2004) 172; Stevens, *Torts and Rights*, above n 7, 59; A Ripstein, 'As if it Never Happened' (2007) 48 *William and Mary Law Review* 1968. The best long treatment of the idea is J Gardner 'What Is Tort law For? Part 1: The Place of Corrective Justice' (2011) 30 *Law and Philosophy* 1.

no difference in principle between the assessment of damages for torts and breach of contract.[9] The remedial principles underlying both are identical. All that differs is the nature of the primary obligation, which thereby determines the form the duty of next best compliance takes.

It is sometimes said that contract damages are assessed on an 'expectation' basis, whilst damages in the law of torts are assessed on a 'reliance' basis. This is quite wrong. For most claims in the law of torts no 'reliance' is necessary for the claimant to succeed. If I pollute your land, or punch you on the nose or call you an axe-murderer in print you may be entitled to damages, but you have not relied upon anything I have done or said. The view that damages in the law of torts are in some sense 'reliance' based has come from a focus upon claims based upon misrepresentation which commonly arise as a concurrent possibility with a claim for breach of contract. A simple and standard example is as follows:[10]

> *P* purchases a boat from *D*. *D* both represents as fact and gives a contractual warranty that the boat is one year old. In fact it is four years old. *P* pays $10,000. The market value of a one-year-old boat is $11,000. The actual value of the boat, given its age, is $5,000.

If we assume that the defendant knew or was reckless as to the truth of his statement of the boat's age, then two wrongs have been committed. *D* has breached his duties (i) to tell the truth and (ii) to keep his promise. Neither duty can any longer be conformed to. An award of damages that seeks to achieve the next best thing will seek to place the parties in the position they would have been in if no breach had occurred. In relation to these different duties, this gives different results. Let it be assumed that *P* wishes to keep the boat and does not wish to rescind. If the truth had been told, and *P* can show that he would not have entered into the contract but for the misrepresentation, then he is entitled to damages that will place him into the position he would have been in as if he had never done so, so that damages will be $10,000 − $5,000 = $5,000. If the promise had been kept, the boat would have been worth $11,000, giving rise to damages of $6,000.

If the bargain had been a bad one so that the market value of a one-year-old boat had been lower than the contract price, say $9,000, then a claim based upon the misrepresentation would give rise to greater recovery ($10,000 − $5,000) than a claim based upon the failure to comply with the warranty ($9,000 − $5,000).

What gives rise to the different results is not any difference between the principle governing damages in contract and the law of torts; these are identical. Rather, because the content of the primary duties is different, the next best position that an award of damages seeks to achieve also differs. This may be further illustrated by those cases where the content of the defendant's duty is the same in contract and the law of torts. If, for example, *D* contractually undertakes to take care not to injure *P*, but negligently does so, *P* may have a claim both for breach of the contractual undertaking and independently for breach of the standard *Donoghue v Stevenson*[11] duty that we owe to other persons independently of contract. Here,

---

[9] Or, indeed, equitable wrongs. The debate here concerns whether *some* awards, such as for an account, are properly characterised as enforcing secondary obligations, or as more straightforwardly compelling perfect compliance. See for a surprising view on this debate *AIB Group (UK) plc v Mark Redler & Co Solicitors* [2014] UKSC 58, [2014] 3 WLR 1367.

[10] The example is lifted from the exemplary discussion in AS Burrows, *Remedies for Torts and Breach of Contract*, 3rd edn (Oxford, Oxford University Press, 2004) 33–34.

[11] *Donoghue v Stevenson* [1932] AC 562.

as the content of the duty is the same, no difference in assessment of damages will arise. Regardless of whether the claim is brought for breach of contract or for the tort, damages will seek to put *P* in the position they would have been in if they had not been wronged.

II. From Caterpillar to Butterfly

Unlike the duty to deliver a lecture slightly later than the advertised time, the duty to pay damages for a wrong can look radically different from the original duty of perfect compliance. A duty to pay hundreds of thousands of dollars of compensation for injury is very different in its content, and may be more onerous for the particular defendant than the original duty that has been breached.

The form the duty of next best compliance takes after breach is, in part, determined by post-breach events. If, upon arriving late at the lecture hall, I discover that nobody has shown up to hear it in any event, I am no longer under any obligation to deliver it. If my negligently injuring you unluckily requires you to attend hospital, then I should offer to take you there, but if it does not, then I do not have to do so. Again, the same is true in law: the content of the obligation to pay damages is determined in part by what happens subsequent to the breach.

That the secondary obligation may be very different in content from the primary obligation, and that it may vary according to the seriousness of the consequences of breach, does not however mean that it can be anything at all. If (as I have argued) the obligation to pay damages is the monetised form that the primary duty takes once breached, this places limits on what it can be. If I agree to pay a window cleaner $10 to wash the windows of my house, this contractual obligation to clean cannot be transformed into an obligation to pay $1,000,000 for failing to do so.

Remoteness: Are We French?

If your violation of my rights has caused me to be worse off, who should bear the loss? The loss cannot be made to disappear, and, as between the two of us, I am the more deserving party. That some losses that I suffer because of your wrong are irrecoverable poses a mystery. Why should it be the innocent party who has to foot the bill?

There is a tension in the common law's rules for remoteness of damage for breach of contract between our adopting the approach of French or German law. The leading case, throughout the common law world, is *Hadley v Baxendale*.[12] The rule adopted came indirectly from Pothier, which would indicate that we are French.

> When the debtor cannot be charged with any fraud, and is merely in fault for not performing his obligation, either because he has incautiously *engaged* to perform something which it was not in his power to accomplish, or because he has imprudently disabled himself from performing

---

[12] *Hadley v Baxendale* (1854) 9 Exch 341.

his engagements; *the debtor is only liable for the damages and the interest which might have been contemplated at the time of the contract; for to such alone the debtor can be considered as having intended to submit.*[13]

This rule, which was incorporated into the French Civil Code[14] and from there adopted by the court in *Hadley v Baxendale*, takes its justification from the 'will theory' that Pothier championed.[15] As the obligations to perform must be the product of the promisor's will, so must be the obligation to pay damages for non-performance. There are several problems with this justification for the rule.

First, and most obviously, the will theory upon which it is based is almost universally rejected today. In treating the existence and content of a promise as a product of the subjective will of the promisor, Pothier treated them as having the same moral basis as a vow.

Like many I often employ vows in an attempt to perform unpleasant tasks. When presented each summer with a pile of exams to mark, I have a number of tricks to try and induce myself to perform the task. So, I resolve that I will only be allowed a cup of tea, a small piece of chocolate and a look at the newspaper once I have managed to mark five papers. I can only break for lunch once I have finished one-fifth of the total. And so on.

I weaken every time. My future self chafes at the restrictions I have imposed. Boredom and despair at my ability to teach anyone anything set in. I find myself doing less awful tasks, such as descaling the kettle, or regrouting the bathroom. The marking is always done in the end, but not without more pain than is necessary. Summer marking that coincides with major international football tournaments is especially problematic.

This is a very bad way to behave. Being resolute is an important virtue. A better version of myself would be able to stick to the resolutions that I make, save where there subsequently appear other better reasons not to do so. We teach our children the importance of setting goals for themselves and to persevere. Stickability is important but the existence and meaning of the vows I make is solely a product of my subjective will. Promises, unlike vows, cannot be subjectively willed into existence. They must be *done*.

If I say 'I promise to buy your small black dog for $100', the existence and meaning of my promise is not determined by my subjective intent. That in my head I intended to offer to sell my large white cat for $50 is neither here nor there. The meaning of promises, just as with words in general, is not determined by the subjective intent of those who use them, and both as a matter of morality and law we are bound by the promises for which we are responsible, regardless of whether we subjectively intended to make them. Promises, as actions in the world, do not take place in our heads. We cannot just will them to be.

Second, it is not, and has never been, the case in English law that the damage must have been within the reasonable contemplation of the parties at the time of contracting. This is because the breach itself need not be foreseeable.[16] The true test is: *given the breach* is the loss too remote? If, for example, I sell you my car, and it is subsequently discovered that I had no title to it, I am liable for the consequential loss that you suffer, that is not too remote. It does not matter that I neither knew nor could reasonably have known of my lack of title.

---

[13] RJ Pothier, *A Treatise on the Law of Obligations or Contracts*, Evans edn (London, Strahan, 1806) 181, pt I, ch 2, art 3, para 160 (emphasis added).

[14] French Code Civil, Art 1150.

[15] RJ Pothier, *A Treatise on the Contract of Sale*, Cushing edn (Boston, Little and Brown, 1839) pt 1, art 3, paras 31–39.

[16] See *Parsons (Livestock) Ltd v Uley Ingham & Co Ltd* [1978] QB 791, 802 (Lord Denning MR).

This legal rule is reflected in the moral position. If I am running late for a lecture my obligation of next best compliance is not dependent upon whether I could have contemplated my non-performance at the time of the original promise. My non-performance may be the result of the most extraordinary combination of factors that I could not reasonably foresee; this does not relieve me of my obligation to do the next best thing within my power.

This objection is fatal not only to Pothier's claim that the obligation to pay damages is a product of the promisor's will, but also to the claims of modern theorists that the obligation to pay damages is voluntarily assumed in the same manner as the primary obligations of performance.[17] Contractual obligations arise because we are responsible for the assumption of these duties, and the secondary obligations to do the next best thing by way of payment of damage would not arise absent such assumption of responsibility. It does not follow that the secondary obligations are *themselves* voluntarily assumed.

The idea that the obligation to pay damages for breach of contract arises because it has been itself agreed to will appeal to those, such as the great Oliver Wendell Holmes, who argued that there was no duty to perform a contract, merely a duty to perform *or pay* damages if you do not.[18] For Holmes, as was natural, the remoteness rule was a matter of determining 'terms which it fairly may be presumed [the defendant] would have assented if they had been presented to his mind'.[19] This zombie idea, coming back each generation after we thought it killed in the last, has had a malign impact upon our law of contract.

Third, as is well known, the rule enunciated in *Hadley v Baxendale* has a poor fit with many decided cases. Unforeseeable consequential loss has therefore been held recoverable so long as it is of the *type* that is foreseeable,[20] and foreseeable losses have been held irrecoverable in a number of cases.[21] Whatever the merits of *Hadley v Baxendale* as a rough-and-ready guide, it cannot represent the whole truth.

Or are We German?

German law never adopted Pothier's foreseeability approach. Instead it has adopted two methods for the limitation of recoverable damages: the first (discussed below) is to ask whether the breach caused the loss. Causation here is not confined to 'factual' causation (*Aquivalenztheorie*) but also includes what English lawyers recognise as issues of 'legal' causation.

More importantly for present purposes, the correct interpretation of the *purpose* of the primary duty breached has been used to delimit the extent of responsibility (the *Shuttzzweck der Norm* theory).[22] It is this approach that the English courts have in recent years moved

---

[17] See, eg, A Kramer, *The Law of Contract Damages* (Oxford, Hart Publishing, 2014) 290; A Kramer, 'An Agreement-Centred Approach to Remoteness and Contract Damages' in N Cohen and E McKendrick (eds), *Comparative Remedies for Breach of Contract* (Oxford, Hart Publishing, 2005) 249, 274. cf A Robertson, 'The Basis of the Remoteness Rule in Contract' (2008) 28 *Legal Studies* 172.

[18] OW Holmes, *The Common Law* (Boston, Little Brown 1881) 301.

[19] *Globe Refinancing Co v Landa Cotton Oil Co* 190 US 540, 543 (1903); Holmes, above n 18, 302–03.

[20] See, eg, *Vacwell Engineering Co ltd v BDH Chemicals Ltd* [1971] 1 QB 88 (CA).

[21] eg *South Australia Asset Management Corp v York Montague Ltd* [1997] AC 191 (HL) 214; *Transfield Shipping Inc v Mercator Shipping Inc (The Achilleas)* [2008] UKHL 48, [2009] 1 AC 61.

[22] See generally, Markesinis, Unberath and Johnston, above n 1, 473–75.

towards. The purpose of the primary right limits the extent of the secondary obligation to pay damages. We have become more German, and less French.

The mere fact that a loss is within the reasonable contemplation of the parties at the time of contracting is insufficient to enable it to be said that it falls within the purpose of the primary duty to perform. An old example of the purposive approach in the context of breach of a statutory duty is the decision in *Gorris v Scott*.[23] The Contagious Diseases (Animals) Act 1869 required animals shipped at sea to be kept in pens of certain dimensions. In breach of this statutory obligation, the defendant did not do this. Some of the claimant's sheep, which the defendant had contracted to ship, were washed overboard, which would not have occurred if they had been kept in pens. The claim failed. Although the defendant's conduct had increased the risk of the sheep being swept overboard, avoiding this was not the purpose of the duty. The statutory duty was imposed in order to prevent the spread of contagious disease, not in order to prevent sheep being lost at sea. Consequently the loss was not recoverable.

Lord Hoffmann in *South Australia Asset Management Corp v York Montague Ltd*[24] ('*SAAMCo*') gave a classic but slightly more difficult example:

> A mountaineer about to undertake a difficult climb is concerned about the fitness of his knee. He goes to a doctor who negligently makes a superficial examination and pronounces the knee fit. The climber goes on the expedition, which he would not have undertaken if the doctor had told him the true state of his knee. He suffers an injury which is an entirely foreseeable consequence of mountaineering but has nothing to do with his knee.

The doctor's negligence does result in the mountaineer running a risk which he otherwise would not have done, but this is insufficient. The purpose of the duty to take care that the doctor has assumed to his patient is to protect the mountaineer against injuries caused by the failure of the knee, not rock falls. If the doctor had been employed under a contract the purpose of the duty would be ascertained by construction of the bargain. The process of construction is precisely the same where the doctor's duty to carefully examine arises from a non-contractual undertaking. The loss is irrecoverable, even though reasonably foreseeable.[25]

SAAMCo itself was more difficult.[26] What fell was a market rather than rocks or the claimant. The (simplified) facts were that the defendant valuer negligently valued a property at £15 million when its true value was £5 million. The claimant lender, in reliance upon the inaccurate valuation, lent £12 million secured upon the property. The borrower defaulted. If the value of the property had not declined, the loss consequent on the negligent valuation would have been £7 million (£12 million − £5 million). However, the market fell so that the property was only worth £1 million. Again the purpose of the contractual duty assumed is a matter of construction. The duty the valuer assumed was not to protect against market falls as such. If the lender would not have lent the money on other properties in the same market,

---

[23] *Gorris v Scott* (1874) LR 9 Ex 125. See also *Ward v Hobbs* (1878) 4 App Cas 13 (HL); *Reeman v Department of Transport* [1997] 2 Lloyd's Rep 648 (CA); *R v Secretary of State ex p Factortame* (No 7) [2001] 1 WLR 942 (QBD); *Environment Agency (Formerly National Rivers Authority) v Empress Car Co (Abertillery) Ltd* [1999] 2 AC 23 (HL) 31–32 (Lord Hoffmann).

[24] *South Australia Asset Management Corp. v York Montague Ltd* [1997] AC 191 (HL) 214.

[25] cf J Stapleton, 'Occam's Razor Reveals an Orthodox Basis for *Chester v Afshar*' (2006) 122 LQR 426, 438.

[26] cf *Andrews v Barnett Waddingham LLP* [2006] EWCA Civ 93.

the full loss due to the careless valuation is £11 million (£12 million − £1 million).[27] The House of Lords correctly held that the full loss was not recoverable. However, part of the purpose of the valuation was to enable the lender to know what its 'cushion' against market falls was. The lender thought it had a cushion of £3 million (£15 million − £12 million) when in fact it had no cushion at all. The lender should be able to recover not only for the loss attributable to the difference between the money lent and the actual value of the property (£7 million) but also for the loss caused by the market fall attributable to the lack of any cushion (£3 million). It was this figure of £10 million (£7 million + £3 million), which is always the same as the difference between the negligent valuation and a careful valuation (£15 million − £5 million), which the House of Lords correctly awarded.[28] A lender who would have been prepared to lend to the borrower 100 per cent of the valuation would have had no interest in a cushion and should recover nothing for the loss caused by the market fall. Where the purpose of the duty undertaken is to protect against market falls, for example where advice is sought as to whether to lend at all, the full loss attributable to the fall is recoverable, as the House of Lords subsequently held.[29]

Lord Hoffmann originally described the rule as being concerned to ascertain the 'scope of the duty' owed. This is, however, a misnomer. There was no debate in *SAAMCo* as to what the duty was, or whether it has been breached, the issue was whether the defendant was responsible for the consequences of breach. Lord Hoffmann, following criticism from Professor Stapleton, adopted a different label, one of 'extent of liability',[30] which is also the term adopted by the US Third Restatement of Tort Law. Unfortunately, this is considerably worse. There are many rules that determine the extent of a defendant's liability (ie the extent to which he is subject to the power of the plaintiff to sue for damages). The expiry of a limitation period, the failure to put a contract in a required form, the minority of the promisee, contributory fault and contractual exclusion all limit the extent of a defendant's liability.

The mistake arises from treating liability and responsibility as if they were synonyms, which they are not. The *SAAMCo* rule concerned the extent of the defendant's *responsibility* for the consequential loss suffered as a result of his wrong. This is, in part, determined by the *purpose* of the duty assumed, and this is ascertained through the ordinary principles of construction.

SAAMCo is sometimes thought of as a case in the law of torts. In the context of the standard duty familiar in *Donoghue v Stevenson* no question of the proper construction of the purpose of the duty arises. A moment's reflection tells us that this was not the kind of duty that the court was concerned with in *SAAMCo*. I am under a general duty to all others I can reasonably foresee may be so injured not to poison them, whether through the use of snails or otherwise. I am under no general positive duty to provide others with

---

[27] The decision proceeded on the basis that the money lent would not have been lent on other properties in the same market. The result cannot be explained on the basis that the loss suffered as a result of the market fall would have been suffered by the claimant in any event. Against: J Stapleton, 'Negligent Valuers and Falls in the Property Market' (1997) 113 *LQR* 1.

[28] L Hoffmann, 'Causation' (2005) 121 *LQR* 592; Against: Stapleton, above n 27. cf Stapleton, above n 25, 445.

[29] *Aneco Reinsurance Underwriting Ltd v Johnson & Higgins Ltd* [2001] UKHL 51, [2002] 1 Lloyd's Rep 157; cf *Blue Circle Industries plc v Ministry of Defence* [1999] Ch 289 (CA).

[30] Hoffmann, above n 28, 596; *Transfield Shipping Inc v Mercator Shipping Inc (The Achilleas)* [2008] UKHL 48, [2009] 1 AC 61 [23].

valuations of property, and certainly under no duty to take care in doing so. What then was the source of this positive duty of the valuer to the plaintiff? The answer, as our legal fore-bears would have recognised, is that the duty owed by the valuer was an assumed duty. The claim was what in old money would have been recognised as an action in assumpsit. Absent a contract, such a duty can be disclaimed by making it clear that it is not being assumed,[31] something that cannot of course be done in relation to our general duties to take care not to injure others. I cannot avoid my general duty to take care not to poison you by telling you that I am assuming no responsibility not to do so. What the purpose of an assumed duty is is always a matter of construction, whether we are within or without contract law. So the result in the mountaineer case does not vary according to whether there is a contract between patient and doctor or not.

A nice illustration of the way in which this purposive approach may give rise to greater liability than the reasonable contemplation test, and why it is to be preferred, is *Supershield Ltd v Siemens Building Technologies FE Ltd*.[32] The defendant was employed to install a valve in a storage tank in an office building to prevent flooding. The work was done unsatisfacto-rily, and the tank overflowed causing substantial damage to electrical equipment. However, this damage was ex ante very unlikely to have occurred. There was in place another safety feature; drains that should have taken the water away. However, very unfortunately (and improbably) these drains were blocked.

Was the damage by flooding irrecoverable because outside of the purpose of the duty undertaken? The answer is, of course, no as the Court of Appeal held. The entire point of the installation of the valve was to prevent damage of this kind, however improbable and unforeseeable the damage caused by flooding may have been.

This approach of seeking to explain the operation of contract law through the ordi-nary rules of construction of the primary obligation of performance, rather than through imposed rules of law determined by (unarticulated) notions of fairness, has found favour in other areas, such as common mistake or frustration. It should not, however, be pushed too far.

Can *The Achilleas* itself be explained using this purposive approach? Under a time char-ter, on 20 April 2004 the charterer gave notice to the owner of redelivery by 2 May 2004. The owner immediately entered into a four- to six-month follow-on charter with a third party, which was subject to cancellation if the vessel was not delivered by 8 May 2004. The charterer's voyage was delayed, and by 5 May 2004 the owners realised that the vessel was not going to be returned by 8 May. They were forced to renegotiate the follow-on charter, which in a volatile market was at a rate $8,000 per day lower than that already agreed. The owners claimed the loss in value of the follow-on charter for its entire 191-day duration resulting from the late return. The charterer argued successfully that they were only liable for the difference between the market and charter rates for the overrun period.

Lord Rodger and Baroness Hale based this result on the *Hadley v Baxendale* rule that such loss was outside the parties' reasonable contemplation at the time of contracting.[33] This is very difficult to understand.[34] The market for charters at that time was, as everyone

---

[31] *Hedley Byrne & Co Ltd v Heller & Partners Ltd* [1964] AC 465.
[32] *Supershield Ltd v Siemens Building Technologies FE Ltd* [2010] EWCA Civ 7, [2010] 1 Lloyd's Rep 349.
[33] Lord Walker agreed with everyone.
[34] Lord Hoffmann, 'The Achilleas: Custom and Practice or Foreseeability' (2010) 14 *Edinburgh Law Review* 47, 54.

knew, volatile. As a result losses of this kind were clearly reasonably within the parties' contemplation.

Although Lord Hoffmann relied upon the principle adopted in *SAAMCo* to explain this result,[35] this cannot be accepted. Was part of the purpose of the duty of the charterer to redeliver by 2 May to enable the owner to perform follow-on charters? Yes of course. Indeed, in most cases this will be the *entire* reason for the duty to redeliver on time. There is no plausible construction of the purpose of the defendant's duty to perform that takes the loss suffered outside of that which should be recoverable. This is a case of the sheep falling ill, not of their being swept overboard.

Instead of basing the result on the construction of the *primary* duty of performance, as had been done in *Gorris v Scott* and *SAAMCo*, Lords Hoffmann and Hope based their decision on an implied agreement to limit the *secondary* obligation to pay damages.[36] This is a return to the Pothier/Holmes fallacy that the obligation to pay damages is itself voluntarily undertaken, rather than its being the form the undertaken obligation to perform takes once it is breached.

It was argued that losses of the order suffered could not have been voluntarily undertaken, first because the volatility of the market made this unlikely unless done expressly, and second because the general market expectation was that liability was limited to the difference in value between the market rate and the charter rate for the overrun period. The former, on its own, clearly cannot suffice. Commodities markets are often extremely volatile and it has never been suggested that this creates a limit on the damages recoverable. Even if we accepted that there was evidence supporting the latter market expectation, this view seems to have come from a mistake as to the law. The claimant should indeed be entitled to the difference in value between the market rate and the charter rate for the overrun period regardless of whether they in fact suffer any loss as a result of late redelivery (eg because they intended to use the vessel for a non-commercial purpose during that period). This figure was a floor under what was recoverable.[37] This does not mean that where the plaintiff in fact suffers loss greater than this figure that that amount is irrecoverable. It should not have been thought a ceiling. Is it really to be the case that in subsequent litigation a trawling exercise of the general view in the market as to the damages payable is to be undertaken, and used to limit the damages recoverable?

The approach of Lords Hoffmann and Hope amounts to the implication of a limitation clause into the parties' agreement, an approach that the House of Lords had previously (and rightly) deprecated in *Jackson v Royal Bank of Scotland plc*,[38] a decision where the substantive judgments were given by Lords Hope and Walker (Lord Hoffmann concurring).

As so often, we find that the Germans were right all along and we should follow their purposive approach of construing the parties' undertaken obligation in limiting the damages recoverable. Unfortunately, the most important judge to give prominence to this idea in the common law world, Lord Hoffmann, pushed this principle beyond its limits. Other jurisdictions should not follow *The Achilleas*.

---

[35] *Transfield Shipping Inc v Mercator Shipping Inc (The Achilleas)* [2008] UKHL 48, [2009] 1 AC 61 [16].
[36] ibid [22] (Lord Hoffmann), [31] (Lord Hope).
[37] See generally, Stevens, above n 7.
[38] *Jackson v Royal Bank of Scotland plc* [2005] UKHL 3, [2005] 1 WLR 377.

We should also follow the Germans in understanding that the scope of responsibility is not solely determined by this process of construction. Outside of the realm of voluntarily assumed obligations and statutory duties, such an approach is not meaningful. There is still an anterior question of the attribution of losses to a particular wrong. This question of responsibility is answered neither in law nor morality by simply asking whether a loss would not have occurred but for the wrong. In the law of torts the dominant modern-day approach following *The Wagon Mound (No 1)*[39] has been to ask whether the loss is reasonably foreseeable at the time of the tort. Elsewhere,[40] I have argued (following others) that the supposed logic of the rule in *The Wagon Mound*, that the test for the existence of liability should determine its scope, is deeply flawed, that there was nothing unjust about the law before it was decided, and that subsequent case law has (rightly) circumvented it with such rules as the 'type of loss' and 'eggshell skull' exceptions. This issue of causal responsibility must still, however, be answered.

Within contract damages, this leads us to a two-stage test. First, is the consequential loss the causal responsibility of the wrongdoer? Second, is the loss within the purpose of the primary duty assumed? The two-stage *Hadley v Baxendale* test may be seen as a rough-and-ready proxy for this, the true rule.

Disproportion

The US Restatement of Contracts disallows recoverability of consequential loss if this would give rise to 'disproportionate compensation'.[41] Although it is difficult to point to clear authority, it is generally assumed that a similar principle applies throughout the common law world. The well-worn example is that of the taxi driver asked to drive a businessperson to the airport to catch a flight in order to clinch a lucrative deal. The taxi driver negligently crashes on the way, the flight is missed and the multimillion-pound deal lost. If the driver had been told in advance as to why it was necessary to get to the airport in time, would this loss be recoverable?

Can the obligation to drive to the airport on time be transformed into an obligation to pay hundreds of millions of dollars? This appears to be an example of trying to transform a caterpillar into a water buffalo. Once we accept that the law of damages is concerned not with compensating for losses in full, but with achieving the next best thing to compliance now possible, this places a restriction on what the driver's obligation can become. Notice that what must be proportionate is the original obligation to perform and the secondary obligation to pay damages, not the consideration paid and the damages payable. If the law were concerned with the relation between consideration and damages, no damages would ever be payable for the breach of a bare covenant contained in a deed as any figure compared to zero is disproportionate to it. The consideration payable is relevant to the question of the value to be placed on the primary obligation (eg has an above market price been paid in order to get a first-class service?) but it is not the sole determinative factor.

---

[39] *Overseas Tankship (UK) Ltd v Morts Dock & Engineering Co (The Wagon Mound)* [1961] 1 AC 388 (PC).
[40] Stevens, *Torts and Rights*, above n 7.
[41] Restatement 2d of Contracts § 351(3).

The Achilleas cannot be explained upon this basis either, as the damages claimed were far lower than the overall value of either the original or the follow-on charter.

In the law of personal injuries it is arguable that we have lost sight of the idea of proportionality.[42] The law's commitment to full compensation for loss of earnings for those injured can mean that a duty to take care not to injure can be transformed into a duty to pay tens of millions of dollars if one is unlucky enough to hit and disable (rather than kill) a young high earner. If we accept (as I do) that the duty is one to take care not to injure, and not merely a duty to take care not to expose to the risk of injury, then the disproportion may appear less acute. If the wrong is constituted by the negligent disabling of the victim it is possible to accept that the anterior duty can be transformed into a very onerous obligation to pay a large sum by way of damages. However, it cannot be anything without limit. It may be that it is only the existence of liability insurance that allows us to accept the law as it is. The law here is close to the idea with which this part began, that if the loss has to be borne by someone, better that it falls on the wrongdoer rather than the innocent victim.

III. Penalty Clauses

Many attempts have been made to rationalise the law against penalties, and I cannot assess the merits of each here. So, it has been argued that it is part of the law's more general concern with ensuring that transactions are substantively fair;[43] or that like Antonio when promising the pound of flesh[44] human beings suffer from a flaw that we are systematically overoptimistic about the future and that this vitiates our consent to certain promises we make;[45] or that enforcing penalty clauses would be self-defeating, as damaging the bonds of trust which underlies why promises should be kept in the first place;[46] or that refusing to enforce penalty clauses is economically efficient;[47] or that the rule is a prophylactic one to prevent unconscionable exploitation of one party by another;[48] or that there are limits on our power to bind our future selves so as to destroy our liberty of action, such as by selling ourselves into slavery, and that the penalties rule reflects this concern to protect liberty. It is also possible to think that there could be more than one reason in play, and that to look for a single one is a mistake.[49] However, as each of these justifications pulls the law towards rules of different scope it would be better if we could at least pinpoint one that has priority

---

[42] See further N McBride and R Bagshaw, *Tort Law*, 4th edn (Harlow, Pearson, 2012) 783–84.

[43] M Chen-Wishart, 'Controlling the Power to Agree Damages' in P Birks (ed), *Wrongs and Remedies in the Twenty-First Century* (Oxford, Clarendon Press, 1996) ch 12.

[44] W Shakespeare, *The Merchant of Venice*.

[45] P Birks, *An Introduction to the Law of Restitution*, rev edn (Oxford, Clarendon Press, 1989) 213–16.

[46] S Smith, 'Performance, Punishment and the Nature of Contractual Obligation' (1997) 60 *MLR* 360.

[47] R Posner, *Economic Analysis of Law*, 9th edn (New York, Aspen, 2014) xx; KW Clarkson, RL Miller and TJ Muris, 'Liquidated Damages v Penalties: Sense or Nonsense?' [1978] *Wisconsin Law Review* 351. But see CJ Goetz and RE Scott, 'Liquidated Damages, Penalties and the Just Compensation Principle' (1977) 77 *Columbia Law Review* 554.

[48] Made as an historical claim by DJ Ibbetson, *A Historical Introduction to the Law of Obligations* (Oxford, Oxford University Press, 1999) 255–56.

[49] See more generally for the defence of this view in private law, S Waddams, *Dimensions of Private Law: Categories and Concepts in Legal Reasoning* (Cambridge, Cambridge University Press, 2003).

where they conflict. Judicial consideration of the question of justification for the rule in the modern era usually takes the form of despair.[50]

It is, at least, arguable that the rule is an historical anachronism, and this suspicion will be for some confirmed when it is observed that civilian jurisdictions do not recognise the same rule, at least not in the same form.[51] For a judge confronted with an irrational rule that has become too well established to be excised, the best course of action is to place it in as small a box as is possible so as to confine the damage. We find this approach in other areas, such as proprietary estoppel, where the law has long since lost touch with the rule's original doctrinal justification but where the weight of decisions is now too great to be overturned. It is inelegant to confine these rogue rules within more or less arbitrary limits, but given the limits of judicial power this may be the best that can be done given where we are.

None of the justifications above fits very well with the formal, and easily circumvented, rule that prevails in England. Consider the following example:

> In exchange for a motorbike, D promises P1 that he will clean P1's windows on Monday. D promises that if he fails to do so he will pay P1 $1 million as damages.

Unless there are special circumstances where $1 million could plausibly be a genuine pre-estimate of P1's loss, or where there is some other good commercial reason for such a large sum to be payable upon breach, such a sum appears to be *in terrorem*, and will be unenforceable as a penalty.[52]

If, however, we change the scenario in a formal but commercially irrelevant way, the result differs.

> In exchange for a motorbike, D promises P2 that he will clean P2's windows on Monday or, failing that, pay P2 $1 million.

Here the obligation to pay $1 million has been framed not as a sum payable upon breach, but as a sum of money payable upon a contingency. If D pays the money, he is never in breach of contract. The claim by P2 is an action for the agreed sum, a claim that does not depend upon proof of breach of contract. The action for the agreed sum, not damages for breach, is easily the most common claim brought before courts everywhere. Sellers must be paid the price, employees must be paid their wages, landlords must be paid their rent, and so on. This may be contrasted with a claim based upon a liquidated damages clause, which is dependent upon proof of breach, the clause fixing the quantum of damages. There is nothing to stop D buying a motorbike for $1 million, however foolish his bargain, and there is nothing to prevent the obligation to pay $1 million from being subject to a contingency.

Commercially, there is no difference between these two agreements, and some will conclude that a rule drawing a distinction between them cannot be supported. Indeed it can be argued that there is a paradox involved in placing the party who is in breach (and thereby within the scope of potential relief) in a better position than the party who is not. Should it be for the defendant to argue that he breached his contract by leaving the windows uncleaned?

---

[50] See, eg, the judgments in *Widnes Foundry (1925) Ltd v Dellulose Acetate Silk Co Ltd* [1931] 2 KB 393 (CA).

[51] See R Zimmermann, *The Law of Obligations: Roman Foundations of the Civilian Tradition* (Oxford, Oxford University Press, 1996) 95–113.

[52] See for the most recent formulation *Makdessi v Cavendish Square Holdings BV* [2013] EWCA Civ 1539, [2014] BLR 246 and *Parkingeye Ltd v Beavis* [2015] EWCA Civ 402. Appeals of both these decisions are pending before the Supreme Court at the time of writing.

The English authority for the rule that the penalties doctrine only applied to sums payable upon breach is surprisingly thin. It is at least arguable that the formulation of the rule in the leading decision, *Dunlop Pneumatic Tyre Co Ltd v New Garage & Motor Co Ltd*,[53] implicitly assumes that it only applies to sums payable upon breach. The decision that adopts the rule as part of its ratio is the extremely brief decision of the House of Lords in *Export Credits Guarantee Department v Universal Products Co.*[54] However, although Lord Roskill relied upon breach rule for the result, the claim was an exceptionally weak one, a claim for indemnification for the sum paid out under a guarantee that nobody could characterise as in terrorem. How the case got as far as the House of Lords is something of a mystery. Earlier, the majority of the House of Lords (save Lord Denning) had in *Bridge v Campbell Discount*[55] assumed that the rule was only triggered upon breach, but this formed no part of the ratio as the result was to find the clause penal. A long run of cases subsequently assumed without substantive argument the existence of the rule,[56] although in *Parkingeye Ltd v Beavis*[57] Moore-Bick LJ doubted the existence of such a limitation, albeit in obiter dicta. The Uniform Commercial Code and the Restatement of Contracts both treat breach as a prerequisite.[58]

When, therefore, in *Office of Fair Trading v Abbey National Plc*[59] the question arose as to whether bank charges for account holders who have exceeded an authorised limit on borrowing were potentially penal, the conclusion that they were not (as not payable upon any breach) stirred little controversy in England and the point was not appealed in the litigation's progress to the Supreme Court.[60]

In a judgment that is simultaneously impressive and maddening the High Court of Australia rejected this limitation.[61] They did so by relying upon the history of the rule. Reasoning of this kind had also appealed in England to Lord Denning in *Bridge v Campbell Discount* and to Millett LJ (as he then was) in *Jervis v Harris*.[62] The origin of the jurisdiction arose in the context of penal bonds. Such bonds, which were not contractual, were obligations to pay a sum of money that was released if a condition was met. This condition need not be (indeed originally would not have been) promissory. So, the condition could be 'convey Blackacre to me' or 'repair the property you have leased' but there need not be any promise to do these things. If the condition was met, the bond was released. The courts of equity intervened to prevent the enforcement of such bonds if they were penal, where compensation could be made for non-fulfilment of the condition to which the bond was subject. As these bonds were never sums of money payable upon breach, nor was the

---

[53] *Dunlop Pneumatic Tyre Co Ltd v New Garage & Motor Co Ltd* [1915] AC 79 (HL).
[54] *Export Credits Guarantee Department v Universal Products Co* [1983] 1 WLR 399 (HL).
[55] *Bridge v Campbell Discount Co Ltd* [1962] AC 600 (HL).
[56] eg, *Euro London Appointments Ltd v Claessens International Ltd* [2006] EWCA Civ 385, [2006] 2 Lloyds Rep 437; *M&J Polymers Ltd v Imerys Minerals Ltd* [2008] EWHC 344, [2008] 1 Lloyd's Rep. 541; *General Trading Company (Holdings) Ltd v Richmond Corporation Ltd* [2008] EWHC 1479 (Comm), [2008] 2 Lloyd's Rep 475).
[57] *Parkingeye Ltd v Beavis* [2015] EWCA Civ 402.
[58] Uniform Commercial Code § 2-178; Restatement 2d of Contracts § 356.
[59] *Office of Fair Trading v Abbey National Plc* [2008] EWHC 875 (Comm); [2008] 2 All ER (Comm) 625 (Andrew Smith J).
[60] *Office of Fair Trading v Abbey National Plc* [2009] UKSC 6, [2010] 1 AC 696.
[61] *Andrews v Australia and New Zealand Banking Group Ltd* [2012] HCA 30, (2012) 247 CLR 205. The court is clearly influenced by WH Lloyd, 'Penalties and Forfeitures' (1915) 29 *Harvard Law Review* 117.
[62] *Jervis v Harris* [1996] Ch 195 (CA).

condition to which they were subject necessarily promissory, we can see that the modern English rule is contrary to its historical origins. These earlier decision were never overruled, and following the Judicature Acts any wider equitable rule should prevail. The court is to be congratulated for an impressive piece of archaeology, but it is puzzling that a century of development, in Australia[63] as well as elsewhere, pointing to the opposite conclusion is not discussed.

However impressive as a work of historical scholarship, *Andrews* is maddening in its failure to articulate what the purpose of the penalties doctrine might be.[64] In order to answer whether the penalties doctrine *ought* to turn upon breach, and if not what its correct scope *ought* to be, it is necessary to articulate what the basis for the rule is. The mechanical citation of authority is rarely sufficient at the highest appellate level, where judges are not bound by prior judicial authority.

We are told:

> [A] stipulation *prima facie* imposes a penalty on a party ('the first party') if, as a matter of substance, it is collateral (or accessory) to a primary stipulation in favour of a second party and this collateral stipulation, upon the failure of the primary stipulation, imposes upon the first party an additional detriment, the penalty, to the benefit of the second party.[65]

The uncertainty of when a stipulation will be characterised as collateral or accessory to a primary stipulation has attracted criticism, but this problem has its source in the failure to identify what the purpose of the rule might be. Presumably *D*'s promise to pay $1 million is collateral to the promise to clean *P2*'s windows (a promise to do *X*, or failing that *Y*). However, commercially identical agreements can be structured where one promise is not conditional upon the non-performance of the other:

> In exchange for a motorbike, *D* promises *P3* that he will pay *P3* $1 million, or in the alternative clean *P3*'s windows on Monday.

Here neither obligation is expressed as collateral to the other, they are expressed as alternatives (a promise to do *X* or *Y*). In commercial substance, however, the agreement is identical to those we have already seen.

One might think that a clear example where the promise to pay was not collateral would be as follows:

> In exchange for a motorbike, *D* promises *P3* that he will pay *P3* $1 million. It is agreed that the obligation to pay $1 million is released if *P3*'s windows have been cleaned by Monday.

Here, it might be thought, the promise to pay is not expressed to be collateral to a primary promise to clean, but vice versa. The promise to pay is not subject to a condition precedent that the work is not done, but rather is defeasible upon the condition subsequent of it being done. Commercially the agreement is still identical to the other hypotheticals we have considered. *D*'s choice is still clean or pay.

---

[63] Prior decisions of the High Court of Australia that had seemed to adopt the breach rule include *IAC (Leasing) Ltd v Humphrey* (1972) 126 CLR 131, 143 (Walsh J); *O'Dea v Allstates Leasing System (WA) Pty Ltd* (1983) 152 CLR 359, 390 (Brennan J).

[64] For forthright criticism, see JW Carter, W Courtney, E Perden, A Stewart and GJ Tolhurst, 'Contractual Penalties: Resurrecting the Equitable Jurisdiction' (2013) 20 *Journal of Contract Law* 99. For a (rare) defence of *Andrews*, see PS Davies and PG Turner, 'Relief Against Penalties Without a Breach of Contract' (2013) 72 *CLJ* 20.

[65] *Andrews v Australia and New Zealand Banking Group Ltd* [2012] HCA 30, (2012) 247 CLR 205 [10].

However, this last kind of case is exactly the form penal bonds originally took. They were obligations to pay a sum of money that were defeasible if a certain condition was fulfilled. We cannot say that the promise to pay is collateral to the promise to clean because what the promisee 'really' in substance wants is clean windows, with the promise to pay $1 million just fallback security. P1, P2 and P3 would all much prefer $1 million, just as the banks would much rather have customers pay charges than never go overdrawn.

Perhaps all four of the examples above are potentially penalties in Australia because the obligation in the alternative to cleaning the windows is much more onerous.

The point is put into a further state of confusion by the endorsement of the views of the majority in *Metro-Goldwyn-Mayer Pty Ltd v Greenham*[66] and the dictum by Lord St Leonards in *French v Macale*:

> [I]t appears, that the question for the Court to ascertain is, whether the party is restricted by covenant from doing the particular act, although if he do it a payment is reserved; or *whether according to the true construction of the contract, its meaning is, that the one party shall have a right to do the act, on payment of what is agreed upon as an equivalent.* If a man let meadow land for two guineas an acre, and the contract is, that if the tenant choose to employ it in tillage, he may do so, paying an additional rent of two guineas an acre, no doubt this is a perfectly good and unobjectionable contract; the breaking up the land is not inconsistent with the contract, which provides, that in case the act is done the landlord is to receive an increased rent.[67]

If this is true, why cannot the last three examples all be characterised as alternative stipulations: *D* having the right not to clean the windows, on payment of a sum agreed by the parties as an equivalent? If this is a question of substance, what is the substance we are looking for? Perhaps all we can say is that where the payment is in exchange for some kind of *quid pro quo*, eg extra land for tillage, it will not constitute a penalty.[68]

Can the Breach Rule be Justified?

We cannot show that the High Court of Australia is wrong simply through criticisms of the antiquity of the law relied upon, the roughshod treatment of more modern authority, the ignoring of the position in other jurisdictions and the difficulty of drawing the line adopted. Only through giving a rationale for the penalties doctrine that explains the breach rule can the position of other jurisdictions be truly defended.

Now, it may be that the penalties rule is a hopeless anachronism, and the breach rule is an arbitrary restriction upon it. If so, however, the breach rule would be no better than confining the rule's application to agreements concluded on Mondays and Wednesdays.

None of the theoretical justifications for the rule given above would confine it to cases of breach. All are principles of substantive justice, and none can, without more, justify drawing a distinction between the commercially identical forms of agreement set out above.

However, just as there is a logical constraint on what the positive law can be, there is a constraint on the content of the obligations parties may agree to. I cannot simultaneously

---

[66] *Metro-Goldwyn-Mayer Pty Ltd v Greenham* [1966] 2 NSWR 717 (CA) (Jacobs JA and Holmes JA).

[67] *French v Macale* (1842) 2 Drury & Warren 269, 275–76 (emphasis added in *Andrews*).

[68] See also *Jervis v Harris* [1996] Ch 195 (CA) where the payment was not a penalty for the tenant not having repaired the premises, but a payment for the work done by the landlord in doing so.

promise you two inconsistent things at the same time. I can promise you to be in Oxford at a certain time, and I can promise you to be in Hong Kong at a certain time, but I cannot promise you to be in Oxford and Hong Kong at the same time.

If the obligation to pay damages is a monetised form of the primary obligation of performance, the parties should, and do have, considerable latitude in determining what this obligation may be. It cannot however, be anything. An obligation to clean the windows of my modest Oxford terraced house cannot be transformed into an obligation to pay $1 million. Such a penalty clause, in purporting to put a figure on the value of the promised work, is inconsistent with the parties' agreement as to the content of the primary obligations. By contrast a promise to pay a sum of money on the failure of a condition does not purport to be the instantiation of any anterior obligation, and no necessary incoherence arises.

The advantage of this justification is that it justifies a purely formal rule, so that only the first of the four examples set out above is within its scope. Further it does not matter that the parties are well informed commercial people on an equal bargaining footing, bargaining with their eyes open as to the possibility of default. We are unconcerned with questions of procedural or substantive fairness, but rather with the coherence of the agreement. That sensible drafting allows the rule to be easily evaded is in its favour, not a criticism. The breach rule makes sense because it is dependent upon the idea that the secondary obligation to pay damages is in an important sense the same obligation, but in a different form, as the primary obligation to perform.

Other jurisdictions should not follow *Andrews v ANZ*.

Compatibility with Exclusion and Limitation of Liability

Fifty years ago, Professor Brian Coote argued that exemption clauses were definitive of the parties' primary obligations of performance.[69] On one view this entailed that a contract that purported to create an obligation to deliver goods, but to exclude liability for failure to do so, was incoherent. If the latter was excluded, the former could not exist.

This view of exemption clauses did not find favour. Lord Diplock, famously, relied upon the distinction between primary obligations of performance and secondary obligations to pay damages that I have relied on in this chapter.

> Breaches of primary obligations give rise to substituted or secondary obligations on the part of the party in default, and, in some cases, may entitle the other party to be relieved from further performance of his own primary obligations. These secondary obligations of the contract breaker and any concomitant relief of the other party from his own primary obligations also arise by implication of law.[70]

This enabled him to conclude that the termination of a contract for breach merely brought to an end the parties' primary duties of performance, both the secondary obligations to pay damages and any exclusion or limitation clause survived.

---

[69] B Coote, *Exception Clauses* (London, Sweet & Maxwell, 1964).
[70] *Photo Production Ltd v Securicor Transport Ltd* [1980] AC 827 (HL).

As to modifications of these rules he said:

> An exclusion clause is one which excludes or modifies an obligation, whether primary, general secondary or anticipatory secondary, that would otherwise arise under the contract by implication of law. Parties are free to agree to whatever exclusion or modification of all three types of obligations as they please within the limits that the agreement must retain the legal characteristics of a contract; and must not offend against the equitable rule against penalties; that is to say, it must not impose upon the breaker of a primary obligation a general second obligation to pay to the other party a sum of money that is manifestly intended to be in excess of the amount which would fully compensate the other party for the loss sustained by him in consequence of the breach of the primary obligation.

If the argument supporting the breach limitation upon the penalties rule is correct, how can it be squared with respecting clauses that reduce, rather than increase, the defendant's liability for breach of contract (or indeed for any other wrong)? Just as a caterpillar cannot become a water buffalo, a water buffalo cannot become a caterpillar. How can the parties coherently agree that an obligation to deliver 100 million barrels of oil is transformed into an obligation to pay $5 for not doing so?[71]

They cannot. However, what they can do is agree that certain obligations either cannot be enforced at all, or are enforceable only to a limited extent. Clauses excluding or limiting *liability* do just that. It is the promisee's power of enforcement that is cut back, not the obligation itself. Just as the parties may agree that their entire agreement is to be unenforceable, they may agree that certain obligations are to be unenforceable. We cannot have liabilities in the air. When courts through orders compel us to act in certain ways, they do so because of the duties that the law imposes upon us, which exist prior to the judge opening her mouth. These orders create new obligations which did not exist before, into which the old obligations usually merge. A penalty clause is an agreement to increase the obligations we would otherwise be under, not merely the liabilities.

We can, however, have legal obligations absent any liability to their enforcement. Familiar examples are contractual obligations contained in agreements that have not been put into a required form, or obligations to pay damages that have ceased to be enforceable because of the expiry of a limitation period. Legal obligations are not a nullity because unenforceable, and may still have legal effects (eg third parties may be liable for procuring their breach, if performed restitution of benefits conferred may be irrecoverable).

There is therefore no requirement of symmetrical treatment of penalty clauses that seek to increase the *obligation* to pay damages, and exclusion clauses that seek to restrict the *liability* to pay them.

IV. Conclusion

The role of the academic lawyer is not solely that of a diligent journalist, reporting the law as posited by those in authority (although that is an important task). Our more difficult

---

[71] For the argument that exclusion clauses *are* incompatible with the treatment of penalty clauses, see P Saprai, 'The Penalties Rule and the Promise Theory of Contract' (2013) 26 *Canadian Journal of Law and Jurisprudence* 443.

task is to explain why the positive law makes ethical sense (if it does). When confronted by decisions from the ultimate appellate courts of different jurisdictions that are incompatible with one another, only some kind of theory from outside the positive law itself can determine which is right and which is wrong. It is not a strength of a legal theory that it purports to claim that all rules and decisions from all jurisdictions are equally correct, but a terrible weakness.[72]

---

[72] Against: J Goudkamp and J Murphy, 'Tort Statutes and Tort Theories' (2015) 131 *LQR* 133.

10

The Methods and Madness
of Unjust Enrichment

I. Introduction

Can we continue to assert a *common* law of obligations when each of the near 40 so-called 'common law' nations has its own substantive legal doctrines and principles regarding property, contract, tort and unjust enrichment; and when the statutes and judicial decisions of the birthplace of the common law no longer bind its colonial offspring? If neither substance nor authority unites the common law, what, if anything, remains common about it? This chapter explores two potential sources of common law unity: (i) its distinctive mode of legal reasoning, inductive reasoning, and (ii) its shared underlying political philosophy, liberal individualism.

Matters of legal reasoning and political philosophy are fairly abstract; therefore, to focus the inquiry, this chapter assesses their unification potential in the concrete context provided by a single branch of the law of obligations, the law of unjust enrichment, of a specific common law jurisdiction, Canada.[1] The chosen context is not random: in recent years, much ink has been spilled over the supposed shift in Canadian unjust enrichment law from a common law to a civilian orientation.[2] In support of this alleged shift, scholars have invoked a number of essential distinctions between common and civil law, including opposing modes of legal reasoning and alternative political philosophies. As such, the law of unjust enrichment in Canada provides a promising, if not ideal, window onto the larger question of common law unity.

---

[*] Thanks are owed to Elise Bant and Anne Schuurman for their insightful comments on and gentle corrections of earlier drafts.

[1] For the purposes of this paper, references to Canadian law apply only to the common law part of Canada's bijural legal system.

[2] C Hunt, 'The Civilian Orientation of Canadian Unjust Enrichment Law: A Reply to Professor McCamus' (2009) 48 *Canadian Business Law Journal* 498; C Hunt, 'The Decline of Juristic Reasons? Unjust Enrichment and the Supreme Court of Canada' (2010) 43 *University of Brithish Columbia Law Review* 173; J McCamus, 'Mistake, Forged Cheques and Unjust Enrichment: Three Cheers for *BMP Global*' (2009) 48 *Canadian Business Law Journal* 76; M McInnes, *The Canadian Law of Unjust Enrichment and Restitution* (Markham, LexisNexis Canada Inc, 2014) 16–24; M McInnes, 'The Reason to Reverse: Unjust Factors and Juristic Reasons' (2012) 92 *Boston University Law Review* 1049; M McInnes, 'A Return to First Principles in Unjust Enrichment: *Kerr v Baranow*' (2011) 51 *Canadian Business Law Journal* 275; M McInnes, '*BMP Global Distributions Inc v Bank of Nova Scotia*: The Unitary Action in Unjust Enrichment' (2009) 48 *Canadian Business Law Journal* 102; M McInnes, 'Making Sense of Juristic Reasons: Unjust Enrichment After *Garland v Consumers' Gas*' (2004) 42 *Alberta Law Review* 399; L Smith, 'Demystifying Juristic Reasons' (2007) 45 *Canadian Business Law Journal* 281.

The now dominant Canadian position is that we do one thing in common law and another in civil, and that, in the Canadian law of unjust enrichment, we are now being 'civil'. The thesis of this scholarship constitutes a threat to the commonality of the common law of obligations.[3] Responding to this threat, this chapter queries whether the distinctions relied upon withstand scrutiny and concludes that, for the most part, their importance is overstated. Moreover, it highlights a particular deleterious effect of this exaggerated focus, namely that it encourages neglect of unjust enrichment's core question concerning the normative justification for the defendant's legally imposed restitutionary obligation to the plaintiff. When, in the spirit of the current trend, we inquire into *how* to approach the question of 'unjust'—what makes an enrichment unjust, ie whether it should be unpacked in terms of the common law's unjust factors or according to the civil law's absence of basis— we believe we address unjust enrichment's central question, but, instead, we answer a question of only peripheral significance.

The arguments herein principally amount to a cautionary tale about relying on black-and-white distinctions between the common law and the law of civilian jurisdictions; nonetheless, through these very distinctions we may learn something about the two potential unifying themes mentioned at the outset. We learn that the former—the distinctive modes of legal reasoning—is overstated if not totally inaccurate, while the latter—the different underlying political philosophies—has received insufficient attention and can help illuminate the normative foundations of the cause of action. As this chapter primarily aims to clear our desks and minds of this ultimately distracting methodology dispute, it forbears from saying too much about precisely what the rational explanation of the defendant's duty might look like. Yet, as the rivalry between the types of reasons that ground the restitutionary obligation points us in a potentially fruitful direction, it closes with a suggested reconceptualisation of the nature of unjust enrichment—one that places it outside of the law of obligations, properly-so-called.

II. Two Unjust Enrichment Models

A successful cause of action in unjust enrichment consists of (i) an enrichment of one party, (ii) at the expense of the other, (iii) the retention of which is unjust.[4] While questions relating to enrichments and corresponding deprivations invite rich scholarship and debate,[5] the heart of unjust enrichment resides in the third question: *what does it mean for an enrichment to be unjust?* The question of injustice is central as its response supplies the normative explanation for the remedial duty.

---

[3] A quick note about jurisdiction: this analysis particularly addresses the English and Canadian (common law) approaches to the law of unjust enrichment. It leaves open the possibility that other common law jurisdictions have developed their own approaches. E Bant has suggested to me that Australian law has developed its own approach, see: *Australian Financial Services Leasing Pty Ltd v Hills Industries Ltd* [2014] HCA 14.

[4] Once the plaintiff discharges her burden of proof with respect to these three elements, the burden shifts to the defendant to demonstrate that he has some sort of defence. Defences lie well outside the ambit of this paper, although the defence of change of position has a not uninteresting role to play in the debate between the two competing approaches. See below, n 80 and text to n 92 for further discussion.

[5] Some examples: What is an enrichment? Is a service an enrichment? Can a debt be an enrichment? Does the deprivation have to correspond to the enrichment materially?

While the receipt of a benefit, in a moral or social sense, puts us under an obligation,[6] the merely descriptive facts (of receiving a benefit or of losing an asset) are obviously insufficient to generate or ground a legal obligation. I say 'obviously', but perhaps more should be said. The imposition of an obligation where none existed previously amounts to a *normative* change in the obligee's status vis-à-vis her obligor. Where, at first, she had no obligation, now she is bound. In private law, individuals come under obligations towards other individuals when one has a legally recognised right exercisable against the other. In the sphere of tort law, this right involves the safety and security of one's person or property, while in contract, the right is created by a legally recognised form of voluntary undertaking. In this way, we might say that remedial rights—ie claims a plaintiff might have against a defendant for a court-ordered remedy—can arise from wrongs or consent.[7] It has proven notoriously difficult to identify satisfactorily the source of the plaintiff's right in unjust enrichment. It is neither a straightforward property right nor a contractual right. In addition, the defendant's passivity makes it difficult to assign him any (legal) responsibility to look out for the plaintiff's well-being. It is significant that the fact of receiving a benefit at the expense of another is (i) not a wrong, (ii) not necessarily consented to and (iii) is not an activity at all (at the most, it is passive acquiescence). Therefore, unless we can argue convincingly that unjust enrichment constitutes a conceptually distinct way of coming under a legal obligation (as some have),[8] the most likely candidate for the source of unjust enrichment's remedial obligation is that it is state-imposed.[9] Again, however, we encounter some difficulty. The state normally does not give two hoots about unrequited benefits. Take the following example:

I invite you over for dinner. Most would say that you are now socially obligated to return the invitation at a later date.[10] But we would never imagine that this social obligation is somehow legally

---

[6] 'To have received from one, to whom we think our selves equall, greater benefts than there is hope to Requite, disposeth to counterfeit love; but really secret hatred; and puts a man into the estate of a desperate debtor, than in declining the sight of his creditor, tacitely wishes him there, where he might never see him more. For benefits oblige; and obligation is thraldome; and unrequitable obligation, perpetuall thraldome, which is to one equall, hatefull' (Thomas Hobbes, *Leviathan*, ch XI).

[7] Admittedly, this is a loose way of talking about the genesis of remedial rights. Something is not a wrong unless it is a violation of a prior obligation. By contrast, consent creates the primary legal right–duty relationship. The concept of 'wronging' does not create the relationship in the same way that a voluntary undertaking does. What provides the normative foundation for the primary obligations of tort law, however, lies well outside the scope of this paper. I would like to thank Andrew Robertson for his helpful comments on this point.

[8] The most sophisticated attempt at presenting unjust enrichment as a standalone generator of a legal obligation is Ernest Weinrib's. In brief, Weinrib argues that unjust enrichment possesses the structure of all other private law actions in that it is bilateral. This means that the obligation-creating aspects of the action must correlate to its rights-possessing features. In other words, the reason that the defendant has an obligation is that the plaintiff has a right. The right is correlatively reflected in the defendant's obligation. To counter the apparent one-sidedness of the unjust enrichment transaction (the defendant commits no wrong, does not consent and cannot even be said to act), Weinrib posits the normative category of 'acceptance.' The defendant must accept the transfer from the plaintiff as non-gratuitously given. This correlates to the plaintiff's transferring the value non-gratuitously. See EJ Weinrib, *Corrective Justice* (Oxford, Oxford University Press, 2012) 185–229; EJ Weinrib, 'The Structure of Unjustness' (2012) 92 *Boston University Law Review* 1067; EJ Weinrib, 'The Normative Structure of Unjust Enrichment' in R Grantham and C Rickett (eds), *Structure and Justification in Private Law: Essays for Peter Birks* (Oxford, Hart Publishing, 2008).

[9] Doctrinal support for this can be found in *Deglman v Guaranty Trust Co of Canada*, [1954] SCR 725, 734, in which Justice Cartwright found the plaintiff's right to recover the value of his services was 'based, not on the contract, but on an obligation imposed by law'.

[10] Absent certain (limited) circumstances: the inviter is your senior colleague, the invitee is only in town visiting for a short while, the inviter invites the invitee solely to entertain another guest. For a detailed discussion of this

enforceable, at least not in our present legal system. You might say that my dinner invitation was a gift and therefore could be legally cognisable as such. Even in the case of social gifts, however, I incur an obligation, although not a legal one, to return in kind. The law, perhaps infamously, is unwilling to impose positive obligations to act for the sake of others.[11] Other positive legal duties— to pay damages, to perform one's contract—are grounded in anterior actions (wrongdoing or consent, respectively) of the obligee. Neither of these obligation-creating circumstances is present in situations of unjust enrichment: the defendant has done no wrong—he is merely a passive recipient of a benefit—and he does not need to have made an undertaking with respect to the transfer.[12] Nevertheless, liability in unjust enrichment attaches.

The key to understanding unjust enrichment lies in discovering the normative basis for the defendant's remedial obligation of restitution. I would suggest that we have yet to come up with a completely satisfactory answer to this question. Fortunately, while we struggle with unjust enrichment *in theory*, *in practice*, we have little difficulty imposing the duty. Here, as well, we are clear that mere receipt of a benefit is an insufficient basis for a legal obligation:

> The common law has never been willing to compensate a plaintiff on the sole basis that his actions have benefited another. Lord Halsbury scotched this heresy in the case of *The Ruabon Steamship Company, Limited v London Assurance* with the words: '… I cannot understand how it can be asserted that it is part of the common law that where one person gets some advantage from the act of another a right of contribution towards the expense from that act arises on behalf of the person who has done it.' Lord MacNaghten, in the same case, put it this way: 'there is no principle of law which requires that a person should contribute to an outlay merely because he has derived a material benefit from it'. It is not enough for the court simply to determine that one spouse has benefited at the hands of another and then to require restitution. It must, in addition, be evident that the retention of the benefit would be 'unjust' in the circumstances of the case.[13]

To summarise, then, as a general rule, when one receives a gratuitous benefit (when one is (i) enriched at (ii) the expense of another), no legal obligation demanding the benefit's return attaches; more is required: one's retention must be unjust.

The question of precisely what makes retention unjust attracts rival approaches.[14] The first, historically associated with the common law, looks to see whether a specific kind of reason exists to reverse the transfer, ie whether something is wrong with the plaintiff's intention or ability to transfer the benefit effectively to the defendant. The second, associated with civilian legal systems, views transfers as falling into one of two categories—those with or those without legal basis—reversing the latter while upholding the former.

As I will explain below, because it looks to juristic reasons and not to unjust factors, the Canadian approach is said to possess a civilian orientation.[15] Let us now look at the rival approaches in more detail.[16]

---

everyday yet fascinating social ritual, see W Miller, *Humiliation and Other Essays on Honor, Social Discomfort, and Violence* (Ithaca, Cornell University Press, 1993) 25–35.

[11] Somewhat infamously, absent a special relationship, there is no duty to rescue at common law: *Osterlind v Hill*, 160 NE 301 (Mass SC 1928).

[12] Notably, sometimes the defendant has made an undertaking, but the contract's basis subsequently fails due to the operation of an unjust factor. This situation is not necessary, however, for the cause of action to arise. Moreover, the failure of consideration can be seen in some cases as evidence of consent's negation.

[13] *Pettkus v Becker* [1980] 2 SCR 834, 848 (Dickson J), citing *The Ruabon Steamship Company Ltd v London Assurance* [1900] AC 6, 10 (Lord Halsbury) and 15 (Lord Macnaghten).

[14] P Birks, *Unjust Enrichment*, 2nd edn (Oxford, Oxford University Press, 2005) ch 5.

[15] Hunt, 'The Decline of Juristic Reasons?', above n 2, 173: 'Canada, unique among common law jurisdictions, has shifted from a common law approach to a civilian model.'

[16] Despite the promise of more detail, this necessarily remains a very general overview.

The Common Law Approach—Unjust Factors

Lord Mansfield in *Moses v Macferlan* provides the classic statement regarding the common law approach to unjust enrichment:

> [The action] lies for money paid by mistake; or upon a consideration which happens to fail; or for money got through imposition (express or implied) or extortion; or oppression; or an undue advantage taken of the plaintiff's situation, contrary to laws made for the protection of persons under those circumstances.[17]

According to the common law approach, the question of unjustness turns on particular factors associated with the impugned transaction. Peter Birks, the leading influential private law scholar and taxonomist, organised the unjust factors into three categories: impaired intention, unconscientiousness and miscellaneous policy factors.[18] The first concerns the state of mind of the plaintiff;[19] the second refers to the defendant's shoddy conduct or behaviour;[20] and the last is a grab bag of factors with no unifying theme other than discrete policy-based reasons to reverse the transfers.[21] In the instantly more accessible language of the playground, the plaintiff in the first category says, 'I didn't mean for you to have it'; in the second, she avers, 'It was bad for you to take it'; while the third-category plaintiff pleads, 'Mother says give it back!'[22]

To summarise, the common law cause of action in unjust enrichment requires that the plaintiff establish (i) an enrichment to the defendant (ii) at her expense (iii) that it would be unjust for him to retain *due to* the operation of one of the recognised or analogous unjust factors.

The Civilian Approach—Juristic Reasons

By contrast, the civilian approach

> begin[s] from the proposition that every enrichment at another's expense either has an explanation known to the law or has not. Enrichments are received with the purpose of discharging an obligation or, if without obligation, to achieve some other objective as for instance the making of a gift, the satisfaction of a condition, or the coming into being of a new contract. These outcomes

---

[17] *Moses v Macferlan* (1760) 2 Burr 1005, 97 ER 676 (KB).

[18] P Birks and R Chambers, *Restitution Research Resource 1997* (Oxford, Mansfield Press, 1997) 3. It is important to note that Birks, above n 14, moved away from the unjust factor approach, endorsing an absence of basis understanding as the best interpretation of English law.

[19] Examples of factors that impair intent are: mistake, duress, undue influence, ignorance, powerlessness, incapacity and failure of consideration.

[20] Here we find the unjust factors of free acceptance and knowing receipt. Notably, Birks changed his mind with respect to this category as well, preferring to place it under the law of wrongs, not autonomous unjust enrichment. The result: the cause of action of unjust enrichment no longer quadrates with the remedy of restitution; restitutionary relief can arise from wrongs as well as unjust enrichments (not to mention contracts). For further discussion, see M McInnes, 'The Measure of Restitution' (2002) 52 *University of Toronto Law Journal* 163; M McInnes, 'At the Plaintiff's Expense: Quantifying Restitutionary Relief' (1998) 57 *CLJ* 472.

[21] Examples from the case law of miscellaneous policy factors include: emergency intervention, ultra vires taxation, common liability and withdrawal from illegality.

[22] According to Lionel Smith, Peter Birks used these labels mainly in person, not in print: Smith, above n 2, 303, n 73.

succeeding, the enrichment is sufficiently explained. An enrichment which turns out to have no such explanation is inexplicable and cannot be retained.[23]

Thus, the civilian approach to unjust enrichment tackles the question of injustice differently from the common law. The plaintiff need not establish an unjust factor, but must instead demonstrate the transfer's lack of legal basis. In the words of the German Civil Code: 'He who obtains something through somebody else's performance or in another way at his expense *without a legal cause*, is obliged to make restitution to the other.'[24] The operative legal idea is that unless there is a legal cause for a transaction, the transacted goods, services (value) cannot remain where they are and must be returned; the defendant cannot keep an enrichment to which he is not legally entitled. Without a legal basis (a juristic reason, legal cause or legal ground) to explain the enrichment, how can a defendant complain if asked (or is legally compelled) to return it?[25] Legally, he has *no ground* for complaint.

The Canadian Approach

Prior to the landmark case of *Garland v Consumers' Gas Co*[26] it was unclear which approach—unjust factors or juristic reasons—the Canadian law of unjust enrichment endorsed. As a matter of history, Canada initially appears to have followed the traditional unjust factors approach.[27] The first case in Canada (not to mention the Commonwealth) to recognise the autonomous action and general principle of unjust enrichment, *Deglman v Guaranty Trust Co of Canada*,[28] referred neither to 'unjust factors' nor 'juristic reasons', deciding the matter on the basis that if a party renders services under an unenforceable contract, he has a right (granted by law, not by contract) to the return of the value of those services. Under a traditional common law analysis, the case turns on the unjust factor of failure of consideration. On the facts, the plaintiff's elderly aunt made an oral promise to leave her nephew real property in exchange for his agreeing to perform domestic services for her during her lifetime. The nephew was good to his word, but his aunt died without making the necessary changes to her will. In the language of unjust factors, the consideration (the grant of land) for which the defendant performed his promised services failed utterly.[29] In playground terms, the nephew's complaint is 'I didn't do the work for nothing!' We should note, however, that *Deglman* is perhaps equally amenable to a juristic reason analysis: there was no juristic reason for his aunt's estate to retain the value of the nephew's

---

[23] Birks, above n 14, 102–03.

[24] Bürgerliches Gesetzbuch (BGB), §812(1) (emphasis added).

[25] In Lionel Smith's modified playground terminology, the *defendant* asserts, 'You meant for me to have it', with respect to the consent-based juristic reasons. With respect to juristic reasons that fall outside of consent, the defendant states, 'Mother says I get to keep it.' Notably, there seems to be no civilian equivalent to the second category of claims, according to which the defendant's shoddy behaviour disentitles him to the enrichment. We might imagine it to be something along the lines of: 'I didn't make you hand it over.' This omission, moreover, aligns with Birks' later disavowal of this category of unjust factors as part of the law of unjust enrichment.

[26] *Garland v Consumers' Gas Co* 2004 SCC 25, [2004] 1 SCR 629.

[27] Hunt, 'Civilian Orientation', above n 2, 502; PD Maddaugh and JD McCamus, *The Law of Restitution* (Aurora, Canada Law Book, loose-leaf) 3:200.40; M McInnes, 'Unjust Enrichment, Juristic Reasons and Palm Tree Justice: *Garland v Consumers' Gas Co*' (2004) 41 *Canadian Business Law Journal* 103, 103.

[28] *Deglman v Guaranty Trust Co of Canada* [1954] SCR 725, [1954] 3 DLR 785.

[29] The aunt's promise was unenforceable because it was not in writing: *Statute of Frauds*, RSO 1950, c 371 s 4.

services. He did not gift the services and his aunt did not provide consideration for his performance (other than the oral—and so unenforceable—promise of a bequest of land) and therefore no contract existed either.

Some 20 years after *Deglman* the Canadian landscape experienced its first civilian tremor. In his concurring opinion in *Rathwell v Rathwell* Dickson J (as he then was) introduced new terminology to the Canadian unjust enrichment lexicon: 'juristic reason'.[30] According to Dickson J, the third element of the test for unjust enrichment required proof of the 'absence of any juristic reason for the enrichment'.[31] Two years later in *Pettkus v Becker*, this time for the majority, Dickson J identified the following as the necessary three elements for the action in unjust enrichment: 'an enrichment, a corresponding deprivation and *absence of any juristic reason* for the enrichment'.[32] Despite using the language of juristic reasons, Dickson J ultimately decided the case on the basis of an unjust factor: free acceptance.[33] According to at least one commentator, in the years and cases following *Pettkus v Becker*, '[i]n one decision after another *almost* without fail, the Supreme Court of Canada resolved restitutionary claims on the basis of unjust factors'.[34] The italicisation refers to a 'slim line' of authority that took Dickson J at his word(s) and applied a civilian understanding.[35]

Following years of debate (in academic circles), the Supreme Court of Canada's decision in *Garland* settled the issue: Canada's approach to unjust enrichment is that of juristic reasons, not unjust factors.[36] Iacobucci J viewed his contribution to the Canadian law of unjust enrichment as a matter of 'redefinition and reformulation',[37] not as a radical departure from the common law.[38] This perhaps reflected Justice Iacobucci's belief that prior to *Garland* Canadian unjust enrichment law already embodied the juristic reason, not the unjust factors, approach. In this spirit, he formulated the Canadian test for unjust enrichment:

> As a general matter, the test for unjust enrichment is well established in Canada. The cause of action has three elements: (1) an enrichment of the defendant; (2) a corresponding deprivation of the plaintiff; and (3) an *absence of juristic reason* for the enrichment.[39]

Recognising that it is the third element of the test that 'has been the subject of much academic commentary and criticism',[40] Iacobucci J aimed to clarify the distinctive Canadian

---

[30] *Rathwell v Rathwell* [1978] 2 SCR 436, 455. For insight into why Dickson J might have chosen this particular phrase, see L Smith, 'The Mystery of "Juristic Reasons"' (2000) 12 *Supreme Court Law Review* 211, 218.

[31] *Rathwell v Rathwell* [1978] 2 SCR 436, 455.

[32] *Pettkus v Becker* [1980] 2 SCR 834, 848 (emphasis added).

[33] ibid 849.

[34] McInnes, *Canadian Law*, above n 2, 21. McInnes provides the following cases (and others) in support of the following unjust factors: *Nepean (Township) Hydro Electric Commission v Ontario Hydro* [1982] SCJ No 15, 132 DLR (3d) 193 (SCC) for mistake; *Re Eurig* [1998] SCJ No 72, 165 DLR (4th) 1 (SCC) for compulsion; *Air Canada v British Columbia* [1989] SCJ No 44, 59 for ultra vires demand; *Kiss Estate v Kiss* [1983] SCJ No 41, 146 DLR (3d) 385 (SCC) for failure of consideration; *Sorochan v Sorochan* [1986] SCJ No 46, 29 DLR (4th) 1 (SCC) for free acceptance; and *Citadel General Assurance Co v Lloyds Bank Canada* [1997] SCJ No 192, 152 DLR (4th) 411 (SCC) for knowing receipt.

[35] In this regard, see *Peter v Beblow* [1993] 1 SCR 980; 101 DLR (4th) 621 (McLachlin J).

[36] *Garland v Consumers' Gas Co* 2004 SCC 25, [2004] 1 SCR 629, 650: 'In my view, … there is a distinctive Canadian approach to juristic reason which should be retained.'

[37] ibid.

[38] See below, text to n 46 for the view that while *Garland* does not represent a departure from the common law, Canada's approach to unjust enrichment is not principally that of juristic reasons analysis. See Maddaugh and McCamus, above n 27, 3:200.40; McCamus, above n 2.

[39] *Garland v Consumers' Gas Co* 2004 SCC 25, [2004] 1 SCR 629, 645 (emphasis added).

[40] ibid 648.

approach by way of a two-part analysis. First, the plaintiff must show that no juristic reason, from an established list of such reasons, exists.[41] The list is established by precedent and includes the following: contract; disposition of law; donative intent; and 'other valid common law, equitable or statutory obligations'.[42] If the plaintiff satisfies this first part of the juristic reason analysis by showing the absence of a recognised category of juristic reason analysis, she or he has made out a prima facie case for restitution (provided that the other two elements, enrichment and corresponding deprivation, have also been made out). The plaintiff's case may be rebutted, however, if the defendant can establish under the second part of the juristic reason analysis that a *novel* juristic reason exists. To determine whether a new juristic reason exists, both the reasonable expectations of the parties as well as public policy considerations should be considered.[43] In the words of the Court, 'This stage of analysis thus provides for a category of residual defence in which courts can look to all of the circumstances of the transaction in order to determine whether there is another reason to deny recovery.'[44]

To summarise, Canada's common law courts appear to have endorsed a civilian model for an important cause of action in the law of obligations. Alone, this could undercut the common law's claim to comprehensive commonality. If one of the three principal causes of action in the law of obligations departs starkly from common law principles, can we say that there is a *common* law of obligations? More to the point, if civilian and common law approaches to unjust enrichment are as oppositional as commentators would have one believe, then this area of law, at least with respect to Canada, can no longer be deemed as part of the common law narrative. Rather than look to other common law courts for guidance, as our courts do in other spheres of private law, Canadian courts should instead look to civilian legal systems.[45] For many, this conclusion is unpalatable. It would mean, for Canadian law at least, that we would look to civilian jurisdictions for help in the law of unjust enrichment, but common law jurisdictions for contracts, torts and property. Given that the law of unjust enrichment often intersects with property, tort and contract doctrines—eg if a benefit is transferred pursuant to a valid contract, then the law of unjust enrichment is excluded—this threatens incoherence within the law of obligations.

Can we avoid this conclusion? Logic gives us two hypothetical solutions. The first endorses the differences drawn between common and civil law treatment of unjust enrichment and denies the potential for reconciliation, but insists that the Canadian law of unjust enrichment has not changed from a common law to a civilian orientation. According to this solution, statements in *Garland* notwithstanding, Canadian courts have not in fact shifted to a juristic reason approach in all cases, but only in a rare subset. By contrast, the second solution denies the difference between civilian and common law approaches to the law of unjust enrichment and argues that they are reconcilable.

---

[41] ibid 651.

[42] ibid.

[43] ibid. In *Kerr v Baranow* 2011 SCC 10, [2011] 1 SCR 269 the SCC has, post-*Garland*, analysed the application of the second part of the juristic reason test, in particular in the context of whether mutual benefits constitute a juristic reason.

[44] *Garland v Consumers' Gas Co* 2004 SCC 25, [2004] 1 SCR 629, 651.

[45] Notably, this is *not* what Canadian courts in the wake of *Garland* have done. For example, in the relatively recent case of *BMP Global Distribution Inc v Bank of Nova Scotia* 2009 SCC 15, [2009] 1 SCR 504, the Court decided the case on the well-established common law principle of mistake of fact. See below, text to n 52.

Let us look at the first solution first. According to John McCamus, the Canadian law of unjust enrichment only uses the civilian model when confronted with a novel claim for restitution. In all other cases, the doctrine of precedent applies and with it the unjust factors.[46] Others have persuasively argued that McCamus' position simply is not in line with what the courts see themselves as doing, and, therefore, ought to be rejected.[47] In *Garland* Justice Iacobucci is explicit that 'there is a distinctive Canadian approach to juristic reasons which should be retained'.[48] Nowhere in the case relied upon by McCamus as evidence of Canada's retention of the traditional common law approach, *BMP Global Distribution Inc v Bank of Nova Scotia*,[49] does Justice Deschamps say anything like this with respect to the unjust factor approach. Indeed, nowhere in her 94-paragraph decision does she even identify a cause of action.[50] Instead, she confidently asserts that the case can be 'resolved by applying the common law rules on mistake of fact'.[51] Which rules are these? The rules of mistake of fact in contract? Those of tort? Those of unjust enrichment? Deschamps J subsequently clarifies her statement by importing Goff J's (as he then was) test for the recovery of money paid under mistake of fact in *Barclay's Bank Ltd v WJ Simms Son & Cooke (Southern) Ltd*.[52] McCamus relies on Deschamps' use of *Barclay's Bank* as evidence that we are returning to the common law approach to unjust enrichment. McCamus, however, like Deschamps J, appears to ignore the fact that *Barclay's Bank* was decided 11 years *before* English law explicitly recognised the standalone cause of action in unjust enrichment in *Lipkin Gorman v Karpnale Ltd*.[53] McCamus relies heavily on the fact that in *BMP* 'no reference is made to the juristic reason analysis in *Garland*. No mention is made of the absence of basis reasoning that one might draw from the civil law.'[54] Of course, he fails to acknowledge that no mention is made of the unjust factors approach either, let alone the cause of action of unjust enrichment.

In sum, we ought to reject both McCamus' insistence that *BMP* is 'one of the most important restitution decisions to come down from the court in recent years' and his related belief that it signifies Canadian unjust enrichment law's rejection of the juristic reason approach. An explicit judicial recognition of juristic reasons should weigh more heavily than a single judgment that seems solely by implication or omission to support the traditional common law approach. One further point on the relevance of *BMP*: while *Garland* has been cited 562 times, out of which it has been expressly followed 48 times, *BMP* has been cited only 34 times and never expressly followed.

In the spirit of taking judges at their word, in what follows, we will take up the second possible solution: that the distinctions between the approaches are overemphasised and that reconciliation is possible.

---

[46] McCamus, above n 2.

[47] McInnes, 'The Unitary Action of Unjust Enrichment', above n 2; Hunt, 'The Decline of Juristic Reasons?', above n 2; Hunt, 'The Civilian Orientation of Canadian Unjust Enrichment', above n 2. For McCamus's response, see McCamus, above n 2, 97–98.

[48] *Garland v Consumers' Gas Co* 2004 SCC 25, [2004] 1 SCR 629, 650.

[49] *BMP Global Distribution Inc v Bank of Nova Scotia* 2009 SCC 15, [2009] 1 SCR 504.

[50] For criticism of this feature of *BMP*, see Z Sinel, 'Causes of Action and Self-Help Remedies: *BMP Global v Bank of NS*' [2009] 17 *Restitution Law Review* 122, 126.

[51] *BMP Global Distribution Inc v Bank of Nova Scotia* 2009 SCC 15, [2009] 1 SCR 504, [19].

[52] *Barclay's Bank Ltd v WJ Simms Son & Cooke (Southern) Ltd* [1980] 1 QB 677, 695; *BMP Global Distribution Inc v Bank of Nova Scotia* 2009 SCC 15, [2009] 1 SCR 504 [21]–[22].

[53] *Lipkin Gorman v Karpnale Ltd* [1991] 1 AC 548.

[54] McCamus, above n 2, 99.

III. Distinctions … Without Difference?

It is largely accepted that, while normally supplying identical results, the two approaches are alternatives: 'Juristic reasons and unjust factors operate in opposite directions.'[55] Against the position that the Canadian law of unjust enrichment employs both common law and civilian approaches,[56] Mitchell McInnes avers, 'the distinction between those two approaches is profound'.[57] In this, McInnes is likely influenced by Peter Birks' point about classification: that absence of basis cannot simply be integrated into the unjust factors approach by calling it another unjust factor.[58] Birks was surely correct that, taxonomically, absence of basis could not be considered the same as an unjust factor because unjust factors 'cannot stand beside absence of basis, only under it'.[59] In other words, unjust factors tell us why there is no basis, but are not equivalent to absence of basis. In the same way, absence of basis does not tell us *why* there is no basis for the enrichment. The two approaches operate on different levels of abstraction, with unjust factors identifying the particular reasons a transfer is defective and absence of basis indicating, more generally, that a lack of legal basis warrants the remedy of restitution. In a more forceful vein, Birks asserts, '[i]n the end, therefore, there is no question of integrating absence of basis anywhere in the list of unjust factors. … They [ie unjust factors and absence of basis] are incompatibly *alternative methods of deciding which enrichments are unjust.*'[60]

As already discussed, one commonly referenced distinction is that the unjust factors approach belongs to the common law, while the juristic reason (or absence of basis) belongs to civilian legal systems, but the following instances of opposition can be found in the literature as well: the involvement of contrasting operative reasons and the related imposition of different burdens of proof; the use of different modes of legal reasoning; and the implication of rival political philosophies. These last two distinctions, recall, are commonly thought to unify the common law when substance and authority do not. Through the following analysis of these potential distinctions in the context of the Canadian law of unjust enrichment, we may better see the appeal (or the lack thereof) of these formal and genealogical differences.

Genesis

One obvious distinction between the unjust factor and juristic reason approaches is their historical and geographical origins: the former belongs to the common law system whereas the latter finds its home in civil law.[61]

---

[55]   McInnes, 'The Unitary Action of Unjust Enrichment', above n 2, 123.
[56]   This is McCamus's position, discussed above, text accompanying n 46.
[57]   McInnes, 'Making Sense of Juristic Reasons', above n 2, 402.
[58]   Birks, above n 14, 114.
[59]   ibid.
[60]   ibid 115 (emphasis added).
[61]   McInnes, 'The Reason to Reverse', above n 2, 1054. But see Smith, above n 2, for doubt that any civilian system has ever functioned solely on the basis of a juristic reason approach.

But what are we to make of this distinction? Do different historical provenances tell us anything substantive about the two approaches? Not necessarily. In themselves, their separate histories tell us nothing other than that they have different historical origins. What matters is how and in what way this historical context might have shaped the substance of the cause of action, not the historical context itself. Moreover, it is doubtful that any civilian system has ever really had a pure juristic reasons account of unjust enrichment. As Lionel Smith asserts, 'no legal system of which I am aware has a law of unjust enrichment that functions entirely on the basis of juristic reasons';[62] the conclusion that a transfer is without legal ground 'is only part of the story'.[63] According to Smith, absence of legal ground only operates with respect to purposive enrichments—ie cases in which the plaintiff intends to enrich the defendant, but the purpose (the legal ground) for the enrichment fails. While an 'important category of cases',[64] it does not include 'cases in which the plaintiff improves the defendant's property thinking it belongs to the plaintiff', cases in which the plaintiff discharges another's debt under a guarantee or cases in which the plaintiff is wholly unaware of the defendant's enrichment at her expense.[65] Furthermore, there is room for the continued relevance of unjust factors in Canadian law. As evidence, a recent Supreme Court of Canada case, *BMP Global Distribution Inc v Bank of Nova Scotia*, was decided on mistake,[66] and in *Garland* mistake was relevant to establish the lack of juristic reason.[67]

We may safely conclude that the fact of distinct historical origin does little more than restate the allegation that the approaches are alternative. It tells us little about *how* they might differ. If Sam is from the United States and Jean from Canada, stating that Sam is American and Jean is Canadian does not help us understand the ways in which Sam and Jean are different, ie what makes Americans different from Canadians. For this, we must delve deeper.

Method of Legal Reasoning

We are told that common law reasoning is inductive and civilian, deductive:

> Common-law courts historically worked inductively, from the ground up. The common law—that wondrous 'heap of good learning'—consists of the accumulated wisdom of the ages. Its lawyers proceed 'downward-looking to the cases,' rather than upwards to 'an unknowable justice in the sky.' Civilians, in contrast, proceed deductively, drawing down from broad principles.[68]

---

[62] Smith, above n 2, 286.

[63] ibid.

[64] ibid 288.

[65] ibid.

[66] *BMP Global Distribution Inc v Bank of Nova Scotia* 2009 SCC 15, [2009] 1 SCR 504, [18].

[67] For an argument that consequence of *Garland* test is the nullification of the legal significance of mistake, see L Smith, 'Public Justice and Private Justice: Restitution after *Kingstreet*' (2008) 46 *Canadian Business Law Journal* 11, 14–15.

[68] McInnes, 'The Reason to Reverse', above n 2, 1054 (footnotes omitted). See also McInnes, 'The Unitary Action', above n 2, 107–08. In a similar vein, according to Thomas Krebs: 'The German law of unjust enrichment operates *deductively*, its starting point is a wide general principle, which is limited and narrowed down both by the codification itself and by subsequent academic analysis and interpretation. English law, on the other hand, has chosen to extend the incidence of restitution for unjust enrichment little by little, case by case, always, until now, on the basis that there must be some good reason why restitution should be available.' T Krebs, 'In Defence of Unjust Factors' in D Johnston and R Zimmermann (eds), *Unjustified Enrichment—Key Issues in Comparative Perspective*

Some venture that this difference in legal reasoning suggests a fundamental difference in temperament between continental Europeans and those across the Channel:

> If we may generalize, the European is given to making plans, to regulating things in advance, and therefore, in terms of law, to drawing up rules and systematizing them. He approaches life with fixed ideas, and operates deductively. The Englishman improvises, never making a decision until he has to: 'we'll cross that bridge when we come to it.' As Maitland said, he is an empiricist. Only experience counts for him; theorizing has little appeal; and so he is not given to abstract rules of law. Convinced, perhaps from living by the sea, that life will controvert the best-laid plans, the Englishman is more at home with case-law proceeding cautiously step-by-step than with legislation which purports to lay down rules for the solution of all future cases.[69]

In the law of unjust enrichment, this distinction can be cashed out quite easily: the unjust factors are discrete instances exhibiting the same legal phenomenon, the principle of unjust enrichment. At first, common law courts recognised separately each type of unjust factor—eg the court in *Barclay's Bank* provided restitution on the basis of money paid over under mistake. In England in 1991 the courts perceived from these particular instances a common thread and the law of unjust enrichment was recognised. In a similar vein, the first US Restatement on the law of restitution did not *create* the law of unjust enrichment.[70] As McCamus writes, 'it will be obvious that the law of restitution existed for years—indeed hundreds of years—prior to the publication of the *Restatement* in 1937. The *Restatement* merely reorganized the doctrine and restated it in a more convenient form.'[71] By contrast, or so the story goes, civilians begin with a general principle that unjustified enrichments—ie enrichments without legal or moral basis—must be returned. This principle is then applied, top-down, to discrete potential factual instantiations of it.

This alleged contrast between inductive and deductive modes of reasoning reflects a further distinction between the so-called 'man on the street' and his generally reviled foil, the philosopher in the clouds:

> Had unjust enrichment clung to its unjust factors, it would have been an untidy heap, like tort, but its one compensating merit would have been that, in any one case, it was *accessible to ordinary intelligence*. The *layman* who wants restitution says 'It was a mistake', 'I was forced to hand it over', 'I was under his thumb', 'it was for a purpose which never came off', and so on. In *1990 the common law still spoke much the same language as the Clapham omnibus.* ... [By contrast,] [n]o passenger on the Clapham omnibus ever demanded restitution for want of legally sufficient basis.[72]

(Cambridge, Cambridge University Press, 2002) 99. For a famous articulation of the distinction between top-down and bottom-up legal reasoning, see R Posner, 'Legal Reasoning from the Top Down and from the Bottom Up: The Question of Unenumerated Constitutional Rights' (1992) 59 *University of Chicago Law Review* 433.

[69] T Weir (tr), K Zweigert and H Kotz, *An Introduction to Comparative Law*, 3rd edn (Oxford, Oxford University Press, 1998) 70. Another way to understand the difference between inductive and deductive approaches to the law is that the unjust factors approach can be said to be specific and particular, while the juristic reasons approach is general and abstract. The former focuses on discrete reasons for the enrichment to be reversed, while the latter at its heart asks a unitary question: whether there is a legal basis for the transfer. For an argument that unjust enrichment is pluralistic like tort law, not unitary like contract, see S Smith, 'Unjust Enrichment: Nearer to Tort than Contract' in R Chambers, C Mitchell and J Penner (eds), *Philosophical Foundations of the Law of Unjust Enrichment* (Oxford, Oxford University Press, 2009).

[70] American Law Institute, *Restatement of the Law of Restitution: Quasi-Contracts and Constructive Trusts* (American Law Institute Publishers, Philadelphia 1937).

[71] McCamus, above n 2, 90.

[72] Birks, above n 14, 107–08 and 115 (emphasis added).

In Australia the courts treat this difference as a knock against the overly philosophical civilian approach:

> To the lawyer whose mind has been moulded by civilian influences, the theory may come first, and the source of the theory may be the writings of jurists not the decisions of judges. However, that is not the way in which a system based on case law develops; over time, general principle is derived from judicial decisions upon particular instances, not the other way around.[73]

While it is likely the case—and this chapter is not the place to tackle this—that deductive and inductive approaches are distinct modes of reasoning, it is unclear that judges ever in either legal system (common or civil) do just one or the other. Rather, judges reason simultaneously in both directions, applying general abstract principles to discrete facts and reasoning by analogy (a common deductive reasoning strategy) to fit new cases within established precedent and under the umbrella of a more general principle. As Carmine Conte has recently urged:

> Interpreted in this way, there is no such thing as pure 'top-down' or pure 'bottom-up' reasoning. If there were, the pure 'bottom-up' adjudicator seeking practical justice without an organizational theory would be lost in Tennyson's wilderness of single instances.[74]

Sophisticated judges in sophisticated legal systems will make use of whatever legal reasoning tools they have available. Sometimes this will involve drawing out a general principle from particular instances that are united by it. At other times judges will apply this general principle to a discrete factual instantiation of it, incrementally changing the scope of the common law. More often, however, judges will do both at once, recognising a general principle and testing to see if a case fits under it by comparing it to other like cases that seem to exhibit the general principle.

Burden of Proof and Operative Reasons for Restitution

One apparently striking way in which the approaches diverge involves the plaintiff's burden of proof. Under the unjust factors approach, she must establish a *positive* factor to reverse an enrichment, alleging that the benefit was transferred in the circumstance of an operative unjust factor: mistake, free acceptance, compulsion, etc. By contrast, the juristic reasons approach demands that she prove the existence of a *negative*, a lack of juristic reason, demonstrating that a just factor (a juristic reason), such as a contract, a gift, a disposition of law or some other legal obligation, does not exist.[75]

---

[73] *Roxborough v Rothmans of Pall Mall Australia Ltd* [2001] HCA 68, (2001) 208 CLR 516, [73] (Gummow J). Notably, Gummow J's remarks were intended as a criticism of Peter Birks' methodology. This was later endorsed by the entire court in *Farah Constructions Pty Ltd v Say-Dee Pty Ltd* [2007] HCA 22, (2007) 230 CLR 89, [154]. But see K Mason, 'Do Top-down and Bottom-up Reasoning Ever Meet?' in E Bant and M Harding (eds), *Exploring Private Law* (Cambridge, Cambridge University Press, 2010); C Conte, 'From Only the "Bottom-up"? Legitimate Forms of Judicial Reasoning in Private Law' (2015) 35 *OJLS* 1.

[74] Conte, above n 73, 14.

[75] Smith, above n 30, 228. Pre-*Garland*, Smith suggested that to counter the obvious difficulty in asking a plaintiff to prove a negative, 'one would need a closed list of such reasons'. In *Garland*, Iacobucci J directly responded to Smith's criticism by establishing, in part one of the juristic reason analysis, a category of recognised juristic reasons for the plaintiff to demonstrate: 2004 SCC 25, [2004] 1 SCR 629, 651.

Even if we ignore the practical difficulties associated with it, what could be more differ-ent from proving a positive than proving a negative? Many things, it turns out. Logically, proving a positive and proving a negative are neither oppositional nor alternative. One way to establish the existence of a negative is to demonstrate a positive reason for its non-existence. If we know that certain features of a putative transaction vitiate the basis of that transaction, then the existence of one of these features supports our proof of a negative: the absence of legal ground to support the transfer of value. This relationship between unjust factors (positive features) and absence of basis (negative feature) undergirded Birks' 'limited reconciliation' of the two approaches, pursuant to which

> [a] pyramid can be constructed in which, at the base, the particular unjust factors such as mistake, pressure, and undue influence become reasons why, higher up, there is no basis for the defendant's acquisition, which is then the master reason why, higher up still, the enrichment is unjust and must be surrendered.[76]

In sum, despite initial appearances, according to Birks, the negative and positive proof aspects of the approaches are not necessarily opposed. Rather, they support one another in determinations of absence of basis. Far from being mutually exclusive, they might be seen as two sides of the same coin.

Perhaps the unjust factors work this way. Perhaps they are the particular reasons that support or explain the 'master reason' that there is no reason (no basis) for the benefit's retention by the defendant. The significance of unjust factors, therefore, should be limited to their evidential effect only. It is not the normative fact of undue influence that renders a transfer unjust to retain, but rather undue influence makes it so that there is no longer a valid reason for retention and the absence of this reason to retain is what grounds the claim in unjust enrichment. I have to admit that there is something a little odd in grounding a positive obligation to return on the basis of a non-existent reason to retain. This ten-sion is aptly brought out in McInnes' repeated characterisation of the positive and negative aspects of unjust enrichment: that while the common law unjust factors approach says 'no restitution unless …', the civilian juristic reason approach says 'restitution unless …'.[77] This signals a markedly different perspective with respect to entitlements. While the unjust factors approach treats transfers as presumptively valid such that a positive reason must be established to justify their unwinding, the juristic reason approach looks at transactions more suspiciously, as requiring legal explanation.

In the language of reasons, the presumption about entitlements amounts to a distinction between reasons for reversing transfers and reasons for keeping transfers:

> The English formulation is understood to imply that the plaintiff must establish some positive reason which makes the enrichment unjust or reversible. Such reasons include that the plaintiff was mistaken or compelled in conferring the enrichment, or that the defendant's conduct can be characterized as 'free acceptance' of the enrichment. These are reasons for *reversing* transfers of wealth. The Canadian formulation suggests a different outlook: that the enrichment will be revers-ible unless some 'juristic reason' is established which will allow the defendant to retain the enrich-ment. Examples might be that the plaintiff was obliged to confer the enrichment, or did so as a gift. These are reasons for *keeping* transfers of wealth.[78]

---

[76] Birks, above n 14, 116.
[77] McInnes, 'Making Sense of Juristic Reasons', above n 2, 402; McInnes, 'A Return to First Principles in Unjust Enrichment', above n 2, 279; McInnes, 'The Unitary Action in Unjust Enrichment', above n 2, 106–07.
[78] Smith, above n 30, 214.

Lionel Smith insists that '[t]here is a tremendously important issue here', and that '[a] list of reasons for reversing enrichments will look very different from a list of reasons for keeping them'.[79] If we understand the operative reasons for keeping and reversing enrichments as premised on certain default rules about the status of entitlements, then Smith is correct and these reasons are not amenable to reconciliation. According to this interpretation, they directly implicate and reflect a choice concerning our default rules about transfers. They reflect the legal status of transfers, specifically, whether a transfer of value creates either a defeasible or a conditional entitlement.[80] The unjust factors approach aligns with a system of private law that considers all transfers to be prima facie justified, leaving it to the interested parties to establish that they are not. Entitlements are defeasible, but prima facie justified. By contrast, the juristic reasons approach treats transfers as conditional on the establishment of a legal basis.

In this vein Kit Barker asks: '[A]re the gains we make at the expense of others something we need to justify, or something we are presumptively entitled to keep?'[81] The mere fact of gain does not in itself provide sufficient ground for a remedial obligation. In much the same way, the mere fact of causation does not provide sufficient ground for compensation in tort law. That I am the cause of your loss is not sufficient for liability. It must also be shown that my action was wrongful in a particular sort of way.[82] If gain in itself is not suspect and entitlements are thus considered prima facie just, then 'it makes no moral sense for it [the common law] to ask as its primary super-structural question whether a defendant's gain is justifiable by reference to some legal ground or, as the Canadians say, "juristic reason".'[83] This is because that which is prima facie morally and legally justified does not require further justification. For Barker, this confuses negative and positive justifications for liability. In the context of standard competitive norms that pervade commercial dealings, we do not have to explain our gains. This is why in the common law approach to unjust enrichment the plaintiff must show why the defendant's gain is unjust:[84]

> The onus must lie on those who wish to claim them to provide a good reason for doing so, by showing not just that they are related to some harm they have suffered, but also that the way in which they have been made violates some behavioral (or possibly distributive) norm.[85]

The purpose of this section is not to take sides with respect to which default rule (operative reason) is better. Rather, its aim is to show that these approaches are in fact *opposed*. The approaches cannot be reconciled as they concern alternative default rules for a legal system.

---

[79] ibid.

[80] This raises interesting questions concerning the role our understanding of rescission might play in informing our grasp of the law of unjust enrichment. Some transfers can be rescinded, provided the principle of *restitution in integrum* is satisfied. To what extent does this help our understanding of the role of unjust enrichment in grounding restitutionary relief? How does it help our comprehension of the defense of change of position? For deeper analyses of the issues related to rescission, see B Häcker, 'Proprietary Restitution after Impaired Consent Transfers: A Generalised Power Model' (2009) 68 *CLJ* 324; E Bant, 'Rights and Value in Rescission: Some Implications for Unjust Enrichment' in D Nolan and A Robertson (eds), *Rights and Private Law* (Oxford, Hart Publishing, 2012) 609.

[81] K Barker, 'Responsibility for Gain: Unjust Factors or Absence of Legal Ground? Starting Points in Unjust Enrichment Law' in C Rickett and R Grantham (eds), *Structure and Justification in Private Law: Essays for Peter Birks* (Oxford, Hart Publishing, 2008) 47.

[82] ibid 55, accepting Peter Cane and Tony Honoré's thesis that gain and causation are not sufficient for liability.

[83] ibid 57.

[84] ibid 73.

[85] ibid.

Does our legal system treat transfers as prima facie just or as prima facie justifiable? Furthermore, if it treats some types of transfers as putatively just, but not others, what accounts for the difference? The former puts the onus on the plaintiff to establish the unjustness (and this can be done through either an unjust factors or juristic reasons approach); the latter places the onus on the defendant to prove he is entitled to keep the entitlement.

Notwithstanding the approaches' opposition and despite Canadian law's civilian overtones, we may still doubt whether Canada has indeed fully adopted the latter. Canadian law does not ask the defendant to furnish a juristic reason for the transferred benefit. It does not treat all enrichments, in other words, as prima facie unjustified. Rather, the plaintiff must show the absence of a juristic reason. If she succeeds, her prima facie case in unjust enrichment is made out subject to the defendant's ability to raise a *new* juristic reason as a defence. As such, Canadian law maintains its commitment to the default rule concerning entitlements that is adopted elsewhere in the common law.

Political Philosophy

Default rules concerning entitlements can be said to reflect a deeper distinction in political philosophy between liberalism and communitarianism. Flying under the radar of most unjust enrichment commentators, this philosophical distinction grounds the other differences in a principled way.[86] Commenting on Hayek's argument that the English legal tradition of the common law was superior to the French civilian system, Mahoney explains that: '[T]he common law is historically connected to strong protection for property rights against state action, whereas the civil law is connected to a strong and less constrained central government.'[87] Thus, while the English common law 'was principally a law of property',[88] the civil code was an expression of a 'desire to sacrifice all rights to political ends'.[89] Viewed in this light, the different orientation of the two approaches has political significance. Systems such as English common law (ie systems that are principally about protecting individual property not only from other individuals who might interfere with it, but also from a state that cannot be trusted) would naturally develop an outlook that property transfers are prima facie justified. In the common law world, one must be secure in the possession of property one has. (Of course, in the context of unjust enrichment, this works against the property interests of the mistaken transferor). Rather than say 'property' is key, we might then better say that 'possession' is the significant interest in question. A positive reason is required to divest one of the things of value in one's possession. By contrast, in a system where individual rights are enjoyed only as a means to a common good or end, the receipt of property and its retention may always be defeasible to the common interest.[90]

---

[86] A notable exception can be found in McInnes, 'The Reason to Reverse', above n 2, 1054: 'It also has been suggested that whereas the common law was concerned with the individual, the civil law was communitarian and hence more inclined to become involved in day-to-day life.'

[87] P Mahoney, 'The Common Law and Economic Growth: Hayek Might Be Right' (2001) 30 *Journal of Legal Studies* 503, 507.

[88] ibid 508.

[89] ibid 510 (quoting the code's principal drafter).

[90] This distinction between underlying political philosophies might also explain why Kantian legal theorists such as Ernest Weinrib within the common law system have few difficulties accepting the absence of basis approach to the law of unjust enrichment given Kant's civil law environment.

The communitarian flavour of civilian understandings of unjust enrichment, I suggest, is one hitherto unexplored explanation for why Canada's law of unjust enrichment possesses the civilian undertones it does. The legal context of the leading unjust enrichment cases in Canada that introduced the terminology of 'juristic reason' into its lexicon—*Rathwell v Rathwell* and *Pettkus v Becker*—is family law. In family law scenarios it is conceivable that the common law's narrow focus on individual autonomy and its concomitant presumption of the justice of transfers ought not apply. Rather, in family law, the better focus is on the common good (as between the spouses). As such, enrichments transferred between spouses are conditional on the common good of that relationship rather than presumed to be the products of individual autonomous actions meriting legitimacy. This is merely a suggestion. Clearly, this hypothesis about the intersection of family law and unjust enrichment requires careful doctrinal analysis to determine whether transfers are treated differently in family law contexts from other private law contexts.

The Canadian Law of Unjust Enrichment: More Common than Civil

The Canadian law of unjust enrichment has provided fertile ground for those obsessed, perhaps unhealthily, with drawing binary distinctions between the civil and common law of obligations. As we have seen, however, the majority of these differences have been overstated. Further, the important and irreconcilable difference concerning a legal system's entitlement default rules (operative reasons for restitution), a distinction that perhaps arises from the additionally true, although admittedly not very nuanced, distinction between underlying political philosophies, does not map perfectly onto the current interpretation of Canadian unjust enrichment law, which, on its first branch, requires the plaintiff to provide a reason to reverse the transfer. Thus, Canadian law appears for the most part to retain the common law's emphasis on the prima facie justness of entitlements as well as the liberal individualism at the heart of the common law, despite its foray into the language of juristic reasons. Therefore, if it is the case that my premises regarding common law unity with respect to form and genealogy are correct, then the Canadian law of unjust enrichment, despite its civilian language and leanings, is no true threat to a limited common law commonality.

We might further say that to the extent that Canadian law gestures toward a civilian, communitarian approach to unjust enrichment, this actually reflects rather than subverts the nature of the common law as the mixing of elements of common and civil reflects Canada's mixed colonial heritage of England and France. Let me explain. Common law reasoning is said to be inductive because *common* law refers not to commonality in the sense of unity or universality, but to its basis in the commons—it is the law of the people. Therefore, if its relevant people, its commons, is composed of a mixed Anglo-American individualism alongside, perhaps tempered by, a French communitarianism,[91] then it is only natural that the treatment of unjust enrichment in the Canadian context will come to reflect these uniquely Canadian political and cultural features.

---

[91] We should also not ignore the influence of First Nations legal and social structures. Knowledge of this subject falls well outside the ambit of this author's bailiwick, but it is an interesting and important subject for future work.

IV. The Bigger Picture: How Method Distracts
from Substance

So far we have seen that the putative differences between the common and civil law approaches to the question of unjustness in unjust enrichment either are not all that different or do not fully apply to the Canadian situation and, therefore, are not as challenging to the unity of the common law as we might initially have suspected. What more is there to say? I think this: when we focus on methodology, on the type of approach we take to whether an enrichment is 'unjust', we fail to inquire into the nature of the injustice that justifies the defendant's legally imposed restitutionary obligation. Because the war between the approaches focuses on unpacking the issue of 'unjust', we think we answer this question. In reality, however, it receives superficial attention. Instead of asking what justifies the defendant's restitutionary obligation, we focus on justifying our preferred method.

A response that what makes the transfer unjust is either an unjust factor or a lack of juristic reason does not answer the fundamental question of what substantively makes the enrichment *sufficiently unjust* to warrant imposing a duty on the defendant to restore it to the plaintiff.

First, the presence of an unjust factor is not sufficient to explain the restitutionary duty. If I mistakenly pay $100 into your bank account and you, thinking the money is rightfully yours, spend it on a delicious dinner out, I have no claim against you in unjust enrichment.[92] The descriptive fact of mistake simply is not enough to ground a normative obligation in you—at least not in situations where you have changed your position. If it were the case that the plaintiff had a right to the return of his or her transferred benefit (and thus the defendant was under a correlative duty to return), then the fact of the defendant's change of position should not change the plaintiff's entitlement. How can an action of one party, independent of the other, somehow change the normative relations between them? Actions that change the normative status of another are commonly referred to as powers, but it seems odd to say that the defendant has a power over the plaintiff to change her relationship to him vis-à-vis the mistaken transfer.

Second, absence of basis is similarly an insufficient normative foundation for the duty. Birks' often-cited example of the freeloading tenant shows why:

> If I live in a flat, and you live above me, in winter my central heating will cut your fuel bills. Heat rises. Investment in insulation may minimize the escape of warmth for which I am paying, but it is true in a sense that I am powerless to prevent this benefit accruing to you. You are enriched in that you are saving heating expenditure which you would inevitably incur if I turned my heating off, and the enrichment is coming from me.[93]

The upstairs tenant cannot point to any juristic reason for his enrichment, but the downstairs tenant has no right of restitution. Birks explains this situation as one of gift, but this is

---

[92] Stephen Smith refers to a situation of dropping money down a hole. In such a situation, no new normative relationship is created by virtue of my mistake. Without some further argument, mistaken payment to another is normatively identical to dropping money down a bottomless pit. In neither scenario can the plaintiff's loss be described as normative. If no new normative relationship is generated when we merely lose possession of money, how can the normative significance of the loss change merely because the hole I dropped my money down turns out to be someone else's bank account? S Smith, 'Justifying the Law of Unjust Enrichment' (2001) 79 *Texas Law Review* 2177, 2189–90.

[93] Birks, above n 14, 158.

unsatisfactory as it stretches the meaning of gift too far: plainly, the downstairs tenant does not intend to benefit his neighbour. In Birks' own words, he is 'powerless to prevent' it.[94] A further example of the insufficiency of lack of juristic reason arises in cases of officious intermeddlers. A stranger armed with a squeegee and a bucket full of soapy water washes my car window while I am stopped at a red light. There is no juristic reason for this transfer. It is not a gift. I know this because he has requested $2 for his troubles. Still, we would not think I am bound to pay him once the work is accomplished.[95]

My point is that talk about proper unjust enrichment methodology has obscured the question of fundamental importance. By spending time and intellectual energy on determining whether Canada's approach is civilian or common law with respect to the issue of unjustness, we have lost sight of what it means for a transaction to be unjust, ie what injustice in the context of unjust enrichment means. Neither the presence of an unjust factor nor the absence of a juristic reason answers this fundamental question.

This is not to say that the scholarship on this issue has been a total waste of time and energy. In fact, at least one of the commonly drawn distinctions between the approaches can help us shape our inquiry into the restitutionary obligation's nature, namely that concerning entitlement default rules of entitlements: 'restitution unless …' versus 'no restitution unless …'. When the plaintiff mistransfers something of value (whether tangible or not—eg a service) to the defendant, the common law is clear that legal title passes to the defendant.[96] The defendant is thus free to dispose of the thing (or enjoy the service) as he sees fit, provided he is not reasonably aware of the transfer's inadequacy. This explains the common law position of 'restitution unless …'. Some have taken this to mean that the defendant has a *right* to the enrichment. While legal title bestows certain rights—right to continued possession, good against everyone except someone with better title—it does not furnish a right against the plaintiff, such that the plaintiff has an obligation not to interfere with the defendant's use and enjoyment of the object of the mistransfer. While the plaintiff cannot directly, ie independently of judicial say-so, retake the object of her mistransfer, the defendant is nonetheless powerless to prevent her from claiming its full value following a successful action in unjust enrichment. Whatever 'right' or title that the defendant may have can be defeated by the plaintiff's exercise of her legal rights.

Faced with a judicial order of restitution to the plaintiff, the defendant cannot assert a right of retention; instead, it is said he has an *obligation* to retransfer the mistransferred value back to the plaintiff. Yet, it is very difficult to understand the defendant's payment of restitution to the plaintiff as an obligation, properly understood.[97] Obviously, since the

---

[94] I question whether in fact the downstairs tenant is really as powerless as Birks suggests. In *Victoria Park Racing & Recreation Grounds Co Ltd v Taylor* (1937) 58 CLR 479, the plaintiff racetrack owner complained that the defendant was profiting unjustly off its races by airing live radio broadcasts of the races. The defendant was able to observe the races by peering over the plaintiff's fence. The court responded that the plaintiff was free to prevent the defendant's visual access should he so desire by simply erecting a higher fence. Similarly, in Birks' heating example, the downstairs neighbour is at liberty to insulate her home such that her upstairs neighbour derives no benefit from her central heating. The upstairs neighbour, in other words, has no ground to complain should the plaintiff do so or even should she decide to wear extra sweaters and forego heat entirely.

[95] Notably, this is easier to understand on the unjust factors approach, as the squeegee kid cannot point to an unjust factor to justify the duty of restitution. (In this situation the facts are such that we cannot interpret my behaviour as free acceptance.)

[96] Traditionally, three types of mistake prevent title from passing: as to identity (*R v Middleton* (1873) LR 2 CCR 38), subject matter (*R v Ashwell* (1885) 16 QBD 190), and quantity (*Ilich v R* (1987) 162 CLR 110).

[97] See D Klimchuk, 'The Normative Foundations of Unjust Enrichment' in R Chambers, C Mitchell and J Penner (eds), *Philosophical Foundations of the Law of Unjust Enrichment* (Oxford, Oxford University Press, 2009).

restitutionary action of the defendant is mandated by the court, it is a *legal* obligation—this almost goes without saying. The defendant, in this sense, is *obliged* to retransfer the value back to the plaintiff. But the important question is not whether the defendant is legally obligated or not (clearly, he is); rather, the question is what *grounds* this legal obligation. Many, although not all, of our legal obligations are grounded in and justified by underlying moral obligations. Legal obligations, on at least some accounts, serve to concretise and in other ways define moral obligations we already happen to have.[98] This not the case in claims of unjust enrichment. If we adopt a Hohfeldian perspective and understand obligations as correlatives of rights,[99] there is no right of the plaintiff that correlates to the defendant's obligation of restitution. We can see this in cases where the defence of change of position is successfully invoked. In these situations, the plaintiff is unable to reobtain her mistakenly transferred asset or the value of her services *solely because* the defendant has disenriched himself (without objective knowledge of the transfer's defect). This is not how rights work. If the plaintiff has a right to the restoration of her thing or service of value, then *no matter what anyone does*, she still has that right.

Let me explain what I mean by 'how rights work'. There is a difference between the normative idea of a right and the mundane object that is its subject matter. If I own a potted plant, say, this means I have a right against you that you do not carelessly or intentionally smash it. It does not mean, however, that I have a right to its continued survival or current level of intactness. If a gust of wind blows it over, my dog uses it as her source of fibre for the day, or my overly solicitous attentions give it root rot, this is just my bad luck, poor dog training or shoddy plant husbandry. And, if you do smash it, then I continue to have a right—the right that you not smash it, although clearly I no longer have the intact thing to which the right initially applied.[100] Rights, in other words, do not disappear by means of the say-so of someone who is not the right-holder. Perhaps objects of the right do, but the relationship of right-duty persists.

The difficulty with understanding the relationship of the plaintiff and defendant in unjust enrichment scenarios as one of right-obligation leads me to suspect a different legal relation at work. I suggest that what the defendant has (prior to a court's order) vis-à-vis the plaintiff is a Hohfeldian liability to return the enrichment. Correlatively, the plaintiff (vis-à-vis the defendant) has a Hohfeldian power to reobtain the enrichment. This power is conditional on the value of the enrichment remaining with the defendant among other things, not the least of which is the requirement that a court intercede on her behalf. If the defendant possesses a liability, then he cannot complain when he is compelled by law to return the benefit's value.[101] The legal obligation imposed by the court of law in the form

---

[98] J Gardner, 'Obligations and Outcomes in the Law of Torts' in P Cane and J Gardner (eds), *Relating to Responsibility: Essays for Tony Honoré* (Oxford, Hart Publishing, 2001).

[99] That is, not as duties. Duties, like obligations, can be grounded by rights—ie the reason for their existence in one person is the right of another. However, unlike obligations, rights are not the only grounds for duties. To take the obvious example, we can sensibly talk about duties toward the environment or our pets without necessarily presupposing either the environment or our dog has a right against us.

[100] As Arthur Ripstein explains with respect to one's coat: 'The coat which is the object of the right is …, like all natural objects, subject to generation and decay, and your right to it is not a right to its persistence or even your continued possession of it; it is a right that *others* not use the coat or damage or destroy it in certain ways.' A Ripstein, 'Civil Recourse and Separation of Wrongs and Remedies' (2011) 39 *Florida State University Law Review* 163, 178.

[101] See Häcker, above n 80.

of a remedial duty is thus not based on an antecedent moral duty as it might be in the case of contract and tort, but rather on an antecedent liability. It is not the case that the defendant has a positive reason to pay the plaintiff restitution, but rather that he has no reason (provided he has not, in good faith, changed his position to his detriment) to object to being compelled to do so.

A further interesting upshot of viewing the unjust enrichment relationship as a power-liability instance of Hohfeldian correlativity is its contrasting relationship to self-help. The difference in unjust enrichment, however, is that a plaintiff is not privileged to help herself to her unjustly transferred value. Rather she must seek a court's intervention. Why this is so is an interesting question. Why can't a plaintiff, knowing she mistakenly gave me $40 rather than $20 and seeing my wallet with the two bills lying on a table, simply grab the one mistakenly transferred bill back? Why must she go to court? Moreover, if the plaintiff has a good claim to the retransfer of her $20, how is it the case that I, the defendant in this scenario, would be able to sue her successfully for trespass to chattels for her non-consented-to interference with my wallet? My suspicion is that this has something to do with the law's distrust of unilateral actions determining bilateral relationships. In this sense, therefore, the 'restitution unless …' approach has the better side of things because the idea of absence of basis implicates necessarily a relationship between the two parties in a way that 'no restitution unless …' does not. Mistakes can be unilateral, but the failure of a transfer by definition must be transactional. The relationship between unjust enrichment and self-help remedies (in particular, rescission) is an exciting field for future scholarship, but one that we cannot more fully explore until we retrain our focus from methodology and form back to substance.

V. Conclusion

This chapter had three main objectives: one narrow, one critical and one aspirational. The first, narrow, aim was to defend the Canadian law of unjust enrichment from the criticism that it no longer could be said to be part of the common law, properly so-called, as it had taken a turn for the civilian. In defence, I suggested that, notwithstanding its civilian language of 'juristic reasons', the Canadian law of unjust enrichment remains in essence true to the common law, broadly understood as the law of the commons. The particular 'commons' of Canada simply happens to reflect a dual common–civil law heritage. Its second, critical, branch questioned our current unhealthy obsession with unjust enrichment methodology. For the most part, it is irrelevant in practice and theory whether a court adopts a traditional common law unjust factor approach or a civilian juristic reason tactic. In practice, the result is normally identical and, as I have argued, most of the theoretical distinctions have been overemphasised. Moreover, our focus on the methodological issues regarding the question of what makes an enrichment unjust has had the unhappy consequence that we ignore the substantive normative problem about what makes it unjust sufficiently to impose an obligation on the passive, non-wrongdoing defendant. Finally, in its aspirational moments, this chapter suggested a reconceptualisation of the defendant's restitutionary 'obligation', proposing that the relationship between unjust enrichment defendants and plaintiffs might be better understood as one of power-liability rather than right-obligation.

11

Recovery of Non-Gratuitously Conferred Benefit Under Section 70 of the Indian Contract Act 1872

ALVIN W-L SEE[*]

I. Introduction

The Indian Contract Act 1872 (ICA 1872), although primarily a statute of contract law, contains a number of sections dealing with situations that have no immediate relevance to contracts. The most curious among them is section 70, which provides:

> Where a person lawfully does anything for another person, or delivers anything to him, not intending to do so gratuitously, and such other person enjoys the benefit thereof, the latter is bound to make compensation to the former in respect of, or to restore, the thing so done or delivered.

The section is also accompanied by two statutory illustrations, which the courts are obliged to take into account in its interpretation.[1] The statutory illustrations read:

(a) A, a tradesman, leaves goods at B's house by mistake. B treats the goods as his own. He is bound to pay A for them.

(b) A saves B's property from fire. A is not entitled to compensation from B, if the circumstances show that he intended to act gratuitously.

The curiosity of the section lies in the absence of an obvious English equivalent, despite the fact that the ICA 1872 was based mainly on mid-nineteenth-century English law. It is as though Indian law was made to inherit something that did not take root in English law. With no directly relevant English case law to rely on, the Indian courts are compelled to begin afresh in understanding and applying the section. In India, section 70 is frequently invoked as a possible basis for recourse due in large part to its seemingly broad scope. This results in an abundance of case law addressing the section, which in turn reflects ample opportunity for its judicial consideration. Despite this, the existing attempts to fine-tune the elements

[*] I would like to thank the conference participants, particularly Andrew Burrows, Birke Häcker, Duncan Sheehan and Graham Virgo, for their insightful suggestions, as well as my colleague, Yip Man, for her helpful comments on an early draft of this chapter. I am also grateful to Tan Jia Hui and Sean Lee Lie Yong for their excellent research assistance. All errors are, of course, my own.
[1] The duty of the courts to consider statutory illustrations was emphasised by the Privy Council in *Mohamed Syedol Ariffin v Yeoh Ooi Gark* [1916] 2 AC 575.

of the section, which would in turn determine its scope, remains largely unsatisfactory. The section is often applied based on vague notions of justice and fairness, and is made to do too much work, applying to too many theoretically dissimilar cases. The root of the problem is clearly the failure to identify a rationale underlying the section and develop it on the basis of such rationale. This chapter suggests that section 70 is best regarded as based on the principle of unjust enrichment and should be developed by reference to the modern law of unjust enrichment. Particular attention will be paid to identifying the unjust factor(s) that underlies the right of recovery, which has been elusive thus far. This attempt at modern reinterpretation of the antique section is made in the hope of injecting structure and clarity of purpose into it, making it more certain for practical and modern use.

II. Section 70: Past, Present and Future

The ICA 1872

Prior to India's independence, four differently constituted Indian Law Commissions were appointed in London. They were tasked with preparing a corpus of substantive law for British India. The draft contract code upon which the ICA 1872 was based was the work of the Third Indian Law Commission appointed in 1861. Five years after its appointment, in 1866, the Third Law Commission submitted the *Second Report on the Substantive Law for India*, which sets out a draft contract code containing 269 sections.[2] It was an attempt to present a simplified statement of English contract law modified in some ways to suit local circumstances. After going through various amendments and rearrangements, the draft law was eventually enacted as the ICA 1872 by the Imperial Legislative Council in India.

The success of the ICA 1872 could be reflected in three broad ways. Firstly, in terms of longevity, the ICA 1872 has been applied for almost one and a half centuries.[3] Secondly, in terms of geographical reach, it applies to almost a quarter of the present world population. Outside India, localised versions of the ICA 1872 are presently in force in Bangladesh, Brunei, Malaysia, Myanmar, Pakistan and Tanzania. Thirdly, in terms of scholarly influence, the ICA 1872 been the subject of study for codification projects elsewhere.[4] These are good reasons for why the ICA 1872 should be afforded serious attention.

Codification of Certain Quasi-Contractual Claims

Although the ICA 1872 was clearly intended to be a contract statute,[5] chapter V, which consists of sections 68–72, is titled 'Of Certain Relations Resembling those Created by

---

[2] *Parliamentary Papers, House of Commons and Command*, vol 49 (London, HMSO, 1868).

[3] However, in Kenya and Uganda, the ICA 1872 was repealed in the early 1960s.

[4] See, eg, Jersey Law Commission, *Report: The Law of Contract* (Topic Report No 10, 2004); W Swain, 'Contract Codification and the English: Some Observations from the Indian Contract Act 1872' in J Devenney and M Kenny (eds), *The Transformation of European Private Law: Harmonisation, Consolidation, Codification or Chaos?* (Cambridge, Cambridge University Press, 2013) ch 9.

[5] The purpose of the ICA 1872, as set out in its preamble, is to 'to define and amend certain parts of the law relating to contracts'.

Contract'.[6] The word 'resembling' indicates that the rights/duties arising from these sections are not strictly contractual. In fact, they are non-contractual in the sense that they may arise independently of any contract. It is most likely that the drafters intended to set out in this chapter certain quasi-contractual claims recognised by mid-nineteenth-century English law. As history tells us, the alleged resemblance between quasi-contract and genuine contract was merely in form, not in substance.[7] From the sixteenth century onwards, the preferred form of action for money claims was the assumpsit, which was premised upon the defendant's promise to pay. Despite its contractual overtone, the assumpsit was extended to accommodate certain non-contractual claims by implying a promise to pay although none actually exists. This marked the birth of the law of quasi-contracts. Although it was well known that the promise was fictitious, and despite the abolition of the forms of action in 1852, quasi-contracts were afforded treatment in most major contract textbooks well into the twentieth century.[8] It is therefore not surprising that the drafters of the ICA 1872 decided to include quasi-contractual provisions in a contract statute.

Importantly, the drafters appear to have been aware about the difficulties with the forms of action, and to have taken steps to simplify things. Section 70, for example, applies to a payment of money, the delivery of goods and the conferral of other forms of benefit, thus cutting across the various forms of assumpsit (*indebitatus assumpsit, quantum meruit* and *quantum valebat*). There is also no mention of a promise to pay by the defendant, hence it is free of contractual overtone. Thus, in the important case of *State of West Bengal v M/S BK Mondal & Sons* the Supreme Court of India said, in specific reference to section 70, that the section was framed in such a way as 'to avoid the niceties of English law on the subject, arising largely from historical reasons and to make the position simple and free from fictions of law and consequent complications'.[9] The Court also made it plain that chapter V has nothing at all to do with rights and liabilities accruing from a contract.[10]

The Origin of Section 70

With the exception of section 70, every other provision in chapter V has a clear root in English law, even though some of these provisions deviate slightly from their English counterparts. Curiously, neither the Third Indian Law Commission's *Second Report* nor the discussions that followed shed any light on which English legal principle section 70 was intended to replicate, improve upon or depart from. Even when the section was presented before the Privy Council for consideration, the court merely applied it in accordance with its wording without considering its underlying rationale.[11] In this part of the chapter, two suggestions will be considered.

---

[6] In the Law Commission's original draft law, the chapter contained eight sections, three of which were eventually omitted. The omitted sections concerned misrepresentation and estoppel.

[7] See generally AWL See, 'An Introduction to the Law of Unjust Enrichment' (2013) 5 *Malayan Law Journal* i.

[8] See, eg, S Leake, *Elements of the Law of Contracts* (London, Stevens and Sons, 1867); J Russell (ed), *A Treatise on the Law of Contracts, and Upon The Defences to Actions Thereon; by Joseph Chitty Jr*, 6th edn (London, S Sweet, 1857).

[9] *State of West Bengal v M/S BK Mondal & Sons* (1962) AIR SC 779 (SC) 794. See also *Badr-un-nisa v Muhammad Jan* (1880) ILR 2 All 671, 674.

[10] ibid. See also *Mulamchand v State of Madhya Pradesh* (1968) AIR SC 1218 (SC).

[11] *Palinivelu Mudaliar v Neelavathi Ammal* (1937) 39 Bomb LR 720 (PC); *Siow Wong Fatt v Susur Rotan Mining Ltd* [1967] 2 AC 269 (PC) (on appeal against the decision of the Federal Court of Malaysia).

Whitley Stokes, who was then the Assistant Secretary to the Home Department (Legislative) in British India, had taken some part in reviewing the content of the draft law. In his book, published more than 15 years after the enactment of the ICA 1872, he wrote: 'Section 70 confers a right resembling that of the Roman *negotiorum gestor*; but under the Indian law compensation is not payable unless the principal actually derives benefit from the *gestio*.'[12] This doctrine of civilian origin confers on a person who managed the affair of another a right of recovery in many situations. In so far as the doctrine forms part of English law, however, it tends to be restricted to situations where the plaintiff conferred the benefit out of necessity, eg to save the defendant's property from destruction or deterioration.[13] This is to some extent reflected in statutory illustration (b). Although this narrow form of the doctrine may be given effect to by section 70, it is unlikely to form the sole basis of the section. Section 70 is clearly wider, capable of applying even to cases where the benefit conferred does not consist of management of the defendant's affair and where there is no situation of necessity.

Another view is offered by the Madras High Court in *Damodara Mudaliar v Secretary of State for India*: 'There can be little doubt that the statement of the law [in section 70] is derived from the notes to *Lampleigh v Brathwait* [in Smith's *Leading Cases*].'[14] This assertion has been subsequently affirmed[15] as well as disputed.[16] Curiously, no authority was cited in support of the assertion. Even the most persistent investigation could trace the assertion no further than to *Damodara* itself. In terms of authenticity, therefore, it qualifies as a myth. And the myth is dangerous because of its contractual overtone. The scenario contemplated by the cited portion of Smith's notes was this. A does something for B, after which B promises to remunerate A for it. In *Lampleigh v Brathwait* it was held that B's promise is enforceable in contract only if it relates back to a prior request by B.[17] Smith noted, and this was cited in *Damodara*, that in the absence of an express request, one could be implied '[w]here [B] has adopted and enjoyed the benefit of [A's] consideration'.[18] Looked through the modern lens, this would appear to be an extension of the rule in *Lampleigh v Brathwait*, which falls squarely within the province of contract law. Thus, it has been suggested that section 70 is related to the doctrine of consideration by providing a broad exception to the

[12] W Stokes, *The Anglo-Indian Codes*, vol I (Oxford, Clarendon Press, 1887) 533.

[13] See generally C Mitchell, P Mitchell and S Watterson (eds), *Goff & Jones: The Law of Unjust Enrichment*, 8th edn (London, Sweet & Maxwell, 2011) ch 18; A Burrows, *The Law of Restitution*, 3rd edn (Oxford, Oxford University Press, 2011) ch 18; J Kortmann, *Altruism in Private Law: Liability for Nonfeasance and Negotiorum Gestio* (Oxford, Oxford University Press, 2005); D Sheehan, 'Negotiorum Gestio: A Civilian Concept in the Common Law?' (2006) 55 *ICLQ* 253. See below, text to nn 106–09.

[14] *Damodara Mudaliar v Secretary of State for India* (1895) ILR 18 Mad 88, 91. This was noted by the Federated Malay States Court of Appeal in *Mohamed Yusoof v Murugappa Chettiar* [1941] MLJ 240, 244.

[15] In *Yogambal Boyee Ammani Ammal v Naina Pilai Markayar* (1909) 3 Ind Cas 110 the Madras High Court explicitly affirmed the assertion. The assertion was also cited with apparent approval in F Pollock and DF Mulla, *The Indian Contract Act, with a Commentary, Critical and Explanatory* (London, Sweet & Maxwell, 1905) 244–45; and formed part of the appellant counsel's submission in *State of West Bengal v M/S BK Mondal & Sons* (1962) AIR SC 779 (SC) 794, 784 although the Supreme Court expressed no view on it.

[16] *Jog Narain Singh v Badri Das* (1912) 13 Ind Cas 144, 146; *Sri Sri Sri Gajapathi Kristna Chandra Deo Garu v P Srinivasa Charlu* (1913) 25 Mad LJ 433, 438.

[17] *Lampleigh v Brathwait* (1615) Hob 105, 80 ER 255.

[18] J Smith, *A Selection of Leading Cases on Various Branches of the Law: With Notes* (London, A Maxwell, 1837) 70. For the same proposition, see E Jenks, *The History of the Doctrine of Consideration in English Law* (London, CJ Clay & Sons, 1892) 64–65.

rule against past consideration.[19] However, in light of the Supreme Court's decision in *State of West Bengal* any attempt to explain section 70 based on contractual principles must be rejected. In fact, a non-contractual explanation of section 70 is more consistent with the general framework of the ICA 1872. Matters of contract formation, including the doctrine of consideration, have already been comprehensively dealt with in chapter I; it is unlikely that the drafters would revisit the same subject matter in chapter V.

Having said the above, the assertion in *Damodara* may not be entirely off target. As explained earlier, the distinction between contract and quasi-contract was not clearly defined during Smith's time, and it appears that he incorporated both in his notes. If the implication of a request is factually justified, then it is no doubt a matter of contract law. However, if the implication is one of law and not of facts (eg because a request is improbable on the facts), and serves only to bring the claim within certain sub-forms of the assumpsit, then the claim is clearly a non-contractual one.[20] The possibility of a non-contractual version of Smith's statement is hinted in Winfield's book on quasi-contracts, where he wrote that a claim for *quantum meruit* would lie where the defendant accepts work done by the plaintiff, for the acceptance 'raises a presumption of request'.[21] Importantly, he distinguished this from the prior request rule in *Lampleigh v Brathwait*, which he saw as belonging 'wholly within the domain of contract'.[22] If one insists that section 70 is based on Smith's notes, then it can only be based on its quasi-contractual dimension. Even so, in *Falcke v Scottish Imperial Insurance Co* Bowen LJ opined that the principle was 'stated too widely'.[23] In any case, given that the contractual overtone of Smith's notes has the tendency to overshadow its quasi-contractual explanation, its reference is best abandoned to avoid confusion.

The above discussion, unfortunately, brings us no closer to understanding the precise basis and scope of section 70. The origin of the section remains a mystery. However, given the general belief that the section was intended to go beyond the then-existing English law,[24] and in light of its quasi-contractual origin, it is suggested that the best way forward is to understand and develop its elements by reference to the modern law of unjust enrichment, which succeeds the now-obsolete law of quasi-contracts.

The Principle of Unjust Enrichment

The term 'quasi-contract' tells us nothing about the substance of the cause of action. It merely tells us what it is not. By the mid-twentieth century Anglo-American legal scholars had come to accept that the bulk of quasi-contracts were based on the principle of unjust enrichment. This influenced the First Law Commission of India, established post-independence in 1955, to form the view that chapter V of the ICA 1872 is also based on

---

[19] APB Leong, *Cheshire, Fifoot and Furmston's Law of Contract*, 2nd Singapore and Malaysian edn (Singapore, Butterworths Asia, 1998) 158. cf P Daruvala, *The Doctrine of Consideration Treated Historically and Comparatively* (Calcutta, Butterworth, 1914) 222.

[20] *Lampleigh v Brathwait* is arguably such a case: see D Ibbetson, '*Lamplugh v Brathwaite* (1615)' in C Mitchell and P Mitchell (eds), *Landmark Cases in the Law of Restitution* (Oxford, Hart Publishing, 2006) 1, 15.

[21] PH Winfield, *The Law of Quasi-Contracts* (London, Sweet & Maxwell, 1952) 56–57.

[22] ibid 59–60.

[23] *Falcke v Scottish Imperial Insurance Co* (1886) 34 Ch D 234, 239.

[24] See, eg, *Jarao Kumari v Basanta Kumar Roy* (1904) 32 ILR Cal 374; *Nellie Wapshare v Pierce Leslie & Co Ltd* (1960) AIR Mad 410; *Govindarajulu Naidu v SS Naidu* (1958) 2 Mad LJ 148.

the same principle. In its *Thirteenth Report*, published in 1958, the Commission proposed to make chapter V more comprehensive by explicit acceptance of the principle of unjust enrichment and the creation of a catch-all section, which reads:

> In any case not coming within the scope of sections 68 to 72A, where there is no contract, but a person is unjustly benefitted at the expense of another person, the former is bound to restore the benefit to the latter or to make compensation therefor.[25]

Although the proposal was never adopted, the idea that chapter V is based on the principle of unjust enrichment began to find judicial support.[26] However, there has been no real progress in terms of understanding and developing the contents of the provisions in chapter V by reference to the modern unjust enrichment analysis. The principle of unjust enrichment has been recognised and understood only at a very superficial level. In *State of West Bengal* the Supreme Court merely said cursorily that the purpose of section 70 is to prevent unjust enrichment but made no attempt to explain why exactly the defendant's enrichment was unjust.[27]

One might find it curious that, despite the underdevelopment of the law of unjust enrichment in India, the courts have warned against importing principles of English common law in aid of interpreting section 70. In *State of West Bengal* the Supreme Court said:

> If the words used in the Indian statute are obscure or ambiguous perhaps it may be permissible in interpreting them to examine the background of the law or to derive assistance from English decisions bearing on the point; but where the words are clear and unambiguous it would be unreasonable to interpret them in the light of the alleged background of the statute and to attempt to see that their interpretation conforms to the said background. That is why, in dealing with the point raised before us we must primarily look to the law as embodied in s. 70 and seek to put upon it a fair and reasonable construction.[28]

While the suggested interpretive approach is not incorrect, it appears to assume that section 70 is sufficiently clear and straightforward.[29] Clearly it is not so. There were several instances where the Indian courts have admitted difficulties with the section's interpretation due to its broad wording.[30] In *Saptharishi Reddiar (Now Minor) v The Secretary of State for India* the Madras High Court made the following observation about two earlier cases that applied section 70: '[T]he judgment[s] in these cases indicate a very substantial difference of opinion between the learned Judges who disposed of them. The wording of Section 70 is very wide indeed.'[31] More importantly, it is necessary to appreciate that the Supreme Court's caution was given at a time when the law of unjust enrichment was still underdeveloped in England, offering little assistance to the understanding of section 70.

---

[25] Law Commission of India, *Thirteenth Report (Contract Act, 1872)* (New Delhi, Ministry of Law, 1958) 13, 84.

[26] See, eg, *Mulamchand v State of Madhya Pradesh* (1968) AIR SC 1218 (SC); *Govindarajulu Naidu v SS Naidu* (1958) 2 Mad LJ 148.

[27] (1962) AIR SC 779 (SC) 789. See also *Mulamchand v State of Madhya Pradesh* (1968) AIR SC 1218 (SC); *Dominion of India v Preety Kumar Ghosh* (1958) AIR Pat 203, 209.

[28] (1962) AIR SC 779 (SC) 891. See also *Sri Sri Sri Gajapathi Kristna Chandra Deo Garu v P Srinivasa Charlu* (1913) 25 Mad LJ 433.

[29] See also *Zulaing v Yamethin District Council* (1932) AIR Rang 176; *Secretary of State v GT Sarin & Co* (1930) AIR Lah 364; See also *Jarao Kumari v Basanta Kumar Roy* (1904) 32 ILR Cal 374.

[30] See, eg, *Damodara Mudaliar v Secretary of State for India* (1895) ILR 18 Mad 88.

[31] *Saptharishi Reddiar (Now Minor) v The Secretary of State for India* (1915) 28 Mad LJ 384, 386. See also *Raja Viswanadha Vijia Kumara v RG Orr* (1918) 45 Ind Cas 786, 788.

In fact, the Indian courts regarded the older English cases that embraced the fiction of implied contract as a hindrance. In *Ram Nagina Singh v Governor-General in Council* the Calcutta High Court said: 'Section 70 has to be construed in the light of the words employed in the section & [*sic*] that no fiction of English Law should be invoked to restrict its operation.'[32]

In the past 30 years, however, the law of unjust enrichment has undergone tremendous developments in other major Commonwealth jurisdictions. Its basic framework and detailed elements have been incrementally worked out such that it now qualifies as a mature branch of the law. Under the prevailing common law framework, a right to restitution arises where: (i) the defendant is enriched; (ii) it is at the plaintiff's expense; and (iii) it is unjust. Upon satisfying these elements, the plaintiff is entitled to a prima facie right to restitution. If the defendant fails to raise a defence to defeat or limit the prima facie right, it will crystallise into an absolute one. This basic framework ensures some certainty in determining the parties' rights and liabilities and allows proper balancing of the parties' interests. In light of this development, it is helpful to draw on the experience of the common law of unjust enrichment to clarify and develop section 70.[33] The remaining parts of this chapter will demonstrate the utility of this approach by examining each of the elements of section 70 within the appropriate inquiry under the modern unjust enrichment framework of analysis. In doing so, however, it must be remembered that we are necessarily constrained by the statute's wording, thus preventing any attempt at full legal transplant.

III. Defendant's Enrichment

It has been argued that section 70 'does not contemplate the case of payment of money and it will be doing violence to the language of the section to hold that the words "lawfully does anything" mean payment of money'.[34] To address this issue, the Law Commission recommended amendment of the existing wording to make specific reference to money payment.[35] However, it is submitted that this is unnecessary as the existing wording is in fact wide enough to include most forms of valuable enrichment.

The provision operates where a person 'delivers anything' to the defendant. There seems no reason why 'anything' may not consist of any valuable asset, including money. The doing of 'anything' for the defendant is obviously much wider. It may refer to a service, which includes discharging the defendant's debt, or procuring a service for, or delivery of goods to, the defendant. The wording of section 70 is thus consistent with the modern view that enrichment consists of anything that has market (monetary) value.[36]

Once it is established that the benefit received by the defendant is objectively enriching due to it having market value, the attention shifts to whether the particular defendant is

---

[32] *Ram Nagina Singh v Governor-General in Council* (1952) AIR Cal 306, 313.

[33] For a similar project, see AWL See, 'Restitution of Mistaken Enrichment under Section 73 of Malaysia's Contracts Act 1950' (2014) 31 *Journal of Contract Law* 206 (addressing the Malaysian equivalent of ICA 1872, s 72).

[34] *Sheo Nath Prasad v Sarjoo Nonia* (1943) AIR All 220, 232. See also *Perumal Chettiar v Kamakshi Ammal* (1938) AIR Mad 785. cf Pollock and Mulla, above n 15, 245.

[35] Law Commission, *Thirteenth Report*, above n 25, 42.

[36] See *Peter v Beblow* [1993] 1 SCR 980 (SC of Canada) 990.

enriched by it, ie subjectively enriched, and if so, to what extent.[37] This is reflected by the statutory requirement that the defendant 'enjoys the benefit thereof'. However, as section 70 does not prescribe any test for determining whether the defendant has enjoyed the benefit, the task of formulating such a test (or tests) is left to the courts. In *Yogambal Boyee Ammani Ammal v Naina Pilai Markayar* the Madras High Court held that 'a person can be said to "*enjoy*" a benefit under this section only by accepting a benefit when he has the option of declining or accepting it'.[38] Under the modern law, however, the element of acceptance does not form the main determinant of whether the defendant has been enriched. Where the defendant receives a money payment or equivalent (eg having his necessary debt discharged), for example, he cannot reasonably argue that he is not enriched even if the benefit is conferred on him without his knowledge. He is incontrovertibly enriched.[39] Thus, even the court in *Yogambal* was forced to concede: 'No doubt, in one sense, when a person has the benefit of an act of another person even against his will, in fact, forced upon him, he may be said to have "enjoyed" [the] benefit thereof.'[40]

In the case of benefits in kind, however, the law looks beyond mere receipt of the benefit. Indeed, it is only fair that the value of the benefit is assessed not by reference to the market but based on the defendant's personal value system.[41] Thus, the law allows him to raise the argument of subjective devaluation, ie to show that he would not have paid for the thing delivered or service rendered, or would not have paid for it at the market price.[42] The plaintiff is, of course, allowed to challenge the argument of subjective devaluation. If the defendant has requested the benefit, that itself is evidence that he values the benefit. The same can be said if the defendant refuses to return a readily returnable benefit. In *Piloo Dhunjishaw Sidhwa v Municipal Corporation of the City*, where the defendant received certain goods from the plaintiff, the Supreme Court said:

> Compensation would normally be the market price of the goods. By refusing to return the goods, the person to whom the goods have been delivered cannot improve his position and seek to pay less than the market value of the goods.[43]

The question, then, is whether the defendant's acceptance of the benefit has the same effect. According to statutory illustration (a), section 70 would apply if B, the defendant, 'treats the goods as his own'. Despite this, it is submitted that 'acceptance' must be given a more restrictive meaning. Suppose that a parcel is left on the defendant's doorstep and the defendant brings it into his house. It would be unrealistic to say that he values the parcel merely because he took possession of it. He may have done so merely to identify the sender or to inspect the parcel's content. Even if he does open the parcel and enjoy what is contained therein, he may do so thinking that it is a gift, and may not have done so if it were clearly not a gift. However, if the defendant is aware that the parcel is not given free of charge, and

---

[37] *Sempra Metals Ltd v IRC* [2007] UKHL 34, [2008] 1 AC 56, [119].
[38] *Yogambal Boyee Ammani Ammal v Naina Pilai Markayar* (1909) 3 Ind Cas 110, 112, followed in *Challa Appayya v Desetti Chandra Ayya* (1950) AIR Mad 817, 818.
[39] *BP Exploration Co (Libya) Ltd v Hunt (No 2)* [1979] 1 WLR 783, 799.
[40] *Yogambal Boyee Ammani Ammal v Naina Pilai Markayar* (1909) 3 Ind Cas 110, 112.
[41] *Sempra Metals Ltd v IRC* [2007] UKHL 34, [2008] 1 AC 56, [119].
[42] ibid; *Benedetti v Sawiris* [2013] UKSC 50, [2013] 3 WLR 351.
[43] *Piloo Dhunjishaw Sidhwa v Municipal Corporation of the City* (1970) 3 SCR 415 (SC) 422. See also *Cressman v Coys of Kensington (Sales) Ltd* [2004] EWCA Civ 47, [2004] 1 WLR 2774.

yet he proceeds to enjoy its content, it is not unfair to impose on him a liability to pay for it. He has forgone the opportunity to reject the benefit (in this case by not using it) which he knows is conferred on him non-gratuitously. This is a case of free acceptance, which we shall explore in more detail later.[44] Although free acceptance is not conclusive proof that the defendant values the benefit, for he could simply be indifferent,[45] it has been convincingly argued that in such a case subjective devaluation should be denied on the basis of the defendant's unconscientious conduct.[46]

Subjective devaluation may also be denied where a benefit in kind is turned into money. In *Manoharlal Radhakrishna v The Union of India* the plaintiff wanted to obtain a lease over the defendant's land.[47] Pending formal agreement, the plaintiff was allowed to begin work on the land. The plaintiff filled up the existing ditch, raised boundary pillars, and constructed two culverts and two gates. Unfortunately, the necessary approval was not forthcoming and the agreement fell through. The plaintiff then sought to recover the cost of work done on the land. The Patna High Court rejected the plaintiff's claim, refusing to infer that the improvement to the land is beneficial to the defendant in the absence of clear evidence. However, if it could be shown that the plaintiff's work has increased the land's value and the defendant has either sold it, or is reasonably certain to sell it, so as to realise the benefit in money form, then surely the defendant should not be allowed to deny that he has benefited.[48] An alternative approach is to require the plaintiff to prove only that the improvement to the land is objectively enriching. The burden then shifts to the defendant to establish subjective devaluation of the objective enrichment.

The above discussion shows that the modern approach to the enrichment inquiry, which strikes a fair balance between the parties' interest, could be given effect to by the broad wording of section 70. Although this chapter will later suggest that free acceptance should be adopted as the core case of the section, the possibility that the section may apply in cases involving no acceptance remains open. For these reasons, the Indian courts are implored to rethink the approach that is presently adopted.

IV. At the Plaintiff's Expense

The purpose of the 'at the plaintiff's expense' inquiry is to identify the necessary link between the plaintiff and the defendant, more specifically between the plaintiff's loss and the defendant's enrichment.[49] Although this inquiry is not apparent from the wording of section 70, it could be inferred from the statutory requirement that the plaintiff has delivered something to, or done something for, the defendant, which serves the same purpose.

---

[44]   See below, text following n 66.

[45]   A Burrows, 'Free Acceptance and the Law of Restitution' (1988) 104 *LQR* 576.

[46]   P Birks, 'In Defence of Free Acceptance' in A Burrows (ed), *Essays on the Law of Restitution* (Oxford, Oxford University Press, 1991) 105; *Goff & Jones*, above n 13, [4-29].

[47]   *Manoharlal Radhakrishna v The Union of India* (1974) AIR Pat 56.

[48]   Burrows, *Restitution*, above n 13, 48–49; G Virgo, *The Principles of the Law of Restitution*, 2nd edn (Oxford, Oxford University Press, 2006) 78–81; P Birks, *Unjust Enrichment*, 2nd edn (Oxford, Oxford University Press, 2005) 61–62. cf *Cressman*, above n 40, [34]–[36]; *Goff & Jones*, above n 13, [4-14]–[4-17].

[49]   Burrows, above n 13, 68–69.

According to the traditional view, the defendant is enriched at the plaintiff's expense if there is a transfer of value from the latter to the former.[50] In a two-party case, the rule is obvious and is rarely debated. Things are more complicated in three-party cases. On one view, there must be a *direct* transfer of value between the plaintiff and the defendant. In other words, the defendant must be enriched directly at the plaintiff's expense.[51] On another view, it is sufficient that a but-for causal test is satisfied, ie if it could be shown that C would not have been enriched but for A's initial conferral of benefit.[52] The second view is clearly broader than the first. To understand these issues better, two common scenarios involving three parties shall be drawn upon for illustrations. The aim is to identify the best possible approach that section 70 could adopt.

Suppose that A has paid Rs 200,000 into B's bank account. When B checks his account balance he is surprised, but is genuinely unaware that someone else had deposited money into his account. Feeling financially well off, B gives Rs 50,000 to C. By the time A discovers the mistake, B has become bankrupt and is therefore not worth suing. Can A leapfrog B and claim Rs 50,000 from C? As A delivered the money to B, not to C, and there is nothing to suggest that A's payment to B was for C (ie on C's behalf), leapfrogging is not allowed. For this scenario, therefore, the statutory wording renders unavailable any wriggle room for importing the second view.

Now consider a second scenario. Pursuant to a contract between A and B, A delivers something to C. If B fails to perform his part of the promise, eg to remunerate A, can A bring a section 70 claim against C? As the thing is delivered from A to C, the necessary link required by section 70 is satisfied. However, A's claim against C would have been denied under the common law. Although it is accepted that C could be enriched at the expense of both A and B, thus lending support to the but-for causal test which underlies the second view, A's claim against C is denied for it would allow A to escape the risks that he has assumed by contracting with B.[53] It is, of course, possible to give effect to the common law position by a narrow interpretation of section 70. It may be said that the delivery of the thing was not for C, but for B. This approach presupposes that the delivery of a thing to the defendant does not always amount to doing something for the defendant, and entails the further argument that section 70 only applies if the delivery of a thing to the defendant also amounts to doing something for the defendant. However, this method of limiting A's claim against C is arguably too crude. Suppose that the contract between A and B turns out to be void or is avoided due to a vitiating factor. Since the contract is legally non-existent, the policy concern about the parties' assumption of risks becomes irrelevant.[54] If we wish to allow section 70 to apply in this modified scenario, and indeed we should, then we must accept that A's delivery of the thing was for C (and B), contradicting the position adopted for the original scenario. On the question of for whom the delivery was made, there should be no difference between the two scenarios. It would be absurd to suggest that the delivery

---

[50] ibid ch 4; *Goff & Jones*, above n 13, ch 5.

[51] J Edelman and E Bant, *Unjust Enrichment in Australia* (Melbourne, Oxford University Press, 2006) 138–41.

[52] *Goff & Jones*, above n 13, 142–62; Birks, above n 48, 89, 93–98.

[53] *MacDonald, Dickens & Macklin v Costello* [2011] 3 WLR 1341; [2011] EWCA Civ 930. See also *Lumbers v W Cook Builders Pty Ltd (in liq)* [2008] HCA 27, (2008) 232 CLR 635. cf R Williams, 'Three Quarrelling Parties, Two Oral Contracts and a Claim in Restitution?' [2010] *Restitution Law Review* 51.

[54] See See, above n 33, 219–21.

was for C in one case but not so in the other. A better solution is to adopt the more lenient but-for causal test for the phrase 'does anything for' such that in both cases the delivery was for C, but accept that in the original scenario A's statutory right to recovery is constrained by an external policy consideration.

The question of whether something was done for the defendant was afforded some attention in the case of *Raja Viswanadha Vijia Kumara v RG Orr*, where the plaintiff carried out necessary repairs to a water tank in his land, which irrigated both his and the defendants' lands.[55] The plaintiff demanded that the defendants contribute to the cost of the repairs but the defendants refused. The Madras High Court held that section 70 did not apply because the repairs were not for the defendants. As the area of the plaintiff's land irrigated by the water tank was three times as large as the defendants', the natural inference is that the repairs were solely for himself, benefiting the defendants only incidentally. The burden lies on the plaintiff to show otherwise.[56] Oldfield J, while finding it undesirable to state any general test, nonetheless went on to say that 'what is done cannot be described as done by one person for another, unless it can be shown that, but for the existence of that other's interest, it would not have been done'.[57] This aspect of the decision, which is somewhat premised on the plaintiff's motive for doing the thing, is overly restrictive for a number of reasons. It appears to assume that the repairs could only be performed for either party, but not for both. In two other 'water tank' cases, however, the same court found that the repairs were carried out for both the plaintiff and the defendant.[58] Moreover, in such cases it may be that the plaintiff's interest is itself sufficiently strong such that the repairs would have been carried out even if the defendant's interest did not exist, thus failing Oldfield J's test. Yet if the plaintiff's action was indeed motivated in part by the defendant's interest, however small, it is counterintuitive to say that it was not also for the defendant.

It is submitted that it is best to abandon any approach that focuses on the plaintiff's motive in doing the thing. There are clearly cases where the plaintiff's claim should be allowed even though he is completely uninterested in the defendant's interest. In the second scenario above A may only be interested in fulfilling his contractual obligation owed to B without caring about C's interest. Yet, it was argued that A's claim against C should sometimes be allowed. Similarly, in a case of mistaken enrichment, which according to statutory illustration (a) may attract the application of section 70, the mistaken plaintiff cannot be said to have any real intention to do the thing for the defendant. The better approach is to focus on the transfer of value between the plaintiff and the defendant, applying a but-for causal test, following the common law approach. This would avoid the phrase 'does anything for' from being interpreted too narrowly so as to deny rightful claims. There is no real danger in adopting a wide interpretation of the phrase for the plaintiff's claim could still be denied on other grounds.

---

[55] *Raja Viswanadha Vijia Kumara v RG Orr* (1918) 45 Ind Cas 786.

[56] ibid 792. See also *Yogambal Boyee Ammani Ammal v Naina Pilai Markayar* (1909) 3 Ind Cas 110, 113; *Lakshmanan Chetti v Arunachalam Chetti* (1932) AIR Mad 151.

[57] *Raja Viswanadha Vijia Kumara v RG Orr* (1918) 45 Ind Cas 786, 792.

[58] *Damodara Mudaliar v Secretary of State for India* (1895) ILR 18 Mad 88; *Saptharishi Reddiar (Now Minor) v The Secretary of State for India* (1915) 28 Mad LJ 384.

V. Unjust Factors

Introduction

The unjust inquiry focuses on the precise injustice that justifies restitution of the defendant's enrichment. This is perhaps the most difficult inquiry in so far as section 70 is concerned. The many types of situations in which section 70 has been held to apply suggest that the section encompasses a variety of unjust factors. However, given that the other provisions in chapter V are fairly specific in their respective subject matters, it is unlikely that the drafters intended section 70 to address a wide variety of situations involving theoretically dissimilar unjust factors. Hence, this part of the chapter hopes to identify a primary unjust factor for the section and to expel unnecessary materials from its scope.

Acceptance of a Non-Gratuitously Conferred Benefit

Non-Gratuitous Intent

A person who does something non-gratuitously does so expecting remuneration. The difficulty with this requirement of section 70 lies in the burden of proof. In *AV Palinivelu Mudaliar v Neelavathi Ammal* the plaintiff provided certain services to the defendants at their request.[59] When he demanded remuneration, the defendants could not pay and so they executed a promissory note in his favour. When they later refused to honour the promissory note, the plaintiff sued. The Privy Council found that the promissory note was voidable due to undue influence (because one of the defendants was the plaintiff's wife), but held in the plaintiff's favour on the basis of section 70. On the issue of whether the plaintiff acted gratuitously or not, the court said: '[The plaintiff] is, obviously, the proper person to state what his intention was; and his testimony on this matter deserves consideration. What does he say?'[60] If the court is understood to mean that the attention is entirely on the plaintiff's testimony, then we run into a difficulty. A plaintiff who is determined to claim will surely say that he did not intend to act gratuitously, even if it were in fact otherwise. Unless he has acted in a way that is contrary to a non-gratuitous intention, he will invariably succeed on this point. This approach leans too far in the plaintiff's favour. A better balance could be achieved by imposing a requirement that the defendant knows, or ought to have known, about the plaintiff's non-gratuitous intent. In the present case, the court also took into account the defendants' conduct, specifically the fact that they did not object when the plaintiff first demanded remuneration. The court found the defendants' conduct to be consistent with the plaintiff's expectation:

> Their conduct at that time is compatible only with the hypothesis that the demand did not come to them as a surprise, and that they knew that he must be paid, and this knowledge must have come to them from him.[61]

---

[59] *AV Palinivelu Mudaliar v Neelavathi Ammal* (1937) 39 Bomb LR 720.
[60] ibid 724.
[61] *AV Palinivelu Mudaliar v Neelavathi Ammal* (1937) 39 Bomb LR 720, 725.

Similarly, in *State of West Bengal*, where the plaintiff contractors did work for the defendant government, the Supreme Court said: '[The Government] was plainly fully aware that the work was done for it by a party whose trade was to work for remuneration and who had previously done similar work and had been paid for it by the Government.'[62] Besides addressing the difficulty in rebutting the plaintiff's claim of non-gratuitous intent, the suggested approach also serves to prevent section 70 from applying too widely to the extent of forcing goods or services onto unwilling recipients. The defendant may have accepted the benefit thinking that it is a gift, regardless of the plaintiff's state of mind. If this were indeed a reasonable inference, it would surely be unfair to require him to pay for it.

Acceptance

Clearly aware of the danger of forcing goods or services onto unwilling recipients, a further measure adopted by the Indian courts is to impose a requirement that the defendant must have accepted the benefit while having a choice as to whether to accept or reject it.[63] Although this requirement has sometimes been stated in specific reference to the phrase 'enjoys the benefit',[64] on other occasions the courts have stated it more generally having a broader policy concern in mind.[65] Clearly, the element of acceptance goes also to establish the unjustness of the defendant's enrichment. It would be helpful to postpone examination of how the Indian courts have approached the element of acceptance until after we consider treatment of the same under English law and legal scholarship. This would allow us to perceive better how the prevailing approach under Indian law is inadequate, and how it could be refined by drawing from the English experience. It is only necessary to add that, despite the courts' emphasis on the element of acceptance, the possibility that section 70 may encompass non-acceptance-based unjust factors remains open.

Free Acceptance

A Coincidental Resemblance

The two elements of section 70 that we have just examined appear to point to a familiar (albeit controversial) concept in the law of unjust enrichment: free acceptance. A free acceptance arises where the defendant is aware that a benefit is being offered to him non-gratuitously, and, having an opportunity to reject it, forgoes that opportunity, leaving the plaintiff to confer the benefit.[66] It would indeed be far-fetched to claim that the drafters intended section 70 to address a case of free acceptance, especially since not all the elements of free acceptance were included in its wording. Moreover, the English cases that were relied upon in support of the principle of free acceptance mostly post-dated the ICA 1872, and they were not so relied upon until the latter half of the twentieth century. However, since

---

[62] *State of West Bengal v M/S BK Mondal & Sons* (1962) AIR SC 779 (SC) 793.

[63] *Damodara Mudaliar v Secretary of State for India* (1895) ILR 18 Mad 88; *Yogambal Boyee Ammani Ammal v Naina Pilai Markayar* (1909) 3 Ind Cas 110; *Challa Appayya v Desetti Chandra Ayya* (1950) AIR Mad 817, 818.

[64] *Yogambal Boyee Ammani Ammal v Naina Pilai Markayar* (1909) 3 Ind Cas 110.

[65] See, eg, *State of West Bengal v M/S BK Mondal & Sons* (1962) AIR SC 779 (SC).

[66] R Goff and G Jones, *The Law of Restitution* (London, Sweet & Maxwell, 1966) 4; P Birks, *An Introduction to the Law of Restitution* (Oxford, Oxford University Press, 1985) ch VIII.

the Indian courts clearly prefer an acceptance-based analysis of section 70, it is argued that the best way forward is to adopt free acceptance as the section's core case. This would supply section 70 with a much-needed rationale to facilitate its necessary refinement.

Before proceeding to examine the elements of free acceptance, it is apt to make a few more preliminary points. Firstly, free acceptance is unique in that it has a dual function within the modern unjust enrichment framework. Its role in the enrichment inquiry has been explained earlier. Here, we focus on its quality as an unjust factor. Secondly, free acceptance does not belong to the family of intent-based unjust factors, which focus on the plaintiff's impaired or qualified intent in benefiting the defendant.[67] Instead, it belongs to the family of policy-motivated unjust factors, which justify restitution by reference to specific policy reasons.[68] In the case of free acceptance, the reason for allowing restitution is the unconscientiousness in the way in which the defendant accepts the benefit.[69] Thirdly, free acceptance has yet to receive clear judicial blessing. Its development was mainly fuelled by academic debates, drawing on a number of early cases for indirect support.[70] Goff and Jones coined the term in 1966,[71] and Birks worked hard to fine-tune its elements in the mid-1980s to 1990s.[72] Although Birks eventually expressed regret for advocating free acceptance as an unjust factor,[73] the principle continues to occupy a prominent place in *Goff & Jones*, the latest edition of which went as far as to devote a separate chapter to it.[74] As the editors explained, this decision 'was partly prompted by a sense that the subject was significant enough to call for such treatment, and was also partly a response to the case law which has relatively recently emerged in this area'.[75] Only recently, the English High Court said in *Benedetti v Sawiris*:

> The question of whether there has, properly speaking, been a free acceptance of the services is likely in practice to be the determining factor as to whether it is regarded as unjust for a defendant to retain the benefit of services without paying for them.[76]

It is, of course, not the intention of this chapter to speculate on the future of free acceptance in English law. Instead, it seeks to draw upon existing work on this topic to refine and develop the content of section 70.

Elements, Rationale and Scope of Free Acceptance

The elements of free acceptance can be briefly explained. Firstly, the defendant must have an opportunity to accept or reject the benefit. If the benefit is already conferred on the

---

[67] Established intent-based unjust factors include mistake, duress and failure of condition.

[68] See S Degeling, 'Understanding Policy Motivated Unjust Factors' in C Rickett and R Grantham (eds), *Structure and Justification in Private Law: Essays in Memory of Peter Birks* (Oxford, Hart Publishing, 2008) 267.

[69] Birks, above n 46, 105; *Goff & Jones*, above n 13, [4-29].

[70] See notably *Leigh v Dickeson* (1884) 15 QBD 60; *Falcke v Scottish Imperial Insurance Co* (1886) 34 Ch D 234; *Re Cleadon Trust Ltd* [1939] 1 Ch 286. Although the judgments of these cases contain statements broadly supporting free acceptance, restitution was denied on the facts.

[71] Goff and Jones, above n 66, 4.

[72] Birks, above n 66, ch VIII; Birks, above n 46, 111.

[73] Birks, above n 48, 42–43. Despite his change of heart, his earlier works remain insightful in approaching this topic. This chapter will therefore continue to rely on them.

[74] *Goff & Jones*, above n 13, ch 17.

[75] ibid [17-01].

[76] *Benedetti v Sawiris* [2009] EWHC 1330, [574]. See also *Rowe v Vale of White Horse DC* [2003] 1 Lloyd's Rep 418.

defendant without his knowledge, he cannot be said to have such an opportunity. In the latter case, it is insufficient that the defendant afterwards decides to enjoy the benefit even if this conduct may be understood as acceptance in the ordinary sense.

Secondly, the defendant must know, or ought to have known, that the plaintiff acted non-gratuitously. Where the plaintiff does not expressly demand payment, whether he has or has not acted gratuitously must necessarily be determined by reasonable inference from the surrounding facts. For example, if the plaintiff is in the business of providing the goods or services in question, the reasonable inference is that he intended to charge for these.

Thirdly, the defendant must have neglected to avail himself of an opportunity to reject the benefit, allowing the benefit to be conferred upon him. Whether the said opportunity exists is to be determined by a simple test. If there is a reason for the defendant to believe that the plaintiff's conduct was influenced by a wrong estimate of probability that the defendant will pay, such that the plaintiff would have desisted if told that he would not be paid, failure to reject the benefit amounts to free acceptance. But the defendant is not required to undertake onerous effort to reject the benefit.[77] He is only required to do what is reasonably necessary, although this would seem to exclude any steps that require incurring expenses.[78] On the other hand, if there is a reason to believe that the plaintiff's conduct was uninfluenced by any estimate of probability that the defendant will pay, failure to reject the benefit does not amount to free acceptance. For example, it is reasonable to assume that a busker, while expecting payment for his performance, will continue to perform even if told that he will not be paid. He will continue to try his luck, hoping that some of the other audiences will pay. Thus, a miserly bystander who watches the performance but refuses to pay cannot be held liable on the basis of free acceptance.

From its three elements it is clear that free acceptance is concerned with the unconscientiousness of the defendant's conduct, specifically his failure reasonably to avail himself of an opportunity to save the plaintiff from the risk of non-payment. Opponents of free acceptance argue that the defendant should nonetheless be left to bear any loss resulting from his own risk-taking.[79] Against this the editors of *Goff & Jones* provide a convincing reply, drawing on the classic window cleaner example:

> Certainly such a claimant takes the risk that, having cleaned the windows without the householder's knowledge, the householder will refuse to pay; but it is not so clear that he also takes the risk that a householder who realises that his windows are being cleaned will not warn him that he is wasting his time. In other words, the window cleaner could be said only to take the risk of the work being rejected once the recipient is aware of what is happening.[80]

A final hurdle confronting proponents of free acceptance is how potential overlaps with more established unjust factors should be dealt with. In the celebrated Australian case of *Pavey and Matthews Pty Ltd v Paul* the plaintiff contractors had renovated a cottage for the defendant pursuant to an oral contract, according to the terms of which the defendant had to pay reasonably for the work according to prevailing rates.[81] When the work

---

[77] *Goff & Jones*, above n 13, [17-13].
[78] ibid. See also GH Mead, 'Free Acceptance: Some Further Considerations' (1989) 105 *LQR* 460, 464–66.
[79] Burrows, above n 45; Mead, above n 78.
[80] *Goff & Jones*, above n 13, [17-05].
[81] *Pavey and Matthews Pty Ltd v Paul* (1987) 162 CLR 221.

was completed the defendant paid $36,000, but the plaintiff demanded nearly twice that sum. Against the plaintiff's claim the defendant argued that the contract was unenforceable for it was not in writing as required by statute. The High Court of Australia held that although the contract was unenforceable the plaintiff could succeed under the law of restitution and unjust enrichment. While no specific unjust factor was identified, the judgment hinted that the defendant's acceptance of the work played an important role in the decision to order restitution.[82] One would have thought that proponents of free acceptance would jump at this opportunity to seize authoritative support for the principle. However, although Birks initially thought that free acceptance applies to a case of this kind,[83] he later admitted that 'free acceptance cannot be the unjust factor on the *Pavey* facts' and 'even the friend of free acceptance may find himself convinced that it cannot cope with many of the request cases'.[84] In *Pavey* there is nothing unconscientious in the defendant's acceptance or receipt of the benefit. It was pursuant to an agreement between the parties, and the defendant intended to pay what she thought was a reasonable sum. The unconscientiousness on the defendant's part only arose subsequently when she refused to pay the demanded amount, but this 'has little or no weight in breaking the balance between a risk-taking intervener and the initially innocent recipient'.[85] Free acceptance is only concerned with a defendant's unconscientiousness at the time of receipt of the benefit, specifically the neglect to avail himself reasonably of an opportunity to save the plaintiff from his risk-taking.

As Burrows has set out to show, many of the cases from which free acceptance allegedly found support could in fact be explained by the concept of failure of condition (or failure of consideration, as it is more commonly known as), an intent-based unjust factor.[86] In *Pavey* the plaintiff's intention to benefit the defendant with the construction work is qualified by a condition that the defendant pays for it. The defendant, being a party to the agreement, clearly shared this expectation. When the defendant refused to pay, the condition for performing the work failed, rendering the defendant's enrichment unjust.

Even where a case could be explained by both free acceptance and failure of condition, Birks conceded that the former should give way to the latter.[87] Free acceptance 'should be regarded as a longstop, not to be called upon until the inquiry into the plaintiff-sided factors has produced a negative result'.[88] The editors of *Goff & Jones* share the same sentiment:

> The situations in which recourse to the principle of free acceptance will be necessary will partly depend on where the boundaries of other unjust factors are drawn. In particular, the need to rely on a principle of free acceptance will depend on how broadly the principle of failure of basis is understood.[89]

The effect of all these fine-tunings is to confine the operation of free acceptance to 'only a handful of cases'.[90] The subject matter is now specific and clear. It is precisely the kind of certainty that section 70 lacks and needs.

---

[82] ibid 228, 263.
[83] Birks, above n 66, 272–75.
[84] Birks, above n 46, 111.
[85] ibid.
[86] Burrows, above n 45.
[87] Birks, above n 46, 116–20.
[88] ibid 145.
[89] *Goff & Jones*, above n 13, [17-06].
[90] ibid 144.

Lessons from Free Acceptance

Unconscientious Acceptance

It is clear that not every acceptance of a non-gratuitously conferred benefit should trigger a right of recovery. Given the judicial preference for an acceptance-based analysis of section 70, one would expect the Indian courts to be meticulous in identifying the kind of acceptance that is required. Unfortunately, the notion of acceptance presently adopted by the Indian courts is largely inadequate. It is sometimes too wide, and at other times too narrow.

In *State of West Bengal* the plaintiff constructed a warehouse for the defendant's use.[91] The Supreme Court said that the defendant was not compelled to accept it, but nonetheless held that acceptance was established because the defendant eventually put the warehouse to use. The judgment appears to assume that an acceptance must be overt, in the sense the word is normally understood. The discussion on free acceptance, however, reminds us that acceptance can be passive. The neglect to avail oneself of an opportunity to reject the plaintiff's conferral of benefit amounts to acceptance. Thus, in *State of West Bengal* acceptance in fact occurred when the defendant allowed the benefit to be conferred without any protest. There was no need to rely on the fact that the defendant afterwards put the warehouse to use.

The overemphasis on the defendant's subsequent enjoyment of the benefit has sometimes stretched the notion of acceptance too widely. In *Saptharishi* the plaintiff intended to carry out repairs to a water tank that irrigated both his and the defendant's land to prevent floods.[92] The defendant was informed of this intention and was asked to contribute a proportionate share of the repair cost. The defendant replied that he did not object to such repairs but refused to contribute to the repair cost.[93] The plaintiff nonetheless went on to repair the water tank and brought a proceeding against the defendant. The Madras High Court held that the defendant's subsequent enjoyment of the benefit without objection amounted to an acceptance.[94] This is incorrect. The defendant clearly rejected the benefit. If the plaintiff decided to confer the benefit anyway, as he did, the fact that the defendant later enjoyed the benefit does not amount to acceptance in any meaningful sense.

Even if one insists that the defendant in *Saptharishi* could be regarded as having accepted the benefit, that should not, by itself, be sufficient to attract any liability. In what way was the defendant's conduct unconscientious? The defendant, having clearly expressed a refusal to pay, cannot be said to have failed to avail himself of an opportunity to save the plaintiff from the risk of non-payment. To decide otherwise would amount to forcing the cost of the benefit onto the defendant, which is counterintuitive. The same point arises in another water tank case. In *Damodara* the plaintiff government, having made necessary repairs to a water tank that irrigated seven of its villages as well as four villages under the jurisdiction of the defendant *zamindar*, claimed from the latter the costs of such repairs.[95] The court

---

[91] *State of West Bengal v M/S BK Mondal & Sons* (1962) AIR SC 779 (SC).

[92] *Saptharishi Reddiar (Now Minor) v The Secretary of State for India* (1915) 28 Mad LJ 384.

[93] See also *Raja Viswanadha Vijia Kumara v RG Orr* (1918) 45 Ind Cas 786.

[94] Following Miller J's view in *Sri Sri Sri Gajapathi Kristna Chandra Deo Garu v P Srinivasa Charlu* (1913) 25 Mad LJ 433.

[95] *Saptharishi Reddiar (Now Minor) v The Secretary of State for India* (1915) 28 Mad LJ 384.

held that the defendant was liable to pay (presumably 4/11 of the costs) under section 70. The exact reasoning of the court was unclear, but an important factor that it took into account was that the defendant 'knew of the intention to execute the repairs and did not disapprove'.[96] Although the facts of the case came very close to illustrating free acceptance, they failed to fulfil an important requirement. Given that the government was under a duty to carry out the repairs for the benefit of its villages, chances are that it would have done so even if the defendant indicated his refusal to pay. In this sense the government's action was most likely uninfluenced by any estimate of probability that the defendant will pay. As such, even if the defendant did not expressly object, there was no unconscientiousness on his part.

Excluding Failure of Condition Cases

In *State of West Bengal* the plaintiff contractors undertook certain construction work for the defendant, a local government department, at the request of its officers. When the work was completed, the defendant refused to pay. The plaintiff thus sued the defendant for payment. The Supreme Court held that there was no enforceable contract between the plaintiff and the defendant because the department officers who requested the work were not authorised to execute the contract, as required under section 175(3) of the Government of India Act 1935. However, for reasons already mentioned, the court held that section 70 applied.[97] The obvious similarity between *State of West Bengal* and *Pavey* is that both cases concerned benefits conferred under a contract that was unenforceable for want of formality. As explained earlier, the *Pavey* facts do not support the finding of free acceptance because the defendant was not unconscientious in accepting the benefit. It may, however, be possible to distinguish the facts of the two cases. In *Pavey* the defendant did make a payment, which implies that she intended to pay all along. The fact that she eventually paid less than the demanded sum does not affect her conscience at the time of accepting the benefit, for that was what she genuinely believed she had to pay. In contrast, it is impossible to tell on the facts of *State of West Bengal* whether the defendant's refusal to pay was intended at the outset or only subsequently. Since it was the defendant who was at fault for not paying, it is perhaps fair to presume against the defendant unless proven otherwise. It is therefore possible for a *State of West Bengal*-type case to be understood as concerning free acceptance.

Having said the above, a section 70 claim may sometimes offer no help to the plaintiff even though his claim appears well-grounded. Suppose in *State of West Bengal* the plaintiff was asked to paint a building belonging to the defendant. However, the plaintiff painted the building only at night when all of the defendant's officers were away and unaware. While the defendant has received the benefit of the plaintiff's service, it may be argued that there is no acceptance of the benefit on the defendant's part. The plaintiff's only hope is to rely on a non-acceptance-based claim. One option is the doctrine of failure of condition, which

---

[96] ibid 389.
[97] For other *State of West Bengal*-type cases, see *Piloo Dhunjishaw Sidhwa v Municipal Corporation of the City* (1970) 3 SCR 415 (SC); *The New Marine Coal Co (Bengal) v Union of India* (1964) AIR 152 (SC); *Union of India v JK Gas Plant* (1980) AIR 1330 (SC); *Union of India v Sita Ram Jaiswal* (1977) AIR SC 329 (SC); *Hansraj Gupta & Co v Union of India* (1973) AIR SC 2724 (SC).

is recognised by case law. A more convenient option is to rely on section 65 of the ICA 1872, which states:

> When an agreement is discovered to be void, or when a contract becomes void, any person who has received any advantage under such agreement or contract is bound to restore it, or to make compensation for it to the person from whom he received it.

As to whether a contract unenforceable for want of formality could be regarded as void, section 2(g) provides a clear answer: 'An agreement not enforceable by law is said to be void.' In several *State of West Bengal*-type cases the courts have held that both sections 65 and 70 applied.[98] There were also such cases where only section 65 was applied.[99] In order to avoid unduly restricting rightful claims, and in keeping with the goal of discarding unnecessary materials from section 70, it is submitted that the *State of West Bengal*-type cases are best dealt with by section 65 alone.

Excluding Contribution and Reimbursement Cases

Where a plaintiff discharges the defendant's debt, or a debt for which the plaintiff and defendant are jointly and severally liable, the plaintiff could in some cases recover from the defendant. The most relevant provision which governs the plaintiff's right of recovery is section 69 of the ICA 1872, which reads:

> A person who is interested in the payment of money which another is bound by law to pay, and who therefore pays it, is entitled to be reimbursed by the other.

The core case is set out in an illustration accompanying the section:

> B holds land in Bengal, on a lease granted by A, the zamindar. The revenue payable by A to the Government being in arrear, his land is advertised for sale by the Government. Under the revenue law, the consequence of such sale will be the annulment of B's lease. B to prevent the sale and the consequent annulment of his own lease, pays the Government the sum due from A. A is bound to make good to B the amount so paid.[100]

Despite the existence of a specific provision for dealing with such cases, the Indian courts have sometimes chosen to rely solely on section 70,[101] and at other times apply both sections 69 and 70.[102] In an attempt to limit the plaintiff's recovery in such cases, the Calcutta High Court clarified that section 70 only applies if the plaintiff has an interest in making the payment so that the payment is lawful, as required by the section.[103] This,

---

[98] See, eg, *Dominion of India v Preety Kumar Ghosh* (1958) AIR Pat 203; *Madura Municipality v K Alagiri Swami Naidu* (1939) AIR Mad 957; *State of Madras v K Periaswami Gounder* (1963) AIR 1963 Mad 154; *Hindustan Construction Co v The State of Bihar* (1963) AIR Pat 254; *AKTKM Sankaran Namboodiripad v State of Kerala* (1963) AIR Ker 278; *BD Naithani v State of UP* (1966) AIR 53 All 507.

[99] See, eg, *KCA Arunachala Nadar & ors v Srivilliputtur Municipal* (1934) AIR Mad 480.

[100] For a real life example, see *K Chengalroya Reddi v Udai Kavour by her agent Mohanmull Choreda (deceased)* (1936) 71 Mad LJ 1a.

[101] See, eg, *Jarao Kumari v Basanta Kumar Roy* (1904) 32 ILR Cal 374; *KRSV Muthayya Chetti v Narayanan Chetti* (1928) AIR Mad 317. In *Sri Sri Sri Gajapathi Kristna Chandra Deo Garu v P Srinivasa Charlu* (1913) 25 Mad LJ 433, 435, the court found it 'safer' to rely on s 70.

[102] *Lala Ram Rattan Lal v Musammat Gaura* (1930) 122 Ind Cas 765; *K Chengalroya Reddi v Udai Kavour by her agent Mohanmull Choreda (deceased)* (1936) AIR Mad 752; *Ram Rachhpal v Banwari Lal* (1935) AIR Lah 981; *Mt Savitribai v Nanhelal* (1934) AIR Nag 84.

[103] *Raja Baikuntha Nath Dey Bahadur v Udai Chand Maiti* (1905) 2 Cal LJ 311; *Panchcouri Ghose v Haridas Jati* [1916] 25 Cal LJ 325; *Gopeswar Banerjee v Brojo Sundari Devi* (1922) AIR Cal 353; *Nagendra Nath Roy v Jugal Kishore Roy* (1925) AIR Cal 1097.

however, is to import an important characteristic of section 69 into section 70, resulting in unnecessary duplication. These cases are best excluded from the scope of section 70 and should be left to the exclusive purview of section 69. As Doss J of the Calcutta High Court rightly said in *Suchand Ghosal vs Balaram Mardana*:

> [N]otwithstanding the apparent generality of the language of Section 70 of the Contract Act, it: seems to me reasonable to presume that it was not the intention of the Legislature that this section should be invoked where relief might be obtained under any other section of the Act.[104]

> … A too liberal construction of the section would render the enactment contained in Section 69 almost a surplusage, and the qualifying words 'who is interested in the payment of the money' entirely nugatory. The particular rule embodied in Section 69 would, on such hypothesis, be included in the more general.[105]

Other Unjust Factors?

Although this chapter argues that section 70 should embrace free acceptance as its core case, there is no denying that the broad wording of the section is capable of encompassing non-acceptance-based unjust factors. In this part we shall examine two other unjust factors that are hinted at by the two statutory illustrations.

Necessity

Let us recall illustration (b), where A saves B's property from fire. If B is aware of A's attempt to put out the fire, it could be said that there is free acceptance, provided that the other requirements are satisfied. However, the possibility of the section applying even where B is unaware is not excluded by the wordings of the section and the statutory illustration. In fact, there are suggestions that section 70 extends beyond free acceptance. In *Gajapathi Kristna Chandra Deo Garu v P Srinivasa Charlu* Aiyar J of the Madras High Court gave an example involving two owners of neighbouring agricultural lands.[106] While one owner was away, his land was at risk of drying up. The other owner irrigated said land under the reasonable belief that he would be repaid the cost of doing so. Aiyar J opined that section 70 could apply in this case even though the absent owner had no option of accepting or rejecting the benefit.[107] In *Saptharishi*, which we have examined earlier, the court, in allowing the section 70 claim, placed some emphasis on the finding that 'the repairs were urgently necessary for the tank and that but for the repairs the tank was in danger of breaching and of overflooding the lands of the defendant'.[108] As explained earlier, the facts of the case do not support the finding of free acceptance. However, it is possible that the decision is explicable on the principle of necessitous intervention, which is based on the policy of encouraging intervention to preserve health or property of others in situations of emergency.[109] While this policy may appear to be in conflict with the statutory requirement of non-gratuitous

---

[104] *Suchand Ghosal vs Balaram Mardana* (1911) ILR 38 Cal 1, 11–12.
[105] ibid 12.
[106] *Sri Sri Sri Gajapathi Kristna Chandra Deo Garu v P Srinivasa Charlu* (1913) 25 Mad LJ 433, 441.
[107] ibid.
[108] *Saptharishi Reddiar (Now Minor) v The Secretary of State for India* (1915) 28 Mad LJ 384, 391–92.
[109] Burrows, above n 13, 480–83.

intent, it is in fact not the case. It is only logical that a truly altruistic intervener, ie one who intervenes without the expectation of payment, should be denied from claiming just as a person who makes a gift is disallowed from reclaiming it. It is important, however, that the requirement of non-gratuitous intent should be relaxed to avoid undermining this policy concern. In response to the suggestion in *Re Rhodes* that the plaintiff must show that he intended to charge for the benefit,[110] the editors of *Goff & Jones* said:

> [I]t is illogical to conclude from the fact that it is good public policy to encourage intervention, that the burden of proving an intention to charge should be imposed on the intervener; the burden should rather lie on the assisted person to prove that the intervener intended to act gratuitously.[111]

In the absence of evidence contradicting a non-gratuitous intent, the plaintiff would invariably win on this point. The necessary counterbalance lies in the requirement that the plaintiff must have acted in a situation of sufficient urgency, which would necessarily depend on the actual facts as well as the kind of interests the law seeks to protect.

Mistake and Duress?

Illustration (a) refers to a mistake on A's part in delivering goods to B. This is rather curious because the right to recover for a mistaken conferral of benefit is already provided for under section 72, which reads: 'A person to whom money has been paid, or anything delivered, by mistake or under coercion, must repay or return it.' There is, however, a situation in which section 70 may play a supplementary role. It is where the benefit in question could not be forced within the meaning of 'anything delivered', eg services and use value, such that section 72 does not apply. Where section 72 is applicable, however, it should apply to the exclusion of section 70.

VI. Restitution

Upon satisfying the requirements of section 70, the defendant is required to make compensation in respect of, or to restore, the thing so done or delivered by the plaintiff. It is interesting that the word 'restitution' does not appear anywhere in the ICA 1872. This is likely because the term had not gained currency in legal usage in the mid-nineteenth century.[112] The phrase 'restore' clearly refers to restitution in the 'giving back' sense. Given that 'restore' and 'compensation' are used as alternatives, and in light of the judicial recognition that 'compensation' does not refer to an award of damages as traditionally understood,[113] 'compensation' in this context is best understood as also referring to restitution, specifically monetary restitution.[114] The amount of money recoverable by the plaintiff correlates with

---

[110] *Re Rhodes* (1884) 44 Ch D 94.

[111] *Goff & Jones*, above n 13, [18-82]. cf *Bartholomew v Jackson* 11 Am Dec 237 (Sup Ct of NY, 1822), which favoured a presumption in the opposite direction.

[112] The term 'restitution' was first referred to extensively in Abbot's review of Keener's treatise: EV Abbot, 'Keener on Quasi-Contracts II' (1897) 10 *Harvard Law Review* 479.

[113] See, eg, *Union of India v JK Gas Plant* (1980) AIR 1330 (SC).

[114] See, eg, *Mulamchand v State of Madhya Pradesh* (1968) AIR SC 1218 (SC); *Govindarajulu Naidu v SS Naidu* (1958) 2 Mad LJ 148.

the extent to which the defendant is enriched. It only remains to be said that the difficult issue of proprietary restitution appears to be sidestepped as the plaintiff is given the choice of how to effect restitution: restitution in specie or restitution in value.

VII. Defences

Illegality

The plaintiff's act of doing something for, or delivering something to, the defendant must be 'lawful'. Although this requirement appears at the beginning of the section's wording, this chapter prefers to examine it at the end since it is, in essence, an illegality defence. This way of understanding the requirement is also consistent with its judicial treatment. The plaintiff is not under any positive duty to prove that his conduct is lawful. Instead, the issue of lawfulness arises only when the defendant raises it to resist the plaintiff's claim.[115]

Due to the generality of the word 'lawful' the courts have held different views as to what it actually requires and its true function. In *State of West Bengal* the Supreme Court merely said that 'the thing delivered or done must not be delivered or done fraudulently or dishonestly'.[116] In *KRSV Muthayya Chetti v Narayanan Chetti* the Madras High Court defined 'lawful' as 'not unlawful', which is in turn said to mean not for a fraudulent purpose, not without proper care, not with any improper or ulterior motive, not for any gain to the plaintiff and not against the will of the defendant.[117] In other cases the courts said that 'lawful' means 'bona fide', which unfortunately adds little to identifying the precise meaning of the term.[118]

The preferable approach, it is submitted, is to be found in *Rakurti Manikyam v Medidi Satyanarayana*.[119] The plaintiff entered into an oral agreement to sell to the defendant 64 bags of rice at the rate of Rs 34.25 per bag. When the defendant failed to pay after receiving the goods, the plaintiff sued to enforce the agreement. The Andhra Pradesh High Court held that the agreement was void for illegality. It contravened the Rice (Andhra Pradesh) Price Control Order, 1963, which prescribed the maximum price at which paddy may be sold (Rs 18 per bag at that time). The plaintiff's alternative claim based on section 70 was also rejected on the same ground. The court explained that the word 'lawful' is to be understood by reference to section 23 of the ICA 1872, which reads:

> The consideration or object of an agreement is lawful, unless—
>
> it is forbidden by law; or
> is of such nature that, if permitted it would defeat the provisions of any law; or

---

[115] See, eg, *Ajodhya Prasad Singh v Narain Prasad Jalan* (1963) AIR Pat 326; *The Life Insurance Corporation of India v KA Madhava Rao* (1972) AIR Mad 112.

[116] *State of West Bengal v M/S BK Mondal & Sons* (1962) AIR SC 779 (SC) 788.

[117] *KRSV Muthayya Chetti v Narayanan Chetti* (1928) AIR Mad 317.

[118] *Challa Appayya v Desetti Chandra Ayya* (1950) AIR Mad 817; *Venkatakrishnamacharlu v Arunachala Pillai* [1919] MWN 244.

[119] *Rakurti Manikyam v Medidi Satyanarayana* (1972) AIR AP 367.

is fraudulent; or

involves or implies, injury to the person or property of another; or

the Court regards it as immoral, or opposed to public policy.

Although section 23 refers to an agreement, which section 70 is not concerned with, it is likely that the drafters of the ICA 1872 intended some coherence in the use of terms. More importantly, the definition set out by section 23 reflects the broad meaning of illegality adopted by modern scholars.[120] The only problem with section 23 is that it does not appear to leave any room for familiar common law exceptions, eg *non in pari delicto* and *locus poenitentiae*.[121] However, since section 23 is not expressly referred to in section 70, the possibility of importing these exceptions remains open.

Negligence?

In *The New Marine Coal Co (Bengal) v Union of India* the Supreme Court suggested that a section 70 claim could be defeated by 'estoppel on the ground of negligence'.[122] The facts of the case need not concern us, for it involved a dispute that is better dealt with under section 65. The suggestion relating to negligence, however, raises a general issue, for a careless conferral of benefit could occur also in cases involving other unjust factors that may come within section 70. Under the common law, negligence is not a recognised defence to an unjust enrichment claim. In *Kelly v Solari* it was held that a mistaken payer could recover 'however careless [he] may have been'.[123] There is even judicial support for adopting this approach for the right to recovery under section 72.[124] The desirability for coherence in the law would demand that section 70 adopts the same approach.

Change of Position, Bona Fide Purchase, etc

Established restitutionary defences such as change of position and bona fide purchase are unlikely to apply in a case of free acceptance due to the unconscientiousness of the defendant's conduct. However, where section 70 applies to supplement section 72 in a case of mistake, such defences should apply. Although they are not explicitly set out in the ICA 1872, it has been argued that in certain cases their importation is necessary to ensure fairness.[125] There is in fact ample judicial support for this suggestion. In *Sri Sri Shiba Prasad Singh v Maharaja Srish Chandra Nandi* the Privy Council qualified the right of recovery in section 72 despite the absence of a statutory defence: '[Not] every sum paid under mistake is recoverable no matter what the circumstances may be. There may in a particular case be

---

[120] See, eg Burrows, above n 13, 488; *Goff & Jones*, above n 13, ch 35.

[121] But see *Sundara Gownder v Balachandran* (1990) AIR Ker 324.

[122] *The New Marine Coal Co (Bengal) v Union of India* (1964) AIR 152 (SC).

[123] *Kelly v Solari* (1841) 9 M & W 54, 59.

[124] See the decisions of the Malaysian High Court in *Bank Bumiputra (M) Bhd v Hashbudin bin Hashim* [1998] 3 MLJ 262; *Green Continental Furniture (M) Sdn Bhd lwn Tenaga Nasional Bhd* [2011] 8 MLJ 394; *The Royal Bank of Scotland Bhd v Seng Huah Hua* [2013] 9 MLJ 681.

[125] See See, above n 33.

circumstances which disentitle a plaintiff by estoppel or otherwise.'[126] Later, in *Mafatlal Industries v Union of India*, the Supreme Court held that change of position is an available defence in a section 72 claim. In that case, Reddy J said: 'Section 72 of the Contract Act is based upon and incorporates a rule of equity. In such a situation, equitable considerations cannot be ruled out while applying the said provision.'[127] Although both cases were concerned with section 72, the courts are likely to be equally willing to import these common law defences into section 70.

VIII. Conclusion

Lord Wright once commented that chapter V of the ICA 1872 dealt with its subject matter 'in a very unsatisfactory manner'.[128] While his criticism is not entirely unjustified, especially given the use of broad and vague wordings, the real problem lies in the inadequate efforts in developing the content of chapter V, which is most evident in the case of section 70. The solution proposed by this chapter is that section 70 should be understood and developed by reference to the modern law of unjust enrichment. Building on the Indian courts' preference for an acceptance-based unjust factor, this chapter argues that the best way forward is to adopt free acceptance as the core case of section 70. Although free acceptance finds no firm footing in the common law, legal scholarship of the past 30 years has moulded the concept into a principled and useable one. The proposed suggestion is also motivated by the belief that the scope of section 70 could only be meaningfully determined by identifying what it could do which other legal provisions could not, which explains the emphasis on expelling unnecessary materials from the section. Only time will tell whether the proposed suggestions will find favour with the Indian courts. In the mean time, it is perhaps worth pondering whether section 70 is any indication that, in the process of modernising the English law of unjust enrichment, something important has been accidently left behind.

---

[126] *Sri Sri Shiba Prasad Singh v Maharaja Srish Chandra Nandi* (1949) AIR PC 297 (PC) 302.
[127] *Mafatlal Industries v Union of India* (1997) 5 SCC 536 (SC) 634.
[128] Lord Wright, 'Restatement of the Law of Restitution' (1937) 51 *Harvard Law Review* 369.

12

Revisiting Canada's Approach to Fiduciary Relationships

ERIKA CHAMBERLAIN

I. Introduction and Background

The Supreme Court of Canada's approach to recognising fiduciary relationships has been the subject of considerable derision in other common law jurisdictions, especially Australia. Its extension of protection to non-economic interests has been characterised as results- or remedy-driven, and a distortion of the traditional bases for finding fiduciary obligations.[1] This chapter will examine whether the unorthodox Canadian approach to fiduciary relationships can be explained on the basis of social, policy, constitutional or other considerations that are more prevalent in Canada. In addition, it suggests that the Supreme Court of Canada has been bolder and more creative than its counterparts elsewhere in the common law world, and has been willing to apply the spirit of equity in ways that appropriately meet the perceived needs of modern society.

Criticism of the Supreme Court's approach to fiduciary relationships is typically aimed at a series of decisions from the late 1980s and early 1990s, which took an expansionist position on the types of conduct and losses that could form the basis of a claim. The foundation for this approach was laid in Wilson J's dissenting opinion in *Frame v Smith*,[2] where she provided a description of the principal characteristics (sometimes called 'criteria') of fiduciary relationships. Wilson J wrote:

> Relationships in which a fiduciary obligation have been imposed seem to possess three general characteristics:
>
> (1)   The fiduciary has scope for the exercise of some discretion or power.
> (2)   The fiduciary can unilaterally exercise that power or discretion so as to affect the beneficiary's legal or practical interests.
> (3)   The beneficiary is peculiarly vulnerable to or at the mercy of the fiduciary holding the discretion or power.[3]

---

[1] See, eg, PD Finn, 'The Fiduciary Principle' in TG Youdan (ed), *Equity, Fiduciaries and Trusts* (Toronto, Carswell, 1989) 25; P Parkinson, 'Fiduciary Law and Access to Medical Records: *Breen v Williams*' (1995) 17 *Sydney Law Review* 433; L Hoyano, 'The Flight to Fiduciary Haven' in P Birks (ed), *Privacy and Loyalty* (Oxford, Clarendon Press 1997); A Duggan, 'Fiduciary Obligations in the Supreme Court of Canada: A Retrospective' (2011) 50 *Canadian Business Law Journal* 85.

[2] *Frame v Smith* [1987] 2 SCR 99.

[3] ibid [60].

Wilson J's test was cited with approval by both judgments in *Lac Minerals Ltd v International Corona Resources Ltd*,[4] and was adopted by the majority in *Hodgkinson v Simms*.[5] In the latter case, LaForest J clarified that Wilson J's three-part description provided 'indicia that help recognize a fiduciary relationship rather than the ingredients that define it'.[6] There has been considerable debate, in this vein, about whether vulnerability is a crucial component of fiduciary relationships; for example, a corporation is hardly in a vulnerable position, but its directors nevertheless owe it fiduciary obligations.[7]

While much has been written about the appropriateness of the power/vulnerability criteria, the cases discussed in this chapter are more significant for their liberal use of Wilson J's phrase, 'legal or practical interests'. A main point of distinction for the Canadian approach to fiduciary relationships is that they have extended beyond financial and proprietary interests to encompass, for example, physical and psychological well-being, access to medical records[8] and minority language rights.[9] In the Crown–Aboriginal context, fiduciary obligations have also been used to restrict the government's ability to enforce laws that limit the practice of Aboriginal rights.[10]

Having reached its apparent zenith in the 1990s, the Supreme Court's expansive approach to fiduciary obligations has diminished in the last decade. The Court has retrenched its position on the Crown–Aboriginal relationship[11] and other public fiduciary duties[12] in particular. The Court has also downplayed the importance of vulnerability and has placed more emphasis on the need for an undertaking by the alleged fiduciary to act in the best interests of the plaintiff. In *Galambos v Perez*,[13] for example, Cromwell J wrote:

> [T]o assert that the protection of the vulnerable is the role of fiduciary law puts the matter too broadly. … Fiduciary law is more concerned with the position of the parties that *results* from the relationship that gives rise to the fiduciary duty than with the respective positions of the parties *before* they enter into the relationship.[14]

Nevertheless, the Court in *Galambos* did not resile from its earlier decisions; it simply clarified their appropriate application.

---

[4] *Lac Minerals Ltd v International Corona Resources Ltd* [1989] 2 SCR 574.
[5] *Hodgkinson v Simms* [1994] 3 SCR 377.
[6] ibid [30].
[7] See, eg, *Lac Minerals International Corona Resources Ltd* [1989] 2 SCR 574, where the majority (Sopinka J) found that there was no fiduciary duty owed by a large mining company toward a smaller mining company that disclosed the location of potentially valuable deposits in an effort to engage in a joint venture. Sopinka J found that there would rarely be fiduciary obligations in commercial dealings between arm's length parties, who are presumably capable of protecting their own interests. The minority, LaForest J, found a fiduciary duty based on the relationship of trust and confidence between the parties and the vulnerability of the smaller mining company. For commentary on the LaForest–Sopinka debate, see JD McCamus, 'Prometheus Unbound: Fiduciary Obligation in the Supreme Court of Canada' (1997) 28 *Canadian Business Law Journal* 107.
[8] *McInerney v MacDonald* [1992] 2 SCR 138.
[9] *Commission Scolaire Francophone du Yukon No 23 c Procureure Générale du Territorie du Yukon* 2011 YKSC 57 rev'd 2015 SCC 25 (new trial ordered on account of reasonable apprehension of bias by the trial judge). See F Larocque, M Power and M Vincelette, 'L'élargissement du concept d'obligation fiduciaire au profit des communauteés de langue française en situation minoritaire dans leurs relations avec l'État' (2012) 63 *University of New Brunswick Law Journal* 363.
[10] *R v Sparrow* [1990] 1 SCR 1075.
[11] *Wewaykum Indian Band v Canada* [2002] SCC 79, [2002] 4 SCR 245.
[12] *Alberta v Elder Advocates of Alberta Society* 2011 SCC 24, [2011] 2 SCR 261.
[13] *Galambos v Perez* 2009 SCC 48, [2009] 3 SCR 247.
[14] ibid [67]–[68].

Critics of the Canadian approach have argued that fiduciary obligations are limited in three primary ways, all of which have been disregarded by the Supreme Court.[15] Firstly, fiduciary obligations protect only proprietary or pecuniary interests. Secondly, fiduciary obligations are proscriptive, and include only the duty not to profit personally from one's fiduciary position, the duty of confidence and the duty to avoid conflicts of interest. And thirdly, the remedies available for breach of fiduciary duty are the account of profits and disgorgement (in personal or proprietary form). The Supreme Court of Canada has expanded on all of these principles, allowing for prescriptive duties that protect non-economic interests, breach of which results in equitable compensation and perhaps punitive damages.

This chapter will review the most unorthodox of the Supreme Court's decisions on fiduciary relationships, and will examine whether their departure from conventional principles can be justified by factors that are unique to Canada, such as its social environment or constitutional framework. Alternatively, it suggests that the Canadian approach is not as unorthodox as it has been characterised to be: unlike other Commonwealth courts, the Supreme Court of Canada has embraced equity's role and has modernised the concept of fiduciary obligations as a means of regulating relationships that are important to society.

II. Protecting Important Relationships

One of the traditional rationales for recognising and enforcing fiduciary obligations is to protect relationships that society considers to be valuable. Finn explained that the fiduciary principle is

> an instrument of public policy. It has been used, and is demonstrably used, to maintain the integrity, credibility and utility of relationships perceived to be of importance in a society. And it is used to protect interests, both personal and economic, which a society is perceived to deem valuable.[16]

This idea was similarly expressed by LaForest J in *Hodgkinson v Simms*,[17] where he wrote:

> The desire to protect and reinforce the integrity of social institutions and enterprises is prevalent throughout fiduciary law. The reason for this desire is that the law has recognized the importance of instilling in our social institutions and enterprises some recognition that not all relationships are characterized by a dynamic of mutual autonomy, and that the marketplace cannot always set the rules.

Historically, this fiduciary protection was limited to relationships in the private sphere, such as trustees and agents. It is not unreasonable to argue, however, that the relationships valued by society have changed over time. The Supreme Court of Canada's jurisprudence on fiduciary relationships can thus be viewed as a reflection of changing social mores. This is evident, for example, in the context of healthcare and familial relationships.

---

[15] See especially *Breen v Williams* (1996) 186 CLR 71, 95, where Dawson and Toohey JJ wrote that the Canadian approach is marked 'by assertion rather than analysis and, whilst it may effectuate a preference for a particular result, it does not involve the development or elucidation of any accepted doctrine'. See also the New South Wales Court of Appeal's decision in the same case: (1994) 35 NSWLR 522, 570.

[16] Finn, above n 1, 26.

[17] *Hodgkinson v Simms* [1994] 3 SCR 377, [48].

The Healthcare Context

The Supreme Court of Canada is unique in imposing a fiduciary duty on physicians to disclose medical records to patients.[18] In *McInerney v MacDonald*[19] the Court described the physician–patient relationship as one of trust and confidence, entailing a duty 'to act with utmost good faith and loyalty, and to hold information received from or about a patient in confidence'.[20] LaForest J, writing for a unanimous court, described a patient's medical information as being held

> in a fashion akin to a trust. While the doctor is the owner of the actual record, the information is to be used by the physician for the benefit of the patient. The confiding of the information to the physician for medical purposes gives rise to an expectation that the patient's interest in and control of the information will continue.[21]

LaForest J continued the trust analogy when justifying the fiduciary obligation to disclose medical records. For example, he explained that it would be difficult for a patient to assess whether a physician is fulfilling his or her obligation of good faith and loyalty without access to his or her medical records. This is similar to the reasoning supporting the access of trust beneficiaries to trust documents.[22] Further, the duty of confidentiality serves to support the frank disclosure of information between the patient and physician, which is necessary to promote treatment that is in the patient's best interests. Finally, the equitable nature of the obligation affords the court the discretion to deny access to medical records in circumstances where it is not in the patient's best interests.[23] All of these factors serve to support the trust and confidence that are critical to an effective physician–patient relationship.

The Canadian position was considered and ultimately rejected by the High Court of Australia in *Breen v Williams*.[24] While the Court was prepared to acknowledge fiduciary aspects of the physician–patient relationship, it would not accept that this extended to the disclosure of medical records to the patient. Rather, a physician's fiduciary obligations are limited to a prohibition on profiting from his or her position, 'if, for example, the doctor has a financial interest in a hospital or a pathology laboratory',[25] or 'the medical practitioner prescribed one of a number of equally suitable pharmaceutical drugs for the undisclosed reason that this assisted the practitioner to obtain undisclosed side-benefits from the manufacturer'.[26]

---

[18] This obligation is now overtaken by legislation. See, eg, Personal Health Information Protection Act, 2004, SO 2004, c 3, Sched A, s 52.

[19] *McInerney v MacDonald* [1992] 2 SCR 138.

[20] ibid [20].

[21] ibid [22]. LaForest J did not go so far, however, as to accept that the patient had a proprietary interest in his or her own medical records.

[22] That is, the right to seek disclosure of trust documents is part of the courts' inherent jurisdiction to supervise the administration of trusts. Disclosure may be necessary to determine whether the trustees are fulfilling their obligations with respect to trust property. See *Schmidt v Rosewood Trust Ltd* [2003] UKPC 25, [2003] 2 AC 709 (Isle of Man).

[23] *McInerney v MacDonald* [1992] 2 SCR 138, [29]. LaForest J stressed that these circumstances would be rare, and that the onus of justifying a denial of disclosure would rest with the physician.

[24] *Breen v Williams* (1996) 186 CLR 71.

[25] ibid 94.

[26] ibid 136.

Gaudron and McHugh JJ were particularly forceful in expressing their view that a patient does not in any way own his or her medical records. They wrote:

> The records are the property of the doctor. He or she may be restrained from using the informa-tion in them to make an unauthorised profit or from disclosing that information to unauthorised persons. But otherwise the records are his or hers to save or destroy. The idea that a doctor who shreds the records of treatment of living patients is necessarily in breach of fiduciary duties owed to those patients is untenable.[27]

With respect, it is not obvious how such a view is untenable. Leaving aside the legislation that now governs health information in most jurisdictions, it seems rather outdated to sug-gest that a physician can do as he or she pleases with a patient's medical records, so long as no unauthorised profits are made. Surely the fiduciary obligations of a physician must extend beyond this. A patient's trust and confidence in his or her physician depends a more vigorous concept of loyalty than a mere avoidance of conflicts.

Nevertheless, the court in *Breen* adopted a generally paternalistic attitude toward the physician–patient relationship. For instance, in finding that a patient's medical records belonged to the physician, Dawson and Toohey JJ indicated that, for the physician 'to have given the [patient] free access to all the matters contained in her medical records may not have been in her interests'.[28] This is essentially a variation on therapeutic privilege, which has been eliminated in Canada because it is paternalistic, condescending and inconsist-ent with patient autonomy.[29] The English Court of Appeal has also adopted a paternalistic attitude to patient information. In *R v Mid Glamorgan Family Health Services, ex parte Martin*[30] the Court found that disclosure of medical records to a patient might not be in the patient's best interests, quoting Lord Templeman in *Sidaway v Governors of Bethlem Royal Hospital* that '[s]ome information might confuse, other information might alarm a particular patient'.

The Supreme Court's decision in *McInerney v MacDonald* reflects a more robust notion of patient autonomy than other common law courts were willing to accept. This may be attributable, in part, to the prominence of the issue in Canadian public discourse. In partic-ular, the *Report of the Commission of Inquiry into the Confidentiality of Health Information*,[31] which was cited by the Court in *McInerney v MacDonald*, addressed at length a patient's right of access to his or her own health records. Notably, the Commission was critical of the medical profession's condescending attitude toward patients:

> While society's attitude toward access to information generally has changed in recent years, profes-sional attitudes have changed much more slowly. Patients are much more knowledgeable about their health care than they were 50 years ago. Many physicians who appeared at the hearings

---

[27] ibid 112.

[28] ibid 91.

[29] Therapeutic privilege is only allowed 'where a patient is unable or unwilling to accept bad news from his or her physician. In those circumstances, a physician is obliged to take reasonable precautions to ensure that the patient has communicated their desire not to be told, or that the patient's health is so precarious that such news will undoubtedly trigger an adverse reaction that will cause further unnecessary harm to the patient.' *Pittman Estate v Bain* (1994) 112 DLR (4th) 257 (Ont SCJ), [708].

[30] *R v Mid Glamorgan Family Health Services, ex parte Martin* [1995] 1 All ER 356 (CA) 363, citing *Sidaway v Governors of Bethlem Royal Hospital* [1985] UKHL 1, [1985] AC 871, 904.

[31] H Krever, *Report of the Commission of Inquiry into the Confidentiality of Health Information* (Toronto, Queen's Printer for Ontario, 1980) vol 2, ch 23.

stressed that good patient care depended upon complete frankness on the part of the patient. While I believe that statement to be incontrovertible, it is my opinion that good medical care requires a reciprocity in which the physician … is completely frank with the patient. If the patient asks to see his or her record … no amount of paternalism should stand in the way of the right of access.[32]

With respect to the argument that access to health records may not be in a patient's best interests, the Commission noted that it had not heard convincing examples of harm that might ensue if a patient viewed his or her records. To the extent that the patient might misinterpret jargon (eg SOB meaning 'shortness of breath' rather than the more common obscenity), the Commission indicated that a re-evaluation of record-keeping methods might be necessary.[33] Ultimately, the Court reasoned that the best interests of the patient would be served by the mutual, frank disclosure of information, and that the patient's right to self-determination was an important aspect of his or her well-being.

Thus, the Supreme Court's decision in *McInerney v MacDonald* seems to have been heavily influenced by widespread discussion about patient autonomy and the right of patients to be fully informed of matters affecting their health and care. That said, *Breen* was decided in the context of similar public debate,[34] so the Supreme Court of Canada's unorthodox approach cannot be fully explained on this basis. Generally speaking, however, the Supreme Court has a different conception of its role in shaping public policy, and is less troubled at taking a proactive stance. As discussed below, the Supreme Court has no qualms about using equitable principles to achieve results that it perceives to be just.

The Family Law Context

Fiduciary principles were introduced into the family law context by Wilson J's dissenting opinion in *Frame v Smith*.[35] The plaintiff in that case alleged that his former wife and her current husband had engaged in an extensive course of conduct to impede his access to his children, in violation of a court order. This included forbidding telephone contact, intercepting letters, regularly moving to new cities, changing their surname and religion, and telling the children that he was not their father. The majority rejected the plaintiff's tort claims on the basis that the Children's Law Reform Act[36] provided a comprehensive scheme for dealing with claims arising out of custody and access disputes and that the legislature clearly intended to abolish any common law actions that had previously existed.[37]

Wilson J agreed that the proposed tort actions (eg conspiracy, intentional infliction of mental suffering) would be inappropriate, but allowed the plaintiff to proceed with a claim for breach of fiduciary duty. Using her now familiar three characteristics of fiduciary relationships, Wilson J concluded that the relationship between a custodial parent and a non-custodial parent fitted within fiduciary principles. She wrote that a custody and access order

---

[32] ibid 470.

[33] ibid 469.

[34] See Parkinson, above n 1.

[35] *Frame v Smith* [1987] 2 SCR 99.

[36] Children's Law Reform Act, then RSO 1980, c 68 (now RSO 1990, c C.12).

[37] See Family Law Reform Act, RSO 1980, c 152, s 69(4), which provided, 'No action shall be brought by a parent for the enticement, harbouring, seduction or loss of services of his or her child or for any damages resulting therefrom.'

puts the custodial parent in a position of power and authority which enables him or her, if so motivated, to affect the non-custodial parent's relationship with his or her child in an injurious way. The selfish exercise of custody over a long period of time without regard to the access order can utterly destroy the non-custodial parent's relationship with his child. The non-custodial parent (and of course, the child also) is completely vulnerable to this.[38]

Obviously, the interests affected in an access dispute are primarily non-pecuniary. Wilson J stressed that they are nonetheless worthy of protection by fiduciary duties. She explained:

The non-custodial parent's interest in the relationship with his or her child is without doubt of tremendous importance to him or her. To deny relief because of the nature of the interest involved, to afford protection to material interests but not to human and personal interests would, it seems to me, be arbitrary in the extreme.[39]

She noted that the protection of non-pecuniary interests is already recognised in equity, most notably through the remedy of specific performance.

Finally, Wilson J explained why the action for breach of fiduciary duty is a preferable way to deal with a 'sustained course of conduct' that severely damages the relationship between a child and a non-custodial parent, to their mutual detriment.[40] In particular, by situating the claim in equity, the court is able to craft a remedy that fosters the best interests of the children. Unlike common law remedies, which typically arise as of right when a cause of action has been proved, equitable remedies allow the courts to exercise discretion and to consider whether the plaintiff's own conduct disentitles him to relief, or whether relief should be awarded on terms, keeping in mind what is in the best interests of the child. For example, a plaintiff who has previously abused access rights may not have the 'clean hands' necessary to obtain a remedy in equity. Wilson J further suggested that the action for breach of fiduciary duty 'can proceed only if there is no risk that the support of the children will be impaired and no risk of a harmful conflict of loyalties arising in the children'.[41]

While Wilson J's analysis in *Frame v Smith* has been highly influential and is commendable from an analytical standpoint, its factual context probably represents the weakest case for application of fiduciary principles. There is clearly a need to protect the parent–child relationship and to deter custodial parents from maliciously impeding access by non-custodial parents; however, to suggest that the custodial parent owes fiduciary obligations to the non-custodial parent seems to stretch the fiduciary principle beyond intuition and logic. Parents who are separated have an obvious conflict of interests, and it is highly counterintuitive to find that the custodial parent must act in a selfless way. A more reasonable argument might have been made that the custodial parent owes a fiduciary obligation to the child not to unduly interfere with his or her relationship with the non-custodial parent, as such interference would be contrary to the child's best interests.[42]

---

[38] *Frame v Smith* [1987] 2 SCR 99, [65].
[39] ibid [68]. See also *Szarfer v Chodos* (1988) 66 OR (2d) 350 (CA), where the Ontario Court of Appeal upheld an action for breach of fiduciary duty against a lawyer who used confidential information about his client's marital difficulties to seduce the client's wife, thereby causing him psychological harm. The Court wrote: 'There is no reason in principle why the loss has to be of a commercial or business nature.'
[40] *Frame v Smith* [1987] 2 SCR 99, [73].
[41] ibid.
[42] See ES Scott and RE Scott, 'Parents as Fiduciaries' (1995) 81 *Virginia Law Review* 2401, 2442–50.

III. Achieving Policy Goals: Sexual Abuse

The Supreme Court of Canada's approach to recognising fiduciary relationships has been motivated, more or less explicitly, by the desire to achieve certain policy goals. This was evident in the cases situated in the healthcare and family law contexts, but is even more obvious in the cases dealing with sexual abuse. Various members of the Court have argued that fiduciary principles better capture the nature of the defendant's wrong in these cases; they have also been used for more tactical advantage, such as expanding the scope of remedies and avoiding the strict application of limitations legislation.

In the well-known decision of *Norberg v Wynrib*[43] the concurring opinion of L'Heureux-Dubé and McLachlin JJ found that a physician had breached his fiduciary duty to a drug-dependent patient by agreeing to prescribe painkillers to her in exchange for sexual favours. While the majority had allowed the plaintiff's action in battery on the basis that her consent to sex was vitiated as a matter of public policy, the concurring judges argued that only breach of fiduciary duty captured the 'essential nature of the wrong done to the plaintiff'.[44] Applying Wilson J's three criteria from *Frame v Smith*, McLachlin J stressed that the arrangement had the potential to affect vital non-legal and practical interests:

> Society has an abiding interest in ensuring that the power entrusted to physicians by us, collectively and individually, not be used in corrupt ways. ... On the other side of the coin, the plaintiff, as indeed does every one of us when we put ourselves in the hands of a physician, has a striking personal interest in obtaining professional medical care free of exploitation for the physician's private purposes. These are not collateral duties and rights created at the whim of an aggrieved patient. They are duties universally recognized as essential to the physician–patient relationship.[45]

McLachlin J also stressed the particular vulnerability of women to abuse by their physicians. Citing the College of Physicians and Surgeons of Ontario's *Final Report on the Task Force on Sexual Abuse of Patients*,[46] she noted that female patients are disproportionately targeted for sexual exploitation, constituting 287 of the 303 reports the Task Force received, and that the paternalistic model of the physician–patient relationship correlates to norms of behaviour for men and women.[47] Patients tend to defer to the expertise of their physicians and comply unquestioningly with their requests, for example, to disrobe and submit to intrusive physical examinations. Further, there is evidence that complaints of sexual abuse are often discounted on the basis that the patient mistook therapy for sexual advances, that complainants are discredited on account of their addictions or psychiatric illness, and that physicians have successfully avoided liability by pointing to a career in a caring profession.[48]

While the concurring decision in *Norberg* did not explicitly refer to the Charter of Rights and Freedoms,[49] it reflected the values of the Charter's equality provision (section 15) in so

---

[43] *Norberg v Wynrib* [1992] 2 SCR 226.

[44] ibid 269.

[45] ibid 277.

[46] M McPhedran, Chair, *Final Report of the Task Force on the Sexual Abuse of Patients* (Toronto, The College of Physicians and Surgeons of Ontario, 1991) 10.

[47] ibid, Legal Appendix, 2, cited in *Norberg v Wynrib* [1992] 2 SCR 226, 280.

[48] See S Rodgers, 'Health Care Providers and Sexual Assault: Feminist Law Reform?' (1995) 8 *Canadian Journal of Women and the Law* 159, 171–75.

[49] Part I of the Constitution Act 1982, being Schedule B to the Canada Act 1982 (UK), 1982, c 11 [*Charter*].

far as it recognised that the existing law had a disproportionately negative effect on women. Indeed, following her retirement from the court, L'Heureux-Dubé J described *Norberg* as an instance where the principle of substantive equality had been introduced into common law.[50] She explained, 'even though constitutional rights may not be directly in issue, the principle of substantive equality requires that the law take into account women's experiences where they have been ignored or excluded in the course of the law's development'.[51]

Accordingly, L'Heureux-Dubé and McLachlin JJ were critical of the lower courts and their own colleagues, who had adopted a 'closed, commercial view of fiduciary obligations' that focused only on the physician's duty of confidence,[52] and some of whom had rejected the plaintiff's claim on account of her 'illegal' behaviour and failure to come to court with clean hands. McLachlin J described the latter argument as a means of 'blaming the victim' of sexual assault, and adopted the more progressive position that

> where such a power imbalance exists it matters not what the patient may have done, how seductively she may have dressed, how compliant she may have appeared, or how self-interested her conduct may have been—the doctor will be at fault if sexual exploitation occurs.[53]

In this respect L'Heureux-Dubé and McLachlin JJ were undoubtedly influenced by the arguments of the Legal Education and Action Fund (LEAF), which intervened in *Norberg v Wynrib* before the Supreme Court. LEAF's factum stressed, inter alia, the position of power held by physicians, the need to recognise social hierarchies, and the interaction of sex, disability and confidentiality that led to the plaintiff's exploitation.[54] LEAF was also highly critical of the lower courts' decisions to dismiss the plaintiff's claims on account of her own illegal or immoral behaviour: LEAF introduced the concept of 'blaming the victim' that was ultimately adopted by McLachlin J.[55] Finally, LEAF argued that the lower courts failed to recognise the nature and extent of the damage suffered by victims of sexual assault, and that the compensatory awards should be 'equal to, if not higher than, those associated with the protection of property'.[56]

It is not surprising, then, that while McLachlin J explained several advantages of treating the plaintiff's claim as one for breach of fiduciary duty, she seemed especially convinced by the question of remedy.[57] Adopting the 'generous, restorative remedial approach' of equitable damages, McLachlin J argued that the plaintiff was entitled to damages for both sexual exploitation ($25,000) and prolongation of her addiction ($20,000). She would also have awarded $25,000 in punitive damages on account of the defendant's 'purposefully

---

[50] C L'Heureux-Dubé, 'It Takes a Vision: The Constitutionalization of Equality in Canada' (2002) 14 *Yale Journal of Law and Feminism* 363, 373.

[51] ibid. The Supreme Court has held that the common law should be developed 'in accordance with "*Charter* values"' (*RWDSU v Dolphin Delivery Ltd* [1986] 2 SCR 573, 592–93).

[52] *Norberg v Wynrib* [1992] 2 SCR 226, 283.

[53] ibid 287.

[54] Factum of LEAF in *Norberg v Wynrib*, Supreme Court of Canada File No 21924, [23] (available at leaf.ca/wordpress/wp-content/uploads/2013/02/1992-norberg.pdf). See also the analysis in L Zhou, 'Fiduciary Law, Non-economic Interests and Amici Curiae' (2008) 32 *Melbourne University Law Review* 1158.

[55] LEAF Factum, above n 54, [44].

[56] ibid [51]. Locke JA, who was the only lower court judge who would have awarded any damages to the plaintiff, would have limited them to $1,000, and expressed disbelief that the plaintiff 'would be so overtaken by these human feelings as to sustain mental damage' (quoted ibid [49]).

[57] It is noteworthy that McLachlin J had expounded on the distinctive principles of equitable compensation not long before in *Canson Enterprises Ltd v Boughton & Co* [1991] 3 SCR 534.

repugnant' behaviour and the need for specific and general deterrence.[58] She found that this was necessary in order to uphold high standards of professional conduct, noting that:

> [T]he sexual exploitation of patients by physicians is more widespread than it is comfortable to contemplate. Its damaging effects extend not only to those persons who are directly harmed, but also to the image of the profession as a whole and the community's trust in physicians to act in our best interests.[59]

L'Heureux-Dubé and McLachlin JJ would accordingly have awarded much higher damages than the majority, which based the claim in sexual battery and awarded $20,000 in general (aggravated) damages and $10,000 in punitive damages. Even less generous was Sopinka J, who based the claim in breach of contract and would have awarded only $20,000. In Sopinka J's view the wrong was a failure to provide appropriate medical treatment for the plaintiff's addiction. The sexual episodes were 'an element of damage', rather than 'the basis of liability'.[60] Not surprisingly, the female judges found this characterisation of the wrong to be a gross understatement: the plaintiff did not just receive poor medical treatment, she was subjected to 'degrading and dehumanizing' contact that 'caused her humiliation and robbed her of her dignity'.[61] She would likely suffer permanent psychological damage, and would presumably have difficulty establishing a relationship of trust with another physician. Punitive damages were warranted not only because the defendant's conduct was repugnant toward the plaintiff's best interests, but also because his behaviour was motivated by his own self-interest.[62]

As indicated, the award of punitive damages was also meant to achieve general deterrence. On this note, Tamar Frankel has argued that the move to characterising physicians as fiduciaries may be influenced by the perceived lack of adequate alternative controls over their behaviour.[63] It was historically accepted that physicians were supervised by medical associations and were loyal to the Hippocratic Oath; however, Frankel observes that the image of the medical profession has changed and that, 'in the courts' opinions, the alternative monitors and control over the professions have weakened substantially'.[64] In the absence of effective regulation, the courts may be willing to use fiduciary principles and punitive damages to enforce the high ethical standards expected of physicians.

While remedial principles were thus at the heart of the concurring judgment in *Norberg v Wynrib*, the majority of the Supreme Court of Canada in *M(K) v M(H)* used the fiduciary approach, in part, to avoid a strict application of limitations legislation in a case of incestuous abuse.[65] The plaintiff alleged that her father had sexually abused her during her pre-teen and teenage years, but she did not commence an action until she was 28. The bulk of the Court's decision discussed the application of limitations statutes to cases of incest, and addressed how the psychological effects of such abuse would frequently lead victims

---

[58] *Norberg v Wynrib* [1992] 2 SCR 226, 299.
[59] ibid 300.
[60] ibid 317.
[61] ibid 297.
[62] ibid 298.
[63] T Frankel, 'Fiduciary Relationship in the United States Today' in DWM Waters (ed), *Equity, Fiduciaries and Trusts* (Toronto, Thomson Carswell, 1993) 173.
[64] ibid 184.
[65] *M(K) v M(H)* [1992] 3 SCR 6.

to delay bringing actions against their abusers.[66] While the Court found that the plaintiff's tort action was not statute-barred, it nevertheless addressed the alternative argument that incest constitutes a breach of fiduciary duty, which at the time was not subject to limitations legislation in Ontario. LaForest J, for the majority, viewed incest as a self-evident breach of fiduciary duty:

> It is intuitively apparent that the relationship between parent and child is fiduciary in nature, and that the sexual assault of one's child is a grievous breach of the obligations arising from that relationship. Indeed, I can think of few cases that are clearer than this. For obvious reasons society has imposed upon parents the obligation to care for, protect and rear their children. The act of incest is a heinous violation of that obligation.[67]

Agreeing with Wilson J's view in *Frame v Smith*, LaForest J found that equitable protection extended to non-economic interests, including those of incest victims.[68]

The extension of fiduciary principles to govern a child's non-economic interests distinguishes the Supreme Court of Canada's approach from those of other common law jurisdictions. Other courts had found that parents owe fiduciary obligations to their children in terms of their financial interests.[69] This typically means that the parental fiduciary obligation is limited to avoiding conflicts of interest or profiting from transactions wherein the child confers a benefit on the parent. In other words, to the extent that other jurisdictions have recognised parental fiduciary obligations, they have been largely proscriptive in nature.

Those who argue that parental fiduciary obligations should be limited to proscriptive duties often refer to the difficulty of defining what are the 'best interests' of a child. As Lionel Smith explains, the duty to act in another's best interests 'is entirely open-ended. Any fiduciary could always do something more in the interests of his beneficiary; not only would that be asking too much, but in any event we could never know that the duty had been fulfilled.'[70] In this respect, it is worthwhile to note that the Supreme Court of Canada, while sometimes using the language of 'best interests', has not imposed such open-ended duties on parents in practice. In *KLB v British Columbia*,[71] for example, the Supreme Court of Canada acknowledged that a fiduciary duty to act in a child's best interests did not provide a workable or justiciable standard.[72] Rather, a parent's fiduciary duty 'is to act loyally, and not to put one's own or others' interests ahead of the child's *in a manner that abuses the child's trust*'.[73] Thus, while a parent who relocates the family for the purposes of employment may be preferring his or her own interests ahead of the children's, it is not an act of fiduciary disloyalty. However, a parent who abuses a child for his own sexual gratification is acting disloyally in a way that breaches his parental fiduciary obligation.[74] Such conduct

---

[66] Again, the Factum of LEAF played an influential role in the court's decision. See Zhou, above n 54.

[67] *M(K) v M(H)* [1992] 3 SCR 6, 61.

[68] ibid 64.

[69] See the discussion in *Paramasivam v Flynn* [1998] FCA 1711, (1998) 90 FCR 489, [67]–[69].

[70] L Smith, 'Can We Be Obliged to Be Selfless?' in AS Gold and PB Miller (eds), *Philosophical Foundations of Fiduciary Law* (Oxford, Oxford University Press, 2014) 143.

[71] *KLB v British Columbia* 2003 SCC 51, [2003] 2 SCR 403.

[72] ibid [46]–[47]. The court suggested that the 'best interests' standard was more helpful in the context of family law and child welfare legislation.

[73] ibid [49] (emphasis added).

[74] Similarly, in *J(LA) v J(H)* (1993) 13 OR (3d) 306 (SCJ), a mother who turned a blind eye to the sexual abuse of her daughter by her stepfather was found to have acted disloyally by putting her own interests (a desire to preserve her marriage) ahead of her daughter's well-being.

places the parent's desires above the well-being of the child through an abuse of the child's trust.[75]

The Canadian courts also have used fiduciary principles to address the wrongs of sexual abuse in other contexts involving abuse of trust. In the British Columbia Supreme Court decision of *FSM v Clarke*,[76] Dillon J found that the Anglican Church had breached its fiduciary duty to a student who was sexually abused by a dormitory supervisor at an Indian residential school run by the Church; specifically, the Church failed to properly investigate and report the abuse and to provide counselling and care to the victim after the fact. Dillon J stressed the vulnerability of the plaintiff, whose day-to-day life was controlled in almost every respect by the school. The religious nature of the school enhanced the relationship of trust and reliance:

> The fact of Anglicanism lent a superior moral tone to the residence that created an additional level of assurance. The Bishop of the Diocese knew that dormitory supervisors were in a position to affect the plaintiff's intimate personal and physical interests and encouraged this position of trust through insistence that child care workers be Anglican and follow Anglican practice.[77]

Moreover, when the abuse was revealed to the Church, it assumed a duty to investigate and take action in the plaintiff's best interests. It breached this duty by failing to take action and by failing to disclose the abuse to the government, which might have pursued a more vigorous investigation.[78]

These decisions may be usefully contrasted with the Federal Court of Australia's decision in *Paramasivam v Flynn*,[79] where the plaintiff's claim for sexual abuse by his legal guardian was found to be time-barred. The court was clear that the scope of fiduciary obligations owed by a guardian was limited to the protection of economic interests; for example, property transferred as a result of undue influence or unconscionable conduct, unauthorised profits or unauthorised commercial advantage. There was no need for equity to enter an area that was adequately protected by tort, simply because the plaintiff may otherwise run afoul of limitations legislation. While the court granted that parents have a legal obligation not to commit incest, they did not believe that the obligation was a fiduciary one, 'still less that equitable intervention is necessary, appropriate or justified by any principled development of equity's doctrine'.[80]

One of the difficulties with the Federal Court's position is its assumption that childhood incest is adequately addressed by the law of tort. Leaving aside whether sexual battery truly captures the nature of the wrong, it is precisely the application of limitations statutes to tort actions that demonstrates the inadequacy of common law (tort) principles

---

[75] But see JE Penner, 'Is Loyalty a Virtue?' in AS Gold and PB Miller (eds), *Philosophical Foundations of Fiduciary Law* (Oxford, Oxford University Press, 2014) 173–74. Penner argues that it belittles the wrong of incest to refer to it as a conflict of interest. In his view, sexual assault is a wrong, no matter who commits it.

[76] *FSM v Clarke* [1999] 11 WWR 301 (BCSC).

[77] ibid [196].

[78] See also *Blackwater v Plint* 2005 SCC 58, [2005] 3 SCR 3 [60], where the plaintiff suffered similar abuse and alleged that Canada and the Anglican church breached their fiduciary duties toward him. The Supreme Court found that no such breach was apparent on the facts, as neither defendant had been dishonest or intentionally disloyal.

[79] *Paramasivam v Flynn* [1998] FCA 1711, (1998) 90 FCR 489.

[80] ibid [72]. See also *Cubillo v Commonwealth* [2001] FCA 1213, (2001) 112 FCR 455, where similar arguments were made regarding fiduciary duties owed to Aboriginal children who were forcibly removed from their families and taken into institutional care.

in these situations. As the Supreme Court of Canada's decision in *M(K) v M(H)* explained, incestuous abuse is committed in such a way that it prevents victims from recognising the wrongness of their parents' conduct and/or reporting that abuse. Through threats, rewards or other forms of manipulation (not to mention the child's dependency on the parent), the abuser convinces the victim to keep silent. The strict application of limitations legislation in these cases protects this behaviour in the name of doctrinal purity.

The same difficulty is evident in England, where even the relatively recent decision in *A v Hoare* will likely leave many incest victims uncompensated.[81] *Hoare* overruled the notorious decision in *Stubbings v Webb*,[82] which had found that the discoverability (or 'knowledge') rule applied to claims in negligence but not to claims for intentional trespass to the person, such as incest. The decision in *Stubbings* meant that incest victims were restricted to the standard six-year limitation period, or three years after attaining the age of majority, in the Limitation Act 1980.[83] This had the anomalous result that an action commenced ten years after an incestuous assault was time-barred as against the perpetrator (the father), but not against the mother, who was sued for failing to protect the plaintiff from abuse.[84] Lord Griffiths justified the inflexibility of the limitation period for intentional torts by stressing that a victim of an intentional tort knows immediately that a wrong has occurred. He wrote, 'I have the greatest difficulty in accepting that a woman who has been raped does not know that she suffered a significant injury.'[85] This ignores that the harms associated with incest are latent and are more often psychological or intangible than purely physical; and that the reason many incest victims do not recognise until well into adulthood that the parent's behaviour was wrong is because the parent led them to believe that it was a normal expression of love within families.[86]

Hoare reduced the harshness of *Stubbings* by finding that the discoverability principle could also apply to intentional torts. However, it maintained that the standard of discoverability is an objective one: 'not whether the claimant himself would have considered the injury sufficiently serious to justify proceedings but whether he would "reasonably" have done so'.[87] Baroness Hale was critical of this objective approach, which fails to take into account the victim's circumstances and the reality that incest perpetrators exploit their authority over their victims in order to keep them quiet.[88] As Godden has explained, 'it is often the impact of abuse that causes claimants to delay brining a civil suit'.[89] The objective standard, therefore, disregards factors such as 'blocked memory syndrome' that plague

---

[81]   *A v Hoare* [2008] UKHL 6, [2008] 1 AC 844.

[82]   *Stubbings v Webb* [1993] 1 All ER 322 (HL). The application of this limitations regime was found not to violate European Convention for the Protection of Human Rights and Fundamental Freedoms in *Stubbings and Others v UK* [1996] ECHR 44.

[83]   Limitation Act 1980 (UK), s 2.

[84]   *S v W (Child Abuse: Damages)* [1994] EWCA Civ 35, [1995] FLR 862.

[85]   *Stubbings v Webb* [1993] 1 All ER 322 (HL), 328.

[86]   See generally N Clevenger, 'Statute of Limitations: Childhood Victims of Sexual Abuse Bringing Civil Actions Against Their Perpetrators after Attaining the Age of Majority' (1991–92) 30 *Journal of Family Law* 447; KE Rodgers, 'Childhood Sexual Abuse: Perceptions on Tolling the Statute of Limitations' (1992) 8 *Journal of Contemporary Health Law & Policy* 309; E Somer and S Szwarcberg, 'Variables in Delayed Disclosure of Childhood Sexual Abuse' (2001) 71 *American Journal of Orthopsychiatry* 332;

[87]   *A v Hoare* [2008] UKHL 6, [2008] 1 AC 844, [34] (Lord Hoffmann).

[88]   ibid [58].

[89]   N Godden, 'Sexual Abuse and Claims in Tort: Limitation Periods after *A v Hoard (and Other Appeals)* [2008] and *AB and Others v Nugent Care Society; GR v Wirral MBC* [2009]' (2010) 18 *Feminist Legal Studies* 179, 181.

some incest survivors, and may leave victims at the mercy of the court's discretion under section 33 of the Limitation Act 1980 to extend time where it is 'equitable' to do so. This discretionary provision allows the court to balance the plaintiff's circumstances against the injustice that may result to the defendant on account of the delay, and thus runs the risk of inconsistent application.[90]

IV. How Can the Canadian Approach be Explained or Justified?

The Canadian courts' departure from orthodox fiduciary principles is an obvious divergence from other common law jurisdictions. To what can this divergence be attributed? Three potentially influential factors are considered below: the Canadian jurisprudence on fiduciary obligations owed by the Crown; the equality provisions of the Charter of Rights and Freedoms; and the Supreme Court of Canada's own perception of its role in public discourse.

Fiduciary Obligations Owed by the Crown

Quite apart from the cases discussed above, the Supreme Court of Canada has been relatively unique in the common law world in imposing fiduciary obligations on the Crown. While these obligations are sui generis, they have helped to shape the overall development of fiduciary doctrine in Canada.

The Crown's fiduciary obligation toward Canada's Aboriginal peoples was first established in *Guerin v The Queen*,[91] where the plaintiff Indian Band had surrendered a portion of its reserve to the Crown pursuant to the Indian Act.[92] The statutory scheme, traceable back to the Royal Proclamation of 1763,[93] provided that Aboriginals could not alienate their real property directly to third parties, but first had to surrender it to the Crown. Dickson J, for the majority, explained that this inalienability of the Aboriginal interest in land gives rise to a fiduciary obligation on the Crown 'to deal with the land for the benefit of the Indians'.[94] He wrote:

> The fiduciary relationship between the Crown and the Indians has its roots in the concept of aboriginal, native or Indian title .… . An Indian Band is prohibited from directly transferring its interest to a third party. Any sale or lease of land can only be carried out after a surrender has taken place, with the Crown then acting on the Band's behalf. The Crown first took this responsibility upon itself in the Royal Proclamation of 1763. … The surrender requirement, and the responsibility it entails, are the source of a distinct fiduciary obligation owed by the Crown to the Indians.[95]

---

[90] ibid 186–89.
[91] *Guerin v The Queen* [1984] 2 SCR 335.
[92] Indian Act, now RSC 1985, c I-5, s 18(1) (Can)13833.
[93] Royal Proclamation of 1763, RSC 1985, App II, No 1.
[94] [1984] 2 SCR 335, 376.
[95] ibid.

The purpose of this arrangement was to prevent Aboriginals from being exploited.[96] Although it did not properly give rise to a trust, it was 'trust-like in character'.[97] On the facts of the case, the fiduciary obligation was breached because the Crown had induced the Band to surrender by promising that it would obtain a lease for the land on certain terms, but then negotiated the lease on less favourable terms. The Crown was accordingly liable for the Band's loss.[98] Following the decision in *Guerin*, the Crown's fiduciary obligation toward Aboriginals was affirmed in various contexts, including treaty interpretation,[99] the creation of reserves[100] and the exercise of Aboriginal rights.[101]

Outside of the Crown–Aboriginal relationship, the Canadian courts have shown some willingness to extend fiduciary principles to other public authorities.[102] This has primarily occurred in situations of asset management (and thereby involving 'trust-like' arrangements): the federal Crown's control of pension funds for disabled veterans,[103] and mismanagement of federal funds intended to support French-language schools.[104] The Supreme Court of Canada has recently sought to confine public fiduciary obligations to situations that closely resemble established fiduciary relationships, and has stressed that there must be a government power that 'affects a legal or significant practical interest' of the plaintiff.[105]

While the concept of public fiduciary duties is too extensive to be discussed here, an important aspect of such duties in Canada is their prescriptive character. For example, the Crown's fiduciary obligation to Aboriginal peoples includes a duty of consultation,[106] and may require the government to enact legislation.[107] In contrast to the conventional view that fiduciary obligations are limited to avoidance of conflicts of interest, the Crown's duty to Aboriginal peoples extends to active protection of their interests. As Leonard Rotman has argued, 'In addition to being required to positively exercise a power where its exercise is in their beneficiaries' best interests, where fiduciaries possess the power to contravene their beneficiaries' best interests, they are bound not to exercise those powers.'[108] This attitude toward the Crown–Aboriginal relationship has crept into the Supreme Court of Canada's more general jurisprudence on fiduciary relationships, and thus may explain its willingness

---

[96] ibid 383.

[97] ibid 386.

[98] The court upheld the trial judge's global damages assessment of $10 million. See also *Blueberry Indian Band v Canada* [1995] 4 SCR 344, where the court found that the Crown had breached its fiduciary duty to the plaintiff by failing to reserve mineral rights when it sold the land that the Band had surrendered.

[99] *R v Badger* [1996] 1 SCR 771.

[100] *Ross River Dena Council Band v Canada* 2002 SCC 54, [2002] 2 SCR 816, [68].

[101] *R v Sparrow* [1990] 1 SCR 1075 (Aboriginal right to fish).

[102] For an extended and persuasive discussion of the concept of public fiduciary obligations, see E Fox-Decent, *Sovereignty's Promise: The State as Fiduciary* (Oxford, Oxford University Press, 2011).

[103] *Authorson v Canada (Attorney General)* (2002) 58 OR (3d) 417 (CA) 73–74, rev'd on other grounds 2003 SCC 39, [2003] 2 SCR 40 (at the Supreme Court of Canada, the Crown conceded that it owed a fiduciary duty, so the issue was not argued before or decided by the court).

[104] *Commission Scolaire Francophone du Yukon No 23 c Procureure Générale du Territorie du Yukon* 2011 YKSC 57, rev'd on other grounds 2015 SCC 25.

[105] *Alberta v Elder Advocates of Alberta Society* 2011 SCC 24, [2011] 2 SCR 261, [51].

[106] See, eg, *Delgamuukw v British Columbia* [1997] 3 SCR 1010.

[107] *Alexander Band No 134 v Canada (Minister of Indian Affairs and Northern Development)* [1991] 2 FC 3. The plaintiffs in that case alleged that the government's failure to enact certain regulations at a particular time led to a significant loss of oil revenue from surrendered lands.

[108] L Rotman, *Parallel Paths: Fiduciary Doctrine and the Crown–Native Relationship in Canada* (Toronto, University of Toronto Press, 1996) 263.

to impose prescriptive duties in other situations. In addition, in protecting the practice of Aboriginal rights, such as the right to subsistence hunting and fishing, this branch of jurisprudence has freed the Canadian courts from thinking of fiduciary principles in the sphere of purely financial or proprietary interests.

The Equality Provisions of the Charter of Rights and Freedoms

If we consider the cases where the Canadian courts have taken their most unorthodox positions on fiduciary relationships (ie the sexual abuse and incest cases), it seems evident that sex discrimination, both individually and systemically, is a prominent concern. This is most obvious in *Norberg v Wynrib*, where the two women judges, L'Heureux-Dubé and McLachlin JJ, characterised the relevant wrong differently from their male colleagues.

Granted, the majority in *Norberg* was at least willing to conclude that the plaintiff's consent to sex was vitiated by her drug addiction and by the defendant's exploitation of the power imbalance in the physician–patient relationship. Sopinka J, however, found that the sex was consensual, and instead grounded liability in breach of the contract to provide appropriate medical treatment.[109] He stressed that the plaintiff was not under the influence of drugs at the times when the sexual encounters occurred, and portrayed her as a seductress 'who played on the respondent's loneliness in order to continue obtaining prescriptions'.[110] The most generous assessment of Sopinka J's view of consent to sex is that it is highly technical.

In contrast, L'Heureux-Dubé and McLachlin JJ took a more sensitive view of the plaintiff's capacity to give meaningful consent and the defendant's exploitation of her addiction. Indeed, they expressed shock that so many of the other judges who had dealt with the case declined to find a breach of fiduciary duty.[111] They were particularly critical of Sopinka J's breach of contract approach, asking 'what of the patient whose medical needs are fully met but who is sexually exploited? On Sopinka J's reasoning she has no cause of action.'[112] Somewhat ironically, while L'Heureux-Dubé and McLachlin JJ have been criticised for extending fiduciary principles beyond their logical scope, it seems an equally (if not greater) adulteration of principle and logic to suggest that sexual exploitation of a drug-dependent patient by a physician is a breach of contract. It is not too bold to suggest that few women would agree with such a characterisation.

It is probably no coincidence that the concurring opinion in *Norberg v Wynrib* made substantial use of the College of Physicians and Surgeons of Ontario's *Final Report on the Task Force on Sexual Abuse of Patients*,[113] which was released following the oral hearing but prior

---

[109] In fairness to Sopinka J, his view on the plaintiff's consent was shared by the trial judge and the British Columbia Court of Appeal. See (1988) 27 BCLR (2d) 240 (SC) 244 (Oppal J), and (1990) 44 BCLR (2d) 47 (CA) 51, 56.

[110] *Norberg v Wynrib* [1992] 2 SCR 226, 306.

[111] ibid 281–82. McLachlin J wrote, 'None of the appellate judges who have written on the case offers a convincing demonstration of why it is wrong to characterize the relationship between Dr Wynrib and Ms Norberg as a fiduciary relationship. … This closed, commercial view of fiduciary obligations is neither defended nor reconciled with the authorities' (ibid 283).

[112] ibid 290.

[113] *Final Report*, above n 46.

to judgment in the case. Sexual abuse by physicians was at the forefront of public discourse. The Report indicated that sexual abuse by physicians was not uncommon, and was over-whelmingly perpetrated by male physicians on female patients. The Task Force expressly concluded 'that the strongest basis for challenging a doctor who has taken advantage of an unequal relationship lies in the law of fiduciary relationships'.[114] They stressed that the power imbalance between physicians and patients meant that it was always the physician's responsibility not to engage in sexual conduct with the patient:

> Physicians need to recognize that they have power and status, and that there may be times when a patient will test the boundaries between them. However, because the physician has more power than the patient in the relationship, it is always the *physician's* responsibility to know what is appropriate and never to cross the line into sexual activity.[115]

Hence the Task Force recommended a 'zero tolerance' approach to sexual abuse of patients by physicians.

L'Heureux-Dubé and McLachlin JJ supported this principle in their decision. Indeed, this is one of the reasons why the fiduciary approach is to be preferred to the sexual battery approach adopted by the majority. The sexual acts in *Norberg v Wynrib* appeared to be consensual. In the battery action, it was thus up to the plaintiff to show that the consent was not 'legally effective'.[116] This was a two-step process based on the test for unconscionable transactions in contract: the plaintiff had to establish that there was a power-dependency relationship and that it involved exploitation. She had to bring evidence of her limited education and drug dependence. On the majority's approach, a more educated or less fragile patient might well be left without a remedy.

Conversely, the fiduciary approach employed by the concurring judges recognised the inherent power imbalance in the physician–patient relationship, particularly where the physician is a man and the patient is a woman, and found a breach whenever that power was abused. It did not matter whether the plaintiff gave apparent consent or even acted seductively; the responsibility for avoiding sexual relations was the physician's alone.

Further, the female concurring judges in *Norberg v Wynrib* were alone in recognising that sexual abuse by a person in a position of trust or authority is typically more damaging than sexual abuse by a stranger. This was acknowledged by the majority in *M(K) v M(H)*, where LaForest J stated that '[a]ssault and battery can only serve as a crude legal description of incest'.[117] LaForest J discussed at length the social science evidence concerning incest victims, and quoted a US decision that found:

> As a practical matter a young child has little choice but to repose his or her trust with a parent or parental figure. When such a person abuses that trust, he commits two wrongs, the first by sexually abusing the child, the second by using the child's dependency and innocence to prevent recognition or revelation of the abuse.[118]

Thus, while the Canadian approach was at times motivated by certain procedural advantages in equity, such as avoidance of limitations legislation, this in fact has a logical basis

---

[114] ibid 80.
[115] ibid 81 (emphasis in original).
[116] *Norberg v Wynrib* [1992] 2 SCR 226, 256.
[117] *M(K) v M(H)* [1992] 3 SCR 6, 26.
[118] ibid 44, citing *Evans v Eckelman* 265 Cal Reptr 605 (Cal App 1 Dist 1990) 608–09.

in the nature of the wrong committed by the defendant. It is the abuse of trust inherent in incest that often causes the victim to either block memories of the abuse or fail to recognise the wrong that was committed. The victim's delay is inextricably linked with the nature of the wrong.

Given its decision on fiduciary obligations, the majority in *M(K) v M(H)* found it unnecessary to rule on the constitutionality of the limitations legislation, ie whether it violated the equality provisions of the Charter of Rights and Freedoms.[119] LEAF had argued that, to the extent that the legislation barred actions by victims of child incest, it was discriminatory on the basis of sex.[120] (LEAF noted that approximately 90 per cent of victims of childhood sexual assault are female.)[121] But even if the Charter were not directly applicable, LEAF argued that the 'filter of Charter values magnifies the aptness' of the equitable approach that the court ultimately adopted.[122] In LEAF's view, framing the wrong as breach of fiduciary duty helped to promote access to justice for child incest victims and deterred those in authority from exploiting children.

A Broader Conception of the Courts' Role in Society

This leads to the final contextual factor behind the Supreme Court of Canada's divergent approach toward the recognition of new fiduciary relationships, namely the Court's perception of its own role in society. The Charter of Rights has often placed the Court at the centre of controversial public debates, so it is more comfortable addressing social problems through its decisions.[123]

This is in sharp contrast to other leading courts in the common law world. In *Breen v Williams*,[124] for instance, Gaudron and McHugh JJ were adamant that the Australian courts should not design a remedy to address changing societal views, especially by recognising prescriptive fiduciary obligations. In an apparent criticism of the Supreme Court of Canada's approach in *McInerney v MacDonald*, they wrote that: 'Judges have no authority to invent legal doctrine that distorts or does not extend or modify accepted legal rules and principles. … The judges of Australia cannot, so to speak, "make it up" as they go along.'[125] Constitutionally, they viewed the role of the common law courts as being more modest; any legal changes 'that cannot logically or analogically be related to existing common law rules and principles are the province of the legislature'.[126]

---

[119] *M(K) v M(H)* [1992] 3 SCR 6, 25.
[120] Factum of LEAF in *M(K) v M(H)*, Supreme Court of Canada file no 21763 (available at leaf.ca/wordpress/wp-content/uploads/2011/01/1992-km-hm.pdf).
[121] ibid [5]–[6].
[122] ibid [26].
[123] See generally JB Kelly and M Murphy, 'Confronting Judicial Supremacy: A Defence of Judicial Activism and the Supreme Court of Canada's Legal Rights Jurisprudence' (2001) 16 *Canadian Journal of Law & Society* 3; and G Huscroft, 'Political Litigation and the Role of the Court' (2006) 34 *Supreme Court Law Review* 35. For a highly critical perspective, see RI Martin, *The Most Dangerous Branch: How the Supreme Court of Canada Has Undermined Our Law and Democracy* (Montreal, McGill University Press, 2003).
[124] *Breen v Williams* (1996) 186 CLR 71.
[125] ibid 290–91.
[126] ibid.

In comparison, the Supreme Court of Canada seems to have embraced its role as reformer of common law/equitable rules to resolve contemporary problems. Shortly after the expansionist cases of 1992, McLachlin J (as she then was) expressed her view extra-judicially that equity had an important role to play in supplementing the common law.[127] She saw the expansion of equitable remedies as part of the modern courts' role:

> First, as society changes, new situations have emerged where redress is required but where the rules of tort, contract and statute provide no remedy. Second, the public perception of justice and what the legal system should be doing has shifted in many areas.[128]

While she acknowledged the need for certainty, predictability and coherence, she embraced the flexibility and justice that equity could inject into the law of civil wrongs.[129] Consistent with her opinions in *Canson Enterprises v Boughton & Co*[130] and *Norberg v Wynrib*, she also stressed that equitable damages serve a deterrent function and aim to hold fiduciaries to their strict obligations of loyalty.[131]

While doctrinal purists may be dismayed by the Canadian position, it is reasonable to suggest that the Supreme Court of Canada's decisions are consistent with the underlying values of equity. Equity has always been a court of conscience, providing relief from the strictures of the common law. Thus, for example, if the strict application of limitations legislation serves to disadvantage certain classes of plaintiffs, it is not inconceivable that the Supreme Court of Canada would use equitable principles to provide relief. This is especially true when the strict application of the law systematically harms a historically disadvantaged group, such as women, Aboriginals or victims of child sexual abuse. In a similar way, the Canadian courts used equity to provide relief to disadvantaged women in matrimonial and cohabitational property disputes in the 1970s and 1980s.[132] The courts' willingness to use equitable principles in such situations is bolstered by its express policy of developing the private law in accordance with Charter values.

V. Conclusion

The Supreme Court of Canada's distinctive approach to recognising fiduciary relationships demonstrates an openness to the use of equitable principles to address perceived societal needs. Both *McInerney v MacDonald* and *Norberg v Wynrib* were decided in the midst of heightened public debate about the responsibility of physicians with respect to patient records and sexual abuse. The decisions also reflect the Charter's imperative for substantive

---

[127] The Hon BM McLachlin, 'The Place of Equity and Equitable Doctrines in the Contemporary Common Law World: A Canadian Perspective' in D Waters (ed), *Equity, Fiduciaries and Trusts* (Toronto, Thomson Canada, 1993) 37.

[128] ibid 39. She referred to the remedial constructive trusts that were imposed by the courts on marital breakdown as an illustration of the courts responding to changing public mores.

[129] ibid 40.

[130] *Canson Enterprises v Boughton & Co* [1991] 3 SCR 534.

[131] McLachlin, above n 127, 52.

[132] eg, *Murdoch v Murdoch* (1974) [1975] 1 SCR 423; *Rathwell v Rathwell* [1978] 2 SCR 436; *Pettkus v Becker* [1980] 2 SCR 834; and *Peter v Beblow* [1993] 1 SCR 980.

equality, using equity to avoid procedural strictures that have a disproportionate effect on women and children.

For all the criticism the Canadian approach has received, it has not led to significant practical or doctrinal difficulty. Breach of fiduciary duty has not, as some had feared, come to swallow up the law of tort or contract.[133] Nor has it created unwieldy or unfulfillable fiduciary obligations, or paralysed physicians in the performance of their duties. And if it has provided somewhat greater recovery to victims of incest or sexual abuse by those in positions of power, it is not clear that this is a bad thing. Given the choice between a court that is willing to act creatively to provide compensation to victims of sexual abuse and incest, and one that is paternalistic, doctrinally rigid and wilfully blind toward the realities of sexual exploitation, the creative court has substantial appeal.

---

[133] See McCamus, above n 7, 136–40, where he takes a benevolent reading of the Supreme Court's jurisprudence, suggesting that 'equitable compensation could provide an effective instrument of doctrinal reform without, at the same time, unattractively destabilizing vast areas of contract and tort'.

13

The Presumptions of Resulting Trust and Advancement Under Singapore Law: Localisation, Nationalism and Beyond

MAN YIP*

I. Introduction

[T]he application of the presumption of advancement must be considered against the backdrop of the particular community; there should not be a blind adherence or slavish application of the presumption simply to dovetail with the English approach. ... In the case of Singapore, the differences between our local climate and the English system are not as stark and the presumption of advancement still accords with the community's contemporary societal norms and expectations in particular situations. Nevertheless, there will inevitably be certain inherent divergences in the attitudes and norms of any two countries, especially where one is oriental and the other, occidental; in fact, these divergences would also exist even amongst different communities within a society.[1]

The presumptions of resulting trust and advancement, derived from English equity and imported through historical colonial links, are part of Singapore law. Relevantly, section 3 of the Application of English Law Act 1993 (AELA)[2] has made it clear that the English common law (including the equitable rules and principles) that had formed part of the law of

* This chapter was substantially completed while I was a visiting scholar at the University of Birmingham, School of Law during the summer of 2014. I would like to thank Mr James Lee for reading an earlier draft, as well as our discussions on some of the issues addressed in this chapter. I am indebted to Associate Professor Yihan Goh and Assistant Professor Alvin See for their very helpful comments on the earlier drafts of this chapter. An earlier version of this chapter was presented at the Obligations VII conference held at the University of Hong Kong in July 2014. I am grateful to all who attended my presentation, and, in particular, I am very thankful for the insightful comments, questions and encouragement from Miss Tatiana Cutts, Mr Jamie Glister, Professor Virgo Graham, Dr Birke Häcker, Professor Lusina Ho, Associate Professor Rebecca Lee, Miss Rachel Leow, Associate Professor Kelry Loi, Associate Professor Kelvin Low, Professor Catherine Macmillan, Professor John Mee, Professor Nicholas Hopkins and Associate Professor Pauline Ridge. Finally, I gratefully acknowledge the excellent research assistance provided by Xuan Lang Teo. All views and errors are my own.

[1] *Lau Siew Kim v Yeo Guan Chye Terence* [2007] SGCA 54, [2008] 2 SLR(R) 108, [61] (VK Rajah JA, delivering the judgment of the Singapore Court of Appeal) (hereinafter '*Lau Siew Kim*').

[2] Application of English Law Act 1993, Cap 7A, 1994 rev edn (Singapore).

Singapore prior to the commencement of the legislation shall continue to apply, subject to modification to suit local circumstances and conditions. This chapter has two objectives. The first objective is to scrutinise the modern developments of the twin presumptions under Singapore law within the domestic context, in the light of three recent Singapore Court of Appeal decisions that unreservedly affirmed their continued relevance. The examination of recent Singapore cases is undertaken in Part II. In Part III, I focus on the application of the presumptions between spouses as the core case to highlight the 'localisation' of the twin presumptions in Singapore as well as identify the internal factors contributing to the present state of development under Singapore law. The spousal presumption is one area where gender distinctions remain, and it is thus important to investigate the reasons for maintaining the gender bias in modern Singapore. For completeness, Part IV considers the likely trend of development for the twin presumptions in the future.

The second objective is to consider the implications for related areas of the law ensuing from the affirmation of the twin presumptions in Singapore. In Part V we look at these related areas of law, which include the future developments of constructive trusts (notably, the common intention constructive trust and the *Pallant v Morgan* equity) as well as the enforcement of equitable interests transferred under illegal transactions. The Singapore experience shows that the convergence or divergence at one point may (but not necessarily will) lead to convergence or divergence in other areas of the law. The dynamism and sustainability of the 'common law' both as a term and an enterprise are closely tied in with the incremental developments within each jurisdiction and the resultant convergence and divergence across the jurisdictions.

II. The Twin Presumptions: Convergence and Divergence

Modern English Law: Declining Importance

In present-day England, the strength of both presumptions of resulting trust and advancement has weakened over the years.[3] Their practical utility is further depreciated in practice.[4] It has been generally observed that the English courts are increasingly inclined towards resolving disputes on their own facts, instead of relying on presumptions.[5] In *Vandervell v IRC* Lord Upjohn said that the 'presumption of a resulting trust is no more than a long stop to provide the answer when the relevant facts and circumstances fail to yield a solution'.[6]

Two major recent developments also further reduce the role and relevance of the two presumptions in the English domestic context. First, when section 199 of the English

---

[3] L Tucker et al, *Lewin on Trusts*, 18th edn (London, Sweet & Maxwell, 2008) [9-05].

[4] See, for a recent example, *Favor Easy Management Ltd v Wu* [2011] EWHC 2017 (Ch); affirmed [2012] EWCA Civ 1464, noted M Yip and J Lee, '"Less than Straightforward" People, Facts and Trusts: Reflections on Context: *Favor Easy Management Ltd v Wu*' (2013) 77 *Conveyancer and Property Lawyer* 431.

[5] See discussion in E Fung, 'The Scope of the Rule in *Shephard v Cartwright*' (2006) 122 LQR 651, 678–80; R Chambers, 'Is There a Presumption of Resulting Trust' in C Mitchell (ed), *Constructive and Resulting Trusts* (Oxford, Hart Publishing, 2010) 267, 268–76.

[6] *Vandervell v IRC* [1967] 2 AC 291, 313.

Equality Act 2010 comes into effect, the presumption of advancement in respect of transfers from husband to wife will be abolished.[7] Second, in the landmark case of *Stack v Dowden*[8] the majority of the House of Lords abolished the presumption of resulting trust as the starting point of analysis in domestic consumer cases (or, at least, where domestic occupation is the primary purpose),[9] on the basis that the assumptions underlying the presumption of resulting trust are not generally suited for familial dealings.

According to *Stack*, in a domestic consumer case, the default starting presumption is that the equitable interests follow the legal interests. The party asserting otherwise bears the burden to rebut the default position, and it would take an exceptional case to depart from that. The appropriate tool of analysis to determine the beneficial interests in a property in such cases is the common intention constructive trust. The approach was affirmed and clarified in *Jones v Kernott*.[10] In that case, the Supreme Court advanced the law further by endorsing an imputation of intention at the stage of quantification of interests where an inference of intention as to the parties' respective shares proves impossible.[11] Both *Stack* and *Jones* have generated intense debates, and subsequent cases applying the *Stack* and *Jones* principles have not escaped academic scrutiny.

Modern Singapore Law: Affirmation and Modernisation

By contrast, the continued relevance of the twin presumptions of resulting trust and advancement has been recently affirmed in two Singapore Court of Appeal decisions, and clarified in a third Court of Appeal judgment.

Low Gim Siah

The earlier case of *Low Gim Siah v Low Geok Khim*[12] concerned a dispute over the deceased father's monies in bank accounts that were in the joint names of the father and his youngest son. The father's estate contended that the monies belonged to the estate by the operation of the presumption of resulting trust because the father had solely contributed the monies in the accounts. The youngest son argued that the monies belonged beneficially to him by the operation of the presumption of advancement, followed by the operation of the right of survivorship upon the father's death. Based on the evidence, the Singapore Court of Appeal ruled that the presumption of advancement had been successfully rebutted.

---

[7] The UK government has thought it necessary to abolish the presumption of advancement before acceding to Protocol 7 of the European Convention on Human Rights. cf J Glister, 'Section 199 of the Equality Act 2010: How Not to Abolish the Presumption of Advancement' (2010) 73 *MLR* 785.

[8] *Stack v Dowden* [2007] UKHL 17, [2007] 2 AC 432 (hereinafter 'Stack').

[9] In *Laskar v Laskar* [2008] EWCA Civ 347, [2008] 1 WLR 2695, 2700, Lord Neuberger held that even though the case concerned a joint purchase between a mother and a daughter, the property was purchased primarily for investment and therefore the *Stack* principles did not apply.

[10] *Jones v Kernott* [2011] UKSC 53, [2012] 1 AC 776 (hereinafter 'Kernott').

[11] For a case where the English court resorted to an imputation of intention, see *Aspden v Elvy* [2012] EWHC 1387 (Ch), [2012] 2 FCR 435 (Ch D); noted J Lee, '"And the Waters Began to Subside": Imputing Intention under *Jones v Kernott*' (2012) 76 *Conveyancer and Property Lawyer* 421.

[12] *Low Gim Siah v Low Geok Khim* [2006] SGCA 54, [2007] 1 SLR(R) 795, noted K Low, 'The Presumption of Advancement: A Renaissance?' (2007) 123 *LQR* 347.

Notably, the Singapore Court of Appeal affirmed the presumption of advancement in traditional relationships between father and child as well as between husband and wife, where only one party is under a moral or equitable obligation to provide for the other.[13] It confined modern English cases[14] which indicated the declining importance of the presumption of advancement to situations concerning joint contributions by married couples in acquiring the matrimonial home or properties purchased with joint savings.[15] It explained that traditional categories of relationships are unaffected by social change, and the obligations of fathers and husbands have not changed so radically in modern Singapore to justify not applying the presumption of advancement. It further observed that there are still many women who are financially dependent on their husbands, and infants are inevitably dependent on their parents for provision.

Lau Siew Kim

In *Lau Siew Kim*[16] the Singapore Court of Appeal sought to develop the law on the twin presumptions further. The dispute concerned two properties purchased in the joint names of Yeo and Lau, a married couple. Upon Yeo's death, by the operation of the rule of survivorship, Lau became the sole registered owner of the properties. Yeo's sons brought proceedings in court, seeking a declaration that Lau (their stepmother) held the properties on a resulting trust for Yeo's estate. At trial, it was found that an unrebutted presumption of resulting trust in favour of Yeo arose over the properties and, accordingly, Lau held them on trust for both herself and Yeo's estate in proportions that corresponded to their respective direct contributions to the purchase price.[17] The High Court also held that the spousal presumption no longer applies in modern times unless there is evidence to support it.[18] The Court of Appeal, however, allowed Lau's appeal and affirmed her sole and absolute ownership of the properties. Disagreeing with the first instance judgment, the Court of Appeal affirmed the modern relevance of the spousal presumption of advancement, and said that its strength ought not to be diminished, save in instances of contrary evidence of intention.[19]

In rationalising the juridical basis of the presumption of resulting trust, Rajah JA (delivering the unanimous judgment of the Court) seemingly endorsed both Chambers' thesis as well as Lord Browne-Wilkinson's judgment in *Westdeutsche Landesbank Girozentrale v Islington LBC*,[20] the two main conflicting schools of thought on the subject.[21] Chambers' thesis advocates the theory that resulting trusts arise in situations of an absence of the

---

[13] ibid [43]–[44].
[14] See eg *Pettitt v Pettitt* [1970] AC 777; *McGrath v Wallis* [1995] 2 FLR 114.
[15] *Low Gim Siah v Low Geok Khim* [2006] SGCA 54, [2007] 1 SLR(R) 795, [43].
[16] *Lau Siew Kim* [2007] SGCA 54, [2008] 2 SLR(R) 108.
[17] *Yeo Guan Chye Terence v Lau Siew Kim* [2007] SGHC 7, [2007] 2 SLR(R) 1.
[18] ibid [65].
[19] *Lau Siew Kim* [2007] SGCA 54, [2008] 2 SLR(R) 108, [77].
[20] *Westdeutsche Landesbank Girozentrale v Islington LBC* [1996] AC 669 (hereinafter '*Westdeutsche*').
[21] See a probing analysis of the decision in K Low, 'Apparent Gifts: Re-examining the Equitable Presumptions' (2008) 124 *LQR* 369.

transferor's intention to benefit the transferee.[22] Lord Browne-Wilkinson, on the other hand, supported the view that the presumed resulting trust arises in response to the parties' presumed intentions.[23] The debate was resolved in a later Singapore Court of Appeal judgment, which we will examine below.

Rajah JA discussed three further points of practical interest concerning the twin presumptions. First, Rajah JA clarified that the strength of the presumptions varies with changes in societal conditions and attitudes[24] Where real property is concerned, owing to the statutory presumption of joint tenancy in cases of joint-name purchase in the absence of specification of the manner of holding, he explained that equitable intervention through the presumption of resulting trust is still required to ensure fairness as between the parties in instances where they do not appreciate or intend the legal significance of joint tenancy.[25] Section 53(1) of the Land Titles Act provides:

> In every instrument affecting registered land, co-tenants claiming under the instrument shall, unless they are described as tenants-in-common, hold the land as joint tenants; and if they are described as tenants-in-common, the shares in the registered land to be held by them shall, subject to subsection (2), be specified in the instrument.[26]

Accordingly, Rajah JA also affirmed the relevance of the presumption of advancement—for it arises to mitigate the injustice occasioned by the rigidity of the presumption of resulting trust—but confined its application to a 'last resort' device in cases where there is no direct evidence of the parties' intentions.[27] Rajah JA indicated obiter that if the legislation was amended to require co-owners to specify the manner of holding for registration, and also included a simple explanatory note on the legal distinction between joint tenancy and tenancy-in-common,[28] there would be no need, generally, for equitable intervention. But he added that the twin presumptions are so well entrenched in Singapore law that any major reform or abolition must be undertaken by the legislature.[29]

Second, Rajah JA observed that the weight of authorities in other common law jurisdictions appear inclined towards applying a pragmatic approach to the presumption of resulting trust in cases involving married couples.[30] That is, the strength of the presumption of resulting trust is much weaker in cases where the spouses contribute jointly (whether equally or not) to the purchase of a property, especially if it is their matrimonial home.

---

[22] R Chambers, *Resulting Trusts* (Oxford, Clarendon Press, 1997) 32.

[23] *Westdeutsche* [1996] AC 669, 708.

[24] *Lau Siew Kim* [2007] SGCA 54, [2008] 2 SLR(R) 108, [52]–[61] and [67].

[25] ibid [92] and [95]. The Singapore Court of Appeal noted that the presumption should be displaced in cases where cogent evidence demonstrates that the registered co-owners 'had in fact exercised their informed and voluntary intention to hold land as legal joint owners'. Such cogent evidence includes a sworn testimony from the solicitor assisting the purchase or one of the co-owners attesting to the completion of the land transfer form.

[26] Land Titles Act, Cap 157, 2004 rev edn (Singapore), s 53(1).

[27] *Lau Siew Kim* [2007] SGCA 54, [2008] 2 SLR(R) 108, [59].

[28] cf RS Yeo, 'The Presumptions of Resulting Trust and Advancement in Singapore: Unfairness to the Woman?' (2010) 24 *International Journal of Law, Policy and Family* 123, 139. Although not entirely against it, Yeo pointed out that the suggestion to include an explanation 'may not be the optimal solution' as it would be difficult to decide how much needs to be explained. More information could potentially confuse while less information might not serve its purpose.

[29] *Lau Siew Kim* [2007] SGCA 54, [2008] 2 SLR(R) 108, [47]–[51].

[30] ibid [101].

The presumption in these cases is that the parties intended to be joint owners in equity as well. Whilst agreeing that the presumption usually accords with reality, Rajah JA was of the view that such pragmatism is more appropriately accommodated within the second stage of considering the presumption of advancement. Importantly, Rajah JA highlighted that a presumption of equal sharing is not consistent with local matrimonial cases that have rejected equal sharing of matrimonial assets as either the default starting point or the norm under Singapore law.[31] He went on to articulate two crucial elements for measuring the strength of the presumption of advancement in general: (a) the nature of the relationship; and (b) the state of the relationship.[32] The former relates to the legal or moral obligation of one party towards the other or the dependence between the parties. The latter relates to how close and caring the relationship is. Overall, therefore, the Court of Appeal in *Lau Siew Kim* agreed with the views expressed in *Low Gim Siah*, but stressed that financial dependence of the transferee on the transferor is merely one consideration in the fact-sensitive approach advocated.[33]

Finally, Rajah JA said obiter that the categories of relationships to which the presumption of advancement applies are not closed. In particular, after considering different developments in England, Australia and Canada, he expressed willingness to apply the presumption of advancement to transfers from mother to child,[34] parent to adult child[35] as well as from fiancé to his fiancée.[36] Other than the traditional 'legal/moral obligation' rationale, he endorsed 'love and affection' as a proper basis upon which to find new advancement relationships.[37] As for de facto relationships, taking into account the positions in England and Australia,[38] Rajah JA did not think the time had come to extend the presumption of advancement to cohabiting couples, as there is presently no domestic legislative recognition and public consensus on this kind of relationship.[39]

To sum up, the factors highlighted by the aforementioned cases in relation to the retention of the twin presumptions include the default statutory presumption of joint tenancy under section 53(1) of the Land Titles Act where real property is concerned, as well as the fact that the twin presumptions are so firmly entrenched in Singapore law that abolition requires legislative action. More specifically, in light of the general factors, the retention of the spousal presumption of advancement under Singapore law is justified by the fact that there are still wives who are financially dependent on their husbands. Gender differences are thus maintained in respect of transactions between spouses.

---

[31] ibid [98], citing *NK v NL* [2007] SGCA 35, [2007] 3 SLR(R) 743.

[32] ibid [77]–[78]. Whilst these two elements will be of guidance in simple cases, one can imagine some difficult scenarios where the two factors pull in opposite directions: see Low, above n 21, 371–72.

[33] *Lau Siew Kim* [2007] SGCA 54, [2008] 2 SLR(R) 108, [78].

[34] ibid [62]–[67].

[35] ibid [68].

[36] ibid [69]–[72]. Rajah JA took note of this development in both England and Australia and did not express any disagreement with the extension to this new category.

[37] ibid [68].

[38] In particular, Rajah JA had noted Gibbs J's minority view in *Calverley v Green* [1984] HCA 81, (1984) 155 CLR 242, 250–51.

[39] *Lau Siew Kim* [2007] SGCA 54, [2008] 2 SLR(R) 108, [74]. Neither English law nor Australian law has extended the presumption of advancement to cohabitees.

Cases after Low Gim Siah *and* Lau Siew Kim

Cases after *Low Gim Siah* and *Lau Siew Kim*, generally emanating from the Singapore High Court,[40] continue to apply the twin presumptions, following the contemporary approach enunciated in *Lau Siew Kim*.[41] Three cases are worthy of mention.

Neo Hui Ling

Neo Hui Ling v Ang Ah Sew[42] involved a dispute between an adult child and her mother over their respective beneficial entitlements to a property that the daughter had paid for and registered in their joint names. In that case, the Singapore High Court considered the question of whether a presumption of advancement should arise in respect of transfers from an adult child to the parent.[43] Although the Court refrained from a determination without the benefit of full arguments, it made two obiter comments indicating that such a development is unwarranted. The Court noted that under Singapore law, by virtue of the Maintenance of Parents Act,[44] children in Singapore are under a legal duty to provide for their aged parents. According to section 3 of the Act, a parent who is of or above the age of 60 and unable to maintain himself/herself adequately can apply for a maintenance order that one or more of his/her children pay maintenance. The Court, as a matter of qualifying the first observation, nevertheless said that a child's 'inclination' to provide for his/her parent should not be confused with his/her intention to make a gift.[45] Ultimately, the Court accepted the daughter's evidence that her intention was for the right of survivorship to apply so that her mother would be provided for when she passed on, instead of giving the mother an inter vivos half interest in the property.[46]

The comments were evidently sensible, but considered more broadly they potentially weaken the oft-cited traditional foundation upon which the presumption of advancement arises, that is, the legal/moral obligation to provide for the transferee. Indeed, in *Lau Siew Kim* the Court of Appeal considered that the obligation rationale coexists with the rationale based on probability of donative intent.[47] Hence, a legal obligation to maintain does not

---

[40] See, eg, *Lim Geok Swan v Lim Shook Luan* [2012] SGHC 18 (a case on the distribution of proceeds of sale of a property bought in the joint names of mother and adult child); *United Overseas Bank Ltd v Giok Bie Jao* [2012] SGHC 56 (an interpleader action which raised an issue as to property ownership between siblings); *Yong Shao Keat v Foo Jock Khim* [2012] SGHC 107 (reference to *Lau Siew Kim* in the discussion of the couple's interests in the property before they were married); *Quek Hung Heong v Tan Bee Hoon (executrix for estate of Quek Cher Choi, deceased)* [2014] SGHC 17 (domestic property dispute).

[41] It is noteworthy that in *Neo Hui Ling v Ang Ah Sew* [2012] SGHC 65, [2012] 2 SLR 831, [44], the Singapore High Court described the *Lau Siew Kim* approach to presumption of advancement as 'a flexible and dynamic application'.

[42] ibid [44]–[47], noted Tang HW, 'Equity and Trusts' in Teo KS (ed), *Singapore Academy of Law Annual Review of Singapore Cases 2012* (Singapore, Academy Publishing, 2013) [15.8]–[15.10].

[43] The defendant did not raise this argument.

[44] Maintenance of Parents Act, Cap 167B, 1996 rev edn (Singapore).

[45] The choice of the word 'inclination' is interesting. It might be that the court did not wish to say directly that a legal obligation to maintain does not translate into an intention to make a gift.

[46] An intention for only the right of survivorship to apply had been previously affirmed and applied by the British Columbia Court of Appeal in *Clelland v Clelland* [1945] 3 DLR 664 which decision was approved in *Lau Siew Kim* [2007] SGCA 54, [2008] 2 SLR(R) 108, [154]. Tang commented that this 'additional gloss to the law of resulting trusts' makes it even harder for lawyers to explain the complexity of this area of the law to their clients. See Tang, above n 42, [15.10].

[47] *Lau Siew Kim* [2007] SGCA 54, [2008] 2 SLR(R) 108, [78]. See also Low, above n 21, 370–71.

automatically translate into an equitable presumption of a gift; at least not all legal obligations of maintenance, as it appears. Perhaps we should reflect more deeply the precise nature of legal/moral obligation that would give rise to a presumption of advancement. Where parental presumption of advancement is concerned, it has been suggested that the presumption arises not from the obligation to maintain, but from the equitable obligation to advance and set up one's child in life.[48]

What *Neo Hui Ling* had not considered was whether the presumption of advancement could be extended to transfers from an adult child to his/her parent on the basis of love and affection, a basis that has been endorsed by the Court of Appeal in *Lau Siew Kim* in respect of converse transfers.[49] *Neo Hui Ling* would have been a good occasion for the court to elucidate upon how the 'love and affection' rationale could be employed to find new advancement relationships, and its interplay with the 'obligation' rationale. Endorsing different rationales underpinning the presumption of advancement renders application and justification more complex. It is thus all the more imperative that the operation and interplay between the different rationales are carefully worked out. Perhaps we are also trying to achieve too much with a device that was developed for a much simpler task.

See Fong Mun (High Court)

In *See Fong Mun v Chan Yuen Lan*[50] the Singapore High Court addressed the question of whether the presumed resulting trust is the best tool of analysis in respect of a domestic property dispute where both parties are alive and could give evidence on their intentions at the time of purchase. In that case, husband and wife each claimed the full beneficial ownership of a property registered in the wife's sole name that was substantially paid for by the husband.[51] The wife signed a power of attorney three days before the completion of the purchase of the property, granting her husband and their eldest son full powers to take charge of, manage and improve the property. Unusually, the couple had lived apart for over 20 years at the time of trial,[52] although they remained married and had no intention to initiate matrimonial proceedings. On the evidence, the High Court found in favour of the husband, accepting his argument that the parties had an agreement prior to the acquisition of the property that he would be the full beneficial owner. In particular, the High Court was satisfied that the power of attorney was executed pursuant to the agreement.[53]

---

[48] See a general discussion of this issue under English law in J Glister, 'The Presumption of Advancement' in C Mitchell (ed), *Constructive and Resulting Trusts* (Oxford, Hart Publishing, 2010) ch 10, esp 310–12.

[49] *Lau Siew Kim* [2007] SGCA 54, [2008] SLR(R) 108, [68]. Rajah JA did not agree with the majority approach in the Canadian case of *Pecore v Pecore* (2007) 279 DLR (4th) 513 in not applying the presumption of advancement in respect of transfers from a parent to his/her *adult* child. Instead, he was persuaded by Abella J's judgment in the same case that the presumption of advancement emerges from affection as much as from financial dependency.

[50] *See Fong Mun v Chan Yuen Lan* [2013] SGHC 99, [2013] 3 SLR 685 (hereinafter 'See Fong Mun (HC)').

[51] Both at trial and on appeal, the issue of contributions had been fiercely fought. The trial judge held that the husband had paid for the entire purchase price (see ibid [8]–[10]), but this was overturned in part on appeal: see *Chan Yuen Lan v See Fong Mun* [2014] SGCA 36, [2014] 3 SLR 1048, [72]–[88] (hereinafter 'See Fong Mun (CA)'), noted Tang Hang Wu, 'A Dispute in Chancery Lane: Re-considering the Resulting and Common Intention Constructive Trust' (2015) 78 *Conveyancer and Property Lawyer* 169.

[52] The husband had an affair and moved out of the property in 1980s, retaining a room and a study in the property.

[53] *See Fong Mun (HC)* [2013] SGHC 99, [2013] 3 SLR 685, [12].

See Fong Mun (HC) was fought on the battle of presumptions. The husband claimed the presumption of resulting trust on the basis that he paid the entire purchase price;[54] and the wife relied on the spousal presumption of advancement, arguing that the property was a gift to her. Whilst acknowledging that *Lau Siew Kim* was the authority on the law of presumed resulting trust, the High Court remarked that the twin presumptions ought not be raised as a matter of course, especially in cases where the parties are present and competent to give evidence as to their intentions and knowledge regarding the purchase of the property.[55] The High Court stated on record that its conclusion was arrived at based on the direct evidence adduced before it, without recourse to the twin presumptions. It was of the view that the facts of the case indicated a 'classic situation of common intention constructive trust',[56] and the ratio of *Lau Siew Kim* should be confined to a situation 'where properties were held by husband and wife as legal joint tenants, and where there was no direct evidence as to whether the properties formed part of the deceased's estate'.[57] It pointed out that *Lau Siew Kim* did not explicitly address a sole-name scenario where both parties could give direct evidence on their intentions at the time of acquisition. Nor did *Lau Siew Kim* discuss what is the legal analysis to follow after the displacement of the twin presumptions or where direct evidence is plentiful, rendering an analysis based on the presumptions unnecessary in the first place. The High Court was doubtful that the presumed resulting trust was the most appropriate analysis for the case at hand, but it noted that the outcome would have been the same had it applied the common intention constructive trust analysis.[58] In other words, the Court did not think that the presumed resulting trust ought to be the exclusive or even a default tool of analysis in all instances of domestic property disputes.

See Fong Mun (Court of Appeal)

The wife appealed the decision of the High Court, contending that the trial judge had erred in his evaluation of the evidence and his further finding that the spousal presumption of advancement had been rebutted by direct evidence. The Court of Appeal allowed the wife's appeal in part, and declared that the wife held 84.17 per cent of the beneficial interest in the property on a resulting trust for the husband as she was found to have made some contribution to the purchase price. Although the Court disagreed with the High Court's conclusion that the power of attorney was evidence of the parties' agreement that the husband was the sole beneficial owner of the property, it nevertheless found that the wife had failed to discharge the burden of proving that the property was a gift to her.[59] It also added that any presumption of advancement (which was weak given that the couple's marriage only existed in name) would have been negated by evidence that the husband had no intention to benefit the wife by his direct contributions to the purchase of the property.[60]

---

[54] The wife conceded that she did not provide the entire purchase price.
[55] *See Fong Mun (HC)* [2013] SGHC 99, [2013] 3 SLR 685, [15].
[56] ibid [17].
[57] ibid [18].
[58] ibid [19].
[59] *See Fong Mun (CA)* [2014] SGCA 36, [2014] 3 SLR 1048, [92].
[60] ibid [93]. The Court said (ibid [92]) that 'there was no convincing reason why Mr See, a man nearing retirement who had just begun an affair, would make the biggest purchase of his life, only to gift it to someone who was his wife in name only'.

Importantly, the Court of Appeal made three points of clarification regarding the resulting trust. First, in respect of the juridical basis of resulting trusts, Chambers' 'lack of intention' analysis was affirmed to be the 'more sensible basis for the principled yet pragmatic development of this equitable doctrine'.[61] But the Court was mindful that accepting such an account of resulting trusts could potentially blur the distinctions between unjust enrichment claims and claims based on resulting trusts, and that this could adversely affect third parties' rights and the security of commercial transactions.[62] It was also clarified that *Westdeutsche* was cited in *Lau Siew Kim* for the limited purpose of setting out the situations in which a resulting trust is presumed to arise.[63]

Second, the Court broadly agreed with the view expressed in *Neo Hui Ling* that the equitable presumptions of resulting trust and advancement should only be invoked where there is no evidence from which to prove or infer the transferor's intention.[64] However, the Court stressed that the question remains whether there is any direct evidence 'that may adequately reveal the intention of the transferor',[65] pointing out that in the case of *Lau Siew Kim*, the husband was deceased and was therefore unavailable to give evidence. That being said, the Court affirmed the continued relevance of the presumption of advancement in Singapore, but recognised that society might one day evolve to a point where departure from the equitable presumption would be justified.[66] As the parties in *See Fong Mun* pleaded their respective cases based solely on the resulting trust, the Court decided the dispute strictly on that basis.

Finally, the Court addressed the High Court's comment that the *Stack/Kernott* framework of common intention constructive trust was a better solution than the resulting trust analysis. Having reviewed the English cases, the Court endorsed[67] Lord Neuberger's minority view in *Stack*,[68] inter alia, that the resulting trust analysis remains the starting point of analysis in a domestic property dispute; but the resulting trust may be rebutted by the common intention constructive trust where the evidence discloses an agreement or understanding between the parties as to their beneficial interests in the property.[69] The Court further said that if there is no such common intention or direct evidence of an intention to benefit the other party on the part of the person who paid the larger part of the purchase price, the presumption of advancement may be invoked to rebut the presumption of resulting trust where the parties are in a recognised relationship of advancement.

Mak Saw Ching

The final case of note is *Mak Saw Ching v Yam Hui Min, Barbara Rebecca*.[70] The case concerned a dispute between a grandmother and her granddaughter over the beneficial

---

[61] ibid [44].
[62] ibid [48].
[63] ibid [43].
[64] ibid [49].
[65] ibid [52].
[66] ibid [152].
[67] ibid [153].
[68] *Stack* [2007] UKHL 17, [2007] 2 AC 432, [123]–[124].
[69] For the full framework of legal analysis to be applied in a domestic property dispute under Singapore law, see *See Fong Mun (CA)* [2014] SGCA 36, [2014] 3 SLR 1048, [160]. Regarding the common intention constructive trust analysis under Singapore law, see discussion below, text to and around nn 141–54.
[70] *Mak Saw Ching v Yam Hui Min, Barbara Rebecca* [2014] SGHC 212.

ownership of a flat that the grandmother had gratuitously transferred into their joint names as joint tenants. After the conveyance the parties' relations deteriorated, which led to the grandmother severing the joint tenancy. Thereafter, the grandmother applied to court for a declaration that the granddaughter held her half-share on trust for her. The grand-mother's primary case was based on an express trust but it failed on the unchallenged evidence before the Court. As for her alternative case based on the presumption of resulting trust, the High Court following *See Fong Mun (CA)*, said that the equitable presumption ought not to be invoked in the present dispute because both parties had the opportunity to and had indeed tendered evidence of the grandmother's actual intention at the time of conveyance.[71] And even if the equitable presumption was rightly invoked, the Court said that it would be rebutted.[72] In this connection, the Court suggested that the modern societal expectation is that a gratuitous transfer is intended as a gift,[73] and courts should thus apply the presumption of resulting trust with 'circumspect[ion] in cases of gratuitous transfers'.[74] The case is going to appeal, and it remains to be seen whether the Court of Appeal will endorse the High Court's observations.

III. Spousal Presumption of Advancement: Domestic Factors

This part of the discussion offers some reflections on the Singapore developments in respect of the application of the twin presumptions in the context of property disputes between spouses. The analysis seeks to go a little deeper, beyond the various internal factors identified by the Singapore courts as justifying the retention and modernisation of the twin presumptions and the maintenance of the one-way operation of the spousal presumption. Using the spousal presumption as the core case of study, this part of the discussion seeks to explain the refinements adopted by the Court in *Lau Siew Kim* as well as the maintenance of its gender-biased operation, by reference to domestic factors.

Refinement of the Presumption of Advancement: Intention v Policy Considerations

Where married couples choose to terminate their marriage by court proceedings, section 112 of the Women's Charter[75] confers on the Singapore courts a broad discretion to divide 'matrimonial assets'[76] between the couple. The statutory regime is underlined by the principle of 'deferred community of property'. Who has acquired or paid for the property does not conclusively determine ownership; but the parties' respective financial contributions towards the acquisition, improvement and maintenance of the asset are relevant factors in

---

[71] ibid [45].
[72] ibid [52].
[73] ibid [48].
[74] ibid [49].
[75] Women's Charter, Cap 353, 2009 rev edn (Singapore).
[76] See ibid s 112(10) for the definition of 'matrimonial asset'.

the exercise.[77] Equitable doctrines like the presumed resulting trust or the common intention constructive trust, however, apply during the subsistence of the marriage, which period is governed by the principle of 'separation of property'.[78] Accordingly, the presumed resulting trust is typically invoked in cases involving a spouse who had died intestate and where there is a property dispute between his estate and the surviving spouse (see *Lau Siew Kim*); or where creditors seek to claim properties owned by spouses.[79] Or, more unusually, in a scenario like *See Fong Mun (CA)* where there is a property dispute between parties who remain married but whose relationship has long broken down. The impact of the presumption of advancement in spousal relationships is thus extremely limited.

Within the limited circumstances in which the spousal presumption is invoked, the Court of Appeal in *Lau Siew Kim* rejected two other ways of aligning the equitable presumptions in accordance with modern practices and expectations of marriage. As discussed above, owing to the inconsistency with family law cases on division of matrimonial assets in the context of divorce, the Court did not wish to adopt a pragmatic approach of readily presuming equal sharing in cases of both spouses contributing jointly (whether equally or not) to the purchase of properties.[80] Family law is relevant.

Yet, family law is also irrelevant. The Court in *Lau Siew Kim* did not think that the approach under the Women's Charter—characterised by notions of fairness to the homemaker spouse and equality of marriage—ought to be relevant in the application or modification of the presumption of advancement.[81] It was not fully explained how the Women's Charter approach, if relevant, should impact the application of the presumption of advancement. The Court in *Lau Siew Kim* did explain that its view was based on the fact that the presumption of advancement is concerned with the parties' intentions, and the intentions are presumably different when the marriage subsists between the spouses.[82] Accordingly, the 'community of property' principle is only brought into play at the termination of marriage by matrimonial proceedings.[83] In any event, for cases involving the intestate demise of a spouse, the Court said that the just determination of the property rights between the parties on the basis that marriage is an equal partnership is sufficiently catered for within the intestate succession regime under Singapore law: the surviving spouse is entitled to at least half of the deceased spouse's estate.[84]

The relevance and irrelevance of family law are nevertheless consistent in that the Court in *Lau Siew Kim* was decidedly against reforming the operation of twin presumptions in a way that would be inconsistent with its view of the legislative intent underpinning section 112 of the Women's Charter. In the Court's view the legislative regime of property division is enacted for a specific purpose, and underlined by a specific principle. And the resulting trust cannot be applied more generously than the expansive statutory regime of division of

---

[77] ibid s 112(2).
[78] ibid ss 51 and 52.
[79] See *Teo Siew Har v Lee Kuan Yew* [1999] SGCA 70, [1999] 3 SLR(R) 410.
[80] See text to and around nn 30–31 above. In *See Fong Mun (CA)* [2014] SGCA 36, [2014] 3 SLR 1048, [159], however, the Court of Appeal 'accepted that the resulting trust analysis may require further refinement'.
[81] *Lau Siew Kim* [2007] SGCA 54, [2008] 2 SLR(R) 108, [79]–[82].
[82] ibid [82].
[83] ibid [82].
[84] See Intestate Succession Act, Cap 146, 2013 rev edn (Singapore), s 7.

matrimonial assets.[85] Importantly, the judgment in *Lau Siew Kim* could be taken to suggest that the equitable presumptions are doctrinally constrained from taking on board family law policy considerations, which are more appropriately addressed via legislation. The impression is further reinforced by the fact that the Court in *Lau Siew Kim* would not extend the presumption of advancement *to de facto* relationships unless there is *legislative recognition or public consensus* on this type of relationship. This reveals a little about the Singapore legal culture: a sharp distinction is drawn between adjudication and politics.[86] The concerns of political legitimacy are usually more acute where property rights are concerned, as courts do not wish to be seen as engaging in an exercise of distribution of proprietary interests that could cause concerns of uncertainty.[87] Although policy considerations can, on a broad level of operation, influence the refinement of general law doctrines,[88] family law type of considerations involve a lot more intricate extra-legal thinking that a court may not feel confident to take on within the limits of litigation. Hence, the Court in *Lau Siew Kim* chose to refine the presumption of advancement in a way that is consistent with intention by admitting considerations of the nature of the relationship, instead of having regard to general notions of fairness. Such moderate reform is also applicable to other types of advancement relationships, rendering the application more uniform. These sentiments are in fact broadly reflected in the later case of *See Fong Mun (CA)* where the Court of Appeal said: '[S]ubjective fairness may not be the most appropriate yardstick to apply in resolving property disputes, and that each party's share of the beneficial interest in the property concerned ought to be determined in a principled and fairly predictable manner.'[89]

There are also several finer points that deserve fuller consideration. First, a very recent Singapore High Court decision has taken a renewed interest in relation to the debate on the appropriate approach to division of matrimonial assets under the Women's Charter. In *Sim Kim Heng Andrew v Wee Siew Gee* George Wei JC commented that although equal sharing is not the norm for division of matrimonial assets under section 112 of the Women's Charter, there is no bias against equality of division and that could well be the just and equitable outcome in many cases involving long marriages with children.[90] If the attitude progressively

---

[85] See, eg, the expansive definition of 'matrimonial assets' under s 112(10) of the Women's Charter which includes assets acquired before the marriage subject to the non-owner spouse's enjoyment or substantial improvement of the assets as well as assets acquired during the marriage by one party.

[86] Beyond trusts, the Singapore High Court had also said that creating a tort of harassment is properly a legislative exercise, to be done through the parliamentary process of deliberation and debates amongst members accountable to the public: see *AXA Insurance Singapore Pte Ltd v Chandran s/o Natesan* [2013] SGHC 158, [2013] 4 SLR 545.

[87] See generally C Rothernam, 'Property and Justice' in M Kramer (ed), *Rights, Wrongs and Responsibilities* (New York, Palgrave, 2001) ch 5. Even with Singapore's recognition of the remedial constructive trust, the availability of this form of proprietary remedy is pinned down to 'fault' (see *Wee Chiaw Sek Anna v Ng Li-Ann Genevieve* [2013] SGCA 36, [2013] 3 SLR 801, [182]). See also M Yip, 'Singapore: Remedialism and Remedial Constructive Trust' [2014] *Trust & Trustees* 373; M Yip, 'Singapore's Remedial Constructive Trust: Lessons from Australia?' (2014) 8 *Journal of Equity* 77.

[88] In *Pettitt v Pettitt* [1970] AC 777, 793, Lord Reid said: 'I do not know how this presumption first arose, but it would seem that the judges who first gave effect to it must have thought either that husbands so commonly intended to make gifts in the circumstances in which the presumption arises that it was proper to assume this where there was no evidence, or that *wives' economic dependence on their husbands made it necessary as a matter of public policy to give them this advantage*' (emphasis added).

[89] *See Fong Mun (CA)* [2014] SGCA 36, [2014] 3 SLR 1048, [159].

[90] *Sim Kim Heng Andrew v Wee Siew Gee* [2013] SGHC 271, [2014] 1 SLR 1276, [57].

gains traction, could this have an impact on the operation of equitable doctrines such as the resulting trust[91] or the common intention constructive trust?

Second, in saying that the equality of partnership in a marriage is sufficiently addressed by the intestate succession legislation in cases of demise of a spouse, the Court in *Lau Siew Kim* was implicitly affirming that the ideology prevails even during the subsistence of the marriage and continues when it is 'terminated' by the death of a spouse. The converse would appear illogical.[92] Indeed, in *NK v NL* the Singapore Court of Appeal said that the 'prevailing ideology of marriage as an equal co-operative partnership' recognises equally the contributions of both spouses and these contributions 'are translated into economic assets in the distribution according to s 112(2) of the [Women's Charter]'.[93] But under Singapore law, at least, to say that a marriage is about an equal partnership is not the same as saying marriage is about equal sharing. This makes it all the more difficult to meaningfully translate the ideology of a marriage being an equal co-operative partnership in terms of an adequate outcome within the doctrinal set up of the equitable presumptions.

Third, the Court in *Lau Siew Kim* had not contemplated a scenario of marriage that involves neither matrimonial proceedings nor the demise of a spouse. *See Fong Mun (CA)* is such a case. This is clearly an area where equity stands on its own, without the aid of family law legislation to give effect to the modern ideology of marriage. The Court of Appeal in *See Fong Mun (CA)* did not address this issue explicitly, but it did accept that the resulting trust may require further refinement.[94] Of course, cases such as *See Fong Mun (CA)* are extremely rare, and other equitable doctrines such as the common intention constructive trust or proprietary estoppel are potentially available. The interface between these various doctrines as well as the specific application of each doctrine must be carefully worked out. There has been some debate regarding the ambit of application of these doctrines and their interplay under English law.[95] The Singapore Court of Appeal has similarly recognised that all issues concerning the 'difficult and intricate' relationships between the three doctrines cannot be readily worked out.[96]

Maintenance of Gender-Biased Operation of the Spousal Presumption: Competing Domestic Policies

In this section we attempt to unravel the reason behind the gender-biased operation of the spousal presumption of advancement. In *Lau Siew Kim* the Court recognised the general 'increasing diversity and decreasing homogeneity' of societies and that blanket

---

[91] Whilst the length of the marriage might be an indication of love and affection between the couple, it is not by itself conclusive of the nature of the relationship.

[92] See generally WK Leong, *Elements of Family Law in Singapore*, 2nd edn (Singapore, LexisNexis, 2012) 3–4.

[93] *NK v NL* [2007] SGCA 35, [2007] 3 SLR(R) 743, [20].

[94] *See Fong Mun (CA)* [2014] SGCA 36, [2014] 3 SLR 1048, [159].

[95] See *Thorner v Major* [2009] UKHL 18, [2009] 1 WLR 776, [20] (Lord Scott of Foscote); *Crossco No 4 Unlimited v Jolan Ltd* [2011] EWCA Civ 1619, [2012] 2 All ER 754, [89].

[96] *See Fong Mun (CA)* [2014] SGCA 36, [2014] 3 SLR 1048, [159]. In *Buthmanaban s/o Vaithilingam v Krishnavanny d/o Vaithilingam (administratrix of the estate of Ponnusamy Sivapakiam, deceased)* [2015] SGHC 35, [98], the Singapore High Court commented that the doctrines of proprietary estoppel and common intention constructive trust are conceptually similar, whilst noting that one difference between them is that '[a]n inchoate equity arising from a proprietary estoppel may not result in a proprietary interest in equity and may be satisfied in other ways'.

presumptions might well not be suitable for certain familial relations.[97] Accepting the limits of judicial power to abolish the twin presumptions, however, the Court affirmed that the one-way spousal advancement is still relevant in modern times.[98] It is, however, interesting that the Court had not thought about equalising the advancement obligations as between spouses, especially since it was willing to equalise the advancement obligations as between parents towards their children, notwithstanding that not all mothers are financially independent.[99] In fact, in *Re Estate of Chong Siew Kum* the Singapore High Court commented (in respect of a mother's parental obligation) that the status of women has changed over the years, and they now 'assume equal importance as providers for the family'.[100] As such, the affirmation of the gender-biased spousal presumption cannot be solely explained based on the need to protect homemakers. Moreover, if the presumption of advancement takes into account the modern societal values as expressed in contemporary parental duties, why is the presumption of advancement not extended to transfers from wives to husbands, so as to take on board modern values of a marriage being an equal co-operative partnership?

It is also important to note that the unequal legal treatment between spouses is not only found in equity. It is mirrored in the law of maintenance under the Women's Charter. Whilst there is clear provision for an able husband to provide maintenance to his dependent wife under the Women's Charter,[101] there is no provision for the reverse, no matter how able the wife and how dependent the husband. It has been observed that this goes against the exhortation underlined by section 46(1) of the Women's Charter which provides that '[u]pon the solemnisation of the marriage, the husband and the wife shall be mutually bound to co-operate in safeguarding the interests of the union'.[102] Pleas for reform to make the maintenance provisions less gender biased have, however, been rejected. The reason given by the Ministry of Community Development, Youth and Sports was essentially that 'a gap still exists between men and women on the socio-economic front' because fewer women participate in the workforce as compared to men, and women are the primary caregivers at home as well as for children post-divorce.[103] Professor Leong has argued that the exceptionality of women being financially more able than the husbands does not justify the law of maintenance being one-sided.[104] This argument is reinforced by the fact that the law does not discriminate between men and women in respect of their statutory maintenance obligations towards their children, despite the financial gap.[105]

---

[97] *Lau Siew Kim* [2007] SGCA 54, [2008] 2 SLR(R) 108, [50].

[98] In *See Fong Mun (CA)* [2014] SGCA 36, [2014] 3 SLR 1048, [152], the Singapore Court of Appeal commented that there is no reason or basis to depart from the view that presumption of advancement 'still accords with the community's contemporary societal norms and expectations in particular situations', but it also accepted that the view could change as the Singapore society evolves.

[99] Glister, above n 48, 313–14.

[100] *Re Estate of Chong Siew Kum* [2005] SGHC 41, [2005] 2 SLR(R) 324, [18].

[101] See s 69(1) (during the subsistence of the marriage) and s 113 (upon the termination of the marriage by court judgment) of the Women's Charter.

[102] See an excellent discussion of the issue in Leong WK, 'The Next Fifty Years of the Women's Charter: Ripples of Change' [2011] *Singapore Journal of Legal Studies* 152, 169.

[103] The Ministry of Community Development, Youth and Sports (MCYS), 'Public Consultation on Women's Charter Amendments: Response to Feedback', app.msf.gov.sg/Portals/0/Summary/pressroom/Response%20to%20 Feedback%20on%20Women's%20Charter%20Amendments.pdf, accessed 29 May 2015.

[104] Leong, above n 102, 170.

[105] Women's Charter, ss 68 and 69(2). See Leong, above n 102, 170.

Professor Leong is not alone in her views. In *ADB v ADC* the Singapore High Court said that a truly equal and independent woman does not require or desire the patronising gestures of maintenance from her husband, which 'belie deep chauvinistic thinking'.[106] The Court, however, explained that the maintenance provisions emanated from the general sentiment prevailing even up until 1996 that the Women's Charter was promulgated for women's protection.[107] It nevertheless took the view that such attitude is anachronistic in present-day Singapore and urged for the Women's Charter to be replaced by a wider and more encompassing regime, as well as to be more appropriately titled the 'Marriage Charter'.[108] In this regard it is noteworthy there have been a number of cases where an application by a financially independent wife for maintenance was denied.[109]

The arguments against retaining the law of maintenance for wives under the Women's Charter apply with equal force to the spousal presumption of advancement. Importantly, a divergence between the judicial sentiments towards the position of women in modern society under statutory matrimonial law on the one hand and within equity on the other might well develop, resulting in an inexplicable inconsistency. Regretfully, however, neither the law on statutory maintenance nor the law on the equitable presumptions could be reformed without legislative action. In fact, it might be said that the one-sided spousal presumption of advancement is legislatively endorsed, or at least, in line with legislative direction. But this does not tell us why the positions of men and women should differ in the marital context. Here, I offer a more fundamental reason for the retention of the one-sided spousal presumption under Singapore law that is not entirely linked to the inferior financial position of the wives.[110] The inconsistency and tension between the advancement obligations as between spouses and their obligations towards children; the view of marriage underlined by the one-way operation of the spousal presumption and the legislative view of marriage under the Women's Charter; the judicial sentiments towards a woman's role and status in society under matrimonial law and within the law of equitable presumptions could well emanate from an increasing conflict between two equally championed domestic policies in Singapore.

As Teo, a sociologist, explained: Singapore, as a modern developed state, is facing problems of a declining birth rate and an ageing population, and yet it remains 'anti-welfare' and focused on economic development.[111] As such, there is a national policy to maintain the traditions within the family and division of labour as between the genders. This national policy is translated into various family-oriented policies that are aimed at promoting marriage,[112]

---

[106] *ADB v ADC* [2014] SGHC 76, [11] (hereinafter 'ADB').

[107] In the Parliamentary debates concerning the 1996 amendment bill for the Women's Charter (see *Singapore Parliamentary Debates, Official Report* (2 May 1996) vol 66, col 95), Mr Abdullah Tamugi (Minister for Community Development) agreed with maintaining the one-sided operation of the statutory spousal maintenance regime and said: 'Call me old-fashioned if you will; call me a male chauvinist if you must, but my upbringing and my background tell me that it is the duty of the husband to maintain the wife. And I think I speak for most, if not all, the husbands in this House.'

[108] *ADB* [2014] SGHC 76, [11].

[109] See, eg, *Chan Choy Ling v Chua Che Teck* [1994] SGHC 194; *AAE v AAF* [2009] SGHC 104, [2009] 3 SLR(R) 827; *Anthony Guo Ninqun v Chan Wing Sun* [2014] SGHC 56.

[110] This is not to say that all wives in Singapore are financially less able than their husbands.

[111] YY Teo, 'Inequality of the Greater Good—Gendered State Rule in Singapore' (2007) 39 *Critical Asian Studies* 423. See also L Thio, 'The Impact of Internationalisation of Domestic Governance: Gender Egalitarianism & the Transformative Potential of CEDAW' (1997) 1 *Singapore Journal of International & Comparative Law* 278.

[112] Public housing regulations generally favour married couples over unmarried couples.

encouraging childbirth to replenish the population[113] and ensuring that the old are taken care of in a way that is not solely dependent on state welfare.[114] On the other hand, driven by domestic economic imperatives, there is also the national policy to encourage women to participate actively in the workforce. In other words, there is a tension between 'tradition' and 'modernisation'. Teo further argues that '[t]hrough its gendered approach toward the family, the Singapore state therefore establishes itself as an agent of change concerned with bringing about economic prosperity while at the same time establishing itself as "protector" of the people's treasured "values"', the 'family values' that have weakened as a result of the socioeconomic changes.[115]

The sociological analysis by Teo on the general level offers an important insight into the law of equitable presumptions that seemingly entrenches the traditional gender roles at home. The inconsistency and paradoxes at the specific level of equity could well be a reflection of the same at the broad level of national imperatives.[116] I am not suggesting that the courts are consciously and actively pushing forward a set of national policies through the spousal presumption, but rather, there are national family policies that continue to entrench certain gender roles at home which could have influenced the courts' view of contemporary societal norms. The same could be the underlying reason for the resistance to amending the one-sided statutory maintenance provisions under the Women's Charter. Of course, I am merely offering an explanation for the gender-biased approach under Singapore law; this is not meant to be a justification, much less a good justification for it.

Asian Family Values?

Related to the preceding discussion but proceeding on a slightly different strand of rationalisation is that the one-way operation of the spousal presumption of advancement is no more than a reflection of the Asian values of family, often said to be rooted in Confucianism, that emphasises the family as the basic unit of a society. Indeed, the Singapore government had at one time actively promoted Confucian ideals,[117] but to what extent these values truly represent the beliefs of the modern multicultural, non-homogenous Singapore society is a separate question. In this regard, it is noteworthy that in a recent work on the law of undue influence in Singapore, Chen-Wishart argues that the divergence between Singapore law

---

[113] Various tax incentives and monetary benefits aimed at encouraging women to give birth.

[114] Housing grants to reward young married couples who live near their parents. See also the Maintenance of Parents Act. It had been explained before that the Maintenance of Parents Act 'stands for the values of the society—it stands for our belief that the first port of call for help is the family; that the law should be used to enforce such values', as well as the fact that this piece of legislation is used to address the issue 'that the very institution of family is now under more stress than ever with an ageing population and smaller families'. See *Singapore Parliamentary Debates, Official Report* (23 November 2010) vol 87, cols 1676–77.

[115] Teo, above n 111, 424.

[116] Even with the removal of the gendered distinction in benefits for spouses and children given to civil servants in 2004, Prime Minster Lee Hisen Loong had urged women to 'make sure your husband looks after you'. See Prime Minister Lee Hsien Loong, 'National Day Rally 2004 Speech' speech at [132] (speech in Singapore, 22 August 2004) www.nas.gov.sg/archivesonline/speeches/view-html?filename=2004083101.htm, accessed 29 May 2015.

[117] Instances of Confucianism permeating public policy include the White Paper, *Shared Values* (Singapore National Printers, Cmd 1 of 1991) and the Confucian Ethics campaign in 1982. See further E Kuo, 'Confucianism as Political Discourse' in Tu Wei-ming (ed), *Confucian Traditions in East Asian Modernity: Moral Education and Economic Culture in Japan and the Four Mini-Dragons* (Cambridge, MA, Harvard University Press, 1997) ch 15.

and English law in the application of the doctrine in family guarantee cases is explicable by reference to the differences between an Asian society and a Western society, underpinned by different cultural values, customs and expectations.[118] Notably, Chen-Wishart has carefully detailed how the modern Confucian values continue to influence Singapore as a society in terms of both its political system and its legal system.

My analysis above, in a way, also draws upon the 'Asian family values' and the fact that the government actively promotes them through various means. But instead of relying on the concept of 'Asian family values' or Confucianism in itself as the *sole* fundamental explanation for the retention of the one-way operation of the spousal presumption, my analysis goes a step further to argue that the 'Asian family values' are championed as a means to an end.[119] The end is the resolution of problems that plague a developed state such as Singapore. For instance, whilst the Maintenance of Parents Act is often seen as an instrument to enforce filial piety, the parliamentary debates both in relation to its enactment as well as the subsequent amendments reveal that there was no agreement as to whether the Act was intended to enforce Asian filial piety or merely to ensure aged dependent parents are provided for.[120] In fact, there was clearly stronger support for the latter view. In *LKC on behalf of LYS v LKY* the Tribunal commented that '[t]he Act [did] not empower the Tribunal to order filial piety'.[121] Professor Leong, the leading family law scholar in Singapore, fully supports this proposition, and has emphasised that 'the purpose of the Act is strictly to order financial assistance for an aged dependent parent'.[122] The Maintenance of Parents Act is thus brought into force to resolve issues arising from an ageing population.

My analysis also explains the equalisation of the parental presumptions of advancement in relation to transfers from parents to children. A Confucian view of the family would see the husband/father as the economic head of the household, and would thus not necessarily support finding that mothers have a duty to support their children. This is not to say that the values undergirding Singaporean society are exactly the same as Western values, or that the values of an Asian society will not lead to a different application or modification of English equity.[123] But it might not be appropriate to characterise Singaporean society as being underpinned by Confucianism.[124] Whilst the Chinese population constitutes a great majority of Singapore's population, the overemphasis on one set of cultural values associated with one particular race would be detrimental to the harmonious coexistence

---

[118] M Chen-Wishart, 'Legal Transplant and Undue Influence: Lost in Translation or a Working Misunderstanding?' (2013) 62 *ICLQ* 1. I am grateful to Mr William Swadling for drawing my attention to this article.

[119] See JB Tamney, *The Struggle over Singapore's Soul: Western Modernisation and Asian Culture* (Berlin, Walter de Gruyter, 1996) pp 181–88. But my arguments in this chapter are not intended in any way to diminish Chen-Wishart's analysis of the doctrine of undue influence under Singapore law, an area where her observations have provided insights.

[120] See *Singapore Parliamentary Debates, Official Report* (25 July 1994) vol 63; *Singapore Parliamentary Debates, Official Report* (23 November 2010) vol 87.

[121] *LKC on behalf of LYS v LKY* [2002] SGTMP 2 (unreported).

[122] Leong, *Elements of Family Law in Singapore*, above n 92, 445.

[123] For example, in Hong Kong, the Hong Kong Court of Final Appeal extended the presumption of advancement to a relationship between a man and his 'concubine', a concept of Chinese customary law. See *Cheung v Worldcup Investments Inc* [2008] HKCFA 78. See also *Favor Easy Management Ltd v Wu* [2012] EWCA Civ 1464, [51] where the English Court of Appeal acknowledged the challenge of giving 'English legal content to Chinese cultural arrangements'. The case involved two parties formerly involved in a culturally Chinese type of sexual relationship, contesting over the beneficial ownership of a commercial property.

[124] See Tamney, above n 119, 181–88.

of all races. Nor would such emphasis facilitate a smooth integration of new immigrants. The recent movement in Singapore is to enforce the 'Singaporean' identity that embraces all races living within its borders.[125] Whilst the values of Singaporean society might resemble Confucian values, they are also the values of other racial/religious communities. As former Chief Justice Chan Sek Keong remarked: 'Multiculturalism is here to stay because we do not have and cannot afford a dominant or a homogeneous culture. The espousal of any racial or religious community will destroy Singapore.'[126]

IV. Real Property: Diminishing Role for the Resulting Trust

As mentioned above, the role of the presumption of advancement in the spousal context has extremely limited impact in view of the circumstances in which they arise. Moreover, a scrutiny of the facts of *Lau Siew Kim* reveals that the case could have been resolved based on direct and circumstantial evidence, without any real need to have recourse to the twin presumptions.[127] This is probably true of a majority of cases. Indeed, the Court of Appeal affirmed in *See Fong Mun (CA)* that the equitable presumptions should only be invoked where there is no direct evidence on the parties' intentions at the time of purchase/transfer.[128] This affirmation underscores the more limited role of the resulting trust in modern times. Even if the twin presumptions are to be raised as a matter of course, their significance in respect of transfers of real property—a key context in which the twin presumptions operate—is further diminished in reality by a confluence of domestic factors, including conveyancing practices and public housing rules.

Informed Choice in a Majority of Cases

Based on a recent qualitative study undertaken by Yeo consisting of a sample of 18 senior conveyancers practicing in Singapore with 10–30 years' experience,[129] the actual conveyancing approach in Singapore is such that a vast majority of purchasers do exercise an informed choice with regards to the manner of holding after having been advised by their lawyers.[130] Such an outcome is unsurprising. 84 per cent of Singaporeans live in Housing Development Board (HDB) flats and the HDB makes it mandatory for all purchasers to

---

[125] See eg *Population White Paper: A Sustainable Population for a Dynamic Singapore* (January 2013) http://population.sg/whitepaper/downloads/population-white-paper.pdf, accessed 29 May 2015.

[126] SK Chan (Chief Justice of Singapore), 'Multiculturalism in Singapore: The Way to a Harmonious Society' (2013) 25 *Singapore Academy of Law Journal* 84.

[127] Tan SY et al (eds), *Tan Sook Yee's Principles of Singapore Land Law*, 3rd edn (Singapore, LexisNexis, 2009) [7.58].

[128] In the framework of analysis proposed by the Court of Appeal (*See Fong Mun (CA)* [2014] SGCA 36, [2014] 3 SLR 1048, [160]), however, one would start off with the presumption of resulting trust if there is sufficient evidence of the parties' financial contributions to the purchase, although the presumption may be rebutted by direct evidence. The presumption of advancement, on the other hand, only applies where there is no direct evidence to rebut the presumption of resulting trust.

[129] Drawn from the 17 leading conveyancing firms listed on the Central Provident Fund's Conveyancing Panel.

[130] Yeo, above n 28, 135–38.

sign a manner of holding form which requires them to choose between joint tenancy or tenancy in common. The form is coupled with an explanatory note highlighting the essential distinctions between the two types of co-ownership. As for the remaining 16 per cent of the population residing in private housing, Yeo's sample survey with 16 conveyancers shows that at least 14 of them issue a manner of holding form for their clients to sign and confirm their choice.[131] Although the sample survey cannot conclusively establish that this is the prevailing practice in Singapore in respect of conveyancing of private housing, it at least shows that some lawyers are minded to advise and ensure that their clients have carefully considered their choice of type of co-ownership.

Hence, it might be that there are not so many cases where the default presumption of joint tenancy under section 53(1) of the Land Titles Act does not accurately reflect the purchasers' actual intentions. Further, as Lady Hale had said in *Stack*:

> [I]t will almost always have been a 'conscious' choice to put the house into joint names. Even if the parties have not executed the transfer, they will usually, if not invariably, have executed the contract that precedes it. Committing oneself to spend large sums of money on a place to live is not normally done by accident or without giving it a moment's thought.[132]

No doubt, the Court of Appeal in *Lau Siew Kim* was minded to protect those who might have made an active choice but one that is uninformed as to the legal implications, but such cases are probably uncommon. In *Lau Siew Kim* the Court of Appeal had said that cogent evidence is required to show that the co-owners have exercised an informed and voluntary choice to hold land as legal joint tenants and such evidence could take the form of sworn testimony from the conveyancing practitioner assisting the purchase or even from one of the co-owners concerned.[133] But perhaps we should also reflect more deeply just how paternalistic the law should be in protecting non-commercial parties. Overzealous paternalism in this instance could render the law more complex and therefore even less readily comprehensible to the lay purchasers, thereby cementing (or, even exacerbating) the very problem that equity is invoked to resolve.

Limited Operation of the Resulting Trust over HDB Flats

In respect of HDB flats, the resulting trust has an even more limited role owing to numerous legislative attempts to banish the doctrine of resulting trust from applying vis-à-vis public housing.[134] The current version of the legislative prohibition is set out in section 51(10) of the Housing and Development Act,[135] which provides that '[n]o person shall become entitled to any protected property (or any interest in such property) under any resulting trust or constructive trust whensoever created or arising'.

---

[131] ibid 136–37.
[132] *Stack* [2007] UKHL 17, [2007] 2 AC 432, [66].
[133] *Lau Siew Kim* [2007] SGCA 54, [2008] 2 SLR(R) 108, [95].
[134] See a very good discussion in Tang HW, 'Housing and Development Board Flats, Trust and Other Equitable Doctrines' (2012) 24 *Singapore Academy of Law Journal* 470, 478–84.
[135] Housing and Development Act, Cap 129, 2004 rev edn (Singapore).

The Singapore courts have, however, resisted adopting a strictly literal interpretation of the relevant provision.[136] Instead, they interpret the relevant provision to mean that no resulting trust or constructive trust in favour of persons who would otherwise have been ineligible to acquire an interest in an HDB flats. In other words, it is to prevent persons from acquiring an interest in a HDB flat through the backdoor by simply contributing towards the purchase price. This more limited prohibition as interpreted by the courts nonetheless has the effect of further reducing the operation of the resulting trust over HDB flats.

Electronic Conveyancing

From January 2006 conveyancing of private property has been made fully electronic via the Singapore Land Authority's electronic lodgement system. Under this electronic system it is mandatory for all purchasers of private property to elect their manner of holding, and the transaction cannot be completed without the election. From 2011 onwards conveyancing of HDB housing has also been executed through this form of electronic conveyancing. The mandatory election exercise will no doubt allay concerns of the lack of an active choice on the part of the purchasers, but to what extent the election requirement helps to address concerns of an *uninformed* choice is a separate matter. Certainly, it would turn the purchasers' attention to considering the distinctions between the two types of co-ownership. It follows that the distinction between legal and equitable title is likely to be diminished.[137]

V. Implications for Related Areas of Law

The limited and diminishing role of the twin presumptions in Singapore law notwithstanding, there appears to be no immediate reason or external pressure to legislatively abolish their operation. By contrast, the abolition of the spousal presumption within English domestic law is necessitated by its prospective accession to international treaty obligations. Where a jurisdiction is situated geographically and politically would thus have an impact on its domestic laws. Importantly, the retention of the twin presumptions under Singapore law will have some implications for related areas of law, which are examined below.

Constructive Trusts: Importation of the *Stack* Framework?

As highlighted above, under English law, the default starting point for domestic consumer cases (or at least where that is the primary purpose) is the common intention constructive trust framework laid down in *Stack*, and clarified in *Kernott*.[138] Notably, under English

---

[136] Regarding the interpretation of s 51(10), see *Koh Cheong Heng v Ho Yee Fong* [2011] SGHC 48, [2011] 3 SLR 125.

[137] Yeo, above n 28, 137.

[138] The lack of legislative intervention to address the financial consequences of the breakdown of cohabitees' relationship had been a strong reason behind the development of the *Stack* framework under English law (see *Gow v Grant* [2012] UKSC 29, 2012 SLT 829, [47] (Lady Hale)).

law, the *Stack* framework applies (as opposed to the presumption of advancement) even as between married couples during the subsistence of their marriage.[139] There is some obiter suggestion that there is still a residual role for the resulting trust in domestic cases but it is likely to be very limited.[140]

The common intention constructive trust is certainly part of Singapore law.[141] Before the case of *See Fong Mun (CA)*, Singapore cases followed the pre-*Stack* approach endorsed by the House of Lords in *Lloyds Bank plc v Rosset*.[142] *See Fong Mun (HC)* was the first case to consider *Stack* seriously.[143] Instead of suggesting that the *Stack* framework would exclusively apply in domestic consumer cases as under English law, the High Court in *See Fong Mun (HC)* took a more considered position that does not directly conflict with *Lau Siew Kim*.[144] It did, however, suggest that the resolution of the juridical underpinning of the presumed resulting trust would have certain doctrinal implications. If Singapore law endorses the 'presumed intention' account of resulting trust (as opposed to the 'absence of intention' account), the Singapore courts would then need to grapple with the inconsistency between the presumed resulting trust and the common intention constructive trust.[145] This perceived inconsistency proceeds from the Court's adherence to Lord Browne-Wilkinson's slightly unfortunate language of 'common intention' in *Westdeutsche*.[146] Language issues aside, the overall tenor of the High Court judgment in *See Fong Mun (HC)* was disinclined from applying the resulting trust as the default tool of analysis in all domestic cases.

The Singapore Court of Appeal in *See Fong Mun (CA)*, however, took a different view. It fully endorsed Lord Neuberger's minority view in *Stack v Dowden*, and rejected the majority's approach. The Court pointed out that the English developments arose from 'changing economic and social conditions in England', which included rises in both property prices and the number of unmarried cohabitees.[147] Yet, there has been no legislative reform to deal adequately with property disputes arising from such conditions. Moreover, the Court commented that the diminished application of the presumption of advancement under English law was also a driver for the *Stack/Kernott* developments, as the retention of

---

[139] *Gibson v Revenue and Customs Prosecution Office* [2009] EWCA Civ 645, [2009] 2 WLR 471, [27].

[140] In *Stack* [2007] UKHL 17, [2007] 2 AC 432, [32], Lord Walker noted that the resulting trust 'may still have a useful function in cases where two people have lived and worked together in what has amounted to both an emotional and a commercial partnership'.

[141] See, eg, *Tan Thiam Loke v Woon Swee Kheng Christina* [1991] SGCA 32, [1991] 2 SLR(R) 595 (hereinafter '*Tan Thiam Loke*').

[142] *Lloyds Bank plc v Rosset* [1991] 1 AC 107. *Rosset* concerned a sole name case. Where joint names cases are concerned, the English law before *Stack* was not entirely clear; under Singapore law, see *Tan Thiam Loke* [1991] SGCA 32, [1991] 2 SLR(R) 595.

[143] *Stack* was first cited in *Lee Kim Kiat v Lee Biow Neo* [2007] SGHC 213, [2008] 2 SLR(R) 174 but for a point that has nothing to do with the common intention constructive trust.

[144] See above, text to n 57.

[145] See Lord Neuberger's two-stage analysis in *Stack* [2007] UKHL 17, [2007] 2 AC 432, [123]–[124].

[146] *Westdeutsche* [1996] AC 669, 708.

[147] *See Fong Mun (CA)* [2014] SGCA 36, [2014] 3 SLR 1048, [127]. It is noteworthy that cohabitation is presently not as prevalent in Singaporean society. Further, many of the Singapore domestic property cases involve disputes between parent and child as well as between siblings. This is the case in Singapore because more than 80% of the population resides in HDB flats (government housing), and these flats are generally made available to members of formally recognised family structures. It is much more difficult for unmarried cohabitees to meet the eligibility requirement to purchase HDB flats. See www.hdb.gov.sg/fi10/fi10321p.nsf/w/BuyResaleFlatEligibility-tobuy?OpenDocument, accessed 29 May 2015. I am very grateful to Associate Professor Kelvin Low for pointing this out to me.

the resulting trust alone would only put more emphasis on direct contributions to purchase price which the English courts consider to be too narrow.[148]

The Singapore Court of Appeal then went on to set out reasons for not adopting the *Stack/Kernott* framework of analysis.[149] In the Court's view, the *Stack/Kernott* analysis is productive of litigation because of the subjectivity and uncertainty inherent in the approach. It therefore follows that, owing to the difficulty for solicitors to advise their clients on the prospects of their dispute, there is a risk of increased and disproportionate litigation costs. Moreover, the Court pointed out that the domestic/commercial distinction, which determines the applicable tool of analysis, might be difficult to apply in some instances. Instead, it preferred Lord Neuberger's approach,[150] which it thought provides pragmatic and clear guidance on when the different trusts apply, without being dependent on the rigid domestic/commercial classification. The Court also agreed with Lord Neuberger's adamant rejection of judicial imputation of intentions at the stage of quantification of interests,[151] which prevents courts from utilising the doctrine of common intentions constructive trust to effect 'palm tree' justice. Further, Lord Neuberger's approach allows a consistent approach to be applied in both domestic and commercial contexts: the common intention constructive trust would apply in both instances to rebut the presumption of resulting trust. Finally, the Court thought that using the resulting trust as the default tool in the absence of any common intention between the parties to determine their respective shares would be consistent with the 'lack-of-intention' analysis discussed above.

As the parties did not raise any argument based on the common intention constructive trust, the Court did not go on to discuss the specifics of the Singapore framework, or if refinements to the *Rosset* 'direct contributions' approach would be necessary. In this connection, it is noteworthy that some English cases after *Stack* and *Kernott* have treated the two landmark decisions as endorsing a holistic approach of considering all contributions, financial or otherwise, at the stage of acquisition of interest.[152] Such a development under Singapore law could afford greater latitude for Singapore law to accommodate contemporary values of marriage in the exercise, as well as balance the interests of justice between unmarried cohabitees based on the nature of the relationship. However, it is also clear that the Singapore courts will not have recourse to imputation of intention at the stage of quantification of interests, which would constrain judicial activism in trying to resolve a case based on notions of fairness and justice. This means that Singapore courts could well take a more robust approach towards the concept and limits of 'inference of intention', given the methodological similarities between inference and imputation of intentions.[153] But in more exceptional cases, where credible evidence of the parties' contributions is scant but it

---

[148] *See Fong Mun (CA)* [2014] SGCA 36, [2014] 3 SLR 1048, [132].

[149] ibid [152].

[150] ibid [153]–[158].

[151] See also *Chia Kum Fatt Rolfston v Lim Lay Choo* [1993] SGHC 203, [1993] 3 SLR 833 in which the Singapore High Court held that parties' interests under a common intention constructive trust are commensurate with their financial contributions, rejecting non-financial contributions as being 'difficult to quantify'—this could be read as rejecting an exercise of imputation of intention. See an excellent discussion in *Tan Sook Yee's Principles of Singapore Land Law*, above n 127, [7.59]–[7.64].

[152] See eg *Singh v Singh* [2014] EWHC 1060 (Ch), [116].

[153] See N Piska, 'Intention, Fairness and the Presumption of Resulting Trust after *Stack v Dowden*' (2008) 71 *MLR* 120, 127–28.

could be shown that the parties had a common intention to share the property that is registered in one party's name,[154] an exercise of inference of intention might prove impossible or artificial if vigorously applied. In such cases, the Singapore courts might need to apply the equitable maxim that 'equality is equity'.

Constructive Trusts: Recharacterisation of the *Pallant v Morgan* Equity?

The fact that Singapore law rejects the *Stack/Kernott* framework would also mean that a sharp commercial/domestic distinction will not emerge within local jurisprudence, as has happened in English law. One immediate implication is that there is no reason to reconsider the jurisprudential basis of the *Pallant v Morgan* equity, which has been accepted as part of Singapore law,[155] following Chadwick LJ's decision in *Banner Homes Group Plc v Luff Developments Ltd*.[156] By contrast, in the recent English Court of Appeal decision in *Crossco No 4 Unlimited v Jolan Limited*[157] Etherton LJ, having regard to the developments of the common intention constructive trust in the domestic context, concluded that the *Pallant v Morgan* equity cases should be reinterpreted as based on a breach of fiduciary duty. However, Arden and McFarlane LJJ did not think that the Court, for reasons of *stare decisis*, could depart from the common intention constructive trust characterisation as enunciated in *Banner Homes*, a decision delivered by a court of equal jurisdiction. The issue of characterisation has yet to be conclusively reviewed under English law.[158] There is therefore potentially further divergence between Singapore law and English law in respect of constructive trusts.

Illegality

A key context in which the equitable presumptions continue to matter is the enforcement of equitable interests in illegal transactions. The effect of the technical 'reliance' principle in *Tinsley v Milligan*[159] is that the presumptions are determinative of whether property could be recovered in cases of illegality.[160] The outcome depends on whether the parties are in a relationship of advancement,[161] as opposed to the merits of the case. The *Tinsley v Milligan* rule has thus been criticised as arbitrary, producing inconsistent results in essentially like cases.[162] The 'reliance' principle has been endorsed by the Singapore Court of Appeal in the case of *Shi Fang v Koh Pee Huat*,[163] although the dicta endorsement of the majority view

---

[154] English law provides such an instance in the case of *Aspden v Elvy* [2012] EWHC 1387 (Ch), [2012] 2 FCR 435 (Ch D), see esp [127].
[155] *Ong Heng Chuan v Ong Boon Chuan* [2002] SGHC 285, [2003] 2 SLR(R) 469 (the dispute arose between two sibling shareholders of a family company). See also *See Fong Mun (CA)* [2014] SGCA 36, [2014] 3 SLR 1048, [157].
[156] *Banner Homes Group Plc v Luff Developments Ltd* [2000] Ch 372.
[157] *Crossco No 4 Unlimited v Jolan Limited* [2011] EWCA Civ 1619, [2012] 2 All ER 754.
[158] See M Yip, 'The *Pallant v Morgan* Equity Reconsidered' (2013) 33 *Legal Studies* 549. Later English cases did not pick up on this issue again: see, eg, *Achom v Lalic* [2014] EWHC 1888 (Ch).
[159] *Tinsley v Milligan* [1994] 1 AC 340.
[160] See generally RA Buckley, *Illegality and Public Policy*, 3rd edn (London, Sweet & Maxwell, 2013) [16-06]–[16-20]. See reform recommended by the Law Commission in its report *The Illegality Defence* (Law Com No 320, 2010). The UK Parliament has, however, decided not to introduce the suggested legislative reform.
[161] See *Chettiar (ARPL Palaniappa) v Chettiar (PLAR Arunasalam)* [1962] AC 294.
[162] See, eg, H Stowe, 'The "Unruly Horse" has bolted' (1994) 57 *MLR* 441, 446.
[163] *Shi Fang v Koh Pee Huat* [1996] SGCA 28, [1996] 2 SLR 221.

in *Tinsley v Milligan* was given without the consideration of an earlier Singapore Court of Appeal decision in *Suntoso Jacob v Koh Miao Ming*.[164] The judgment in *Suntoso Jacob* was consistent with the minority view in *Tinsley v Milligan*:[165] a property is not recoverable if it is transferred under an illegal transaction.

Since *Stack*, however, there is some uncertainty as to the fate of the *Tinsley v Milligan* rule under English law,[166] as domestic consumer cases will no longer be subject to the presumed resulting trust analysis. It has been commented that 'it seems not unlikely that the [*Stack*] approach will render the avoidance of illegality issues by the "proprietary interest" technique favoured in *Tinsley v Milligan* more problematic and less readily applicable'.[167] The *Tinsley v Milligan* rule will further diminish in significance under English law when section 199 of the Equality Act 2010 is finally brought into force, although its effect is likely to remain for a while given that the provision is not meant to affect transactions entered into before the provision is effective.[168]

By contrast, the retention of the equitable presumptions under Singapore law is likely to further entrench the *Tinsley v Milligan* principle (and its problems) within local jurisprudence. On a broader level, the retention of the *Tinsley v Milligan* rule also presents an obstacle to undertaking a more uniform and consistent approach towards illegality in general, whether involving enforcement of equitable interests, seeking restitution, etc. Australian jurisprudence, which rejected the *Tinsley v Milligan* principle in *Nelson v Nelson*,[169] is now moving towards a more uniform approach of determining the effects of illegality,[170] based on the technique of statutory interpretation where the illegality is sourced in a statute. Of course, given the problems of the *Tinsley v Milligan* principle, the Singapore courts could well decide to abolish the principle and adopt a more principled approach, whilst retaining the twin presumptions. But *Nelson v Nelson* has yet to be properly considered by the Singapore courts.[171] And a legislative reform exercise (which identified the problems with the *Tinsley v Milligan* rule) undertaken some years ago was abandoned. Nevertheless, it is not entirely hopeless. In *Ting Siew May v Boon Lay Choo*, a case on contractual illegality, the Singapore Court of Appeal clarified that the 'reliance principle'[172] is a 'legal principle with normative elements', and the question is thus not whether the illegality had to be specifically pleaded by one party, but whether the party is seeking to enforce an illegal contract.[173]

---

[164] *Suntoso Jacob v Kong Miao Ming* [1986] SGCA 2, [1986] SLR 59. The 'reliance' principle in *Tinsley v Milligan* was later applied in *Chee Jok Heng Stephanie v Chang Yue Shoon* [2010] SGHC 153, [2010] 3 SLR 1131; *Guillaume Levy-Lambert v Goh See Yuen Pierre* [2010] SGDC 482; *Lim Leong Huat v Chip Hup Hup Kee Construction Pte Ltd* [2010] SGHC 170, [2011] 1 SLR 657. None of these cases discussed the implication of the ruling in *Suntoso Jacob*.

[165] See Lord Goff of Chieveley's judgment in *Tinsley v Milligan* [1994] 1 AC 340, 351–64 (with whom Lord Keith of Kinkel concurred).

[166] Indeed, the UK Supreme Court has yet to address the proper approach to the defence of illegality or the fate of the *Tinsley v Milligan* rule. See *Jetivia SA v Bilta (UK) Limited (in liquidation)* [2015] UKSC 23, [2015] 2 WLR 1168, [13–17].

[167] See Buckley, above n 160, [16–19].

[168] See Equality Act 2010, s 199(2).

[169] *Nelson v Nelson* [1995] HCA 25, (1995) 184 CLR 538.

[170] See, eg, *Miller v Miller* [2011] HCA 9, (2011) 242 CLR 446; *Equuscorp Pty Ltd v Haxton* [2012] HCA 7, (2012) 246 CLR 498.

[171] *Nelson v Nelson* was briefly cited in *Lee Kim Kiat v Lee Biow Neo* [2007] SGHC 213, [2008] 2 SLR(R) 174 without proper consideration of its significance.

[172] The rule is generally associated with the decision of the English Court of Appeal in *Bowmakers v Barnet Instruments* [1945] KB 65. See generally Buckley, above n 160, [16–04]–[16–05].

[173] *Ting Siew May v Boon Lay Choo* [2014] SGCA 28, [2014] 3 SLR 609, [127].

The Court explained that the law of illegality and public policy is underpinned by considerations of wider public interest.[174] One could thus remain optimistic that when the *Tinsley v Milligan* is next argued before the Singapore Court of Appeal, a comprehensive review and perhaps significant reform is likely.

VI. Conclusion

That the common law with English origins has taken root and flourished in other common law jurisdictions, evolving and morphing to suit the needs of its new home, is an exciting phenomenon,[175] providing interesting reference points for all common law jurisdictions. This chapter has addressed the importation and 'localisation' of the presumptions of resulting trust and advancement in the spousal context, as an example of such phenomenon. Unlike the contributions to this topic before, I have argued that a primary factor leading to the divergence between English law and Singapore law is the political situation of each jurisdiction. But I have also pointed out that that the retention of the twin presumptions in Singapore law might not be so significant in view of internal factors that progressively limit its role in the domestic context. Perhaps what is more interesting is how this point of divergence could potentially lead to more points of divergence in related areas of law between Singapore law and English law.

In modern times, therefore, the 'common law' ought not be approached merely as a study of the relationship between English law and the laws of its former colonial states. The incrementalism of its development, a hallmark of this body of law, has also taken on a new form of dynamism. Within each common law jurisdiction, the indigenous common law must be also appreciated against the backdrop of domestic legislation.[176] Even in respect of points of convergence, we should pause to investigate the reasons. For example, where commercial matters are concerned, the legal alignment between the various common law jurisdictions might be attributable to a desire to keep pace with the laws of major financial hubs (of which London is one) to ensure consistency and simplicity, as opposed to a deferential relationship to English law based on vestigial colonial ties. As Chief Justice Sundaresh Menon of Singapore has recently commented:

> [I]n the field of business and commercial law, the courts can perhaps better serve national interests as well as the interests of their users by avoiding divergence where possible so as to develop the law in a commercial sensible way which does not detract from the transnational character of the prevailing environment.[177]

---

[174] ibid [128].

[175] For Australian law, see Hon Justice J Douglas, 'England as a Source of Australian Law: For How Long?' (2012) 86 *Australian Law Journal* 33.

[176] See generally the importance of studying the relationship between common law and statutes: A Burrows, 'The Relationship between Common Law and Statute in the Law of Obligations' (2012) 128 *LQR* 232. See also J Lee, 'A Civil Law for the Age of Statutes' in TT Arvind and J Steele (eds), *Tort Law and the Legislature* (Oxford, Hart Publishing, 2013) ch 5.

[177] The Honourable the Chief Justice Sundaresh Menon, Keynote Address at Singapore Academy of Law and Chancery Bar Conference 2013 'Finance, Property and Business Litigation in a Changing World' (speech in Singapore, 25 April 2013) www.sal.org.sg/Lists/Speeches/Attachments/113/CJ%20Menon's%20Keynote%20 Address%20(SAL-ChBA%20Conference).pdf, accessed 29 May 2015.

14

Divergence in the Australian and English Law of Undue Influence: Vacillation or Variance?

ROBYN HONEY[*]

I. Introduction

Although Australia inherited the English doctrine of undue influence, the English and Australian doctrines have diverged significantly. Given that the issues of human behaviour and public policy, which drive the doctrine and justify its role in the law of contract and property, do not vary between the jurisdictions, perhaps the current differences are superficial and likely to be temporary. This chapter describes and analyses doctrinal trends in recent English and Australian undue influence cases, in order to assess whether the current discrepancy constitutes true doctrinal variance or is merely a consequence of judicial vacillation. It also appraises the likelihood that the doctrines will realign over time.

The chapter traces the origin and progression of the dissimilarity, so as to attain an understanding of how and why divergence occurred. It then looks to recent English and Australian cases in order to assess whether, and to what extent, this dissonance affects the way that the doctrine currently operates. To this end, it draws from cases decided in Australia and England over the past five years, which consider the equitable doctrine of undue influence *inter vivos*.[1] Observations will be made about the way that the doctrine of undue influence is operating in England and Australia with a view to gauging whether the two versions are growing toward one another or moving further apart. It will be shown that, when employing the doctrine, the English and Australian courts continue to be moved by similar concerns, so that an impetus for convergence exists. However, it will be suggested that differences between the legal landscapes currently existing in England and Australia are acting to obstruct convergence. It will be argued that, unless fundamental changes occur, there can be no realistic expectation that the English and Australian doctrines will realign.

[*] The author thanks Professor Elise Bant and Professor Matthew Harding of the University of Melbourne for their invaluable guidance and also Dr Katy Barnett, Dr Jeannie Patterson and Dr Sirko Harder for their encouragement and feedback.

[1] This chapter does not consider the doctrine of undue influence that operates in the context of testamentary dispositions.

II. Undue Influence in England and Australia

Shared Origins

The foundations of the doctrine of undue influence were laid by the Court of Chancery in the nineteenth century.[2] Seminal cases such as *Huguenin v Baseley*,[3] *Bainbrigge v Browne*[4] and *Allcard v Skinner*[5] disclose three key features of the doctrine:

— a relationship of trust and confidence between the benefactor and the influential party;
— vitiated consent on the part of the benefactor; and
— unacceptable conduct (such as active coercion or passive exploitation) by the influential party.

Initially, the English doctrine was law in the Australian colonies, and even after federation, the Australian law of undue influence developed in parallel with its English counterpart.[6] Thus, the three critical features of undue influence were also built into the Australian doctrine.

However, this configuration carried with it an inherent ambiguity. The facets did not always feature equally. One or other might figure more prominently as the basis for equitable relief. This has intrigued legal scholars, because undue influence appears to differ in nature and operation depending on which of its aspects is in focus.[7] The debate concerning the 'true' (definitive) rationale of the doctrine has produced several competing models of undue influence. It is submitted that three such models—the fiduciary model,[8] the vitiated consent model[9] and the unconscionable conduct model[10]—have influenced

---

[2] Although equitable relief for undue influence can be found in 18th-century cases (see below n 12), the doctrine as we know it today was formed in: *Huguenin v Baseley* (1807) 14 Ves 273, 33 ER 526; *Griffiths v Robins* (1818) 3 Madd 191, 56 ER 480; *Dent v Bennett* (1839) 4 My & Cr 269, 41 ER 105; *Smith v Kay* (1859) 7 HLC 750, 11 ER 299; *Sharp v Leach* (1862) 31 Beav 491, 54 ER 1229; *Bainbrigge v Brown* (1881) 18 Ch D 188; *Allcard v Skinner* (1887) 36 Ch D 145 and *Morley v Loughnan* [1893] 1 Ch 736.

[3] *Huguenin v Baseley* (1807) 14 Ves 273, 33 ER 526, 536 (Lord Eldon).

[4] *Bainbrigge v Brown* (1881) 18 Ch D 188, 197–98 (Fry J).

[5] *Allcard v Skinner* (1887) 36 Ch D 145, 172 (Cotton LJ), 177 and 181–82 (Lindley LJ) and 190–91 (Bowen LJ).

[6] The High Court decisions, upon which most of the Australian law of undue influence is based, cite English authorities almost exclusively. See *Spong v Spong* (1914) 18 CLR 544; *Watkins v Combes* (1922) 30 CLR 180; *Johnson v Buttress* (1936) 56 CLR 113; and *Bank of New South Wales v Rogers* (1941) 65 CLR 42.

[7] Professor Rick Bigwood has referred to this 'shape shifting' feature of undue influence as a 'gestalt shift': R Bigwood, 'Undue Influence: "Impaired Consent" or "Wicked Exploitation"?' (1996) 16 *OJLS* 503.

[8] See, eg, LS Sealy, 'Fiduciary Relationships' [1962] *CLJ* 69, 78–79; P Finn, *Fiduciary Obligations* (Sydney, Law Book Company, 1977) ch 16; D Tiplady, 'The Limits of Undue Influence' (1985) 48 *MLR* 579, 580–82; R Flannigan, 'The Fiduciary Obligation' (1989) 9 *OJLS* 285, 292–96; P Finn, 'The Fiduciary Principle' in T Youdan (ed), *Equity, Fiduciaries and Trusts* (Toronto, Carswell, 1989) 1; Bigwood, above n 7, 510; PJ Millett, 'Equity's Place in the Law of Commerce' (1998) 114 *LQR* 214, 219–21; R Bigwood, 'Contracts by Unfair Advantage: From Exploitation to Transactional Neglect' (2005) 25 *OJLS* 65; R Bigwood, 'Ill-Gotten Contracts in New Zealand Parting Thoughts on Duress, Undue Influence and Unconscionable Dealing Kiwi-Style' (2011) 42 *Victoria University of Wellington Law Review* 83.

[9] See, eg, P Birks and Chin NY, 'On the Nature of Undue Influence' in J Beatson and D Friedmann (eds), *Good Faith and Fault in Contract Law* (Melbourne, Oxford University Press, 1995) 57.

[10] See, eg, J Hardingham, 'Unconscionable Dealing' in PD Finn (ed), *Essays in Equity* (North Ryde, NSW, Law Book Company, 1985) 18 and 19; and D Capper, 'The Unconscionable Bargain in the Common Law World' (2010) 126 *LQR* 403. This might otherwise be termed 'the abuse of influence model' or the 'improper means of

the development of English and Australian law and, further, that the divergence under consideration has come about because English and Australian courts have adopted different models of the doctrine.

Divergence

Australia—The Emergence of a Fiduciary Model of Undue Influence

During the course of the past century,[11] Australian courts have developed a distinctive model of undue influence as the breach of a 'fiduciary-like' duty.[12] The locus classicus of this view is to be found in the judgment of Dixon J in *Johnson v Buttress*.[13] This model is epitomised in cases where, due to the existence of a 'relation of influence',[14] the influential party 'falls under a duty in which fiduciary characteristics may be seen'.[15] In such cases, the influential party must 'use his position of influence in the interest of no one but the man who is governed by his judgment, gives him his dependence and entrusts him with his welfare'.[16] Endorsed by influential scholars[17] and followed in many subsequent decisions,[18] the fiduciary model became orthodoxy in Australia.

persuasion' model—the critical feature being that undue influence is explained by reference to the unacceptable nature of the conduct of the influential party.

[11] The association between fiduciary relationships and relationships of influence outside the established categories was acknowledged by the High Court in *Spong v Spong* (1914) 18 CLR 544, 551 (Isaacs J) and 552 (Rich J).

[12] It is not suggested that this was a novel or uniquely Australian approach. The association between fiduciary obligation and the doctrine of undue influence has a long heritage. It is discernible in judgments dating back to the 18th century. See, eg, *Walmesley v Booth* (1739) 2 Atk 25, 26 ER 412 as to a presumption of undue influence between solicitor and client and *Ayliffe v Murray* (1740) 2 Atk 58, 26 ER 433 with respect to trustee and beneficiary. Furthermore, several English decisions referred to in *Johnson v Buttress* had described undue influence in such a way as to emphasise its fiduciary aspect. See, eg, *Billage v Southee* (1852) 9 Hare 534, 540, 68 ER 623, 626 (Sir George J Turner VC); *Smith v Kay* (1859) 7 HLC 750, 779, 11 ER 299, 310–11 (Lord Chelmsford); and *Morley v Loughnan* [1893] 1 Ch 736, 756 (Wright J).

[13] *Johnson v Buttress* (1936) 56 CLR 113, 134–36.

[14] ibid 136.

[15] ibid 135.

[16] ibid. On this basis, undue influence constitutes the breach of an equitable duty. As such it is an equitable wrong. However, like breach of fiduciary obligation, this wrong may be committed notwithstanding that the influential party has been guilty of no reprehensible behaviour. This is possible because the duty that is breached exists to serve public policy.

[17] In the Australian context, the two most influential proponents of a fiduciary model have been Professors Paul Finn and Rick Bigwood. See Finn, *Fiduciary Obligations*, above n 8; Finn, 'The Fiduciary Principle', above n 8, 1 and P Finn, 'Fiduciary Reflections' (2014) 88 *Australian Law Journal* 127. See also, Bigwood, above n 7, at 510 and Bigwood, 'Contracts by Unfair Advantage', above n 8, 83. It is not suggested that a fiduciary model enjoyed the unanimous support of Australian commentators.

[18] See *Bank of NSW v Rogers* (1941) 65 CLR 42, 51 (Starke J) and 61 (McTiernan J); *Union Fidelity Trustee Co v Gibson* [1971] VR 573, 576 (Gillard J). Justice Dixon's 'fiduciary like' principle was cited with approval in: *Urane v Whipper* [2001] NSWSC 796, [23] (Windeyer J); *Harrison v Schipp* [2001] NSWCA 13, [100] (Giles JA with whom Handley JA agreed); *Hartigan v International Society for Krishna Consciousness Incorporated* [2002] NSWSC 810, [32]–[33] (Bryson J); *Burrawong Investments Pty Ltd v Lindsay* [2002] QSC 82, [63] (Muir J); *Hillston v Bar-Mordecai* [2003] NSWSC 89, [32] (Bryson J); *Woodland v Rodriguez* [2004] NSWSC 1167, [42] (Master MacLaughlin); *Da Yun Xu v Fang Lin* [2005] NSWSC 569, [26] (Barrett J); *Sleboda v Sleboda* [2007] NSWSC 361, [3] (Gzell J); *Maher v Honeysett & Maher Electrical Contractors Pty Ltd* [2007] NSWSC 12, [131] (Barrett J); *Janson v Janson* [2007] NSWSC 1344, [73] (Biscoe AJ); *Lai See Law by her Tutor the Protective Commissioner of New South Wales v Yan Mo* [2009] NSWSC 639, [78] (Bergin in Eq); *Christodoulou v Christodoulou* [2009] VSC 583, [71] (Kaye J); *Calvo v Sweeney* [2009] NSWSC 719, [250] (White J); *Creswick v Creswick* [2010] QSC 339, [351]–[352] (Daubney J); *Western v Male* [2011] SASC 75, [253] (Nyland J).

On this model, undue influence constitutes an equitable wrong in that it is the breach of an equitable duty. However, consistent with its fiduciary-like character, this duty can be breached notwithstanding that the influential party has acted in 'good faith'.[19] In such instances, relief is justified on the basis that the doctrine serves public policy in protecting the vulnerable and safeguarding socially valuable relationships of trust.[20] On the fiduciary model, undue influence is not primarily concerned with the quality of the benefactor's consent to the impugned transaction. There is certainly no necessity to prove or presume that the benefactor's will was 'overborne'.

Australia—Distinguishing Unconscionable Dealing and Vitiated Consent

Matters became more complicated with the emergence of the equitable doctrine of unconscionable dealing. It became necessary to distinguish that doctrine from undue influence. In a series of important decisions delivered during the 1980s and 1990s, the High Court asserted that unconscionable dealing could be distinguished from undue influence on the basis that the latter responds to the inadequacy of the benefactor's consent. In *Commercial Bank of Australia Ltd v Amadio* ('*Amadio*'), Deane J famously asserted that:

> The equitable principles relating to relief against unconscionable dealing and the principles relating to undue influence are closely related. [They] are, however, distinct. Undue influence, like common law duress, looks to the quality of the consent or assent of the weaker party … Unconscionable dealing looks to the conduct of the stronger party in attempting to enforce, or retain the benefit of, a dealing with a person under a special disability in circumstances where it is not consistent with equity or good conscience that he should do so.[21]

This dictum was cited with approval in *Bridgewater v Leahy*.[22] Notwithstanding that both of these statements were obiter dicta,[23] the dichotomy that they assert has been enthusiastically accepted and frequently reiterated.[24]

During the interval between *Amadio* and *Bridgewater v Leahy*, the seminal work 'On the Nature of Undue Influence' by Professors Peter Birks and Chin Nyuk Yin was published.[25] Birks and Chin offered a plausible doctrinal basis for a 'plaintiff-sided' model of undue influence founded on vitiated consent. They identified the doctrine's closest relatives as 'personal disadvantages' and other manifestations of impaired autonomy.[26] This work

---

[19] Indeed, this was so in *Johnson v Buttress*. The trial judge, Nicholas J, found that Mrs Johnson had been kind to Mr Buttress and his wife and that there had been 'ample reason for gratitude to her': see *Johnson v Buttress* (1936) 56 CLR 113, 122 (Latham CJ). There was no evidence that Mrs Johnson had used her influence to procure the transfer and, indeed, this was inessential, because the basis of the doctrine 'is the prevention of an unconscientious use of any special capacity or opportunity' to affect the will or freedom of judgment of another: ibid 134 (Dixon J).

[20] ibid 135.

[21] *Commercial Bank of Australia Ltd v Amadio* (1983) 151 CLR 447, 474 (citations omitted). See also the dictum of Mason J (ibid 461) in which his Honour enunciated the distinction in similar terms. cf *Louth v Diprose* (1992) 175 CLR 621, 627 (Brennan J): 'Gifts obtained by unconscionable conduct and gifts obtained by undue influence are set aside by equity on substantially the same basis.'

[22] *Bridgewater v Leahy* (1998) 194 CLR 457, 478–79 (Gaudron, Gummow and Kirby JJ).

[23] Each of these cases was decided on the basis of unconscionable dealing, not undue influence.

[24] In the past five years, the dictum of Deane J was cited with approval in 12 undue influence cases and the dictum of Mason J was cited with approval in six. See n 53 below.

[25] Birks and Chin, above n 9, 57.

[26] Such as 'minority, mental illness and socio-economic disability': ibid 62. As such on the vitiated consent model, undue influence is not a wrong, but rather might be categorised as the basis for restitution of unjust enrichment.

was very influential in Australia. In 1998 it was endorsed by Sir Anthony Mason in the *Anglo-American Law Review*,[27] an endorsement that has frequently been cited by Australian judges as validation of the vitiated consent model.[28] Pursuant to this model, relief is granted on the basis of matters connected solely with the benefactor. Therefore, like the fiduciary model, it allows the claimant to succeed even where the influential party has acted in good faith. Unlike the fiduciary model, however, breach of equitable duty by the influential party is *not* a prerequisite for relief.

England—Royal Bank of Scotland Pty Ltd v Etridge (No 2)

Notwithstanding that Australian courts had developed their own body of case law on undue influence, until *Royal Bank of Scotland Pty Ltd v Etridge (No 2)* (*'Etridge'*)[29] there was no obvious inconsistency between the English and Australian conceptions of undue influence. Both English and Australian courts used fiduciary language to describe the circumstances in which a defendant would be obliged to disprove undue influence. Furthermore, both charged such a defendant to acquit herself by proving that the benefactor's quality of consent had not been impaired at the time of the transaction.

However, with the watershed decision in *Etridge*, it became evident that the English and Australian doctrines had diverged. The House of Lords mandated a wholly 'defendant-sided' model of undue influence, which is not reconcilable with Australian law. Pursuant to *Etridge*, the rationale of the doctrine is to set aside transactions procured by 'unacceptable forms of persuasion'.[30] The quality of the benefactor's consent is beside the point. Breach starts and ends with the influential party's conduct. The transaction is set aside because it would be unfair to *treat* it as a product of the benefactor's free will.[31]

On this view, the doctrine constitutes an equitable wrong—ie the breach of an equitable duty not to misuse influence. However, this duty has no fiduciary character or significance. It does not look beyond the parties, operate prophylactically or seek to serve wider policy objectives. Nor is there scope for 'innocent' breach. Undue influence always involves (to a greater or lesser extent) morally culpable or unconscionable behaviour by the influential party.[32] The claimant must prove (or demonstrate that it may justly be inferred) that the

---

[27] A Mason, 'The Impact of Equitable Doctrine on the Law of Contract' (1998) 27 *Anglo-American Law Review* 1, 6–7. Sir Anthony also cited with approval the dicta of Deane and Mason JJ in *Amadio*.

[28] See n 54 below.

[29] *Royal Bank of Scotland Pty Ltd v Etridge (No 2)* [2001] UKHL 44, [2002] 2 AC 773.

[30] ibid [7] (Lord Nicholls). A similar expression—'insidious techniques of persuasion'—was used by Lord Clyde: ibid [93].

[31] According to Lord Nicholls, it is the means used to procure the claimant's consent—not the quality of the consent itself—to which equity objects. Where unacceptable means are used, then the consent 'ought not fairly to be treated as the expression of a person's free will': ibid [7].

[32] It is acknowledged that this assertion runs counter to the later decisions of the Court of Appeal in *Hammond v Osborn* [2002] EWCA 885 and *Niersmans v Pesticcio* [2004] EWCA Civ 372. In the latter case, a conveyance was set aside as against an 'innocent' defendant on the basis that the solicitor engaged to provide independent legal advice had failed in her duty to do so. Citing *Hammond v Osborn*, Mummery LJ (with whom Jacob and Pill LJJ agreed) stated that: '[T]he basis of the court's intervention is not the commission of a dishonest or wrongful act by the defendant, but that, as a matter of public policy, the presumed influence arising from the relationship of trust and confidence should not operate to the disadvantage of the victim, if the transaction is not satisfactorily explained by ordinary motives.' However, it is submitted that this position cannot be reconciled with the statements made by the House of Lords in *Etridge* that, where a relationship of trust and confidence is proven on the facts, an abuse of influence may be inferred as a matter of fact from the relationship and the nature of the transaction: *Etridge* [2001] UKHL 44, [2002] 2 AC 773, [16]–[18] (Lord Nicholls), [92]–[93] (Lord Clyde), [107]

influential party dealt unfairly with her, whether by pressuring her to transact or by exploiting influence over her to that end.

III. Recent Developments: Convergence Impeded

The explanation of undue influence given by Lord Nicholls in *Etridge* carried the support of all the members of the House.[33] However, a review of recent decisions in each jurisdiction suggests that concern for the same three factors (consent, conduct and relationships of trust and confidence) is still discernible.

Australia

Recent cases reveal tensions emerging within the Australian law of undue influence. In summary, the fiduciary model retains support, but there is now a well-entrenched line of authority which asserts that undue influence is concerned with the quality of the benefactor's consent. Furthermore, one may discern the emergence of a 'duress-like' model of undue influence, which looks for coercive or exploitative behaviour by the influential party, but offers relief only if the court accepts that the benefactor's will was overborne as a result of that conduct. Virtually no interest has been expressed in an '*Etridge*-style', wholly defendant-focused, model of undue influence and it will be submitted that this is not likely to change.

Support for a Fiduciary Model Endures

Cases decided during the past five years confirm that Australian courts continue to employ the fiduciary model—treating undue influence as the misuse of power or opportunity afforded by an entrusted position. This conception of the doctrine retains a particularly strong following in New South Wales.[34] The decisions in *Courtney v Powell*[35] and *Calvo v Sweeney*[36] provide useful examples of the operation of the fiduciary model in a twenty-first-century Australian context.

Courtney v Powell concerned the transfer by an elderly man of his home to his daughter for nominal consideration and without the benefit of adequate independent legal advice.

(Lord Hobhouse) and [152]–[153] (Lord Scott). Thus, according to *Etridge*, abuse of influence, whether proven or inferred, is always the basis for relief for undue influence.

[33] ibid [3] (Lord Bingham), [91] (Lord Clyde), [100] (Lord Hobhouse) and [192] (Lord Scott). This was notwithstanding Lord Bingham's observation that 'the opinions of Lord Nicholls and Lord Scott show some difference of expression and approach': ibid [3].

[34] See, eg, *Courtney v Powell* [2012] NSWSC 460; *Calvo v Sweeney* [2009] NSWSC 719; *Simpson v RBM* [2010] NSWSC 166; and *Brown v Barkley Brown* [2009] NSWSC 76. See also *James Harry Allaway as Trustee for the James and Andy Allaway Superannuation Fund v Joel Daniel Steel as Trustee for the Steel Family Trust* [2014] WADC 83, [156].

[35] *Courtney v Powell* [2012] NSWSC 460.

[36] *Calvo v Sweeney* [2009] NSWSC 719.

Neither the quality of Mr Courtney's consent, nor misconduct on the part of Mrs Powell, was critical to the outcome of this case. Notwithstanding that Mr Courtney had been 90 years old and 'physically, mentally and … emotionally frail'[37] when he made the transfer and that he had not been adequately or independently advised,[38] Ball J did not direct his attention primarily to the adequacy of Mr Courtney's consent.[39] Nor, it is clear, did his Honour consider it to be necessary for the claimants to prove that Mrs Powell had employed improper means of persuasion. Indeed, his Honour's reasoning suggests that, notwithstanding that Mrs Powell had not sought the gift and had been 'a loving and devoted daughter',[40] the transfer would have been set aside had she not actively sought to avoid benefiting from her position.

Ball J maintained a fixed focus on undue influence as a means of preventing the exploitation of influence emanating from a position of trust. His Honour reaffirmed the dictum of Cotton LJ in *Allcard v Skinner* that

> the Court interferes, not on the ground that any wrongful act has in fact been committed by the donee, but on the ground of public policy, and to prevent the relations which existed between the parties and the influence arising therefrom from being abused.[41]

Mrs Powell was obliged, by reason of the fact that she was in a position to influence her father, to prove that she had not taken advantage of her position of trust by using her influence for an improper *purpose*.[42] The case turned on the fact that Mrs Powell had not put her own interests ahead of those of her father, but had used her influence over her father only for *his* benefit. This is evident from the emphasis that his Honour placed on the fact that Mrs Powell had sought to dissuade her father from making the gift and had asked his solicitor to transfer no more than a half interest in the property.[43] Ultimately, the claim of undue influence failed here,[44] because his Honour was satisfied that Mrs Powell had not attempted to exploit her influence for her own advantage.

In another New South Wales case, *Calvo v Sweeney*,[45] undue influence was again presented and applied in such a way as to suggest that it is akin to the fiduciary obligation of loyalty. Indeed, White J observed that similar principles apply.[46] Mr Sweeney, a chartered accountant, was retained to find investors for the Calvos' company, Australian Institute of Music Ltd, which was in serious financial difficulty. Dr and Mrs Calvo claimed inter alia

---

[37] *Courtney v Powell* [2012] NSWSC 460, [48].

[38] The only legal assistance given to Mr Courtney was given by Mrs Powell's solicitor in her presence and did not extend to the risks involved in, or alternatives to, making the gift.

[39] In the absence of adequate independent legal advice, it is arguable that there was scope to question whether the gift was the product of an 'informed exercise of judgment'. cf *Hewitt v Gardner* [2009] NSWSC 1107.

[40] *Courtney v Powell* [2012] NSWSC 460, [20].

[41] ibid [39], quoting *Allcard v Skinner* (1887) 36 Ch D 145, 171 (Cotton LJ).

[42] ibid [48].

[43] ibid [23]–[25].

[44] Although the gift was ultimately reversed by way of a claim under s 59 of the Succession Act 2006 (NSW).

[45] *Calvo v Sweeney* [2009] NSWSC 719.

[46] Citing the dictum of Dixon J in *Johnson v Buttress*, his Honour stated that '[s]imilar principles which apply to a fiduciary also apply where one party has "*an ascendency or influence over* [the] *other*", or a dependence or trust on the other, where it is incumbent on he who takes a substantial gift from the person over whom an ascendency or influence exists to show that it is not the product of the exercise of that influence': ibid [249] (citation omitted). Breach of fiduciary duty was also pleaded and proven in this case. However, his Honour expressly stated that undue influence would have succeeded, even if this had not been a fiduciary relationship: ibid [253].

that Mr Sweeney had, by undue influence over them, procured shares from the company which the Calvos had formerly controlled. White J held that an antecedent relationship of trust and influence had existed by virtue of the plaintiffs' faith in Mr Sweeney to 'do his best for them' and to rescue their business.[47] His Honour went on to uphold their claim, because Mr Sweeney failed to prove that he had not, in procuring the transaction, breached obligations to the Calvos that had arisen from the trusting nature of the relationship.[48]

Although Dr Calvo had suffered a stroke, it was Mr Sweeney's conduct and not impairment to the Calvos' capacity to consent that was the focus of his Honour's attention. Furthermore, although it was shown that Mr Sweeney had taken advantage of existing time constraints to increase the pressure on Dr Calvo, unacceptable means of persuasion were not decisive. What rendered the exercise of influence undue was the fact that Mr Sweeney had employed the trust reposed in him to his own advantage.[49]

Finally, it is noteworthy that the relief granted in this case was also consistent with a fiduciary characterisation. The Calvos had not transferred shares to Mr Sweeney; they had acquiesced to the issue of shares with the consequence that their own shareholding had thereby been diluted.[50] His Honour did not reverse the transaction by declaring the share issue to be invalid on the basis of impaired consent. Instead, White J declared that the new shares were held by Mr Sweeney on trust for the Calvos, because 'equity requires the party who has acquired property as the result of the exercise of undue influence to account for it and that account is achieved by declaring that the shares are held on constructive trust'.[51] This resembles the remedial response to an acquisition of property in breach of fiduciary duty.

Concern for Vitiated Consent is Entrenched as Integral to Undue Influence

It is evident that a vitiated consent model now sits alongside the fiduciary model of undue influence in Australia. Recent cases demonstrate that the vitiated consent model is thriving, especially where (as is commonly the case) undue influence is pleaded alongside unconscionable dealing.[52] Judgments in at least 18 of the undue influence cases decided in the last five years affirmed the vitiated consent model—citing either (or both) of the dicta from *Amadio*[53] and/or Sir Anthony Mason's extra-curial endorsement of Birks and Chin's

---

[47] ibid [251].

[48] ibid [243]–[246] and [253].

[49] ibid [251].

[50] White J said that this was tantamount to a voluntary transfer: ibid [254].

[51] ibid [254].

[52] In all except two of the cases cited below at nn 53, 54 and 55, both undue influence and unconscionable dealing were pleaded. Moreover in almost every instance the outcome was the same for both doctrines, ie either both undue influence and unconscionable dealing succeeded or both failed.

[53] In the past five years, the dictum of Deane J was cited with approval in at least 12 undue influence cases— albeit, sometimes in the course of distinguishing the doctrine of unconscionable dealing. See: *Johnson v Johnson* [2009] NSWSC 503, [97]; *Hewitt v Gardner* [2009] NSWSC 1107, [108]; *Darmanin v Cowan* [2010] NSWSC 1118, [319]; *Varma v Varma* [2010] NSWSC 786, (2010) 6 ASTLR 153, [535]; *Pascot v Pascot* [2011] FamCA 945, [259] and [266]; *Stone v Registrar of Titles* [2012] WASC 21, [197]; *Anderson v McPherson [No 2]* [2012] WASC 19, (2012) 8 ASTLR 321, [242]; *Langford v Reddy* [2012] NSWSC 289, [130], [137]; *Commercial Base P/L v Watson* [2013] VSC 334, [37]; *Anderson v Anderson* [2013] QSC 8, [65]; *Hay v Hay* [2014] FCCA 775, [131]; and *Daunt v Daunt* [2015] VSCA 56, [63]. The dictum to the same effect by Mason J in that case was cited with approval in at least six cases. See *Tillett v Varnell* [2009] NSWSC 1040, [49]; *Darmanin v Cowan* [2010] NSWSC 1118, [318];

thesis.[54] More importantly, in many of these cases, the claim of undue influence was decided on the basis of whether the benefactor had been in a position to bring her mind to bear on the transaction in question.[55]

This approach is exemplified by *Hewitt v Gardner*.[56] Mrs Gardner had lived with her mother, Mrs Lipscombe, in the latter's home for 20 years before Mrs Lipscombe's death. During the last 10 of these years, Mrs Gardner had been her mother's primary carer and had held her power of attorney. Mrs Gardner formed the view that her siblings planned to evict her from the house when Mrs Lipscombe died and she communicated this to her mother. Two years before she died Mrs Lipscombe transferred the house (her only asset) to Mrs Gardner for consideration of one dollar. After Mrs Lipscombe's death, her other children sought to have the transfer set aside.

Even though the facts lent themselves to a fiduciary analysis, none was employed here. It was a 'relationship of dependence', rather than a 'relationship of influence', which gave rise to the presumption of undue influence in this case.[57] Furthermore, in ascertaining whether such a relationship existed, Ward J made no reference to the fact that Mrs Gardner held her mother's power of attorney and had acted as her agent in banking and other matters. Instead, her Honour took a claimant-focused approach consistent with the vitiated consent model advocated by Birks and Chin. In deciding whether a presumption of undue influence arose, her Honour concentrated on Mrs Lipscombe and her state of dependency, rather than looking for ascendancy on the part of Mrs Gardner or even for 'a relationship of trust and confidence'. She noted that Mrs Lipscombe had been 'frail, in a deteriorating condition, elderly and had been in a position of dependence and reliance on Mrs Gardner for some years'.[58] No assessment was made of Mrs Gardner's position relative to her mother, as might have been expected pursuant to *Union Fidelity Trustee Co of Australia Ltd v Gibson*.[59] Her Honour did not consider whether Mrs Gardner had been in sound physical and mental health, nor whether her strength of personality and character (relative to that of her mother) were such as to arm her with power over her mother. Concentrating exclusively on

---

Brown v NSW Trustee & Guardian [2011] NSWSC 1203 [35]; *Mango Media Pty Ltd v Comitogianni* [2011] NSWSC 152, [236]; *Pascot v Pascot* [2011] FamCA 945, [266]; and *National Australia Bank Ltd v Wehbeh* [2014] VSC 431, [43] (Macaulay J).

[54] Nine judgments included within their restatement of the applicable legal principles Sir Anthony's declaration that 'it is the ... impairment of the judgment of the weaker party that is the critical element in the grant of relief on the ground of undue influence'. See above n 27. See *Brown v Barkley Brown* [2009] NSWSC 76, [142]; *Hewitt v Gardner* [2009] NSWSC 1107, [61]; *Darmanin v Cowan* [2010] NSWSC 1118, [323]; *Varma v Varma* [2010] NSWSC 786, (2010) 6 ASTLR 153, [532]; *A v N* [2012] NSWSC 354, [475]; *Langford v Reddy* [2012] NSWSC 289, [131]; and *Anderson v Anderson* [2013] QSC 8, [65]. See also *Anderson v McPherson [No 2]* [2012] WASC 19, (2012) 8 ASTLR 321, [242]; *Birtwell v Sands* [2012] QSC 396, [127] which cite the passage of *Bridgewater v Leahy* [1998] 194 CLR 457, 478 [75] (Gaudron, Gummow and Kirby JJ) in which Sir Anthony's words were reiterated.

[55] See the following cases, in which the claim of undue influence was upheld: *Johnson v Johnson* [2009] NSWSC 503, [104]; *Pascot v Pascot* [2011] FamCA 945, [255]. And see the following cases, in which the claim of undue influence was rejected: *Christodoulou v Christodoulou* [2009] VSC 583, [105]–[110]; *Varma v Varma* [2010] NSWSC 786, [17](vii) and [187]; *Langford v Reddy* [2012] NSWSC 289, [169]–[170]; *Anderson v McPherson [No 2]* [2012] WASC 19, [252]; *Stone v Registrar of Titles* [2012] WASC 21, [213]–[214]; *White v Wills* [2014] NSWSC 1160, [513]–[514]; and *Thorn v Boyd* [2014] NSWSC 1159, [127].

[56] *Hewitt v Gardner* [2009] NSWSC 1107.
[57] ibid [70].
[58] ibid [68].
[59] *Union Fidelity Trustee Co of Aust Ltd v Gibson* [1971] VR 573, 577 (Gillard J).

the benefactor's position, her Honour concluded that Mrs Lipscombe had been in a 'clear position of dependency'.[60]

It is evident that Ward J did not equate undue influence with coercive or even exploitative behaviour. The facts lent themselves to a finding that Mrs Gardner had used improper means of persuasion to procure the gift. It was arguable that Mrs Gardner had placed pressure on Mrs Lipscombe by sharing her conviction that her siblings were 'out to get her'. Indeed, this conduct was deemed to be significant, but only insofar as it informed her Honour's assessment as to whether the transaction was the product of Mrs Lipscombe's fully informed mind.[61] It is clear from her Honour's reasoning that the transfer was not set aside, because Mrs Gardner's actions constituted a breach of any duty owed to her mother or because this behaviour was deemed to be unconscionable in view of her position of trust. In deciding whether the presumption of undue influence had been rebutted, her Honour's focus remained fixed on Mrs Lipscombe and the quality of her consent to the transfer.[62] She formed the view that Mrs Lipscombe had made a hasty and ill-informed decision motivated by a desire to protect her daughter from a perceived threat of homelessness. While Mrs Lipscombe's difficulty in making a free and informed exercise of judgment was exacerbated by Mrs Gardner's actions, ultimately equitable relief was granted because Ward J was not satisfied that the transfer was 'the product of a fully informed mind' on Mrs Lipscombe's part.[63]

Beyond Vitiated Consent: The Movement Towards a 'Consent Overborne' Model

On a vitiated consent model, undue influence responds to impaired consent; it does not require proof that the benefactor's consent was wholly ineffective.[64] So it is interesting to note that recent Australian decisions evince a strong movement towards a conception of undue influence which posits that restitution is to be made on the basis that the benefactor's will was 'overborne'. These judgments use language of compulsion reminiscent of that which had been associated with the legal doctrine of duress[65] and which is still employed in relation to the doctrine of undue influence used in the context of probate.[66] It is not asserted that these cases equate equitable undue influence with common law duress or probate undue

---

[60] *Hewitt v Gardner* [2009] NSWSC 1107, [70].

[61] ibid [92].

[62] ibid [91]–[97].

[63] ibid [91]. Note that her Honour did not require the claimant to prove that Mrs Lipscombe's will had been overborne.

[64] eg, Birks and Chin, above n 9, 87–88 argue that the transaction is voidable, because the benefactor's autonomy was 'seriously impaired'. Some recent Australian decisions took an approach that is consistent with this view. See, eg, *Hewitt v Gardner* [2009] NSWSC 1107, [70] and [94] (Ward J) and *Stone v Registrar of Titles* [2012] WASC 21, [212] (Simmonds J).

[65] In cases such as *Occidental Worldwide Investment Corp v Skibs A/S Avanti, The Siboen and the Sibotre* [1976] 1 Lloyds Rep 293, 336 (Kerr LJ); *Universal Tankships of Monrovia v International Transport Workers Federation* [1983] 1 AC 366, 400 (Lord Scarman). Note that the 'will overborne' rationale is generally considered to have been rejected even in the context of duress. See *Crescendo Management Pty Ltd v Westpac Banking Corp* (1988) 19 NSWLR 40, 45 (McHugh JA).

[66] See *Hall v Hall* [1868] LR 1 P & D 481, 482 (Sir JP Wilde); *Wingrove v Wingrove* (1885) 11 PD 81, 82 (Hannen P); *Boyse v Rossborough* (1857) 6 HLC 2, (1857) 3 PD 151; *Buckley v Maddocks* (1891) 12 LR (NSW) Eq 277, 282 (Stephen J); *Winter v Crichton* (1991) 23 NSWLR 116, 121–22 and more recently *Trustee for the Salvation Army (NSW) Property Trust v Becker* [2007] NSWCA 136, [62]–[64] (Ipp JA, with whom Mason P and McColl JA agreed) and *White v Wills* [2014] NSWSC 1160, [71] (Sackar J).

influence. However, they do suggest an understanding of undue influence that is similar to those doctrines in that it is directed at the quality of the claimant's consent, but requires proof of a very high degree of impairment in order to render the transaction voidable.

On this approach, courts treat the presumption of undue influence as contingent upon the existence of a relationship in the nature of 'dominion' or 'dominance' and will hold that the presumption has been rebutted upon proof of a very little independence on the part of the benefactor. Interestingly, where *Johnson v Buttress* has been cited in recent cases, there has been a defection from the 'position of trust and confidence' formula laid out by Dixon J in favour of the notion of 'dominion' emphasised by Latham CJ. Thirteen recent Australian undue influence cases stipulated that the benefactor was required to prove the existence of 'dominion' or 'dominance' in order to access the benefit of the presumption.[67]

Furthermore, recent cases indicate that there has been a resurgence of the view that restitution for undue influence is offered on the basis that the benefactor's will was overborne by the defendant's influence.[68] For instance, in *Anderson v McPherson*[69] Edelman J cited, apparently with approval, the famous dictum in *Tufton v Sperni*, which stated that in order to prove undue influence a claimant must demonstrate that that she had been in a position 'in which it could fairly be said that … [her] mind was in effect a mere channel through which the will of the defendant operated'.[70] On this reasoning, it is not enough to have misused a power to affect the benefactor's consent or that the benefactor's consent was thereby 'skewed'. It assumes that the transaction which is reversible for undue influence was not truly the product of the benefactor's consent at all. It follows that, where an invalidating presumption arises, it will be rebutted by the slightest proof of choice by the benefactor. It is it is beyond the scope of this paper to speculate as to why judges in the twenty-first century should be attracted to expressions that hark back to duress and undue influence cases decided at a time when the will theory of contract and the doctrine of freedom of contract were at the height of their popularity.[71] However, it may be observed that, should this trend continue, it is likely that access to relief on the basis of undue influence will contract.

---

[67] See *Brown v Barkley Brown* [2009] NSWSC 76, [114] (Ward J); *Darmanin v Cowan* [2010] NSWSC 1118, [320] and [322] (Ward J); *Tulloch v Braybon (No 2)* [2010] NSWSC 650, [43] (Brereton J); *Varma v Varma* [2010] NSWSC 786, [533] (Ward J); *A v N* [2012] NSWSC 354, [476] (Ward J); *Anderson v McPherson [No 2]* [2012] WASC 19, (2012) 8 ASTLR 321, [247] (Edelman J); *Anderson v Anderson* [2013] QSC 8, [54] (Dalton J); *White v Wills* [2014] NSWSC 1160, [85] (Sackar J); and *Thorn v Boyd* [2014] NSWSC 1159, [124] (Robb J). See also: *Goldie v Getley [No 3]* [2011] WASC 132, [4], [65], [140], [145] (Simmonds J) and *Mango Media Pty Ltd v Comitogianni* [2011] NSWSC 152, [244] (Davies J); *Brown v NSW Trustee & Guardian* [2011] NSWSC 1203, [46] and [47]; and *McIvor v Westpac Banking Corporation* [2012] QSC 404, [15], [18], [25], [35], [37] and [115] (Applegarth J), in which 'dominion' (rather that trust and confidence) is presented as the requisite source of influence.

[68] Eight recent Australian cases have made reference to a 'will overborne' requirement: *Tillett v Varnell* [2009] NSWSC 1040, [49] (Brereton J); *Anthony v Vaclav* [2009] VSC 357, [126] (Vickery J); *Tulloch v Braybon (No 2)* [2010] NSWSC 650, [76], [83] and [84] (Brereton J); *Brown v NSW Trustee & Guardian* [2011] NSWSC 1203, [35]; *Mango Media Pty Ltd v Comitogianni* [2011] NSWSC 152, [247] (Davies J); *Langford v Reddy* [2012] NSWSC 289, [168] (Sackar J); *McIvor v Westpac Banking Corporation* [2012] QSC 404, [85] and [118] (Applegarth J); and *Anderson v McPherson [No 2]* [2012] WASC 19, (2012) 8 ASTLR 321.

[69] *Anderson v McPherson [No 2]* [2012] WASC 19, (2012) 8 ASTLR 321, [248]. His Honour went on to reject the claim of undue influence, because the claimant was unable to prove that the defendant had had a 'dominance and ascendancy over her will': ibid [247] and [250]–[252].

[70] *Tufton v Sperni* [1952] 2 TLR 516, 530 and 532 (Jenkins LJ), 532 (Morris LJ). Approved in *Bank of Credit & Commerce International SA v Aboody* [1990] 1 QB 923, 969 (Slade, Balcombe and Woolf LJJ).

[71] See O Black, *Agreements: A Philosophical and Legal Study* (Cambridge, Cambridge University Press, 2012) 220–21, citing P Atiyah, *The Rise and Fall of Freedom of Contract* (Oxford, Oxford University Press, 1979) 212 and

No Move to a Defendant-sided Model

Within the context of the vitiated consent model, raising the threshold of impairment that must be proven will tend to give the doctrine a more defendant-sided appearance. Requiring the claimant to prove 'subjection' or that the benefactor's will had been overborne is likely to inhibit the application of the doctrine in 'innocent defendant' cases. It may be conjectured that seldom will the will of a legally competent person be overborne by an acceptable amount of pressure or method of persuasion. Therefore, although a 'will overborne' version of the vitiated consent model is structurally plaintiff-sided, it might have the effect of restricting the application of the doctrine to circumstances where the defendant has behaved reprehensibly.

That said, even where the influential party has used unacceptable means of persuasion, Australian courts tend to look past the defendant's conduct to focus on its effect on the quality of the benefactor's consent. There is no momentum in Australia towards a wholly defendant-sided model of undue influence, such as that described in *Etridge*.[72] Moreover, from a doctrinal perspective, there is probably no place in Australia for a doctrine of undue influence which comprises the breach of an equitable duty not to employ improper means of persuasion, as this ground is already adequately covered by the doctrine of unconscionable dealing.

England

Complying with Etridge

If Australian judges are spoilt for choice, their English brethren are evidently in no doubt about their obligation to apply the law laid down in *Etridge*.[73] Judges dutifully demonstrate that they have applied Lord Nicholls' formulation to the letter—typically by quoting verbatim from, or very closely paraphrasing and assiduously referencing, Lord Nicholls' speech. As a result, after more than a decade, the *Etridge* model remains intact in England. Yet recent cases reveal that there is trouble beneath the surface. It is evident that the conception of undue influence as grounded in vitiated consent has not been eradicated and, furthermore, that an attachment to the fiduciary notion of undue influence lingers.

Concern for the Quality of Consent Endures

Etridge provides a template for undue influence that bypasses the question of consent entirely and permits a transaction to be set aside, notwithstanding the fact of consent, on the basis that the consent was unfairly obtained.[74] However, recent cases confirm that concern for consent is seeping into the *Etridge* formula. For example, in *Evans v Lloyd*, even

---

S Whittaker, 'Introductory' in HG Beale (ed), *Chitty on Contracts*, 30th edn (London, Sweet & Maxwell, 2008) vol 1 [1–010].

[72] Indeed, very few recent Australian cases refer to modern English case law on undue influence.

[73] Note the caution issued by Lord Hobhouse against treating Lord Nicholls' guidance with respect to the role of the burden of proof, the steps to be taken by lenders who have been put on inquiry and the duties of solicitors 'as optional, to be watered down when it proves inconvenient': [2001] UKHL 44, [2002] 2 AC 773, [100].

[74] See above n 31.

in the course of applying *Etridge*, Judge Keyser QC declared that '[t]he concern of the doctrine of undue influence is directed to the question of independence of will'.[75]

More significantly, in *Daniel v Drew*[76] the Court of Appeal stated that the critical question in every case of undue influence is whether the influence has invaded the free volition of the donor to withstand the influence. Ward LJ, with whom Buxton and Wilson LJJ agreed, put it thus:

> The donor may be led but she must not be driven and her will must be the offspring of her own volition, not a record of someone else's. There is no undue influence unless the donor if she were free and informed could say 'This is not my wish but I must do it'.[77]

Moreover, this reasoning evidently strikes a chord with judges, because it is frequently cited with approval and applied.[78]

There are four points at which this concern about the quality of consent has been apparent: (1) as the basis of 'proven' undue influence; and in the context of inferred undue influence, in ascertaining whether: (2) an antecedent relationship of trust and confidence exists; (3) the transaction calls for explanation;[79] and (4) an inference of abuse of influence can be refuted. It is submitted that the multiplicity of contexts in which this concern is being manifested indicates the strain of maintaining a wholly defendant-sided model.

(1) Proven Abuse of Influence

The Court of Appeal in *Daniel v Drew* made it clear that all instances of undue influence, including actual undue influence, are grounded in vitiated consent. Ward LJ described actual undue influence as a twisting of the benefactor's mind, reasoning that actual undue influence requires proof that the influential party brought this about by her own actions.[80] On this view, the impropriety of the influential party's behaviour—ie whether it amounts to abuse of influence—is assessed on the basis of its impact on the benefactor's state of mind.

(2) Inferred Abuse of Influence—An Antecedent Relationship of Trust and Confidence

Lord Nicholls held in *Etridge* that, where a benefactor has reposed 'trust and confidence' in the influential party in the management of the benefactor's financial affairs, the court will draw an inference of abuse of influence in relation to any transaction that 'calls for

---

[75] [2013] EWHC 1725 (Ch), [58] (Judge Keyser QC).

[76] [2005] EWCA Civ 507.

[77] ibid [36]. Note the similarity of this language to that used in cases pertaining to probate undue influence, which is certainly grounded in vitiated consent. See the authorities noted in n 66 above, especially *Wingrove v Wingrove* (1885) 11 PD 81, 82 (Hannen P).

[78] *Hewett v First Plus Financial Group Plc* ('*Hewett*') [2010] EWCA Civ 312, [20] (Briggs J with whom Leveson and Jacob LJJ agreed); *Howard v Howard-Lawson* [2012] EWHC 3258 (Ch), [85] (Norris J); *Evans v Lloyd* [2013] EWHC 1725 (Ch), [39] (Judge Keyser QC); *Hart v Burbidge* [2013] EWHC 1628 (Ch) (Sir William Blackburne J) [39]; and *Thompson v Foy* [2009] EWHC 1076, [101] (Lewison J) which was in turn cited with approval in *Gorjat v Gorjat* [2010] EWHC 1537, [142] (Sarah Asplin QC).

[79] So that, where the parties were in a relationship of trust and confidence, it raises an inference that the influence was abused to procure the transaction: *Etridge* [2001] UKHL 44, [2002] 2 AC 773, [14] (Lord Nicholls).

[80] [2005] EWCA Civ 507, [31]. Ward LJ went on to say that presumed undue influence is concerned with 'what has not been done namely ensuring that independent advice is available to the donor.'

explanation'.[81] His Lordship did not explain what sort of 'trust and confidence' is required to raise the inference. Remarks made in some recent cases indicate that judges tend to look for an antecedent relationship that suggests a threat to the benefactor's free volition.

For instance, in *Evans v Lloyd*, notwithstanding that the parties were extremely close and that the benefactor, a 70-year-old man, depended on the defendants for his accommodation, employment, food and transport, the relationship between them did not give rise to an inference of abuse of influence. Judge Keyser QC held that the claimants had not established dependence 'in the relevant sense', because there had been no threat to Mr Evans' ability to exercise 'independence of will'.[82] Furthermore, his Honour looked primarily at the benefactor and placed importance on the fact that he had been strong-willed and an independent thinker. Thus, the first prerequisite for an inference of abuse of influence—ie an antecedent relationship of trust and confidence—was not met, because his Honour was satisfied that there had been no threat to the benefactor's independence of will. If this is so, it is consistent with the dictum in *Daniel v Drew*, but not with *Etridge*.[83]

(3) Inferred Abuse of Influence—A Transaction Calling for Explanation

On Lord Nicholls' reasoning, an inference of undue influence pertains to the conduct of the influential party and not to the benefactor's state of mind. In order to provide the basis for an inference of this nature, the explanation that is called for should also pertain to the conduct of the influential party. A transaction that calls for an explanation as to the benefactor's state of mind should not be used to justify an inference about the influential party's conduct. Put simply, the question prompted must be: 'What did she (the influential party) do to secure this?' and *not* 'What was she (the benefactor) thinking?' In assessing whether the nature of the transaction in the context of the parties' relationship is such as to prompt that question, the focus ought to be on those aspects of the transaction itself which might generate suspicion as to how it was procured. Lord Nicholls and Lord Scott offered some suggestions in *Etridge*. A transaction will call for explanation, if it is: immoderate;[84] irrational;[85] not readily explicable by the relationship of the parties;[86] or '*so large* as not to be reasonably accounted for on the ground of friendship, relationship, charity, or other ordinary motives on which ordinary men act'.[87] However, it is submitted that aspects of the transaction which go to its significance to the individual benefactor, so as to raise questions as to her motivation or state of mind at the time, do not serve this purpose.

Yet the cases reveal a tendency to use this stage of the inquiry to gauge the likelihood that the benefactor freely consented to the transaction. Frequently, judges direct their attention to those features of the transaction which shed light on its significance to the benefactor.

---

[81] [2001] UKHL 44, [2002] 2 AC 773, [14].

[82] [2013] EWHC 1725 (Ch), [58].

[83] According to Lord Nicholls, it is not the quality of the benefactor's consent itself, but only the 'means used' to procure it, to which equity objects. Where unacceptable means are used, then the consent 'ought not fairly to be treated as the expression of a person's free will': *Royal Bank of Scotland Pty Ltd v Etridge (No 2)* [2001] UKHL 44, [2002] 2 AC 773, [7].

[84] ibid [22] (Lord Nicholls), citing *Bank of Montreal v Stuart* [1911] AC 120, 137 (Lord Macnaghten) and, by implication, [156] (Lord Scott).

[85] ibid [22] (Lord Nicholls), citing *Bank of Montreal v Stuart* [1911] AC 120, 137 (Lord Macnaghten).

[86] ibid [21] (Lord Nicholls).

[87] ibid [22] (Lord Nicholls) (emphasis added), citing *Allcard v Skinner* (1887) 36 Ch D 145, 185 (Lindley LJ). See also ibid [13] (Lord Nicholls) and [220] (Lord Scott).

The characteristics and circumstances of the individual benefactor and her motivation for entering into the transaction are commonly placed at the centre of the inquiry. This draws attention away from the influential party's method of persuasion and lends itself to a slide into conjecture about quality of the benefactor's consent.

In *Hackett v Crown Prosecution Service*[88] the transfer by an elderly and disabled person of her 'sole major asset' and source of income should have been sufficient to justify a finding that this was a transaction which called for explanation. Silber J looked further, however, and also took into account the fact that, in making the gift, Mrs Hackett had favoured one of her three sons to the exclusion of the others.[89] Similarly, in *Evans v Lloyd*[90] Judge Keyser QC found that an ostensibly disadvantageous voluntary transfer by an elderly man of his only property to his employers did *not* call for explanation in light of the singular character of the donor. His Honour determined that it was not surprising that Mr Evans, who was 'a farmer through and through' and who had 'no interest in … property or … wealth',[91] might make such a substantial gift of farmland to the defendants, because they too were farmers and would be able to look after the land.[92]

In each of those instances, the circumstances that the court took into account in deciding whether or not the transaction 'called for explanation' included matters that had little to do with the nature of the transaction per se or with the motives of 'ordinary people'. Included within the ambit of analysis were facts better suited to laying the evidentiary groundwork for an inference as to the adequacy of the benefactor's consent, rather than to an inference that the influential party had behaved unfairly or had preferred her own interests. The tendency to be drawn to consider circumstances of this nature suggests an inquiry that is, at least to some extent, directed at the quality of the benefactor's consent.

Proponents of a purely defendant-sided approach might argue that such considerations go to context, citing *Turkey v Adawh*.[93] In applying the law as laid down in *Etridge*, Buxton LJ insisted that the transaction had to be considered in context.[94] However, it should be noted that, later in that case, Chadwick LJ stated that the claimant was obliged to produce 'facts … which persuade the court that the transaction in question is of such a nature that a person in the position of … [the claimant], acting in the way that such a person might ordinarily be expected to act, would not have entered into the transaction, unless *his or her will was overborne*'.[95] Moreover, this was followed by *Smith v Cooper*, in which Lloyd LJ asserted that 'a transaction calling for explanation' was 'short hand for the formula in *Allcard v Skinner*', ie that 'the transaction must be one which is "not to be reasonably accounted for on the grounds of friendship, relationship, charity or other ordinary motives on which ordinary men act"'.[96] This has been interpreted as requiring the claimant to prove 'a transaction arising out of the relationship that calls for evidence of the free exercise of the will of the

---

[88] *Hackett v Crown Prosecution Service* [2011] EWHC 1170.
[89] ibid [59].
[90] *Evans v Lloyd* [2013] EWHC 1725 (Ch).
[91] ibid [64] and [65].
[92] ibid [17].
[93] *Turkey v Adawh* [2005] EWCA Civ 382, [2005] All ER 131.
[94] ibid [32].
[95] ibid [39] (emphasis added).
[96] *Smith v Cooper* [2010] EWCA Civ 722, [58]–[60] (Lloyd LJ with whom Wilson and Jacob LJJ agreed), citing *Allcard v Skinner* (1887) 36 Ch D 145, 185 (Lindley LJ).

claimant as a result of full, free and informed thought'.[97] In other words, the transaction must be such as to raise questions primarily about the benefactor's motivation for transacting, and only secondarily as to the defendant's conduct in affecting that motivation. In this way, concern for consent has been built into the prerequisites for an inference of abuse of influence.

(4) Disproving an Inference of Abuse of Influence

Finally, where an inference would otherwise be drawn that the influential party had procured the transaction by the misuse of her influence, the defendant must 'produce evidence to counter the inference which otherwise should be drawn'.[98] This ought to entail the presentation of such evidence of the behaviour of the influential party leading up to the transaction as will prove that there was no misuse of influence on her part. Where the nature of the influence is such that it may be wielded without specific overt acts of persuasion, it may be necessary to refute an inference of exploitation with evidence that speaks to the absence of constraint *emanating from the influential party* upon the benefactor's free will. Following the reasoning in *Etridge*, it is the exploitation of influence that must be measured—albeit sometimes by reference to its impact on the benefactor's capacity to consent—not the diminution of consent itself.[99]

Yet courts continue to frame this task in terms that focus on the benefactor. For example, *Hackett* turned on the fact that Silber J was satisfied that Mrs Hackett's decision to transfer the property to her son was 'based upon "full, free and informed thought"'.[100] Similarly, in *Evans v Lloyd* Judge Keyser QC said that the question is 'whether the gift, though not adequately explained by ordinary motives, was the product of an independent will'.[101] In *Hart v Burbidge*[102] Sir William Blackburne upheld a claim of undue influence in circumstances where there was no suggestion that pressure had been applied or unacceptable methods of persuasion had been used, because 'at the end of the day' he was 'left … with a real concern as to whether … [the benefactor] really understood' the transaction.[103] This speaks to the difficulty of eradicating from consideration concerns about the quality of the benefactor's consent and of maintaining an exclusively defendant-focused model.

Fiduciary Traits Still Discernible

The *Etridge* formulation of undue influence differs significantly from the fiduciary model. It is primarily transactional, rather than relational. It is directed at acts of coercion and exploitation—neither of which requires the existence of a relationship between the parties. According to *Etridge*, the existence of a relationship of trust and confidence has no special significance beyond providing justification, in certain circumstances, for an inference that

---

[97] *Hackett v Crown Prosecution Service* [2011] EWHC 1170, [53] (Silber J).
[98] *Royal Bank of Scotland Pty Ltd v Etridge (No 2)* [2001] UKHL 44, [2002] 2 AC 773, [14] (Lord Nicholls).
[99] The nature of this task is well described by Buxton LJ in *Turkey v Adawh* [2005] EWCA Civ 382, [2005] All ER 131, [15]. His Lordship there states that 'the burden then shifts to the claimant to show that in fact, and despite the terms and nature of the agreement, he did not in truth abuse the position that he held'.
[100] *Hackett v Crown Prosecution Service* [2011] EWHC 1170, [81].
[101] *Evans v Lloyd* [2013] EWHC 1725(Ch), [71].
[102] *Hart v Burbidge* [2013] EWHC 1628 (Ch).
[103] ibid [129].

the influence arising from it has been abused.[104] It does not give rise to a 'fiduciary-like' duty.[105] Indeed, the inference itself constitutes no more than recognition that the influence arising from such relationships is readily exploited and that such exploitation can be achieved without resort to overt acts of persuasion.[106] Therefore, according to *Etridge*, relief is premised on the fact that influence has been abused.[107] Whether that abuse of influence is proven or inferred, the claimant is obliged to provide some factual basis for a finding that improper means of persuasion were actually used. Abuse is not imputed to serve public policy objectives[108] and there is no scope for good faith breach.[109]

However, several English cases since *Etridge* have used reasoning that is evocative of a fiduciary principle. The Court of Appeal has twice declared that the presumption of undue influence arises from the trust and confidence of the parties' relationship, and that the court intervenes on the basis of public policy, so that a transaction may be set aside notwithstanding that the influential party did not behave in a reprehensible manner.[110] Furthermore, in several recent cases relief was granted notwithstanding the absence of any factual basis for a finding that improper means of persuasion were used. These cases suggest support for the view that, in the context of undue influence, a position of trust and confidence carries with it a duty to ensure that the benefactor is emancipated from that influence. Such a duty might be likened to a fiduciary duty in that the influential party is required to look to the benefactor's best interests and may be liable even though she acted in good faith.

For instance, in *Smith v Cooper*[111] a claim made by a woman of diminished mental capacity to set aside two transactions, by which she had transferred considerable benefit to her de facto spouse, was upheld. Miss Cooper had not been reluctant to enter into this arrangement—indeed she had persisted with it in the face of warnings from her father. However, she had not been independently advised. In upholding the appeal, Lloyd LJ (with whom Wilson and Jacob LJJ agreed) reasoned that, even if Miss Cooper had understood the effect of the transactions and had reached a conclusion in favour of them as a result of her own thought processes, once the presumption had been raised, the defendant was obliged to prove that it resulted from her free unconstrained will. In the absence of independent

---

[104] *Royal Bank of Scotland Pty Ltd v Etridge (No 2)* [2001] UKHL 44, [2002] 2 AC 773, [9] and [14] (Lord Nicholls), [93] (Lord Clyde), [104] (Lord Hobhouse) and [153]–[154] (Lord Scott). The relevant circumstances are those in which the transaction in question 'calls for explanation'.

[105] cf ibid [104] (Lord Hobhouse).

[106] ibid [9] (Lord Nicholls).

[107] ibid [6]–[7] and [13] (Lord Nicholls), [93] (Lord Clyde), [103]–[104] (Lord Hobhouse).

[108] The 'protective' operation of the doctrine is restricted to the presumption of influence emanating from trust and confidence, which arises only in relation to certain types of relationship, eg parent–child, solicitor–client and doctor–patient. See *Etridge*, ibid [18] (Lord Nicholls) and [158] (Lord Scott). cf *Hammond v Osborn* [2002] EWCA 885, [60]–[61] (Ward LJ); *Niersmans v Pesticcio* [2004] EWCA Civ 372, [20] (Mummery LJ, with whom Pill and Jacob LJJ agreed).

[109] It is acknowledged that this assertion runs counter to the later decisions of the Court of Appeal in *Hammond v Osborn* [2002] EWCA 885 and *Niersmans v Pesticcio* [2004] EWCA Civ 372. However, it is submitted that these cases cannot be reconciled with the statements made by the House of Lords that, at least in those cases in which actual undue influence or a relationship of trust and confidence must be proven (ie outside the established categories), liability is premised on a finding (whether proven or inferred) that the influential party did in fact abuse or exploit her influence. *Royal Bank of Scotland Pty Ltd v Etridge (No 2)* [2001] UKHL 44, [2002] 2 AC 773 [16] (Lord Nicholls), [93] (Lord Clyde); [104] (Lord Hobhouse), [158] (Lord Scott).

[110] *Hammond v Osborn* [2002] EWCA 885, [60]–[61] (Ward LJ) and [32] (Sir Martin Nourse LJ) and *Niersmans v Pesticcio* [2004] EWCA Civ 372, [20] (Mummery LJ, with whom Pill and Jacob LJJ agreed).

[111] *Smith v Cooper* [2010] EWCA Civ 722.

legal advice, there was no evidence to demonstrate that Miss Cooper had made these decisions 'independent of the influence that Mr Smith *was able* to exercise over her'.[112] In effect, Mr Smith's position of ascendancy placed him under a duty to ensure that Miss Cooper was properly advised and allocated to him the risk that there might be doubts about what influenced her decision to transact.

The decision in *Hart v Burbidge* demonstrates a similar approach.[113] Susan Burbidge and her mother, Phyllis Hart, had been very close. Susan was a loving and supportive daughter. As a consequence, theirs was a relationship of 'trust and confidence, reliance and dependence'.[114] There was no evidence that Susan had done anything to coerce Phyllis. Nevertheless, the transactions in question were set aside, because Susan could not prove that she had discharged a duty which attended her position as her mother's 'mainstay'. Sir William Blackburne stated that:

> At the end of the day it is for Susan to persuade me that her mother was acting fully independently of this undue influence when she entered into the impugned transactions. I am not persuaded that she was. I am not willing to give Susan the benefit of any doubts.[115]

This resembles the fiduciary reasoning seen in *Johnson v Buttress* and *Inche Noriah v Shaik Allie Bin Omar*.[116] It is arguable that what truly lies behind the decisions in *Smith v Cooper* and *Hart v Burbidge* is not any real apprehension of misconduct with respect to the means persuasion, but the failure by an influential party to discharge a duty, acquired by virtue of her position of trust, to ensure that the benefactor had been properly advised or otherwise emancipated.[117]

Lastly, in the interesting case of *Hewett v First Plus Financial Group plc*[118] ('*Hewett*') the Court of Appeal upheld a claim of undue influence based on the breach of a fiduciary-like duty of disclosure. Finding himself in financial difficulty, primarily because he was unable to meet credit card repayments, Mr Hewett approached his wife to co-sign a mortgage over her share of the matrimonial home to secure his personal debts. Although she was reluctant to sign and thereby put the family home at risk, she complied because she believed that the mortgage was 'the only way of keeping the house'.[119] No allegation of coercion or pressure was levelled against Mr Hewett. Nor was this a case of morbid dependency—Mrs Hewett was able to make financial decisions and was cognizant of the risks entailed in executing the mortgage.[120] Yet, the mortgagee was prevented from enforcing the mortgage as against

---

[112] ibid [71] (emphasis added).

[113] *Hart v Burbidge* [2013] EWHC 1628 (Ch).

[114] ibid [111].

[115] ibid [132].

[116] *Inche Noriah v Shaik Allie Bin Omar* [1929] AC 127.

[117] That is not to say that Susan had in no way behaved reprehensibly. Both Sir William Blackburne and the Court of Appeal considered it to be significant that she had written a misleading letter to Phyllis' solicitors, probably for the purpose of preventing them from advising Phyllis. See *Hart v Burbidge* [2013] EWHC 1628 [101] and [2014] EWCA Civ 992 [23] and [57] (Vos LJ with whom Richards and Black LJJ agreed). However, it is submitted that such misconduct more closely resembles a breach of duty to ensure that Phyllis was properly advised than an unacceptable form of persuasion.

[118] *Hewett v First Plus Financial Group plc* [2010] EWCA Civ 312.

[119] ibid [14].

[120] ibid [10].

her, on the basis that it had been fixed with constructive notice of undue influence by Mr Hewett.

The abuse of influence in this case was Mr Hewett's failure to meet an obligation of candour,[121] which arose because Mrs Hewett had reposed trust and confidence in him.[122] At the time that she signed the mortgage, Mrs Hewett believed that she had a happy and stable marriage. Unbeknown to her, Mr Hewett had been having an affair and had already decided to leave the marriage. Briggs J (with whom Leveson and Jacob LJJ agreed) made it clear that the equitable wrong committed by Mr Hewett, and of which the mortgagee was deemed to have had constructive notice, consisted of an 'abuse of confidence' by virtue of the 'breach of his duty of fairness and candour' in failing to disclose his decision to leave the marriage.[123] Insofar as undue influence is presented (at least in this instance) as the breach of an obligation of candour arising by virtue of the fact that trust and confidence has been reposed, its resemblance to breach of fiduciary obligation is striking.[124]

IV. Analysis: Divergence or Convergence?

Doctrinal Divergence

As matters stand, the Australian and English doctrines of undue influence have diverged and it is unlikely that this will be undone. Australian case law has produced two models of undue influence: the fiduciary model and the vitiated consent model. It appears that the latter is breaking down into a disability-like 'impaired consent' model and a duress-like 'overborne consent' model. Ample dicta can be found to support each of the three. Thus, Australian judges are faced with a 'trilemma'. As the problem is unacknowledged, there is nothing to direct, and little to guide, their choice. English judges have no such problem. In England, there is only one model of undue influence—the abuse of influence model, mandated by the House of Lords in *Etridge*. This model differs from both the vitiated consent and fiduciary varieties. In essence, the English doctrine of undue influence is directed at remedying the effects of coercive and exploitative behaviour, whereas the Australian doctrine operates to alleviate the claimant from responsibility for transactions to which she did not freely consent. Even where it is concerned with the defendant's behaviour, the Australian doctrine specifically addresses the exploitation of influence derived from a position of trust.

Substantive Convergence

Yet a tendency towards convergence is perceptible. In both England and Australia, undue influence cases manifest an abiding concern for the same three matters that have always

---

[121] ibid [34]–[35].
[122] ibid [30].
[123] ibid [34]–[35].
[124] eg, *McKenzie v McDonald* [1927] VLR 124, in which Dixon J held that a fiduciary had a duty not to purchase from or sell to the principal without making full disclosure of all that he knew with respect to the transaction.

driven the doctrine. Attempts to isolate the one true rationale have been unsuccessful, because the other two aspects can be neither subsumed nor severed. England has opted for an abuse of influence model. However, despite conscientious effort made by the judiciary to demonstrate a high degree of fidelity to the *Etridge* formula, concern for impaired consent is trickling back into the doctrine through multiple points of ingress. Moreover, it is clear that fiduciary characteristics, derived from the doctrine's heritage, have not been eradicated. As we have seen, Australian undue influence law runs both a fiduciary model and a vitiated consent model[125] simultaneously. Theoretically, it is not necessary in Australia to use the doctrine of undue influence to deal with cases in which the chief concern lies with the defendant's conduct, because the doctrine of unconscionable dealing is available to do this work. Yet, despite the best efforts of Mason and Deane JJ, in practice, the line between these doctrines is not as bright as might be hoped. Unconscionable dealing tends to be pleaded as well as, rather than instead of, undue influence in such cases. Furthermore, where this happens, the outcome for both causes of action is usually the same.[126]

Vacillation or Variance?

On this basis, one might be inclined to dismiss present differences between the English and Australian doctrines as mere vacillation, rather than true variance. However, the legal landscape in each jurisdiction has changed too fundamentally to allow any real prospect of convergence without radical change. Firstly, it is not to be expected that the law so carefully and emphatically laid down in *Etridge* will be reversed and, even if English courts were to refine or revise the doctrine, the core of *Etridge* is that undue influence consists of wrongful abuse of the power to influence. In Australia, the High Court has made it clear that this kind of behaviour is to be dealt with by the separate and distinct equitable wrong of unconscionable dealing.[127] Secondly, a vitiated consent model cannot be accommodated within the conception of undue influence minted in *Etridge*. Yet concern for the quality of the benefactor's consent is integral to the Australian doctrine—indeed it is what distinguishes undue influence from unconscionable dealing. Thus, it would seem that convergence has been irreversibly obstructed.

Looking for a Solution

Perhaps the best way forward, in both jurisdictions, is to break from the past and desist from trying to use one doctrine to do two different jobs. In both England and Australia,

---

[125] Indeed, it is arguable that there are two vitiated consent models.

[126] This is because facts which provide the basis of a relationship of influence for the purposes of undue influence can readily be used to prove the existence of a special disadvantage for the purposes of unconscionable dealing. The 'overlap' between the doctrines was greatly enlarged when the High Court accepted that strong emotional attachment can create a special disadvantage. See *Louth v Diprose* (1992) 175 CLR 621 and *Bridgewater v Leahy* (1998) 194 CLR 457.

[127] *Amadio* (1983) 151 CLR 447, 446 (Mason J) and 474 (Deane J); *Bridgewater v Leahy* (1998) 194 CLR 457, 478–79 (Gaudron, Gummow and Kirby JJ).

undue influence serves as an equitable wrong in that it corrects a breach of equitable duty by the influential party—whether that duty is a straightforward obligation not to use unacceptable means of persuasion or has a more rigorous fiduciary character. It has also been employed, in both jurisdictions, as one of the means by which consent is used to define the limits of obligation and qualify the concept of property.[128] In Australia and (albeit less openly) in England, undue influence is used as a justification for declining to enforce what would otherwise have been a binding contractual promise, and even for reversing what would otherwise have been a completed conveyance, in cases where the quality of the benefactor's consent to the transaction has been called into question.

Perhaps a better solution might be to uncouple concerns about consent from those relating to the conduct of the influential party, allowing each to be addressed by a separate doctrine. A bifurcated approach has been suggested by a number of commentators.[129] Typically, it has been advocated that intervention on the basis of impaired consent constitutes restitution for unjust enrichment. However, this characterisation is inessential to an argument in favour of bifurcation. As matters stand, the English and Australian courts face the same problem, which they have attempted to solve using irreconcilably different, but equally ineffective, means. Separating the equitable wrong of exploitation of influence from the vitiating factor of excessive dependence would clear the path towards a more rational and authentic doctrine. It would facilitate discussion about the nature and content of the duties entailed in a wrong of undue influence—for example, in what circumstances and to what extent are they 'of a fiduciary character'? It would also provide a firmer basis for decisions about the appropriate remedial response. At a minimum, it would have the advantage that neither in England nor in Australia would the culpability of the defendant's conduct be tested by reference to the quality of the claimant's consent.

V. Conclusion

The apprehensions which arise when one person has very great influence over another do not differ significantly between Australia and England. We worry that the influential party will abuse her power by pressuring the other to conform to her will or by exploiting her position of trust. We are concerned that a transaction procured in such circumstances might not be supported by consent the quality of which is sufficient to found a legally binding obligation. We also perceive a broader threat to our ability to form relationships that foster trust and in which we can allow ourselves to be dependent. These concerns lie at the core of the doctrine of undue influence. In both England and Australia, its development has

---

[128] Historically the concept of consent has been fundamental in obligations and property law—especially contract law. See Black, above n 71, 220.

[129] J Edelman and E Bant, *Unjust Enrichment in Australia* (Oxford, Oxford University Press, 2006) 219; A Burrows, *A Restatement of the English Law of Unjust Enrichment* (Oxford, Oxford University Press, 2012) 75–82; J Edelman, 'Fraud, Undue Influence and Unconscionable Transactions' in J McGhee QC (ed), *Snell's Equity*, 32nd edn (London, Sweet & Maxwell, 2013) 243; W Swadling, 'Undue Influence: Lessons from America?' in C Mitchell and W Swadling (eds), *The Restatement Third: Restitution and Unjust Enrichment, Critical and Comparative Analyses* (Oxford, Hart Publishing, 2013) 119–120 and 131.

been shaped by the courts' responses to each of these apprehensions. Furthermore, recent cases indicate that all three remain operative in both jurisdictions today.

However, during the past 30 years, the interplay between these rationales has become problematic. English and Australian courts have dealt differently with this problem and this has resulted in doctrinal divergence. There can be no realistic expectation that the English and Australian doctrines will realign in the natural course of events. Yet cases in both jurisdictions indicate that an impetus for convergence exists. They also show that, as matters stand, neither the English nor the Australian doctrine is satisfactory, because neither adequately describes the work that undue influence actually does. It is concluded that, without a radical change of course, convergence is highly improbable. However, it may be that radical change is required in each jurisdiction anyway. Finally, it is suggested that bifurcation may offer the best hope for convergence and for authentic doctrines of undue influence in each jurisdiction.

15

Whose Conscience? Unconscionability in the Common Law of Obligations

GRAHAM VIRGO[*]

I. The Nature of the Problem

Unconscionability has been described as the 'universal talisman'[1] that underpins equity. It is the golden thread that ties together the common laws of equitable obligations in many jurisdictions. It is a word that is often used by judges, legislatures[2] and commentators, but it hides a myriad of meanings. The different uses of this single word in various jurisdictions means that, whilst there may appear to be a convergence of equitable principles and remedies in the common law, on closer inspection there is significant divergence; we are divided by a common equitable language. At the heart of the debate about the use and abuse of 'unconscionability' is confusion about whose conscience is relevant to determine what is against conscience. Is it the conscience of the court or the conscience of the defendant determined either objectively or subjectively? Two decisions of the UK Supreme Court handed down one fortnight in May 2013 reveal very different interpretations of conscience.

Pitt v Holt[3] concerned a claim to set aside a voluntary disposition by deed on the ground of a mistake relating to inheritance tax liability. Lord Walker held that the equitable jurisdiction to rescind a deed would be engaged if the mistake was sufficiently serious[4] so that the assertion of the legal rights of donees under the deed would be unjust or unconscionable.[5] This 'unconscionableness', as Lord Walker called it, is to be evaluated objectively,[6] and requires close examination of the facts, including 'the circumstances of the mistake and

[*] I am grateful to Simon Lee and Ajay Ratan for helpful comments on the subject of this chapter.
[1] A Mason, 'Themes and Prospects' in P Finn (ed), *Essays in Equity* (Australia, Thomson Reuters, 1985) 44.

[2] See, eg, Australia, Trade Practices Act 1974, Part IVA: Competition and Consumer Act 2010, Sch 2, Part 2-2; England, Land Registration Act 2002, s 110; United States, Uniform Commercial Code, § 203-2 (2002), 'Unconscionable Contract or Clause' (see A Leff, 'Unconscionability and the Code: The Emperor's New Clause' (1967) 115 *University of Pennsylvania Law Review* 485). The American Law Institute's ongoing project on the Restatement of Consumer Contracts will incorporate a restatement of the US doctrine of unconscionability.

[3] *Pitt v Holt* [2013] UKSC 26, [2013] 2 AC 108. See further P Davies and G Virgo, 'Relieving Trustee's Mistakes' [2013] *Restitution Law Review* 74; B Häcker, 'Mistaken Gifts and *Pitt v Holt*' [2014] *Current Legal Problems* 333.

[4] *Pitt v Holt* [2013] UKSC 26, [2013] 2 AC 108, [114].

[5] ibid [124], relying on *Ogilvie v Littleboy* (1897) 13 TLR 399, 400 (Lindley LJ). Affirmed by the House of Lords: *Ogilvie v Allen* (1899) 15 TLR 294.

[6] *Pitt v Holt* [2013] UKSC 26, [2013] 2 AC 108, [125].

its consequences for the person who made the vitiated disposition', change of position, and 'other matters relevant to the exercise of the court's discretion'.[7] Lord Walker used the language of 'unconscionableness' interchangeably with that of 'injustice' and 'unfairness'.[8] This appears simply to turn upon the exercise of judicial discretion without regard to any obvious underlying principles. Lord Walker rejected the suggestion that this is 'susceptible to judicial manipulation' on the ground that the Court ought to form a judgment about the justice of the case.[9]

In that case the deed was rescinded even though the mistake related to the payment of tax which was lawfully due. A matter of particular significance was that the disposition did not form part of an artificial or abusive tax avoidance scheme and had in fact been authorised by the Court of Protection. Had the equitable jurisdiction been invoked in the consolidated appeal in *Futter v Futter*,[10] which also involved a disposition to a trust, it is likely that the donee's receipt would have been characterised as unconscionable, because the disposition did form part of an artificial tax avoidance scheme. Lord Walker described such schemes as 'a social evil',[11] and emphasised that the Court might refuse to award equitable discretionary relief on the ground of public policy, suggesting that there are moral questions which need to be examined by the court in determining unconscionability.

Two weeks after *Pitt v Holt* the Supreme Court decided *Vestergaard Frandsen v Bestnet Europe Ltd*,[12] a case concerning accessorial liability for breach of the equitable duty of confidence. The claimant company had sued the defendant, a former employee, for breach of confidence, arising from the manufacture and sale of insecticidal mosquito nets which involved the use of the claimant's trade secrets. The defendant had not breached any duty of confidence herself, but was associated with a consultant who had deliberately breached his own duty of confidence which was owed to the claimant. In considering the nature of the liability for breach of the equitable duty of confidence, Lord Neuberger emphasised that the action 'is based ultimately on conscience'.[13] A defendant who learns of a trade secret in circumstances where she reasonably does not appreciate that it is confidential might be liable to respect the confidentiality from the moment she is told or otherwise appreciates that it is confidential, since from 'that moment, it can be said that her conscience is affected in a way which should be recognised by equity'.[14] Lord Neuberger interpreted conscience as encompassing knowledge, wilful blindness, reckless disregard of another's rights and dishonesty, all of which he considered focus on the defendant's own state of mind.[15] The defendant was not considered to be party to a common design to exploit trade secrets because she did not know that they were being misused and so did not share with the other participants one of the features of the common design which rendered it wrongful, namely the necessary state of mind.[16]

---

[7] ibid [126].

[8] ibid.

[9] ibid [128].

[10] This had not been invoked initially and the Supreme Court refused to permit the appellants to raise it on appeal.

[11] *Pitt v Holt* [2013] UKSC 26, [2013] 2 AC 108, [135].

[12] *Vestergaard Frandsen v Bestnet Europe Ltd* [2013] UKSC 31, [2013] 1 WLR 1556.

[13] ibid [22].

[14] ibid [25].

[15] ibid [26].

[16] ibid [34].

The different contexts of *Pitt v Holt* and *Vestergaard* might be sufficient to explain the variable objective and subjective interpretations which were adopted. The different uses of the words 'unconscionability' and 'conscience' might also be regarded as justifying the different interpretations, although there is no reason to think that the two words are other than different sides of the same coin. But what is especially significant is that the obvious difference of approach was not acknowledged, and this is symptomatic of the contemporary use of this ancient equitable language. As Kelvin Low has correctly recognised:

> Whereas every species of conduct that justified equitable intervention may be described, perhaps not inaccurately, as 'unconscionable', they are themselves unconscionable in different ways. The flexibility of the word robs it of any stable meaning. To say that someone's conduct is unconscionable does not tell us whether he is dishonest, untrustworthy or merely lacking in grace.[17]

If unconscionability is to be interpreted in different ways, a taxonomy needs to be developed to explain when different interpretations are being used and why. An important part of that taxonomy will be the development of more accurate vocabulary to reflect the different meanings.

II. The Language of Conscience and Unconscionability

The Meaning of Conscience and Unconscionability

Gleeson CJ has said that the use of the word 'unconscionable' 'may be merely an emphatic method of expressing disapproval of someone's behaviour, but its legal meaning is considerably more precise'.[18] But identifying that precise legal meaning is not easy. The words 'conscience' and 'unconscionability' are typically used to justify a particular decision without further explanation and so might be criticised for vagueness. But are these words any different from other vague legal concepts, such as reasonableness, legitimate expectation or rule of law, around which much jurisprudence and commentary has developed? Indeed, in *Elders Pastoral Ltd v Bank of New Zealand*[19] Somers J recognised that 'words such as unconscionable and inequitable have drawn closer to more objective concepts such as fair, reasonable and just'. Further, according to Richard Nolan, open-ended evaluative concepts such as 'reasonableness' do not attract the same hostility as 'unconscionability'.[20] He notes that 'Australia, which has done most in the common law world of recent decades to re-affirm the importance of conscience as a criteria of judgment, has not, as a result, slid into some predicted juridical dystopia.'[21] Conscience might even be considered to be the equitable equivalent of the rule of law, which has been described as 'vague and amorphous' hence its appeal,[22] since conscience provides a 'hedge against tyranny and high-handed governance'[23]

---

[17] K Low, 'Nonfeasance in Equity' (2012) 128 *LQR* 63, 67.

[18] *Australian Competition and Consumer Commission v CG Berbatis Holdings Pty Ltd* [2003] HCA 18, (2003) 214 CLR 51, [7].

[19] *Elders Pastoral Ltd v Bank of New Zealand* [1988] 2 NZLR 180, 193.

[20] R Nolan, 'Fiduciaries and their Flawed Decisions' (2013) 129 *LQR* 469, 473.

[21] ibid.

[22] AC Hutchinson, *Is Eating People Wrong?* (Cambridge, Cambridge University Press, 2011) 61.

[23] ibid.

by enabling equity to regulate the exercise of power by fiduciaries. Nevertheless, it is note-worthy that much less attention has been paid to the philosophical foundations and prin-cipled interpretation of conscience, compared to the voluminous literature involving rigorous analysis of the rule of law.

In order for such theoretical and doctrinal work to be replicated in equity, attention needs to be paid to the definition of conscience and unconscionability. Basic questions lack definitive answers, such as whether unconscionability is the antithesis of conscience. The preferable view is that it is, in the sense that unconscionability means 'contrary to good conscience'.[24] A further vital issue relates to the use of synonyms for unconscionability, to determine whether they might assist in determining what contrary to good conscience means. Common synonyms include bad faith, equitable fraud,[25] injustice and unfairness.[26] But other words and phrases have been used as well, including dishonesty and improper or commercially unacceptable conduct.[27] In determining the taxonomy of conscience it will be vital to consider to what extent these words and phrases can be used to supplement or even replace the orthodox equitable language.

But the fact that the words 'conscience' and 'unconscionability' are used by themselves or in conjunction with other words and phrases betrays a fundamental uncertainty as to what conscience is actually about. For example, is unconscionability a state of mind or does it relate to a normative standard for evaluating conduct, to morality or simply to a sense of guilt? The significance of such confusion was highlighted by Karl Llewellyn in *The Bramble Bush*, albeit not referring specifically to unconscionability, but his comments are apt:

> Legal usage of technical words has sinned, and does still, in two respects: it is involved in ambiguity of two kinds: multiple senses of the same term, and terms too broad to be precise in application to the details of single disputes. First, it does not use terms in single senses, but uses the same term in several senses; and in several senses, indiscriminately, without awareness. This invites confusion, it makes bad logic, almost inevitable, it makes statement of clear thought difficult, it makes clear thought itself improbable. ... Surely one can find smaller common *elements* whose varied combi-nations make up these larger complexes.[28]

To avoid bad logic and to facilitate clear thought, attention needs to be paid to the core meaning of what constitutes conscience and unconscionability, with particular reference to the smaller common elements which comprise the larger concept.

The History of Conscience

Conscience and unconscionability have been used for hundreds of years, so it is vital to identify their origins to see if they can be of assistance in understanding their contemporary

---

[24] J McConvill and M Bagaric, 'The Yoking of Unconscionability and Unjust Enrichment in Australia' (2002) *Deakin Law Review* 225, 249.

[25] *Earl of Chesterfield v Janssen* (1751) 2 Ves Sen 125, 157 (Lord Hardwicke).

[26] *Pitt v Holt* [2013] UKSC 26, [2013] 2 AC 108, [126] (Lord Walker).

[27] *Yam Seng Pte Ltd v International Trade Corporation Ltd* [2013] EWHC 111 (QB), [2013] 1 Lloyd's Rep 526, [138] (Leggatt LJ).

[28] K Llewellyn, *The Bramble Bush* (Oxford, Oxford University Press, 2008) 89.

application. The history of conscience in equity is complex and uncertain.[29] Although what follows is a gross simplification of rigorous historical scholarship, it is possible to identify six different stages in the development of conscience as an equitable construct in broadly chronological order.

(1) The Chancellor's Conscience

Conscience originally referred to the conscience of the Chancellor as the measure of equity, with conscience being a reference to the individual moral judgment of the judge,[30] albeit one influenced by theological learning and canon law, since the Chancellor was typically a cleric.[31] Conscience in this moral sense was criticised for its inherent uncertainty being, as Selden famously acknowledged, like making the Chancellor's foot the measure of the standard foot.[32]

(2) Personal Knowledge

As Chancery procedure developed, references to conscience involved the ascertainment of legally relevant facts from the judge's personal knowledge or belief rather than by reference to what was alleged and proved.[33]

(3) The Defendant's Conscience

The focus then shifted to the assessment of the defendant's conscience, as determined by the court, but with reference to what the defendant knew or believed to be true, rather than what he believed to be morally right. This interpretation of conscience derived from the ability of equity to compel the defendant's appearance and to examine the defendant on oath with a view to extracting a confession.[34] It also reveals a focus of the Chancery court on intervening to purge or purify what was considered to be the corrupt conscience of the defendant, and has been described as a 'cathartic jurisdiction'.[35] This was recognised by Lord Ellesmere in *Earl of Oxford's Case*:[36]

> The office of the Chancellor is to correct men's conscience for frauds, breaches of trust, wrongs and oppressions of what nature soever they be …

(4) The Foundation of Equitable Doctrine

Under the influence of Lord Chancellors, notably Lord Eldon, who were lawyers rather than clerics, equitable principles were identified and were often justified with reference to

---

[29] See D Klinck, 'The Unexamined "Conscience" of Contemporary Canadian Equity' (2001) 46 *McGill Law Journal* 571; R Havelock, 'The Evolution of Equitable Conscience' (2014) 8 *Journal of Equity* 128.

[30] C St German, *Doctor and Student* (1523, 1531).

[31] J Baker, *An Introduction to English Legal History*,4th edn (Oxford, Oxford University Press, 2002) 99.

[32] J Selden, *Table Talk of John Selden* (London, Selden Society, 1927) 43.

[33] M McNair, 'Equity and Conscience' [2007] *OJLS* 659.

[34] ibid 676.

[35] W Ashburner's *Principles of Equity*, ed D Browne, 2nd edn (London, Butterworths, 1933) 39.

[36] *Earl of Oxford's Case* (1615) 1 Ch R 1, 6. See also *Allcard v Skinner* (1887) 36 Ch D 145, 189 (Bowen LJ).

conscience. Through the development of a doctrine of precedent, categories of like cases were identified which were informed by past decisions and past values. So, rather than seeking to identify unconscionability in each case, it was sufficient that a case fell within a particular category of liability, the existence of which could be justified by reference to the old language of conscience.[37] Here unconscionability operates as a matter of opinion, but one that has been 'formed and inferred by considered decisions in similar but not identical cases, by the values of the community, that is by the palimpsest of past legal and community traditions'.[38]

(5) Chancery is Conscience

Conscience has also been used simply to describe the Chancery jurisdiction, but without providing any justification for the exercise of that jurisdiction.[39] Arguably it is this sense of conscience that was recognised by Lord Nottingham in *Cooke v Fountain*:[40]

> With such a conscience as is only *naturali et interna* this Court has nothing to do; the conscience by which I am to proceed is merely *civilis et politica* and tied to certain measures; and it is infinitely better for the public that a trust, security, or agreement, which is wholly secret, should miscarry, than that men should lose their estates by the mere fancy and imagination of a chancellor.

(6) Rhetorical Conscience

Throughout the history of equity the language of conscience and unconscionability has also been used simply as a rhetorical device which the judge could hide behind to exercise discretion without reference to principle.[41] The wheel may appear to have gone full circle, with the modern judge who seeks to interpret conscience in this way[42] appearing to act like the former Lord Chancellor and exercising judgment without reference to principle. But that is not the case. For the first interpretation of conscience was highly principled, with reference to theological interpretations of conscience, with very close attention to biblical text and commentary by scholars. Modern approaches to conscience, which actually hide behind the language of conscience, do not reflect the original, principled notion of conscience.

Summary

This review of the history of conscience reveals a variety of different interpretations over time, although a general trend can be identified away from conscience as a test of morality, to conscience underpinning equitable principle. At times conscience has referred explicitly

---

[37] CJ Rossiter and M Stone, 'The Chancellor's New Shoe' (1988) 11 *University of New South Wales Law Journal* 11, 24.

[38] ibid 26. See also P Finn, 'Unconscionable Conduct' (1994) 8 *Journal of Contract Law* 37.

[39] G Watt, *Equity Stirring* (Oxford, Hart Publishing, 2009) 106.

[40] *Cooke v Fountain* (1676) 3 Swanst 585, 600.

[41] D Klinck, *Conscience, Equity and the Court of Chancery in Early Modern England* (Farnham, Ashgate, 2010) 10.

[42] See, eg, *Pitt v Holt* [2013] UKSC 26, [2013] 2 AC 108, [126] (Lord Walker). See also *National Westminster Bank v Morgan* [1985] AC 686, 703 (Lord Scarman).

to the conscience of the defendant, but typically it has been interpreted objectively, albeit in the light of the defendant's own knowledge and belief of the facts and circumstances.

III. Contemporary Interpretations of Conscience

It does not necessarily follow that the historical understanding of conscience must rule the interpretation of conscience and unconscionability today. But reviewing contemporary equitable doctrines reveals four different interpretations, most of which are clearly influenced by the different stages in the historical development of conscience: (1) The subjective conscience of the defendant with reference to his or her own knowledge and suspicions. Here conscience refers to a state of mind.[43] (2) The objective conscience of the defendant with reference to what he or she should have known or suspected. (3) The court's conscience, whereby the court determines on the facts of the case and with reference to recognised principles what the defendant ought to do as a matter of good conscience. Here conscience relates to an assessment of the defendant's behaviour.[44] (4) The judge's conscience, whereby conscience is used as a rhetorical device behind which the judge can hide by asserting that a particular result is justified by good conscience but without needing to go further by explaining what that might mean.

Each of these interpretations can be illustrated by a variety of different equitable doctrines. The following survey does not purport in any way to be comprehensive, but seeks to show how each of these four interpretations is reflected in contemporary equity. But, in doing so, it will be seen that the boundaries between the interpretations are fluid and controversial, which will indicate how a new taxonomy of conscience and unconscionability might be developed.

Subjective Conscience of the Defendant

There are a variety of contexts where a subjective interpretation of conscience, with reference to what the defendant knew or suspected, influences the operation of equitable doctrine.

Creation of Equitable Proprietary Interests

Where a defendant has received an asset in circumstances where the claimant has a restitutionary claim for its value, the defendant will hold the asset on constructive trust for the claimant if the defendant's retention of it can be characterised as unconscionable.[45] Here unconscionability is assessed with reference to the defendant's knowledge or suspicion

---

[43] *Yeoman's Row Management Ltd v Cobbe* [2008] UKHL 55, [2008] 1 WLR 1752, [91] (Lord Walker).
[44] ibid.
[45] *Westdeutsche Landesbank Girozentrale v Islington LBC* [1996] AC 669, 714 (Lord Browne-Wilkinson), interpreting *Chase-Manhattan Bank NA v Israel-British Bank (London) Ltd* [1981] Ch 105.

concerning the circumstances of the receipt.[46] So, for example, if the claimant has paid money to the defendant in the mistaken belief that she was discharging a liability, that money will be held on constructive trust if the defendant knew that it had been paid by mistake. This is because, once the defendant was aware of the mistake, he should have repaid the money and the failure to do so constitutes the unconscionable conduct which justifies the recognition of the constructive trust.[47] It is sufficient that the defendant believes or suspects that the claimant was mistaken or that the transaction was invalid.[48]

Unconscionable Receipt

Where the defendant has received an asset transferred in breach of trust, he or she will be liable to pay its value to the claimant if the defendant was at fault at the time of receipt. It has been a matter of controversy as to what the appropriate level of fault to trigger such personal liability should be. This claim was originally called 'knowing receipt', and the language of 'knowledge' is still used.[49] It has sometimes been held that an objective test of knowledge applies, described as 'constructive knowledge', so that it is sufficient that the defendant failed to make such inquiries as a reasonable person would have made as to whether the asset had been transferred in breach of trust.[50] Other cases have held that a subjective test applies, so it must be established that the defendant knew or suspected that the asset had been received in breach of trust.[51] The applicable level of fault was considered by the Court of Appeal in *Bank of Credit and Commerce International (Overseas) Ltd v Akindele*,[52] which held that the appropriate test is one of unconscionability,[53] namely whether the defendant's knowledge of the circumstances relating to the breach of trust made it unconscionable for him or her to retain the benefit of the property that had been received; constructive knowledge would not suffice. Although the Court of Appeal gave no real guidance as to what constitutes 'unconscionable conduct' for these purposes, it appears that a subjective test was contemplated.[54] Clearly, a defendant's receipt will be considered to be unconscionable if he or she knew of the breach of trust and, presumably, also if he or she turned a blind eye to the breach. It is not, however, clear whether the receipt of a defendant who was suspicious about the breach is unconscionable.

It cannot be stated with absolute certainty, however, that the law necessarily requires unconscionability for this receipt-based claim to be interpreted in a subjective sense.

---

[46] *Westdeutsche Landesbank Girozentrale v Islington LBC* [1996] AC 669, 705 (Lord Browne-Wilkinson).

[47] In *Fitzalan-Howard (Norfolk) v Hibbert* [2009] EWHC 2855 (QB), [49], Tomlinson J suggested that the conscience of the recipient of a mistaken payment might not be affected when he suspected or learned of the mistaken payment, but rather when he could reasonably be required to have acted by making repayment.

[48] Although in *Papamichael v National Westminster Bank plc* [2003] 1 Lloyd's Rep 341, 373, Judge Chambers QC said that actual knowledge is required.

[49] See, eg, *Williams v Central Bank of Nigeria* [2014] UKSC 10, [2014] AC 1189, [35] (Lord Sumption).

[50] See *Belmont Finance Corp Ltd v Williams Furniture Ltd (No 2)* [1980] 1 All ER 393, 405 (Buckley LJ) and 412 (Goff LJ).

[51] *Re Montagu's Settlement Trust* [1987] Ch 264.

[52] *Bank of Credit and Commerce International (Overseas) Ltd v Akindele* [2001] Ch 437.

[53] ibid 455 (Nourse LJ).

[54] See also *Criterion Properties plc v Stratford UK Properties LLC* [2003] EWCA Civ 1783, [2003] 1 WLR 2108. Compare P Birks, 'Receipt' in P Birks and A Pretto (eds), *Breach of Trust* (Oxford, Hart Publishing, 2002) 227, who considered that unconscionability involved an unreasonable failure to appreciate the trust provenance of the property received, which involves an objective test.

In *Armstrong DLW Gmbh v Winnington Networks Ltd*,[55] for example, Stephen Morris QC held that unconscionability for these purposes encompassed both subjective awareness by the defendant of possible impropriety and also where, on the facts actually known to the defendant, a reasonable person would have appreciated that the transfer was in breach of trust or would have made such inquiries or sought advice which would have revealed the probability of breach of trust. In *Arthur v Attorney-General of the Turks and Caicos Islands*[56] Sir Terence Etherton described knowing receipt as 'involving unconscionable conduct amounting to equitable fraud. It is a classic example of lack of *bona fides*.' But this confirms the ambiguity of unconscionability, since equitable fraud and absence of good faith can incorporate objective notions of fault.

Rectification for Unilateral Mistake

Where one party (A) mistakenly believes that the written contract to which she is a party contains a term, that contract may be rectified to accord with A's belief where the other party (B) has acted unconscionably in some way. For these purposes unconscionability is interpreted subjectively as involving actual knowledge,[57] but also includes wilful blindness, suspicion as to the mistake, as well as wilfully and recklessly failing to make such inquiries as an honest and reasonable person would make.[58] B must also have failed to draw the mistake to the notice of A and calculated that this would benefit him.[59] In such circumstances it would be inequitable or unconscionable to allow B to resist rectification. Etherton LJ has described the defendant's conduct in denying rectification as dishonest in a subjective sense.[60] It has, however, been suggested that it should be sufficient to trigger rectification if B ought to have been aware of A's mistake.[61]

Trustee Exemption Clauses

In *Armitage v Nurse*[62] a clause in a trust instrument stated that no trustee should be liable for any loss suffered by the trust fund save where it was caused by the trustee's 'own actual fraud'. In determining the validity of this clause the Court equated fraud with dishonesty. A trustee would be considered to have acted dishonestly if he or she intended to pursue a course of action either knowing that it was contrary to the best interests of the beneficiaries or being recklessly indifferent to their interests, regardless of whether the trustee intended to benefit from the conduct.[63] This is a subjective test of fault, with reference to the trustee's

---

[55] *Armstrong DLW Gmbh v Winnington Networks Ltd* [2012] EWHC 10 (Ch), [2013] Ch 156, [132].

[56] *Arthur v Attorney-General of the Turks and Caicos Islands* [2012] UKPC 30, [4].

[57] *A Roberts and Co Ltd v Leicestershire County Council* [1961] Ch 555, 570 (Pennycuick J); *Riverlate Properties Ltd v Paul* [1975] Ch 133, 140 (knowledge involving a degree of sharp practice); *Agip SpA v Navigazione Alta Italia SpA* [1984] 1 Lloyds Rep 353.

[58] *Commission for the New Towns v Cooper (Great Britain) Ltd* [1995] Ch 259, 280 (Buckley LJ).

[59] *Thomas Bates Ltd v Wyndham's (Lingeries) Ltd* [1981] 1 WLR 505, 515 (Buckley LJ).

[60] *Daventry District Council v Daventry and District Housing Ltd* [2011] EWCA Civ 1153, [2012] 1 WLR 1333, [96].

[61] ibid [184] (Toulson LJ). See also D McLauchlan, 'The "Drastic" Remedy of Rectification for Unilateral Mistake' (2008) 124 *LQR* 608; A Burrows 'Construction and Rectification' in A Burrows and E Peel (eds), *Contract Terms* (Oxford, Oxford University Press, 2007).

[62] *Armitage v Nurse* [1998] Ch 241.

[63] ibid 251.

intention, knowledge and recklessness, which means suspicion of adverse consequences arising from the trustee's actions.[64] It follows that if the trustee knew or suspected that the breach of trust would, or might, have a detrimental effect on the beneficiaries, the liability for breach could not be excluded.

There are, however, circumstances where dishonesty for these purposes is interpreted objectively, by reference to the standards of reasonable people. In *Walker v Stones*[65] the trustees of a discretionary trust were the partners in a firm of solicitors. The trust instrument included a clause that exempted trustees from all liability other than for 'wilful fraud or dishonesty'. The beneficiaries alleged that the trustees had acted in breach of trust by benefiting people who were not objects of the trust. The Court of Appeal accepted that a trustee-solicitor could have acted dishonestly, even if he or she thought that he or she was acting in the best interests of the beneficiaries, if this belief was so unreasonable that no reasonable trustee acting in that profession could have held it. This stricter objective test of dishonesty was justified because of the higher standards expected of trustees who are solicitors.[66]

It follows that whether dishonesty is interpreted subjectively, as in *Armitage v Nurse*, or objectively, as in *Walker v Stones*, will depend on the circumstances of the trustee, with higher standards of conduct expected of professional trustees, such as solicitor-trustees.

Objective Conscience of the Defendant

The objective interpretation of conscience defines unconscionability with reference to what the defendant should have known or suspected.

Dishonest Assistance

Where the defendant has assisted or induced a breach of trust or fiduciary duty, he or she will be liable to the trust or the principal. Such liability will only be imposed where the defendant is at fault in some way. Various tests of fault have been recognised, including knowledge of the breach, constructive notice,[67] want of probity[68] and dishonesty.[69] The requirement of dishonesty has been confirmed by the House of Lords,[70] but its meaning has proved controversial. In *Twinsectra Ltd v Yardley*[71] dishonesty was defined by reference to whether the defendant considered that his or her conduct was dishonest by the standards of reasonable and honest people. This is a subjective test of dishonesty, which

---

[64] *Barnes v Tomlinson* [2006] EWHC 3115 (Ch), [2007] WTLR 377; *Spread Trustee Co Ltd v Hutcheson* [2011] UKPC 13, [2012] 2 AC 194, [60] (Lord Clarke).

[65] *Walker v Stones* [2001] QB 902.

[66] See also *Barnes v Tomlinson* [2006] EWHC 3115 (Ch), [79] (Kitchin J); *Fattal v Walbrook Trustees (Jersey) Ltd* [2010] EWHC 2767 (Ch), [81] (Lewison J).

[67] *Selangor United Rubber Estates Ltd v Cradock (No 3)* [1968] 1 WLR 1555, 1590 (Ungoed-Thomas J).

[68] *Carl Zeiss Stiftung v Herbert Smith & Co (No 2)* [1969] 2 Ch 276.

[69] *Re Montagu's Settlement Trusts* [1987] Ch 264, 286 (Sir Robert Megarry V-C).

[70] *Twinsectra Ltd v Yardley* [2002] UKHL 12, [2002] 2 AC 164.

[71] ibid.

is also applied in the criminal law for the crimes of theft and fraud.[72] The House of Lords considered this to be the definition of dishonesty which had been adopted by the Privy Council in *Royal Brunei Airlines v Tan*,[73] but an objective test of dishonesty was recognised in that case, namely whether the reasonable person would consider the defendant's conduct to be dishonest, albeit that this was to be assessed in light of the facts as the defendant knew them to be. In *Tan* dishonesty was equated with a want of probity and commercially unacceptable conduct. Lord Millett in *Twinsectra* recognised that the Privy Council in *Tan* had adopted an objective test of dishonesty, which he considered was focused on dishonest conduct rather than a dishonest state of mind, which is why a different test of dishonesty is used in the criminal law where the focus is on criminal culpability. Lord Millett analysed the approach of the Privy Council as involving

> an objective standard of dishonesty by which the defendant is expected to attain the standard which would be observed by an honest person placed in similar circumstances. Account must be taken of subjective considerations such as the defendant's experience and intelligence and his actual state of knowledge at the relevant time. But it is not necessary that he should actually have appreciated that he was acting dishonestly; it is sufficient that he was.[74]

In assessing this standard of honesty, the court will have regard to the defendant's personal attributes and the reason why the defendant acted as he or she did. So, if the defendant is a professional, such as a solicitor, the objective standard of honesty will be more rigorous.

This objective test of dishonesty was subsequently confirmed by the Privy Council in *Barlow Clowes International Ltd v Eurotrust International Ltd*,[75] was recognised by Arden LJ in *Abou-Rahmah v Abacha*[76] and followed in *Starglade Properties Ltd v Nash*.[77] In that case Morritt LJ recognised that '[t]here is a single standard of honesty objectively determined by the court. That standard is applied to specific conduct of a specific individual possessing the knowledge and qualities he actually enjoyed.'[78]

It is notable that the language of dishonesty rather than unconscionability has been used for this claim. That is surprising, since the language of objective dishonesty could readily be replaced with that of unconscionability, especially in the light of the long tradition of conscience being interpreted objectively in equity. Most recently in *Williams v Central Bank of Nigeria*[79] Lord Sumption called this accessorial liability 'knowing assistance'[80] and considered it to be based on fraud, but also added that the 'liability of a knowing assister has always depended on the unconscionability of *his* conduct'.[81] In the space of one paragraph the whole gamut of equitable fault is encompassed without any apparent awareness that these terms might bear different meanings.

---

[72] See *Ghosh* [1982] QB 1053.

[73] *Royal Brunei Airlines v Tan* [1995] 2 AC 378.

[74] *Twinsectra*, above n 70, [121].

[75] *Barlow Clowes International Ltd v Eurotrust International Ltd* [2005] UKPC 37, [2006] 1 WLR 1476.

[76] *Abou-Rahmah v Abacha* [2006] EWCA Civ 1492, [2007] 1 All ER (Comm) 827, [65].

[77] *Starglade Properties Ltd v Nash* [2010] EWCA Civ 1314.

[78] ibid [26].

[79] *Williams v Central Bank of Nigeria* [2014] UKSC 10, [2014]AC 1189, [35].

[80] See also *Vestergaard Frandsen v Bestnet Europe Ltd* [2013] UKSC 31, [2013] 1 WLR 1556, [26] (Lord Neuberger).

[81] ibid (emphasis in original).

Unconscionable Transactions

A transaction can be set aside where the claimant's consent to enter into it can be considered to have been procured by unconscionable conduct.[82] The essential features of unconscionable conduct was identified by Lord Hardwicke in *Earl of Chesterfield v Janssen* as involving

> fraud presumed or inferred from the circumstances or conditions of the parties contracting: weakness on one side, usury on the other, or extortion or advantage taken of that weakness. There has always been the appearance of fraud from the nature of the bargain.[83]

The equitable jurisdiction to vitiate a transaction[84] for unconscionability is engaged where the claimant suffered from a special disability or was in a disadvantageous position as against the defendant, so that there is a reasonable degree of inequality between the parties.[85] The defendant must have acted unconscionably[86] in exploiting the claimant's disadvantage. This has been described as involving equitable, or constructive, fraud.[87] In *Hart v O'Connor* Lord Brightman recognised that equitable fraud involved the defendant acting in bad faith or taking advantage of the claimant in some way.[88] Simple exploitation of gross inequality of bargaining power between the parties is not unconscionable.[89] The defendant needs to have acted in a morally reprehensible manner,[90] either because he or she actually knew of the claimant's special disability or disadvantage or should have known of it, since the defendant was aware of particular facts which would have put the reasonable person on notice that the claimant had a special disability or disadvantage.[91] So this encompasses an objective test. But fault of the defendant is not sufficient to characterise the transaction as unconscionable; it must also be overreaching and oppressive in that there is a significant imbalance in the substance of the transaction to the disadvantage of the weaker party,[92] such as where the transaction is at a gross undervalue. A transaction will not be oppressive simply because it turns out to a party's disadvantage[93] or that, in the eyes of the court, it was unreasonable.[94]

---

[82] *Hart v O'Connor* [1985] AC 1000; *Crédit Lyonnais Bank Nederland NV v Burch* [1997] 1 All ER 144, 151 (Nourse LJ).

[83] *Earl of Chesterfield v Janssen* (1751) 2 Ves Sen 125, 157.

[84] Which might be a bargain or a gift: *Evans v Lloyd* [2013] EWHC 1725 (Ch).

[85] *Blomley v Ryan* (1956) 99 CLR 362, 405.

[86] *Alec Lobb (Garages) Ltd v Total Oil Great Britain Ltd* [1985] 1 WLR 173, 182 (Dillon LJ); *Louth v Diprose* (1992) 175 CLR 621, 637 (Deane J); *Kakavas v Crown Melbourne Ltd* [2013] HCA 25, (2013) 250 CLR 392.

[87] *Earl of Chesterfield v Janssen* (1751) 2 Ves Sen 125, 157 (Lord Hardwicke); *Hart v O'Connor* [1985] AC 1000, 1028.

[88] ibid.

[89] *National Westminster Bank plc v Morgan* [1985] AC 686, 708 (Lord Scarman).

[90] *Boustany v Pigott* (1995) 95 P & CR 298, 302 (Lord Templeman); *Yorkshire Bank plc v Tinsley* [2004] EWCA Civ 816, [2004] 1 WLR 2380.

[91] *Owen and Gutch v Homan* (1853) 4 HLC 997, 1035 (Lord Cranworth LC); *The Commercial Bank of Australia Ltd v Amadio* (1983) 151 CLR 447, 467 (Mason J); *Nichols v Jessup* [1986] 1 NZLR 226, 236 (Somers J). In *Kakavas v Crown Melbourne Ltd* [2013] HCA 25, (2013) 250 CLR 392 the High Court of Australia recognised that 'wilful ignorance' of the disability or disadvantage suffices, [156], but this is assessed with reference to the facts of which the defendant was aware.

[92] *Alec Lobb (Garages) Ltd v Total Oil GB Ltd* [1983] 1 WLR 87, 95; *Strydom v Vendside Ltd* [2009] EWHC 2130 (QB), [39] (Blair J).

[93] *Irvani v Irvani* [2000] 1 Lloyd's Rep 412, 425.

[94] *Multiservice Bookbinding Ltd v Marden* [1979] Ch 84, 110 (Browne-Wilkinson J).

Breach of Confidence

The action for breach of confidence is founded on the obligation of conscience[95] and responds to wrongdoing in the form of unconscionable conduct. Megarry J recognised in *Coco v Clark*:

> The equitable jurisdiction in cases of breach of confidence is ancient; confidence is the cousin of trust. The Statute of Uses, 1535, is framed in terms of 'use, confidence or trust'; and a couplet, attributed to Sir Thomas More, Lord Chancellor avers that;

> 'Three things are to be helpt in Conscience; Fraud, Accident and things of Confidence'. (See 1 Rolle's Abridgement 374).[96]

Although Lord Neuberger in *Vestergaard Frandsen A/S v Bestnet Europe Ltd*[97] assumed that the mental state to trigger liability for breach of confidence is subjective,[98] this is inconsistent with a significant line of authorities, many of which he did not consider.[99] Liability should in fact depend on whether the defendant was aware of the duty of confidence, or should have been aware of it because the reasonable person standing in the defendant's shoes would have realised that the information was being given in confidence, so that the defendant has notice that the information was confidential.[100]

Principled Conscience of the Court

Whereas subjective and objective interpretations of conscience assess unconscionability from the perspective of the defendant, the notion of principled conscience refers to the conscience of the court, in that the judge determines on the facts of the case and with reference to recognised principles whether the defendant ought, as a matter of good conscience, to be liable to the claimant. Many equitable doctrines can be analysed in this way, but two in particular illustrate how conscience can influence principled decision-making.

Recognition of Constructive Trust

Equity might recognise that an asset is held on constructive trust to ensure that the defendant does not profit from what is characterised as unconscionable conduct in a principled sense. This was recognised by Millett LJ in *Paragon Finance plc v DB Thakerar and Co*:

> A constructive trust arises by operation of law whenever the circumstances are such that it would be unconscionable for the owner of property ... to assert his own beneficial interest in the property

---

[95] *Moorgate Tobacco Co Ltd v Philip Morris Ltd (No 2)* (1984) 156 CLR 414, 438 (Deane J); *Stephens v Avery* [1988] Ch 449, 455 (Sir Nicolas Browne-Wilkinson V-C).

[96] *Coco v Clark* [1968] FSR 415, 419.

[97] *Vestergaard Frandsen A/S v Bestnet Europe Ltd* [2013] UKSC 31, [2013] 1 WLR 1556, [25].

[98] As recognised in some cases, eg, *Thomas v Pearce* [2000] FSR 718 (honesty); *R v Department of Health, ex parte Source Informatics Ltd* [2001] QB 424, [31] (Simon Brown LJ) ('the defendant's own conscience, no more and no less').

[99] Including *Seager v Copydex Ltd* [1967] 1 WLR 923; *Coco v Clark* [1969] RPC 41, 48 (Megarry J); *Attorney-General v Guardian Newspapers Ltd (No 2)* [1990] 1 AC 109, 281 (Lord Goff); *Campbell v Mirror Group Newspapers Ltd* [2002] EWCA Civ 1373, [2003] QB 633, [66]–[71] (Lord Phillips); [2002] UKHL 2, [14] (Lord Nicholls), [44] (Lord Hoffmann).

[100] *Primary Group (UK) Ltd v Royal Bank of Scotland plc* [2014] EWHC Ch 1082, [211] (Arnold J).

and deny the beneficial interest of another. ... In these cases the plaintiff does not impugn the transaction by which the defendant obtained control of the property. He alleges that the circumstances in which the defendant obtained control make it unconscionable for him thereafter to assert a beneficial interest in the property.[101]

So, for example, where the claimant has transferred an asset to the defendant in circumstances where the defendant was subject to a legally binding obligation to deal with the asset for the benefit of a particular person and the defendant breached that undertaking, he would hold the asset on constructive trust for that other person.[102] This principled constructive trust has also been used to perfect an imperfect gift, where the donor sought to make a gift of property to the donee but failed to transfer legal title. The donor would hold the property on constructive trust for the donee if it would be unconscionable for the donor to revoke the gift, where, for example, the donor had represented to the donee that the gift would be made and the donee had relied on this representation in some way.[103]

Proprietary Estoppel

The equitable doctrine of proprietary estoppel is triggered by unconscionable conduct,[104] but this does not involve any assessment of the defendant's mental state, whether assessed objectively or subjectively, as was recognised by Oliver J in *Taylor Fashions Ltd v Liverpool Victoria Trustees Co Ltd*:

> [P]roprietary estoppel ... is directed rather at ascertaining whether, in particular individual circumstances, it would be unconscionable for a party to be permitted to deny that which knowingly, or unknowingly, he has allowed or encouraged another to assume to his detriment than to inquiring whether the circumstances can be fitted within the confines of some preconceived formula serving as a universal yardstick for every form of unconscionable behaviour.[105]

Whilst this may appear to involve the determination of unconscionability on the facts through the exercise of unprincipled judicial discretion, the operation of unconscionability is founded on principles,[106] as was recognised by Lord Scott in *Yeoman's Row Management Ltd v Cobbe*:

> [U]nconscionability of conduct may well lead to a remedy but, in my opinion, proprietary estoppel cannot be the route to it unless the ingredients for a proprietary estoppel are present. To treat a

---

[101] *Paragon Finance plc v DB Thakerar and Co* [1999] 1 All ER 400, 408. See also *Westdeutsche Landesbank Girozentrale v Islington London Borough Council* [1996] AC 669, 705 (Lord Browne-Wilkinson).

[102] *Ashburn Anstalt v Arnold* [1989] Ch 1; *Ollins v Walters* [2008] EWCA Civ 782, [2009] Ch 212, [37] (Mummery LJ) (mutual will); *Pallant v Morgan* [1953] Ch 43 (joint venture); *Banner Homes Group plc v Luff Developments Ltd* [2000] Ch 372. See B McFarlane, 'Constructive Trusts Arising on a Receipt of Property *sub Conditione*' (2004) 120 *LQR* 667.

[103] *Pennington v Waine* [2002] EWCA Civ 227, [2002] 1 WLR 2075.

[104] *Blue Haven Enterprises Ltd v Tully* [2006] UKPC 17, [24] (Lord Scott) (the 'key which unlocks the door' to equitable relief). See generally B McFarlane, *The Law of Proprietary Estoppel* (Oxford, Oxford University Press, 2013), ch 5.

[105] *Taylor Fashions Ltd v Liverpool Victoria Trustees Co Ltd* [1982] QB 133, 151. See also *Gillett v Holt* [2001] Ch 210, 225 (Robert Walker LJ); *Ramsden v Dyson* (1866) LR 1 HL 129, 141 (Lord Cranworth) (test of dishonesty); *Willmott v Barber* (1880) 15 Ch D 96, 105 (Fry J) (test of fraud).

[106] See for example the 'five probanda' identified by Fry J in *Willmott v Barber*, ibid, which the Privy Council consider to be a 'highly convenient and authoritative yardstick for identifying' unconscionable behaviour without being necessarily determinative: *Blue Haven Enterprises Ltd v Tully* [2006] UKPC 17, [23] (Lord Scott).

'proprietary estoppel equity' as requiring neither a proprietary claim by the claimant nor an estoppel against the defendant but simply unconscionable behaviour is, in my respectful opinion, a recipe for confusion.[107]

He added:

Proprietary estoppel requires … clarity as to what it is that the object of the estoppel is to be estopped from denying, or asserting, and clarity as to the interest in the property in question that that denial, or assertion, would otherwise defeat. If these requirements are not recognised, proprietary estoppel will lose contact with its roots and risk becoming unprincipled and therefore unpredictable, if it has not already become so.[108]

The essential elements of proprietary estoppel were recognised by Oliver J in *Taylor Fashions Ltd v Liverpool Victoria Trustees Co Ltd*:

[I]f A under an expectation created or encouraged by B that A shall have a certain interest in land, thereafter, on the faith of such expectation and with the knowledge of B and without objection by him, acts to his detriment in connection with such land, a court of equity will compel B to give effect to such expectation.[109]

In *Yeoman's Row* itself, even though the defendant's conduct was characterised as unconscionable or unattractive in withdrawing from an oral agreement to sell property immediately after planning permission had been obtained, no equitable remedy was recognised to satisfy the claimant's expectations.[110] Crucially, Lord Walker emphasised that careful analysis should not be abandoned in favour of 'unprincipled and subjective judicial opinion'.[111] Particularly pertinent to the recognition of the principled conscience of the court, Lord Walker emphasised that conscience was being used in this context as an 'objective value judgment on *behaviour* (regardless of the state of mind of the individual in question)'.[112]

Discretionary Conscience of the Judge

The final interpretation of conscience is to treat it simply as a rhetorical device behind which the judge can hide, by asserting that a particular result is justified by good conscience but without needing to go further by explaining what that might mean. This is an approach to Equity which can be traced back to Sir Thomas More's *Utopia*:

The law and Judges should avoid arcane interpretations and debates about law but should instead judge the overall equity or justice of a situation and decide accordingly.[113]

It is an approach that enables the judge to reach a judgment about what he or she considers to be a just result on the facts, but without explicit reference to recognised principles, it

---

[107] *Yeoman's Row Management Ltd v Cobbe* [2008] UKHL 55, [2008] 1 WLR 1752, [17]. See also ibid [46] (Lord Walker) and *Blue Haven Enterprises Ltd v Tully* [2006] UKPC 17, [24] (Lord Scott).

[108] ibid [28].

[109] *Taylor Fashions Ltd v Liverpool Victoria Trustees Co Ltd* [1982] QB 133, 144. See also *Sidhu v Van Dyke* [2014] HCA 19, (2014) 251 CLR 505, [77].

[110] A claim in unjust enrichment for the value of the claimant's services in obtaining the planning permission was successful.

[111] *Yeoman's Row Management Ltd v Cobbe* [2008] UKHL 55, [2008] 1 WLR 1752, [59].

[112] ibid [91].

[113] T More, *Utopia* (1516) Book 1, 45.

being sufficient to hide behind the smoke-screen of what might be considered to be ancient language which incorporates its own principles, but without identifying what those principles might be. Rather, discretionary conscience permits a holistic analysis of the facts, by enabling the court 'to look at the matter in the round'.[114]

It is this discretionary interpretation of conscience which underlay the so-called 'new constructive trust' which was developed in the 1970s by a number of judges, led by Lord Denning MR, who used the constructive trust as a mechanism to create equitable property rights where justice and good conscience demanded it.[115] But this was subsequently rejected because it is unprincipled and uncertain.[116] Similarly, the notion of 'public conscience' was used in the 1980s in England to temper the perceived rigidity of the *ex turpi causa* rule, by virtue of which claims would be defeated if the claimant was tainted by illegality. This rule was reformulated so that the illegality defence applied only where the public conscience would be affronted if relief was granted. This test was recognised in equity,[117] but was also applied more generally in tort.[118] It was rejected by the House of Lords in equity, on the ground that it was inconsistent with the authorities and too uncertain,[119] and was eventually also rejected for tort cases.[120] The courts were surely right to do so. The public conscience test was vague and resulted in inconsistent decisions,[121] often turning on judicial outrage arising from the facts of the case.[122] Justice is dependent on a high degree of predictability, which is lacking under the public conscience test.

Experimentation with discretionary judicial conscience in the late twentieth century appears to have been short-lived, both as regards the new model constructive trust and the public conscience test. But the decision of the Supreme Court in *Pitt v Holt*[123] resurrects this approach, since 'unconscionableness' lacks any reference to underlying principle and essentially permits the judge to reach the result which he or she considers to be just and fair. Indeed, Lord Walker specifically recognised that, when determining whether the donor's mistake is sufficiently grave to vitiate the disposition, close examination of the facts is required with reference to all the circumstances and consequences of the mistake.[124] Conscience interpreted in its purely discretionary sense consequently continues to operate.

IV. A New Taxonomy of Conscience

This brief survey of the use of conscience and unconscionability reveals disparate interpretations of apparently similar concepts. What is particularly concerning is the apparent assumption amongst many judges and commentators that conscience has a consistent

---

[114] *Pitt v Holt* [2013] UKSC 26, [2013] 2 AC 108, [126] (Lord Walker).
[115] *Hussey v Palmer* [1972] 1 WLR 1286; *Eves v Eves* [1975] 1 WLR 1338.
[116] *Burns v Burns* [1984] Ch 317, 342 (May LJ).
[117] *Tinsley v Milligan* [1992] Ch 310 (Court of Appeal).
[118] See, eg, *Thackwell v Barclays Bank plc* [1986] 1 All ER 676.
[119] *Tinsley v Milligan* [1994] 1 AC 340.
[120] *Stone and Rolls Ltd (In Liquidation) v Moore Stephens (a firm)* [2009] UKHL 39, [2009] 1 AC 1391, [97] (Lord Scott).
[121] *Tinsley v Milligan* [1994] 1 AC 340, 363 (Lord Goff).
[122] *Hewison v Meridian Shipping Services Pte Ltd* [2002] EWCA Civ 1821, [2003] ICR 766, 788 (Ward LJ).
[123] [2013] UKSC 26, [2013] 2 AC 108.
[124] ibid [126].

meaning. That is clearly not the case. In order to ensure precision of analysis, consistency of application and appropriate communication of meaning a new taxonomy of conscience needs to be adopted, involving a fundamental distinction between the defendant's conscience and the conscience of the court.

The Defendant's Conscience

When the defendant's conscience is assessed, a further distinction needs to be drawn between conscience as a state of the defendant's mind and conscience as an assessment of the defendant's behaviour, which essentially reflects subjective and objective interpretations of conscience.

As has been seen, conscience is sometimes assessed with reference to the defendant's own state of mind, having regard to what the defendant intended, knew or suspected. But subjective conscience is increasingly rare as a test of fault, with evidence in some doctrines that it is being displaced in favour of the objective interpretation. Even subjective interpretations of conscience have objective undertones, since determining the defendant's state of mind inevitably involves considerations of what a reasonable person would have thought in the circumstances of the case.

In fact, the preferable interpretation of the defendant's conscience is that it refers to an assessment of the defendant's conduct, albeit in light of the facts as the defendant knew, believed or suspected them to be. Conscience is to be assessed not by reference to the defendant's own assessment of his or her conduct, but by reference to an external, objective assessment. This is consistent with the historical development of conscience in equity, in the sense that the court determines what the defendant's conscience should require him or her to do in the light of his or her own awareness of the facts. It is also consistent with moral and theological interpretations of conscience, on which equitable notions are founded.[125]

Perhaps, in order to distinguish between different interpretations of unconscionability, this objective assessment of the defendant's behaviour should be called 'dishonesty', which is preferable to the language of constructive knowledge or notice which does not reflect the significance of the defendant's subjective awareness in establishing fault. Dishonesty is a word, however, which is not free from difficulty. Indeed, the objective definition of dishonesty in the action for dishonest assistance provides no definition of what dishonesty itself is. Sometimes the language of honesty has been qualified. For example, in *George Wimpey UK Ltd v VI Construction Ltd*[126] Sedley LJ preferred to use the language of 'honourable' rather than 'honest', but he also wanted to incorporate the language of reasonableness. As he said:

> The phrase 'honest and reasonable' is not a term of art. It is a judicial attempt to sketch a line beyond which conduct may be regarded as unconscionable or inequitable. Its duality, however, is a recognition that honesty alone is too pure a standard for business dealings because it omits legitimate self-interest; while reasonableness alone is capable of legitimising Machiavellian tactics.[127]

This dual standard of honesty and reasonableness might usefully identify the core sense of the objective interpretation of the defendant's fault. Where, in the light of the defendant's

---

[125] See, eg, *Augustine: Confessions*, C Hammond (trans) (Cambridge, MA, Harvard University Press, Loeb Classical Library, 2014); M Svensson, 'Augustine on Moral Conscience' (2013) *The Heythrop Journal* 42; J Ratzinger, 'Conscience and Truth' (1991) http://www.ewtn.com/library/curia/ratzcons.htm.

[126] *George Wimpey UK Ltd v VI Construction Ltd* [2005] EWCA Civ 77, [56].

[127] ibid [60].

awareness of the facts, his or her action or failure to act can be considered to be dishonest and unreasonable, it follows that the defendant's conduct is properly characterised as unconscionable. It is appropriate simply to call this 'dishonest'.

Dishonesty in this objective sense should constitute the essence of equitable fault. It does not follow that unconscionability as a subjective state of mind has no role to play in contemporary equity, although, as will be seen, its role is much less significant than previously thought.

The Court's Conscience

Conscience alternatively refers to the conscience of the court. This can be interpreted as the exercise either of principled or unprincipled discretion. The exercise of judicial discretion with reference to identified principles is not in fact fundamentally different from objective dishonesty, since the identification of such fault determined by the judge on the evidence can be characterised as a principle which triggers equitable intervention. But principled conscience is much more extensive in its operation as it responds to many different principles.

In fact, the dichotomy between uncontrolled discretion and principled discretion is false. HLA Hart[128] recognised that discretion is fundamentally different from arbitrary choice: discretion is 'a certain kind of wisdom or deliberation guiding choice',[129] so that a decision which is not susceptible to principled justification is not an exercise of discretion at all. Hart rejected arbitrary choice as a basis for judicial decision-making. He was right to do so. Whilst the role of judicial discretion involves a choice and is essential to ensure that justice is achieved, if the resort to justice is to be defensible and predictable, there needs to be identifiable principles or recognised factors to guide that discretion and to ensure that like cases are treated alike, for the benefit of the parties, their advisers and, if the case goes to trial, the judge.

A principle is appropriately defined as a reason of general application.[130] The problem, of course, relates to the identification of those principles, but they have emerged over time through the constant evolution of equity. Such principles are typically founded on what the judge considers to be just and fair, not determined through the exercise of arbitrary choice, but rather as an external normative standard against which the defendant can be judged. Some of these equitable principles can be identified at a high-level of abstraction, such as fair dealing, trust and confidence, but then various sub-branches can be identified from them,[131] often influenced by the particular context.[132] So, for example, Toulson LJ has said of the equitable remedy of rectification that:

> [I]ts origins lie in conscience and fair dealing, but those origins cannot be invoked to justify an unprincipled approach: far from it. Particularly as rectification is normally invoked in a contractual

---

[128] HLA Hart 'Discretion', written in 1956 and published in (2013) 127 *Harvard Law Review* 652.
[129] ibid 658.
[130] J Gardner, 'Ashworth on Principles' in L Zedner and P Roberts (eds), *Principles and Values in Criminal Law and Criminal Justice: Essays in Honour of Andrew Ashworth* (Oxford, Oxford University Press, 2012) 9.
[131] *Shearer v Spring Capital Ltd* [2013] EWHC 3148 (Ch), [250] (Daniel Alexander QC).
[132] Watt, above n 39, 109.

context, it seems to me that its principles should reflect the approach of the law to contracts, in particular to the formation and interpretation of contracts. Similarly, as rectification most commonly arises in a commercial context, it is plainly right that the applicable principles should be as clear and predictable in their application as possible.[133]

Gleeson CJ summarised eloquently the proper approach to this notion of principled conscience, namely that the relevant conscience is one 'properly formed and instructed with respect to the conduct in question'.[134]

It follows that the taxonomy of conscience and unconscionability is threefold:

1. The defendant's subjective state of mind.
2. The defendant's behaviour assessed with reference to the defendant's awareness of the circumstances.
3. The conscience of the court exercised with reference to recognised principles at various levels of abstraction.

V. Implications

Whether this taxonomy is sufficiently robust to explain the state of the law and, if it is found wanting, to justify reform, requires careful consideration of disparate aspects of contemporary equity. Suffice for now to consider three potential implications: the role of fault in equitable claims; the role of conscience in the law of restitution and the exercise of remedial discretion.

The Determination of Fault in Equitable Claims

In assessing the appropriate level of fault in equitable claims, reference is sometimes made to the *Baden* classification.[135] Although this has been subject to much criticism from judges[136] and commentators, it remains of some use, if only as a way of identifying the range of fault recognised in equity. Traditionally, equitable receipt-based and accessorial liability claims have required proof of knowledge, which is what the *Baden* classification refers to. In that case, five different types of knowledge were identified:

1. actual knowledge;
2. wilfully shutting one's eyes to the obvious;
3. wilfully and recklessly failing to make such inquiries as an honest and reasonable person would have made;

---

[133] *Daventry District Council v Daventry and District Housing Ltd* [2011] EWCA Civ 1153, [2012] 1 WLR 1333, [196].

[134] *Australian Broadcasting Corporation v Lenah Game Meats Pty Ltd* [2001] HCA 63, (2001) 208 CLR 199, [45].

[135] *Baden v Société Générale pour Favoriser le Développement du Commerce et de l'Industrie en France SA* [1993] 1 WLR 509, 575 (Peter Gibson J).

[136] In *Royal Brunei Airlines Sdn Bhd v Tan* [1995] 2 AC 378, 392, the Privy Council indicated that, for accessorial liability at least, the *Baden* classification is best forgotten. It was expressly adopted by the High Court of Australia in *Farah Constructions Pty Ltd v Say-Dee Pty Ltd* [2007] HCA 22, (2007) 230 CLR 89.

4. knowledge of circumstances that would indicate the facts to an honest and reasonable person; and
5. knowledge of circumstances that would put an honest and reasonable person on inquiry.

This classification must be treated with caution, particularly because the distinctions between the categories are difficult to draw in practice and may be too refined.[137] Indeed, they have been described as differences of degree rather than kind.[138]

The *Baden* language of knowledge used to form the defining fault component of both receipt-based and accessorial personal liability claims. That language has been replaced by unconscionability and dishonesty, respectively. In reality, however, the line between the two fault elements is difficult to draw. In *Dubai Aluminium Co Ltd v Salaam*[139] Lord Millett described the claim for knowing receipt as founded on allegations of dishonesty and then described it as dishonest receipt, and most recently Lord Neuberger emphasised three times in the space of one paragraph that the liability of the recipient is founded on dishonesty.[140] This is consistent with the analysis of the defendant's conscience as involving conduct objectively assessed in the light of the defendant's own knowledge or suspicion of the facts. In a receipt-based claim the defendant's behaviour is unconscionable (or dishonest) when he or she should have made restitution of the value of the property received in the light of the facts involving breach of trust which the defendant knew or suspected. The defendant will be liable for assisting or inducing a breach of trust when his or her conduct is characterised as dishonest (or unconscionable) in the light of the facts involving the breach which the defendant knew or suspected.

A similar approach to the assessment of fault can be identified in the defence of change of position to an unjust enrichment claim. That defence will not be available where the defendant acted in bad faith in changing his or her position. Bad faith for these purposes has been equated with unconscionability and has been interpreted as including dishonesty, a failure to act in a commercially acceptable way, sharp practice falling short of outright dishonesty,[141] and wilfully and recklessly failing to make such inquiries as an honest and reasonable person would make,[142] but not negligence.[143] There is no reason to think that this is anything other than an objective assessment of the defendant's conduct, but in the light of the facts as the defendant knew or suspected them to be. It would, in fact, be possible to replace the language of bad faith with that of dishonesty.

---

[137] *Agip (Africa) Ltd v Jackson* [1990] Ch 265, 293 (Millett J).
[138] *Royal Brunei Airlines v Tan* [1995] 2 AC 378, 390.
[139] *Dubai Aluminium Co Ltd v Salaam* [2002] UKHL 48, [2003] 2 AC 366.
[140] *Williams v Central Bank of Nigeria* [2014] UKSC 10, [2014] AC 1189, [64]. See also *Vestergaard Frandsen v Bestnet Europe Ltd* [2013] UKSC 31, [2013] 1 WLR 1556, [42] (Lord Neuberger). Although in *Williams* Lord Sumption asserted that liability for knowing receipt does not require proof of dishonesty on anybody's part: [2014] UKSC 10, [2014] AC 1189, [35]. Whilst he did not explain what he meant by dishonesty for these purposes, he appeared to relate it to fraud.
[141] *Niru Battery Manufacturing Co v Milestone Trading Ltd* [2002] EWHC 1425 (Comm), [2002] 2 All ER (Comm) 705, 741. This was endorsed in the Court of Appeal: [2003] EWCA 1446 (Civ). See also *Abou-Rahmah v Abacha* [2006] EWCA Civ 1492, [2007] 1 All ER (Comm) 827.
[142] *Papamichael v National Westminster Bank* [2003] Lloyd's Rep 341, 369 (Judge Chambers QC); *Armstrong DLW GmbH v Winnington Networks Ltd* [2012] EWHC 10 (Ch), [2013] Ch 156, [110] (Stephen Morris QC); *Jeremy D Stone Consultants Ltd v National Westminster Bank* [2013] EWHC 208(Ch), [247] (Sales J).
[143] *Maersk Air Ltd v Expeditors International (UK) Ltd* [2003] 1 Lloyd's Rep 491, 499.

That unconscionability for the equitable receipt-based claim and for change of position should be interpreted in the same way was recognised by the Court of Appeal in *Abou-Rahmah v Abacha*,[144] in which it was held that general suspicions on the part of the defendant about the nature of the trustee's conduct does not constitute unconscionability; the defendant must be suspicious about the particular transaction involving the transfer of property.

It follows that unconscionability in its objective sense should be the appropriate fault for both equitable receipt-based and accessorial liability. In fact, this can be considered to embody all aspects of the *Baden* test, since, in the light of the defendant's knowledge (which should encompass belief and suspicion) the question is whether the defendant's behaviour was appropriate, which will be assessed objectively with reference to what the reasonable person would have done.

The Role of Conscience in Unjust Enrichment

Relevance of Conscience in the English Law of Unjust Enrichment

The foundations of the modern law of unjust enrichment in England can be traced back to various judgments of Lord Mansfield, who based the action for money had and received to the use of the payer on the idea that retention of the money by the payee would be against conscience.[145] So, in *Sadler v Evans*[146] he recognised that money had and received was 'founded upon large principles of equity, where the defendant can not conscientiously hold the money'. The significance of conscience to the law of restitution was emphasised subsequently. So, in *Kelly v Solari*[147] it was recognised that money paid by mistake could be recovered, even though the claimant had made the mistake negligently, specifically because it would be against conscience for the payee to retain it. Further, in *Fibrosa Spolka Akcyjna v Fairbairn Lawson Combe Barbour Ltd*[148] Lord Wright, in an influential dictum, said:

> It is clear that any civilised system of law is bound to provide remedies for cases of what has been called unjust enrichment or unjust benefit, that is to prevent a man from retaining the money of or some benefit derived from another which it is against conscience that he should keep.

Even in *Lipkin Gorman (a firm) v Karpnale Ltd*,[149] where the unjust enrichment principle was incontrovertibly recognised in England for the first time, Lord Goff explicitly related the defendant's unjust enrichment resulting from retention of money paid by mistake to Lord Mansfield's contention that it would be against conscience for the defendant to retain the money.

But restitution is not tied to vague notions of conscience, enabling the judge to exercise an arbitrary choice depending on perceived notions of justice on the facts of the case.[150]

---

[144] *Abou-Rahmah v Abacha* [2006] EWCA Civ 1492, [2007] 1 All ER (Comm) 827.
[145] Most famously in *Moses v Macferlan* (1760) 2 Burr 1005, 1011.
[146] *Sadler v Evans* (1766) 4 Burr 1984, 1986. See also *Dale v Sollet* (1767) 4 Burr 2133, 2134; *Clarke v Shee* (1774) 1 Cowp 197, 199.
[147] *Kelly v Solari* (1841) 9 Mand W 54, 58 (Parke B).
[148] *Fibrosa Spolka Akcyjna v Fairbairn Lawson Combe Barbour Ltd* [1943] AC 32, 61.
[149] *Lipkin Gorman (a firm) v Karpnale Ltd* [1991] 2 AC 548, 572.
[150] A concern of Hamilton LJ in *Baylis v Bishop of London* [1913] 1 Ch 127, 140.

Instead the unjust enrichment formula is applied,[151] relating to whether the defendant has been unjustly enriched at the claimant's expense.[152] This is a principle rather than a cause of action, namely that the defendant was enriched at the claimant's expense in circumstances which fall within an identified and recognised ground of restitution.[153] Since 1991 the language of conscience is only rarely used when examining unjust enrichment.[154]

Conscience in Australia

In Australia the law of restitution has taken a different course, albeit from a starting point similar to the existing English approach.[155] In *Pavey and Matthews Pty Ltd v Paul*[156] the High Court explicitly recognised unjust enrichment. Refinement of principle followed. But it was Gummow J, in particular in *Roxborough v Rothmans of Pall Mall Australia Ltd*,[157] who put the law on a different course. In rejecting the role of unjust enrichment as a unifying principle, he emphasised instead the equitable origins of restitution in *Moses v Macferlan*, from which he concluded that the law of restitution should be founded on unconscionability. Confirmation of this volte face followed in a number of decisions,[158] most significantly in *Australian Financial Services and Leasing Pty Ltd v Hills Industries Ltd*.[159] As the plurality in that case recognised:[160] '[T]he concept of unjust enrichment is not the basis of restitutionary relief in Australian law.' Rather, the 'enquiry is conducted by reference to equitable principles', namely whether the retention of monies paid to the defendant can be considered to be unconscionable. But which of the four interpretations of conscience applies here? Conscience as a fault element seems inappropriate to the law of restitution, even in Australia, since liability to make restitution does not require proof of the defendant's fault. The plurality recognised that 'conscience' does not involve the judge's subjective evaluation of the justice of the case,[161] and purported to identify equitable principles to assess conscience. But the only indication as to what these principles are involved reference to 'a construct of standards and values',[162] or, as Chief Justice French recognised,[163] a legal standard 'informing guiding criteria for particular classes of case'. But there was no attempt to identify what these standards, values or criteria might be. Since the High Court appears

---

[151] *Banque Financière de la Cité v Parc (Battersea) Ltd* [1999] 1 AC 221, 227 (Lord Steyn).

[152] A formula which should not be treated as though it has statutory force: *Investment Trust Companies v The Commissioners for Her Majesty's Revenue and Customs* [2012] EWHC 458 (Ch), [39] (Henderson J).

[153] *Uren v First National Home Finance Ltd* [2005] EWHC 2529 (Ch).

[154] See, eg, *Vedatech Corp v Crystal Decisions (UK) Ltd* [2002] EWHC 818 (Ch), [74] (Jacob J). In *Banque Financière de la Cité v Parc (Battersea) Ltd* [1999] 1 AC 221, 237 Lord Clyde described the action as equitable but emphasised that it did not follow that it was entirely discretionary in its application.

[155] See W Swain, 'Unjust Enrichment and the Role of Legal History in England and Australia' (2013) 36 *University of New South Wales Law Journal* 1030.

[156] *Pavey and Matthews Pty Ltd v Paul* (1987) 162 CLR 221.

[157] *Roxborough v Rothmans of Pall Mall Australia Ltd* [2001] HCA 68, (2001) 208 CLR 516.

[158] Including *Farah Construction Pty Ltd v Say-Dee Pty Ltd* [2007] HCA 22, (2007) 230 CLR 89 and *Lumbers v W Cook Builders Pty Ltd (in liq)* [2008] HCA 27, (2008) 232 CLR 635. *Equuscorp Pty Ltd v Haxton* [2012] HCA 7, (2012) 246 CLR 498, [30] (French CJ, Crennan and Kiefel JJ) appeared to signal a return to the recognition of unjust enrichment as having a significant taxonomical role in Australian law.

[159] *Australian Financial Services and Leasing Pty Ltd v Hills Industries Ltd* [2014] HCA 14.

[160] ibid [78].

[161] ibid [76].

[162] ibid.

[163] ibid [16].

unwilling to identify such principles to establish liability, it may be that conscience is simply a cipher for the exercise of arbitrary choice by the judge after all.

But might the unjust enrichment principle have an appropriate role in constructing what conscience demands? On the same day that the High Court handed down judgment in *Hills Industries*, Edelman J handed down judgment in *Lampson (Australia) Pty Ltd v Fortescue Metals Group Ltd (No 3)*,[164] and sought to carve out a role for unjust enrichment in the light of what was said in *Hills Industries*. He considered that unjust enrichment is not a direct source of liability in Australia, but has a useful function as a taxonomic category in assisting understanding, in the same way as 'torts' is a useful descriptive category but does not identify the underlying cause of action of a particular tort. Nevertheless, he went on to identify the core features of the unjust enrichment formula, involving enrichment that is unjust and at the plaintiff's expense, which provides the reason for restitution to be awarded. But does this not constitute the essence of an underlying cause of action, albeit with the additional need to identify recognised factors which render the enrichment unjust? Without the elements of this cause of action, what is it that triggers the restitutionary response? If it is unconscionability in the unprincipled fourth sense, then we are left with a claim without definition, save for the judge being given carte blanche to determine the just result by reference to standards and values which he or she is allowed to determine. If it is unconscionability in the principled third sense, we are still left with the need to identify what those principles are. The principle of unjust enrichment would serve that purpose, but then that is elevating unjust enrichment beyond a mere 'label', 'concept' or 'notion' to something else which gives meaning to what is unconscionable. That still preserves the equitable foundation of the claim, but makes sense of it by incorporating an unjust enrichment principle.

The High Court in *Hills Industries* did identify some principles to assist in the interpretation of the change of position defence with reference to conscience, notably by considering whether the defendant had relied on the receipt and thereby suffered an irreversible detriment.[165] It followed that the defendants' decisions not to pursue claims against the claimant following the receipt of a mistaken payment constituted a complete defence to the restitutionary claim because it involved an irreversible detriment. There is no reason to think that an English court would have reached a different result.[166] Of course, in England the elements of the unjust enrichment claim would need to be established first, but they were clearly satisfied since the defendant had been enriched by the receipt of money paid as a result of the claimant's mistake. Although in Australia it was necessary to show that the defendant's receipt of the money was against conscience, surely that could only be established by proving that the defendant had received money paid by the claimant as a result of a mistake. In both jurisdictions change of position would be established as a complete defence and in both cases this would render an obligation to make restitution unjust or, to put it another way, against conscience.

As a matter of form, the divide between English and Australian restitution law seems more significant than ever following the decision of the High Court in *Hills Industries*, with England relying on unjust enrichment and Australia on conscience. But, as a matter

---

[164] *Lampson (Australia) Pty Ltd v Fortescue Metals Group Ltd (No 3)* [2014] WASC 162.
[165] *Australian Financial Services and Leasing Pty Ltd v Hills Industries Ltd* [2014] HCA 14, [24] (French CJ).
[166] Although the defence of change of position is interpreted more widely in England.

of substance, the difference is vanishingly small. In England unjust enrichment operates to establish whether the receipt of the enrichment is unconscionable in a principled sense, whereas in Australia unconscionability can only be interpreted in a principled way with reference to unjust enrichment. As French CJ rightly said,[167] 'legal principles of restitution or unjust enrichment can be equated with seminal equitable notions of good conscience'. It follows that, if it is necessary to explain the law of restitution with reference to conscience, it is vital that the principle of unjust enrichment be used to justify what conscience demands. The language of conscience might be considered to have no useful function in this context, so it can be ignored, as now appears to be the case in England. Nevertheless, and against the trend of analysis in England, there may be a useful role in linking unjust enrichment to unconscionability to explain the existence and operation of restitutionary relief and defences, but not if there is any danger that conscience will be interpreted as allowing the judge to exercise arbitrary choice on the facts. That is the danger now facing the Australian courts if it fails to control conscience by constraining it within the bounds of unjust enrichment.

Remedial Discretion

Conscience may also assist in the exercise of the court's discretion when determining the appropriate remedy to be awarded, either with reference to the defendant's fault or the principled conscience of the court. This can be illustrated by three contexts where judges have a discretion to determine the appropriate remedy to be awarded.

Breach of Confidence

In the action for breach of confidence two personal remedies are available, depending on the state of the defendant's conscience as a standard of fault. One is account of profits and the other is the negotiation measure, which is assessed with reference to what the claimant could reasonably have demanded from the defendant to waive the obligation of confidence. Account of profits is typically available where subjective unconscionability can be established, in that the defendant deliberately or recklessly breached a duty of confidence.[168] Where the defendant unconsciously breached the duty of confidence the negotiation measure will be awarded.[169] The award of these remedies can be justified with reference to unconscionability. Where the subjective test of unconscionability is engaged the more extensive remedy of account of profits can be justified, whereas the negotiation measure is justified where the defendant's breach of duty can be characterised as objectively unconscionable.

Proprietary Estoppel

The remedial consequences of proprietary estoppel involve the exercise of discretion by reference to the court's conscience, but in a principled way. It was recognised by the High

---

[167] *Australian Financial Services and Leasing Pty Ltd v Hills Industries Ltd* [2014] HCA 14, [16].
[168] *Peter Pan Manufacturing Corp v Corsets Silhouette Ltd* [1964] 1 WLR 96.
[169] *Seager v Copydex* [1967] 1 WLR 923, 931 (Lord Denning MR), 935 (Salmon LJ), 939 (Winn LJ). See also *Vestergaard Frandsen A/S v Bestnet Europe Ltd* [2013] UKSC 31, [2013] 1 WLR 1556, [24] (Lord Neuberger).

Court of Australia in *Waltons Stores (Interstate) Ltd v Maher*[170] that 'the court, as a court of conscience, goes no further than is necessary to prevent unconscionable conduct'. Whilst superficially vague, this does provide a basis from which principles have been identified. So, for example, the relief usually reflects the value of what the promisor has promised,[171] although this may not always be the just measure of relief.[172]

Remedial Constructive Trust

Unconscionability should be relevant to the award of proprietary remedies as well. Whilst the remedial constructive trust is not recognised in England,[173] a compelling case can be made for its recognition, but only if the court's discretion is exercised with reference to the principled notion of unconscionability. One of the significant objections to the recognition of the remedial constructive trust is that it would involve unrestrained judicial discretion. Birks was strongly opposed to its recognition for that reason. He said:

> The law of remedies is not exempt from the demands of certainty and predictability: nor is the law as a whole intellectually respectable if, even at the level of remedies, it takes refuge in an inscrutable case to case empiricism. Practising lawyers need to be able to advise their clients as to the likely results of litigation. The judges on whom these results depend need the insulation from personal criticism which only objectively ascertainable rules and principles can provide.[174]

Whilst it is undoubtedly the case that unrestricted discretion is unacceptable, in part for the reasons identified by Birks, as Hart argued this does not involve the exercise of discretion at all, but arbitrary choice; discretion demands principles to guide and justify the judicial decision. There is no reason why such principles cannot be identified for the remedial constructive trust,[175] such that the judge should be able to decide that assets or profits are held on constructive trust where that is consistent with recognised principles. This would also enable the judge to fashion the constructive trust appropriately. As Deane J recognised in *Muschinski v Dodds*:

> The fact that the constructive trust remains predominantly remedial does not, however, mean that it represents a medium for the indulgence of idiosyncratic notions of fairness and justice. As an equitable remedy, it is available only when warranted by established equitable principles or by the legitimate processes of legal reasoning, by analogy, induction and deduction, from the starting point of a proper understanding of the conceptual foundations of such principles … proprietary

---

[170] *Waltons Stores (Interstate) Ltd v Maher* (1988) 164 CLR 387, 419.

[171] *Sidhu v Van Dyke* [2014] HCA 19, (2014) 251 CLR 505, [85] (French CJ, Kiefel, Bell, Keane JJ).

[172] ibid [83]. See A Robertson, 'Unconscionability and Proprietary Estoppel Remedies' in E Bant and M Harding (eds), *Exploring Private Law* (Cambridge, Cambridge University Press, 2010), 402 who argues that the only role of unconscionability is to ensure that the relying party is completely protected from harm arising from their reliance.

[173] *FHR European Ventures Ltd v Cedar Capital Partners LLC* [2014] UKSC 45, [2015] AC 250, [47] (Lord Neuberger). See also Lord Neuberger, 'The Remedial Constructive Trust—Fact or Fiction', lecture delivered on 10 August 2014 to the Banking Services and Finance Law Association Conference, New Zealand: www.supremecourt.uk/docs/speech-140810.pdf.

[174] P Birks, 'The Remedies for Abuse of Confidential Information' [1990] *LMCLQ* 460, 465.

[175] An attempt to do so was made by Hammond J in *Butler v Countrywide Finance Ltd* [1993] 3 NZLR 623, 632, having regard to factors such as economic efficiency, the nature of the right to be supported and the conduct of the parties.

rights fall to be governed by principles of law and not by some mix of judicial discretion, subjective views about which party 'ought to win' … and 'the formless void' of individual moral opinion.[176]

The key question, then, will be what principles should be relevant when determining whether a remedial constructive trust should be recognised. In fact, the preferable analysis of the constructive trust is that, rather than there being two diametrically opposed camps of institutional and remedial constructive trust,[177] the trust should be regarded essentially as institutional, arising by operation of law, but it should be possible to modify the proprietary implications of recognising the trust with regard to principles grounded on the state of the recipient's conscience.

The most important principle underpinning the constructive trust is that it should be triggered with regard to the court's characterisation of the defendant's conduct. Dishonesty is an objective standard of unconscionability, albeit one which is assessed with references to the defendant's knowledge or suspicion about the relevant facts. That standard is appropriate to justify the imposition of a personal liability. But something more should be needed for the recognition of proprietary rights in equity and that is why subjective unconscionability, involving deliberate or reckless conduct, should be the standard for the recognition of the constructive trust. This will not be an absolute standard, however, since there will be circumstances where an objective test of unconscionability can be justified, especially where a fiduciary is liable for breach of duty, because of the high standard of conduct expected of fiduciaries. That would be consistent with what Hayton has called the 'good person' philosophy, namely that fiduciaries are expected to act as good people for the benefit of their principals.[178] For that reason we can justifiably deem a fiduciary to have acted unconscionably where they have acted in breach of fiduciary duty, which should be sufficient to recognise a constructive trust.

Why should the defendant's fault be relevant to create a proprietary interest? This can be justified because an unconscionable defendant should be deprived of all benefits arising from their unconscionable conduct; the claimant's claim to the assets is stronger than that of the defendant; the defendant should be purged of his or her unconscionability by disgorging all benefits obtained from the unconscionable conduct; and all those claiming through the defendant should likewise have their conscience purged from all possible unconscionability. Of course, these justifications become more absurd and unconvincing, but that is why the constructive trust should not be absolute but can be modified. There may be other considerations to take into account, such as whether other remedies can do the same work more effectively or third party recipients have pure consciences which do not need to be purged.

The appropriate model of the constructive trust consequently is one where the trust arises by operation of law where the defendant's receipt or retention of property is unconscionable, actual or deemed, but this trust can be modified with reference to recognised

---

[176] *Muschinski v Dodds* (1985) 160 CLR 583, 615. See also *State Trustees Ltd v Edwards* [2014] VSC 392, [143] (McMillan J).

[177] See Deane J in *Muschinski v Dodds* (1985) 160 CLR 583, 614: '[F]or the student of equity, there can be no true dichotomy between the two notions.'

[178] D Hayton, 'The Development of Equity and the "Good Person" Philosophy in Common Law Systems' (2012) 76 *Conv* 263, 272.

principles, such that the trust might be defeasible. The operation of this model of the constructive trust can be tested by reference to a particularly controversial problem, namely whether a fiduciary who has received a bribe from a third party should hold that bribe on constructive trust for the principal. In England the Supreme Court has held that the fiduciary will hold the bribe on an institutional constructive trust for the principal.[179] This is justified because the fiduciary should be treated as though he or she had acquired the bribe on behalf of the principal, who therefore has a proprietary interest in it. This result can be justified with reference to unconscionability,[180] which is deemed because of the high standards we expect of fiduciaries, such that the fiduciary should not profit from the breach of duty, so any increase in the value of the bribe should be transferred to the principal. But what about those who claim through the fiduciary? In particular, where the asset which has been held on constructive trust has been transferred to a volunteer recipient whose conscience is not tainted, why should the principal be able to vindicate his or her proprietary right against the recipient? Here it would be appropriate to modify the constructive trust so that the equitable proprietary right is defeated by the innocent receipt. It would be different, however, if the recipient's conscience was tainted by knowledge or suspicion about the bribe,[181] for then the principal's proprietary right should be vindicated in equity.

VI. Conclusions

To understand the true function of conscience and unconscionability it is vital to distinguish between the conscience of the defendant and the conscience of the court. The former involves an assessment of fault, interpreted subjectively or objectively. When fault forms a necessary part of the equitable claim, usually the defendant's conscience is to be assessed objectively, in the light of what the defendant knew or suspected, and this can legitimately be described as dishonesty. The subjective assessment of the defendant's conscience should be exceptional and preferably is only relevant to the recognition, and potential modification, of equitable proprietary rights. In *Vestergaard Frandsen v Bestnet Europe Ltd*[182] the reference to conscience for purposes of establishing the claim for breach of confidence was a reference to the defendant's fault. Since this did not involve any proprietary implications, the objective interpretation of conscience should have been adopted, in accordance with the general trend of the authorities, and not the subjective interpretation as adopted by Lord Neuberger.

Alternatively conscience refers to the conscience of the court, which enables the judge to determine the justice of the case but only in a principled way and not by reference to an arbitrary choice. It is this sense of conscience which was adopted by Lord Walker in *Pitt v Holt*,[183] but since he did not identify any principles to underpin the exercise of the

---

[179] *FHR European Ventures Ltd v Cedar Capital Partners LLC* [2014] UKSC 45, [2015] AC 250.
[180] *Tanwar Enterprises Pty Ltd v Cauchi* [2003] HCA 57, (2003) 217 CLR 315, [20].
[181] Such as the wife and solicitor of Reid in *Attorney General of Hong Kong v Reid* [1994] 1 AC 324, who appear to have known that the assets which were transferred to them were purchased with bribe money.
[182] *Vestergaard Frandsen v Bestnet Europe Ltd* [2013] UKSC 31, [2013] 1 WLR 1556.
[183] *Pitt v Holt* [2013] UKSC 26, [2013] 2 AC 108.

discretion, this reference to conscience was inappropriate. In fact, any reference to conscience and unconscionability in the context of equitable rescission for mistake was unnecessary, it being sufficient that the mistake was sufficiently serious before a disposition could be rescinded. If it is considered to be desirable to retain the language of conscience to explain the operation of the equitable jurisdiction, this needs to be explicitly linked to the seriousness of the mistake as the underlying principle which enables the court to conclude that the defendant's receipt of a mistaken payment can be characterised as unconscionable.[184] In other words, unconscionability is the conclusion rather than the test to trigger equitable intervention.

Any suggestion that the use of the language of conscience is only relevant to enable the judge to secure the perceived just result on the facts of the case should be rejected. The reason for doing so was expressed powerfully by Llewellyn:

> [U]nless the appellate courts consciously awaken to what their duty is in this regard ... they are threatened with loss of their own souls, and we are threatened with loss of the greatest asset of the common law. Every opinion must be directed forward. It must make sense and give guidance for tomorrow for the *type of situation* in hand. Only in the light of that are the equities and decencies of the particular case to be attended to, for in the working out of that forward-looking guidance two things occur: first, the authoritative material at hand to work with exercises in due restraint ... and that gives a court firmness of heart and rock-solidity of work; second, no pressure of the particular case can readily mislead into sentimentality when all is judged against right guidance through the *type* of situation for the future.[185]

Ultimately, and fundamentally, the true role of conscience in contemporary equity reflects a battle over the nature of private law. There is a spectrum of approaches. At one end, characterised by Birks's position, is the pure logic of the law, founded on reason, principle and predictability where there is no role for conscience. At the other end, reflected in the approach of many judges, is the desire to reach the just result on the facts behind the smoke-screen of conscience. The preferable approach falls somewhere between the two extremes. Principled justice is justifiable; principled conscience has a legitimate role to play in explaining the equitable jurisdiction. That way conscience is not higher than the law, but is an essential part of it.

---

[184] For reasons of consistency with the analysis of the constructive trust, it might be considered that where an asset has mistakenly been transferred to the defendant by a deed which is sought to be rescinded, so that the asset will be held on constructive trust for the claimant, this can only occur where the defendant's conscience is affected in a subjective sense. But, where the claimant seeks to rescind the deed, this will inevitably notify the defendant of the restitutionary claim, such that the failure to make restitution can be characterised as unconscionable. But the prior question is whether the deed can be rescinded. This should not depend on unconscionability, but simply on whether the mistake was sufficiently serious.

[185] KN Llewellyn, *The Bramble Bush* (Oxford, Oxford University Press, 2008) 15.

16

Form and Substance in Equitable Remedies[*]

STEPHEN A SMITH

I. Introduction

Today—nearly a century and a half after the Judicature Acts—is it helpful to describe specific performance and injunctions ('specific relief') as 'equitable' remedies?[1] Does this label tell us anything useful about specific relief? It is of course true that the contemporary rules governing specific relief originated in the Chancery Court, ie in the court of 'equity'. But legal rules are rarely described according to their court of origin. We do not have textbooks on 'Rules Originating in the Court of Appeal' or 'Rules Originating in Lord Atkin's Court'. So why have textbooks on 'Remedial Rules Originating in the Chancery Court'? It is also true that the rules governing specific relief are equitable in the Aristotelian sense that they were introduced and developed as exceptions, in particular as exceptions to the remedial rules in force in the Royal Courts. But this history is hardly a justification for describing the law on specific relief as equitable since much of the contemporary law, whatever its origins, began as an exception. Vicarious liability is an exception to the general rule that we are not liable for the acts of others. Punitive damages are an exception to the general rule that damages are not meant to punish. The tort of negligence was at one time an exception to the general rule that tort liability was strict.

Writers who defend what I will call the 'traditional' practice of describing specific relief as equitable would presumably respond to these observations by arguing that the description identifies an important feature of specific relief beyond its origins in the Chancery Court. This chapter examines two suggestions as to what this feature might be. The first suggestion is that the traditional label identifies an important feature of the form of specific

[*] I am grateful to Jeff Berryman for comments on an earlier version of this paper and to Brodie Noga for research assistance.

[1] Writers on remedies commonly describe specific performance and injunctions as equitable remedies; see, eg, DB Dobbs, *Law of Remedies*, 2nd edn (St Paul, West Group, 1993); and J Berryman, *The Law of Equitable Remedies*, 2nd edn (Toronto, Irwin Law, 2013). This description is the basis for discussing specific performance in books on 'equitable remedies'; see, eg, ICF Spry, *The Principles of Equitable Remedies*, 6th edn (Agincourt, Carswell Company, 2001); Berryman, *Equitable Remedies* (cited above); and in books on 'equity'; see, eg, J Martin, *Modern Equity*, 18th edn (London, Sweet & Maxwell, 2009); G Virgo, *The Principles of Equity and Trusts* (Oxford, Oxford University Press, 2012). An important counter-example is A Burrows, *Remedies for Torts and Breach of Contract*, 3rd edn (Oxford, Oxford University Press, 2004).

rulings. In particular, it identifies the fact that, unlike rulings that originated in the Royal Courts, 'specific' rulings are personal directives: a specific ruling is an order commanding the defendant to do or not do something. The second suggestion (which may be combined with the first) is that the traditional label identifies an important feature of the substance of specific relief or at least of the rules governing their availability, namely that they have a distinctive moral quality.

The chapter's conclusion is that neither the form nor the substance of specific relief justifies the traditional terminology. Admittedly, some aspects of the contemporary law governing specific relief cannot be understood apart from their equitable origins. But to describe specific relief in general as equitable is unhelpful and a barrier to understanding the main features of the law governing specific relief—features that could easily have developed in a unitary legal system. Indeed, I will suggest that it is not just the term 'equitable' that is unhelpful, but also terms such as 'injunction', 'specific performance' and 'specific relief'. Within the class of rulings that contemplate future states of affairs ('directive' rulings),[2] the most important distinction is between executable and non-executable rulings. The historical distinction between 'legal' relief and equitable (or 'specific', or 'injunctive') relief broadly tracks the distinction between executable and non-executable relief. This congruence explains why the historical labels have survived. But it does not justify them: the labels impede understanding the logic behind the distinction.

In light of this book's theme, it is appropriate to close these introductory remarks by mentioning that this chapter was motivated by a recent development exclusive to English common law. In 1997 the Civil Procedure Rules (CPR)[3] abolished the traditional form in which rulings originating from the Royal Courts were expressed. Today in England all directive rulings are expressed as orders.[4] For reasons discussed below, this change could be seen as either a radical reordering of the basic foundations of English law or a trivial linguistic clean-up. But on either interpretation, contemporary English law has rejected the idea that a distinctive feature of so-called equitable rulings is their personal form. This rejection raises the question of whether there are other reasons—reasons that apply to common law jurisdictions generally—to abandon the traditional terminology.

II. Form

Specific rulings are traditionally expressed as personal orders commanding the defendant to do or not do a certain act: 'It is this day adjudged and ordered that the defendant John Jones, before 1 o'clock in the afternoon of Jan 1, 2015, pull down and remove the structure located …'.[5] By contrast, directive rulings that originated in the Royal Courts (namely

---

[2] Directive rulings thus include specific performance, injunctions and the main rulings originating from the Royal Courts: rulings for the recovery of damages, debts or land. Excluded from this category are rulings that, by their issuance, bring about a new legal state of affairs ('constitutive' rulings) or rulings that merely declare an existing state of affairs or legal right and that are not enforceable as such ('declaratory' rulings). This essay is concerned exclusively with directive rulings, in particular directive rulings that provide for the final disposition of disputes in which plaintiffs seek to uphold rights recognised by the law of tort, contract, unjust enrichment and property.

[3] Civil Procedure Rules 1998 (UK), c12.

[4] I discuss this change in section III.

[5] T Chitty and J Jacob, *Chitty & Jacob's Queen's Bench Forms*, 19th edn (London, Sweet & Maxwell, 1965) no 1350 ('Judgement or Order for Injunction at Trial').

rulings to pay damages, a debt,[6] or to recover land) are traditionally expressed as impersonal 'judgments' that a certain state of affairs shall happen: 'It is this day adjudged that the plaintiff shall recover $100 from the defendant.'[7]

As just mentioned, this difference in form has recently been abolished in England. But for many writers the distinction between personal and impersonal rulings is fundamental to understanding specific relief—even in jurisdictions where the distinction has been abolished.[8] Two propositions are usually advanced in support of this view. The first, which lies outside this chapter's direct concerns, is that the difference in the form of specific rulings and judgments explains an important difference in how these rulings are enforced. A failure to comply with a judicial order, it is said, is a direct affront to the court's (originally the Chancellor's) authority—it is a contempt of court—and so is 'enforced' by punishing the defendant, typically by imprisonment, though sometimes by a fine or sequestration of goods. By contrast, not bringing about the state of affairs stipulated in a judgment is not an act of disobedience since a judgment does not command the defendant (or anyone else) to do anything. A judgment does, however, stipulate a legally required state of affairs, and so in this view a judgment implicitly authorises the plaintiff to bring about the stipulated state of affairs directly, which is typically done by engaging the assistance of a sheriff or bailiff. In the case of a monetary judgment, the sheriff or bailiff will normally try to achieve the desired result by execution against the defendant's assets, ie by seizing and selling such assets as needed to satisfy the judgment.[9]

The second proposition, which is directly relevant to this chapter, is that the traditional difference in the form of specific rulings and judgments reflects a fundamental difference in the relationship of specific rulings and judgments with substantive law.[10] According to what I will call the 'formal separation thesis', a judgment is basically a declaration or statement of the law applicable to the litigants' situation. In this view, a judgment that the plaintiff 'shall recover $100 from the defendant' is fundamentally a judicial declaration that, as a matter of law, the defendant owes the plaintiff $100. By contrast, a specific ruling that orders the defendant 'to deliver the cow Betsy to the plaintiff' says nothing, in this view, about the parties' legal rights and duties. The order is simply an expression of the Chancellor's (or his contemporary representative's) view that the defendant ought, as a matter of morality (or 'conscience'), to deliver the cow to the plaintiff. According to the formal separation thesis an order is fundamentally an act of the executive, which leaves the parties' legal relationship unaffected. In its most extreme version, the thesis supposes that orders have nothing to do with the 'law', strictly defined.[11]

---

[6] For convenience, I include within rulings to pay a debt those rulings originating in the Royal Courts that would today be described as 'restitutionary'. The form and content of restitutionary awards is the same as that of awards to pay debts or damages.

[7] Chitty and Jacob, *Forms*, above n 5, no 688 ('Judgement for Plaintiff for Debt or Damages and Costs after Trial by Judge Alone').

[8] See, eg, Spry, above n 1, 26–35, 323; Dobbs, above n 1, 6, 12–13, 62–63.

[9] In the case of an order for recovery of land, execution may be brought about by taking possession of land, with or without the assistance of a legal official.

[10] See, eg, Spry, above n 1, 26–35, 323; Dobbs, above n 1, 5–6, 12–13, 62–63.

[11] See Dobbs, above n 1, 63: 'The difference between the judgment at law, which declared rights in things—*in rem*—and the decree in equity which commanded the defendant's conscience to act—*in personam*—was thus a very considerable one. The chancellors used it constantly to explain why they could be apparently contradictory systems at work on English soil, yielding different results: one was law, the other was merely a personal matter.'

The suggestion that personal orders are fundamentally non-legal fits neatly with the standard account of the Chancery Court's historical evolution. In this account, the Chancery Court's practice of issuing orders (not judgments) developed so as to ensure that its rulings did not conflict with the judgments issued by the Royal Courts. By confining itself to issuing personal orders, the Chancery left the 'law' to the Royal Courts, and so made possible the two courts' coexistence. The formal separation thesis also fits neatly with the fact that, even today, judgments and orders (in systems that maintain the distinction) have different effects on litigants' substantive rights. It is orthodox law that the legal rights a plaintiff asserts in order to obtain a judgment are replaced by (or 'merged with') the judgment, allowing no further action to be taken on the original rights.[12] Thus, a plaintiff who obtains a judgment for the payment of a contractual debt cannot later sue for damages for losses arising from late payment (whether those losses arose before or after the judgment). By contrast, an order is said to leave the parties' substantive rights untouched, such that the plaintiff may rely upon them in a further action.[13] Thus, a plaintiff who has obtained an order that the defendant perform a contract may bring a subsequent action for damages if performance is late or becomes impossible.[14]

The formal separation thesis appears, then, to be supported by both the historical and contemporary practice of common law courts. Nonetheless, it is vulnerable to two significant objections. The first, which strictly speaking applies only to England, is the already-mentioned fact that today in England all directive rulings are expressed as orders. The general form for an English award of damages or payment of a debt reads: 'It is ordered that the defendant: (1) pay the claimant the sum of £...'.[15] Given this language, it is not possible in England to defend the description of specific relief as equitable on the basis that specific rulings have a distinctive equitable form. Both specific rulings and rulings that originated in the Royal Courts ('non-specific rulings') are expressed as personal orders that command the defendant to perform or not perform an act. If expressing a ruling in the form of an order indicates that the ruling has nothing to do with the law, then rulings to pay damages, debts, or recover land—each of which originated in the Royal Courts—also have nothing to do with the law in England today. This objection cannot be avoided on the ground that the just-described change is merely 'formal' since the formal separation thesis is entirely about the form of rulings.

There is no counterpart to the CPR's reforms in other common law jurisdictions. Yet the English reforms should give even non-English defenders of the formal separation thesis reason to pause. England has overturned a distinction that, if the defenders are correct, lies at the core of the common law. Yet England made this change with little fuss or fanfare. The adoption of a common form for all directive rulings appears to have attracted no attention or controversy in the proceedings leading up to the CPR or afterwards. The change appears to have been regarded merely as part of the CPR's general cleaning-up of archaic language.[16]

---

[12] See *Re European Central Railway Co* (1876) 4 ChD 33 (CA), 37–38.

[13] See *Austins of East Ham ltd v Macey* [1941] Ch 338 (CA), 341.

[14] The full story is more complex because the order determines how the defendant's duty must be performed: see *Singh v Nazeer* [1979] Ch 474 (Ch), 480.

[15] See, eg, Forms No 45 and No 46 which CPR 40B PD 14.1 refers to as general forms of a trial judgment.

[16] No doubt part of the reason the changes attracted little attention is that they had few practical consequences. Orders that trace their origins to the Chancery Court are still subject to the special preconditions traditionally applied to such orders, eg inadequacy of damages and clean hands, and, with a few small exceptions, are still enforced in the same way (namely by the threat of punishment).

This observation leads to a second, and more general, objection to the formal separation thesis: the traditional difference between orders and judgments can be explained without reference to equity. The states of affairs contemplated by orders and judgments are, in each case, states of affairs that ordinary legal rules—the 'law' developed by the Royal Courts— suppose are legally required. Both an order to deliver goods due under a contract and a judgment stipulating that a sum of money due under a contract shall be recovered contemplate the satisfaction of an ordinary contractual duty—a duty first recognised in the Royal Courts.[17] A plaintiff who obtains an order 'not to trespass' and, at the same time, a judgment for damages for losses arising from past trespasses is awarded the latter because the defendant did the very thing that the order prohibits. Although orders, unlike judgments, may be issued before a breach has occurred, the states of affairs that such orders contemplate—eg, not trespassing or causing a nuisance—are still legally required. The actions required by an injunction not to trespass are the same regardless of whether the defendant trespassed in the past: in each case the required action is 'not trespassing'.

The suggestion that orders are somehow outside of the law or that they do not deal with the law must therefore be rejected: the states of affairs contemplated by orders have the same relationship to the substantive law as those contemplated by judgments. But the states of affairs contemplated by orders are admittedly different in one respect from those contemplated by judgments. They differ in the means by which they can be realised. This difference explains the traditional difference in their forms.

The states of affairs contemplated by judgments can in principle be brought about without the defendant's participation. The transfer of money that is contemplated by a judgment to pay a debt or damages can in principle be achieved by execution against the defendant's assets. By seizing and selling the defendant's property and then transferring the appropriate sum to the plaintiff, a third party (or even the plaintiff) can in principle bring about the result contemplated by a monetary judgment. Similarly, the state of affairs contemplated by a judgment for the recovery of land can be brought about simply by the plaintiff taking possession. Of course, in either case the defendant can attempt to obstruct efforts to bring about the desired result. And in the case of a monetary judgment, the defendant may lack the assets needed to satisfy the judgment. However, in principle the states of affairs contemplated by judgments can be brought about without the defendant's participation.

Seen in this light, judicial pronouncements stating that plaintiffs shall 'recover' money or land appear to be a natural (albeit linguistically awkward) way to make clear that it is not strictly necessary that the defendants themselves hand over the relevant money or land. True, if it were important as a matter of principle that defendants personally bring about the states of affairs contemplated by judgments this locution would require further explanation. But there is no such principle. Once defendants have failed to pay a debt, committed a wrong, or taken possession of another's land, then by definition they have failed to follow

---

[17] I have argued elsewhere that there is no substantive duty to pay damages or to make certain kinds of restitutionary payments: see S Smith, 'Duties, Liabilities, and Damages' (2012) 125 *Harvard Law Review* 1727; S Smith, 'A Duty to Make Restitution?' (2013) 26 *Canadian Journal of Law and Jurisprudence* 157. In this specific respect, then, there is a difference between how judgments to pay damages or to make restitution relate to the substantive law, and how judgments to pay a debt or to recover land relate to that law. However, to avoid constant qualification this difference is ignored in this chapter. The argument advanced above only requires that the states of affairs contemplated by orders relate to the substantive law in the same way as at least some of the states of affairs contemplated by judgments.

the guidance provided by the substantive law. The question for a court contemplating a ruling in such cases is (merely) how to bring about the desired state of affairs. In cases where that state of affairs can be brought about by either the defendant or a third party, a judicial ruling declaring that this state of affairs 'shall happen' makes clear that either method is acceptable.

By contrast, the states of affairs contemplated by orders (in systems that continue to distinguish orders from judgments) generally cannot be brought about by a third party, or at least not easily. Short of throwing defendants in jail the only way to stop them from trespassing, causing nuisances or breaching restrictive covenants is to convince them to decide not to trespass, commit a nuisance, etc. Similarly, an order to convey title to land cannot be fulfilled unless the defendant decides to sign the necessary documents.[18] The states of affairs contemplated by orders to tear down buildings or to deliver specific goods can in theory be brought about by third parties, but not easily and not without a risk of violence. It follows that courts that wish to bring about the states of affairs contemplated by traditional orders have a good reason to enlist the defendant's assistance. The obvious way to try to obtain this assistance is to order the defendant to bring about the desired state of affairs. And the only way to enforce such orders is by external incentives, such as the threat of committal or a fine.

These observations suggest that the distinction between judgments and orders should not be seen as a distinction between rulings that stipulate what the law requires and rulings that stipulate what equity requires, but, more mundanely, as a distinction between rulings stipulating states of affairs that can be brought about or 'executed' by third parties ('executable rulings') and rulings stipulating states of affairs than cannot be so executed ('non-executable rulings'). Naturally, some rulings fall near the borderline of this distinction. Examples include rulings contemplating the tearing-down of a building constructed by the defendant or contemplating the transfer of specific goods in the defendant's possession. As just noted, the states of affairs contemplated by such rulings can in principle be realised by third parties, but for practical reasons it is generally preferable that they be brought about by the defendant. In such cases, the modern law generally provides that defendants should in the first instance be ordered to bring about the desired state of affairs, but gives plaintiffs the option of enforcing the order by third-party execution.[19] Other borderline cases include rulings that require the payment of a sum of money on a future date or on the occurrence of a future event. An example is the ruling made in cases where the buyer in a land-sale contract has refused to pay the price.[20] In principle, the buyer's obligation to pay the price is executable by third parties. However, in practice execution is complicated because in a typical land-sale contract the obligation to pay is conditional on the vendor being able and willing to convey good title. The consequence of this condition is that other than in the rare cases where the vendor has already performed, any ruling that contemplates the buyer's payment must make that payment conditional on the vendor being able and willing to perform. A third party attempting to execute such a ruling would therefore need

---

[18] Note that contemporary courts are often given powers to order the execution of a document where the defendant refuses to comply with an order to do so; see, eg, Supreme Court Act 1981 (UK), c 54, s 39.

[19] RSC Ord 45, rr 4(1), 5, 8.

[20] See *Johnson v Agnew* [1980] AC 367 (HL). The separate question as to why courts do not restrict claimants to awards of damages in such cases is discussed in the text accompanying nn 33–35.

to obtain the relevant sum from the defendant (typically by seizing and selling the defend-ant's assets) without knowing whether the claimant will remain ready and willing to convey title. If the claimant changes her mind, the execution process would presumably need to be reversed. Ordering the defendant personally to pay on the condition stipulated in the contract—namely that the plaintiff remains able and willing to convey title—is a simpler solution. A ruling to pay a sum of money in the future is also relatively common when the defendant is in breach of an obligation to make periodic payments, for instance under an annuity policy.[21] Again, the monetary result contemplated by such an obligation can in principle be brought about by third parties. However, in practice third-party execution is again complicated, or at least burdensome, because it must occur repeatedly (ie each time the sum is due and not paid). It is simpler to issue a single order commanding the defend-ant to make the payments. And if the threat of contempt proceedings does not persuade the defendant to pay voluntarily, the claimant retains the option to bring an action in debt or damages once the sum is actually due.

Admittedly, some traditionally available orders cannot be explained in this way. For example, the difficulties associated with third-party execution do not explain why courts are willing to specifically enforce buyers' obligations to pay the price in land-sale cases where title has passed.[22] There seems no reason to prefer an order to a judgment in these circum-stances. But in general the distinction between executable and non-executable rulings lines up with the traditional distinction between judgments and orders. In legal systems that continue to employ both judgments and orders, judgments are generally used to stipulate executable states of affairs, while orders are generally used to stipulate non-executable states of affairs. It is not necessary to know anything about equity to understand this distinction. But in general the distinction between executable and non-executable rulings lines up with the traditional distinction between judgments and orders. In legal systems that continue to employ both judgments and orders, judgments are generally used to stipulate executable states of affairs, while orders are generally used to stipulate non-executable states of affairs. It is not necessary to know anything about equity to understand this distinction.

This explanation of the difference in form between orders and judgements is supported by the way in which the English reforms described earlier were introduced and received. The explanation supposes that the difference in form between orders and judgments (in systems that maintain the distinction) is today largely a matter of administrative con-venience. In this view, it does not particularly matter whether courts order defendants to pay debts subject to the condition that if they do not comply their assets may be seized or, instead, if courts issue impersonal judgments stating that debts shall be paid subject to the understanding that if they are not paid voluntarily the defendant's assets may be seized.[23]

---

[21] *Evans Marshall & Co v Bertola SA* [1973] 1 WLR 349 (CA).

[22] The explanation (not justification) appears to be the idea that it would be inequitable if only one contracting party's obligations were specifically enforceable ('positive mutuality'). While there might have been some practical justification, in these circumstances, for mutuality of specific performance in the time prior to the Judicature Act (see Berryman, above n 1, 186), the idea has never been applied widely and is today largely discredited: Berryman, above n 1, 235–39; Burrows, above n 1, 459. The only explanation for the contemporary availability of specific performance in these circumstances appears to be historical.

[23] Of course it matters how rulings are enforced. But as the English reforms illustrate, the form in which a ruling is expressed does not determine how it may be enforced. Although monetary awards are now expressed in England as 'orders' they are normally enforceable only by execution against assets; see A Zuckerman, *Zuckerman on Civil Procedure*, 2nd edn (London, Sweet & Maxwell, 2006) 822.

Judgments and orders are alternative routes to the same result, and it is that result—eg payment of a debt—that matters, not how it is brought about. Seen in this light, the English reforms reflect nothing more than the mundane decision that even in cases where it is not strictly necessary for the defendant to personally bring about the desired result, it is generally preferable that the defendant do so—if for no other reason than to avoid involving third parties—and so this preference should be made explicit. Of course, if it were the case that orders could only be enforced by punishment the English reforms would have significant practical implications. But there is no reason that orders to perform executable tasks cannot be enforced directly by execution. The English reforms sensibly provide for just this result: under the CPR, executable orders are generally enforceable only by execution while non-executable orders are generally enforced by punitive measures.[24] Admittedly, in some cases it will be clear that the defendant is unlikely to comply with an order to bring about an executable state of affairs—and thus where such an order would have little point—but in such cases judges can set a short time period for compliance. Under the old system, judges dealt with the parallel situation (namely cases where judgments were issued notwithstanding that the defendant was willing to bring about the result voluntarily) by restraining third-party execution until the defendant had time to act. The main advantage of the contemporary English system is uniformity and simplicity of expression. It is not surprising, then, that the English changes attracted almost no attention: far from disrupting the common law's foundations, they were largely a matter of housekeeping.

The conventional rule that orders leave litigants' legal rights unchanged while judgments replace those rights can also be explained without invoking equity. The main significance of the first half of this rule is that plaintiffs who have obtained orders can be awarded damages for losses arising from further delays or total non-performance. This result makes sense as plaintiffs should generally be able to recover damages for losses arising from non-performance whether or not the defendant has been ordered to perform. In principle, all that matters when assessing a claim for damages is if and when performance happened. The explanation of the second half of the rule, which precludes plaintiffs who have obtained a judgment from later suing for damages, is more complex. In the case of judgments to pay damages, no explanation is needed since damages are generally unavailable for non-payment of damages, regardless of whether a judgment has been issued. In the case of judgments to pay debts the answer is partly historical—money traditionally had a constant value so being deprived of it for a period of time caused little loss. While the value of money is not constant today, the availability in modern times of pre- and post-judgment interest means that the most common foreseeable form of loss—loss of the time-value of money—is implicitly compensated. In addition, defendants are generally given a short period to pay judgments, and those judgments can be quickly executed by attentive plaintiffs. Against this background, the traditional rule that a duty to pay a debt merges with the judgment can be justified on the ground that it avoids the cost of additional litigation. Finally, judgments for the recovery of land are typically executable immediately, so any losses arising from delay in taking possession may generally be attributed to the plaintiff. As well, losses that plaintiffs suffer from trespassing typically do not arise from trespassers merely being on the plaintiff's property but rather from trespasser damaging or using that property or from restricting the plaintiff's access. The plaintiff's ability to sue for such losses, even when

---

[24] ibid 817–30.

the losses arise post-judgment, is not affected by a judgment. For example, plaintiffs can recover damages for lost profits or rents arising from dispossession ('mesne profits') even with respect to losses that arise subsequent to a judgment for possession.[25]

These observations on the traditional distinction between orders and judgments are not meant to deny that the distinction arose in a dual system and that at least part of the reason it arose was to avoid a conflict between the systems. The fact that the Chancery Court issued orders, not judgments, is an important part of its history. But whatever the historical genesis of the distinction, its application today (in systems that maintain it) can be explained without resort to that history. Impersonal directives—judgments—are a natural (though not inevitable) way to try to bring about states of affairs that do not require the defendant's participation. Personal directives—orders—are a natural way to try to bring about states of affairs that require the defendant's involvement. The formal distinction between orders and judgments could easily have arisen in a unitary legal system.

III. Substance

Rules that originated in the Chancery Court are often said to share a particular substantive aim. This aim is typically described by saying that equity is concerned above all with preventing 'unconscionable conduct' or, slightly more narrowly, preventing the unconscionable insistence on legal rights (ie rights derived from Royal Courts).[26] Such descriptions have not gone unchallenged. It is widely accepted that many of the rules relating to trusts have little to do with preventing unconscionable behaviour, notwithstanding their Chancery Court origins. On the other hand, many of the rules that originated in the Royal Courts appear to have just such an aim—for example many of the rules governing damages.[27] I will put these broader arguments to the side; my concern is exclusively for the rules governing specific relief. Are these rules explained by a concern to prevent unconscionability, in particular the unconscionable assertion of legal rights? The answer, I suggest, is that at most only a small and relatively insignificant number of these rules can even potentially be explained this way.

The Possibility of Specific Relief

The most important objection to explaining specific relief in terms of a concern for unconscionability is that the most basic fact about specific relief—namely that it is awarded at

---

[25] See D Elvin and J Karas, *Unlawful Interference with Land* (London, Sweet & Maxwell, 2002) [4–017], [4–022]; *Ministry of Defence v Ashman* [1993] 2 EGLR 102 (CA).

[26] See, eg, Spry, above n 1 ('Equitable principles have above all a distinctive ethical quality, reflecting as they do the prevention of unconscionable conduct'); Virgo, *Equity and Trusts*, above n 1 ('Equity ... restrains injustice by stopping the unconscionable conduct of a particular person'). This view is not shared by all equity textbooks; see, eg, R Meagher, J Heydon and M Leeming, *Equity: Doctrines & Remedies*, 4th edn (Sydney, Butterworths, 2002) 3 ('Equity can be described but not defined. It is the body of law developed by the Court of Chancery in England before 1873').

[27] See, eg, S Worthington, *Equity* (Oxford, Oxford University Press, 2003) 26.

all—has nothing to do with unconscionability. An order to perform a contract or to cease a trespass is not an order to refrain from acting unconscionably. Like other specific rulings, these orders (merely) command defendants to comply with their ordinary legal duties. It is of course wrong to break a contract or commit a trespass, but there is nothing distinctively unconscionable about such wrongdoing. The wrong in such cases is the wrong of breaching an ordinary legal duty—the same wrong that gives rise to awards of damages. Specific rulings thus do exactly what is traditionally assumed to be the particular concern of the Royal Courts, namely to uphold legal rights. Another way of making this point is to observe that specific relief is related to the substantive law in an entirely different way than are those institutions that were developed as part of the Chancery Court's 'exclusive' jurisdiction, such as the trust. The trust can plausibly be described as an institution that restrains defendants from doing things that the substantive rules of contract, tort and property— rules developed in the Royal Courts—allow them to do. By contrast, specific rulings require defendants to do the very things that the substantive rules of contract, tort and property require them to do.

Adequacy of Damages

Perhaps unsurprisingly, defenders of the distinctiveness of equitable remedies have said little about why defendants should do the things that specific rulings require them to do; instead defenders focus on the rules governing the availability of specific rulings. Yet most of these rules—and certainly the most important of them—also have nothing to do with unconscionability.

According to the conventional view, the most important rule governing specific relief is that it is not available except where damages are inadequate. It has been queried whether in practice this rule is as significant a bar to specific relief as the conventional view assumes.[28] But for present purposes the important point is that whatever the rule's significance in practice, it has nothing to do with preventing unconscionability. On any interpretation of 'inadequacy of damages' the concept is unconcerned with the parties' behaviour. The simplest explanation for why specific relief is not granted when damages are adequate (assuming specific performance is even possible)[29] is that damages often are a reasonable, even if not perfect, substitute for specific relief *and* because damages generally impose fewer costs on the legal system. Damages are frequently an adequate substitute in the sense that plaintiffs can often purchase substitute identical or near-identical performance from a third party. An award of damages provides money that can often be used (or relied upon in advance) to purchase the same performance that a specific ruling would require. The cost-advantage of damages arises from the fact that damages are a monetary remedy while specific rulings, with rare exceptions, are non-monetary. It is generally simpler for courts to specify the actions required and to determine if those actions have been carried out in the case of monetary rulings as opposed to non-monetary rulings. Monetary rulings thus

---

[28] See D Laycock, *The Death of the Irreparable Injury Rule* (Oxford, Oxford University Press, 1991).

[29] Typically, specific relief is not possible because it is too late—the contract has been terminated, the trespass is over—and even where specific relief is possible it is rarely desired, either because the plaintiff can bring an action in debt (the most common private law action) or for the recovery of land (the second most common action) or because the plaintiff wants nothing further to do with the defendant.

raise a smaller risk of further litigation between the parties. Finally, but crucially, the costs of enforcing monetary rulings are typically significantly less than the cost of enforcing non-monetary rulings. In most cases the only practical way to enforce a non-monetary ruling is to punish the defendant—which entails an additional trial and, in most cases, incarcerating the defendant.[30] By contrast, monetary rules can be executed by third parties if necessary.

If the only thing that mattered when contemplating rulings was achieving perfect justice, then the practical advantages of damages over specific relief would be irrelevant. But justice is only one of many services the state provides; it also builds hospitals, educates children, defends borders, and so on. All these services cost money—public money. It is because judges do not work for free that their number is limited and that there are usually long queues to get to court. Given the scarcity of judicial resources, it would be irresponsible for the courts to ignore the costs of the services they provide—including the cost of providing and enforcing rulings. Whatever arguments might be made for the irrelevance of economic considerations when determining how citizens ought to treat one another, ie when determining the substantive law, such considerations are clearly relevant when determining how judges and other state officials ought to act.

Of course, the extent to which damages should be awarded in preference to specific relief depends not just on the comparative administrative costs of these rulings but also on the extent to which damages are an adequate substitute for specific relief. It is no surprise, then, that the standard case in which damages are found inadequate is where it is not possible for the defendant to purchase or otherwise bring about the state of affairs contemplated by the relevant duty. For example, damages are typically held to be inadequate in cases involving negative duties, such as duties not to trespass or cause a nuisance or not to compete with a co-contractor, because only the defendant can perform a negative duty. Damages are also inadequate where the defendant's duty is to deliver unique goods or convey title to land because by definition unique goods and particular parcels of land cannot be purchased elsewhere. In all these cases the reason that, notwithstanding its administrative convenience, a monetary award is an inadequate substitute for a non-monetary award, is that money cannot purchase what the duty is meant to achieve.

In rare cases courts will order specific performance of monetary duties. Probably the most common such order—specific performance of a duty to make periodical payments[31]—is consistent with the above explanation because such rulings are issued precisely to avoid repeat litigation.[32] The explanation of the other main instance of monetary specific

---

[30] A ruling to pay a debt is of course a monetary ruling. It is consistent with the above explanation, then, that litigants seeking such rulings do not need to prove that damages are inadequate. The other main category of ruling not subject to the adequacy of damages requirement, a ruling for the recovery of land, is also straightforward to administer though it is admittedly more difficult to enforce than a monetary remedy (since force may be needed to remove a determined trespasser). The marginally higher costs associated with such rulings were, and no doubt still are, considered reasonable given the importance that the common law accords to property rights. Some rights are more valuable than others—and so worth spending more to protect perfectly. Whether the common law correctly identifies such rights is another question.

[31] *Evans Marshall & Co v Bertola SA* [1973] 1 WLR 349 (CA).

[32] This explanation was advanced in *Beswick v Beswick* [1968] AC 58, 81, 88, 97 (HL) [*Beswick*], where the duty was to pay an annuity to a third party. Notice, however, that damages would have been inadequate in *Beswick* even if the payment were a one-off, since damages would have been nominal and so insufficient to pay for alternative performance. The alternative, and preferable, solution to cases involving payments to third parties—to allow the plaintiff to bring an action in debt—is precluded because an action in debt is only possible when the relevant sum is owed to the plaintiff. This limitation seems explicable only on historical grounds.

relief—specific performance of a buyer's duty to pay the price in a sale of land[33]—is more complex. In cases where the vendor has conveyed title to the land, the explanation appears to be historical. As noted earlier, a judgment to pay the price (or, equally, to pay damages) is a perfectly satisfactory award in such circumstances.[34] At one time, the availability of specific performance in these circumstances may have avoided procedural problems arising from a bifurcated court system,[35] but their availability today seems explicable only as an historical anachronism. However, there may be a justification for the rule in the more typical land-sale case in which the parties' obligations are concurrent. If the buyer refuses to pay in such a case, the vendor normally cannot bring an action in debt because he has not passed title to the buyer. The vendor could attempt to convey title notwithstanding the buyer's unwillingness to pay, but doing so raises the very risks that the concurrency requirement was meant to avoid (eg insolvency). An action for damages is arguably also inadequate in these circumstances because the buyer cannot be certain to find another buyer or least to find one in a reasonable (and predictable) time period. Admittedly, there are established markets for certain kinds of land—not all land is unique—but a rule restricting disappointed vendors (or buyers) to specific performance in cases where land is unique is impractical because there is no simple test for uniqueness. Vendors who wrongly assume that their land is unique will be penalised under such a rule if the market price of land drops between the time of breach and the time of judgment.[36] The solution to this dilemma is to order recalcitrant buyers to comply with their future monetary obligations, and to back up those orders with the threat of contempt charges. Historically, such orders were available only from the Chancery Court.

The common law's preference for damages over specific relief has been explained on grounds other than administrative convenience. For example, damage awards have been defended on the ground that they facilitate efficient breaches,[37] give effect to the parties' true intentions,[38] or promote detached relationships.[39] These and related explanations seem unnecessarily complicated, but for present purposes the important point is that none of them link the 'adequacy of damages' rule to a concern for unconscionability.

Difficulty of Supervision

Even if damages are inadequate in the sense just described a court may refuse a request for specific relief and award damages instead. In the vast majority of cases, such refusals are made for either of two overlapping reasons (or for both reasons). The first reason is that specific relief would be difficult to 'supervise'. Of course, courts do not literally supervise

---

[33] *Johnson v Agnew* [1980] AC 367 (HL).

[34] See n 23 above and accompanying text.

[35] See Berryman, above n 1, 186.

[36] Vendors of land can almost certainly find buyers, and find them quickly, if they drop their price low enough, but it is not clear that courts could determine the appropriate price in advance or, if the vendor has already made the sale, assess the fairness of the price.

[37] RL Birmingham, 'Breach of Contract, Damage Measures and Economic Efficiency' (1970) 24 *Rutgers Law Review* 273.

[38] D Markovits and A Schwartz, 'The Myth of Efficient Breach: New Defenses of the Expectation Interest' (2012) 98 *Virginia Law Review* 143.

[39] D Kimel, *From Promise to Contract: Towards a Liberal Theory of Contract* (Oxford, Hart Publishing, 2003) 83.

the carrying-out of their rulings. They may, however, be called upon to intervene if the defendant fails to comply and, more generally, if disputes arise in connection with carrying out a ruling. The concern for supervision is thus a concern for avoiding future litigation—and so for avoiding rulings that are especially likely to give rise to disputes. Courts are rightly hesitant to issue orders whose satisfaction requires the litigants' future co-operation or—what usually amounts to the same thing—if it is not possible to state precisely the outcome contemplated by the order. It was on this basis that the House of Lords refused to order a supermarket located in a shopping mall to comply with its contractual obligations to stay open, serve customers, and so on.[40]

It is sometimes suggested that the common law takes the 'difficulty of supervision' condition too seriously, but so far as I am aware it has never been suggested that the condition should be eliminated entirely. The latter suggestion would indeed be surprising since the condition's rationale is merely an extension of the general argument in favour of monetary rulings. The administrative costs that are associated with non-monetary awards generally are supervision costs. The rationale for a distinct 'difficulty of supervision' bar is that some non-monetary orders raise a heightened supervision risk. An order to operate a supermarket raises a significantly greater risk of future litigation than an order to deliver goods. Thus, for the same reason that courts should worry generally about supervision—namely that judicial resources are scarce, publicly funded goods—they should worry particularly about rulings that raise special supervision issues, and they should do this even if damages are an imperfect substitute. It may be debated how much weight this concern should be given in a modern legal system, but that it should be given some weight seems incontrovertible. In any event, the supervision condition has nothing to do with unconscionability. If anything, this condition provides potential wrongdoers with increased opportunities to exploit their potential victims since it eliminates one of the sanctions for breach.

Personal Duties

The other main reason specific relief may be refused, notwithstanding the inadequacy of damages, is that the relevant duty cannot be fulfilled without non-trivial personal involvement by the defendant. This is the standard explanation for the common law's long-standing refusal to order employees to fulfil their employment obligations. The 'personal duty' condition could be viewed as a sub-category of the supervision condition (since orders to perform personal duties invariably raise supervision issues), but it is generally assumed that a distinct reason for refusing such orders is that they give rise to a kind of servitude. More needs to be said to explain how ordering compliance with a valid legal duty, even if it is personal, can amount to servitude (the explanation, I suggest, turns on the fact that court-ordered duties are owed to the state),[41] but in any case a concern for servitude has nothing to do with unconscionability. It may well be undesirable to permit courts to order the performance of personal duties, but there is nothing unconscionable about personal duties nor is it unconscionable for those owed such duties to seek their performance.

---

[40] *Co-operative Insurance Society Ltd v Argyll Stores (Holdings) Ltd* [1998] AC 1, 12 (HL).

[41] See S Smith, 'Rule-Based Rights and Court-Ordered Rights' in A Robertson and D Nolan (eds), *Rights and Private Law* (Oxford, Hart Publishing, 2011) 221, 250.

Whatever its ultimate foundation, the concern for servitude, like the concern for supervision, is a concern raised by particular features of non-monetary orders. There is no need to ask whether orders to pay debts or damages or to recover land could amount to servitude because fulfilling such orders requires little or no personal involvement by the defendant.[42]

The Traditional Bars

In addition to refusing specific relief because damages are an adequate substitute, supervision is difficult or the duty is personal, courts may also refuse specific relief on the basis of what are conventionally described as the 'equitable bars' (or 'equitable defences' or 'equitable maxims'), but which I will call the 'traditional bars'. For example, specific relief may be refused because the plaintiff does not have 'clean hands', delayed unduly in bringing the application or because the order would cause special hardship.

As might be expected given their conventional label, the traditional bars are typically highlighted in discussions of the allegedly equitable nature of specific relief. I will argue below that most of the traditional bars can be understood without knowing anything about their equitable origins. But the first—and the most important—thing to know about the traditional bars is that they play a small role in the law governing specific relief and are rarely relevant in litigation. Even taken as a group, the traditional bars are minimally significant in comparison to any one of the three conditions described above. It is true that many rarely invoked rules are important for understanding broader legal concepts. The rules on offer and acceptance are rarely invoked in litigation yet they are crucial to understanding the nature of contractual obligations. The traditional bars, however, are negative conditions; they are reasons for not awarding specific relief. As such, even if they were invoked frequently it is unlikely that they could tell us much about the general nature of specific rulings or the reasons for issuing them. The traditional bars are comparable in this respect to the historically 'equitable' reasons for setting aside contracts, such as undue influence and unconscionability. Like the traditional bars to specific relief, the doctrines of undue influence and of unconscionability originated in the Chancery Court. Yet no one has ever suggested that the existence of these doctrines justifies describing contractual duties as equitable or describing contract law as an equitable body of law. It is rightly recognised that the existence of these doctrines provides at most a reason to describe a small sub-set of the grounds for invalidating prima facie valid contracts as equitable.

There is little agreement amongst writers or courts as to the number of traditional bars, their names or the borders between them. The discussion below focuses on what are arguably the most important and widely accepted bars (albeit they are sometimes listed under other labels).

Clean Hands

It is orthodox law that specific relief may be refused if the plaintiff has 'unclean hands'. In broad terms, plaintiffs have unclean hands if they have engaged in behaviour that, while

---

[42] The defendant does not strictly need to do anything in response to such orders because the only consequence of non-performance is that a third party may seize and sell the defendant's assets.

not strictly a legal wrong or a reason to deny a substantive right (eg a contractual right), is undesirable and is linked to the right the plaintiff is seeking to enforce.[43] For example, a plaintiff's bad faith failure to disclose important information in the proceedings leading to a contract of sale may constitute unclean hands.[44] In other cases, the concept of uncleanliness is interpreted more broadly, as when Scientologists were denied an injunction against defamatory publications because their own activities and beliefs were, in the judge's view, deplorable.[45]

The clean hands bar is less important today than previously because of the expansion of general defences such as illegality, duress, undue influence, unconscionability and misrepresentation. Indeed, it may be queried whether the bar serves any useful role today. Nonetheless the clean hands bar seems defensible in principle—and for reasons that have nothing to do with unconscionability. The clean hands doctrine is closely related to the general defence of illegality, especially insofar as this defence allows courts to refuse relief to plaintiffs whose behaviour, though not strictly unlawful, is considered immoral or otherwise contrary to public policy. Under the latter doctrine, courts have, for example, refused to enforce prostitution contracts, notwithstanding that entering into such contracts is not unlawful in most common law jurisdictions.[46] By definition, the kinds of behaviour at issue in cases of unclean hands are not sufficiently unclean to invoke the general defence of public policy. They may, however, be sufficiently unclean to invoke a narrower version of that defence.

The most plausible justification for the broader public policy defence is the familiar idea that the courts do not wish to be seen as even indirectly assisting or condoning immoral or otherwise undesirable (even if not strictly unlawful) behaviour. In such cases, the courts are effectively saying to plaintiffs what ordinary citizens often say in similar situations: 'I won't stop you from doing what you are doing, but I also won't help you or get involved in any way.' One could explore the philosophical basis of this principle further, but for the moment my concern is its application outside ordinary public policy cases.

The proper application of this principle depends on two criteria. The first is the degree to which the relevant behaviour is contrary to public policy. The courts rightly do not refuse assistance to plaintiffs engaged in trivial misbehaviour. The second criterion is the nature of the assistance that the misbehaving party seeks from the state. The greater the assistance or involvement that is sought, the greater the risk that the state will be seen as supporting the plaintiff's misbehaviour. It follows that the test for what counts as disqualifying misbehaviour should be easier to satisfy in cases where the plaintiff is seeking a greater degree of assistance from the courts. As we have seen, plaintiffs seeking specific relief are normally seeking more assistance than plaintiffs seeking payment of a debt or damages or the recovery of land. Specific rulings are often more difficult to draw up than other orders, they

---

[43] The traditional maxim 'he who comes to equity must do equity' is similar to clean hands—and raises the same issues—except that it looks to the plaintiff's future conduct. Broadly defined, the clean hands bar covers cases (rare today) in which specific performance is refused on the basis of the plaintiff's breach, the plaintiff's misrepresentation, the defendant's mistake, or the unfairness of the contract's terms.

[44] *Quadrant Visual Communications Ltd and Others v Hutchison Telephone (UK) Ltd and Another* [1993] BCLC 442 (CA); *Falcke v Grey* (1859) 4 Drew 651, 62 ER 250.

[45] *Hubbard v Vosper* [1972] 2 QB 84 (CA).

[46] A similar principle underlies the law's refusal to assist plaintiffs who have issued unlawful threats or engaged in similar behaviour in the process of obtaining contractual rights even if that behaviour had no effect on the defendant's decision to enter the contract: see *Barton v Armstrong* [1976] AC 104 (PC), 121; S Smith, *Contract Theory* (Oxford, Clarendon Press, 2004) 317–22.

may lead to further litigation, and, crucially, they are enforced by criminal prosecutions and punishments. By contrast, rulings for the payment of a debt or damages or for the recovery of land are easy to express, rarely lead to subsequent litigation and can be enforced with little or no involvement by the state.[47] Against this background, it is unsurprising that courts will sometimes refuse a request for specific relief on the basis of the defendant's undesirable behaviour notwithstanding that the behaviour in question is not sufficiently undesirable to refuse all relief entirely. The clean hands defence is an application of the general principle that courts must be careful not to be associated too closely with a plaintiff's undesirable—even if not strictly unlawful—behaviour.

The public policy explanation of the clean hands bar is not meant to suggest that the courts always apply the bar properly or even that the bar is on balance a good thing. Reasonable legal systems might well come to the view that the distinction between 'refusing all relief' and 'refusing specific relief' is too fine to be practically serviceable. However, the bar is not incoherent or patently unreasonable. More importantly, the clean hands bar is at most only indirectly related to a concern for unconscionability. One way of dirtying one's hands is to engage in unconscionable behaviour. But as the Scientology case illustrates, it is not the only way. The clean hands bar is based on the same principles that underlie the traditional common law doctrine of illegality.

Hardship

It is orthodox law that specific relief may be refused if it would cause undue hardship to the defendant. In the conventional understanding, specific relief is said to cause undue hardship if it imposes a burden on the defendant that is out of all proportion to its value to the plaintiff. For example, in *Patel v Ali*[48] the plaintiff was refused specific performance of a contract for the sale of a residential property. Subsequent to the original agreement, the defendant owner's leg was amputated, she bore two more children and her husband was sent to prison—all of which led her to rely heavily on neighbours and nearby relatives for assistance.

It might be thought that the hardship bar is based on a straightforward concern for unconscionability. Demanding specific relief in circumstances where such relief imposes a burden out of all proportion to its value appears an obvious example of unconscionable behaviour. In such circumstances, a fair-minded person would accept compensatory damages in lieu of performance. On closer reflection, however, the link is far from straightforward.[49] The suggestion that the hardship bar is triggered by unconscionable behaviour presumes that the unconscionable behaviour in question is the defendant's decision to seek enforcement of the substantive right. In this view it was not the contract that was unfair in *Patel*, but rather the decision to seek its specific enforcement. Indeed, it is because the contract was perfectly valid that damages were awarded: Mrs Ali had to pay damages because she breached her duty to convey the property. Yet this interpretation leads

---

[47] The 'enforcement officers' employed to enforce High Court (but not County Court) rulings in England are private contractors.

[48] *Patel v Ali* [1984] Ch 283 (Ch) (hereinafter *Patel*).

[49] I explore some of the ideas discussed below in S Smith, 'Rights and Remedies: A Complex Relationship' in K Roach and R Sharpe (eds), *Taking Remedies Seriously* (Ottawa, Canadian Institute for the Administration of Justice, 2010) 31, 55–57.

to the paradoxical conclusion that if, prior to the litigation, Mrs Ali had asked how, as a matter of law, she ought to act, the answer would be that she ought to convey the property. She ought to convey the property because (according to this explanation) she had a legal duty to do so.

The objection to this interpretation of the hardship bar, then, is that it supposes that defendants have legal duties to do things that courts clearly do not believe they ought to do. Courts clearly do not want the Mrs Ali's of the world to quit their properties. Yet the explanation of the hardship bar that supposes the bar is based on the plaintiff's unconscionable attempt to obtain specific relief—and nothing more—must suppose that such a duty exists. It is true that on learning of the judicial unwillingness to order performance of their duties the Mrs Ali's of the world may feel little urgency to perform voluntarily. The law, however, cannot adopt this explanation of the hardship bar since the law must assume that the duties it asserts are meant to be treated as just that—duties.

The question then arises whether it is possible to explain cases such as *Patel* without assuming that the defendants have legal duties to do what the law refuses to order them to do. If we look elsewhere in the law, the obvious, indeed direct, analogies to cases such as *Patel* are necessity cases. In the famous American case of *Vincent v Lake Erie Transportation Co*[50] the court held that a defendant who had tied his ship without permission to the plaintiff's dock to avoid it being destroyed in a violent storm had acted perfectly reasonably, but nevertheless had to compensate for damage caused to the dock. In *Vincent* the plaintiff did not have the opportunity to seek an injunction against trespassing, but had he been able to make such a request the court would undoubtedly have refused, and for the same reason as in *Patel*—the burden of performance was out of all proportion to its value. What *Vincent* makes clear is that the justification for damages in such cases cannot be that the defendant acted wrongly: just like Mrs Ali, the shipowner in *Vincent* acted perfectly reasonably. Why, then, did the defendant in *Vincent* have to pay compensation? The obvious answer—I would suggest the only possible answer[51]—is that there are circumstances in which individuals must compensate for the harm they caused notwithstanding that they did no wrong, moral or legal. Citizens in the position of the defendants in *Vincent* and *Patel* have what Francis Bohlen described in his analysis of *Vincent* as an 'incomplete privilege', meaning that they are allowed to do something that is normally not allowed subject to the condition that they must compensate for any harm they cause.[52] Any other interpretation of cases like *Vincent* or *Patel* must suppose that we have legal duties to do things that the courts in such cases clearly did not think the defendants should have done.

The no-duty explanation of hardship cases does not deny that courts often refuse to enforce valid legal duties. For example, courts will refuse to award any relief if a statutory limitation period has expired, notwithstanding that the statute has no effect on the defendant's substantive duty. And as we have just seen, courts may refuse to order compliance with a non-monetary duty if the plaintiff has unclean hands. In these examples, however, the reason for refusing relief or for refusing a particular kind of relief has nothing to do

---

[50] *Vincent v Lake Erie Transportation Co*, 109 Minn 456, 124 NW 221 (Minn Sup Ct 1910).

[51] Other disagree: see, eg, J Gardner, 'What Is Tort Law For? Part 1: The Place of Corrective Justice' (2011) 30 *Law & Philosophy* 1, 42.

[52] F Bohlen, 'Incomplete Privilege to Inflict Intentional Invasions of Interests of Property and Personality' (1926) 39 *Harvard Law Review* 307.

with the general desirability of the defendant performing his duty. The uncleanliness of the plaintiff's hands or the delay by the plaintiff is a reason for refusing relief, but it is not a reason for denying the defendant's substantive duty. By contrast, the reason for refusing specific relief in cases such as *Patel* is precisely the undesirability of the supposed duty. It is a reason, in other words, for denying the duty entirely.

The conclusion suggested by these observations is that courts refuse specific relief in cases such as *Patel* not because the plaintiff unconscionably sought specific relief, but rather because the alleged duty no longer existed. As in *Vincent*, the only duty that the defendant in *Patel* was under (once the circumstances had changed) was a duty to pay compensation.

Public Interest

A third traditional bar, albeit one less widely accepted than the previous bars, is that specific relief will not be granted where performance is contrary to public interest. This bar was famously—and controversially—applied in *Miller v Jackson* as one of the reasons for refusing an injunction to prevent the playing of cricket on a field next to the plaintiff's property: an injunction, it was held, would be contrary to the local community's interest in playing cricket on the village green.[53]

The controversy surrounding the public interest bar is unsurprising: it is relatively rare that the 'public interest' figures explicitly in judicial reasoning about private law disputes. However, for present purposes the important point is that whatever the bar's substantive merits or practical significance, it has nothing to do with the prevention of unconscionable conduct. It may be petty and selfish to try to shut down the community cricket field, but it is not unconscionable. Moreover, the public interest bar is similar to the hardship bar in that the reasons on which it is founded are not so much reasons to refuse specific relief as reasons to deny the alleged duty entirely. If the public interest is a sufficient reason not to order the cricket club to stop playing, it is a sufficient reason for holding that the cricket club has no duty to stop playing cricket.

Delay (Laches)

A fourth traditional bar to specific relief is delay or 'laches'.[54] The idea that plaintiffs may lose the right to judicial relief because of their delay in seeking relief is unexceptional and given effect throughout the law by statutory limitation periods. However, laches differs from normal limitation periods because while the latter are triggered merely by passage of time, laches cannot be invoked unless the delay has prejudiced the defendant. Because the tests are different, plaintiffs who are denied specific relief on the ground of laches will normally be awarded damages in lieu (the reverse is not true because statutory limitation periods apply to specific and non-specific relief).

The question raised by laches, therefore, is whether there is any explanation, aside from history, for why plaintiffs who have delayed bringing an action may be denied specific relief notwithstanding that the statutory limitation period has not expired. Why is specific relief

---

[53] *Miller v Jackson* [1977] QB 966 (CA) 989 (Cumming-Bruce LJ), 981–82 (Denning LJ).

[54] This bar is closely related to, and arguably indistinguishable from, the bar usually described as acquiescence: see R Sharpe, *Injunctions and Specific Performance*, loose-leaf (consulted on 1 July 2014) (Aurora, Canada Law Book, 2006) [1.860].

subject to an additional limitation period? The answer, it is suggested, is that granting specific relief to plaintiffs who have delayed may cause a special kind of prejudice—a kind of prejudice not normally suffered when plaintiffs seek monetary remedies. The payment of money by way of damages or a debt is rarely made significantly more onerous by the passage of time. The cost of paying money is relatively constant over time; indeed, the cost often decreases because of inflation. By contrast, the cost of complying with an order of specific relief may increase significantly with delay. For example, the cost of removing or repairing a structure may increase if the defendant has added to the structure or begun to use it for new purposes. Likewise, the cost of complying with an order to deliver goods may increase if the defendant has agreed to resell the goods or has put them to a particular use. Of course, the burden of complying with a specific ruling does not always increase over time. And in cases where plaintiffs make clear that they have not relinquished their right to performance defendants can hardly complain that the cost of complying with their duty has increased. It is a crucial feature of the test for laches, then, that it requires courts to determine if the cost of compliance has increased over time and, further, to determine if the plaintiff's actions encouraged the defendant to believe that the plaintiff was acquiescing in the defendant's non-performance.[55] If the defendant's inaction is due solely to his or her decision not to perform, the bar does not apply.

   Understood in this way, the test for laches is admittedly based on a concern for fairness to the defendant and so on a concern for unconscionability in a broad sense. It is unfair to allow plaintiffs to obtain specific relief in circumstances where their own tardiness or other actions have led the defendant to rely detrimentally on an assumption that such relief would not be sought. However, it is not necessary to refer to the Chancery Court origins of specific relief to understand why the laches bar is applied exclusively to specific rulings. An award of specific relief that is issued following a delay can prejudice defendants in ways that granting non-specific relief is unlikely to do.

Other Bars: Volunteers, Mutuality, Election, Impossibility, Specificity, etc.

As mentioned earlier, there is little agreement amongst textbook writers as to the number of traditional bars. However, most writers include in their lists bars that are not mentioned above. Some of the additions, eg the maxim 'he who comes to equity must do equity', seem best understood as variations on the categories discussed above (in the example just given, the category of clean hands).[56] Other possible additions appear best explained as straightforward implications of the nature of specific rulings. For example, the rule that specific relief will not be granted if the relevant duty cannot be specified clearly,[57] or if the duty has become impossible to perform,[58] can be explained on the mundane ground that there is little point in issuing an order that cannot be expressed or performed. Equally straightforward is the rule that specific performance is not available if the plaintiff has 'elected' to pursue relief by way of damages:[59] the plaintiff's election in such cases effectively terminates

---

[55] ibid [1.930].
[56] To the extent that 'mutuality' is a valid bar it appears to operate as an aspect of the clean hands or other bars: see Spry, above n 1, 91–98.
[57] Burrows, above n 1, 493.
[58] ibid 497.
[59] Spry, above n 1, 239.

the contract, and thus the duty to perform. None of these bars have anything remotely to do with unconscionability. Some additional bars are admittedly difficult to explain aside from their historical provenance, notably the bar against awarding specific relief to 'volunteers' and, to the extent that it exists, the bar against awarding specific relief to plaintiffs who could not themselves be subject to a specific ruling (the so-called 'mutuality' defence).[60] However, neither of these rarely applied bars can be justified in terms of a concern for unconscionability; indeed neither seems justifiable on any ground.

Discretion

It is orthodox law that specific relief is not available 'as of right' but only as an exercise of the court's discretion. Like other broad assertions about the nature of specific relief, this proposition is often queried.[61] Assuming the proposition is true, does it reveal anything distinctively equitable about the rules governing specific relief?

An initial observation is that the mere fact that the rules governing specific relief grant courts discretion, even significant discretion, is hardly a distinguishing feature. The contemporary rules for determining the existence of a duty of care in tort provide judges with at least as much discretion as any of the rules governing specific relief. Nor is there anything distinctive about the fact that the courts' alleged discretion with respect to specific relief concerns a decision whether or not to make a ruling: the rules governing the availability and content of punitive damages or damages for pain and suffering again leave judges with as much leeway as any of the rules governing specific relief.

Still, it might be said—and has been said—that the discretion regarding specific relief has a distinctively equitable explanation, namely the idea mentioned earlier that the Chancery Court does not deal in 'law' (or 'legal rights'), strictly understood. Plaintiffs do not have a right to specific relief because all questions of 'rights' were historically within the Royal Courts' exclusive jurisdiction. In the post-Judicature Act world, this explanation is difficult to sustain without some delicate conceptual gymnastics, but for present purposes it is sufficient to note that the preceding discussion suggests an alternative explanation of the courts' alleged discretion with respect to specific relief. The reasons for and against granting relief discussed in the previous sections (adequacy of damages, supervision, personal nature of the duty, clean hands, etc) are all reasons of 'degree'; damages may be more or less adequate, supervision more or less costly, and so on. Further, balancing these reasons involves weighing incommensurables: there is no right answer to the question of whether the savings associated with a substitute monetary award outweighs the minor (or sometimes not so minor) injustice arising from such awards. The question of whether specific relief ought to be awarded is therefore different in principle from questions such as 'did the defendant make a promise?' or 'did the defendant tell a lie?'. Anyone seeking to answer

---

[60] It might be argued that the bar against granting specific performance to 'volunteers' (in practice plaintiffs seeking enforcement of unpaid-for, but valid, promises under seal) is justified on the ground that mere donees do not merit the state's special assistance. But given that it is the state, not the defendant, who is providing the ruling, it is not clear why this should matter. All plaintiffs are volunteers vis-à-vis the state.

[61] Burrows, above n 1, 457; R Zakrzewski, *Remedies Reclassified* (New York, Oxford University Press, 2005) 94–96.

it must balance different and often incommensurable factors. Such balancing unavoidably involves discretion.

Admittedly, the courts could respond to this feature of the tests for specific relief by developing arbitrary 'bright-line' rules. But arbitrary rules impose their own costs and so should only be used where uncertainty is a serious concern. It is significant, then, that certainty is not as important in this area of the law as it is in many others. The rules governing specific relief are not rules about how citizens should treat one another: they are rules about how judges should respond to citizens' requests for assistance. To be sure, courts should not be treat plaintiffs as mere supplicants, praying for relief. But the discretion that courts enjoy with respect to specific relief does not lead to this result. The courts' alleged discretion is limited to a choice between specific relief and damages, and, crucially, when damages are awarded in lieu they are meant to provide, so far as possible, a true substitute for performance (eg by providing funds sufficient to purchase alternative performance). In short, the discretion that judges enjoy with respect to specific relief is limited in scope and significance, and arises because of the kinds of considerations that courts must take into account (for reasons explained earlier) when assessing requests for specific relief.

IV. Conclusion

When judges and scholars explain the law they generally do so by trying to show how it is, or at least might plausibly be thought to be, morally justified. This approach is unsurprising: explaining the law is an attempt to make sense of it, and one of the main features that must be made sense of is the fact that the law presents itself as morally justified. Unless we are to suppose that the law is involved in a giant charade, an explanation that shows the law to be systematically unjustified raises more questions than it answers.

It would be wrong to assume, however, that every aspect of the law can be explained in this way. All that can be said about some features of the law is that they exist because at some moment in history a particular decision or action was taken, and no one subsequently reversed that decision or action. Writers who regard specific relief as a distinctively equitable remedy do not generally go this far. They do, however, assert that the rules governing specific relief were developed and shaped by a court that, for historical reasons, was concerned with a particular aspect of morality. They assert, in other words, that the existence and scope of specific relief can only be explained by reference to the allegedly particular concerns and methods of the Chancery Court.

This chapter offers a different explanation. Specific relief itself hardly needs to be explained at all. It is an interesting historical question why the Royal Courts did not issue specific rulings,[62] but there is no mystery as to why a legal system would employ specific rulings. The only way that the results contemplated by certain kinds of legal duties can be achieved is if the duty-holder acts in compliance with the duty—and the most obvious way

---

[62]   Early in their history the Royal Courts occasionally issued specific rulings; see JH Baker, *An Introduction to English Legal History*, 4th edn (London, Butterworths, 2002) 58. It is not clear why they stopped, but the explanation no doubt has to do at least partly with the administrative convenience of non-specific rulings.

for a legal system to encourage such a decision is to order compliance and back up that order by the threat of punishment. If a legal system wants defendants to comply with their legal duties not to trespass—as any legal system that recognises such duties presumably does—the obvious way to try to bring about this result is to order defendants to perform the duty.

The rules governing the availability of specific rulings can be explained on similarly general grounds. The distinctive feature of specific rulings is that the states of affairs that they contemplate cannot be brought about, or at least not easily brought about, without the defendant's participation. Because of this feature, specific rulings are more costly for the legal system to administer (sometimes much more costly) than non-specific rulings, and so are discouraged where a non-specific ruling can provide a reasonable substitute. This feature also explains why specific rulings may lead to a kind of servitude, taint the legal system in a particular way or lead to special prejudice if delayed—all of which give rise to further reasons for refusing specific relief. It is unnecessary to invoke equity to explain these reasons. Specific rulings are governed by special rules not because they originated in the Chancery Court, but because of the distinctive features of the states of affairs that they seek to bring about. With only a few exceptions, the same rules could easily have developed in a unitary system.

INDEX